BETTER HOMES AND GARDENS®
COMPLETE·GUIDE·TO
FOOD·AND·COOKING

Our seal assures you that every recipe in the *Complete Guide to Food and Cooking* has been tested in the Better Homes and Gardens® Test Kitchen. This means that each recipe is practical and reliable, and meets our high standards of taste appeal. We guarantee your satisfaction with this book for as long as you own it.

WE CARE!

All of us at Better Homes and Gardens® Books are dedicated to providing you with the information and ideas you need to create tasty foods. We welcome your comments or suggestions. Write us at:
Better Homes and Gardens® Books, Cookbook Editorial Department, LS-348,
1716 Locust Street, Des Moines, IA 50336

© Copyright 1991 by Meredith Corporation, Des Moines, Iowa.
All Rights Reserved. Printed in the United States of America.
First Edition. First Printing.
Library of Congress Catalog Card Number: 90-64090
ISBN: 0-696-01911-6

Better Homes and Gardens® Books
Vice President, Editorial Director: Elizabeth P. Rice
Art Director: Ernest Shelton
Managing Editor: David A. Kirchner
Project Editors: James D. Blume, Marsha Jahns
Project Managers: Liz Anderson, Jennifer Speer Ramundt, Angela K. Renkoski

Food and Family Life Editor: Sharyl Heiken
Associate Department Editors: Sandra Granseth, Rosemary C. Hutchinson, Elizabeth Woolever
Senior Food Editors: Linda Henry, Mary Jo Plutt, Joyce Trollope
Associate Food Editors: Jennifer Darling, Heather M. Hephner, Shelli McConnell,
   Heidi McNutt, Mary Major Williams,
Test Kitchen: Director, Sharon Stilwell; Photo Studio Director, Janet Herwig;
   Home Economists: Lynn Blanchard, Kay Cargill, Marilyn Cornelius, Maryellyn Krantz,
   Jennifer Nuese, Colleen Weeden

Associate Art Directors: Neoma Thomas, Linda Ford Vermie, Randall Yontz
Assistant Art Directors: Lynda Haupert, Harijs Priekulis, Tom Wegner
Graphic Designers: Mary Schlueter Bendgen, Michael Burns, Mick Schnepf
Art Production: Director, John Berg; Associate, Joe Heuer; Office Manager, Michaela Lester

President, Book Group: James F. Stack
Vice President, Retail Marketing: Jamie Martin
Vice President, Administrative Services: Rick Rundall

Better Homes and Gardens® Magazine
President, Magazine Group: James A. Autry
Editorial Director: Doris Eby
Food and Nutrition Editor: Nancy Byal

Meredith Corporation Officers
Chairman of the Executive Committee: E. T. Meredith III
Chairman of the Board: Robert A. Burnett
President and Chief Executive Officer: Jack D. Rehm

Complete Guide to Food and Cooking
Project Editors: Rosemary Hutchinson, Joyce Trollope
Editors: Linda Henry, Heather M. Hephner
Graphic Designer: Tom Wegner
Project Manager: Angela K. Renkoski
Publishing Systems Text Processor: Kathy Benz
Food Stylists: Lynn Blanchard, Janet Herwig
Technical Consultants: Lynn Blanchard, Kay Cargill, Marilyn Cornelius, Maryellyn Krantz,
   Sharon Stilwell, Colleen Weeden
Contributing Editors: Marlene Brown, Sandra Day, Lorene Frohling, Sandra Mosley,
   Lynn Hoppe Phelps, Linda Foley Woodrum
Contributing Photographers: Dennis E. Becker, Mike Dieter, M. Jensen Photography

Have you ever been stumped by a cooking question? Often it's hard to know where to go for more information.

Now, help is right here at your fingertips. To answer your cooking questions and provide practical information, the editors of Better Homes and Gardens® Books have put together this storehouse of food and cooking facts. Look here for information on buying and storing food, facts about ingredients and cooking terms, tips on food preparation, plus recipes and more.

Turn to pages 6 and 7 and see what's in this book. Then discover more than 1,000 alphabetically listed entries and two complete indexes—one for recipes and the other for text—to make finding information easy.

Whether your hobby is cooking or you simply enjoy eating good food, this book is for you. Keep the *Complete Guide to Food and Cooking* handy in the kitchen and use it whenever a food or cooking question pops up.

Contents

	What's in this book . . .	6
A-B	Abalone to Butterscotch	8
C	Cabbage to Cutlet	66
D-F	Daikon to Funnel Cake	138
G-I	Game to Italian Seasoning	184
J-N	Jackfruit to Nutrition	218
O-Q	Oat to Quinoa	274
R-S	Rabbit to Syrup	344
T-Z	Taco to Zwieback	400
	Emergency Substitutions	446
	Recipe Index	447
	Text Index	451
	Metric Cooking Hints	480

Golden Delicious Granny Smith Jonagold

What's in this book...

To help you get the most out of the *Complete Guide to Food and Cooking,* we've highlighted the book's major features on these two pages.

■ Charts compare varieties, list cooking directions for basic foods, and provide lots more at-a-glance information.

■ Questions listed in entries describe cooking problems. Answers are provided in an easy-to-find format.

■ Cross-references lead you to additional information about a particular topic.

■ Alphabetically listed entries for ingredients, cooking terms, techniques, and classic recipe names are followed by definitions or explanations. Where helpful, alternate names and spellings also are given.

■ Pronunciations are given for less familiar entries. We've used phonetic pronunciations so you don't need a pronunciation key. Accented syllables are printed in capital letters.

■ Selecting and storing information is included in many ingredient entries.

■ More than 175 recipes are included to help define and clarify certain entries and to provide variations for some basic foods.

■ Math boxes provide equivalent amounts of ingredients.

Selecting Apples

Apple varieties differ in sweetness and skin color. Some varieties are more desirable for eating fresh, others for cooking and baking, and certain varieties are all-purpose. If you can't find a specific variety in your area, check with the supermarket's produce manager for an appropriate substitution.

Type	Appearance	Flavor	Uses
Cortland	Red with green highlights	Slightly tart	Eating, baking
Crispin	Yellow-green	Sweet	All-purpose
Criterion	Yellow with a red blush	Sweet	All-purpose
Empire	Dark red	Mildly tart	Eating, salads
Fuji	Greenish yellow with red blush	Sweet	All-purpose
Gala	Orange-yellow	Sweet	Eating, salads
Golden Delicious	Yellow	Tangy, sweet	All-purpose
Granny Smith	Green	Tart	All-purpose
Jonagold	Yellow with orangish red blush	Tangy, sweet	All-purpose

18 Applesauce

Q: What varieties of apples work best for applesauce?
A: Any tart and juicy cooking apple will work—try Cortland, Granny Smith, Jonathan, McIntosh, or Winesap. If all you have are the sweeter Golden Delicious apples, you may prefer to reduce the sugar slightly.

Nutrition information: A ½-cup serving of unsweetened, canned applesauce has about 50 calories; the sweetened variety of canned applesauce has about 100 calories.

Apricot A small, golden orange, soft-textured fruit with a large brown center pit. It has a rich, sweet flavor similar to a peach with winelike overtones and a hint of lemon.

Market forms: Apricots
Fresh apricots usually are available from late May to mid-August. Throughout the year, you'll find canned apricots, dried apricots, and apricot nectar in the supermarket.

Selecting: Look for plump, firm apricots with a red blush. Avoid fruit that is pale yellow or green-yellow, very firm, very soft, or bruised.

Storing: Store firm fruit at room temperature until it yields to gentle pressure and is golden in color. Refrigerate ripe fruit up to 2 days.

Apricot Math
1 pound apricots	=	8 to 12 whole
	=	2½ cups sliced

Nutrition information: Three medium apricots have about 50 calories. A ½-cup serving of apricots canned in heavy syrup has about 110 calories. Apricots also are a significant source of vitamin A.

(See *Dried Fruit* for the Cooking Dried Fruit chart and storing and preparation hints.)

Arrowroot A fine, dry, white powder that comes from the root of the arrowroot plant and is used as a thickening agent. Because arrowroot thickens at lower temperatures than either flour or cornstarch, it is sometimes used to thicken delicate sauces that should not boil. Arrowroot-thickened mixtures should be cooked using a minimum amount of stirring.

Arroz con Pollo *(ah ROS con POL yo)*
A Spanish or Mexican main dish made with rice, chicken, tomato, green pepper, and seasonings, including saffron. Saffron gives this dish its characteristic yellow color.

Arroz con Pollo

- 2 pounds meaty chicken pieces*
- 1 tablespoon cooking oil
- 1 cup long grain rice
- ½ cup chopped onion
- 1 clove garlic, minced
- 1 7½-ounce can tomatoes, cut up
- ½ cup chopped green pepper
- 1 tablespoon instant chicken bouillon granules
- ⅛ teaspoon saffron, crushed
- 1 cup frozen peas
- 1 2-ounce jar sliced pimiento, drained and chopped

■ Sprinkle chicken lightly with *salt.* In a large skillet brown chicken in hot oil about 15 minutes, turning often. Remove chicken from pan. Add rice, onion, and garlic to drippings in pan; cook till rice is golden. Add *undrained* tomatoes, green pepper, bouillon, saffron, 2 cups *water,* and ⅛ teaspoon *pepper.* Bring to boiling. Stir mixture well. Arrange chicken

Rome Beauty

Stayman

Winesap

Apple-Pear See *Asian Pear.*

Apple Pie Spice A blend of ground cinnamon, cloves, nutmeg or mace, and allspice that's especially good in fruit pies and pastries.

(See *Spice* for selecting, storing, and nutrition information.)

A Tip from Our Kitchen
The difference between making a smooth or chunky applesauce is just a matter of when the sugar is added. For a chunky sauce, add the sugar before cooking the apples. For smooth applesauce, stir in the sugar after the apples are cooked and mashed.

■ Cooking tips present helpful information from our editors and Test Kitchen home economists.

Artichoke **19**

■ Key words help you locate information quickly.

atop rice mixture. Cover and simmer 20 to 25 minutes or till chicken is tender. Sprinkle peas and chopped pimiento on top; cover and cook 5 minutes more. Makes 4 servings.
Note: To save calories and cut fat, remove skin from chicken before cooking.

Nutrition information per serving: 479 calories, 32 g protein, 49 g carbohydrate, 17 g fat (4 g saturated), 81 mg cholesterol, 877 mg sodium, 501 mg potassium.

■ Nutrition information that lists the per-serving amounts of calories, protein, carbohydrate, total fat, saturated fat, cholesterol, sodium, and potassium is included for all recipes. Many ingredient entries also include calorie counts.

Artichoke A globe-shaped bud with sharp, pointed leaves that grows on a tall, thistlelike plant. Artichokes have a subtle, nutty flavor.

Artichokes

■ Color photographs help you identify many ingredients quickly and show you some finished food dishes.

The Art of Eating Artichokes
Use your fingers to pull off the leaves one at a time. Dip the base of the leaf into a sauce or melted butter or margarine, and draw the leaf through your teeth, scraping off the tender meat inside the base of each leaf. Discard the rest of the tough leaf. Once all of the fleshy leaves have been removed, remove the small, thin inner leaves, exposing the fuzzy "choke." Scoop out the choke with a spoon and discard. Eat the meaty bottom portion with a fork, dipping each piece into desired sauce.

flared leaves.) Artichokes should yield slightly to pressure and have large, tightly closed leaves. Avoid any with mottled or spread leaves or shriveled cones. Sometimes leaf edges darken because of chill damage. This darkening, called winter kiss, does not affect the quality of the artichoke.

■ How-to photos show you how to perform a variety of cooking techniques.

Types: There are several types of artichokes, but the *Green Globe,* with a deep green color and a round but slightly elongated shape, is the most common. Green globes are available in baby to large sizes.

Market forms: Artichokes are sold fresh, canned, and frozen. Fresh artichokes are available year-round, but early spring is the peak harvest time. Artichoke hearts and bottoms are available canned and may come marinated, packed in oil, or packed in water. Artichoke hearts also are available frozen.

Selecting: Look for compact, firm globes that are heavy for their size. (Summer and fall artichokes will be more conical with slightly

Storing: Place fresh artichokes in a plastic bag and refrigerate. They are best if used within a couple of days, but will keep for up to a week. Opened, canned artichoke products can be refrigerated for up to 4 days in a storage container.

How to cook: See the Cooking Fresh Vegetables chart under *Vegetable.*

Nutrition information: One medium artichoke has about 60 calories, and ½ cup cooked artichoke hearts has about 40 calories.

To prepare an artichoke, wash, then cut off the bottom stem so the artichoke sits flat. Cut off about 1 inch from the top. Remove loose outer leaves. With kitchen shears, snip off about ½ inch from tips of remaining leaves. Brush cut surfaces with lemon juice to prevent browning.

A-B

Fish Fillets Amandine
(see recipe, page 11)

Mixed Nut Brittle
(see recipe, page 58)

Abalone (*ab uh LOW nee*) A large mollusk with a delicate flavor. The meat is tough, but, once pounded, it becomes tender. Available fresh along the Pacific Coast, elsewhere it's sold frozen and canned.

Al Dente (*ahl DEN tay*) An Italian term, meaning "to the tooth," which is used to describe cooking spaghetti or other pasta to the stage where it offers just a slight resistance when it is bitten.

Alligator A thick-skinned reptile with a long body and tail. Alligators have light (white) and dark (pink) meat. The flavor of alligator meat, which is considered seafood, is similar to chicken or turtle with a slightly fishy flavor. The solid muscle meat has a firm texture.

Market form: Dressed alligator meat is sold frozen in specialty stores and some supermarkets.

Preparation hints: Alligator fat has a strong, unpleasant flavor, so trim excess fat from the meat. The meat needs to be tenderized by marinating it for 24 to 48 hours or by pounding it.

Cooking hints: Deep-fat frying, barbecuing, and poaching are some popular ways to cook alligator. It also can be baked.

Nutrition information: Alligator has less fat than most cuts of beef or pork. A 3-ounce portion of plain, cooked alligator has about 120 calories.

Allspice A pungent, sharply aromatic, reddish brown spice. Although many people think allspice is a combination of different spices, it's actually one spice that tastes predominantly like cloves, except it is sweeter and more mellow, plus it has notes of cinnamon and nutmeg. Allspice berries are sold whole and ground.

(See *Spice* for the Spice Alternative Guide and selecting, storing, and nutrition information.)

Almond The kernel of the fruit of the almond tree. The oval-shaped almond, which is encased in a light tan, pitted shell, is a smooth, flat, white nut covered with a cinnamon-brown skin. Almonds have a rich but mild flavor.

Almonds

Q: **What's the difference between sliced and slivered almonds?**
A: The main difference is the thickness. Slivered almonds are whole almonds halved lengthwise, then halved lengthwise again into pieces thick enough to have a pleasant crunch. Sliced almonds are whole almonds (usually with the skin left on) thinly sliced lengthwise.

Types: Sweet and bitter are the two main types of almonds. Only sweet almonds are sold in the United States. Bitter almonds contain poisonous hydrocyanic acid, and special processes must be used to make them safe to eat. Almond extract is made from processed bitter almonds.

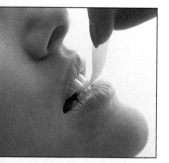

To check for doneness, taste the pasta often near the end of the cooking time. The pasta is al dente when it is tender but still slightly firm when it is bitten.

To toast just a few almonds (or any nut), place them in a small skillet. Cook over medium heat, stirring often, for 5 to 7 minutes or till golden. Toast larger amounts in a shallow baking pan in a 350° oven for 5 to 10 minutes, stirring once or twice.

Storing: Almonds in the shell will keep for several months in a cool, dry place. Refrigerate shelled nuts in an airtight container for up to 6 months or freeze for up to 1 year.

Q: What is almond paste and how is it used in cooking?

A: Almond paste is made from sweet almonds that have been finely ground and combined with sugar. It can be purchased ready to use for fillings in coffee cakes and pastries. Almond paste is a main ingredient in marzipan (see also *Marzipan*).

(See *Nut* for the Selecting Nuts chart and selecting, nutrition, and other information.)

Alum *(AL um)* An astringent mineral salt used primarily to give crisp texture to certain types of pickles. Alum is rarely called for in recipes today.

Amandine A French word for a food made with or garnished with almonds. It is often applied to vegetable or fish dishes.

Fish Fillets Amandine

1 **pound orange roughy, pike, *or* red snapper fillets (½ inch thick)**
⅓ **cup all-purpose flour**
¼ **cup milk *or* buttermilk**
1 **tablespoon cooking oil**
2 **tablespoons margarine *or* butter**
¼ **cup sliced almonds**
1 **tablespoon lemon juice**
1 **tablespoon snipped parsley**

■ Separate fillets or cut into 4 serving-size portions. Rinse; pat dry with paper towels. In a shallow dish combine flour, ¼ teaspoon *salt,* and ¼ teaspoon *pepper.* Place milk in a shallow dish; dip fish into milk. Dip into flour mixture; turn to coat.

■ In a large skillet heat oil and *1 tablespoon* of the margarine or butter over medium heat. Add fish. Fry fish 3 to 4 minutes or till golden. Turn carefully. Fry 3 to 4 minutes more or till golden and crisp and flakes easily with a fork. Drain on paper towels.

■ Drain and scrape coating from skillet and discard. Add remaining margarine and the almonds to skillet; cook and stir over medium heat about 2 minutes or till nuts are golden. Remove from heat. Carefully stir in lemon juice and parsley. Spoon atop fish. Serves 4.

Nutrition information per serving: 305 calories, 20 g protein, 10 g carbohydrate, 21 g fat (2 g saturated), 24 mg cholesterol, 281 mg sodium, 92 mg potassium.

Trout Amandine: Prepare Fish Fillets Amandine as above *except* substitute four 8- to 10-ounce pan-dressed trout for the fillets. Coat trout as above. Increase cooking oil to 3 tablespoons. Heat oil in a 12-inch skillet along with the *1 tablespoon* margarine or butter. Fry 2 of the trout for 5 to 7 minutes or till golden. Turn carefully and fry for 5 to 7 minutes more or till trout flakes easily. Drain trout on paper towels. Keep warm in a 300° oven. Fry remaining trout, adding additional oil and margarine or butter as necessary. Prepare almond mixture and serve as above.

Nutrition information per serving: 320 calories, 25 g protein, 10 g carbohydrate, 20 g fat (3 g saturated), 64 mg cholesterol, 205 mg sodium, 630 mg potassium.

Amaranth

Amaranth *(AM uh ranth)* A high-protein, off-white grain the size of poppy seeds. Amaranth has a nutty taste and contains more protein and fiber than corn, rice, or wheat.

Amaranth should not be eaten raw. The grain is usually combined with other grains or flours because of its assertive flavor and heavy texture. Amaranth flour is added to baked goods and snack foods. It also is available puffed (also called popped). Puffed amaranth, which is milder in flavor than the whole grain or flour, sometimes is included in granola or served as a cooked breakfast cereal. Amaranth is sold at health food stores and some supermarkets.

Storing: Keep in an airtight container in a cool, dry place for up to 6 months.

Nutrition information: Puffed amaranth has about 110 calories per ¾-cup serving.

Ambrosia

Ambrosia A dessert made with shredded or flaked coconut, sugar, and fruit, such as oranges, pineapples, or bananas. Ambrosia also can refer to any food with a very pleasant flavor and aroma.

American Cheese

American cheese

American Cheese A rindless, milky orange process cheese with a mild flavor and smooth texture. American cheese is typically a blend of cow's-milk natural cheeses. During processing, the cheese mixture is shredded, mixed, and heated to keep it from further ripening. This gives American cheese a longer shelf life than natural cheese. American cheese also is referred to as pasteurized process cheese, and often is sold in slices.

(See *Cheese* for the Selecting Cheese chart and selecting, storing, serving, nutrition, and other information.)

Anchovy

Anchovy A small saltwater fish of the herring family. Anchovies are noted for their intense fish flavor.

Market forms: Most anchovies are cured in salt, then canned or bottled in oil or brine, which gives them a salty flavor. You can choose flat fillets or fillets rolled around capers. You also might see imported ones packaged in wine or in a flavored wine sauce. Popular uses for the canned fillets are in Caesar salad and as a pizza topping.

Anchovies also are boned, pounded, and blended into a paste, which is available in tubes. A richer, more concentrated version comes in small jars. In small amounts, the paste enhances the flavor of sauces, gravies, dressings, and hors d'oeuvres.

Q: How much anchovy paste is equivalent to 1 anchovy fillet?
A: Use ½ teaspoon anchovy paste in place of 1 anchovy fillet.

Nutrition information: One anchovy fillet packed in oil has about 10 calories.

Angel Food Cake

Angel Food Cake A moist, velvety, airy cake with fine, even holes and a delicate texture and flavor. It is made from stiffly beaten egg whites combined with sugar, cream of tartar, flour, and flavoring and is usually white inside. The stiffly beaten egg whites allow the cake to rise without baking powder. Angel food cake also can be made from a packaged mix.

Q: Is there a way to dress up plain angel food cake?
A: Yes, there are several ways. One is to add a little flavoring or spice, such as lemon peel, peppermint extract, cinnamon, or cocoa powder, to the batter. Another is to hollow out a baked angel food cake and fill it with your favorite pudding. You also can top cake slices with fresh fruit or chocolate sauce.

Preparation hints: The first step in properly beating egg whites for angel food cake is picking the right bowl. Select one that
continued

Cocoa Angel Food Cake
(see recipe, page 14)

is made of glass or metal, not plastic. Fat and food particles can become trapped in scratched plastic bowls and keep the egg whites from beating properly. Also, choose a bowl that is large enough that the beaters will not become buried in the fluffy whites.

Nutrition information: Because plain angel food cake has no shortening, margarine, butter, or egg yolks, it is relatively low in calories and has no fat or cholesterol. It has about 160 calories in $\frac{1}{12}$ of a 10-inch cake made from scratch.

(See *Cake* for How to Solve Cake Problems, Cake-Making Hints, and baking, storing, and other information.)

Angel Food Cake

1½	cups egg whites (10 to 12 large eggs)
1½	cups sifted powdered sugar
1	cup sifted cake flour *or* ¾ cup plus 2 tablespoons sifted all-purpose flour
1½	teaspoons cream of tartar
1	teaspoon vanilla
1	cup sugar

■ Bring egg whites to room temperature. Sift powdered sugar and flour together 3 times.
■ In a large bowl beat egg whites, cream of tartar, and vanilla with an electric mixer on medium speed till soft peaks form (tips curl). Gradually add sugar, about *2 tablespoons* at a time, beating till stiff peaks form (tips stand straight). Sift about *one-fourth* of the flour mixture over beaten egg whites; fold in gently. (If bowl is too full, transfer to a larger bowl.) Repeat, folding in remaining flour mixture by fourths.
■ Pour into an *ungreased* 10-inch tube pan. Bake on the lowest rack in a 350° oven for 40 to 45 minutes or till top springs back when lightly touched. *Immediately* invert cake, leaving cake in pan; cool thoroughly. Loosen and remove cake from pan. If desired, serve with whipped cream and berries. Serves 12.

Nutrition information per serving: 156 calories, 4 g protein, 36 g carbohydrate, 0 g fat, 0 mg cholesterol, 72 mg sodium, 63 mg potassium.

Cocoa Angel Food Cake: Prepare Angel Food Cake as below left *except* sift ¼ cup *unsweetened cocoa powder* with powdered sugar and flour.

Nutrition information per serving: 161 calories, 4 g protein, 36 g carbohydrate, 0 g fat, 0 mg cholesterol, 73 mg sodium, 84 mg potassium.

Angelica
A sweet, aromatic herb. Its candied stems are used to decorate desserts and to flavor alcoholic beverages, such as Chartreuse, gin, and Benedictine.

Angels on Horseback
A hot appetizer made by wrapping bacon around a shucked oyster and cooking it. Usually served on toast, this appetizer often is accompanied by a lemon wedge or hollandaise sauce.

Anise
(ANN us) Refers to both the herb and the spice aniseed. The small, feathery leaves, used fresh or dried, are not available commercially, but anise is an easy herb to grow at home. The tiny, grayish brown seeds (available whole and ground) are used as a spice. The leaves and the seed have a licoricelike flavor. Anise extract and oil of anise also are available.

A Tip from Our Kitchen
If you grow anise at home, use the leaves in salads and vegetable dishes.

(See *Spice* for the Spice Alternative Guide and selecting, storing, and nutrition information.)

Antipasto   An assortment of hot or cold appetizers commonly served as a first course before an Italian meal. Antipasto is an Italian word meaning "before the food." The array of well-seasoned, savory foods can include Italian cured meats, cheeses, pickled or marinated vegetables, and canned, pickled, or cured fish.

Aperitif   *(ah pear uh TEEF)* An alcoholic beverage served before a meal to stimulate the appetite. Some popular aperitifs are dry or sweet vermouth, dry sherry, dry white wine, and champagne and other sparkling wines.

Appetizer   A small portion of food or drink served as the first course of a multicourse meal to stimulate the appetite.

Appetizer also refers to small portions of food, separate from a meal, served at cocktail parties and receptions. In this case, they're generally referred to as hors d'oeuvres.

Apple   A round, thin-skinned fruit that grows on a tree and has a center core. Apples can have green, red, or yellow skins, sweet to tart flavor, and a crisp, juicy, or mealy texture.

Varieties: Commercial growers produce about 300 varieties of apples, although there are 2,500 varieties grown in the United States. Those listed in the Selecting Apples chart, page 16, are some of the most popular.

Market forms: Thanks to controlled-atmosphere storage, many apple varieties are available fresh throughout the year. Fresh apples are sold in bulk or plastic bags. But nearly half of the entire crop produced is used for processing into various products, such as apple juice or cider, applejack, applesauce, apple pie filling, apples sliced for pies, apple butter, and jams and jellies. Sliced and chopped apples also are available dried.

Selecting: Your choice of apple depends on how you'll be using it. See the Selecting Apples chart, page 16, for suggestions of what varieties are good for eating fresh, cooking, and baking.

Choose firm apples that have smooth, unblemished skins without bruises or breaks. Russeting, or brownish, freckled patches on the skin, generally does not affect the flavor.

Storing: Apples purchased in a plastic bag can be stored that way in your refrigerator crisper. Store apples purchased in bulk in a cool, moist place. Keeping apples at room temperature causes them to loose crispness and flavor and to ripen about 10 times faster.

A Tip from Our Kitchen
Once cut, apples brown easily. Sprinkle apple pieces and slices with lemon, orange, or grapefruit juice mixed with water, or treat them with ascorbic acid color keeper.

Q: **For which kinds of recipes should apples be peeled?**
A: It all depends on how the apples will be used. Peel apples that will be made into pies, but leave the peel on for salad or fruit platter recipes. Baked apples hold together better with the peel left on.

Apple Math
1 pound apples   =   4 small, 3 medium, or 2 large
                        =   2¾ cups sliced
                        =   2 cups chopped

Nutrition information: A medium apple has about 80 calories.

(See *Dried Fruit* for the Cooking Dried Fruit chart and storing and preparation hints.)

continued

Cortland

Crispin

Empire

Golden Delicious

Granny Smith

Jonagold

Selecting Apples

Apple varieties differ in sweetness and skin color. Some varieties are more desirable for eating fresh, others for cooking and baking, and certain varieties are all-purpose. If you can't find a specific variety in your area, check with the supermarket's produce manager for an appropriate substitution.

Type	Appearance	Flavor	Uses
Cortland	Red with green highlights	Slightly tart	Eating, baking
Crispin	Yellow-green	Sweet	All-purpose
Criterion	Yellow with a red blush	Sweet	All-purpose
Empire	Dark red	Mildly tart	Eating, salads
Fuji	Greenish yellow with red blush	Sweet	All-purpose
Gala	Orange-yellow	Sweet	Eating, salads
Golden Delicious	Yellow	Tangy, sweet	All-purpose
Granny Smith	Green	Tart	All-purpose
Jonagold	Yellow with orangish red blush	Tangy, sweet	All-purpose
Jonathan	Red with yellow undertones	Rich, mildly tart	All-purpose
McIntosh	Red and green	Tart	Eating, salads
Newtown Pippin	Green	Mildly tart	Eating, cooking
Northern Spy	Red, striped or blushed	Moderately tart	Eating, baking
Red Delicious	Red; 5 "knobs" on bottom	Rich, sweet	Eating, salads
Rome Beauty	Red, striped; may have green	Slightly tart	Baking, cooking
Stayman	Deep purplish red; sometimes has a russeted hue	Rich, mildly tart	Eating, cooking
Winesap	Deep purplish red	Tangy, winelike	All-purpose
York Imperial	Deep red with green stripes	Slightly tart	Baking, cooking

Jonathan

McIntosh

Red Delicious

Rome Beauty

Stayman

Winesap

Apple-Pear See *Asian Pear.*

Apple Pie Spice A blend of ground cinnamon, cloves, nutmeg or mace, and allspice that's especially good in fruit pies and pastries.

(See *Spice* for selecting, storing, and nutrition information.)

Applesauce A sauce made by cooking apple pieces until they lose their shape. Applesauce usually is lightly sweetened with sugar and often flavored with cinnamon or nutmeg. You can buy applesauce in a can or jar, sweetened or unsweetened, and in regular or chunky style. Applesauce can be a blend of two or more varieties of apples, or it can be flavored with other types of fruit.

A Tip from Our Kitchen
The difference between making a smooth or chunky applesauce is just a matter of when the sugar is added. For a chunky sauce, add the sugar before cooking the apples. For smooth applesauce, stir in the sugar after the apples are cooked and mashed.

How to cook: In a Dutch oven mix 3 pounds *cooking apples* (9 medium), peeled, quartered, and cored; 1 cup *water;* ⅓ to ⅔ cup *sugar;* and, if desired, ¼ teaspoon ground cinnamon. Bring to boiling; reduce heat. Cover and simmer for 8 to 10 minutes or till tender; add more water, if necessary.

Remove from heat. Mash with a potato masher or process in a blender or food processor to desired texture. Serve warm or chilled. Stir before serving. Makes about 4 cups (about 120 calories per ½-cup serving).

continued

Q: What varieties of apples work best for applesauce?
A: Any tart and juicy cooking apple will work—try Cortland, Granny Smith, Jonathan, McIntosh, or Winesap. If all you have are the sweeter Golden Delicious apples, you may prefer to reduce the sugar slightly.

Nutrition information: A ½-cup serving of unsweetened, canned applesauce has about 50 calories; the sweetened variety of canned applesauce has about 100 calories.

Apricot
A small, golden orange, soft-textured fruit with a large brown center pit. It has a rich, sweet flavor similar to a peach with winelike overtones and a hint of lemon.

Market forms:
Fresh apricots usually are available from late May to mid-August. Throughout the year, you'll find canned apricots, dried apricots, and apricot nectar in the supermarket.

Apricots

Selecting: Look for plump, firm apricots with a red blush. Avoid fruit that is pale yellow or green-yellow, very firm, very soft, or bruised.

Storing: Store firm fruit at room temperature until it yields to gentle pressure and is golden in color. Refrigerate ripe fruit up to 2 days.

Apricot Math
1 pound apricots = 8 to 12 whole
= 2½ cups sliced

Nutrition information: Three medium apricots have about 50 calories. A ½-cup serving of apricots canned in heavy syrup has about 110 calories. Apricots also are a significant source of vitamin A.

(See *Dried Fruit* for the Cooking Dried Fruit chart and storing and preparation hints.)

Arrowroot
A fine, dry, white powder that comes from the root of the arrowroot plant and is used as a thickening agent. Because arrowroot thickens at lower temperatures than either flour or cornstarch, it is sometimes used to thicken delicate sauces that should not boil. Arrowroot-thickened mixtures should be cooked using a minimum amount of stirring.

Arroz con Pollo *(ah ROS con POL yo)*
A Spanish or Mexican main dish made with rice, chicken, tomato, green pepper, and seasonings, including saffron. Saffron gives this dish its characteristic yellow color.

Arroz con Pollo

- 2 **pounds meaty chicken pieces***
- 1 **tablespoon cooking oil**
- 1 **cup long grain rice**
- ½ **cup chopped onion**
- 1 **clove garlic, minced**
- 1 **7½-ounce can tomatoes, cut up**
- ½ **cup chopped green pepper**
- 1 **tablespoon instant chicken bouillon granules**
- ⅛ **teaspoon saffron, crushed**
- 1 **cup frozen peas**
- 1 **2-ounce jar sliced pimiento, drained and chopped**

■ Sprinkle chicken lightly with *salt.* In a large skillet brown chicken in hot oil about 15 minutes, turning often. Remove chicken from pan. Add rice, onion, and garlic to drippings in pan; cook till rice is golden. Add *undrained* tomatoes, green pepper, bouillon, saffron, 2 cups *water,* and ⅛ teaspoon *pepper.* Bring to boiling. Stir mixture well. Arrange chicken atop rice mixture. Cover and simmer 20 to 25 minutes or till chicken is tender. Sprinkle peas and chopped pimiento on top; cover and cook 5 minutes more. Makes 4 servings.

Note: To save calories and cut fat, remove skin from chicken before cooking.

Nutrition information per serving: 479 calories, 32 g protein, 49 g carbohydrate, 17 g fat (4 g saturated), 81 mg cholesterol, 877 mg sodium, 501 mg potassium.

Artichokes

Artichoke A globe-shaped bud with sharp, pointed leaves that grows on a tall, thistlelike plant. Artichokes have a subtle, nutty flavor.

The Art of Eating Artichokes
Use your fingers to pull off the leaves one at a time. Dip the base of the leaf into a sauce or melted butter or margarine, and draw the leaf through your teeth, scraping off the tender meat inside the base of each leaf. Discard the rest of the tough leaf. Once all of the fleshy leaves have been removed, remove the small, thin inner leaves, exposing the fuzzy "choke." Scoop out the choke with a spoon and discard. Eat the meaty bottom portion with a fork, dipping each piece into desired sauce.

Types: There are several types of artichokes, but the *Green Globe,* with a deep green color and a round but slightly elongated shape, is the most common. Green globes are available in baby to large sizes.

Market forms: Artichokes are sold fresh, canned, and frozen. Fresh artichokes are available year-round, but early spring is the peak harvest time. Artichoke hearts and bottoms are available canned and may come marinated, packed in oil, or packed in water. Artichoke hearts also are available frozen.

Selecting: Look for compact, firm globes that are heavy for their size. (Summer and fall artichokes will be more conical with slightly flared leaves.) Artichokes should yield slightly to pressure and have large, tightly closed leaves. Avoid any with mottled or spread leaves or shriveled cones. Sometimes leaf edges darken because of chill damage. This darkening, called winter kiss, does not affect the quality of the artichoke.

Storing: Place fresh artichokes in a plastic bag and refrigerate. They are best if used within a couple of days, but will keep for up to a week. Opened, canned artichoke products can be refrigerated for up to 4 days in a storage container.

How to cook: See the Cooking Fresh Vegetables chart under *Vegetable.*

Nutrition information: One medium artichoke has about 60 calories, and ½ cup cooked artichoke hearts has about 40 calories.

To prepare an artichoke, wash, then cut off the bottom stem so the artichoke sits flat. Cut off about 1 inch from the top. Remove loose outer leaves. With kitchen shears, snip off about ½ inch from tips of remaining leaves. Brush cut surfaces with lemon juice to prevent browning.

Arugula

Ascorbic Acid Color Keeper
A granular mixture that includes vitamin C crystals (vitamin C also is called ascorbic acid) and sugar. It is used to keep peeled or cut fruits, such as apples, bananas, peaches, and pears, from darkening when exposed to air. The dry color keeper usually is diluted with water before it is used.

Q: Where do you buy ascorbic acid color keeper and how should it be stored?
A: Look for color keeper with the canning and freezing supplies in your supermarket. Store it in a cool, dry place for up to 1 year.

Asian Pear
A round fruit with thin skin and a core similar to an apple with tiny brown seeds. It also is known as apple-pear, Nashi pear, and Chinese pear. You can find about 10 varieties on the market. Skin color ranges from golden brown to pale yellow-green. The flesh is bright white, and the flavor can range from winelike to tart and rich. Asian pears have a crisp, juicy texture that is not softened by cooking and baking.

Arugula *(uh ROO gyuh luh)*
A peppery and pungent salad green with slender, deep green leaves. Arugula, also known as rocket or roquette, is similar in appearance to dandelion greens.

Use the spicy flavor of arugula to accent milder greens in salads. The yellow flowers that are sometimes still attached to arugula also are edible.

Selecting: Buy fresh, small leaves with good green color and avoid yellow, wilted, overgrown leaves (the older and larger the leaves, the more pungent the flavor).

Storing: Refrigerate arugula in a plastic bag for up to 2 days.

Preparation hints: Wash gently but thoroughly by immersing in cold water (you may have to change the water several times) till there is no trace of grit and sand. Pat dry with paper towels.

Nutrition information: One cup of fresh arugula has about 10 calories.

Asian pears

Selecting: Asian pears usually are sold ripe and ready to eat.

Storing: Because Asian pears generally are ripe when you buy them, store them in the refrigerator until ready to use.

Preparation hints: Don't wait for these fruits to soften as pears do; use them when firm and crisp. Asian pears are best eaten fresh, but they can be poached or used in pies; however, they will take longer to cook than "regular" pears.

Nutrition information: An average Asian pear has about 100 calories.

Asparagus

Asparagus
Long, slender, edible stalks with a tightly closed bud at one end. Asparagus stalks, or spears, have a mild flavor and a delicate texture.

Types: There are two basic kinds of asparagus—green and white. The green asparagus is dark colored, and the buds may be tinged with purple. Green asparagus usually is harvested when the stalks are about 8 inches long.

Creamy white asparagus spears usually are more expensive than green asparagus. They are harvested when their tips just break through the ground (it's the lack of exposure to the sun that keeps the stalks pale). White asparagus rarely is available fresh in the United States.

Market forms: Green asparagus spears or tips can be purchased fresh, frozen, and canned. Grocers' supplies of fresh green asparagus peak from April to May. White asparagus generally is available canned.

Selecting: Choose spears with good color that are crisp, straight, and firm with tightly closed buds. Asparagus with wilted, or very thin or very thick (more than ½ inch thick) stalks may be tough and stringy. If you can, select spears that are all the same size because they'll cook more evenly.

Storing: Wrap the bases of fresh asparagus spears in wet paper towels and keep them tightly sealed in a plastic bag. Refrigerate fresh asparagus for up to 4 days. Cut or break off stem ends; wash spears just before using.

A Tip from Our Kitchen
If desired, you can remove the scales on asparagus stalks. Just use a vegetable peeler when you clean the stalks.

How to cook: See the Cooking Fresh Vegetables chart under *Vegetable*.

Nutrition information: One-half cup of cooked asparagus has about 25 calories. Four medium spears have about 15 calories.

Aspic A savory gelatin mixture, usually made with meat, poultry, or fish stock, that's used to glaze chilled foods. It also refers to a molded (usually tomato-based) gelatin salad.

Au Gratin *(oh GRAT in)* A French term that refers to cooking a food in a hot oven or under the broiler to form a crisp golden crust. The food may be left plain or topped with bread crumbs or cheese to form this crust.

Au Jus *(oh ZHU)* A French term, meaning "with juice," that refers to serving roasted meat with its juices only.

Avocados

A Florida variety

Hass

Fuerte

Cocktail

Avocado A pear-shaped fruit with a large pit, green skin, and yellow-green meat when ripe. Avocados, sometimes nicknamed alligator pears, grow on trees as pears do. The interior fruit is hard like an apple when unripe, but turns to a buttery texture when ripe. An avocado has a delicate, nutty flavor.

Varieties: You may find different varieties in your produce section. Common varieties include the *Hass* and *Fuerte,* both from California. The oval-shaped Hass has a thick, pebbly, deep green skin and tastes rich. The milder-flavored Fuerte has a thin, smooth, green skin and an elongated pear shape. Other avocados include the tiny, seedless *Cocktail* avocados, more than 65 Florida varieties, and other varieties.

Selecting: Before buying avocados, think about how you'll be using them. Firm-ripe avocados are ideal for slicing and chopping; very ripe fruit is perfect for guacamole and mashing in recipes. Buy very firm avocados if you won't be using them for a few days; they'll ripen in 3 to 4 days. Don't buy bruised fruit with gouges or broken skin.

Q: When is an avocado ripe?
A: Firm-ripe avocados yield to gentle pressure. Very ripe avocados feel soft without pressing.

Storing: Keep very firm avocados at room temperature until they soften. To speed ripening, place the avocados in a brown paper bag or next to other fruit. Refrigerate ripe avocados and use them within a few days. Never freeze avocados; freezing them ruins their texture.

Preparation hints: Avocados peel easily when firm-ripe. It's easier to cut them in half, then peel the halves. For very ripe avocados being used for mashing, just scoop the pulp away from the skins.

To seed an avocado, cut lengthwise through the fruit around the seed. With your hands, twist the halves in opposite directions to separate them. Carefully tap the seed with the blade of a sharp knife so it catches in the seed. Rotate the knife to loosen the seed. Lift the knife and remove the seed.

Tips from Our Kitchen

To help keep avocados from turning brown, treat the cut surfaces with lemon juice or ascorbic acid color keeper.

When you plan to use only half an avocado, save the half that contains the pit. Wrap it tightly in plastic wrap and refrigerate. These steps slow browning.

Nutrition information: Avocados are high in fat. A California avocado weighing about 6 ounces has about 300 calories and about 30 grams of fat. However, an 11-ounce Florida avocado has about 350 calories and about 28 grams of fat.

Baba *(BOB ah)* A light-textured cake

made of yeast dough and raisins, soaked with a sugar syrup and rum, brandy, or liqueur. A baba is usually baked in a tall mold or in individual molds. When soaked with rum, it also is called "baba au rhum."

A savarin is similar to a baba, but a savarin has no raisins and is baked in a ring mold. The center may be filled with a puddinglike mixture or fruit.

Bacon Meat cut from the side or back of

a hog that is cured and sometimes smoked.

Types: Various kinds of bacon are made by using different ingredients in the curing. Sugar-cured, maple-cured, and hickory-smoked tell you that sugar, maple flavoring, and hickory wood, respectively, were used to give a distinctive aroma, color, and flavor to the bacon.

Another type of bacon, lower salt bacon, is cured with only about two-thirds of the sodium found in regular bacon.

In some parts of the country, a similar product made from beef is available. Government regulations prohibit it from being called bacon, so the generic name is breakfast beef.

Market forms: Most bacon is sold pre-sliced. You can choose thin-, regular-, and thick-sliced bacon. Bacon that is not sliced is called slab bacon.

Selecting: Good-quality bacon has evenly spaced ribbons of rosy pink meat throughout firm white fat. Too much fat in bacon causes excessive shrinkage during cooking; too little fat means tough, dry bacon.

The best bacon is cut from the center of the side of the hog. Sold as center-cut bacon, it costs a little more. The least expensive bacon is cut from the ends of the hog side. Sold as ends and pieces, these irregular slices are drier and have a heavier smoked flavor than regular bacon.

Q: What can I use when a recipe calls for crumbled bacon?

A: You can use fresh bacon, crisp-cooked, drained, and crumbled (1 slice equals about 1 tablespoon). Or, for more convenience, use cooked bacon pieces or bacon-flavored vegetable protein chips, which are sold in jars.

Storing: See the Storing Meat chart under *Meat.*

continued

Cooking Bacon

Quick to cook, bacon can be baked, panbroiled, or micro-cooked. It is done when the lean is brown and the fat is translucent and lightly browned.

● *Baking:* Place slices on a rack in a shallow baking pan. Bake, uncovered, in a 400° oven for 10 to 12 minutes.

● *Micro-cooking:* Place bacon on a microwave-safe rack or paper plate. Cover with microwave-safe paper towels. Micro-cook 4 slices on 100% power (high) for 2½ to 3½ minutes; cook 6 slices for 4 to 5 minutes.

For panbroiling directions, see the Panbroiling and Panfrying Meat chart under *Meat.*

Nutrition information: A slice of regular-sliced bacon contains about 40 calories and about 3 grams of fat.

Bagel
A nonsweet, doughnut-shaped yeast roll with a chewy texture and a shiny top. Bagels are broiled and boiled before baking. In addition to plain bagels, many flavors, such as egg, onion, garlic, and raisin, are available.

Bagel Toppings

Here are some quick toppings to spread on plain bagels.

● Mix soft-style cream cheese with dried fruit bits, nuts, and a dash ground cinnamon. Spread on split bagels.

● Spread peanut butter on split bagels and top with apple slices. Sprinkle lightly with cinnamon-sugar.

● Mix softened margarine or butter with a little shredded orange peel. Spread on toasted bagels and sprinkle lightly with ground cinnamon; broil just till topping is bubbly.

Nutrition information: One bagel (3½-inch diameter) has about 180 calories.

Baguette
(ba GET) French bread that's shaped into a long, thin loaf that can be up to 2 feet long, and typically is only a couple of inches in diameter (see also *French Bread*).

Bake
To cook food in the indirect, dry heat of an oven. The food may or may not be covered during cooking. Baking meats and poultry uncovered is called roasting.

Baked Alaska
A dessert made of cake and ice cream that is covered with a meringue mixture and browned in the oven. The meringue mixture often is mounded to resemble an igloo. Although sponge cake often is used, you can use any type of cake, from delicate yellow cake to heavy, brownielike chocolate cake.

Because eating slightly cooked eggs may be harmful due to possible bacterial contamination, you may want to avoid baked Alaska because the egg whites are not fully cooked (see Using Eggs Safely under *Eggs*).

Baking Dish
A coverless glass or ceramic utensil used for cooking in the oven. (The same utensil in metal is called a baking pan.) Baking dishes vary in size and may be square, rectangular, or round. The sides of the dish are usually about 2 inches high (see question and answer under *Baking Pan.*) Many, but not all, baking dishes are microwave-safe.

A baking dish can be substituted for a metal baking pan of the same size. However, for baked items, such as breads and cakes, the oven temperature will need to be lowered 25 degrees to prevent overbrowning of the food.

Baking Pan
A coverless metal utensil used for cooking in the oven. (The same utensil in glass or ceramic is called a baking dish.) Baking pans vary in size and may be round, square, rectangular, or a special shape, such as a heart. The sides of the pan are ¾ inch high or more. Because pans are usually made of lightweight aluminum or stainless steel, they're not suitable for micro-cooking.

Q: **How are baking pans measured?**
A: The size of a baking pan or dish is measured across the top of the container from inside edge to inside edge. The depth also is measured on the inside of the pan or dish from the bottom to the top of the rim. Sometimes the dimensions of pans or dishes vary from the standard sizes used in most recipes. Try to use the size pan or dish called for in a recipe.

If your baking pans and dishes are not standard size, you may need to make some adjustments. For example, if your baking pan is larger than the one specified, you will need to reduce the baking time. If the pan is smaller, more time is needed, and be aware that the batter may overflow.

Baking Powder
A chemical leavening agent that is a combination of baking soda, an acid, and starch. In the presence of heat or moisture, the baking soda reacts with the acid to produce carbon dioxide gas bubbles that cause a product to rise and become light and porous. The starch (usually cornstarch) prevents absorption of moisture from the air.

Double-acting baking powder produces gases twice—first during mixing and second during baking. Unless another type of baking powder is specified, current recipes use the double-acting product because it is the most common type on the market. The *single-acting* phosphate and tartrate baking powders, which release most of their gases when mixed with a liquid, are not as common.

Store the airtight tins of baking powder in a cool, dry place and replace every 6 months.

Q: **How can I determine if baking powder has lost its potency?**
A: First, check the can for an expiration date. If it's past or near the date, dissolve ½ teaspoon baking powder in ¼ cup hot water. If it doesn't foam and bubble within a few seconds, or if the reaction is weak, replace your baking powder.

Baking Soda
A chemical leavening agent that, when combined with moisture and an acidic ingredient, releases carbon dioxide gas and causes a product to rise and become light and porous. Buttermilk, soured milk, chocolate, molasses, lemon juice, and cream of tartar are some of the acid-containing foods used with baking soda in baking. Baking soda, also known as bicarbonate of soda or sodium bicarbonate, is an essential ingredient in baking powder (see also *Baking Powder*).

Store baking soda in an airtight container in a cool, dry place for about 6 months.

Q: **What are some other kitchen uses for baking soda?**
A: You can remove a buildup of coffee oils and tea stains from pots and cups by washing them in a baking soda solution. Also, you can set an opened box of soda at the back of your refrigerator to absorb odors and help prevent a transfer of flavors between foods.

Baklava
(bahk luh VAH) A rich, baked dessert made of layers of flaky phyllo dough, nuts, and a honey syrup. Traditionally, baklava is cut into diamond-shaped pieces.

Bamboo Shoot
The cone-shaped shoot from an edible bamboo plant grown in tropical Asia. Ivory-colored bamboo shoots have a slightly crisp and fibrous texture.

Market forms: Canned bamboo shoots are sold whole and sliced. Fresh bamboo shoots are found only in specialty markets in the United States.

continued

Storing: Refrigerate any unused canned shoots in a covered container with water for up to 2 weeks. Change the water daily.

Nutrition information: One-half cup of sliced, canned bamboo shoots has about 15 calories.

(See *Oriental Cooking* for identification photo.)

Banana   Typically a yellow-skinned, crescent-shaped fruit with black or greenish black tips and creamy white meat with tiny edible black seeds. Some varieties have meat with pink or orange overtones.

Varieties: These are some banana varieties you might see at the supermarket.
☐ **Cardaba:** A large, triangular banana with a yellow, waxy skin. The meat is pale salmon in color when fully ripe. It has a sweet, yet tart, flavor.
☐ **Cavendish:** The most familiar variety and the one that's most often commercially available. This yellow banana is firm but moist and creamy inside with a mild, sweet flavor.
☐ **Ladyfinger:** Also known as Mysore. This smaller-sized banana has a slightly tangy flavor and a moist creamy meat. If green, the flavor is puckery.
☐ **Manzano:** A short, chubby banana. It also is called an Apple or Finger banana. A Manzano is green and astringent when underripe. When ripe, the skin is yellow with black spots, and the meat is tart and crunchy with a strawberrylike flavor.
☐ **Red:** A short, fat, red-skinned banana that turns purplish black when ripe. The meat is sweet and creamy with pink overtones. Supplies of red bananas are limited.

Market forms: Bananas are available fresh and in several dried forms.

Selecting: Bananas continue to ripen after picking. You can choose bananas in any stage of ripeness. Green or unripe bananas need to ripen several days before using. For immediate eating, yellow banana varieties are ripe when they have a healthy yellow color with a few brown spots and, possibly, green tips. Use fully ripe bananas, which are soft and yellow but flecked with more brown, in recipes when mashed bananas are specified.

Red bananas ripen more slowly, turning to purplish red. They are soft when ripe.

Bananas

Cavendish

Red

Cardaba

Manzano

Ladyfinger

Banana Math

1 pound bananas	=	3 medium or
		4 small
	=	2 cups sliced
	=	1 cup mashed

Storing: Store bananas at room temperature until ripe. When bananas are the right color for your desired use, place them in the refrigerator until you need them. The peel turns black when the fruit is refrigerated, but the pulp stays at the desired ripeness for a few days.

Q: How do I keep bananas from turning brown in salads or pies?
A: To keep banana pieces from browning, toss them with a mixture of lemon juice and water or treat them with ascorbic acid color keeper.

A Tip from Our Kitchen

Although bananas are usually eaten fresh, they also are delicious cooked. Try broiling peeled bananas, brushing them occasionally with melted margarine or butter. Or, panfry bananas with nuts, margarine or butter, and brown sugar.

Nutrition information: One medium yellow banana contains about 105 calories.

(See *Dried Fruit* for storing hints.)

Barbecue (noun) A piece of equipment, with or without a cover, used to cook food over hot charcoal briquettes or another heat source, such as a gas or electric unit. Barbecue also refers to a food prepared in a highly seasoned sauce and to a social gathering featuring foods cooked over coals or other charcoal-like heat.

Barbecue (verb) To cook food over hot coals or other charcoal-like heat. This process also is referred to as grilling.

Direct vs. indirect grilling: Barbecued foods are cooked by either direct or indirect heat. For direct grilling, food is placed on the grill rack directly over the heat. This is a fast method for small flat foods, such as steaks, hamburgers, and chops. The food must be turned to cook both sides.

For indirect grilling, food is placed on the grill rack over a drip pan. The heat is on the sides of the drip pan, and the barbecue grill must be covered. This method is used for large foods, such as turkeys and roasts. The food does not need to be turned.

For specific directions on direct- and indirect-grilling meat, poultry, fish, and vegetables, see the charts on pages 29–32.

Building the fire: To preheat a gas or electric barbecue grill, follow the directions in your owner's manual.

To start a charcoal fire, if the grill does not have a separate rack for holding the charcoal, line the bottom of the barbecue grill's firebox with heavy-duty foil and add an inch of pea gravel or coarse grit. After using the grill about a dozen times, change the foil and wash and dry the gravel or grit bedding.

To estimate the number of charcoal briquettes needed for what you're grilling, spread them out in a single layer, extending them about an inch beyond the size of the food to be cooked. On windy or very cold days, or for foods that need a longer cooking time, include a few extra briquettes.

Pile the briquettes into a pyramid. Drizzle liquid lighter or jelly fire starter over the entire charcoal surface. Wait for a minute, then carefully ignite with a match. (*Never use gasoline or kerosene to start charcoal.*) Presoaked charcoal also is available; follow label directions for starting these coals.

If you wish to use an electric fire starter, be sure to follow the manufacturer's directions.

Allow 20 to 30 minutes for the briquettes to preheat (they'll glow and look gray with no black showing). Then, using long-handled
continued

tongs, spread the coals. For direct grilling, arrange them in a single layer about ½ inch apart. For indirect grilling, place a disposable foil pan in the center of the firebox and arrange the coals around the pan. For long cooking, add new coals every 30 minutes.

Testing Coal Temperature

To determine the temperature of the coals, carefully hold your hand, palm side down, above the coals at the level the food will be cooked. Start counting the seconds, "one thousand one, one thousand two."

If you need to withdraw your hand after 2 seconds, the coals are *hot;* after 3 seconds, they're *medium-hot;* after 4 seconds, they're *medium;* after 5 seconds, they're *medium-slow;* and after 6 seconds, they're *slow.*

For indirect grilling, *hot* coals will give *medium-hot* heat over the drip pan. *Medium-hot* coals will give *medium* heat over the pan, and so on.

Q: **What can be done if the coals aren't the right temperature when it is time to begin cooking?**

A: If the coals are too hot, you can raise the grill rack, spread the coals apart, close the air vents halfway, or remove coals.

If the coals are too cool, you can tap the ash off the coals with tongs, move the coals closer together, lower the grill rack, or open the vents to allow more air to circulate in the grill.

Q: **What causes flare-ups when barbecuing, and how can they be controlled?**

A: Flare-ups are a result of fat and meat juices dripping on the coals. Trimming the fat from meats or using lean ground meat will help prevent flare-ups.

If there is a flare-up, you can raise the grill rack, cover the grill, or space the

coals farther apart. As a last resort, remove the food from the grill and mist the fire with water from a pump-spray bottle. Then return the food to the grill.

Adding Smoke Flavor

Wood chips or chunks add a delightful smoke flavor to barbecued foods. To use them when you barbecue, first select the wood that gives the flavor you prefer. Keep in mind the flavor should blend with the flavor of the food you're cooking. Here's a list of woods and the foods with which they work best.

Hickory gives an intense, sweet flavor. It is good with beef, pork, poultry, and salmon. *Mesquite* gives a sweet flavor and is good with beef, poultry, pork, duck, and lamb. *Apple, Cherry,* and *Osage Orange* give a delicate, sweet flavor that's good with poultry and fish.

Softwoods, such as pine, should not be used because their resins discolor the food and give it a bitter taste.

Once you've decided on the type of wood chips or chunks to use, soak them in enough water to cover for at least 1 hour, then drain. (If indirect grilling, add an inch of water to the drip pan.) Sprinkle the chips or chunks on the hot coals. Add more chips or chunks every 15 to 20 minutes and more water to the drip pan as necessary.

Cleaning up: When you've finished grilling, soak the rack immediately in a sinkful of hot, sudsy water. Later, use a stiff grill brush for washing and removing stubborn spots. If your grill rack is too large to fit into the sink, remove the rack from the grill and cover both sides with wet paper towels or newspapers; let rack stand for an hour or so. Remove the wet paper and wash off the food.

Don't use abrasive cleaning products on the grill rack without checking the barbecue grill's instruction manual.

Direct-Grilling Meat

Test for the desired temperature of the coals (see tip, page 28). Place the meat on the grill rack directly over the preheated coals. Grill the meat, uncovered, for the time given or till done, turning the meat over after half of the grilling time.

Cut	Thickness (Inches)	Coal Temperature	Doneness	Direct-Grilling Time (Minutes)
Beef Flank steak	¾	Medium	Medium	12 to 14
Steak (chuck, blade, top round)	1	Medium	Rare Medium Well-done	14 to 16 18 to 20 22 to 24
	1½	Medium	Rare Medium Well-done	19 to 26 27 to 32 33 to 38
Steak (top loin, tenderloin, T-bone, porterhouse, sirloin, rib, rib eye)	1	Medium-hot	Rare Medium Well-done	8 to 12 12 to 15 16 to 20
	1½	Medium-hot	Rare Medium Well-done	14 to 18 18 to 22 24 to 28
Veal Chop	1	Medium	Medium to well-done	19 to 23
Lamb Chop	1	Medium	Rare Medium	10 to 14 14 to 16
Pork* Blade steak	½	Medium-hot	Well-done	10 to 12
Canadian-style bacon	¼	Medium-hot	Heated	3 to 5
Chop	¾	Medium-hot	Medium to well-done	12 to 14
	1¼ to 1½	Medium	Medium to well-done	30 to 40
Ham slice	1	Medium-hot	Heated	20 to 25
Miscellaneous Bratwurst, fresh		Medium-hot	Well-done	12 to 14
Frankfurters		Medium-hot	Heated	3 to 5
Ground-meat patties (beef, lamb, pork*)	¾ (4 to a pound)	Medium	Medium to well-done	14 to 18

*Pork should be cooked till the juices run clear.

Indirect-Grilling Meat

In a grill with a cover arrange *medium* coals around a drip pan, then test for *medium-slow* heat above the pan (see tip, page 28), unless chart says otherwise. Insert a meat thermometer into the meat. Place meat, fat side up, on the grill rack directly over the drip pan, not over the coals. Lower the grill hood. Grill for the time given and till meat thermometer registers desired temperature. Add more coals to maintain heat as necessary.

Cut	Weight (Pounds)	Doneness	Indirect-Grilling Time (Hours)
Beef			
Boneless rolled rump roast	4 to 6	150° to 170°	1¼ to 2½
Boneless sirloin roast	4 to 6	140° rare 160° medium 170° well-done	1¾ to 2¼ 2¼ to 2¾ 2½ to 3
Eye round roast	2 to 3	140° rare 160° medium 170° well-done	1 to 1½ 1½ to 2 1¾ to 2¼
Rib eye roast	4 to 6	140° rare 160° medium 170° well-done	1 to 1½ 1½ to 2 2 to 2½
Rib roast	4 to 6	140° rare 160° medium 170° well-done	2¼ to 2¾ 2¾ to 3¼ 3¼ to 3¾

Tenderloin roast
  Half
  Whole
(for both cuts, test for *medium-hot* heat above pan)
	
	2 to 3
	4 to 6
		
		140° rare
		140° rare
			
			¾ to 1
			1¼ to 1½

Round tip roast	3 to 5 6 to 8	140° to 170° 140° to 170°	1¼ to 2½ 2 to 3¼
Top round roast	4 to 6	140° to 170°	1 to 2
Veal			
Boneless rolled breast roast	2½ to 3½	170° well-done	1¾ to 2¼
Boneless rolled shoulder roast	3 to 5	170° well-done	2¼ to 2¾
Loin roast	3 to 5	160° to 170°	1¾ to 3
Rib roast	3 to 5	160° to 170°	1¼ to 2½
Lamb			
Boneless rolled leg roast	4 to 7	160° medium-well	2¼ to 3¾
Boneless rolled shoulder roast	2 to 3	160° medium-well	1½ to 2¼
Rib roast	1¾ to 2½	140° rare 160° medium-well	¾ to 1 1 to 1¼
Whole leg roast	5 to 7	140° rare 160° medium-well	1¾ to 2¼ 2¼ to 2½
Pork*			

Boneless top loin roast
  Single loin
  Double loin, tied
	
	2 to 4
	3 to 5
		
		160° to 170°
		160° to 170°
			
			1 to 1¼
			1¼ to 2¼

Loin back ribs, spareribs Country-style ribs (for these cuts, test for *medium* heat above the pan; brush with sauce last 15 minutes)	2 to 4 2 to 4	Well-done Well-done	1¼ to 1½ 1½ to 2

Note: If you cook beef and lamb to an internal temperature of 140° (rare), be aware that some organisms that cause food poisoning may survive at this temperature.
*Pork should be cooked till the juices run clear.

Cut	Weight (Pounds)	Doneness	Indirect-Grilling Time (Hours)
Pork* *(continued)*			
Loin blade or sirloin roast	3 to 4	170° well-done	1¾ to 2½
Loin center rib roast (backbone loosened)	3 to 5	160° to 170°	1¼ to 2½
Rib crown roast	6 to 8	160° to 170°	2 to 3½
Tenderloin (test for *medium* heat above the pan)	¾ to 1	160° to 170°	½ to ¾
Ham (fully cooked)			
Boneless half	4 to 6	140°	1¼ to 2½
Boneless portion	3 to 4	140°	1½ to 2¼
Smoked picnic	5 to 8	140°	2 to 3

*Pork should be cooked till the juices run clear.

Direct-Grilling Fish

Thaw fish or shellfish if frozen. Test for *medium-hot* coals (see tip, page 28). For fish fillets, place in a well-greased grill basket. For fish steaks and other fish and seafood, grease the grill rack. Place the fish on the rack directly over the preheated coals. Grill, uncovered, for the time given or until the fish just begins to flake easily when tested with a fork; shrimp, lobster, and scallops should look opaque. Turn fish over after half of the grilling time. Brush with melted margarine or butter, if desired.

Form of Fish	Weight/Size	Direct-Grilling Time
Fillets, steaks, or cubes	½ to 1 inch thick	4 to 6 minutes per ½-inch thickness
Dressed	½ to 1½ pounds	7 to 9 minutes per ½ pound
Lobster tails	6 ounces 8 ounces	6 to 10 minutes 12 to 15 minutes
Sea scallops for kabobs	12 to 15 per pound	5 to 8 minutes
Shrimp, peeled and deveined, for kabobs	Medium shrimp (about 20 per pound); jumbo (about 12 to 15 per pound)	6 to 8 minutes for medium; 10 to 12 minutes for jumbo

Indirect-Grilling Poultry

In a grill with a cover arrange *medium-hot* coals around a drip pan, then test for *medium* heat above the pan (see tip, page 28). Place *unstuffed* poultry, breast side up, on the grill rack directly over the drip pan, not over the coals. Lower the grill hood. Grill for the time given or till done, adding coals as necessary. (**Note:** Birds vary in size, shape, and tenderness. Use these times as general guides.)

To test for doneness, cut into the thickest part of the meat near a bone; juices should run clear and meat should not be pink. Or, grasp the end of the drumstick with a paper towel. It should move up and down and twist easily in the socket. For turkeys and larger chickens, insert a meat thermometer into the center of the inside thigh muscle, not touching bone; thermometer should register 180° to 185°. In a whole or half turkey breast, thermometer should register 170°.

Type of Bird	Weight	Indirect-Grilling Time (Hours)
Chicken, whole**	2½ to 3 pounds 3½ to 4 pounds 4½ to 5 pounds 5 to 6 pounds	1 to 1¼ 1¼ to 1¾ 1¾ to 2 2 to 2½
Cornish game hen	1 to 1½ pounds	1 to 1¼
Pheasant	2 to 3 pounds	1 to 1½
Quail	4 to 6 ounces	about ½
Squab	12 to 14 ounces	¾ to 1
Turkey, unstuffed	6 to 8 pounds 8 to 12 pounds 12 to 16 pounds	1¾ to 2¼ 2½ to 3½ 3 to 4
Turkey, boneless, whole	2½ to 3½ pounds 4 to 6 pounds	1¾ to 2¼ 2½ to 3½
Turkey breast, whole	4 to 6 pounds 6 to 8 pounds	1¾ to 2¼ 2½ to 3½

**Choose broiler-fryer or roasting chickens.

Direct-Grilling Poultry

Remove the skin from the poultry, if desired. Rinse poultry and pat dry with paper towels. Test for desired temperature of the coals (see tip, page 28). Place poultry on the grill rack, bone side up, directly over the preheated coals. (For ground turkey patties, use a grill basket.) Grill, uncovered, for the time given or till tender and no longer pink. (**Note:** White meat will cook slightly faster.) Turn poultry over after half of the grilling time. During last 10 minutes, brush often with a sauce, if desired.

Type of Bird	Weight/Size	Coal Temperature	Direct-Grilling Time
Chicken, broiler-fryer, half	1¼ to 1½ pounds	Medium	40 to 50 minutes
Chicken breast, skinned and boned	4 to 5 ounces	Medium-hot	15 to 18 minutes
Chicken breast halves, thighs, and drumsticks	2 to 2½ pounds total	Medium	35 to 45 minutes
Chicken kabobs (boneless breast, cut into 2x½-inch strips and threaded loosely onto skewers)	1 pound	Medium-hot	8 to 10 minutes
Cornish game hen half	½ to ¾ pound	Medium-hot	45 to 50 minutes
Turkey breast tenderloin steak	4 to 6 ounces	Medium	12 to 15 minutes
Turkey drumstick	½ to 1½ pounds	Medium	¾ to 1¼ hours
Turkey hindquarter	2 to 4 pounds	Medium	1¼ to 1½ hours
Turkey patties (ground raw turkey)	¾ inch thick	Medium-hot	15 to 18 minutes
Turkey thigh	1 to 1½ pounds	Medium	50 to 60 minutes

Direct-Grilling Vegetables

Before grilling, rinse, trim, cut up, and precook vegetables as directed. To precook any vegetable, in a saucepan bring a small amount of water to boiling; add desired vegetable and simmer, covered, for the time specified in the chart. Drain well. Generously brush vegetables with *olive oil, margarine, or butter* before grilling to prevent vegetables from sticking to the grill rack. Test for *medium-hot* coals (see tip, page 28). To grill, place the vegetables on the grill rack directly over the preheated coals. Lay vegetables perpendicular to wires on grill rack so vegetables don't fall into coals. Grill, uncovered, till tender and slightly charred, following the timings; turn occasionally. Watch grilling closely; don't overdo the charring.

Vegetable	Preparation	Precooking Time	Direct-Grilling Time (Minutes)
Asparagus	Snap off and discard tough bases of stems. Precook, then tie asparagus in bundles with strips of cooked green onion tops.	3 to 4 minutes	3 to 5
Fresh baby carrots	Cut off carrot tops. Wash and peel carrots.	3 to 5 minutes	3 to 5
Eggplant	Cut off top and blossom ends. Cut eggplant crosswise into 1-inch-thick slices.	Do not precook.	8
Fennel	Snip off feathery leaves. Cut off stems.	Precook whole bulbs for 10 minutes. Cut bulbs into 6 to 8 wedges.	8
Leeks	Cut off green tops; trim bulb roots, and remove 1 or 2 layers of white skin.	10 minutes or till tender. Halve lengthwise.	5
Sweet peppers	Remove stems. Quarter peppers. Remove seeds and membranes. Cut into 1-inch-wide strips.	Do not precook.	8 to 10
New potatoes	Halve potatoes.	10 minutes or till almost tender.	10 to 12
Zucchini	Wash; cut off ends. Quarter lengthwise into long strips.	Do not precook.	5 to 6

Barley   An oblong, beige cereal grain with a mild, starchy flavor and a slightly chewy texture. Barley, one of the earliest plants known to man, can be served as a breakfast cereal or added to soups and casseroles. Barley also is used to make malt, which is used in beer making.

Market forms: Pearl barley is the most popular form for cooking, but barley also comes in several other forms.
□ **Pearl:** Has the outer hull removed and has been polished or "pearled." It is sold in regular and quick-cooking forms. Pearl barley adds a nutty flavor to soups and casseroles (see also *Pearl Barley*).
□ **Scotch or Pot:** Less highly processed than pearl. Scotch barley is not readily available, but you may find it in health food stores. Scotch barley is used in soups and casseroles but requires a long period of soaking before using.
□ **Barley Grits:** Cracked, parboiled product similar to bulgur. Try grits in salads.
□ **Barley Flakes:** Similar to rolled oats but thicker and chewier. Add to cookies, breads, and homemade granola.
□ **Barley Flour:** The finely ground grain. Breads made with barley flour have a cakelike texture and a slight sweetness.

Storing: Store pearl and Scotch barley in an airtight container in a cool, dry place for up to 1 year. Other forms of barley keep for up to 9 months when stored in an airtight container in a cool, dry place.

How to cook: See the Cooking Grains chart under *Grains*.

Nutrition information: A ¾-cup serving of cooked pearl barley contains 145 calories.

Basil   *(BAYZ uhl; BAZ uhl)* An herb whose aroma and flavor range from peppery and robust to sweet and spicy. Its color can be various shades of green or purple. Basil leaves are used either fresh or dried.

Sweet basil

Purple basil

Varieties: The main variety grown, and the one most frequently used in cooking, is *Sweet* basil. Its pleasant, spicy aroma and taste blend well with most foods. Lesser known *Purple* basil makes a striking garnish for foods. *Lemon* basil has a concentrated lemon fragrance and is perfect for fish. *Cinnamon* basil has a sweet, spicy, cinnamon scent that is good in chutneys or fruit salads.

A Tip from Our Kitchen
One of the best ways to use fresh basil is in pesto, a puree that includes basil, olive oil, and Parmesan cheese (see *Pesto* for recipe). Toss it with hot pasta or dollop it on minestrone soup.

(See *Herb* for the Herb Alternative Guide and selecting, storing, preparation, cooking, nutrition, and other information.)

Bass

Bass A general name for a variety of fresh- and saltwater fish with spiny fins and rough scales. Bass are lean fish with a delicate to mild flavor.

Bass vary in size from 8 ounces to more than 100 pounds. Some of the more common types are *Channel, Largemouth, Smallmouth, Striped,* and *Black Sea* bass. The first three species live in fresh water, and the others live in salt water.

Bass is usually sold fresh or frozen as fillets or steaks. You can cook bass by baking, grilling, broiling, micro-cooking, and panfrying. One 3-ounce serving of baked sea bass has about 110 calories.

(See *Fish* for the Cooking Fish chart and selecting, storing, thawing, and other information.)

Baste To flavor, glaze, or moisten a food by brushing or spooning on a liquid during cooking. The liquid can be pan drippings, margarine, butter, broth, fruit juice, marinade, glaze, or sauce.

Q: What kinds of foods usually are basted?
A: Poultry that has the skin removed, meats, and fish are the most common foods that require basting. The basting liquid usually adds flavor while keeping these foods moist. Occasionally pastries also are basted to add flavor and create a crisp, attractive crust.

Batter A mixture usually made with flour and a liquid, such as milk or fruit juice. It also may include egg, sugar, margarine, butter, shortening, cooking oil, leavening, or flavorings. Batters can vary in consistency from thin enough to pour to thick enough to drop from a spoon. Batters are used to make a variety of items, including pancakes, waffles, popovers, muffins, and cakes.

Bavarian Cream A cold, molded dessert made by folding gelatin and whipped cream into a custard. A Bavarian cream may be flavored with fruit, liqueur, or wine.

Bay Leaf The stiff, green leaf of the evergreen bay tree that has slightly serrated edges. Dried whole bay leaves are most commonly used in cooking; however, occasionally you may find fresh leaves.

Q: How, and in what, do you use bay leaves?
A: Bay leaves give a pungent, woodsy aroma and heavy flavor to beef dishes, soups and stews, marinades, and tomato dishes.
Don't crumble bay leaves. Use them whole and always remember to remove them before serving.

(See *Herb* for selecting, storing, preparation, cooking, nutrition, and other information.)

Bay leaves

Bean

Bean   The pod or seed of any of several plants in the legume family. (For dried beans, see *Bean, Dried.*) Beans have a mild flavor and are green, yellow, or purple. They vary in shape from pencil thin to wide and flat. Most beans, such as green and wax beans, are the undeveloped pods of the bean plant and are eaten pod and all. Fresh lima beans, however, are the mature seeds of the plant.

Varieties: There are a number of fresh bean varieties from which you can choose.
□ **Chinese Long or Yard:** A slender green pod, 1 to 2 feet long.
□ **Green:** A slender green pod.
□ **Haricot Verts** *(HAR ih koh VERT):* A pencil-thin, tender, green string bean pod.
□ **Italian Green:** A wide, flat green pod.
□ **Lima:** Broad, flat, light green-white beans.
□ **Purple:** A small purple pod that turns green when cooked.
□ **Yellow Wax:** A slender yellow pod.

Market forms: Depending on the variety, beans are available fresh, frozen, and canned.

Selecting: Choose beans according to the characteristics mentioned above. When beans are bulging and leathery, they are old. Avoid bruised or scarred beans, or ones that are rusty with brown streaks or spots.

Storing: Fresh beans should be washed before you store them. Refrigerate them in airtight plastic bags for 3 to 4 days.

Green Bean Math

1 pound beans	=	4 cups whole
	=	2½ cups cooked, cut

How to cook: To cook fresh green, Italian green, purple, and yellow wax beans, see the Cooking Fresh Vegetables chart under *Vegetable.* Lima beans often are cooked from the frozen or dried state. Cook frozen limas following package directions. To cook dried

continued

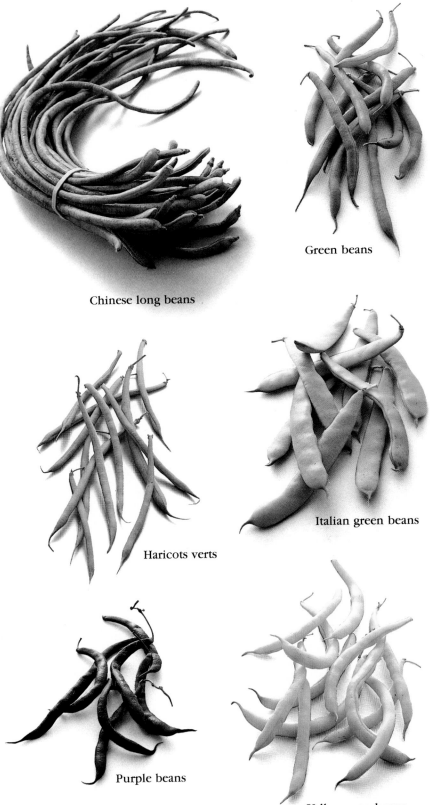

Chinese long beans

Green beans

Haricots verts

Italian green beans

Purple beans

Yellow wax beans

limas, see the Selecting and Cooking Dried Beans chart under *Bean, Dried*.

To cook Chinese long or yard beans, remove ends and cut into 1-inch pieces. Cook, covered, in a small amount of boiling salted water for 4 minutes or till tender. Or, steam beans for 4 minutes or till tender.

For haricots verts, remove ends. Simmer or steam beans for 4 to 5 minutes or till tender.

Nutrition information: Calorie counts vary, depending on the bean. A ½-cup serving of cooked green, Italian, or yellow wax beans has about 20 calories, and ½ cup of cooked frozen lima beans has 85 calories.

Bean, Dried

A dried seed of any of several plants in the legume family. Dried beans come in many sizes and in different colors, including black, brown, red, and white. They can be round, oval, or kidney-shaped.

Varieties: See the Selecting and Cooking Dried Beans chart, opposite.

Market forms: Dried beans are sold in bags at the supermarket. Certain varieties of cooked dried beans are available canned.

Selecting: Choose plump dried beans and discard any shriveled or moldy beans.

Storing: Store at room temperature up to 1 year or in your freezer indefinitely.

Cooking hints: It is best to simmer dried beans slowly to help them retain their shape.

Be aware that if you're using a recipe that calls for an acid food, such as tomatoes or vinegar, these ingredients will slow down the cooking process. Add the acid food as near the end of the cooking time as possible.

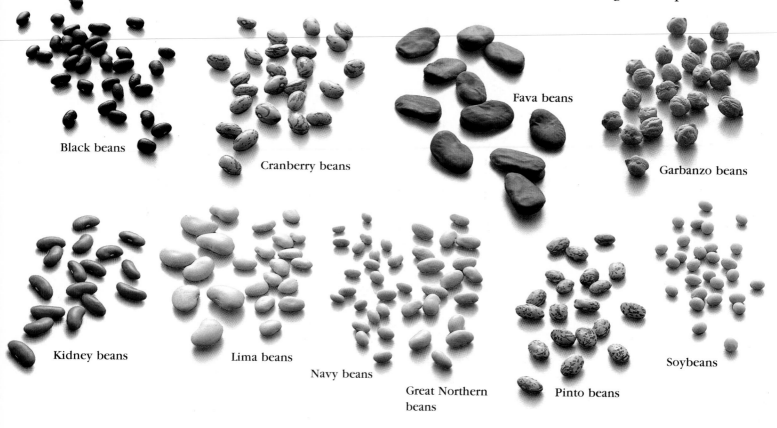

Black beans

Cranberry beans

Fava beans

Garbanzo beans

Kidney beans

Lima beans

Navy beans

Great Northern beans

Pinto beans

Soybeans

Dried Bean Math

1 pound dry beans	=	2½ cups uncooked
	=	6 to 7 cups cooked
1 15-ounce can beans	=	1¾ cups drained

How to cook: See the Selecting and Cooking Dried Beans chart, below.

Nutrition information: Dried beans contain dietary fiber. The calorie counts of dried beans vary depending on the variety, but cooked dried beans average about 120 calories per ½-cup serving.

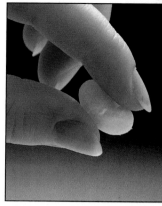

To test the doneness of dried beans, remove a bean from the saucepan. Press the bean between your thumb and finger. The beans are done when they feel soft. If there is a hard core, cook the beans a little longer, then test them again.

Selecting and Cooking Dried Beans*

Rinse beans. In a 4½-quart Dutch oven, combine 1 pound beans and 8 cups cold water. Bring to boiling; reduce heat. Simmer for 2 minutes. Remove from heat. Cover and let stand for 1 hour. (Or, omit simmering; soak beans in cold water overnight in a covered pan.) Drain and rinse. In the same pan combine beans and 8 cups fresh water. Bring to boiling; reduce heat. Cover and simmer for the time listed below or till beans are tender, stirring occasionally.

Variety	Appearance	Cooking Time	Yield
Black	Small, black, oval	1 to 1½ hours	6 cups
Black-eyed pea	Small, cream-colored, oval (one side has a black oval with a cream-colored dot in the center)	Do not presoak beans. Simmer 45 minutes to 1 hour.	7 cups
Chick-pea or Garbanzo	Medium, yellow or golden, round and irregular	1½ to 2 hours	6¼ cups
Cranberry	Small, tan-colored (with specks and streaks of burgundy), oval	1¼ to 1¾ hours	7 cups
Fava	Large, brown, flat oval	Follow these soaking directions instead of those above. Bring beans to boiling; simmer 15 to 30 minutes to soften skins. Let stand 1 hour. Drain and peel. To cook, simmer 45 to 50 minutes or till tender.	7 cups
Great Northern	Small to medium, white, kidney-shaped	1 to 1½ hours	7 cups
Lima: Baby	Small, off-white, wide oval	45 minutes to 1 hour	6½ cups
Large and butter bean	Medium, off-white, wide oval	1 to 1¼ hours	6⅛ cups
Navy or pea	Small, off-white, oval	1 to 1½ hours	7 cups
Pinto	Small, tan-colored (with brown specks), oval	1¼ to 1¾ hours	6½ cups
Red kidney	Medium to large, brownish red, kidney-shaped	1 to 1½ hours	6⅔ cups
Soybean	Small, cream-colored, oval	2 to 2½ hours	7 cups

See special cooking directions for black-eyed peas and fava beans.

Bean Sprout

Bean Sprout   The shoot of a germinated seed of the mung bean. These pale, creamy white, tender shoots are crisp and pleasant-tasting with a nutlike flavor. Both fresh and canned bean sprouts are available. Fresh sprouts also can be grown from seeds in just a few days.

Selecting: Fresh bean sprouts are available year-round. When choosing them, look for ones that are crisp and white with beans attached; avoid dark or slimy-looking sprouts.

Storing: Rinse fresh bean sprouts and pat them dry. Store them in the refrigerator in a plastic bag, with a dry paper towel placed in the bottom of the bag, for up to 3 days. Rinse the sprouts again before using.

Q: **Do the beans and roots have to be removed from fresh bean sprouts?**
A: The roots should be removed before using sprouts in recipes. Just break them off. But the beans can be left on if you like.

Nutrition information: One-half cup of fresh bean sprouts has about 15 calories.

(See *Sprout* for an identification photo.)

Bean Thread

Bean Thread   A thin, almost transparent, flavorless noodle made from ground mung beans. Used in Oriental cooking, bean threads also are called cellophane noodles and bean noodles. They can be cooked in liquid or fried in fat.

A Tip from Our Kitchen

When working with bean threads, keep in mind that they cook quickly. If you're cooking them in a liquid mixture, such as soup, cook them 30 seconds or just until they are soft. Deep-fried bean threads will puff in only a few seconds.

(See *Oriental Cooking* for an identification photo.)

Béarnaise Sauce

Béarnaise Sauce   *(bear NAYZ)*
A rich, tangy, golden sauce made with butter or margarine, egg yolks, and a seasoned vinegar mixture. It is similar to hollandaise sauce, except béarnaise uses vinegar instead of lemon juice. Béarnaise often includes shallots or green onions, tarragon, and sometimes wine. This classic French sauce is served with meat, poultry, and fish.

Beat   To make a mixture smooth and light by briskly whipping or stirring it with a spoon, whisk, rotary beater, or electric mixer.

Béchamel Sauce

Béchamel Sauce   *(BAY shuh mel)*
The French word for a basic white sauce made with butter or margarine, flour, and milk or cream.

Beef

Beef   Red meat from cattle raised for food. Beef, the most popular meat in America, is well-known for its appealing flavor and juiciness and its firm texture.

Grading: The following United States Department of Agriculture grades are the ones you are most likely to see when you shop (see also *Meat*).
☐ **Prime:** The highest grade and the most expensive. The meat is well-marbled with fat.
☐ **Choice:** The most popular grade. The meat is less marbled than prime, but it contains enough fat to be cooked with dry heat and still be tender.
☐ **Select:** Least expensive grade. The meat contains the least marbling and often is sold as a house brand or an economy meat.

Market forms: You have your choice of fresh beef or ready-to-eat, processed beef. You'll find a variety of processed beef—cured, canned, frozen, precooked, freeze-dried, vacuum-sealed, and shelf-stable—at the store.

Selecting: At its best, fresh beef has a bright red to deep red color. Look for beef cuts with a moderate amount of marbling (flecks of fat in the meat) and only a small amount of fat on the edge. Meat usually is trimmed to less than ¼ inch of fat on all surfaces. Since meat is sold by weight, paying for excess fat is a waste of money.

Beef cuts: Knowing the general location of where the various retail cuts come from will give you a clue to their tenderness. For the names and locations of those cuts, see the identification photos, pages 40 and 41.

The most tender cuts come from the lightly used muscles along the upper back of the animal (rib, short loin, and sirloin). The less tender cuts come from the heavily used muscles near the front (chuck) and the back end (round) of the animal. Expect to pay more for the more tender cuts. Less tender cuts generally are cheaper but require longer cooking.

Q: Is it OK to have beef on a low-fat diet?
A: Yes. New breeding and feeding techniques by producers as well as closer trimming of fat by the butcher have resulted in leaner beef. Calories, fat, and cholesterol have been lowered. If you are on a low-fat diet, choose one of the leaner cuts, such as the bottom round roast, top round steak or roast, eye round roast, round tip roast, T-bone steak, top loin steak, sirloin steak, and arm pot roast.

Storing: See the Storing Meat chart under *Meat.*

How to cook: Use low to moderate temperatures for cooking beef for maximum flavor, juiciness, and tenderness. Choose dry-heat cooking methods (roasting, broiling, panbroiling, frying, stir-frying, or panfrying) for tender cuts.

Proper cooking helps meat seem more tender. Use moist-heat cooking (stewing, simmering in liquid, or braising) to prepare less tender beef cuts.

For suggested cooking methods of individual cuts, see the identification photos, pages 40 and 41. For roasting, broiling, panbroiling, and panfrying directions, see the Roasting Meat, the Broiling Meat, and the Panbroiling and Panfrying Meat charts under *Meat.* For grilling directions, see the Direct-Grilling Meat and the Indirect-Grilling Meat charts under *Barbecue.*

Steak Doneness

How can you tell if steaks are cooked just right? Cut into your steaks and use the photos, right, as a guide for determining doneness.

Rare steak is pink on the edges and red in the center.

Medium steak has only a little pink in the center and brown or gray edges.

Well-done steak is completely cooked with no pink remaining.

If you prefer medium-rare doneness, cook your steaks till they look halfway between rare and medium. For medium-well doneness, cook till the steaks appear halfway between medium and well-done.

Serving hints: Proper carving makes meat easier to eat and serve. Always cut across the grain when carving. And remember—successful carving begins with a sharp knife.

Nutrition information: A 3-ounce serving of cooked, trimmed lean beef has less than 200 calories.

(See *Meat* for Using a Meat Thermometer and labeling, preparation, and other information.)

continued

Retail Beef Cuts:
The number listed with each retail cut refers to the wholesale cut marked on the drawing at right. Besides the name of the retail cut, you'll find the best ways to cook each meat cut.

Chuck 1

Rib 2

Short Loin 3

Sir-loin 4

Round 5

Short Plate & Flank 7

Foreshank & Brisket 6

Mock tender roast (1)
Braise

Boneless top blade roast (1)
Braise

Boneless shoulder pot roast (1)
Braise

Boneless arm pot roast (1)
Braise

7-bone pot roast (1)
Braise

Short ribs (1)
Braise; cook in liquid

Rib roast (2)
Roast

Rib eye roast and steak (2)
Roast—roast
Steak—broil; panbroil; panfry

Back ribs (2)
Braise; cook in liquid; roast

Top loin steak (3)
Broil; panbroil; panfry

Tenderloin roast and steak (3)
Roast—roast; broil
Steak—broil; panbroil; panfry

T-bone steak (3)
Broil; panbroil; panfry

Bottom and top sirloin steak (4)
Broil; panbroil; panfry

Sirloin steak (4)
Broil; panbroil; panfry

Top sirloin roast (4)
Roast

Round tip steak (5)
Broil; panbroil; panfry

Round steak (5)
Braise; panfry

Bottom round roast (5)
Braise; roast

Top round roast (5)
Roast

Round tip roast (5)
Roast; braise

Eye round roast (5)
Braise; roast

Corned beef brisket (6)
Braise; cook in liquid

Fresh beef brisket (6)
Braise; cook in liquid

Shank crosscut (6)
Braise; cook in liquid

Flank steak (7)
Broil; braise; panfry

Skirt steak (7)
Braise; broil; panbroil; panfry

Flank steak roll (7)
Braise; broil; panbroil; panfry

Beef Wellington
A dish featuring filet of beef that is roasted only till rare. The meat is then spread with a liver or mushroom pâté, wrapped in pastry, and baked. The dish often is served with a brown sauce.

A Tip from Our Kitchen
To simplify beef Wellington, use a sheet of packaged frozen puff pastry instead of making your own pastry.

Beer
An alcoholic beverage made from fermented malt cereals. Beer's flavor comes mostly from barley malt and hops, although some beers use rice. The alcohol content of beer brewed in the United States ranges from 3 to 6 percent. In cooking, beer adds flavor to stews, sauces, and marinades.

Types: Most beer sold in the United States is *Lager* beer, which is pale, light-bodied, and mellow-tasting. *Light* beer is a lager beer with fewer calories and usually less alcohol. *Ale* has a sharper flavor and more body than lager. Its color ranges from pale gold to amber. *Stout* and *Porter* beers are dark, heavy beers with the strong, sweet flavor of hops.

Beet
A deep red, bulb-shaped root vegetable, topped with graceful, deep green leaves. Beets have a sweet-savory flavor and often are regarded as two vegetables in one because the leaves are as tasty as the roots.

Market forms: Fresh beets are available year-round but are most plentiful from March through July. Canned beets come whole, diced, sliced, and in julienne strips. Jars of pickled beets also are available.

continued

Beets

How to cook: See Beets and Greens on the Cooking Fresh Vegetables chart under *Vegetable.*

Nutrition information: Cooked, sliced beets have about 25 calories per ½ cup. A ½-cup serving of cooked beet greens has about 20 calories.

Beignet *(ben YAY)* The French name for fritters of various types made from a rich yeast dough, cream puff paste, or batter, and deep-fat fried. Beignets sometimes are filled with sweet or savory fillings.

Belgian Endive A small, cone-shaped salad green with 5- to 6-inch-long, slender leaves that are tightly packed. The leaves are creamy white with pale yellow tips. Belgian endive also is known as French endive or witloof chicory. The slightly bitter flavor of Belgian endive complements mild lettuces when mixed in salads. The crunchy leaves make edible containers for all kinds of hors d'oeuvres.

Selecting: Look for well-shaped, firm, small to medium beets with a healthy color and smooth skins. Avoid very large beets, as they may be tough, pithy, and less sweet. Leaves should be deep green and fresh-looking.

Storing: Trim the beet greens, leaving an inch or two of stem; do not cut the long thin root. Store unwashed beets in an open plastic bag or a plastic bag with holes in it. The beets will last for up to 1 week in the refrigerator. Wash beet greens in cold water; pat dry. Place the beet greens in a plastic bag lined with a paper towel, and store in the refrigerator for up to 3 days.

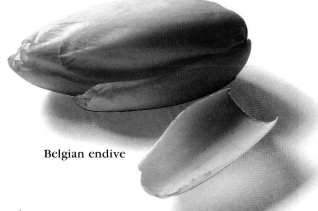

Belgian endive

Selecting: Look for tightly packed heads that are firm and unblemished. The leaves should be creamy white blending to pale yellow at the tips.

Storing: Refrigerate Belgian endive in a plastic bag for up to 3 days.

Preparation hints: To prepare Belgian endive, cut away the bitter core with a knife. Leave whole to cook as a vegetable, or separate into leaves to use raw.

Nutrition information: Belgian endive has about 15 calories per cup.

Berry

Generally a small, plump, rounded fruit that comes in many varieties and colors. Berries generally are soft, juicy, and highly perishable, and their flavors range from sweet to tart.

Varieties: The most popular varieties of berries are listed in the Selecting Berries chart, below. Only a few of the berry varieties are commonly available in supermarkets. Many of the other berries are locally grown and may be purchased at roadside stands and farmer's markets.

Selecting: Look for berries with healthy color for the particular variety. If picking your own, select berries that separate easily from their stems. Avoid bruised or moldy fruit.

Storing: Refrigerate berries in a single layer, loosely covered. Heaping berries in a bowl or container will crush the delicate fruit. Use most berries within a day or two.

Berries can be frozen by arranging washed berries, with stems removed, on a baking sheet. Place in freezer until solid; transfer them to plastic freezer containers or bags, leaving ½-inch headspace. Return to freezer.

Q: Why do berries sink when added to batters?

A: Berries, like chocolate chips or nuts, sink because of their weight. However, the thicker the batter they're in, the less likely they are to sink. Add berries as the last ingredient to help prevent them from being crushed.

Selecting Berries

Berry varieties differ in texture, skin color, and sweetness. How berries are used depends on their sweetness. Naturally sweet berries, such as strawberries and blueberries, can be eaten raw, often without sweetening. Tart and sour berries, such as cranberries and gooseberries, usually are served sweetened with sugar and cooked.

Type	Color	Qualities	Flavor	Calories per ½ cup
Blackberry*	Purplish black to black	Soft, juicy	Sweet, tangy	37
Blueberry*	Purplish blue	Plump, firm	Mildly sweet	41
Boysenberry*	Purplish black	Soft	Sweet, tangy	33
Cranberry*	Glossy red	Plump, firm	Tart	23
Currant*	Red, white, or black	Firm (small berries best)	Tart, tangy	31
Elderberry	Deep purple to black	Soft, juicy	Sweet	53
Gooseberry*	Pale green	Crisp	Tart	34
Huckleberry	Blue or black	Plump, firm	Mildly sweet	45
Lingonberry	Dark red	Firm	Very tart	33
Loganberry	Purplish red	Soft	Tart	40
Mulberry	Bluish purple, red, reddish black, or nearly white	Soft	Mildly sweet to slightly sour	31
Raspberry*	Red, golden, or black	Soft	Mildly sweet	30
Strawberry*	Bright red	Soft	Mildly sweet	23

See individual entries for additional information.

Betty A baked dessert made with a sweetened fruit filling and soft bread cubes and usually served warm. Some of the bread cubes are stirred into the fruit and some are buttered and sprinkled on top before baking.

A Tip from Our Kitchen

To make bread cubes easily, start with frozen, sliced bread. Use a serrated knife to cut the bread into ½-inch cubes.

Beverage Any of a wide variety of drinkable liquids that can be hot or cold, carbonated or noncarbonated, and alcoholic or nonalcoholic.

Soda Fountain Favorites

Although treats from the soda fountain have been with us for many years, it is easy to confuse a shake with a malt or a float with a soda. These descriptions point out the differences.
- **Shake:** A frothy, blended mixture of milk, flavored syrup, and often ice cream.
- **Malted milk:** Similar to a shake, except malted milk powder is added, making it slightly thicker.
- **Float:** A fizzy beverage made by mixing a fruit syrup or other flavored syrup with a carbonated beverage and floating scoops of ice cream on top. Sometimes a plain carbonated beverage is used without flavoring.
- **Ice-cream soda:** A creamy, yet fizzy, beverage made by mixing a flavoring, such as syrup or fruit juice, with ice cream and adding carbonated water.
- **Egg cream:** A foamy beverage made by blending milk, carbonated water, and flavored syrup. Despite its name, egg cream has no egg in it.

Bias-Slice To slice a food—often a vegetable or a partially frozen piece of meat—crosswise into diagonal pieces.

To bias-slice meat, hold a sharp knife or cleaver at a 45-degree angle to the meat and cut it into thin diagonal slices.

Bind To thicken or hold a mixture together. Various items may be used as binders. For example, eggs and bread crumbs can be used to help hold a meat loaf together, and mayonnaise can be used to bind a salad.

Biscuit A small, light, flaky bread, made from a soft dough, that's generally leavened with baking powder or baking soda. Biscuits should be fairly uniform in shape and should double in height during baking. The top crust is crisp-tender and golden brown, with lighter sides. The crumb is creamy white and slightly moist, and should peel off in layers.

Types: Traditional biscuits are rolled out and cut into rounds with a straight-sided biscuit cutter. A quicker kind that doesn't require kneading, rolling, or cutting is drop biscuits. Drop biscuits have a higher proportion of liquid to dry ingredients, so the mixture is a very thick batter rather than a soft dough. The biscuits are dropped by tablespoonfuls onto a baking sheet.

Storing: Wrap leftover biscuits in foil or place them in a plastic bag. Store the biscuits at room temperature for 2 to 3 days. To reheat before serving, wrap them in foil and heat in a 300° oven for 10 to 12 minutes.
To freeze biscuits, wrap them in heavy foil and freeze up to 3 months. To reheat, place the frozen, wrapped biscuits in a 300° oven and heat for 20 to 25 minutes.

continued

Garden Biscuits
(see recipe, page 46)

Q: Can I cut biscuits without a biscuit cutter?

A: Yes, roll the dough into a square or rectangle. Then, using a sharp knife dipped in flour, cut the dough into squares, rectangles, or triangles. Be careful to avoid flattening the dough after it is rolled out, or the biscuits will be uneven after baking. If you want round biscuits, cut them out with a straight-sided glass.

Biscuit-Making Tips

- Mix the fat with the flour just till coarse crumbs form. Overmixing produces mealy biscuits, not flaky ones. If margarine or butter is the fat called for, make sure it is well-chilled so it will be easy to cut into the flour mixture.
- Don't overknead the dough. For most recipes, folding and pressing the dough gently for 10 to 12 strokes are enough.
- Cut out as many biscuits as possible from a single rolling of dough. Too many rerollings of the dough causes biscuits to be tough. The extra flour needed for rerolling also causes biscuits to be dry.
- If you like biscuits with soft sides, arrange the biscuits close together on the baking sheet. For crusty sides, place the biscuits about 1 inch apart.

Convenience products: Commercially prepared biscuit mix is available. This mix also is handy for making coffee cakes, pancakes, and other quick breads. Prepackaged refrigerated biscuits also are on the market and come in various types.

Q: What's the doneness test for biscuits?

A: A biscuit is done when both the top and bottom crusts are golden brown. To check the bottom crust, use a metal spatula to lift the biscuit up slightly.

Biscuits

  2 **cups all-purpose flour**
  1 **tablespoon baking powder**
  2 **teaspoons sugar**
  ½ **teaspoon cream of tartar**
  ¼ **teaspoon salt**
  ½ **cup shortening, margarine, *or* butter**
  ⅔ **cup milk**

■ In a bowl stir together flour, baking powder, sugar, cream of tartar, and salt. Cut in shortening, margarine, or butter till mixture resembles coarse crumbs. Make a well in the center; add milk all at once. Stir just till dough clings together.

■ On a lightly floured surface, knead dough gently for 10 to 12 strokes. Roll or pat dough to ½-inch thickness. Cut with a 2½-inch biscuit cutter, dipping cutter into flour between cuts. Transfer biscuits to a baking sheet. Bake in a 450° oven for 10 to 12 minutes or till golden. Serve warm. Makes 10.

Nutrition information per serving: 195 calories, 3 g protein, 21 g carbohydrate, 11 g fat (3 g saturated), 1 mg cholesterol, 159 mg sodium, 59 mg potassium.

Buttermilk Biscuits: Prepare Biscuits as above, *except* stir ¼ teaspoon *baking soda* into flour mixture and substitute ¾ cup *buttermilk* for the milk.

Nutrition information per serving: 194 calories, 3 g protein, 21 g carbohydrate, 11 g fat (3 g saturated), 1 mg cholesterol, 191 mg sodium, 61 mg potassium.

Garden Biscuits: Prepare Biscuits as above, *except* add 2 tablespoons finely shredded *carrot,* 1 tablespoon finely snipped *parsley,* and 1 tablespoon finely chopped *green onion* to flour mixture with the milk.

Nutrition information per serving: 196 calories, 3 g protein, 21 g carbohydrate, 11 g fat (3 g saturated), 1 mg cholesterol, 160 mg sodium, 67 mg potassium.

Sour Cream Biscuits: Prepare Biscuits as above, *except* reduce milk to *¼ cup* and add ½ cup dairy *sour cream* to the flour mixture with the milk.

Nutrition information per serving: 214 calories, 3 g protein, 21 g carbohydrate, 13 g fat (4 g saturated), 6 mg cholesterol, 160 mg sodium, 59 mg potassium.

Drop Biscuits: Prepare Biscuits as in recipe, opposite, *except* increase milk to *1 cup. Do not knead, roll, or cut dough.* Drop dough from a tablespoon onto a greased baking sheet. Bake as opposite. Makes 10 to 12.

Nutrition information per serving: 199 calories, 3 g protein, 21 g carbohydrate, 11 g fat (3 g saturated), 2 mg cholesterol, 163 mg sodium, 71 mg potassium.

Bismarck A yeast doughnut, either round or pillow-shaped, that's filled with jelly or pudding. Bismarcks often are coated with sugar or frosted with icing.

Bisque *(BISK)* A rich, thick, smooth soup that usually is made with shellfish, such as shrimp or lobster, and cream. Bisque also can be made with poultry or vegetables.

Bitters An aromatic, alcoholic liquid with a bitter taste that is used in small amounts as a flavoring, especially in alcoholic drinks. It is made from a mixture of roots, barks, herbs, leaves, and alcohol.

Blackberry A medium to large, oblong berry that grows on brambles or prickly shrubs. Blackberries have a soft texture and juicy interior and range in color from purplish black to black. Blackberries are larger than raspberries and taste sweet and tangy when ripe.

Blackberries

Varieties: There are many varieties of blackberries, but only a few are marketed commercially. The shiny, purplish black *Olallie Berry* is a blackberry hybrid that is large and slender with a sweet flavor. The purplish black *Marionberry* is a rich, sweet-tasting, medium-size berry with a very soft texture. Other popular varieties include *Evergreen* and *Cherokee* blackberries.

Market forms: Fresh blackberries are plentiful in some parts of this country in the summer. But the most commonly available forms are canned and frozen. Blackberry juice products, jams, and jellies also are available.

(See *Berry* for the Selecting Berries chart, including calories, and selecting and storing information.)

Black Bottom Pie A single-crust pie with a two-layer filling. The dark bottom layer of filling (from which the pie gets it name) is similar to a rich chocolate pudding, and the light top layer is similar to a rum-flavored chiffon pie filling. The crust usually is made from pastry.

(See *Pie* for Pie-Making Hints and storing information.)

Blackened Fish Fish of any kind prepared by a popular Cajun cooking method. The technique involves cooking seasoned fish fillets over high heat in a heavy skillet until the fish is charred or blackened.

A Tip from Our Kitchen
Watch out for the smoke! A great deal of smoke is given off when you blacken fish, so a good exhaust fan over the range is essential. Or, cook the fish outdoors, placing the skillet directly on top of hot coals in your grill.

Black-Eyed Pea A small, oval, cream-colored pea with a black oval "eye" that has a cream-colored dot in the center. Black-eyed peas, also known as cowpeas, have a mealy texture and earthy flavor.

Black-Eyed peas

Selecting: Dried black-eyed peas are available in plastic bags and are sold in bulk. Look for whole, unbroken peas. Black-eyed peas also are available canned and frozen.

Storing: Store dried black-eyed peas in an airtight container in a cool, dry place for up to 1 year.

How to cook: Because you cook black-eyed peas as you would beans, see the Selecting and Cooking Dried Beans chart under *Bean, Dried.*

Nutrition information: A ½-cup serving of cooked, frozen black-eyed peas has about 110 calories, and ½ cup cooked dried peas has about 100 calories.

Blanch To partially cook fruits, vegetables, or nuts in boiling water or steam. The technique is an important step in preparing fruits and vegetables for freezing. Blanching also is used to loosen the skins from foods, such as tomatoes, peaches, and almonds.

A Tip from Our Kitchen
When blanching foods in boiling water, begin timing as soon as the food is plunged into the water. Don't wait for the water to return to boiling, or the food may be overcooked. Cool the blanched food quickly by plunging it into ice water.

Blancmange *(bluh MAHNGE)* A sweet, molded pudding flavored with almonds. Blancmange typically is white and smooth and is served with a sauce or fruit.

Bland A term used to describe food that is unseasoned or lacking in flavor.

Blend To combine two or more ingredients until they are smooth and uniform in texture, flavor, and color. This may be done by hand with a spoon or other similar utensil or with an appliance, such as an electric mixer or blender.

Blintze A dessert made of thin pancakes rolled around a cheese, jam, or fruit filling. The rolled blintze is cooked in margarine or butter and served warm with sour cream or applesauce.

Blueberries

Blueberry
A tiny purplish blue berry that is rounded in shape with a tiny star-shaped cap. Blueberries are firm, plump, mild, and sweet.

Market forms: Fresh blueberries usually are available during summer and very early fall. When fresh berries are not available, look for canned or frozen ones and fruit drinks, jellies, and jams made with blueberries.

Storing: For general storage information, see *Berry.* If properly refrigerated, blueberries will last from 10 to 14 days.

Q: What can be done about blueberries that "bleed" when they are added to a batter?

A: To minimize the problem, use fresh blueberries when possible because they will not bleed unless their skins are broken. When using canned blueberries, drain and carefully blot them with paper towels. When using frozen blueberries, add them to a batter while they're still frozen. No matter what form you use, make them the last ingredient you add and gently stir them into the batter.

(See *Berry* for the Selecting Berries chart, including calories, and selecting information.)

Blue Cheese
A sharp, tangy, and pungent-flavored cheese with a semisoft consistency and crumbly texture.

Blue cheese is the common name for several varieties of blue-veined cheeses. The blue veins are caused by the growth of molds that are incorporated during manufacturing. Aging also is an important part of the manufacturing process. The longer a blue cheese ages, the more pronounced its flavor will be.

Blue cheese

Types: Each type of blue cheese has its own flavor and texture.

☐ **Danish:** Varies from mild to tangy and sharp. This cow's-milk cheese, also called Danablu, can be soft, creamy, and spreadable, or firm and crumbly. Danish blue cheese is heavily laced with greenish blue veins and may have a yellowish white edible crust.

☐ **Domestic:** Has a semisoft body ranging from spreadable to crumbly. It is made from cow's milk and has a piquant flavor that varies from tangy to very sharp.

Gorgonzola cheese

☐ **Gorgonzola** *(gor gun ZOH luh):* Softer, creamier, and less pungent than most other blue cheeses. Gorgonzola is made from cow's milk and is streaked with greenish veins.

☐ **Roquefort** *(ROHK fert):* A very rich cheese with a pungent and salty flavor. Made from unskimmed sheep's milk and aged in rustic limestone caves, Roquefort is exclusively produced within the city of Roquefort, France.

Roquefort cheese

☐ **Stilton:** Milder and less salty than Roquefort and more crumbly than Gorgonzola. Stilton, made from cow's milk and cream, is produced only in England.

Market forms: In addition to wheels, wedges, and blocks of blue cheese, a crumbled form also is sold.

(See *Cheese* for the Selecting Cheese chart and selecting, storing, serving, nutrition, and other information.)

Boil To cook food in liquid at a temperature that causes bubbles to form in the liquid and rise in a steady pattern, breaking on the surface.

Q: What is a rolling boil?
A: When a liquid is boiling so vigorously that the bubbles cannot be stirred down, the liquid is at a full rolling boil. The term often is used in making jelly.

Bok Choy A variety of Chinese cabbage with long, white, celerylike stalks and large, deep green leaves. Crisp like celery, bok choy has a sweet and mild cabbagelike flavor. The leaves and stalks can be used either raw or cooked. Bok choy is as versatile as celery and is popular in Oriental dishes.

Q: What are some other names for bok choy?
A: Bok choy sometimes is called pak choi, celery mustard, Chinese mustard, Chinese chard cabbage, and Chinese white cabbage.

Bok choy

Selecting: Choose bok choy that has crisp leaves and firm stalks. Avoid stalks with wilted, mushy leaves.

Storing: Store bok choy in a plastic bag in the refrigerator. Use within a few days.

Preparation hints: Trim the base and pull stalks apart. Discard any ragged or discolored leaves. Slice or chop the stalks and shred the leaves.

Nutrition information: One-half cup of cooked, shredded bok choy has about 10 calories.

Bombe *(bahm)* A layered, frozen dessert made in a melon-shaped or round mold. The dessert is formed by first spreading a layer of ice cream, sherbet, whipped cream, custard, or mousse around the inside of the mold. This layer is frozen till firm, then a second layer of a different flavor or ingredient is added. The layers are repeated until the mold is filled.

A Tip from Our Kitchen
To unmold a frozen bombe, wrap a warm, damp towel around the mold for a few minutes to loosen it. Cover the bombe with a serving plate and invert the two together. Remove the mold.

Bordelaise Sauce (bor duhl AYZE)
A dark, flavorful sauce made with wine (usually red wine), brown stock, shallots or green onions, and herbs. Traditional recipes often include poached bone marrow. This classic French sauce usually is served with broiled or grilled meats.

Borscht (borsh)
An Eastern European beet soup that is especially popular in Russia and Poland. Borscht can contain meat or meat broth, or it can be made only with vegetables, such as cabbage, leeks, onions, and beet tops. Borscht can be served hot or cold. This magenta-colored soup usually is served with a dollop of sour cream.

Boston Brown Bread
A dark, sweet, steamed quick bread made with rye and wheat flour, cornmeal, molasses, and raisins. Boston brown bread traditionally is cylindrical in shape, but can be baked in a loaf pan or mold. Commercially prepared Boston brown bread also is available.

Boston Brown Bread

- ½ cup whole wheat flour
- ½ cup rye flour
- ½ cup yellow cornmeal
- ½ teaspoon baking soda
- ¼ teaspoon salt
- 1 cup buttermilk *or* sour milk*
- ⅓ cup molasses
- ½ cup raisins

■ In a mixing bowl stir together whole wheat flour, rye flour, cornmeal, baking soda, and salt. In another mixing bowl combine buttermilk or sour milk and molasses. Add to flour mixture, stirring till well-blended. Stir in raisins. Pour batter into a well-greased 7½x3½x2-inch loaf pan. Cover tightly with greased foil, greased side down.

■ Place pan on a rack set in a Dutch oven. Pour hot water into the Dutch oven around the loaf pan till water covers 1 inch of the pan. Bring to boiling; reduce heat. Cover; simmer for 2 to 2¼ hours or till wooden toothpick inserted near the center comes out clean. Add additional boiling water as needed to keep the water around the pan at a depth of 1 inch. Remove pan from the Dutch oven; let stand 10 minutes. Remove bread from pan. Serve warm. Makes 1 loaf (15 servings).

Note: To make sour milk, use 1 tablespoon *lemon juice* or *vinegar* plus enough whole milk to make 1 cup. Stir together and let stand 5 minutes before using.

Nutrition information per serving: 81 calories, 2 g protein, 18 g carbohydrate, 0 g fat, 1 mg cholesterol, 82 mg sodium, 166 mg potassium.

Boston Cream Pie
A dessert made from a single layer of cake that is split horizontally. A thick, creamy filling is spread between the cake layers, and a topping of chocolate glaze or powdered sugar is added.

Bouillabaisse (boo yuh BASE)
A flavorful soup or stew that is traditionally made with a variety of fish and shellfish. Usually, bouillabaisse also contains tomato, garlic, herbs, wine or cognac, and saffron. Bouillabaisse means "fish soup" in French.

Bouillon (BOOL yon)
A seasoned clear broth usually made from the water in which beef has been cooked. Bouillon also can be made using either chicken, vegetables, or fish. Often it is used as a base for soups and sauces. Bouillon is essentially the same thing as broth.

The term often refers to commercially prepared dehydrated products called instant bouillon. Instant bouillon is available in jars as granules or cubes.

To make bouquet garni seasonings easy to remove, use string to tie them together in a 100-percent cotton cheesecloth bag.

Bouquet Garni *(bow KAY gar NEE)*

A bundle of aromatic herbs simmered in soups and stews, stocks, and poaching liquids. In traditional French cooking, a bouquet garni includes thyme, parsley, and bay leaf.

Boysenberry A large, aromatic,

purplish black berry with a sweet and tangy blackberry flavor and soft texture. This berry is a hybrid of a blackberry, a loganberry, and a raspberry. Boysenberries are at their juicy best in pies and jams.

Market forms: Look for fresh boysenberries in the midsummer months. Boysenberries are used in some fruit drinks, jellies, and jams.

(See *Berry* for the Selecting Berries chart, including calories, and selecting and storing information.)

such as breads, breakfast cereals, cookies, muffins, meat loaves, and stuffings.

Q: What does bran do in the diet?
A: Bran is a good source of fiber, although the amount of fiber that bran provides depends upon the grain source.

Types: Here's a rundown on the kinds of bran you're most likely to find at the supermarket and health food store. (For information on soluble and insoluble fiber, see *Fiber.*)

☐ **Corn:** Corn bran provides the highest amount of fiber of these four brans. Most of the fiber in corn bran is insoluble.

☐ **Oat:** Oat bran is high in soluble fiber.

☐ **Rice:** Rice bran contains a fair amount of soluble fiber and a high proportion of insoluble fiber.

☐ **Wheat:** For years, wheat bran was known simply as "bran." Wheat bran contains mainly insoluble fiber.

Boysenberries

Braise To cook food slowly in a small

amount of liquid in a tightly covered pan on the range top or in the oven. This moist-heat method of cooking works well for less tender cuts of meat.

Bran The high-fiber, coarse outer layer of

a grain kernel. The kernels of all grains contain a bran layer, which protects the developing seed inside.

Because of an increased awareness of the advantages of dietary fiber, Americans have come to appreciate bran in a variety of foods,

Tips from Our Kitchen

Here are some tasty ideas for adding bran to your baked foods. (*If using corn bran,* add 2 extra tablespoons of liquid for each ¼ cup of bran.)

● For muffins, substitute ¾ cup of bran for ¼ cup flour in a basic 12-muffin recipe.

● For whole grain breads, substitute 1 cup bran for ¼ cup whole grain flour.

● For meat loaf, substitute ¼ cup of bran for ¼ cup fine dry bread crumbs in a 1-pound meat loaf recipe.

● For oven-fried chicken coating, mix bran with seasonings using 2 tablespoons per two pieces of chicken.

Storing: Store bran in an airtight container in a cool, dry place for up to 1 month. Refrigerate bran for up to 3 months, or freeze it for up to 1 year.

Q: **What type of oat bran is best for cooking and baking?**

A: Be sure to buy 100-percent oat bran for use in recipes. This oat bran looks like coarse powder or flour. It is available in supermarkets and health food stores, usually with the ready-to-cook cereals. Don't confuse oat bran with oat bran flake cereals, which are similar in appearance to wheat and corn flakes.

Nutrition information: All grains have bran, but brans vary in composition. Here's how 100-gram portions (about 3½ ounces) of the brans stack up:
Corn bran—224 calories, 1 g fat, 85 g fiber
Oat bran—246 calories, 7 g fat, 16 g fiber
Rice bran—316 calories, 21 g fat, 22 to 34 g fiber
Wheat bran—216 calories, 4 g fat, 42 g fiber.

Brandied A term that refers to any food soaked in or flavored with brandy.

Brazil Nut The seed of a wild South American tree. The tree grows 3- to 4-pound pods. Inside each pod are numerous three-sided Brazil nuts, encased in very hard, rough, dark brown shells. The large ivory-colored Brazil nut has a thin brown skin and an oily, rich flavor.

Brazil nuts

Storing: Keep unshelled Brazil nuts in a cool, dry place up to 6 months. Refrigerate shelled nuts in an airtight container and use within 3 months; freeze up to 6 months.

Q: **Since Brazil nuts are so hard, what's the best way to crack them?**

A: In a saucepan cover Brazil nuts with cold water. Bring the water to boiling and boil for 3 minutes; drain. Cover the nuts with cold water again and let stand 1 minute; drain. Use a hand-held nutcracker or hammer to open the shells.

(See *Nut* for the Selecting Nuts chart and selecting, nutrition, and other information.)

Bread Any of various baked products made from flour or meal, liquid, salt, and a leavening agent. Bread comes in a variety of shapes and sizes.

The world of bread goes far beyond a loaf of purchased "sandwich bread." It includes everything from a loaf of heavy, dark, coarse rye to a delicate croissant and a moist, golden brown muffin. Breads vary in shape, too—from the familiar loaf to braids and breads molded in special fluted pans.

Nutrition information: One 1-ounce slice of commercial white bread has about 75 calories. A slightly smaller slice of 100-percent whole wheat bread has about 60 calories and contains more fiber than white bread.

(See also *Bread, Quick* and *Bread, Yeast.*)

Bread Crumbs Bread in tiny pieces used as an ingredient for coatings, stuffings, and other mixtures. There are two kinds of bread crumbs. Soft bread crumbs are made from fresh or slightly stale bread that is torn into small pieces. Fine dry bread crumbs are made from very dry bread that is finely crushed. Fine dry crumbs are available commercially in plain and seasoned forms. (To make evenly shaped, soft bread cubes, see tip under *Betty.*)

continued

Tips from Our Kitchen

Here are some handy hints for making bread crumbs.

● To make soft bread crumbs, use a blender or food processor to break the bread into fluffy crumbs. One slice of bread will yield about ¾ cup crumbs.

● When making fine dry bread crumbs, minimize the mess by placing the dried bread in a plastic bag and crushing it with a rolling pin. One slice of bread will yield about ¼ cup fine dry crumbs.

Breadfruit   An edible, oval or round fruit with an average weight of about 1 pound. Its intriguing rind is yellow-green and covered with small rounded spines. The creamy white meat sometimes has seeds. Breadfruit resembles a potato in flavor and usually is boiled to be eaten as a vegetable.

Jackfruit, weighing up to 100 pounds, is a larger cousin of breadfruit. Both breadfruit and jackfruit are staples in South Pacific and Malaysian cuisines.

Selecting: Select firm breadfruit with a bright yellow-green peel to use in potato-type recipes. For recipes calling for a ripe breadfruit, choose fruit with a brown-speckled peel.

Storing: Store wrapped breadfruit in the refrigerator once it is ripe. Try to use the ripened fruit within 2 days.

Nutrition information: A ½-cup serving of breadfruit has about 110 calories.

Breading   A coating of crumbs used on such foods as meat, poultry, fish, and vegetables. Breading made with soft or fine dry bread crumbs is the most common type, but other ingredients, such as crushed crackers, crushed cereal, flour, and cornmeal, also are used.

The term also refers to the process of coating a food with crumbs, usually after dipping the food in egg or milk. The breading adds flavor and texture to the food and helps keep it moist during frying or baking.

A Tip from Our Kitchen

For less mess, place the breading mixture in a plastic bag. Add the food that's been dipped in egg or milk, a few pieces at a time, shaking to coat the pieces thoroughly.

Bread Pudding   A baked dessert made from dried bread cubes and a mixture of eggs, milk, and sugar. Dried fruit, nuts, or chocolate pieces also may be added. The mixture is baked until set and served warm.

Bread Pudding

    4 beaten eggs
    2 cups milk
    ⅓ cup sugar
    ½ teaspoon ground cinnamon
    ½ teaspoon vanilla
    3 cups (4 slices) dry bread cubes
    ⅓ cup raisins *or* other snipped dried
        fruit
    ¼ cup coconut (optional)

■ In a mixing bowl beat together eggs, milk, sugar, cinnamon, and vanilla. Place dry bread cubes in an 8x1½-inch round baking dish. Sprinkle raisins or dried fruit and coconut, if desired, over bread. Pour egg mixture over all. Bake in a 325° oven for 35 to 40 minutes or till a knife inserted near the center comes out clean. Cool slightly. Makes 6 servings.

Nutrition information per serving: 216 calories, 9 g protein, 34 g carbohydrate, 6 g fat (2 g saturated), 149 mg cholesterol, 282 mg sodium, 261 mg potassium.

Bread, Quick The name given to a baked bread or loaf that uses baking powder, baking soda, steam, or air instead of yeast to leaven the dough or batter.

Types: Here are the most common quick breads.

☐ **Biscuit:** A small, light, flaky bread made from a soft dough, with a golden brown, crisp-tender crust. The moist crumb is creamy white and should peel off in flaky layers.

☐ **Coffee Cake:** A rich, sweet bread made from a batter or dough, with a texture more like cake than bread.

☐ **Corn Bread:** A bread made from a batter containing both cornmeal and flour.

☐ **Loaf:** A bread made from a batter and typically baked in a loaf-shaped pan. Common quick bread loaf flavors include zucchini, pumpkin, banana, and nut.

☐ **Muffin:** A small, individual, savory or sweet bread made from a batter. Muffins have a rounded top and a breadlike crumb.

☐ **Pancake:** A thin, flat, tender bread made from a batter and cooked in rounds on a griddle or in a skillet.

☐ **Popover:** A big, puffy, steam-raised bread made from an egg-rich batter.

☐ **Scone:** A plain or sweet, biscuitlike quick bread made from a soft dough. Scones are richer than biscuits because the dough contains eggs.

☐ **Waffle:** A bread with a honeycomb appearance that's made from a batter and cooked in a special appliance called a waffle baker or waffle iron.

Preparation hints: There are two methods used to mix quick breads. For most batters, the dry ingredients are combined, then the liquid ingredients are added all at once. These are quickly and lightly stirred in just till the dry ingredients are moistened. Overbeating the batter can cause coarseness in texture and other undesirable characteristics.

For most doughs, the solid fat is cut into the dry ingredients till the mixture resembles coarse crumbs. The liquid ingredients are added all at once and stirred just till the dough clings together. The dough for biscuits and scones is then kneaded for a few strokes.

Q: **Why do recipes for quick bread loaves say to store overnight before slicing?**

A: Storing the bread overnight serves two functions: It allows the flavors to mellow, and it makes the loaves easier to slice. After baking, let the loaves cool completely on a wire rack, then wrap them in foil or plastic wrap and store at room temperature overnight.

Storing: For storage information on *Biscuits, Muffins,* and *Popovers,* see individual entries.

Place quick bread loaves in a plastic bag; store at room temperature for up to 3 days. To freeze, wrap breads tightly in heavy foil or put them in freezer bags and freeze for up to 3 months.

Tips for Quick Bread Loaves

● After adding the liquid mixture to the flour mixture, stir the ingredients just till they are moistened. If you stir out all the lumps, your loaves will have peaks, tunnels, and a tough texture.

● Avoid getting rims around the edges of quick bread loaves by greasing the baking pans on the bottom and only ½ inch up the sides.

● Check the bread 10 to 15 minutes before the baking time is completed. Cover with foil if it is browning too fast.

● Quick breads are done when a wooden toothpick inserted near the center of the loaf comes out clean.

● Don't consider your quick bread loaf a failure if it has a crack on top. This is characteristic of quick breads.

Bread, Yeast

Bread, Yeast A baked product that uses yeast as the leavening agent. The yeast produces tiny bubbles of carbon dioxide gas that, along with the steam produced by the liquid ingredients during baking, causes dough to expand and rise.

Types: There are two basic types of yeast bread—kneaded and batter. In kneaded breads, the kneading develops the gluten (an elastic protein in flour) that makes the dough stronger and more elastic for better volume. Kneading also produces a finer grain or texture in breads (see also *Knead*). Loaves of frozen bread dough, in white, whole wheat, and rye, are available as well as frozen sweet bread dough.

Batter breads are not kneaded. The first addition of flour is beaten in with a mixer to help develop the gluten; additional flour is stirred in by hand. Because less flour is used, the dough is stickier than kneaded dough. The dough rises in the baking pan, then it is baked.

Q: Does a batter bread look different than a kneaded bread?

A: Batter bread has a more open texture than kneaded bread, and the top probably will have a rough, pebbly appearance and not a smooth crust.

Baking hints: Once your bread has baked for the time specified in the recipe and has turned golden brown, test it for doneness by tapping the top of it with your finger. A hollow sound means the bread is done.

Remove baked bread from the loaf pan or baking sheet as soon as you take it out of the oven so it doesn't get soggy on the bottom. Place it on a wire rack to cool.

Use a serrated knife and a sawing motion to slice bread without squashing it.

Storing: Once the yeast bread is completely cool, wrap it in foil or plastic wrap, or place it in a plastic bag. Store in a cool, dry place for up to 3 days.

To freeze yeast bread, place the completely cooled, unfrosted bread in a freezer bag or container, or tightly wrap it in heavy foil. Freeze for up to 3 months. Thaw the wrapped bread at room temperature for 1 hour (or, wrap in foil and heat in a 300° oven about 20 minutes). Frost sweet breads, if desired.

Q: Where's the best place to let yeast dough rise?

A: Choose a draft-free area with the optimum temperature of 80° to 85°. Don't raise dough in a hot area because excessive heat kills the yeast. Too much cold, on the other hand, stunts the yeast's growth. One good way to raise yeast dough is to place the bowl of dough in an unheated oven, then set a large pan of hot water under the bowl on the oven's lower rack.

Choosing Flour for Breads

The amount of protein in the flour you use can affect how your yeast breads turn out. The more protein in the flour, the more structure-building ability the flour will have, which means the bread will rise higher. All-purpose flours are milled from different classes of wheat— hard wheat, which is high in protein, and soft wheat, which is low in protein. You'll find all-purpose flours that contain anywhere from 9 to 13 grams of protein per cup. When you're baking yeast bread, choose an all-purpose flour that has at least 11 grams of protein per cup. If the all-purpose flour you have has less than 11 grams of protein per cup, save it for quick breads and other non-yeast-bread baking.

Check the nutrition information panel on the bag of flour to find out the protein content. Be sure to look at the part of the panel where the information is listed in grams, not percentages.

Microwave-Proofing Dough

With the help of your microwave oven, you may be able to shorten the time it takes to proof (raise) yeast breads.

● To make sure your oven will work for proofing, use the following test.

Place 2 tablespoons cold stick margarine or butter (do not use corn oil margarine) in a microwave-safe custard cup in the center of your oven. Micro-cook, uncovered, on 10% power (low) for 4 minutes. If the margarine doesn't completely melt, your microwave can proof yeast dough. If, however, the margarine does completely melt, your microwave puts out too much power at this low setting and will kill the yeast before the bread has a chance to rise. In this case, you'll have to let your yeast breads rise conventionally.

● If your oven passed the test, here's how to proceed. While kneading your dough, place 3 cups water in a 4-cup microwave-safe measure. Cook on 100% power (high) for 6½ to 8½ minutes or till boiling. Move measure to back of oven. Place kneaded dough in a greased microwave-safe bowl, turning it over once. Cover with waxed paper and place in microwave oven with the hot water. Heat dough and water on 10% power (low) for 13 to 15 minutes or till dough has almost doubled. Punch dough down; shape as directed.

Then place shaped dough in microwave-safe 8x4x2- or 9x5x3-inch loaf dishes. Return to microwave oven with hot water. Cover with waxed paper. Heat on low for 6 to 8 minutes or till nearly doubled. (For breads or rolls that are shaped on baking sheets or in muffin cups, you'll have to do the second proofing step conventionally.)

Note: For rich breads (those with eggs and a higher proportion of sugar), proofing times will be longer. Allow 15 to 20 minutes for the first proofing and 10 to 14 minutes for the second.

Bread-Making Hints

● When a recipe gives a range for the amount of flour, start by adding the lower amount. Knead in as much of the remaining flour as you can without going over the maximum amount given. Too much flour causes breads to be dry and have a heavy, compact texture.

● Let dough rise till it is nearly doubled in size. But don't let loaves rise all the way to the top of the pan because the dough needs room to rise as it bakes. Dough that rises too much may fall while it is baking or may have holes throughout the inside.

● Always check the expiration date on the yeast package before using it. Dough made with yeast that is inactive because it is old will not rise.

● If you live more than 3,000 feet above sea level, expect your dough to rise faster. See *High-Altitude Cooking* for more information.

Brew To prepare a beverage such as tea or coffee by steeping or boiling. Or, to prepare beer or other alcoholic beverages by steeping or boiling and fermenting. The word also can refer to the beverage made by brewing.

Brick Cheese

A semisoft cheese made from cow's milk. It is mild and sweet when young, but develops a pungency and slight tanginess as it ages. The brick cheese in your dairy case most likely will be young with a smooth, supple texture and creamy white color. It also is sold in an aged form.

Brick cheese

(See *Cheese* for the Selecting Cheese chart and selecting, storing, serving, nutrition, and other information.)

To knead, fold the dough over and push it down with the heel of your hand, as shown. Give the dough a quarter turn, then fold it over and push down again.

Dough should rise till it has doubled in size. You can tell when it is ready to shape by pressing two fingers about ½ inch into the dough. If the indentations remain, the dough is ready.

Punch down the dough by pushing your fist into the center, as shown. Then pull the edges of the dough to the center, turn the dough over, and place it on a lightly floured surface.

Brie cheese

Brie Cheese   *(bree)* A rich cheese with a mild, yet robust, flavor. The snowy white, edible rind encases the pale yellow cheese.

Brie is made from cow's milk and is surface-ripened, which means surface mold ages the cheese from the outside in.

Selecting: Young Brie is creamy and mild-tasting and holds a cut edge when sliced. Ripe Brie is runny when cut and tastes stronger.

When buying Brie, press down on the cheese with your finger to determine its age. If the cheese bounces back, the Brie is young. If your finger leaves an indentation in the cheese, then the Brie is ripe. Another sign of ripe Brie is a slightly bulging package. Avoid buying Brie that smells like ammonia because it may be too ripe for eating, or perhaps this delicate cheese has been mishandled.

(See *Cheese* for the Selecting Cheese chart and storing, serving, nutrition, and other information.)

Brine   A heavily salted water mixture used to pickle or cure vegetables, meats, fish, and seafood.

Brioche   *(BREE oshe)* A soft, slightly sweet yeast roll, rich in butter and eggs. The brioche dough is molded and baked in the shape of fat buns with topknots. Brioche dough also can be baked in one large, fluted, specially designed brioche pan.

Tips from Our Kitchen
● Brioche dough tends to be a little sticky. Chilling it in the refrigerator before shaping makes it easier to work with. Or, you can omit the first rising time and just refrigerate the dough for up to 24 hours.
● Individual brioche pans are round and fluted. If you don't have them, substitute 2½-inch muffin pans.

Brittle   A hard, crunchy candy made by cooking sugar, corn syrup, water, margarine or butter, and nuts (usually peanuts) to a very high temperature. The hot candy mixture is poured out onto large, buttered pans and stretched into thin sheets.

Q: **Why do brittle recipes call for baking soda?**

A: It's the baking soda that makes the brittle porous and tender. Because it's so important that the soda is evenly distributed in the candy mixture and doesn't land in one clump when it is added, some recipes call for sifting the baking soda first.

(See *Candy* for Candy-Making Tips and equipment, storing, and other information.)

Mixed Nut Brittle

    2 cups sugar
    1 cup light corn syrup
    ½ cup water
    ½ cup margarine *or* butter
    1 cup raw peanuts
    1 cup raw cashews, coarsely chopped
    ¾ cup slivered almonds
    1½ teaspoons baking soda, sifted

■ Butter 2 large baking sheets; set baking sheets aside. Butter the sides of a heavy 3-quart saucepan. In the saucepan combine sugar, corn syrup, water, and the ½ cup margarine or butter. Cook over medium-high heat to boiling, stirring constantly with a wooden spoon to dissolve sugar. This should take about 5 minutes. Clip candy thermometer to side of the pan.

■ Cook over medium-low heat, stirring occasionally, till thermometer registers 275°, soft-crack stage (30 to 35 minutes). Mixture should boil at a moderate, steady rate over entire surface. Stir in nuts (this will cause the thermometer temperature to drop some). Continue cooking over medium-low heat, stirring frequently, till thermometer registers 295°, hard-crack stage (15 to 20 minutes). Remove pan from heat; remove thermometer.

■ Quickly sprinkle sifted baking soda over mixture, stirring constantly. Immediately pour mixture onto prepared baking sheets. Stretch candy by using 2 forks to lift and pull candy as it cools. Pull gently to avoid tearing. Cool completely. Break into pieces. Store tightly covered. Makes 2¼ pounds (72 servings).

Nutrition information per serving: 76 calories, 1 g protein, 10 g carbohydrate, 4 g fat (1 g saturated), 0 mg cholesterol, 35 mg sodium, 37 mg potassium.

Broccoli

Broccoli
A vegetable with rigid, thick, green stalks, topped with deep green or purplish green, tightly packed heads of tiny buds. Both the stalks and buds may be eaten either raw or cooked.

Market forms: Fresh broccoli is available year-round. You also can find frozen broccoli spears and cuts as well as chopped broccoli and broccoli frozen in sauces. Frozen broccoli also is available as part of mixed vegetable combinations.

Selecting: Look for firm stalks with deep green or purplish green heads that are tightly packed. Heads that are light green in color or that have tiny yellow flowers are past their prime and should be avoided.

Storing: Keep broccoli in a plastic bag in the refrigerator for up to 4 days. Broccoli also can be blanched and frozen for up to 1 year.

A Tip from Our Kitchen
When broccoli stems seem tough, use a sharp knife to peel away the tough outer portion of the stems to make the broccoli more tender.

How to cook: See the Cooking Fresh Vegetables chart under *Vegetable.*

Nutrition information: One cup of chopped raw broccoli has about 25 calories, and ½ cup of cooked chopped broccoli has about 20 calories.

Broccoli Raab *(rob)* A vegetable with 6- to 9-inch, dark green, leafy stalks and clusters of small buds that look somewhat like those on broccoli. Broccoli raab, which is a member of the cabbage family, also is called broccoli di rape, rape, or rapini. Both the stems and leaves have a somewhat sharp and bitter flavor.

Broccoli Raab

Selecting: Broccoli raab is sold in loose bunches. Look for small, sturdy stems. They should have dark green, fresh-looking leaves.

Storing: Keep broccoli raab in a plastic bag in the refrigerator for up to 4 days.

How to cook: Boil, steam, or stir-fry broccoli raab till it is crisp-tender. It often is served with butter and garlic.

Nutrition information: Broccoli raab has about 20 calories per ½ cup.

Broil To cook food a measured distance below direct, dry heat. Most ovens have a broiler section that's used to cook meats, poultry, and fish, brown or toast other foods, and melt cheese.

Nutrition hints: When broiling, less fat in the meat means less chance of flare-ups—and fewer calories for you. So, trim excess fat from meats and remove the skin from poultry before broiling. For a low-calorie flavor bonus, baste meats, poultry, and fish with calorie-reduced salad dressing instead of higher calorie sauces or glazes.

Position the broiler pan and its rack far enough away from the heat source so the surface of the food, not the rack, is the specified distance from the heat. Use a ruler to measure this distance.

A Tip from Our Kitchen
Preheat the broiler a few minutes before cooking, but don't preheat the pan and rack because that can cause them to warp and may cause foods to stick.

Broth A thin, clear liquid in which meat, poultry, fish, or a vegetable has been cooked. Broth can be used in soups and sauces. Commercially prepared broths are available in cans in regular and concentrated strengths. Broth is essentially the same thing as bouillon.

Brown To cook food in a skillet, broiler, or oven in order to develop a rich, desirable color on the outside, add flavor and aroma, and help seal in natural juices. For more color and flavor, foods such as meat and poultry often are coated with flour and seasonings before browning.

Brown Bread Any leavened bread made with a dark flour, such as whole wheat or rye, along with all-purpose flour.

Brownie A rich bar cookie that's usually chocolate in flavor, but also can be vanilla, butterscotch, or a combination of flavors. Brownie textures range from heavy and chewy to light and cakelike. Nuts, chocolate pieces, or small candies sometimes are added. Brownies can be served plain or frosted. (For a brownie recipe, see page 62.)

(See *Cookie* for Cookie-Making Hints and preparation, baking, storing, and other information.)

Rocky Road Brownies
(see recipe, page 62)

Rocky Road Brownies

  1 6-ounce package (1 cup) semisweet
        chocolate pieces
  1 cup all-purpose flour
  ½ teaspoon baking powder
  ⅓ cup margarine *or* butter
  ¾ cup sugar
  2 eggs
  1 teaspoon vanilla
  ¼ cup chopped nuts
  ½ cup tiny marshmallows

■ In a small, heavy saucepan heat and stir ½ *cup* of the chocolate pieces over low heat till melted. Remove from heat and cool slightly. Meanwhile, mix flour and baking powder.
■ In a small mixer bowl beat margarine or butter till softened. Add sugar and beat till well combined. Add eggs and vanilla and beat well. Beat in melted chocolate. Add flour mixture and beat till well-mixed. Spread in a greased 9x9x2-inch baking pan.
■ Bake in a 350° oven for 20 minutes. Remove from oven; sprinkle remaining chocolate pieces, nuts, and marshmallows atop baked layer. Bake 5 to 10 minutes more or till marshmallows are golden. Cool. Cut into bars or squares. Makes 16.

Nutrition information per serving: 180 calories, 2 g protein, 23 g carbohydrate, 10 g fat (3 g saturated), 27 mg cholesterol, 64 mg sodium, 63 mg potassium.

Brown Sauce
A basic cooking sauce made with margarine or butter, flour, and brown stock or beef broth (see also *Stock*). The sauce is made by browning the flour in melted margarine or butter and adding the brown stock. The mixture is brought to a boil, then simmered several hours (simmering time varies depending on the amount of sauce). Brown sauce is served with meat and poultry and is a base for other sauces.

Q: What is espagnole sauce?
A: Cooks disagree about what goes into an espagnole *(es pun YOLE)* sauce. Some say it is just another name for a basic brown sauce. Others say it is the basic brown sauce with the addition of tomatoes or tomato paste.

Brunch
An informal, late-morning meal featuring an assortment of foods, some that are typically served at breakfast and others normally served at lunch.

Nutrition hints: Brunches often include high-calorie, high-cholesterol, and high-fat foods including pancakes, omelets, quiches, and sausages. To trim calories, cholesterol, and fat, choose lean meats, such as ham or Canadian bacon, instead of sausage or regular bacon. Also, opt for reduced-fat or low-fat cheeses instead of regular cheeses. To make the meal even more healthful, serve whole grain breads or muffins and fresh fruit.

Brussels Sprout
A vegetable that looks like a tiny, compact cabbage with overlapping leaves. Brussels sprouts have a cabbagelike flavor.

Market forms: Brussels sprouts are available fresh and frozen. Fresh brussels sprouts are plentiful between October and April. Frozen brussels sprouts are available plain, in sauces, and as part of vegetable mixtures.

Selecting: Look for firm, compact brussels sprouts. Avoid large, old-looking sprouts, because their flavor will be bitter. The

Brussels sprouts

smaller, vivid green sprouts will be the sweetest. Avoid sprouts that have any odor.

Storing: Refrigerate brussels sprouts, unwashed, in a plastic bag for up to 2 days.

How to cook: See the Cooking Fresh Vegetables chart under *Vegetable.*

Nutrition information: A ½-cup serving of cooked brussels sprouts has about 30 calories.

Buckwheat   A plant that produces
triangular seeds. Though used in much the same way as a grain, technically buckwheat is a fruit.

Market forms: Look for these products at supermarkets and health food stores.
☐ **Buckwheat Flour:** Made from grinding buckwheat groats. There are two grades of flour. Light buckwheat flour is ground with very little hull; it has a delicate flavor and is light in color. Dark-grade buckwheat flour is ground with the hull and has a strong flavor. Buckwheat flour is used to make pancakes, breads, and other baked goods.
☐ **Buckwheat Grits:** Mild-flavored, coarsely ground, unroasted buckwheat kernels. Serve buckwheat grits as a cooked cereal.
☐ **Buckwheat Groats:** Whole, unpolished, unroasted buckwheat kernels. When buckwheat groats are roasted, they are sold as "kasha," an important ingredient in Russian cooking. Kasha has a nuttier, fuller flavor than buckwheat groats. Use in casseroles and as a cooked cereal.

Storing: Store buckwheat in an airtight container in a cool, dry place for up to 3 months. Refrigerate for up to 6 months or freeze for up to 1 year.

How to cook: See the Cooking Grains chart under *Grains.* Or, for a pilaf-type product, in a large skillet, stir ¾ cup *buckwheat groats (kasha)* with 1 beaten *egg.* Stir over medium heat for 4 minutes or till kernels are separate and dry. Add 2 cups hot *water* and ½

teaspoon *instant chicken bouillon granules.* Simmer, covered, over low heat for 10 to 15 minutes or till the grain is tender; stir once. Makes 4 servings (130 calories per serving).

Nutrition information: A ½-cup serving of cooked roasted buckwheat groats (kasha) contains about 90 calories.

Bulgur   *(BULL ger)* A parched, cracked
wheat product. To make it, the whole wheat kernel is soaked, cooked, and dried. Then 5 percent of the bran is removed from the dried, hard wheat kernels, and the remaining kernel is cracked into small pieces. Bulgur is dark tan in color with a delicate nutty flavor.

   Bulgur absorbs twice its volume in water when it is soaked. Because bulgur is precooked, it cooks quickly or needs only a brief soaking before using.

Storing: Store bulgur in an airtight container in a cool, dry place for up to 6 months. Or, it may be stored indefinitely in the freezer.

How to cook: See the Cooking Grains chart under *Grains.*

Nutrition information: A ¾-cup serving of cooked bulgur contains about 130 calories.

Bun   An individual bread, usually made
with yeast, that is shaped by hand or baked in a muffin pan. It may be sweet or plain. The name also is given to the soft rolls eaten with hamburgers and frankfurters.

Burgoo   A thick, hearty soup or stew
made of chicken, beef, bacon, vegetables, and seasonings. It is very popular in the South.

   This term also is used to refer to a cooked mixture of hardtack and molasses as well as to thin oatmeal porridge.

Burnt Sugar   See *Caramelized Sugar.*

Burrito

Burrito   A Mexican or Tex-Mex specialty that consists of a large flour tortilla wrapped around a filling of seasoned meat, refried beans, and/or cheese. Lettuce, tomato, and avocado also may be included. The sides and edges of the tortilla are folded, forming a bundle, which is then baked. If the bundle is fried in hot fat, it is called a chimichanga.

Bean and Cheese Burritos

    6 8-inch flour tortillas
    1 cup chopped onion
    1 tablespoon cooking oil
    1 16-ounce can refried beans
    1 cup shredded cheddar cheese
       Shredded lettuce
       Salsa

■ Stack the tortillas and wrap in foil. Heat in a 350° oven for 10 minutes to soften. In a skillet cook onion in cooking oil till tender. Add refried beans. Cook and stir till the mixture is heated through.
■ Spoon about *¼ cup* of the bean mixture onto *each* tortilla just below center. Divide cheese among the tortillas. Fold edge nearest filling up and over just till bean mixture is covered. Fold in 2 sides just till they meet; roll up. Place on a baking sheet.
■ Bake in a 350° oven about 10 minutes or till heated through. Serve with lettuce and salsa. Makes 3 servings.

Nutrition information per serving: 590 calories, 25 g protein, 73 g carbohydrate, 24 g fat (10 g saturated), 40 mg cholesterol, 1,241 mg sodium, 838 mg potassium.

Butter

Butter   A dairy product made by churning cream skimmed from milk into a solid fat. In the United States, butter must be at least 80 percent milk fat.

Q: Can regular butter be substituted for unsalted butter?
A: Salted and unsalted butter can be used interchangeably. If you use salted butter in baked products calling for unsalted butter, reduce the amount of salt that's called for in the recipe.

Types: There are several butter products available at the supermarket.
☐ **Butter:** Made with fresh cream that is lightly salted. It is often labeled *sweet cream butter.*
☐ **Unsalted:** Made with fresh cream without added salt. Unsalted butter usually is identified as such on the label. Unsalted butter also is known as *sweet butter.*
☐ **Whipped:** Whipped with air or other harmless gases to make it spreadable. It comes salted and unsalted. Whipped butter cannot be substituted for regular butter in recipes.
☐ **Butter-Margarine Blend:** A product that combines butter and margarine into one spread. In a recipe, the stick form can be substituted for regular butter or margarine.

Market forms: Butter and unsalted butter are most often available in 1-pound blocks or in ¼-pound sticks. Whipped butter comes in ½-pound tubs.

Q: What does clarified butter mean?
A: Also known as drawn butter, clarified butter is butter with the milk solids removed. The clear yellow fat that remains doesn't burn easily, so it's often used for quickly browning meats. Perhaps the best use for clarified butter is as a dip for lobster, crab, and artichokes.

To clarify butter, melt it over low heat in a heavy saucepan without stirring. When the butter is completely melted, you will see a clear, oily layer on top of a milky layer. Slowly pour the clear liquid into a dish, leaving the milky layer in the pan. The clear liquid is the clarified butter. Either discard the milky liquid or add it to cream sauces and soups. Clarified butter will keep several weeks in the refrigerator, longer in the freezer.

Storing: Because butter tends to absorb other food's flavors and odors, it is usually sold in protective wrapping. Leave butter in its original wrapping till you're ready to use it. Once opened, store leftovers tightly wrapped in plastic wrap in the refrigerator. Keep salted butter for up to 3 weeks and unsalted butter for up to 2 weeks (salted butter lasts a little longer because the salt acts as a preservative). You also can store salted and unsalted butter in the freezer, tightly wrapped in freezer wrap, for 6 to 9 months.

Butter Math

4 sticks	= 1 pound	= 2 cups
2 sticks	= ½ pound	= 1 cup
1 stick	= ¼ pound	= ½ cup
⅔ stick	= 2⅔ ounces	= ⅓ cup
½ stick	= 2 ounces	= ¼ cup
¼ stick	= 1 ounce	= 2 tablespoons
1 pat	= 1 teaspoon	

Nutrition information: One tablespoon of butter has about 100 calories. One tablespoon of whipped butter has about 75 calories. Butter is high in saturated fat and cholesterol.

Butterfat   A term used to describe the fat content of milk and cream. It is more correctly called milk fat.

Butterfly   To cut a boneless piece of meat or seafood, such as a pork chop or shrimp, almost in half so you can form a butterfly shape. Because this technique exposes twice the surface area of the food, the food cooks more quickly.

Buttermilk   A commercial dairy product made by adding special bacterial cultures to milk (usually skim milk). Salt also is usually added. Buttermilk is a smooth and fairly thick liquid, with a distinctive, slightly sour, tangy flavor. It is used as a beverage and can be used as an ingredient in baking. Dry buttermilk powder also is available.

A Tip from Our Kitchen

If you don't happen to have buttermilk on hand when you need it for baking, or if you run across a recipe that calls for sour milk, here's an easy substitute.

For each cup of buttermilk or sour milk, place 1 tablespoon lemon juice or vinegar in a glass measuring cup. Add enough milk to make 1 cup total liquid; stir. Let the mixture stand 5 minutes before using.

Nutrition information: One cup of buttermilk has about 100 calories and 2 grams of fat.

(See *Milk* for storing and other information.)

Butterscotch   A sweet, mellow flavor produced by cooking margarine or butter and brown sugar together.

The term also refers to a clear, hard candy made with butter and brown sugar.

C

Cream Puffs
(see recipe, page 130)

Chili con Carne
(see recipe, page 99)

Corn Sticks
(see recipe, page 121)

Cabbage

Cabbage A vegetable with a compact head of tightly wrapped leaves. Cabbages range in color from almost white to green or red, and their shapes vary from elongated to round. Cabbage is a versatile vegetable that's crisp and mild when served fresh, and tender and slightly sweet when cooked.

Varieties: Here are the most common types of cabbage available.
☐ **Green:** Round with very tightly packed green leaves. Its flavor is delicate.
☐ **Red:** Round with very tightly packed reddish purple leaves. Red cabbage tastes very similar to green cabbage.
☐ **Chinese:** A name given to several varieties of Oriental cabbages that resemble a cross between celery and lettuce. These cabbages include both Bok Choy and Napa (or Nappa) cabbage (see also *Bok Choy* and *Chinese Cabbage*).
☐ **Savoy:** Round with green, ruffled, deeply ridged, veined leaves. Savoy is milder and less crisp than green cabbage.

Market forms: Supermarkets sell heads of fresh cabbage as well as shredded green cabbage. Sometimes other shredded vegetables are added to the cabbage for use in making coleslaw.

Selecting: Feel the weight of a cabbage in the palm of your hand. It should be firm and heavy for its size. Look for healthy, bright leaves free from withering or brown spots.

Green or Red Cabbage Math

1 small head	=	about 1 pound
1 medium head	=	about 2 pounds
	=	about 12 cups shredded

Storing: Refrigerate cabbage, wrapped tightly in a plastic bag, for up to a week.

How to cook: See the Cooking Fresh Vegetables chart under *Vegetable*.

A Tip from Our Kitchen

Overcooking cabbage results in a pungent odor and strong flavor, so it is best to cook the cabbage only till it is crisp-tender.

Nutrition information: One-half cup of cooked cabbage or 1 cup of raw shredded cabbage has about 15 to 20 calories.

Cabbages

Napa

Red

Green

Savoy

Cactus leaves

Cactus Leaf
The fleshy, oval leaf of the prickly pear cactus. Cactus leaves, sometimes called nopales (*no PAH lays*), are green and have tiny, sharp thorns. The thorns usually are removed before the leaves are sold. Cooked cactus leaves are soft and crunchy and have the slipperiness of okra. They have a flavor reminiscent of green beans with an avocadolike aftertaste.

Q: How are cactus leaves used in cooking?
A: They're sometimes diced or cut into strips, cooked in water until crisp-tender, and added to foods, such as scrambled eggs.

Selecting: Fresh cactus leaves are available year-round. Choose small to medium, thin leaves with no wrinkles. Canned cactus leaves also are sold in some areas.

Storing: Refrigerate cactus leaves in a plastic bag for up to 1 week.

Preparation hints: Carefully remove the base of the thorns, plus any thorns and blemishes. Then rinse the cactus leaves thoroughly before using.

Caesar Salad
A tossed salad combining romaine lettuce, croutons, and Parmesan cheese with garlic, olive oil, vinegar and/or lemon juice, and sometimes anchovies. Traditionally, a coddled egg is added.

Because eating slightly cooked eggs, such as coddled eggs, may be harmful due to possible bacterial contamination, the following recipe using cooked eggs has been developed (see Using Eggs Safely under *Eggs*).

Today's Caesar Salad

1 **egg**
⅓ **cup chicken broth**
3 **anchovy fillets**
3 **tablespoons olive oil**
2 **tablespoons lemon juice**
   Few dashes white wine
      Worcestershire sauce
1 **clove garlic, halved**
1 **large head romaine, torn into**
      bite-size pieces (about 10 cups)
½ **cup garlic croutons**
¼ **cup grated Parmesan cheese**
   Whole black pepper

■ For dressing, in blender container combine egg, chicken broth, anchovy fillets, olive oil, lemon juice, and Worcestershire sauce. Cover; process till smooth. In a small saucepan, cook and stir dressing over low heat for 8 to 10 minutes or till thickened. *Do not boil.* Transfer to a bowl; cool slightly. Cover surface with plastic wrap; chill.
■ Before serving, rub the inside of a wooden bowl with the cut side of garlic; discard garlic. Add romaine, croutons, and Parmesan cheese. Pour dressing over all; toss gently. Transfer to individual salad plates; grind pepper atop each serving. Makes 6 servings.

Nutrition information per serving: 122 calories, 5 g protein, 5 g carbohydrate, 9 g fat (2 g saturated), 40 mg cholesterol, 275 mg sodium, 336 mg potassium.

Caffeine

A colorless, somewhat bitter substance found in coffee, tea, chocolate, and cola. Caffeine, a natural stimulant, is actually a drug rather than a food. Because of the popularity of coffee and cola, caffeine is among the most widely consumed drugs in this country. For many people, caffeine provides a welcome pick-me-up in the morning, but for some it contributes to insomnia and has other side effects.

Levels of caffeine vary from cup to cup and from product to product. In general, a 6-ounce cup of coffee contains anywhere from 64 to 150 mg of caffeine; a 5-ounce cup of tea or a 12-ounce can of cola contains 40 mg caffeine; and a 5-ounce serving of hot cocoa contains 4 mg caffeine.

Cajun Cooking

The cuisine of French-speaking south Louisiana, not to be confused with the more aristocratic Creole cooking of New Orleans. It features simple, one-pot, country fare with southern, French, Italian, Spanish, African, and Indian influences. The word Cajun is an alteration of the word Acadian, the name for the early French-Canadian settlers.

Cuisine highlights: Onion, bell pepper, red pepper, bottled hot pepper sauce, and filé powder are vital Cajun ingredients (see also *Filé Powder*). Many Cajun dishes owe their color and rich flavor to a roux, a browned fat and flour mixture (see also *Roux*). Cajun recipes often feature fish and seafood, game, chicken, pork, crayfish, and sausage. Rice is served at almost every meal.

Specialties: Some celebrated Cajun dishes include étouffée (recipe follows), boudin (rice and liver sausage), rice dressing, fricassee, andouille (smoked pork sausage), and gumbo (see also *Fricassee* and *Gumbo*).

Q: Are all Cajun dishes hot and spicy?
A: No. Well seasoned is a more accurate description of Cajun cooking. Imitations of Cajun cooking might lead you to believe that the recipes are supposed to set the taste buds ablaze. Even though some dishes are spicier than others and some cooks have a heavy hand when measuring the red pepper, true Cajun cooking is not that hot.

Crayfish Étouffée

- 1 **pound fresh** *or* **frozen peeled crayfish tails** *or* **shrimp**
- ¼ **cup cooking oil, margarine,** *or* **butter**
- 2 **large onions, finely chopped (1½ cups)**
- 1 **cup finely chopped celery**
- ½ **cup finely chopped green pepper**
- 2 **cloves garlic, minced**
- 2 **tablespoons crayfish fat, margarine,** *or* **butter**
- 4 **teaspoons cornstarch**
- 1 **cup water**
- ½ **cup tomato sauce**
- ½ **teaspoon salt**
- ¼ **to ½ teaspoon ground red pepper**
- ¼ **teaspoon ground black pepper**
  Hot cooked rice

■ Thaw crayfish tails or shrimp, if frozen.
■ In a heavy 3-quart saucepan, heat cooking oil, margarine, or butter; add finely chopped onions, chopped celery, chopped green pepper, and minced garlic. Cook, covered, about 10 minutes or till tender.
■ Add crayfish fat, margarine, or butter, stirring till melted. Stir in cornstarch.
■ Stir in crayfish or shrimp, water, tomato sauce, salt, red pepper, and black pepper. Bring mixture to boiling. Reduce heat and simmer, uncovered, about 5 minutes or till crayfish are tender or shrimp turn pink. Serve with hot cooked rice. Makes 4 servings.

Nutrition information per serving: 444 calories, 26 g protein, 41 g carbohydrate, 21 g fat (3 g saturated), 100 mg cholesterol, 609 mg sodium, 680 mg potassium.

Cake A baked, sweet dessert with a texture similar to a very tender bread.

Types: Cakes are divided into these kinds:
☐ **Layer-Type:** Cakes that depend on shortening, margarine, butter, or cooking oil and baking powder or soda for their fine texture. These rich cakes are tender but don't crumble excessively when you slice them. Layer-type cake batter can be shaped into circles, rectangles, squares, loaves, and cupcakes. These cakes can be made in a variety of flavors, such as white, yellow, chocolate, and spice. Also, commercial mixes are sold. Pound cake and fruitcake are a part of this group (see also individual entries).
☐ **Angel Food, Chiffon, and Sponge:** Cakes that depend on air beaten into eggs for their airy texture. Angel food, chiffon, and sponge (sometimes called foam) cakes are light, moist, and tender (see also individual entries). A jelly-roll cake is a type of sponge cake. The texture of these cakes is even but less fine than layer-type cakes. Commercial mixes are sold for angel and chiffon cakes.

Baking hints: In general, a layer-type cake is done when its top is domed, it starts to pull away from the sides of the pan, and it springs back when lightly touched. To be sure a cake is baked, insert a toothpick near the cake center. It should come out free of wet batter.

For an angel food, chiffon, or sponge cake, the toothpick test won't work well because its firmer surface can make a toothpick appear clean when the cake is still wet inside. Instead, touch the top lightly. If it springs back, the cake is done.

Q: How should cakes be cooled?
A: Cool a layer-type cake in the pan on a rack for 10 minutes. Then remove the cake from the pan and cool completely.

Cool an angel food, chiffon, or sponge cake by turning it upside down in the pan. Cooling it this way keeps it from falling or losing volume. If your tube pan doesn't have legs, or if the legs are too short, invert the pan on a metal funnel or a glass bottle with a slim neck.

Storing: To freeze an unfrosted layer-type cake, place it on a baking sheet and put it in the freezer till firm. Then place the cake in a plastic freezer bag or an airtight container, seal, and return it to the freezer. Unfrosted layer-type cakes can be frozen for up to 6 months. Fruitcakes can be frozen for up to 12 months.

Angel food, chiffon, and sponge cakes also can be frozen for longer storage. Place the unfrosted cake in a freezer bag or airtight container and freeze it for up to 3 months.

To thaw, remove the cake from the bag or container and let the cake stand at room temperature for 1 to 2 hours.

Cake-Making Hints

Here are some tips for successful cakes.
● Have all of the ingredients at room temperature unless the recipe directs otherwise. (Eggs should only be left out about 30 minutes before using them.) This makes ingredients easier to combine and gives cakes better volume.
● If a recipe calls for cake flour, but you don't have any on hand, use 1 cup minus 2 tablespoons of all-purpose flour for each cup of cake flour. Some cake recipes call for cake flour because it produces a slightly more tender cake, but you'll find all-purpose flour makes a good cake, too.
● Be sure to preheat your oven before baking; otherwise your cakes won't rise properly.
● For angel food, chiffon, and sponge cakes, beat the egg whites until they form stiff peaks that stand up straight.
● Once the batter is in the pan, tap a layer-type cake on a countertop to release any large air bubbles in the batter. But for an angel food, chiffon, or sponge cake, run a metal spatula through the center of the batter to release any trapped air bubbles. Don't tap the pan on the counter because this motion can reduce cake volume.

To remove a cake layer, run a spatula around the sides of the pan. Place a cooling rack atop cake. Invert the pan and rack together; remove pan. To prevent cracking, reinvert the cake onto another rack.

To loosen an angel food cake from its pan, press a metal spatula against the pan side and loosen the cake in a continuous motion (not a sawing motion). Keep pressure against pan to avoid cutting into the cake.

continued

Nutrition hints: While you probably don't want to think about calories when you crave a mouth-watering piece of cake, there is a way you can have your cake and count calories, too. Opt for plain angel food cake. It has about 160 calories in ½12 of a 10-inch cake made from scratch. This compares with about 310 calories for ½12 of a frosted two-layer chocolate or yellow cake from a mix.

(See *High-Altitude Cooking* for Cake Adjustments.)

How to Solve Cake Problems

If your cakes are not turning out as you would like, here are some general tips, as well as information related to specific types of cakes, that will help solve cake problems.
● Measure all ingredients carefully before you start baking (see *Measure* for Measuring Techniques). You'll have less chance of making a mistake in measuring or forgetting ingredients if you check them against your recipe before you begin.
● Before you start baking, check your oven for accuracy using an oven thermometer. An oven temperature that's too high or too low can bake the cake too quickly or too slowly, causing a variety of problems.

Layer-Type Cakes
● **Your cake has a coarse texture:** It might be that you didn't beat the sugar and shortening, margarine, or butter long enough. For a fine, even cake texture, be sure to beat these ingredients together thoroughly.
● **Your cake is heavy and compact:** Perhaps you didn't beat the sugar and shortening, margarine, or butter long enough. For a light texture, beat these ingredients together well.

● **Your cake is dry:** You might have overbaked the cake. Remember to check doneness after the minimum baking time.
Or, you might have overbeaten the egg whites, if they were used. Stiffly beaten egg whites should stand in straight peaks, but should look moist or glossy. When the egg whites have a "curdled" appearance, they are overbeaten. Start again with fresh egg whites instead of folding in the overbeaten ones.
● **Your cake has elongated, irregular holes:** You may have overmixed the batter when the flour was added. Mix until the ingredients are just combined.

Angel Food, Chiffon, and Sponge Cakes
● **Your cake has poor volume:** Perhaps you didn't beat the egg whites long enough or you may have beaten them too long. To beat them to just the right stage, stop when the egg whites stand in straight peaks when the beaters are removed. The egg whites should look moist or glossy.
Or, perhaps you overmixed the batter when the flour was added. Gently fold ingredients together until they are just combined and the batter is smooth.

● **Your cake shrinks or falls:** You may have beaten the egg whites too long; beat them until they're stiff but still look moist or glossy.
Or, you may have forgotten to cool your cake upside down. As soon as you remove it from the oven, invert it in the pan.
● **Your cake is tough:** You may have overmixed the batter when the dry ingredients were added. Gently fold ingredients together just until mixed.
● **Your sponge cake has layers:** Perhaps you didn't beat the egg yolks long enough. To avoid a layered appearance, beat yolks till thick and lemon-colored. This takes several minutes.
● **Your chiffon cake has yellow streaks:** You may have added the egg yolks directly into the dry ingredients. To keep the yolks from forming eggy streaks, first make a well in the dry ingredients. Next add the oil to the dry ingredients. Then add the egg yolks.
● **Your chiffon cake has a layer:** You may have either underbeaten or overbeaten the egg whites. To avoid this eggy layer, beat the egg whites until they're stiff but they still look moist or glossy.

Cake Decorating

Cake Decorating A technique of dressing up cakes and cupcakes with frosting and other trimmings, usually for special occasions and holidays. The same techniques can be applied to decorating cookies.

Simple decorations for frosted cakes, cupcakes, or cookies include sifted powdered sugar, small candies, tinted coconut, nuts, chocolate curls, and edible flowers. Prepackaged decorations also are available.

For more formal decorations, such as borders, leaves, flowers, figures, and writing, a piping bag and decorating tips usually are required. The shape and size of the tips vary with their use. For instance, small round tips are used for writing; star tips make drop flowers, stars, zigzags, and shells; and leaf tips form leaves, stripes, and ruffles.

A Tip from Our Kitchen

An inexpensive, disposable piping bag is easy to make. First snip about ¼ inch from the corner of a plastic freezer bag. Then place the desired tip in the bag so that it pokes out of the hole. Then just add frosting, seal the bag, and decorate.

Calamari *(kahl uh MAR ee)* The Italian name for squid (see also *Squid*).

Calorie The unit of measure for the energy supplied by food. Just as your car needs gas to run, your body needs energy-yielding food to function. The number of calories you need depends on your size, gender, stage of life, and activity level. When a person eats more calories than the body needs, the excess is stored as fat. With each 3,500 extra calories, the body gains 1 pound.

Q: How can I determine how many calories I need each day?
A: The National Research Council has set up guidelines called the Recommended Dietary Allowances (RDAs). Factors for estimating daily calorie needs are published as part of these guidelines. The calorie estimates vary with the amount of activity in a life-style. To estimate your daily calorie needs (for maintaining your weight) use the following calculations.
1. Choose the type of activity level you normally have to determine the calories you burn per pound.
   Very light activity (seated and standing activities, driving, laboratory work, typing, sewing, ironing, cooking)—14 calories per pound.
   Light activity (walking 2.5 to 3 mph, garage work, electrical work, carpentry, restaurant work, housecleaning, child care, golf, sailing)—16 (women) to 17 (men) calories per pound.
   Moderate activity (walking 3.5 to 4 mph, weeding, carrying a load, cycling, tennis, dancing)—17 (women) to 19 (men) calories per pound.
   Heavy activity (digging, soccer, climbing, basketball)—20 (women) to 23 (men) calories per pound.
2. Multiply the calories you burn per pound by your current weight in pounds to estimate your daily calorie needs. For example, a woman weighing 120 pounds, whose normal level of activity is "light," will need about 1,920 calories (120 pounds times 16 calories per pound).

(See *Nutrition* for information on planning a balanced diet, daily recommendations, and hints for losing weight.)

Camembert Cheese *(KAM uhm bear)* A slightly tangy, earthy cheese. This cow's-milk cheese often is confused with Brie. However, Camembert comes in smaller rounds and has a stronger flavor than Brie. When ripe Camembert is cut, the soft, almost fluid, cream-colored interior bulges out from under a gray-white edible crust.

Camembert cheese

(See *Cheese* for the Selecting Cheese chart and selecting, storing, serving, nutrition, and other information.)

Canadian-Style Bacon

Canadian-Style Bacon A cured and smoked boneless pork loin. This round meat cut resembles ham more than bacon in both appearance and flavor. It is available in both fully cooked and cook-before-eating forms. For cooking directions, see the Broiling Meat and the Panbroiling and Panfrying Meat charts under *Meat.*

Nutrition information: A 1-ounce piece of Canadian-style bacon has about 50 calories and 2 grams of fat.

Canapé

Canapé *(CAN uh pay)* A small, open-face sandwich served as an appetizer and eaten as finger food. Canapés commonly have a base, a spread, and a topping. Bases can be bread, pastry, or crackers. Spreads are usually margarine, butter, or mayonnaise mixtures. Toppings can be seafood, meat, or vegetables.

Candied Fruit or Peel

Candied Fruit or Peel A fruit or citrus peel that is cooked in a sugar syrup. Among the types available are candied citron, pineapple, red or green cherries, and orange, grapefruit, or lemon peels. Whole and diced fruits can be purchased as well as mixtures of fruits and peels. Candied fruits and peels often are used in fruitcake and other desserts.

Candy

Candy A confection using sugar, or an ingredient high in sugar, as the basic ingredient. Candy, both homemade and commercially produced, comes in a variety of textures including soft, chewy, and hard. Flavors and fillings, such as chocolate, fruits, and nuts, often are added. (For information on individual candies, see entries listed under *Candy* in the Index.) To help you with your home candy making, here is some of the most important candy-making information.

Equipment: Using the right equipment ensures successful home candy making.
☐ **Candy Thermometers:** These are indispensable because they take the guesswork out of testing candy mixtures. Buy a candy thermometer that's clearly marked and easy to read. One with an adjustable clip that attaches to the pan is especially handy.
☐ **Saucepans:** Heavy aluminum saucepans are your best choice because they conduct heat much more evenly than stainless steel and other types of metal pans, which tend to have hot spots. Using the size of pan specified in the recipe is important, too. A pan that's too small can lead to messy and dangerous boil-overs. A pan that's too big allows the candy mixture to spread out too thin and not cover the bulb of the thermometer, which can give you an inaccurate temperature reading.
☐ **Beating Equipment:** A wooden spoon with a long handle is ideal for beating fudge and pralines—*do not* use an electric mixer because the candy mixture will overtax the mixer motor. On the other hand, you'll need a sturdy, freestanding electric mixer for beating divinity and nougats. Portable mixers and some lightweight freestanding mixers don't have enough power to handle the strain these dense mixtures place on the motor.
☐ **Special Equipment:** Kitchen and candy-making supply stores carry lots of candy-making equipment, such as candy-dipping forks and plastic and metal candy molds.

Q: **Can candy be made successfully without using a candy thermometer?**
A: Yes, but results are more accurate if you use a calibrated candy thermometer. However, if one isn't available, test candy mixtures by using the cold water test. Test the candy shortly before it reaches the suggested minimum cooking time. Working quickly, drop a few drops of the hot mixture from a spoon into a cup of very cold (but not icy) water. Use your fingers in the water to form the drops of candy into a ball. Remove the ball from the water. The firmness of the ball will indicate the temperature of the mixture (see how-to photos, opposite). If the mixture has not reached the correct stage, continue cooking for 2 to 3 minutes. Then, quickly retest the candy.

continued on page 76

Cold Water Tests for Candy

If you don't own a calibrated candy thermometer, test candy mixtures referring to one of these candy-making stages. For more information, see the question and answer, opposite.

**Thread stage
(230°–233°)**
Dip a teaspoon into the pan of hot candy mixture. When you lift the spoon, the mixture will fall off the spoon in a fine, thin thread.

**Soft-ball stage
(234°–240°)**
Shape drops of candy into a ball in the cold water. When removed from the water, the ball will *immediately* flatten and run between your fingers.

**Firm-ball stage
(244°–248°)**
Shape drops of candy into a ball in the cold water. When removed from the water, the ball will be firm enough to hold its shape, but will quickly flatten.

**Hard-ball stage
(250°–266°)**
Shape drops of candy into a ball in the cold water. When removed from the water, the ball will hold its shape, but will flatten when it is pressed.

**Soft-crack stage
(270°–290°)**
When dropped into cold water, the candy mixture will separate into hard, but pliable and elastic, threads.

**Hard-crack stage
(295°–310°)**
When dropped into cold water, the candy mixture will separate into hard, brittle threads that easily snap or break.

A Tip from Our Kitchen

Check the accuracy of your candy thermometer every time you get ready to make candy. To calibrate your thermometer, put it in a pan of boiling water for a few minutes and then read the temperature. If the thermometer registers above or below 212°, calculate the difference; then add or subtract that number to or from the recipe temperature, and cook to the newly calculated temperature. For example, if the thermometer reads 210°, cook the candy 2 degrees *lower* than the recipe temperature specifies. If the thermometer reads 214°, cook the candy 2 degrees *higher* than the recipe states. (In general, at high altitudes, the boiling temperature of water will be approximately 2 degrees lower for every 1,000 feet above sea level.)

Preparation hints: Attach a candy thermometer to the side of the saucepan so the mercury bulb is completely covered by the candy syrup, but it is not touching the bottom of the pan.

Q: How humid is too humid when it comes to making candy?

A: Humidity affects the preparation of all candy. You're likely to have trouble making candy if the humidity in the room is more than 60 percent.

Storing: The secret to keeping candy fresh is proper storage. Most candies keep well for 2 to 3 weeks if stored tightly covered in a cool, dry place. However, avoid storing different types of candy together in the same container because hard candies may get soft and sticky and candies may trade flavors.

Protect taffies, caramels, and nougats from dampness by wrapping them individually in plastic wrap. Keep brittles and toffees from dampness by layering them in an airtight container between sheets of waxed paper.

Stop divinity from drying out by storing it in an airtight container lined with waxed paper.

Fudge, pralines, and caramels freeze well in airtight freezer bags or containers for up to 1 year. After you remove candy from the freezer, let it stand several hours to warm to room temperature before opening or removing the wrapping. This prevents moisture from collecting on the candy surface and causing white speckles or gray streaks.

Candy-Making Tips

● Before you begin making candy, assemble all of the equipment you'll need and prepare all of the ingredients. For example, have the walnuts chopped before the fudge recipe says to beat them in. The time it takes to chop the nuts is too long for the fudge to sit.

● Measure accurately, and don't make substitutions for basic ingredients. *Never* alter quantities in candy recipes—this includes halving and doubling recipes. To double your yield for a specific recipe, make it twice.

● When cooking candy mixtures, it's extremely important to keep the mixture boiling at a moderate, steady rate over the entire surface. Some recipes will suggest range-top temperatures for cooking the candy mixtures (such as medium-high, medium, etc.). Use these suggestions only as a guide because every range top heats differently.

● As you cook candy mixtures to dissolve the sugar, stir constantly but gently, so the mixture doesn't splash on the sides of the saucepan. This precaution helps prevent sugar crystals from forming and clumping together in the saucepan.

● Some candies, such as fudge and pralines, are cooled, undisturbed, till they're lukewarm. Be careful not to move the saucepan or beat the candy mixture while it's hot, or large sugar crystals will form, giving the candy a grainy, coarse texture.

Q: What is candy coating, and why is it used for candy dipping?

A: Candy coating is a general term used for a variety of products. It's sometimes called white chocolate, almond bark, confectioner's coating, or summer coating and is available in 2-pound packages and in blocks or round disks wherever candy-making supplies are sold. The coating comes in vanilla, chocolate, and butterscotch flavors.

It's used for candy dipping because it doesn't require "tempering," which is a process candy makers use to prevent real chocolate from developing speckles or gray streaks as it hardens.

Cannelloni   A type of pasta that is made from noodle dough and is rectangular in shape. Cannelloni are typically cooked in boiling water, drained, rolled around a meat or cheese filling, and baked in a tomato sauce or white sauce.

A Tip from Our Kitchen
To shortcut cannelloni making, substitute tube-shaped, packaged, dried manicotti shells. Cook them according to package directions.

Canning   Preserving food by sealing it in an airtight container using a pressure or boiling-water canner. For quality home-canned products, start with top-quality fruits and vegetables and equipment in very good condition.

It also is essential to follow the latest standard canning procedures. Canning procedures have recently been revised by the United States Department of Agriculture. Check with your county extension agent for recommendations for processing times, pressures to use, headspace, altitude adjustments, and other information.

Fruits and vegetables used for canning should be varieties recommended for canning. They also should be young, tender, and recently harvested (no more than 12 hours old).

Equipment: Using the right equipment is essential for successful canning.
☐ **Canners:** There are two types of canners—a boiling-water canner and a pressure canner. A boiling-water canner is a deep kettle with a lid and rack. A large kettle, with a rack and cover, that is deep enough to allow at least 1 inch of boiling water above the tops of the jars can be improvised for a canner. A boiling-water canner is used only for fruits, tomatoes, pickles, jellies, jams, and preserves, which have a high level of acidity.

A pressure canner is a more elaborate piece of equipment and consists of a large kettle, rack, locking lid with a seal, pressure lock, and a dial or weighted gauge. The higher temperature reached when the food is processed under pressure is essential for low-acid foods, such as vegetables. If your canner has a dial gauge, you should have it checked for accuracy once a year; contact your county extension service office for a testing location.

Steam canners also are available but are not recommended for safe canning.
☐ **Jars and Lids:** Use only standard canning jars, not those from commercially prepared foods. Use screw bands and flat metal lids with a sealing compound. Follow the manufacturer's directions carefully when using the lids since procedures vary from brand to brand. Do not reuse the flat lids.

Using home-canned foods: Before using a home-canned food, always inspect the jar to see if there are signs of spoilage. If there is leakage, patches of mold, a swollen lid, a foamy or murky appearance, or an unusual odor, *do not use the food.* Contact your county extension agent for information on destroying the food and the jar.

Never eat any home-canned foods unless they have been properly processed. And, *never* taste or serve a pressure-canned food until it has been brought to a boil and boiled for 10 to 20 minutes, depending on the food.
continued

(For altitudes higher than 1,000 feet above sea level, add 1 minute for each 1,000 feet of elevation.) If there is an unnatural odor as the food boils, *discard it*.

High-Altitude Canning

Canning directions usually are written for altitudes less than 1,000 feet above sea level. If you live at a higher altitude, contact your county extension agent for changes to make in canning times and pressures.

Cantaloupe

Cantaloupe   A round melon with a cream-colored netting over a yellowish green rind and soft, orange-colored meat. Also called muskmelon, cantaloupe has a sweet fruity flavor reminiscent of peaches and pears. The center of the fruit is filled with small seeds that are not edible.

Selecting: With your index finger, press the blossom end slightly; it should give to gentle pressure when ripe. Then smell the melon; it should have a sweetly aromatic scent. A strong smell indicates overripeness. If you're buying cut melons, look for a deep apricot-colored meat inside—the deeper the color, the sweeter the taste.

Nutrition information: A boon to dieters, half of a cantaloupe contains about 90 calories, and 1 cup of cubed pieces has about 60 calories. This fruit is also a generous source of vitamins A and C.

(See *Melon* for the Selecting Melons chart and storing, preparation, nutrition, and other information.)

Caper   The flower bud of the caper bush that is used to flavor or garnish foods. This small, firm bud has a pungent, slightly bitter flavor and is usually pickled in vinegar or packed in salt.

Carambola   *(care um BOWL uh)* A small, oval fruit with deep lengthwise grooves, waxy-looking, bright yellow skin, and juicy, sweet, yellow meat. Carambola tastes like a combination of lemon, pineapple, and apple. Its flavor ranges from sweet to slightly tart. Carambola is nicknamed star fruit because when it is sliced crosswise, the slices are shaped like stars.

Market forms: Carambola is available fresh and dried.

Carambola

Selecting: Select firm, shiny-skinned, golden fruit. Fruit with more green than gold will taste very tart.

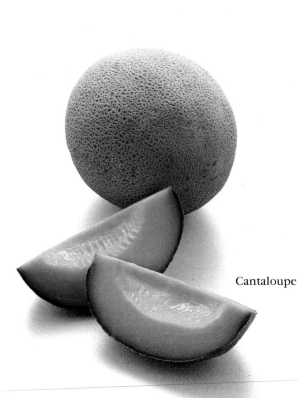

Cantaloupe

Storing: Ripen fresh carambolas with green-tinged skin at room temperature. Refrigerate fully yellowed fruit in a covered container or a plastic bag about 1 week.

Q: **Do carambolas need to be peeled before using?**
A: No, they require only rinsing. You may, however, want to strip the brownish fibers off the top of the fruit's ridges before slicing it. Use carambolas in desserts and salads, or as a garnish.

Nutrition information: One small carambola has about 40 calories.

Caramel
A rich, chewy candy made by boiling sugar, cream, and butter together for a long time. Caramel candies usually are cut into cubes with a buttered knife and then individually wrapped so they hold their shape and don't stick together.

A Tip from Our Kitchen
When time is short, cut your cooking time by using a caramel recipe that calls for sweetened condensed milk instead of cream. Sweetened condensed milk is whole milk to which sugar is added and from which more than half the water is removed. Because some of the water is removed, it will take less time to caramelize.

(See *Candy* for Candy-Making Tips and equipment, storing, and other information.)

Caramelized Sugar
Sugar that has been heated and stirred till it melts and browns. This deep golden syrup also is called burnt sugar. It is used in dessert recipes, such as flan, candy-coated nuts, and burnt sugar cake and frosting.

Tips from Our Kitchen
To caramelize sugar, see the photo at right. Once caramelized, the syrup can be tricky to work with. Here are three tips to make the process easier.
- If your recipe calls for water to be added to the hot sugar syrup, be sure to add the water carefully to avoid steam burns. The syrup may clump as you add the water, but it will dissolve again as you continue to heat it.
- The golden syrup hardens almost immediately upon cooling, so be sure to work quickly once the sugar is melted.
- For easier cleanup, fill your skillet with water and heat it along with the wooden spoon till the hardened syrup dissolves.

Caraway
A hard, brown, crescent-shaped seed with a sharp, slightly sweet flavor reminiscent of anise. Caraway seed gives German-style rye bread its distinctive flavor.

(See *Spice* for selecting, storing, and nutrition information.)

Carbohydrate
Sugars, starches, and certain food fibers. Sugars and starches are excellent sources of energy (food fibers are not used). Although they are found in milk and a few other foods of animal origin, most carbohydrates come from plant sources, such as fruits, vegetables, and grains.

There are two types of carbohydrates. Simple carbohydrates, or sugars, are found naturally in foods such as fruits. When you eat foods containing these carbohydrates, you get vitamins, minerals, and fiber in addition to the sugar. *continued*

To caramelize sugar, heat it in a heavy skillet or saucepan over medium-high heat, without stirring, till the sugar begins to melt. Shake the skillet occasionally. Reduce the heat to low, then cook and stir the mixture with a wooden spoon till the sugar is golden brown and completely melted.

Complex carbohydrates, or starches, consist of chains of sugars linked together; they are found in a wide variety of foods such as breads, cereals, pasta, rice, corn, potatoes, peas, and beans. They differ from simple carbohydrates in that they must be broken down before the body can use the sugar that they contain. Foods containing complex carbohydrates also provide vitamins, minerals, and fiber.

(See *Nutrition* for information on planning a balanced diet.)

Cardamom *(KAR duh muhm)* A
pungent and aromatic spice with a flowery sweetness that's a little like ginger but much more subtle. Cardamom pods are the fruit of a plant in the ginger family. Each pod contains clusters of tiny, hard, black seeds. Whole cardamom pods, whole seeds, and ground cardamom seeds all are available.

A Tip from Our Kitchen
When recipes call for crushed cardamom, you can use either the whole pod or whole seed. Remove the soft shell if using the pods; grind the seeds with a mortar and pestle or crush them between two large spoons.

(See *Spice* for the Spice Alternative Guide and selecting, storing, and nutrition information.)

Cardoon A vegetable that resembles a large bunch of wide, flat celery. Sometimes it is called cardoni. This pale green vegetable has a flavor similar to both celery and artichoke.

Selecting: Fresh cardoons sometimes are available from October to mid-March in specialty markets. Look for fresh, crisp stalks with no signs of wilting or decay.

Storing: Refrigerate in a plastic bag for up to 2 weeks.

Preparation hints: Remove the large, tough outer ribs. The tender inner ribs can be cut into short pieces, boiled, and topped with a sauce or used as a cooked celery substitute.

Nutrition information: One-half cup of boiled cardoon has about 20 calories.

Carob The seeds of the pod of the carob tree that are used in powder or chip form for cooking. Carob products have a mild flavor that is reminiscent of chocolate.

Carrot A root vegetable, generally with a long, slender shape, bright orange color, and feathery green top. Carrots are mild and sweet-flavored with a crisp, crunchy texture.

Varieties: Several hundred varieties of carrots exist, but generally they are sold more by size and shape than variety. Besides the common long and slender orange carrots, baby carrots also are available. Baby carrots

Carrots

may be round or look like miniature versions of regular carrots, and they may be orange or have a creamy white color.

Market forms: Buy carrots fresh (with or without tops), frozen, or canned. Fresh carrots are available year-round. Canned carrots are available whole, sliced, or diced. Frozen carrots come in tiny whole and sliced or crinkle-cut forms. They also are available frozen with seasonings or sauces or as part of vegetable mixtures.

Selecting: Look for straight, rigid, bright orange carrots without cracks or dry spots. If the tops are attached, they should be healthy, green, and fresh-looking. Avoid carrots with many small rootlets because these are old.

Storing: Cut off carrot tops, if attached. Refrigerate the carrots in plastic bags for up to 2 weeks. For longer storage, trim, peel, and blanch tiny whole or cut-up carrots. Then pack them in freezer containers and freeze for up to 1 year.

Q: **Is it necessary to peel carrots?**
A: No. Peeling is a matter of personal preference. If you don't peel them, scrub them clean with a stiff brush.

How to cook: See the Cooking Fresh Vegetables chart under *Vegetable.*

Carrot Math

1 pound	=	6 to 8 medium carrots
	=	3 cups shredded
	=	2¼ cups chopped
3 medium	=	1½ cups thinly bias-sliced
2 medium	=	1 cup sliced

Nutrition information: A raw medium carrot has about 30 calories. A ½-cup serving of cooked, sliced carrots has about 35 calories.

Carving
Cutting or slicing cooked meat, poultry, fish, or game into serving-size portions.

Carving Tips
● Use a long, sharp knife. Sharpen the knife with a butcher steel or a hone before each use. For ease and speed, use an electric knife.
● Place the item to be carved on a cutting board of plastic or other material that can be put into the dishwasher for a thorough cleaning.
● Let cooked meat and poultry stand for 15 to 20 minutes before beginning to carve. This standing time lets the flesh firm up so carving is easier. The carved slices also will hold together better and be more attractive.
● To help keep the carved slices warm, place them on a heated platter and cover them with foil.

How to carve boneless meats: When carving a beef flank steak, hold the steak steady on the board with a carving fork. Starting at the narrow end of the steak, slice with the knife blade at an angle almost parallel to the top of the steak (see Figure 1). Continue cutting very thin slices all at the same diagonal angle across the grain of the flank steak.

Figure 1

Carve a large rolled roast, such as rolled rib, horizontally across the grain.

Carve smaller roasts, such as a sirloin tip, vertically into ¼-inch-thick slices. Do not remove the strings of a tied roast until you come to them, so the meat doesn't fall apart. Also, it is easier to snip the string with scissors than to cut the string with the carving knife.

To carve a beef brisket, cut at a slight angle across the grain, making ⅛- to ¼-inch-thick slices. Rotate the brisket as necessary to continue cutting across the grain.

continued

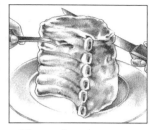

Figure 2

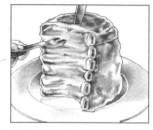

Figure 3

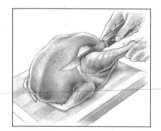

Figure 4

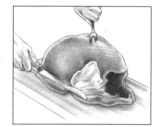

Figure 5

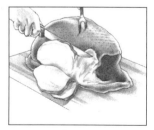

Figure 6

How to carve a bone-in roast: When carving beef rib roast, insert a carving fork between the top two ribs. Slice from the fat side across to the rib bone (see Figure 2). Cut along the rib bone with the knife tip to loosen each slice, keeping the knife close to the bone (see Figure 3).

How to carve a turkey or other whole poultry: If the bird is stuffed, remove the stuffing to a serving bowl. Grasp the tip of one leg and pull it away from the body. Cut through the skin and meat between the thigh and body (see Figure 4). With the tip of the knife, separate the thighbone from the backbone by cutting through the joint. Repeat on the other side.

To separate the thigh and drumstick, cut through the joint where the leg bone and thighbone meet. Serve the legs and thighs of smaller birds whole. To carve the drumstick meat of large birds, hold the drumstick vertically by the tip, with the large end on the cutting board. Slice the meat parallel to the bone and under some tendons, turning the leg to get even slices. Next slice the thigh by cutting slices parallel to the bone. Repeat with the remaining drumstick and thigh.

To carve the breast meat, make a deep horizontal cut into the breast above each wing (see Figure 5). This cut will be the end point of the breast meat slices.

Beginning at the outer edge of one side of the breast, cut slices from the top of the breast down to the horizontal cut (see Figure 6). Make the slices thin and even. Final smaller slices can follow the curve of the breastbone. Repeat on the other side.

Remove wings by cutting through the joint where the wing bone and backbone meet.

Casaba *(kuh SAH buh)* A member of the
melon family, with a wrinkled, golden yellow rind and smooth-textured, creamy white meat. The large, globe-shaped casaba melon has one pointed end and tastes like a mildly sweet mango. Inedible oval-shaped seeds fill the center of the moist, juicy melon.

Casaba

Nutrition information: Rich in potassium, casabas have a modest calorie count—about 40 calories per ⅒ of a melon.

(See *Melon* for the Selecting Melons chart and storing, preparation, nutrition, and other information.)

Cashew The seed of a tropical, applelike
fruit. The kidney-shaped, beige-colored nut is enclosed in a toxic shell and protrudes from the bottom of the fruit. To make cashews safe to eat, the toxic shells are removed and the nuts are cleaned, and they usually are roasted before marketing. Cashews are famous for their rich, buttery flavor.

Cashews

Storing: Roasted cashews will stay fresh in airtight jars or cans for about a month at room temperature. Or, store them in an airtight container in the refrigerator for up to 6 months or in the freezer for up to 1 year.

(See *Nut* for the Selecting Nuts chart and selecting, nutrition, and other information.)

Casserole A round or oval, covered dish used for cooking in the oven. A casserole may be glass, ceramic, or metal. Unlike a baking dish, which is straight-sided, a casserole frequently has curved sides. Often a casserole can double as a serving dish. Many, but not all, glass and ceramic casseroles can be used for micro-cooking. Microwave-safe plastic casseroles also are available.

The term also is used to refer to the food cooked in a casserole.

A Tip from Our Kitchen
Sizes of casseroles vary and, unlike baking dishes and pans, they are measured by volume, not inches. To determine the size of a casserole, measure the amount of water it holds when filled to the top. Casseroles most commonly are sold in 1-, 1½-, 2-, and 3-quart sizes.

Catfish Any of a wide range of scaleless fish found mostly in fresh water. Catfish are noted for their long "whiskers."

In the South, catfish have long been popular for fish fries. But in other parts of the country, these bottom-feeders earned a reputation for being a strong, muddy-tasting fish. Then in the late 1960s, farmers in some southern states began raising catfish in ponds, feeding them on floating grain pellets. Catfish fed this way have an improved mild flavor with firm flesh that is snow white in color. The majority of the catfish on the market today are farm raised. The most commonly eaten kinds are *Channel, Blue,* and *White.*

Market forms: Catfish can be purchased fresh or frozen. They come dressed or cut into steaks and fillets.

How to cook: One of the most popular ways to prepare catfish is panfrying. However, it is also excellent baked, broiled, or grilled.

For panfrying, baking, and broiling directions, see the Cooking Fish chart under *Fish.* For grilling directions, see the Direct-Grilling Fish chart under *Barbecue.*

Nutrition information: One 3-ounce serving of breaded and fried catfish has about 190 calories. The same-size serving of plain, baked catfish has about 130 calories.

(See *Fish* for selecting, storing, thawing, and other information.)

Catsup A smooth, thick sauce with a spicy, sweet-tart flavor that usually is used as a condiment. Tomato catsup, also called ketchup, is the most common type. However, catsup can be made from other ingredients, such as mushrooms, cranberries, or walnuts. Various types of commercially bottled tomato catsup are available, including plain, hot-style, low-calorie, and low-sodium varieties.

Nutrition information: Depending on the brand, 1 tablespoon of plain tomato catsup can contain from 5 to 20 calories and from 5 milligrams of sodium (for low-sodium catsup) to 180 milligrams of sodium (for regular catsup).

Cauliflower A large, globular vegetable, usually with an irregular, creamy white head and small green leaves. Cauliflower has a mild cabbagelike flavor.

Cauliflower

Types: Besides the familiar white or ivory-colored cauliflower, you'll occasionally find a purple or green variety.

Market forms: Fresh cauliflower is available all year. Frozen cauliflower is available in pieces, in sauces, or as part of vegetable mixtures.

Selecting: Look for solid, heavy heads with bright green leaves. Avoid cauliflower heads that have
continued

brown bruises, a speckled appearance, or leaves that are yellowed or withered. The size of the head is not an indicator of quality.

Storing: Refrigerate cauliflower in a plastic bag for up to 4 days.

How to cook: See the Cooking Fresh Vegetables chart under *Vegetable.*

Nutrition information: One-half cup of raw cauliflower has about 10 calories; ½ cup cooked cauliflower has about 15 calories.

Caviar Lightly salted sturgeon eggs (roe). Because fresh caviar is highly perishable and requires special handling, it is very expensive.

Eggs of other fish are used to make less costly caviar substitutes, but the label must list the type of fish. You're likely to find whitefish, lumpfish, salmon (red caviar), tuna, cod, and carp caviar.

Look for caviar in small jars in supermarkets and specialty stores. One tablespoon of caviar has about 40 calories.

A Tip from Our Kitchen

Serve caviar as an appetizer on thin toast with chopped, hard-cooked egg white, snipped chives, or sieved, hard-cooked egg yolk as a garnish.

Celeriac *(suh LER ee ak)* An irregular, brown-skinned, knobby root vegetable with a creamy white interior. Also called celery root, celeriac is grown only for its bulblike root— its stalks are removed. It has a mild, celerylike flavor and a crisp, turniplike texture.

Selecting: Look for small, firm celeriacs. Larger ones tend to be woody and tough. They're generally available October through April.

Storing: Trim off the stringy roots. Refrigerate in a plastic bag for up to 1 week.

Preparation hint: Before using celeriac, peel it, cut it up, and cook it. Use it as you would cooked carrots.

How to cook: See the Cooking Fresh Vegetables chart under *Vegetable.*

Nutrition information: One-half cup of fresh celeriac has about 30 calories.

Celery A leafy green vegetable with long, slender stalks (called ribs) joined at the base. The heart is the center of the celery where the ribs are thin and delicate and have tiny leaves. Celery is crisp with a mild flavor.

Celery

Celeriac

Types: There are two kinds of celery—*Green* and *Golden*, with green being the most common type. Packages labeled celery hearts are the very tender innermost ribs of green celery. Golden celery, which is grown under a layer of soil so it doesn't turn green, is rarely available in stores.

Selecting: Fresh celery is available year-round. Look for crisp ribs that are firm, unwilted, and unblemished. Leaves should be fresh and green, not yellow and droopy.

Storing: Refrigerate celery in a plastic bag for up to 2 weeks.

Q: Can extra celery be stored in the freezer?
A: Celery tends to lose its crispness when frozen, so it usually is not a good vegetable to freeze. If you plan to use sliced or chopped celery in soups, however, you can freeze the cut-up celery pieces in freezer bags or containers for up to 3 months.

A Tip from Our Kitchen
To restore crispness to fresh celery, trim the ribs and soak them in ice water for 10 to 20 minutes.

How to cook: See the Cooking Fresh Vegetables chart under *Vegetable*.

Nutrition information: Celery has only about 5 calories per stalk or about 10 calories per ½ cup sliced.

Celery Salt
A blend of ground celery seed and table salt. Use celery salt to season soups, salads, meats, fish, and vegetables.

Celery Seed
Produced by a plant that is a relative of the green vegetable celery. This tiny seed lends a fresh celery flavor to salad dressings, pickles, and coleslaw.

(See *Spice* for selecting, storing, and nutrition information.)

Cereal
An edible product that is processed from grain and usually is served for breakfast. Cereal also refers to any plant that produces a grain used for food. These plants are known as cereal grains.

Varieties: The most common cereal products are made from wheat, corn, rice, oats, rye, and barley. Buckwheat and soy products, though used as cereals or blended with cereal mixtures, generally do not belong in this group. Other less common cereals include millet, quinoa, and triticale (see also individual entries).

Market forms: Breakfast cereal products are usually categorized according to whether they are served hot as cooked cereals or cold as ready-to-eat cereals.

Cooked cereals include oatmeal, grits, farina, and some grain combinations. Many cooked cereals come in regular, quick-cooking, and instant forms. For quick-cooking versions, the grain kernel is cut into pieces to shorten cooking time. Instant cooked cereals are cut into even smaller pieces so they need no additional cooking at all, just the addition of boiling water.

Ready-to-eat cereals come salted and unsalted; sweetened and unsweetened; flaked, puffed, shaped, and shredded; fortified with vitamins and minerals; and embellished with fruits, nuts, and other grains.

Storing: To maintain quality, store cereals in airtight containers in a cool, dry place. For best flavor and texture, use ready-to-eat cereals within 3 weeks after opening. Store cereals to be cooked for up to a year.

continued

How to cook: See the Cooking Grains chart under *Grain*.

A Tip from Our Kitchen

Cereal products have many uses beyond the breakfast table. Substitute crushed cornflakes or bran flakes for bread crumbs as a coating for fish or chicken or in a meat loaf. You can plan on 3 cups of flakes yielding about 1 cup finely crushed cereal.

Nutrition hints: To select the most nutritious cereals, read labels and compare. Generally, the less processed a cereal is, the more nutritious it is. Those that contain whole grains usually are high in fiber and protein. Others are fortified with vitamins.

Charlotte Russe *(shar luht ROOS)* A

dessert made with layers of ladyfingers or sponge cake and a filling. The ladyfingers or cake may be sprinkled or soaked with rum or a liqueur. Popular fillings are pudding, custard, mousse, and whipped cream.

Chateaubriand *(shaa toe bree ON)* A

thick slice of beef tenderloin that is broiled or grilled and usually served with a béarnaise sauce.

Chayote *(chaw YOTE ee)* A pear-shaped

squash with a delicate, green or white skin that can be peeled as you would an apple. The skin is smooth with slight ridges. The moist flesh tastes like a cross between an apple and a cucumber and surrounds a single flat seed. Chayotes, also known as mirlitons, can be prepared as you would summer squash. Or, they can be cooked and stuffed.

Selecting: Look for small, firm, unblemished chayotes.

Chayotes

Storing: Refrigerate in a plastic bag for up to 2 weeks.

How to cook: See the Cooking Fresh Vegetables chart under *Vegetable*.

Nutrition information: A ½-cup serving of cooked chayote contains about 20 calories.

Cheddar Cheese A firm-textured and

mild- to sharp-flavored natural cheese. Cheddar is made from cow's milk and has a white to orange color. The word cheddar also refers to a step in the cheese-making process. Cheddaring is when the curds are pressed into slabs to form cheese. Then the slabs are turned repeatedly to condense the cheese and give it a smoother, firmer texture.

Types: Cheddar cheeses are classified by age. The longer a cheddar ages, the sharper its flavor. The name longhorn is given to cylindrical pieces of cheddar or Colby that often are cut into half moons.

Cheddar cheese

☐ **Mild Cheddar:** Aged about 3 months.
☐ **Medium Cheddar:** Aged about 6 months.
☐ **Sharp Cheddar:** Aged 6 months or more.

Market forms: Cheddar is sold shredded, in wheels, and in chunks. Some is coated with wax, which should be removed before eating.

(See *Cheese* for the Selecting Cheese chart and selecting, storing, serving, nutrition, and other information.)

Cheese

A dairy product made from heated milk with an enzyme or coagulant added to form curds and whey. The curds are pressed to form various shapes. Whey is used to make some cheeses, such as ricotta.

From milk to cheese: The texture and flavor of cheese is determined by the kind of milk used. The majority of cheese is made from cow's milk, but milk from goats, sheep, buffalo, camels, and reindeer also is used.

Other factors that affect the characteristics of cheese are the additives (enzymes or acids) used for coagulating the milk, the culture used, and the conditions for cooking, cutting, forming, and curing the curd. All these factors combine to produce cheeses that range from fresh, soft, and mild to aged, firm, and robust.

Natural Versus Process

Cheese made directly from the curd of milk and not reprocessed or blended is known as *natural cheese*. Some of the natural cheeses are made from unpasteurized milk. *Process cheese* is made from natural cheese that has undergone additional steps, such as pasteurization. Other ingredients often are added for flavoring, a softer texture, and longer shelf life.

Types of natural cheese: There are dozens of natural cheeses. For specific information on individual cheeses, see the Selecting Cheese chart, pages 88 and 89, and the individual entries.

Types of process and other cheese: Here is a brief description of various cheeses.
☐ **Pasteurized Process Cheese:** Made by grinding, blending, and heating one or more natural cheeses. An emulsifier also is added to it. It melts smoothly when heated.
☐ **Pasteurized Process Cheese Food:** Made the same way as pasteurized process cheese, but other dairy ingredients may be added. The process cheese food has more moisture and less fat than process cheese.
☐ **Pasteurized Process Cheese Spread:** Lower in fat and higher in moisture than pasteurized process cheese food. It is spreadable at room temperature.
☐ **Cold-Pack Cheese:** Made by grinding and mixing one or more natural cheeses. It is not heated during processing. It also is known as club cheese. Cold-pack cheese can be smoked, and other ingredients, including spices and other flavorings, may be added.
☐ **Cold-Pack Cheese Food:** Made the same way as cold-pack cheese except other dairy ingredients are added. Other possible additions include spices or flavorings, artificial colors, and sweeteners.

Q: **What is imitation cheese and how can it be used?**
A: A product must be called an imitation cheese if it does not meet the government standards of the product it is imitating. Some imitation cheeses may melt differently than their counterparts, so you may want to do a little experimenting if you are going to cook with them. Or, use them just for snacking or in salads.

Selecting: When buying cheese, put your senses to work. Look, touch, smell, and, if possible, taste the cheese before you purchase it. If the package is wet and sticky, or if the
continued on page 90

Selecting Cheese

When you're deciding what cheese to select, use this chart for a quick comparison. It helps identify the texture, color, and flavor of a variety of cheeses. Use it also to compare the calories, fat, and cholesterol for a 1-ounce portion (except where noted otherwise). Then look at the suggested ways to use the cheese. Here's a brief explanation of what the how-to-use terms mean.

•*Crumbling:* Breaks easily into small pieces for potato or salad toppings or for use in fillings, dips, and dressings.
•*Cubing:* Cuts nicely into chunks for salads and cheese trays.

•*Grating:* Very fine pieces for use as a topping and in cooking.
•*Shredding:* Long, narrow strips for use as a topping and in cooking.
•*Slicing:* Cuts easily into slices and generally melts well for use in sandwiches.
•*Snacking:* Spreads on crackers and cuts into cubes and slices for eating out of hand.
•*In Cooking:* Generally melts smoothly and combines with other ingredient flavors for use in sauces, casseroles, and other entrées.

Cheese	Characteristics (texture; color; flavor)	How to Use	Nutrition Information (per ounce)
American*	Smooth, semisoft texture; orange; mild, milky flavor	Cubing, shredding, slicing, snacking, in cooking	106 calories 9 g fat 27 mg cholesterol
Asiago *(ah see AH go)*	Semifirm to hard texture, depending on length of curing; light yellow; sharp flavor	Grating, snacking, in cooking	110 calories 9 g fat 35 mg cholesterol
Bel Paese *(bel pa AY zuh)*	Smooth with texture of firm butter; creamy yellow with gray surface; rich and sweet to moderately robust flavor	Snacking	110 calories 8 g fat 27 mg cholesterol
Blue*	Crumbly texture; blue- and green-streaked white interior; sharp, tangy flavor	Crumbling, in cooking	100 calories 8 g fat 21 mg cholesterol
Brick*	Semisoft texture; creamy white; mild and sweet to pungent and slightly tangy flavor	Slicing, snacking, in cooking	105 calories 8 g fat 27 mg cholesterol
Brie* *(bree)*	Creamy to runny texture with soft, thin, edible rind; cream-colored interior; mild yet robust flavor	Snacking, in cooking	95 calories 8 g fat 28 mg cholesterol
Camembert* *(KAM uhm bear)*	Soft, almost fluid inside texture with gray-white edible crust; cream-colored interior; slightly tangy and earthy flavor	Snacking	85 calories 7 g fat 20 mg cholesterol
Cheddar*	Firm, smooth texture; white to orange; mild to sharp flavor	Cubing, shredding, slicing, snacking, in cooking	114 calories 9 g fat 30 mg cholesterol
Cheshire	Hard, crumbly texture; made in red, white, or blue; intense tangy, salty flavor	Crumbling, slicing, snacking	110 calories 9 g fat 29 mg cholesterol
Colby*	Firm body and open texture; light yellow to orange; mild to mellow flavor	Shredding, slicing, snacking, in cooking	112 calories 9 g fat 27 mg cholesterol
Colby-Monterey Jack*	Firm, smooth texture; a blend of orange Colby and white Monterey Jack with mottled appearance; mild, milky flavor	Shredding, slicing, snacking, in cooking	108 calories 9 g fat 29 mg cholesterol
Edam* *(EE duhm)*	Semisoft to hard texture with small holes; light yellow; mild, nutty, and sometimes salty flavor	Slicing, snacking, in cooking	101 calories 8 g fat 25 mg cholesterol
Feta* *(FEHT uh)*	Soft, crumbly texture; white; sharp, salty flavor	Crumbling, snacking, in cooking	75 calories 6 g fat 25 mg cholesterol

*See individual entries for additional information.

Cheese	Characteristics (texture; color; flavor)	How to Use	Nutrition Information (per ounce)
Fontina (fon TEE nuh)	Semisoft to firm texture, depending on the age, with small holes; ivory with a wax rind; pleasant aroma with a delicate to full flavor	Snacking, in cooking	110 calories 9 g fat 33 mg cholesterol
Gjetost (YED ost)	Hard texture; light brownish yellow; sweet caramelized flavor	Slicing, snacking	132 calories 8 g fat cholesterol not available
Gouda* (GOO duh)	Semisoft to hard texture, smooth, with small holes; yellow; mild and nutty to sharp flavor	Cubing, slicing, snacking, in cooking	101 calories 8 g fat 32 mg cholesterol
Gruyère* (groo YEHR)	Firm texture with small holes; ivory; mild, nutty flavor	Shredding, slicing, snacking, in cooking	117 calories 9 g fat 31 mg cholesterol
Limburger*	Soft, creamy texture; pale yellow; very pungent aroma and robust flavor when aged	Snacking	93 calories 8 g fat 26 mg cholesterol
Monterey Jack*	Smooth, semisoft to hard texture; creamy white; mild to mellow flavor	Cubing, shredding, slicing, snacking, in cooking	106 calories 9 g fat 25 mg cholesterol
Mozzarella* (maht suh REHL uh)	Smooth, semisoft, chewy texture; creamy white; mild, delicate flavor	Cubing, shredding, slicing, snacking, in cooking	Whole milk: 80 calories 6 g fat 22 mg cholesterol Part skim milk: 72 calories 5 g fat 16 mg cholesterol
Muenster* (MUHN ster)	Smooth, waxy texture; creamy white with orange-red exterior; mild to pungent flavor	Cubing, shredding, slicing, snacking, in cooking	104 calories 9 g fat 27 mg cholesterol
Parmesan*	Hard, dry texture; pale yellow; sharp, salty flavor	Grating, in cooking	1 tablespoon: 23 calories 2 g fat 4 mg cholesterol
Port du Salut (por duh suh LYOO)	Smooth, semisoft texture; creamy yellow with orange rind; mild to robust flavor	Snacking	100 calories 8 g fat 35 mg cholesterol
Provolone (proh vuh LOH nee)	Firm, smooth texture; creamy yellow; mild to sharp with a light smoky flavor	Cubing, shredding, slicing, snacking, in cooking	100 calories 8 g fat 20 mg cholesterol
Romano*	Hard, dry texture; light yellow; sharp, piquant flavor	Grating, in cooking	110 calories 8 g fat 29 mg cholesterol
Sapsago (sap SAY go)	Hard, dry texture; light green; tangy and spicy with an herb flavor	Grating	Not available
Scamorze (ska MORD zo)	Semisoft texture; light yellow; delicate, nutty flavor	Cubing, shredding, slicing, snacking, in cooking	70 calories 5 g fat 16 mg cholesterol
Swiss*	Smooth, firm texture with large holes; creamy, pale yellow; mellow, nutty flavor	Cubing, shredding, slicing, snacking, in cooking	107 calories 8 g fat 26 mg cholesterol

*See individual entries for additional information.

cheese has shrunk in the rind, don't buy it. In general, avoid cheese with dry and cracked edges, uneven texture, unpleasant odors, and off-flavors.

Storing: Airtight packaging is the key to proper cheese storage. If the cheese has a rind, leave it on during storage to keep the cheese fresh. Wrap unused cheese tightly in foil or plastic wrap, then seal it in a plastic bag or container with a tight-fitting lid. Store the cheese in your refrigerator.

Most cheese comes stamped with a "sell by" date on the package. In general, the softer the cheese is, the shorter the storage life. If there is no date on the container, cheeses such as cottage and ricotta should be stored no longer than 5 days after purchase. Firm and hard cheeses have less moisture and can be stored for longer periods. For instance, sharp cheddar may keep for weeks in your refrigerator, if properly wrapped.

As cheese ages, it naturally develops more flavor and may develop surface mold. Most surface mold is harmless but looks unappealing. For firm cheese, cut away at least 1 inch around the moldy area and use the remaining cheese. Discard soft cheeses, such as cottage cheese, ricotta, and cream cheese, that have mold.

Q: Can cheese be frozen?
A: Yes. For longer storage, cheese can be frozen, but semisoft and hard cheeses will be more crumbly, and soft cheeses may separate slightly. Because of the texture change, it's best to use thawed cheese for cooking in casseroles and sauces.

Cut the piece of cheese (1 pound or less and not more than 1 inch thick), wrap it in freezer wrap, and freeze quickly at 0°. Thaw frozen cheese in the refrigerator and use as soon as possible in cooking. Most soft natural cheeses can be frozen for up to 4 months, and firm and hard natural cheeses may be frozen for up to 6 months.

Serving hints: Cheese tastes best when served at room temperature. Unlock its flavor by allowing firm cheese to stand at room temperature for 1 to 2 hours and soft cheese to stand for 1 hour before serving.

If the cheese has a rind, remove the rind before serving (except for Brie and Camembert). If the rind doesn't peel off easily, use a sharp knife to cut it off.

Tips from Our Kitchen
● When adding cheese to a sauce, use a low temperature and gently heat till cheese melts and combines with other ingredients. If overcooked or heated too quickly, cheese will become tough and stringy. Process cheese is not as likely to string, become rubbery, or develop a grainy texture when heated.
● For speedy melting, shred or cut the cheese into small pieces. If possible, add cheese at the end of cooking and stir or heat just till melted.

Nutrition hints: Cheese is a real powerhouse of important nutrients. But it also contains fat, with 65 to 75 percent of the calories in most cheeses coming from fat. If you're watching your fat intake, you may want to select a full-flavor cheese so you can use less. Or, there are a number of low-fat cheese products available. Look for cheese made with skim milk instead of whole milk. Smart choices include part-skim ricotta and mozzarella and dry-curd or low-fat cottage cheese. Many dairies also are making lower fat (and lower sodium) natural cheeses.

Cheesecake
A rich, dense dessert made with cream cheese or ricotta or cottage cheese; eggs; sugar; and sometimes sour cream. It usually is baked and may have either a crumb or a pastry crust.

continued

Cheesecake Supreme
(see recipe, page 92)

Tips from Our Kitchen

- Beat a cheesecake filling gently, especially after adding the eggs. Beating too vigorously will incorporate too much air, which causes a cheesecake to puff and then fall, creating a crack.
- When using a springform pan for cheesecake, place the pan on a shallow baking pan. If the springform pan leaks, the baking pan will catch the spills.
- Cool a cheesecake for 15 minutes, then loosen the crust from the sides of the pan. This helps prevent the cheesecake from cracking as it cools.

Q: **What is the best way to see if a baked cheesecake is done?**

A: Gently shake the cheesecake. If the cheesecake looks nearly set and only a small circle in the center jiggles slightly, it is done. (The center will firm up during the cooling time.) Using a knife to test a cheesecake may create a crack in the top and will not work for cheesecakes made with a large amount of sour cream because it won't give an accurate test. Cheesecakes made with sour cream should jiggle a little more and will have a larger soft spot in the center.

Cheesecake Supreme

- 1¾ cups finely crushed graham crackers
- ¼ cup finely chopped walnuts
- ½ teaspoon ground cinnamon
- ½ cup margarine *or* butter, melted
- 3 8-ounce packages cream cheese, softened
- 1 cup sugar
- 2 tablespoons all-purpose flour
- 1 teaspoon vanilla
- ½ teaspoon finely shredded lemon peel
- 2 eggs
- 1 egg yolk
- ¼ cup milk
  Fresh berries (optional)

■ For crust, combine crushed graham crackers, walnuts, and cinnamon. Stir in margarine or butter. Reserve ¼ cup of the crumb mixture for topping, if desired. Press remaining crumb mixture onto bottom and about 2 inches up sides of an 8- or 9-inch springform pan.

■ In a mixer bowl combine cream cheese, sugar, flour, vanilla, and lemon peel. Beat with an electric mixer till fluffy. Add eggs and yolk all at once, beating on low speed just till combined. Stir in milk. Pour into crust-lined pan. Sprinkle with reserved crumbs, if any. Place on a shallow baking pan in the oven.

■ Bake in a 375° oven for 45 to 50 minutes for the 8-inch pan (35 to 40 minutes for the 9-inch pan) or till center appears nearly set when shaken. Cool 15 minutes. Loosen crust from sides of pan. Cool for 30 minutes more; remove sides of pan. Cool completely. Chill at least 4 hours. Garnish with fresh berries, if desired. Makes 12 to 16 servings.

Nutrition information per serving: 447 calories, 8 g protein, 34 g carbohydrate, 32 g fat (15 g saturated), 116 mg cholesterol, 378 mg sodium, 153 mg potassium.

Sour Cream Cheesecake: Prepare Cheesecake Supreme as above, *except* reduce cream cheese to *2 packages* and omit the milk. Add three 8-ounce cartons dairy *sour cream* with the eggs. Bake about 55 minutes for the 8-inch pan (about 50 minutes for 9-inch pan).

Nutrition information per serving: 502 calories, 8 g protein, 36 g carbohydrate, 37 g fat (18 g saturated), 120 mg cholesterol, 353 mg sodium, 212 mg potassium.

Chocolate Swirl Cheesecake: Prepare Cheesecake Supreme as above, *except* omit lemon peel. Stir 2 squares (2 ounces) *semisweet chocolate*, melted and cooled, into *half* of the batter. Pour *half* of each batter mixture into crust; repeat. Use a spatula to gently swirl the batters.

Nutrition information per serving: 470 calories, 8 g protein, 36 g carbohydrate, 34 g fat (16 g saturated), 116 mg cholesterol, 379 mg sodium, 168 mg potassium.

Cherimoyas

Cherries Jubilee A dessert featuring ice cream served with a warm, dark cherry sauce accented with flaming brandy.

Cherries

Rainier   Bing   Montmorency

Cherimoya *(cher uh MOY uh)* A fist-sized tropical fruit that is heart-shaped and has a pale green, patterned outer skin. Cherimoyas, also called custard apples, have a creamy white interior with large watermelonlike black seeds. When ripe, this fruit has a creamy, almost custardlike texture. It tastes like a sweet combination of bananas and papaya with a tinge of pineapple.

Selecting: Cherimoyas sold in supermarkets usually are pale green and quite firm. When ripe, some cherimoyas turn a dull brownish green. A ripe cherimoya should be slightly soft.

Storing: Refrigerate ripe fruit in a paper bag for up to 2 days. If the fruit is not ripe, ripen it by leaving it at room temperature, turning the fruit occasionally, until the skin turns a dull brownish green.

Q: How do you serve cherimoyas?
A: Cherimoyas are best served raw. Halve the fruit, then remove the seeds. Cube or slice the fruit, or spoon very soft fruit right from the skin. Mix cherimoyas into fruit salads or compotes.

Nutrition information: Cherimoyas have about 80 calories per 3-ounce serving.

Cherry A small, round to heart-shaped fruit that has a pit, a light golden to deep red, smooth skin, and a stem. The fruit inside clings to the pit and has a juicy texture and sweet to tart flavor.

Types: Most cherries eaten plain are sweet cherries. Cherries used for cooking or canning usually are tart cherries and are known also as sour or pie cherries.
☐ **Sweet:** The most popular dark-colored, sweet cherries are the large, dark red *Bing* and the *Lambert*, also dark red. Other varieties include the *Tartarian*, a small, purplish black cherry, and the *Chapman*, a large, round, red cherry.
   A popular light-colored, sweet cherry is called *Royal Ann* (also known as *Napoleon* and *Queen Anne*). It has a light golden color with a red blush over it. Although mainly used for canning, Royal Anns are sometimes sold fresh. Other light-colored sweet cherries include the *Rainier* and *Golden Bing*.
☐ **Tart:** The red *Montmorency,* which is ideal for canning and baking, is probably the most widely used variety in the United States. Other tart cherries include the *English Morella* and *Early Richmond*. Although some tart cherries are sold fresh, the vast majority
continued

of them are processed into cherry products, such as pie filling.

Market forms: You'll find fresh sweet cherries primarily during the months of May through July; the season for tart cherries is generally limited to June and July. Year-round, cherries are available frozen, canned, candied, dried, and as maraschino cherries. *Dried* cherries can be dried Bing cherries or sweetened tart cherries, and may be used like any other dried fruit for eating and cooking. *Maraschino* cherries usually are yellow cherries that have been preserved and dyed with red or green food coloring and flavored with almond or mint.

Selecting: When shopping for fresh cherries, look for plump, even-colored fruit that is firm, smooth-skinned, and brightly colored for the variety. Avoid bruised, split, or very soft fruit.

Storing: Fresh cherries are meant to be enjoyed as soon as possible. Refrigerate them, covered, for up to 4 days. After opening canned cherries, keep them in a covered container in the refrigerator for up to 1 week. Maraschino cherries last up to 6 months in the refrigerator.

Q: Can I freeze cherries?
A: Yes, you can freeze fresh cherries to enjoy them all year. Rinse and dry the cherries. Then, pit them, if desired. Place the cherries in freezer bags or freezer containers, leaving a ½-inch headspace. Freeze the cherries for 6 to 12 months.
   To thaw frozen cherries, set them out at room temperature for 30 minutes.

Preparation hint: Pit cherries using either a commercially made cherry pitter or the tip of a knife.

Cherry Math
1 pound cherries	=	3 cups whole
	=	2½ cups halved

Nutrition information: One cup of fresh sour cherries (with pits) contains about 50 calories; the same amount of fresh sweet cherries contains about 100 calories.

(See *Dried Fruit* for the Cooking Dried Fruit chart and storing and preparation hints.)

Chervil

Chervil *(CHUR vul)* A delicate herb that resembles parsley and has lacy, fernlike, green leaves. The leaves have a sweet, licoricelike flavor. Chervil is readily available as dried leaves, and fresh chervil may be found in specialty markets.

(See *Herb* for the Herb Alternative Guide and selecting, storing, and nutrition information.)

Chess Pie A single-crust pie with a very sweet, rich custard filling that's flavored with lemon. The filling of this Southern favorite is unusual because it contains cornmeal. Sometimes nuts and raisins also are added. The crust is usually made from pastry.

(See *Pie* for Pie-Making Hints and storing information.)

Chestnut

Chestnut The fruit of the chestnut tree. This mound-shaped, golden nut is encased in a fine brown membrane and a smooth, leathery, mahogany-colored shell. Chestnuts have a sweet, starchy flavor and a moist, crumbly texture. In the United States, chestnut trees were abundant until the 1930s when a blight destroyed most of them. Most of the chestnuts sold are imported, although a few orchards in the U.S. now produce them.

Market forms: Fresh, unshelled chestnuts can be found only during the winter months. You can purchase canned chestnuts year-round, either whole or puréed. Also available are dried chestnuts and "marrons glacés," whole candied chestnuts, from France.

Q: **Can dried chestnuts be substituted for fresh ones?**

A: Yes, but they have to be boiled first. To get the equivalent of 1 cup of fresh chestnuts, start with about 3 ounces of the dried. Cover with water and simmer, covered, for 1½ to 2 hours or till completely rehydrated. Drain well.

Storing: Fresh chestnuts are perishable. They can be kept, unshelled, in the refrigerator in a plastic bag for up to 2 weeks. Or, they may be kept frozen several months. Before using, discard any moldy chestnuts.

Dried chestnuts will keep indefinitely in an airtight container in the refrigerator or freezer.

A Tip from Our Kitchen

To shell fresh chestnuts, cut an X on the flat side of each chestnut. Place in a shallow baking pan and roast in a 400° oven for 15 minutes, tossing them occasionally. Peel the chestnuts while they're still warm from the oven—they get harder to peel as they cool.

(See *Nut* for the Selecting Nuts chart and selecting and other information.)

Chèvre Cheese

Chèvre Cheese *(shev)* Any cheese made from goat's milk. These cheeses often have a distinctive tangy flavor and are made in a number of shapes, such as logs and cones. Chèvre comes plain or coated with herb or ash.

Chicken

Chicken A domestic bird that is well known for its tender white meat and moist dark meat.

Types: Here are the common types of chicken you can buy at your local supermarket.

☐ **Broiler-Fryers:** Young, tender chickens that weigh anywhere from 2½ to 5 pounds, with an average weight of 3½ pounds. You can broil, grill, bake, fry, simmer, roast, or micro-cook these all-purpose birds.

☐ **Capons:** Castrated roosters usually weighing about 9 pounds. Capons have a layer of fat under the skin, making their meat especially tender and flavorful. Capons taste best when they are roasted.

☐ **Roasting Chickens:** Young chickens weighing about 5 pounds. They are a little older and larger than broiler-fryers, and their meat is tender and should be roasted or grilled.

☐ **Stewing Chickens:** Mature female chickens weighing 2½ to 5 pounds. They generally are less tender than other chickens. Simmer stewing chickens in liquid, or use them in stews and soups.

Market forms: You can purchase chickens whole, cut up, and packaged by the piece (for example, all breasts or all thighs). Look for fresh, frozen, and canned products. Some supermarkets also feature cooked chicken in their meat departments or delicatessens.

Selecting: For information, see *Poultry.*

Buying tip: Allow about ½ pound for each serving for chicken with bones or ¼ pound per serving for boneless chicken.

continued

Cutting Up A Whole Chicken

1. To cut up a bird, cut through the skin between the thigh and body. Bend thigh back until hip joint breaks. Cut through joint, separating leg from body. To separate thigh and drumstick, slit skin above knee joint, break joint, then cut apart. Repeat on the other side.

2. To remove a wing, pull it away from the body. Slit the skin between wing and body. Bend the wing back until the joint breaks. Cut through the joint. Repeat on the other side.

3. With a sharp knife or kitchen shears, cut along breast end of ribs on one side, cutting toward neck to separate breast from back. Repeat on the other side. Bend front and back halves apart. Cut through neck joints that connect halves.

4. To divide the back in half, hold the piece at each end. Bend the ends toward the skin side until the bones break. Cut the back in half where the bones are broken. Cut off the tail.

5. To divide breast in half, cut lengthwise along breastbone. *Or,* to divide breast in half crosswise, grasp breast at each end and bend breast toward the skin side to break bones. Cut between wishbone and breastbone, as shown.

Skinning And Boning Chicken Breasts

To skin chicken breasts, place the whole breast, skin side up, on a cutting board. Starting on one side of the breast, use your hand to pull the skin away from the meat. Discard the skin.

To bone chicken breasts, cut the meat away from one side of the breastbone, using a thin, sharp knife. Then move the knife over the rib bones, pulling away the meat. Repeat on the other side.

To remove the long white tendon from each breast half, hold one end of the tendon with your fingers. Use the tip of the knife to scrape the meat away from the tendon as you pull it out.

Refrigerating: Uncooked chicken should be refrigerated promptly after it is purchased and then used within 2 days. Cut-up cooked chicken can be stored in the refrigerator for up to 2 days, and whole cooked chicken for up to 3 days.

Freezing: For longer storage, you can freeze uncooked whole chickens for up to 1 year, chicken pieces for up to 9 months, and cooked chicken that is not in broth or gravy for up to 1 month. See *Poultry* for additional freezing and thawing information.

A word of warning: *Never freeze stuffed chickens.* The stuffing may not reheat to a high enough temperature to kill bacteria that can cause food poisoning. Also, when stuffed chickens thaw, the stuffing provides optimum conditions for the growth of bacteria. If you want to make stuffing ahead, freeze it separately from the bird.

To retain the texture and flavor, do not refreeze thawed uncooked or cooked chicken.

A Tip from Our Kitchen

When cutting chicken or any raw meat or fish, place it on a plastic cutting board, because this type of cutting board is easier to clean than a wooden one. Improperly cleaned wooden cutting boards may retain harmful bacteria that can contaminate other foods and cause food poisoning.

How to cook: For roasting and broiling directions, see the Roasting Poultry and Broiling Poultry charts under *Poultry.*

For grilling directions, see the Direct-Grilling Poultry and Indirect-Grilling Poultry charts under *Barbecue.*

If you need cooked chicken for a recipe, poach some chicken breasts. To get 2 cups of cubed, cooked chicken, start with 2 whole medium chicken breasts (about 1½ pounds), halved and skinned, if desired, or ¾ pound skinned and boned chicken breasts.

Place the chicken breasts in a large skillet with 1⅓ cups water. Bring to boiling; reduce heat. Cover and simmer for 18 to 20 minutes for breast halves with bones (12 to 14 minutes for boneless pieces) or till tender and no longer pink. Drain and cut into cubes.

Q: **Should a dieter eat dark or white chicken meat?**

A: White meat is the better low-calorie choice, especially without skin. Here is a comparison of 3 ounces of roasted light and dark meat with and without skin. (Note that without skin you'll be consuming slightly more meat. That's why the cholesterol is slightly higher but the fat is lower.)

Light meat with skin—189 calories, 9 grams of fat, and 71 milligrams of cholesterol. *Light meat without skin*—147 calories, 4 grams of fat, and 72 milligrams of cholesterol.

Dark meat with skin—215 calories, 13 grams of fat, and 77 milligrams of cholesterol. *Dark meat without skin*—174 calories, 8 grams of fat, and 79 milligrams of cholesterol.

Nutrition hints: By removing the skin and pockets of fat under the skin of the chicken, you can trim off calories and fat.

(See *Poultry* for thawing, cooking, and other information.)

Chicken-Fry
To coat a food, usually beef, with a seasoned mixture and then cook it in a skillet until a brown, crisp crust forms. The coating can be seasoned flour or a covering of egg followed by crumbs. If a less tender cut of meat is used, it may be tenderized by pounding before coating. A creamy gravy often is served with chicken-fried foods.

To test chicken for doneness, grasp the end of a drumstick with a paper towel. It should twist easily in the socket. Or, pierce the thigh meat with a fork. The juices should be clear, not pink.

Chicory

Chicory

Typically, a variety of salad green, also called curly endive, that forms a head with crisp, frilly, narrow, dark green leaves that curl at the edges. Chicory has a pleasantly bitter tang and a prickly texture. Radicchio is a red variety of chicory (see also *Radicchio*).

Chicory roots can be ground into a coffee substitute, which also is called chicory.

(See *Endive* for selecting, storing, and nutrition information.)

Chiffon Cake

A light cake similar to angel food cake in that it depends on beaten egg whites for its airy texture. It is richer than angel food cake, however, because it includes cooking oil and egg yolks. It also contains baking powder to help with leavening.

Plain chiffon cake is pale yellow with a slightly sweet flavor, but it can be dressed up with citrus peel or bottled flavorings. One-twelfth of a 10-inch cake made from scratch has about 290 calories.

(See *Cake* for How to Solve Cake Problems, Cake-Making Hints, and baking, storing, and other information.)

Chiffon Cake

2¼ cups sifted cake flour *or* 2 cups sifted all-purpose flour
1½ cups sugar
1 tablespoon baking powder
½ cup cooking oil
7 egg yolks
1 teaspoon vanilla
2 teaspoons finely shredded orange peel
1 teaspoon finely shredded lemon peel
7 egg whites
½ teaspoon cream of tartar

■ In a large bowl combine flour, sugar, baking powder, and ¼ teaspoon *salt;* make a well in center. Add oil, yolks, vanilla, and ¾ cup *cold water.* Beat with an electric mixer on low speed till combined. Beat on high speed about 5 minutes or till satin smooth. Fold in orange and lemon peels. Thoroughly wash beaters. In a large bowl beat egg whites and cream of tartar on medium to high speed till stiff peaks form (tips stand straight). Pour batter in a thin stream over beaten egg whites; fold in gently. Pour into *ungreased* 10-inch tube pan. Bake in a 325° oven for 65 to 70 minutes or till top springs back when lightly touched. *Immediately* invert cake (leave in pan); cool thoroughly. Serves 12.

Nutrition information per serving: 288 calories, 5 g protein, 40 g carbohydrate, 12 g fat (2 g saturated), 124 mg cholesterol, 160 mg sodium, 58 mg potassium.

Chiffon Pie

A single-crust pie with a fluffy filling that's made with gelatin, egg whites, flavoring, and sometimes whipped cream (see Using Eggs Safely under *Egg.*) The crust can be pastry or crumb based.

Chili con Carne

A Mexican main dish made with beef, onions, sometimes pinto or kidney beans, and seasonings, such as chili peppers, ground cumin, and chili powder. The flavor of the dish varies from hot to mild, depending upon the amount and type of peppers and other seasonings used. Whether it's made with cubed or ground beef and contains beans are two points often debated.

Chili con Carne

- ¾ **pound lean ground beef**
- 1 **cup chopped onion**
- ½ **cup chopped green pepper**
- 2 **cloves garlic, minced**
- 1 **16-ounce can tomatoes, cut up**
- 1 **16-ounce can dark red kidney beans, drained**
- 1 **8-ounce can tomato sauce**
- 2 **to 3 teaspoons chili powder**
- ½ **teaspoon dried basil, crushed**
- ¼ **teaspoon salt**
- ¼ **teaspoon pepper**

■ In a large saucepan cook ground beef, onion, green pepper, and garlic till meat is brown. Drain fat. Stir in *undrained* tomatoes, kidney beans, tomato sauce, chili powder, basil, salt, and pepper. Bring to boiling; reduce heat. Cover; simmer for 20 minutes. Makes 4 servings.

Microwave directions: In a 2-quart microwave-safe casserole, combine beef, onion, green pepper, and garlic. Micro-cook, covered, on 100% power (high) for 6 to 9 minutes or till meat is no longer pink and vegetables are tender, stirring once. Drain. Stir in *undrained* tomatoes, kidney beans, tomato sauce, chili powder, basil, salt, and pepper. Cook, covered, on high for 9 to 11 minutes or till heated through, stirring twice.

Nutrition information per serving: 308 calories, 22 g protein, 31 g carbohydrate, 12 g fat (4 g saturated), 49 mg cholesterol, 1,081 mg sodium, 1,027 mg potassium.

Chili Pepper
A smooth-skinned pod of any of the numerous pepper plants. These peppers range in flavor from mild to fiery and vary in color from yellow to red or green. Some varieties of chili peppers are eaten fresh, and others are used dried.

(See *Pepper* for identification photos, the **Selecting Peppers chart, market forms, and selecting, storing, preparation, and other information.**)

Chili Powder
A ground blend of relatively mild chili peppers, oregano, cumin, garlic, and salt. It has a hot, spicy, and sometimes peppery taste and aroma. Additional seasonings in the blend can include coriander, red pepper, cloves, allspice, and others. Salt-free chili powder also is available.

(See *Spice* for the Spice Alternative Guide and selecting and storing information.)

Chili Sauce
A spicy, tangy, thick sauce made from tomatoes, sweet peppers, chili peppers, onions, celery, and spices. Chili sauces have varying hotness levels and are used as a condiment and as a recipe ingredient. One tablespoon of commercially bottled chili sauce has about 20 calories.

Chill
To cool a food to below room temperature in the refrigerator or over ice.

Tips from Our Kitchen
● To chill foods quickly, place the bowl or saucepan of food in a container of ice water. Or, place the food in the freezer for a short time to start chilling. (Twenty minutes in the freezer equals about an hour in the refrigerator.)
● If the food you are chilling is a gelatin mixture, be sure to stir it frequently for a more even set. If the mixture is a pudding, sauce, or other thickened mixture, cool it without stirring to avoid making the mixture runny.

Chinese Cabbage
A name given to both a category of Oriental cabbages and to a specific variety of Oriental cabbage. Chinese cabbages are nothing at all like head cabbages. They're more like a cross between celery and lettuce.

continued

Varieties: There are basically two kinds of Chinese cabbages available.

☐ **Bok Choy:** Elongated cabbage with long, white, celerylike stalks and large deep green leaves. Bok choy has a sweet, mild, cabbagelike flavor (see also *Bok Choy*).

☐ **Napa (or Nappa):** Elongated, tightly curled leaves with large white ribs and slightly frilly, pale green tips. Napa cabbage, also known as Chinese cabbage, celery cabbage, and Tientsin cabbage, is crunchy and a little sweeter than head cabbage, with a slight zestiness.

Selecting: Pick fresh-looking Chinese cabbages with crisp leaves. Avoid those with discolored, wilted leaves.

Storing: Refrigerate in a plastic bag for up to 4 days.

Q: How is napa cabbage used, and is there a substitute for it?

A: Napa cabbage quite often is used in Oriental stir-fries as well as in salads and in fillings for sandwiches, egg rolls, spring rolls, and wontons. When napa cabbage isn't available, you can try substituting smaller amounts of head cabbage.

Nutrition information: A 1-cup serving of fresh, shredded Chinese cabbage has about 10 calories; ½ cup of cooked, shredded Chinese cabbage also has about 10 calories.

(See *Bok Choy* and *Cabbage* for identification photos.)

Chinese Noodle   Any of a variety of noodles used in Oriental cooking.

Types: Here's what you'll find in the supermarket or at an Oriental food store.

☐ **Cellophane:** Thin, almost transparent, flavorless noodles made from ground mung beans. These noodles can be cooked in liquid or deep-fried in fat. They also are called bean threads or bean noodles.

☐ **Chinese Egg:** Very fine noodles that taste and look much like regular egg noodles.

Chinese egg noodles are made from wheat flour, water, and egg. They are sold either fresh, steamed, or dried.

☐ **Rice Sticks:** Almost transparent, flavorless noodles. Rice sticks are similar to cellophane noodles except that they are made from rice flour. They also are known as rice noodles or rice vermicelli.

Q: Is there a substitute for Chinese noodles?

A: Try using fine egg noodles, thin spaghetti, vermicelli, or angel hair pasta, except in recipes that call for deep-fat fried noodles.

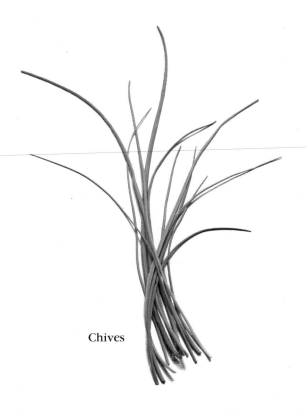

Chives

Chive   An herb that belongs to the onion family. Its long, green, tubular leaves have a mild onion flavor and are used in cooking.

Market forms: Fresh chives are sold year-round—often right in a growing pot so you can snip the leaves as you need them. They grow back after cutting, just as grass does. Frozen and freeze-dried chives also are available.

Q: How do you use fresh, frozen, and freeze-dried chives?

A: Use them as they are—it's not necessary to thaw frozen chives or reconstitute freeze-dried chives. Use the three forms of chives—fresh, frozen, and freeze-dried—interchangeably in recipes. If you're substituting frozen or freeze-dried for the fresh, use the amount that's called for in the recipe, not one-third of the amount as is recommended when substituting other dried herbs for fresh ones. Fresh chives are the best choice for garnishes.

(See *Herb* for the Herb Alternative Guide and selecting, storing, preparation, cooking, nutrition, and other information.)

Chocolate
A rich brown food made from cacao beans. The cacao beans are roasted, shelled, and ground to make pure chocolate. Pure chocolate is about 50 percent cocoa butter, a vegetable fat that gives chocolate its smooth texture. When most of the cocoa butter is pressed out of pure chocolate, the remaining product is cocoa powder (see also *Cocoa*).

Semisweet chocolate

Premelted, unsweetened chocolate product

Unsweetened chocolate

Milk chocolate

White baking bars or pieces with cocoa butter

Sweet chocolate

Types: Following are summaries of the various kinds of chocolate.

□ **Sweet:** A chocolate product made of at least 15 percent pure chocolate, extra cocoa butter, and sugar. It is used in cooking and baking.

□ **Milk:** A chocolate product made of at least 10 percent pure chocolate, extra cocoa butter, sugar, and milk solids. This is the most popular chocolate for eating, but it also is used for cooking and baking.

□ **Semisweet:** A chocolate product made of at least 35 percent pure chocolate, extra cocoa butter, and sugar. It is used for eating, cooking, and baking. It sometimes is called bittersweet chocolate.

□ **Unsweetened:** Pure chocolate with no sugar or flavoring added. It sometimes is called bitter or baking chocolate. Because it is so bitter, it is used almost exclusively for cooking and baking.

□ **Chocolatelike Products:** Foods that are used as chocolate is but cannot be called pure chocolate because they lack chocolate liquor (the thick, rich brown paste resulting from ground cocoa beans) and/or contain another fat, such as vegetable oil.

Premelted, unsweetened chocolate product is semiliquid and made of cocoa powder and vegetable oil. *White baking bars* or *pieces with*
continued

cocoa butter are made of sugar, cocoa butter, dry-milk solids, and flavorings. They often are confused with confectioner's coating, a product made with hardened vegetable fat instead of cocoa butter.

Market forms: Chocolate is available in an array of eating and cooking forms, such as squares, chunks, and pieces of various sizes. There also are numerous chocolate candies and many products made with chocolate, such as chocolate-flavored syrup, ice-cream toppings, and milk.

Although not made from chocolate, imitation chocolate pieces also are available.

Chocolate Substitutions

Although it is always best to use the type of chocolate called for in a recipe, in an emergency you can use the following substitutions:

- For 1 square (1 ounce) *unsweetened chocolate,* use 3 tablespoons unsweetened cocoa powder plus 1 tablespoon shortening or cooking oil.
- For 1 square (1 ounce) *semisweet chocolate,* use 1 square unsweetened chocolate plus 1 tablespoon sugar.
- For 4 ounces *sweet chocolate,* use ¼ cup unsweetened cocoa powder plus ⅓ cup sugar and 3 tablespoons shortening.

Storing: Chocolate should be stored tightly covered in a cool, dry place. The temperature should be between 60° and 78°.

In hot weather, you may want to refrigerate chocolate. Before refrigerating chocolate, wrap it tightly in foil and then seal it in a plastic bag to prevent the chocolate from absorbing odors from other foods. When bringing chocolate to room temperature, leave it wrapped, so moisture doesn't condense on it and cause lumping when the chocolate is melted.

Q: When chocolate looks gray on the surface, can it still be used?

A: Yes. This gray color or "bloom" does not hurt the quality of the chocolate and will disappear when heated. Bloom develops when chocolate is stored in conditions that are too humid or too warm.

Melting hints: Chocolate can be melted either in a pan on the range top or in a microwave-safe container in the microwave oven. To speed melting on the range top, chop or break up the chocolate before putting it into the pan.

To melt chocolate on the range top, use a heavy saucepan or a double boiler. Be sure all the utensils are completely dry, because even a little water will cause the chocolate to stiffen and become grainy and lumpy. Place the saucepan over low heat or place the top of the double boiler over hot, not boiling, water. Stir chocolate frequently to prevent it from scorching.

To melt chocolate in the microwave oven, place 1 cup chocolate pieces or two 1-ounce squares of chocolate in a microwave-safe measuring or custard cup. Micro-cook, uncovered, on 100% power (high) for 1½ to 2 minutes or till soft enough to stir smooth. (Chocolate pieces—as well as squares of chocolate—won't seem melted until stirred.)

Q: Is there a way to "repair" chocolate that has stiffened during melting?

A: Yes. Stir in ½ to 1 teaspoon of shortening or cooking oil at a time, till the mixture becomes smooth and shiny. Do not use margarine or butter.

Nutrition information: The calories and fat vary from one manufacturer's product to another, but in general, a 1-ounce portion of sweet chocolate, milk chocolate, semisweet chocolate, and unsweetened chocolate each contains about 145 calories. Each also contains 9 or 10 grams of fat except for unsweetened chocolate, which has about 15 grams of fat.

Chokecherry A small, tart fruit of the wild cherry tree with red skin and a pit. The fruit is too sour to enjoy plain. Use it sweetened in jam, jelly, and sauce recipes.

Cholesterol A substance produced by the liver that helps blanket nerve fibers and lends durability to cell walls. Although cholesterol is needed in moderate amounts, the body manufactures an adequate supply. Medical experts say that elevated blood cholesterol levels may increase the risk of heart attack and some forms of cancer in some people. Cholesterol is found only in animal foods.

(See *Fat* for the Fat and Cholesterol Primer.)

Chop (noun) A term used to refer to a cut of pork, lamb, or veal taken from the loin or rib area of the animal. Chops can be purchased with or without the bone.

Chop (verb) To cut a food with a knife or cleaver, or with an appliance, such as a food processor, into irregular pieces about the size of peas. Recipes can call for coarsely or finely chopped foods, which are pieces larger or smaller than peas.

A Tip from Our Kitchen
The food processor can make short work of chopping. For pieces that are close to the same size, cut or break up the food somewhat before putting it into the appliance. Then quickly turn the appliance on and off to control the size of the pieces. The longer the food processor runs, the smaller the pieces.

Q: Is cubing the same as chopping?
A: No. The terms chopping, cubing, dicing, and mincing all appear in recipes and may be confusing. To see the difference, compare the foods and descriptions in the photos, below.

Chop Suey A popular Chinese-style main dish that originated in America. Although ingredients vary from recipe to recipe, chop suey usually contains bean sprouts, bamboo shoots, water chestnuts, celery, mushrooms, and soy sauce. It may also include pieces of chicken or pork. Chop suey commonly is served with rice.

Chou Paste *(SHOO)* The French name for a pastry used in cream puffs and éclairs. It also is called choux (see also *Cream Puff*).

Chopping refers to cutting a food into irregular pieces about the size of peas.

Mincing refers to chopping a food into tiny irregular pieces.

Cubing means to cut a food into uniform pieces, usually about ½ inch on all sides.

Dicing is similar to cubing, except the pieces are smaller, ⅛ to ¼ inch in size on all sides.

Chowchow   A zesty relish that is made from chopped vegetables, such as cabbage, peppers, cucumbers, and onions, packed in a sugar-vinegar solution, and seasoned with mustard and pickling spice. Chowchow is served as a condiment with such foods as grilled meats and sausages.

Chowder   A thick soup that usually is milk-based and made with seafood or fish. Clam chowder is perhaps the most common example (see *Clam Chowder*). Other chowders are made with ingredients such as corn, chicken, potatoes, and cheese.

Chow Mein   A Chinese main dish that contains meat or poultry and crisp-tender vegetables, such as celery, mushrooms, and Chinese cabbage. The dish often is similar to chop suey, except that it is served with noodles. The noodles may be Chinese egg noodles, which are cooked in water and then quickly fried, or chow mein noodles.

Chicken Chow Mein

      4   **medium boneless, skinless chicken
            breast halves (12 ounces total)** *or*
            12 ounces lean boneless pork
     ½   **cup water**
      1   **tablespoon cornstarch**
      3   **tablespoons soy sauce**
      1   **teaspoon grated fresh gingerroot** *or*
            ½ teaspoon ground ginger
      2   **tablespoons cooking oil**
      2   **green onions, bias-sliced into 1-inch
            lengths**
      1   **stalk celery, thinly sliced (½ cup)**
      1   **clove garlic, minced**
      1   **cup sliced fresh mushrooms**
      3   **cups chopped Chinese cabbage**
   1½   **cups fresh bean sprouts** *or* **one 14-
            ounce can bean sprouts, drained**
      1   **3-ounce can chow mein noodles**

■ Cut chicken into bite-size pieces or thinly slice pork, across the grain, into bite-size pieces; set aside.

■ For sauce, in a small bowl stir together water, cornstarch, soy sauce, and gingerroot. Set the mixture aside.
■ Pour *1 tablespoon* of the oil into a wok or 12-inch skillet. Preheat over medium-high heat. Stir-fry onion, celery, and garlic for 2 minutes. Stir in mushrooms and stir-fry 2 minutes more. Remove vegetables from wok.
■ Add remaining oil to the wok or skillet. Add the chicken or pork to the wok or skillet. Stir-fry for 2 to 3 minutes or till no pink remains. Push chicken or pork from the center of the wok. Stir sauce. Add sauce to the center of the wok or skillet. Cook and stir till thickened and bubbly. Return cooked vegetables along with Chinese cabbage and bean sprouts to the wok or skillet. Stir ingredients together to coat with sauce. Cook and stir for 2 to 3 minutes or till heated through. Serve over chow mein noodles. Makes 4 servings.

Nutrition information per serving: 325 calories, 25 g protein, 21 g carbohydrate, 17 g fat (3 g saturated), 54 mg cholesterol, 936 mg sodium, 530 mg potassium.

Chow Mein Noodle   A short, crisp, fried noodle. These noodles are primarily served in America as an accompaniment to chow mein. Available in cans and packages, they also can be used as a topping for casseroles or in a snack mix.

Chutney   A fruit or vegetable relish served as an accompaniment to meats and curried foods. This East Indian specialty can range in texture from smooth to chunky and in flavor from sweet to tart. Sometimes chutney also is spicy-hot. Commercially made chutney often contains mangoes, tamarinds, raisins, and spices. Tomatoes, apples, and peaches are common ingredients in homemade chutney recipes.

Cilantro *(sih LON troh)* Small, fragile, green leaves of the coriander plant (see also *Coriander*). This herb also is known as Chinese parsley. Cilantro has a pungent, almost musty odor and taste that give a distinctive flavor to Mexican and other Latin American dishes, as well as to Oriental cuisine. Dried and freeze-dried cilantro leaves are available as well as the fresh herb.

(See *Herb* for the Herb Alternative Guide and selecting, storing, preparation, nutrition, and other information. See also *Oriental Cooking* for an identification photo.)

Cinnamon A dark, reddish brown spice with a strong, spicy-sweet flavor and aroma. Cinnamon is actually the bark of a tropical evergreen tree. When the bark is left to dry, it rolls up into tight curls, called cinnamon sticks. The sticks are pulverized to make ground cinnamon. Cinnamon sticks and ground cinnamon, as well as oil of cinnamon, are available year-round.

Q: How do you use stick cinnamon and oil of cinnamon?
A: Use stick cinnamon as a swizzle stick in hot chocolate, hot rum drinks, and apple cider. Or, use it in a spice bag when making hot punches. Oil of cinnamon often is used in making candy.

(See *Spice* for the Spice Alternative Guide and selecting, storing, and nutrition information.)

Cioppino *(chuh PEA no)* A fish stew first made in California. It typically includes fish, shellfish, tomatoes, onion, and wine. It is similar to the French fish stew, bouillabaisse.

Cioppino

1 pound fresh *or* frozen fish fillets
¾ cup chopped green pepper
½ cup chopped onion
1 clove garlic, minced
1 tablespoon cooking oil
1 16-ounce can tomatoes, cut up
1 8-ounce can tomato sauce
½ cup dry white *or* red wine
3 tablespoons snipped parsley
¼ teaspoon dried oregano, crushed
¼ teaspoon dried basil, crushed
⅛ teaspoon salt
   Dash pepper
1 6½-ounce can minced clams
1 4½-ounce can shrimp, rinsed and drained

■ Thaw fish, if frozen. Cut fish into 1-inch pieces. In a large saucepan cook green pepper, onion, and garlic in hot oil till tender. Add tomatoes, tomato sauce, wine, parsley, oregano, basil, salt, and pepper. Bring to boiling; reduce heat. Cover and simmer 20 minutes. Add fish, *undrained* clams, and shrimp. Bring just to boiling; reduce heat. Cover and simmer 5 to 7 minutes or till fish flakes easily with a fork. Makes 5 servings.

Nutrition information per serving: 208 calories, 28 g protein, 11 g carbohydrate, 5 g fat (1 g saturated), 90 mg cholesterol, 568 mg sodium, 789 mg potassium.

Citron A citrus fruit similar to lemon, but with a thick, yellow-green rind. The rind is candied and used as a baking ingredient. Candied citron is sold in pieces, diced, and as part of mixed candied fruits and peels.

Citrus Fruit A tropical fruit that is high in vitamin C. Citrus fruits include oranges, grapefruit, lemons, limes, and related varieties. They range in taste from tart to sweet and in color from orange and yellow to green.

Types: See the Selecting Citrus Fruit chart, page 106.

continued

Selecting Citrus Fruit

You'll find many kinds of citrus fruit at the supermarket. These fruits vary in flavor from sweet and juicy to bold and tart. They also offer a diversity of color and size, from yellow and orange to bright green, and from small kumquats to large grapefruit.

Type*	Size	Appearance	Flavor	Calories (per fruit)
Grapefruit	1 to 2 per pound	Yellow to pink peel and meat	Sweet-tart, tangy	78 calories
Kumquat	About 20 per pound	Bright orange peel; pale orange meat	Sweet-tart	12 calories
Lemon	3 or 4 per pound	Bright yellow peel; pale yellow meat	Sour	17 calories
Lime	4 or 5 per pound	Bright green peel; pale green meat	Bold, tart	20 calories
Limequat	About 20 per pound	Shiny green peel; pale green meat	Tart lime	Not available
Orange	3 medium or 2 large per pound	Bright orange peel; orange meat	Sweet, juicy	60 calories
Tangelo	3 medium or 2 large per pound	Light to deep orange peel; pale yellow to deep orange meat	Tangy, sweet	Not available
Tangerine	About 4 per pound	Bright orange peel; orange meat	Mild, sweet	37 calories

See individual entries for additional information.

Storing: Citrus fruits keep well—you can store them for 2 to 3 weeks in the crisper of your refrigerator.

Q: Can citrus fruit be frozen?
A: Yes, you can freeze either orange or grapefruit sections or any citrus fruit peel for use later. Store the sections and peel up to 6 months.

To freeze sections, peel and section (see *Section*) the fruit first. Then spread the sections out on a flat baking sheet and freeze them. Place the frozen sections in freezer bags or containers, leaving ½-inch headspace, and return them to the freezer. Use the sections for chilled fruit mixtures. If you add partially frozen sections to a mixture, they'll help chill it.

To freeze peel, remove the peel using a vegetable peeler or shredder. Then spread the peel out on a baking sheet and freeze it. Place the frozen peel in freezer bags or containers, leaving ½-inch headspace, and return it to the freezer. Label and date the packages. Use the peel in recipes.

Tips from Our Kitchen

- If you like to squeeze your own citrus juices, here's how to get the most juice from the fruits you buy. Start by choosing fruits that are heavy for their size; they'll contain more juice.
- Before squeezing the fruit, leave it out at room temperature about 30 minutes. Then roll each piece of fruit on the counter under the palm of your hand a few times. This will encourage more juice to flow.
- Save time by using the microwave oven to warm a lemon, lime, or a small orange before juicing it. Halve the fruit and heat it on 100% power (high) for 30 to 45 seconds.

Nutrition information: All citrus fruits are high in vitamin C. Calorie counts vary somewhat but are fairly low. (See the Selecting Citrus Fruit chart, above.)

  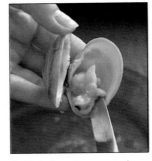

1. To clean and shuck clams, use a stiff brush to scrub the clamshells under cold running water. Then soak the clams in salted water to expel any sand. (A hard-shell clam is shown.)

2. Hold clam with hinged back side against a heavy cloth in the palm of the hand. Working over a plate to catch the juices, insert a sturdy blunt-tipped knife between shell halves.

3. Holding the shell firmly, move the knife blade around the clam, cutting the muscles that hold the shell together. Twist the knife slightly to pry open the shell.

4. Cut the clam muscle free from the shell. Remove the muscle and the juices, and use in the shucked form.

Clam

A shellfish with edible flesh encased in two shells hinged at the back. Clams should be mild with the flavor of fresh salt water.

Types: In the United States, the East Coast is the major source of commercial clams. The Pacific Coast provides less common varieties.

☐ East Coast Clams

Hard-shell: Also called round clams and, in New England, quahogs. Of the different types of hard-shell clams, the smallest are littlenecks, which are the sweetest and most tender. Cherrystones are slightly larger than littlenecks. Still larger are chowder clams. These are tougher than the smaller varieties and are used minced in soups and sauces.

Soft-shell: Also called long-neck clams, steamers, squirt clams, and belly clams. Soft-shell clams have necks that stick out between the shells. These small clams have a very soft texture, and although usually steamed, they're great fried or used in clam chowder.

Surf: Larger and more oval than hard-shells. Surf clams are usually processed into minced clam products or cut into strips for frying.

☐ Pacific Coast Clams

The Pacific *Littlenecks* are hard-shell clams but aren't related to the East Coast variety. The *Razor* clam is a long, narrow soft-shell type. The *Geoduck (GOO ee duck),* found only off the Pacific Northwest coast, is the largest clam in North America. It often is ground for use in soups and chowders.

Market forms: Clams are marketed live in the shell, fresh shucked, canned, and smoked. You'll find fresh shucked clams sold in pint and quart containers.

Q: How many shucked clams come in a pint container?

A: Figure on about 18 shucked clams per pint. That's equal to about two 7½-ounce cans of minced clams.

Selecting: When buying live clams, look for moist shells without cracks and chips. Only buy clams that close when gently tapped.

For shucked clams, look for plump ones with clear juices and no pieces of shell.

continued

Storing: Refrigerate live clams, covered with a moist cloth in an open container, for up to 5 days.

Before cooking, discard any clams that don't close their shells when lightly tapped. Refrigerate shucked clams, covered in their liquor, for up to 3 days. If more liquor is needed to keep them covered, make a homemade brine by mixing ½ teaspoon salt with 1 cup water. Freeze shucked clams, covered in their liquor, for up to 6 months.

Preparation hints: Chilling live clams before shucking makes them easier to open.

See the Preparing and Cooking Shellfish chart under *Shellfish*.

How to cook: See the Preparing and Cooking Shellfish chart under *Shellfish*.

Nutrition information: A 3-ounce serving of steamed clams has about 130 calories.

Clam Chowder
A hearty soup or stew made with clams. New England-style chowders are milk-based and often contain salt pork or bacon and diced potatoes. Manhattan-style chowders are tomato-based and may contain other vegetables in addition to (or in place of) potatoes in a broth.

New England Clam Chowder

    1   pint shucked clams *or* two 6½-ounce
          cans minced clams
    2   slices bacon, halved
  2½   cups finely chopped, peeled potatoes
    1   cup chopped onion
    1   teaspoon instant chicken bouillon
          granules
    1   teaspoon Worcestershire sauce
    ¼   teaspoon dried thyme, crushed
    ⅛   teaspoon pepper
    2   cups milk
    1   cup light cream
    2   tablespoons all-purpose flour

■ Chop shucked clams, reserving juice; set clams aside. Strain clam juice to remove bits of shell. (*Or,* drain canned clams, reserving juice.) If necessary, add water to clam juice to equal *1 cup.* Set clam-juice mixture aside.

■ In a large saucepan cook bacon till crisp. Remove bacon, reserving *1 tablespoon* drippings. Drain bacon on paper towels; crumble. Set aside.

■ In the same saucepan combine reserved bacon drippings, reserved clam-juice mixture, potatoes, onion, bouillon granules, Worcestershire sauce, thyme, and pepper. Bring to boiling; reduce heat. Cover and simmer about 10 minutes or till potatoes are tender. With the back of a fork, mash potatoes slightly against the side of the pan.

■ Combine milk, cream, and flour till smooth. Add to potato mixture. Cook and stir till slightly thickened and bubbly. Stir in clams. Return to boiling; reduce heat. Cook 1 to 2 minutes more. Sprinkle each serving with some of the crumbled bacon. Makes 4 main-dish servings or 6 to 8 side-dish servings.

Nutrition information per side-dish serving: 257 calories, 17 g protein, 24 g carbohydrate, 11 g fat (5 g saturated), 56 mg cholesterol, 323 mg sodium, 678 mg potassium.

Fish Chowder: Prepare New England Clam Chowder as above, except substitute 1 pound fresh or frozen *fish steaks,* cut ¾ inch thick, for the clams. Thaw fish, if frozen, and cut into ¾-inch cubes. Substitute 1 cup *water* for the reserved clam juice and add ½ cup sliced *carrot* with potatoes and onion. Add fish to chowder with milk mixture. Bring just to boiling; reduce heat. Cover; simmer about 3 minutes or till fish flakes easily with a fork.

Nutrition information per side-dish serving: 260 calories, 19 g protein, 23 g carbohydrate, 10 g fat (5 g saturated), 60 mg cholesterol, 330 mg sodium, 586 mg potassium.

Manhattan Clam Chowder

1 pint shucked clams *or* two 6½-ounce
    cans minced clams
3 slices bacon, halved
1 cup chopped celery
1 cup chopped onion
1 28-ounce can tomatoes, cut up
2 cups finely chopped, peeled potatoes
½ teaspoon dried basil *or* marjoram,
    crushed
¼ teaspoon pepper

■ Chop shucked clams, reserving juice; set clams aside. Strain clam juice to remove bits of shell. (*Or,* drain canned clams, reserving juice.) If necessary, add water to juice to equal *1½ cups.* Set clam-juice mixture aside.
■ In a large saucepan cook bacon till crisp. Remove bacon, reserving drippings. Drain bacon on paper towels; crumble. Set aside.
■ Cook celery and onion in reserved bacon drippings over medium heat about 5 minutes or till tender. Drain. Stir in reserved clam-juice mixture, *undrained* tomatoes, potatoes, basil or marjoram, and pepper. Bring to boiling; reduce heat. Cover and simmer for 20 to 25 minutes or till vegetables are tender.
■ With the back of a fork, mash vegetables slightly against side of the pan. Stir in clams. Return to boiling; reduce heat. Cook 1 to 2 minutes more. Sprinkle each serving with some of the crumbled bacon. Makes 4 main-dish or 6 to 8 side-dish servings.

Nutrition information per side-dish serving: 200 calories, 14 g protein, 20 g carbohydrate, 7 g fat (2 g saturated), 40 mg cholesterol, 379 mg sodium, 819 mg potassium.

Clarify To make a cloudy food clear by separating solids from liquid. Foods that are clarified include butter, cooking oil after it has been used for deep-fat frying, and broths for clear soups (see also *Butter*).

Clove A dark, nail-shaped spice with a strong, pungent, almost hot flavor. Cloves are the unopened flower buds of a tropical evergreen tree. Whole and ground cloves are available.

A Tip from Our Kitchen
Make an old-fashioned pomander ball by sticking whole cloves into unpeeled oranges, lemons, limes, tangerines, or apples. You may need to poke the fruit first with a wooden or metal skewer in order to get the clove in without breaking it. Arrange the pomanders in a bowl for a fragrant centerpiece, or add them to your Christmas punch.

(**See** *Spice* **for the Spice Alternative Guide and selecting, storing, and nutrition information.**)

Coagulate To change the form of a food from liquid or semiliquid to semisolid or solid. For example, when an egg is heated, it changes from semiliquid to semisolid.

Coat To evenly cover a food with a substance such as bread crumbs, flour, or a batter. Coating a food usually adds flavor and texture and helps keep the food moist. If both the outer surface of the food and the coating are dry, the food must be dipped into a liquid, such as milk or beaten egg, before it is dipped into the dry coating.

Cobbler A baked dessert made with a fruit filling and a biscuitlike topping.

A Tip from Our Kitchen
For a perfectly done cobbler, drop the cobbler topping in mounds onto a *hot* bubbly fruit mixture. The heat from the fruit helps the topping cook evenly.

continued

Fruit Cobbler

> Desired filling (see below)
> 1 cup all-purpose flour
> ¼ cup sugar
> 1 teaspoon baking powder
> ½ teaspoon ground cinnamon
> (optional)
> 3 tablespoons margarine *or* butter
> 1 beaten egg
> 3 tablespoons milk
> Ice cream (optional)

■ Prepare filling. Keep hot. For topping, stir together flour, sugar, baking powder, and, if desired, cinnamon. Cut in margarine or butter till mixture resembles coarse crumbs. Combine egg and milk. Add to flour mixture, stirring just to moisten.
■ Transfer hot filling to an 8x8x2-inch baking dish. Drop topping into 6 mounds atop hot filling. Bake in a 400° oven for 20 to 25 minutes or till a toothpick inserted into topping comes out clean. Serve warm with ice cream, if desired. Makes 6 servings.

Apple or Pear Filling: Cook and stir 6 cups sliced, peeled *apples or pears,* ⅓ to ⅔ cup *sugar,* 3 tablespoons *water,* and 1 tablespoon *lemon juice* till boiling. Reduce heat. Cover and simmer for 5 minutes or till fruit is almost tender, stirring occasionally. Combine 2 tablespoons *water* and 1 tablespoon *cornstarch;* add to filling. Cook and stir till mixture is thickened and bubbly.

Nutrition information per serving with topping: 287 calories, 4 g protein, 53 g carbohydrate, 7 g fat (2 g saturated), 36 mg cholesterol, 131 mg sodium, 176 mg potassium.

Blueberry or Peach Filling: In a saucepan combine ⅓ to ⅔ cup *sugar* and 1 tablespoon *cornstarch.* Stir in ¼ cup *water.* Stir in 4 cups fresh *or* frozen *blueberries or* unsweetened *peach slices.* Cook and stir till mixture is thickened and bubbly.

Nutrition information per serving with topping: 276 calories, 4 g protein, 50 g carbohydrate, 7 g fat (2 g saturated), 36 mg cholesterol, 136 mg sodium, 134 mg potassium.

Cherry or Rhubarb Filling: In a saucepan combine 6 cups fresh *or* frozen unsweetened pitted *tart red cherries or* sliced *rhubarb,* 1 to 1¼ cups *sugar,* ¼ cup *water,* and 4 teaspoons *cornstarch.* Let stand 10 minutes (20 minutes for frozen fruit). Cook and stir till mixture is thickened and bubbly.

Nutrition information per serving with topping: 381 calories, 5 g protein, 76 g carbohydrate, 8 g fat (2 g saturated), 36 mg cholesterol, 132 mg sodium, 241 mg potassium.

Cockle
A tiny, clamlike mollusk with sweet meat, which is available shucked or canned. It is cooked and eaten in much the same way as a clam.

Cocktail
An alcoholic beverage that consists of a mixture of spirits or of spirits and another liquid, such as fruit juice or carbonated water. A cocktail can be nonalcoholic when it is made with a mixture of fruit juices or a combination of fruit juice and a carbonated beverage.

The term also refers to a fruit or seafood appetizer that's served as a first course.

Cocoa
A brown powdery food made by pressing most of the cocoa butter from pure chocolate. It is also the name of a beverage made with cocoa powder and milk.

Types: Here is a brief description of the various types of cocoa powder.
☐ **Unsweetened Cocoa Powder:** Pure chocolate powder with no ingredients added.
☐ **Dutch-Process Cocoa Powder:** Cocoa powder treated with alkali to partially neutralize the natural acids in the cacao bean. It also is called European-style cocoa powder. The flavor is more mellow and the color darker than unsweetened cocoa powder.
☐ **Presweetened Cocoa Powder:** A powdered drink mix made of cocoa powder, sugar, and flavorings. It usually is combined with milk for a beverage.

☐ **Instant Cocoa Mix:** A powdered drink mix made of cocoa powder, milk solids, sugar, and other flavorings. It usually is combined with water for a beverage. Low-calorie products and those with marshmallows also are available.

Storing: Cocoa will keep for several years if tightly covered and stored in a cool, dry area.

Q: **Can cocoa be substituted for other types of chocolate in a recipe?**
A: Yes. To substitute unsweetened cocoa powder and Dutch-process cocoa powder for chocolate, see tip under *Chocolate.* Other types of cocoa powder, such as presweetened cocoa powder and instant cocoa mix, do not give the same results if substituted in a recipe calling for unsweetened cocoa powder.

Nutrition information: One ounce or ⅓ cup of unsweetened cocoa powder contains about 70 calories and 5 grams fat.

Coconuts

Unsweetened cocoa powder

Instant cocoa mix

Presweetened cocoa powder

Coconut   The large, oval, husk-covered fruit of the coconut palm, filled with a milky liquid and white meat. The outer shell is hairy and tan-colored and has three soft spots, sometimes referred to as eyes. Once it is broken, the "nut" inside has a dark brown skin covering the white, firm-textured meat.

Market forms: Buy fresh, whole coconut or canned or packaged coconut. Canned and packaged coconut is processed and sold shredded, flaked, and grated in sweetened and unsweetened forms. Fresh and dried coconut pieces also may be available.
 Various other coconut products are sold. *Coconut water* is the liquid drawn from a coconut. *Coconut milk* is made from water (sometimes coconut water) and coconut pulp. *Coconut cream* (also called cream of coconut) is a thick, syrupy, sweetened coconut mixture. *Coconut oil* also is available.
 continued

Selecting: Select coconuts that slosh when gently shaken. The more liquid you hear sloshing around, the fresher the coconut. Avoid ones with damp or moldy eyes or cracked shells. One medium coconut, weighing about 1 pound, yields about 3 cups of shredded coconut.

Storing: Store whole coconuts at room temperature for up to 1 month. After the coconut is cracked, tightly wrap the coconut meat and store it in the refrigerator for up to 5 days. Use fresh coconut milk and water within 2 days. You can freeze shredded fresh coconut in a freezer bag for up to 6 months.

After opening, keep canned, packaged, or dried coconut in an airtight container. Canned or packaged coconut keeps 5 to 7 days, and dried coconut keeps 3 to 4 weeks in the refrigerator.

Cracking Coconuts

To open a coconut, locate the three soft eyes at the top of the shell. Pierce them with the tip of a knife or an ice pick; drain off the milk. With a hammer, gently tap the shell all around until it cracks and splits on its own.

Peel the brown husk from the coconut meat, and chop the coconut meat into uniform pieces. Use your food processor or a hand grater to shred or grate the coconut.

Nutrition information: A 2x2x½-inch piece of fresh coconut meat contains about 160 calories; ½ cup canned, sweetened, flaked coconut has about 170 calories.

Cod A lean saltwater fish with a white, delicately flavored, firm flesh that separates into large flakes when cooked.

Market forms: Cod is sold fresh and frozen as steaks and skinless, boneless fillets. Other market forms include frozen breaded sticks, portions, and nuggets as well as frozen prepared entrées. Salt cod also is available.

How to cook: Cod can be prepared in many different ways—baked, poached, broiled, panfried, and grilled. For baking, poaching, broiling, and panfrying directions, see the Cooking Fish chart under *Fish*. For grilling directions, see the Direct-Grilling Fish chart under *Barbecue*.

Nutrition information: Baked cod has about 90 calories in one 3-ounce serving.

Q: What is scrod?
A: Although scrod often is thought of as a separate species of fish, it actually is the name for a small cod or haddock. It's a term that you might see used on restaurant menus.

(See *Fish* for selecting, storing, thawing, and other information.)

Coddle To gently simmer an egg in the shell in water or another liquid just long enough to coagulate some of the white and slightly heat the yolk. Because eating slightly cooked eggs may be harmful due to possible bacterial contamination, we no longer recommend this method of cooking (see Using Eggs Safely under *Eggs*).

Coffee A beverage made from coffee beans that's usually served hot or used to flavor foods, especially desserts.

Types: There are hundreds of different coffees and coffee blends. Coffee flavor and body are determined by the type of bean used, the climate and soil where the coffee is grown, when the coffee is harvested, and the roasting method. Even coffees made from the same type of bean can vary greatly depending on the other factors.

Market forms: Here are the most common forms in which coffee is sold.

Whole beans are available in a regular or dark roast. Dark-roasted beans have been roasted longer, giving them a darker color and stronger flavor. Dark roasting also produces a slightly bitter flavor, which some coffee drinkers like.

Ground coffee is available in different grinds for different brewing. The shorter the brewing method, the finer the beans are ground. For instance, espresso coffee is finer than drip coffee, and drip coffee is finer than percolator coffee. Some coffee connoisseurs prefer buying whole beans and grinding them as they need them for the freshest coffee possible.

Instant coffee comes in powder form and in freeze-dried crystals. Often freeze-dried coffee is preferred because freeze-drying retains more flavor.

Flavored coffee is sold in whole bean, ground, and instant forms. Some popular flavorings that are added include spices, liqueurs, chocolate, and vanilla.

Regular Versus Decaffeinated

Most forms of coffee are available in regular and decaffeinated versions. For regular coffees, the caffeine content varies with the brewing method and the strength of the brew. For example, one 6-ounce cup of drip coffee has 110 to 150 milligrams of caffeine; the same amount of percolated coffee has 64 to 124 milligrams. Instant types of coffee have about half as much caffeine as the brewed types.

Decaffeinated coffee has about 97 percent of the caffeine removed. Decaffeinated whole or ground coffee usually is more expensive than regular coffee because of the additional processing to extract the caffeine.

Specialty Coffee Beverages

Specialty coffee beverages often appear on menus, but you may have wondered what they are and how they're made. Here are descriptions of some of the more popular ones.

● **Cafe au lait** *(ka FAY oh LAY)*: A French coffee drink made with equal parts of regular coffee and hot milk.

● **Cappuccino** *(cop uh CHEE no)*: An Italian version of café au lait made with espresso and frothy milk or cream. (Steam is forced through the milk portion to make it hot and foamy.) Cappuccino is served with a cinnamon stick or a sprinkling of cocoa powder, ground cinnamon, or nutmeg.

● **Demitasse** *(DEM ih tas)*: Double-strength coffee that's served in a small cup. A favorite in France, demitasse is served black with or without sugar.

● **Espresso** *(eh SPRES oh)*: Strong, concentrated black coffee that's brewed under pressure from finely ground, dark-roasted coffee. This Italian favorite is served in a small cup with a sugar cube and lemon peel.

● **Irish coffee:** Slightly sweetened coffee served in a tall, stemmed glass with Irish whiskey and a thick layer of whipped cream. Usually it is sprinkled with ground cinnamon or cocoa powder.

Selecting: Fresh regular and decaffeinated coffees are most readily available in vacuum-packed containers. Specialty coffees usually are not vacuum-packed. For the freshest possible specialty coffees, buy the coffee in small quantities from a store where the coffee is stored in airtight containers. Buying small amounts lets you use up the coffee quickly and also allows you to sample different coffees more often.

continued

Storing: In general, store fresh coffee, whether it is whole bean or roasted and ground, in a covered container in the refrigerator. Both whole beans and ground will stay fresh with no noticeable change up to 2 weeks. For longer storage, keep it in the freezer. (For coffee that isn't vacuum-packed, whole roasted coffee beans will stay fresh slightly longer than ground roasted coffee does.) Store instant and freeze-dried coffee at room temperature.

Unopened packages of vacuum-packed roasted coffee and jars of instant and freeze-dried coffees can be kept at room temperature for at least a year.

Coffee Cake
A rich sweet bread made from a batter or dough that usually is served at breakfast or brunch. Coffee cakes also are known as coffee breads.

Types: Coffee cakes can be leavened with yeast, or with baking powder or baking soda. Those made with yeast resemble bread, but the dough is sweeter and richer. These cakes usually are glazed with a sweet icing.

Coffee cakes made with baking powder or baking soda are more like cake than bread in texture, with an open grain and uneven surface. They often have a fruit filling and/or a streusel topping.

Coffee cakes can be shaped into circles, loaves, rings, pinwheels, and braids. The shape also can be formed by the type of baking pan used—square, rectangular, round, or tube.

Convenience products: Coffee cakes can be made from a variety of convenience products. Biscuit, hot-roll, and muffin mixes make an easy base for cakelike coffee cakes to which fruits, nuts, and spices can be added. Loaves of frozen bread dough and frozen sweet bread dough are available for making more breadlike coffee cakes. Refrigerated biscuit and roll doughs also can be turned into quick coffee cakes. Ready-made frozen coffee cakes are available, too.

Colby Cheese
A mild-flavored, natural cheese with a firm body and tiny holes. Colby is a cow's-milk cheese that has a light yellow to orange color.

(See *Cheese* for the Selecting Cheese chart and selecting, storing, serving, nutrition, and other information.)

Colby cheese   Colby-Monterey Jack cheese

Colby-Monterey Jack Cheese
A blend of orange Colby and white Monterey Jack cheeses with a mild, milky flavor, firm, smooth body, and mottled appearance (see also *Colby Cheese* and *Monterey Jack Cheese*). This cheese often is labeled as Colby-Jack, Co-Jack, marbled, or popcorn cheese.

(See *Cheese* for the Selecting Cheese chart and selecting, storing, serving, nutrition, and other information.)

Colcannon
An Irish dish that is a mixture of mashed cooked potatoes, cabbage or kale, and milk. Scallions, chives, or onion; parsley; and margarine or butter usually are added for flavor.

A Tip from Our Kitchen
For an easy colcannon, simply add chopped cabbage and onion to the water when cooking peeled potatoes. Then drain the cooked vegetables, mash, and season to taste.

Cold Cut   See *Luncheon Meat.*

Coleslaw   A salad mixture containing shredded raw cabbage combined with a flavorful dressing. Either a creamy mayonnaise-type mixture or sweet-tart vinaigrette is used for the dressing. Other crisp, colorful ingredients, such as shredded carrot, chopped green or red pepper, and sometimes raisins, may be added.

Coleslaw

    2 cups shredded cabbage
    1 medium carrot, shredded
    ½ of a small green *or* sweet red pepper,
       finely chopped
    2 green onions, sliced
    ½ cup mayonnaise *or* salad dressing
    1 tablespoon vinegar
    2 teaspoons sugar
    ½ teaspoon celery seed

■ In a mixing bowl combine cabbage, carrot, green or sweet red pepper, and green onions. For dressing, stir together mayonnaise or salad dressing, vinegar, sugar, and celery seed. Pour the dressing over the cabbage mixture; toss to coat. Cover and chill for 1 to 24 hours. Makes 4 servings.

Nutrition information per serving: 224 calories, 1 g protein, 7 g carbohydrate, 22 g fat (3 g saturated), 16 mg cholesterol, 168 mg sodium, 171 mg potassium.

Vinaigrette Coleslaw: Prepare Coleslaw as above, *except* omit mayonnaise, vinegar, sugar, and celery seed. For vinaigrette, in a screw-top jar combine ¼ cup *vinegar,* 3 tablespoons *salad oil,* 2 to 3 tablespoons *sugar,* and, if desired, several dashes *bottled hot pepper sauce.* Cover; shake well. Pour over cabbage mixture; toss to coat. Cover and chill as above.

Nutrition information per serving: 134 calories, 1 g protein, 11 g carbohydrate, 10 g fat (1 g saturated), 0 mg cholesterol, 12 mg sodium, 169 mg potassium.

Collard greens

Collard Green   A leafy vegetable that is actually a type of kale. Its green leaves have an irregular shape and torn-looking edges. Collard greens have a hearty, spinachlike flavor when cooked and are particularly popular in southern cooking.

Selecting: Choose healthy-looking greens with no brown spots.

Storing: Wash greens in cold water; pat dry. Place them in a plastic bag lined with a paper towel; store in refrigerator for up to 5 days.

How to cook: See Greens on the Cooking Fresh Vegetables chart under *Vegetable.*

Q: How can collard greens be cooked so they have a less bitter flavor?
A: Bring the collard greens to boiling in water, then discard water and add fresh water. Cook till collards are tender.

Nutrition information: One-half cup of cooked collard greens has about 15 calories.

Combine   To stir together two or more ingredients till well mixed.

Compote   A mixture of several kinds of bite-size fruits combined with a spice or flavoring or cooked in syrup. A compote can be served chilled or warm as a dessert or as a side dish for breakfast or brunch.

A compote is sometimes served in a stemmed bowl that also is called a compote.

Concentrate   To make less dilute, often by boiling to remove excess liquid.

The term also refers to a food that's sold in undiluted form, such as a frozen fruit juice concentrate.

Conch   (*konk*) A saltwater mollusk found in southern United States waters that has a beautiful, large, spiral shell. Conch has a delicate flavor. Like abalone, it needs to be tenderized by pounding before cooking.

Condiment   A food item, such as salt, pepper, catsup, mustard, pickles, or relish, that is used to add flavor to another food. Condiments most often are added at the table, but they also are used as recipe ingredients.

Conserve   (*KON serv*) A mixture of two or three fruits and sugar that is cooked to a jamlike consistency. Typically one of the fruits is a citrus fruit. Raisins and nuts usually are included. Conserve is used as a spread for breads, a filling for pastries, a topping for desserts, or a glaze for meats or poultry.

Consommé   A French word for a strong, flavorful stock made from the clarified liquid in which meat or poultry and its bones have been simmered. Longer cooking concentrates the liquid and extracts gelatin from the bones.

Q: Can consommé be served cold?
A: Yes. To serve consommé chilled, pour the warm soup into a small flat pan and chill.

Once set, it can be cut into bite-size cubes and served in a soup cup or used as a garnish on a salad plate.

Container Size   The volume of a box, bag, package, or can.

Container Sizes
There are many sizes and types of containers. Use this handy chart to estimate the approximate total volume containers hold.

Size	Total Volume
8-ounce can	= 1 cup
10½- to 12-ounce can	= 1¼ cups
12-ounce vacuum-packed can	= 1½ cups
14- to 16-ounce can (No. 300)	= 1¾ cups
16- to 17-ounce can (No. 303)	= 2 cups
20-ounce can (No. 2)	= 2½ cups
29-ounce can (No. 2½)	= 3½ cups
46-fluid-ounce can (No. 3 cylinder)	= 5¾ cups
6½-pound or 7-pound, 5-ounce can (No. 10)	= 12 to 13 cups
6-ounce can frozen juice concentrate	= ¾ cup
10-ounce package frozen vegetables	= 1½ to 2 cups
16-ounce package frozen vegetables	= 3 to 4 cups
1-pound package brown sugar (packed)	= 2⅓ cups
1-pound package powdered sugar (unsifted)	= 3¼ cups
5-pound bag sugar	= 11¼ cups
5-pound bag all-purpose flour (unsifted)	= 17½ cups
1-pound can coffee	= 5 cups

Cookie

Cookie A small, sweet, baked item that can be different shapes and a variety of thicknesses and textures, from thin and crisp to thick and cakelike. Cookies can be decorated and served with or without frosting. Candylike, no-bake cookies, prepared in a saucepan, also are popular.

Types: Cookies can be made from scratch or prepared from commercial doughs or mixes. Sometimes nuts, fruits, or cereals are added for variety. Here are five basic cookie types.

□ **Bar:** Cookies made from either a fairly stiff dough that's spread or pressed into a pan or a batterlike mixture that's poured into the pan. They range in texture from chewy to cakelike and can be cut into various shapes including diamonds, triangles, and squares. Brownies are familiar bar cookies (see also *Brownie*).

□ **Cutout:** Cookies made from a fairly soft dough that often is chilled and then rolled out. The rolled-out dough is cut into a variety of shapes. Thinly rolled cutout cookies tend to be crisp, and thicker cookies often have a soft interior. Gingerbread people are examples of cutout cookies.

□ **Drop:** Cookies made from a soft dough dropped by the spoonful onto a cookie sheet. Drop cookies can be crisp, chewy, or cakelike. Chocolate chip cookies are perhaps the most well-known drop cookie.

□ **Shaped:** Cookies made from a firm dough that may need to be chilled before shaping. These cookies are molded by hand or shaped with a utensil, such as the bottom of a glass, a fork, cookie stamp, cookie mold, or cookie press. Shaped cookies are generally crisp. Spritz are a popular kind of shaped cookie (see also *Spritz*).

Shaped cookies also include those made from a thin batter, such as rosettes or pizzelles. Rosettes are shaped by dipping a fancy metal mold into the batter and then deep-frying the mold with the batter. Pizzelles are made in the same way as waffles, by pouring batter onto a special iron.

□ **Sliced:** Cookies made from a fairly soft dough that's shaped into rolls and chilled before it is sliced into rounds and baked. These cookies also are called refrigerator cookies and have a crisp but tender texture. A date pinwheel is a popular sliced cookie.

Margarine in Cookies

If you choose to make cookies with margarine, the firmness of the cookie dough may vary depending on the type of margarine. Be sure to choose a stick product that's labeled "margarine," not "spread." A 100-percent corn-oil margarine will make your dough softer than dough made from other margarines. So, you may need to adjust the recipe chilling instructions. For shaped or sliced cookies, chill the dough in the freezer instead of the refrigerator; for cutout cookies, refrigerate the dough at least 5 hours.

Preparation hints: The following general points will ensure success when making all types of cookies. For more information on specific types of cookies, see Cookie-Making Hints, page 118.

□ To avoid any surprises, always read through the recipe first, and then gather the ingredients and equipment you'll need.

□ Next, check that the oven rack is in the middle position in the oven. Remember to preheat the oven.

□ For easy mixing, use room-temperature ingredients unless the recipe says otherwise.

□ For tender cookies, mix the flour with the other ingredients just until combined, unless the recipe says differently. Overmixing cookie dough makes cookies tough.

□ Some cookie doughs are stiff enough to overwork some portable mixers. Stir the last portion of flour into the dough by hand if you're using such a mixer.

continued

Cookie-Making Hints

Because bar, cutout, drop, shaped, and sliced cookies are all very different, there are points to know about making each type. Following are some of the most useful tips.

Bar Cookies
● Be sure to use the right-size pan. If it is too large, the cookies will be thin and overbaked. If the pan is too small, the cookies will be thick and underbaked.
● Glass baking dishes brown bar cookies faster than metal ones. When substituting a glass baking dish for a metal pan, reduce the oven temperature by 25 degrees.
● Bar cookies are done when the edges begin to appear dry and pull away from the pan, and when a slight impression remains when lightly touched. Also, a toothpick inserted near the center of cookies that are cakelike will come out clean when they're done.
● Some bar cookies need to be cut while they're still warm; others need to be completely cooled before cutting. To get perfect-looking bar cookies, follow your recipe for cooling and cutting instructions.
● When making cookies that are cooled in the pan before cutting, line the baking pan with foil to make cookie-cutting easier and reduce cleanup. If recipe directions include greasing the pan, be sure to grease the foil. After baking and cooling, transfer the cookies to a cutting board using the foil. Cut nice even bars without the pan getting in the way.

Cutout Cookies
● To make rolling out the dough easy, work with small amounts at a time. Refrigerate the rest of the dough until you're ready to use it.
● To keep the cookie dough from sticking to the counter when you're rolling it out, lightly sprinkle the surface with flour. Or, use a floured pastry cloth and rolling-pin cover.
● To avoid having the dough stick to the cookie cutter, dip the cutter in flour occasionally.
● To get the most cookies out of each portion of dough, cut cookies as close together as possible.
● Press dough scraps together, trying not to toughen the dough by overhandling it. Then reroll the dough on a lightly floured surface and cut more cookies.
● Cutout cookies are done when the edges are firm and the bottoms are very lightly browned.

Drop Cookies
● Cooling the cookie sheet between batches will keep drop cookie dough from flattening too much during baking.
● Drop cookies are done when the edges and bottoms are lightly browned, or when a slight impression remains when cookies are lightly touched with a fingertip.

Shaped Cookies
● There are many kitchen utensils you can use when you want to flatten balls of dough and give shaped cookies a festive look, but you don't have any wooden or ceramic cookie stamps. For example, fancy flatware handles, patterned backs of spoons, bottoms of glasses, and other items with a design can be used to flatten and imprint shaped cookies.
● Some cookies made from batters are shaped by rolling the very thin baked cookie around a wooden dowel or the handle of a wooden spoon. This needs to be done while the cookies are still warm and flexible. If the cookies become cool and brittle before they're rolled, soften them by briefly reheating them in the oven.
● Shaped cookies are done when the edges and bottoms are lightly browned.

Sliced Cookies
● Finely chop any nuts or fruit that you add to the dough so it will slice easily.
● For clean slices, cut the chilled roll of dough with a thin, sharp knife, cleaning the knife occasionally during slicing.
● To get nice round slices, occasionally turn the roll of dough while you slice it. This prevents flattening on one side of the roll.
● Sliced cookies are done when the edges are firm and the bottoms are lightly browned.

Q: Is it necessary to chill cookie dough?
A: Bar and drop cookie doughs don't have to be chilled, but most sliced and cutout, and some shaped, cookie doughs do. Chilling makes these doughs easier to work with and gives the cookies a better shape. If you don't have time to chill your cookie dough in the refrigerator, speed up the process by placing the wrapped dough in the freezer for one-third of the refrigerator chilling time. If using corn-oil margarine, see tip on page 117 for times.

Baking hints: Here are some tips that good cookie bakers use for delicious results with all types of cookies. For more specific hints on cookie baking, see information opposite.
☐ Select cookie sheets and pans made of heavyweight metal with a dull finish. Light-colored ones are best because dark-colored ones can overbrown the bottoms and sides of cookies before they're completely baked.
☐ When your recipe recommends baking cookies on a greased cookie sheet, use a light coating so the cookies won't spread too much. Use shortening or a nonstick vegetable spray—margarine and butter burn.
☐ To avoid overbaking some cookies and underbaking others, bake one sheet or pan of cookies at a time on a rack in the middle of your oven.
☐ To help cookies keep their shape, let the cookie sheets or pans cool between batches.

Storing: To store cookie dough, place it in a plastic bag or an airtight container. When making sliced cookies, wrap rolls of dough in plastic wrap first. Refrigerate the dough for up to a week, or freeze it in freezer containers for up to 6 months. (Meringue-type and very thin cookie batters don't refrigerate or freeze well.) Thaw most frozen doughs in the container before baking. If it is too firm to work with, let the dough stand at room temperature to soften. For rolls of dough for sliced cookies, thaw the dough until it is just soft enough to slice.

To store baked cookies, it is best to completely cool them and leave them unfrosted so they don't stick together. In an airtight or freezer container, arrange a single layer of cookies and cover them with a layer of waxed paper. Repeat layers of cookies and waxed paper, leaving enough air space to close the container easily. Store at room temperature for up to 3 days or freeze for up to 8 months.

Cooking Oil See *Fat and Oil.*

Cool To allow a hot food to come to room temperature. Mixtures often are cooled before adding ingredients, such as eggs, that cannot tolerate high levels of heat.

Coq au Vin *(coke oh VAN)* A classic French dish in which chicken is cooked in dry red wine, often burgundy, along with onions, mushrooms, bacon, and herbs.

Coquille *(co KEEL)* A French word meaning shell that refers to a scallop shell or scallop-shaped dish in which seafood and other creamed mixtures are baked and served.

A Tip from Our Kitchen
If you don't own coquilles, substitute individual au gratin dishes or other small casserole dishes.

Cordon Bleu *(core dawn BLUE)* A French term meaning blue ribbon that was originally used to refer to a prize given to a graduate of the famous French cooking school of the same name. Today the term is used to refer to any excellent cook.

As a recipe term, cordon bleu refers to veal or another meat or poultry that is pounded and layered with Swiss cheese and ham. The layers are then formed into a roll, coated with crumbs, and cooked.

Coriander

Coriander A lacy-looking plant in the parsley family. The white to yellowish brown seeds, which are considered a spice, taste somewhat like a blend of lemon and sage. Coriander seeds may be purchased either ground or whole.

The leaves of the coriander plant are the herb cilantro (see also *Cilantro*). The flavor of cilantro is distinctively different from coriander seed, so the two definitely are not interchangeable.

Frankfurters and sausages would be at a loss without the flavor of ground coriander. Coriander seed is a major ingredient in curry powder and pickling spice.

(See *Spice* for selecting, storing, and nutrition information. See also *Oriental Cooking* for an identification photo.)

Corn The bright yellow or white seed of a plant that grows in kernels on a cob. The kernels are surrounded by fine silks and a green husk. Corn has a mild sweet flavor.

Corn

Varieties: In addition to yellow corn, you'll also find white corn, which has creamy white kernels that are smaller and sweeter than yellow corn. Corn with both yellow and white kernels also is available. Baby corn is a tiny version that can be enjoyed cob and all.

Market forms: Corn is available in three forms—fresh, frozen, and canned. The peak season for fresh corn on the cob is late spring to summer. Frozen corn is available on the cob, as whole kernels, in sauces, and mixed with other vegetables. Canned corn is available as either whole kernels, plain or mixed with other vegetables, or cream-style. Baby corn is available in cans or jars, frozen in packages, and occasionally fresh.

Selecting: Purchase fresh corn on the cob with bright, healthy-looking, green husks. The more recently the corn has been picked, the better the flavor will be.

Pull the husk back and look for well-filled-out ears. Avoid those with insect or other damage or lots of underdeveloped kernels.

Q: Is it best to buy fresh corn on the cob with or without the husks?
A: It is best to buy corn with the husk on because a healthy-looking husk tells you that the corn is fresh and not too old. If the husk has been removed, it's difficult to tell how recently the corn was picked.

Storing: Use fresh corn on the cob as soon as possible or store it in the refrigerator for no more than 2 days. Certain super-sweet varieties will retain their sweet flavor if stored a few extra days in the refrigerator.

A Tip from Our Kitchen

To freeze fresh, whole kernel corn, blanch cleaned ears, using 1 gallon of water per pound of vegetables. Blanch for 5 or 6 minutes; cool quickly. Cut corn from cobs at ⅔ depth of kernels; don't scrape. Fill freezer containers, shaking to pack lightly, and leave a ½-inch headspace. Freeze up to 10 months.

How to cook: See the Cooking Fresh Vegetables chart under *Vegetable*.

Nutrition information: Cooked corn on the cob has about 85 calories per medium ear, and a ½-cup serving of canned, drained whole kernel corn has about 65 calories.

Corn Bread

A quick bread made with cornmeal and flour that usually has a light and porous texture. Corn bread is commonly made in a square or rectangular pan, but a southern-style variation is baked in a skillet. Corn muffins are made simply by baking the batter in muffin pans. For corn sticks, the batter is baked in heavy shallow metal pans that are shaped like ears of corn. Corn pone is an unsweetened corn bread made without flour. The sweetness level of corn bread varies a bit throughout the country—Southerners tend to like their corn bread less sweet than Northerners.

Corn bread mixes are widely available, as are frozen corn muffins.

Corn Bread

- 1   cup all-purpose flour
- 1   cup yellow, white, *or* blue cornmeal
- 2   to 4 tablespoons sugar
- 1   tablespoon baking powder
- ½   teaspoon salt
- 2   eggs
- 1   cup milk
- ¼   cup cooking oil *or* shortening, melted

■ In a mixing bowl combine flour, cornmeal, sugar, baking powder, and salt. In another bowl beat together eggs, milk, and oil or melted shortening. Add to flour mixture and stir just till batter is smooth (*do not overbeat*).
■ Pour into a greased 9x9x2-inch baking pan. Bake in a 425° oven for 20 to 25 minutes or till golden brown. Makes 8 or 9 servings.

Nutrition information per serving: 228 calories, 6 g protein, 30 g carbohydrate, 9 g fat (2 g saturated), 56 mg cholesterol, 273 mg sodium, 109 mg potassium.

Corn Sticks or Corn Muffins: Prepare Corn Bread as below left, *except* spoon batter into greased corn stick pans or muffin pans, filling pans ⅔ full. Bake in a 425° oven for 12 to 15 minutes or till brown. Makes 24 to 26 sticks or 12 muffins.

Nutrition information for 2 corn sticks or 1 muffin: 152 calories, 4 g protein, 20 g carbohydrate, 6 g fat (1 g saturated), 37 mg cholesterol, 182 mg sodium, 72 mg potassium.

Green Chili Corn Bread: Prepare Corn Bread as below left, *except* fold 1 cup shredded *cheddar cheese or Monterey Jack cheese* and one 4-ounce can diced *green chili peppers*, drained, into the batter.

Nutrition information per serving: 288 calories, 9 g protein, 31 g carbohydrate, 14 g fat (5 g saturated), 71 mg cholesterol, 489 mg sodium, 146 mg potassium.

Corny Corn Bread: Prepare Corn Bread as below left, *except* stir one 12-ounce can *whole kernel corn with sweet peppers*, drained into the batter.

Nutrition information per serving: 261 calories, 6 g protein, 38 g carbohydrate, 9 g fat (2 g saturated), 56 mg cholesterol, 399 mg sodium, 173 mg potassium.

Confetti Corn Bread: Prepare Corn Bread as below left, *except* stir ½ cup shredded *cheddar cheese*, ¼ cup finely shredded *carrot*, and ¼ cup finely shredded *zucchini* into the batter.

Nutrition information per serving: 259 calories, 7 g protein, 31 g carbohydrate, 12 g fat (3 g saturated), 63 mg cholesterol, 319 mg sodium, 137 mg potassium.

Corned Beef

A cured beef product usually made with fresh beef brisket or beef round and cured with spices added to a salt brine. Corned beef tastes slightly salty and has a deep red color.

Preserving beef by "corning" was a necessity before refrigeration. Granular salt the size of wheat kernels—corn to the British—was used in the process. Today, beef is corned for flavor rather than preservation.
continued

Market forms: You'll find ready-to-cook corned beef in the meat case. Or, look in the deli case for cooked, sliced corned beef that's ready-to-eat. Canned, cooked corned beef also is available.

How to cook: Ready-to-cook corned beef can be oven roasted or cooked in water until tender. After cooking, corned beef is sometimes roasted with a glaze, which adds flavor to the meat.

Nutrition information: One 3-ounce portion of cooked, trimmed corned beef contains about 210 calories and 965 milligrams of sodium.

Cornish Game Hen

Cornish Game Hen A specially bred, small chicken that typically weighs 1½ pounds or less. Cornish game hens are prized for their delicate, tender meat. They also are called Rock Cornish hens.

Market forms: Cornish game hens are almost always sold frozen. For thawing information, see *Poultry*.

How to cook: For roasting and broiling directions, see the Roasting Poultry and Broiling Poultry charts under *Poultry*. For grilling directions, see the Direct-Grilling Poultry and Indirect-Grilling Poultry charts under *Barbecue*. Allow half of a Cornish game hen for each serving.

Q: **How can a Cornish game hen be halved, especially if it's still frozen?**
A: Ask your butcher to halve it while it is frozen. Or, once you get the Cornish game hen home, thaw the bird and then use kitchen shears to cut it into halves.

Nutrition information: A 3-ounce serving of cooked Cornish game hen with skin contains about 200 calories, 12 grams of fat, and 75 milligrams of cholesterol.

(See *Poultry* for selecting, refrigerating, freezing, thawing, cooking, and other information.)

Cornmeal

Cornmeal Dried corn kernels that have been finely ground. Traditionally, Southerners prefer their cornmeal from white strains of corn, Northerners like theirs from yellow, and Southwesterners sometimes use the blue variety. Cooked cornmeal has a cornlike taste and can be used in a variety of ways. Serve it as a cooked breakfast cereal, or use it as a coating for fried foods. It also is the main ingredient in corn breads and certain pancake, pudding, and muffin recipes.

Cornmeal labeled "stone ground" is slightly coarser than other cornmeal. The blue variety of cornmeal is sold at specialty food stores.

Corn Flour

In addition to cornmeal, you may find corn flour on your supermarket shelf. Corn flour is corn that has been ground into a fine powder. A special kind of corn flour is Masa Harina tortilla flour, which is used to make tamales and corn tortillas.

Storing: Store cornmeal in an airtight container in a cool, dry place for up to 6 months or in the refrigerator or freezer for up to 1 year.

How to cook: See the Cooking Grains chart under *Grain*.

Nutrition information: A ¾-cup serving of cooked cornmeal has about 110 calories.

Corn Pudding

Corn Pudding A custardlike side dish that combines eggs, milk, and fresh or canned corn. The dish sometimes includes onions and sweet peppers.

Corn Relish

Corn Relish A tangy, colorful corn mixture served as an accompaniment to meats, poultry, sandwiches, and other main dishes. Its flavor ranges from very tangy to mildly sweet and sour. Corn relish often includes other vegetables, such as onions and sweet peppers, and may be thickened.

Corn Relish

> 1 12-ounce can whole kernel corn
> ⅓ cup vinegar
> ¼ cup sugar
> 1 tablespoon finely chopped onion
> ½ teaspoon salt
> ¼ teaspoon celery seed
> ¼ teaspoon mustard seed
> ¼ teaspoon bottled hot pepper sauce
> 1 tablespoon diced pimiento
> 2 tablespoons chopped sweet red *or* green pepper

■ In a medium saucepan combine the *undrained* whole kernel corn, vinegar, sugar, onion, salt, celery seed, mustard seed, and bottled hot pepper sauce. Bring mixture to boiling, stirring occasionally. Reduce heat and boil gently, uncovered, for 2 minutes. Remove from heat and stir in the diced pimiento and sweet red or green pepper. Transfer to a covered container and store in the refrigerator. Serve with a slotted spoon. Makes 2 cups.

Nutrition information per tablespoon: 13 calories, 0 g protein, 3 g carbohydrate, 0 g fat, 0 mg cholesterol, 61 mg sodium, 21 mg potassium.

Cornstarch
A white, powdery thickening agent that comes from corn. Products thickened with cornstarch have a clearer, more translucent appearance than mixtures thickened with flour, which produces a more opaque look. Cornstarch will keep up to 2 years in a cool, dry place.

A Tip from Our Kitchen
Cornstarch has twice the thickening power of flour, so, when substituting cornstarch for flour, use half as much cornstarch.

Q: How do you cook with cornstarch and not get lumps?
A: To prevent lumps when cooking with cornstarch, combine equal parts cornstarch and *cold* liquid. Add this to the hot mixture you wish to thicken and stir constantly till the mixture boils. Cook and stir for 2 minutes after boiling. Stirring frequently during thickening also helps prevent lumps.

Cottage Cheese
A soft, white, unripened, cow's-milk cheese with a delicate, but slightly acidic, flavor.

The name "cottage" comes from early European farmers who made this cheese in their cottages with milk that was left over from making butter. Today, cottage cheese is not made from buttermilk or whey.

Cottage cheese

Types: There are three major types of cottage cheese on the market.

☐ **Creamed Cottage Cheese:** The result of mixing dry curds with a cream mixture. This variety is the richest and creamiest, containing 4 percent or more milk fat.

☐ **Low-Fat Cottage Cheese:** Made the same way as creamed, but with a lower fat cream mixture. It is the most popular choice for dieters and contains not less than ½ percent and not more than 2 percent milk fat.

☐ **Dry-Curd Cottage Cheese:** The curds without added cream. It is the leanest of the cottage cheeses, because it contains less than ½ percent milk fat.

Nutrition information: If you're counting calories, keep in mind that a ½-cup serving of creamed cottage cheese contains 109 calories, 5 grams of fat, and 16 milligrams of cholesterol. Dry-curd cottage cheese has 62 calories, less than 1 gram of fat, and 5 milligrams of cholesterol. Low-fat cottage cheese (2 percent) has 102 calories, 2 grams of fat, and 10 milligrams of cholesterol.

(See *Cheese* for storing and other information.)

Cottage Pudding A cake, usually yellow, that is topped with a sweet fruit, chocolate, or hard sauce.

Court Bouillon *(court BOOL yon)* A seasoned broth used for poaching vegetables or fish. When made for poaching vegetables, it usually contains water, onion, celery, carrot, and seasonings. When made for poaching fish, it usually also contains fish heads and tails, wine, and vinegar. The food that is cooked in the broth absorbs the flavors of the ingredients.

Couscous *(KOOS koos)* A commercially produced grain product in the shape of very tiny beads. Made from ground semolina, it is a staple in North African cooking and can either be used in recipes or served as a mild-tasting side dish in place of rice. It usually is found in the rice or pasta section of the supermarket or at specialty stores, and is available in regular and quick-cooking forms.

Crab A crustacean shellfish with eight legs and a pair of claws, which is prized for its delicately flavored, white, sweet meat. Often it is served with melted butter for dipping.

Types: North America has the largest variety of crabs. Here are six popular ones.
☐ **Blue:** Named for their blue pincers. The blue crab is caught primarily along the East Coast. They have tender meat and weigh from ¼ to 1 pound. They're sold in the hard-shell and soft-shell stages. When the shells are soft, crabs are completely edible except for the face, intestines, and gills.
☐ **Dungeness:** West Coast favorites that weigh from 1½ to 3½ pounds. The meat from the body is white, and the meat from the claws and legs is reddish. They generally are sold as whole cooked crab.
☐ **King:** Alaskan crabs weighing from 6 to 20 pounds. Their legs, up to 3 feet long, are filled with long pieces of red-flecked, white meat.

☐ **Snow:** About half the size of king crabs. They have long spindly legs containing meat. They're also known as spider, tanner, or queen crabs.
☐ **Rock:** Small crabs native to New England and California. They weigh only 5 to 8 ounces and have brownish meat.
☐ **Stone:** Found primarily in the waters off the Florida coast. Only the firm-textured meat from the claws is eaten.

Market forms: Whole crabs are sold live, cooked, and frozen. Legs and claws also are available cooked and frozen. Cooked crabmeat comes frozen, pasteurized (which requires refrigeration), and canned. Canned crab is available as claw meat, lump meat, or flaked meat.

Selecting: Live crabs should be lively and heavy for their size. Their shells should feel hard (except for soft-shell crabs). Frozen crabs should be wrapped well without evidence of ice or frozen juices. Whole crabs and crabmeat should smell sweet, not fishy.

Crab Math
Use these guidelines to determine how much crab to buy per serving.
● ½ to 1 whole Dungeness crab
● 1 pound live blue crabs
● 8 ounces of crab legs
● 3 to 4 ounces of cooked crabmeat

Storing: If possible, cook live crabs the same day you buy them. Otherwise, refrigerate them covered with a damp towel, or place them on damp newspapers in an insulated cooler half-filled with ice. Cook them within 1 day. Before cooking, discard any crabs that aren't alive. Live crabs will become docile under refrigeration, but if they are alive, they should move their legs slightly.

Use freshly cooked crabmeat within 2 days, or freeze the meat for up to 1 month. Once opened, canned crabmeat should be used within 2 days.

How to cook: Live hard-shell crabs are great boiled or steamed. For boiling directions, see the Preparing and Cooking Shellfish chart under *Shellfish.* To crack a cooked crab, see photos, right.

Soft-shell crabs are most commonly batter-coated and fried, but they also can be grilled or stuffed and baked. Cook frozen crab according to package directions.

Nutrition information: Depending on the type of crab, calories range from about 70 to 90 calories for 3 ounces of cooked crabmeat.

Crab Apple

A small, round fruit with tiny seeds within its core. This tiny apple has a red skin and white fruit inside with a very tart flavor and crisp, juicy texture. Crab apples often are used for making jelly.

Crab apples

Market forms: Fresh crab apples are rarely available in supermarkets, but you'll occasionally find them at farmer's markets. Commercially prepared forms include spiced and canned crab apples and jelly.

Selecting: Choose firm fresh apples that have smooth, unblemished skins without bruises or breaks.

Storing: Store fresh crab apples in the refrigerator for up to 2 weeks.

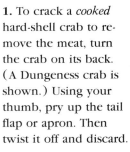

1. To crack a *cooked* hard-shell crab to remove the meat, turn the crab on its back. (A Dungeness crab is shown.) Using your thumb, pry up the tail flap or apron. Then twist it off and discard.

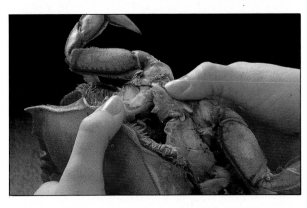

2. Holding the crab with the top shell in one hand, grasp the bottom shell at the point where the apron was removed. Pull the top shell away from the body of the crab and discard.

3. Using a small knife, remove the "devil's fingers" (spongy gills) from each side of the top of the crab. Also discard the internal organs, the mouth, and the small appendages at the front of the crab.

4. To remove the meat, twist off the legs and claws, using your fingers. Use a nutcracker to crack each joint, then pick out the meat. Break the body in half and remove the remaining meat.

Crab Boil A blend of whole and cracked herbs and spices that generally includes bay leaf, mustard seed, allspice, clove, black pepper, dillseed, and red pepper. Crab boil also is known as shrimp spice. The mixture is added to the boiling water in which shellfish are cooked to give the food extra flavor.

Crab Louis A cold salad of crabmeat served on lettuce, often garnished with hard-cooked egg and tomato, and topped with a dressing of mayonnaise, chili sauce, onion, and seasonings.

Crab Louis

1 **medium head iceberg lettuce**
2 **6-ounce packages frozen crabmeat, thawed,** *or* **two 7-ounce cans crabmeat, chilled, drained, and cartilage removed**
2 **large tomatoes, cut into wedges**
2 **hard-cooked eggs, cut into wedges**
   Louis Dressing
   Paprika
1 **lemon, cut into wedges**

■ Remove 4 large leaves from lettuce head. Set aside. Tear remaining lettuce into bite-size pieces. On *each* of 4 salad plates, place *1* lettuce leaf. Top with torn lettuce. Reserve *4* large pieces of crabmeat. Flake remaining crabmeat. Arrange flaked crabmeat, tomatoes, and egg wedges on lettuce. Drizzle with Louis Dressing. Sprinkle with paprika. Garnish with the reserved crabmeat and lemon wedges. Makes 4 servings.

Louis Dressing: Stir together ½ cup *mayonnaise or salad dressing,* ¼ cup finely chopped *green pepper,* ¼ cup finely chopped *green onion,* 2 tablespoons *chili sauce,* 1 tablespoon *milk,* ½ teaspoon *lemon juice,* and a dash *Worcestershire sauce.* Beat ¼ cup *whipping cream* to soft peaks. Fold whipped cream into mayonnaise mixture.

Nutrition information per serving: 423 calories, 24 g protein, 12 g carbohydrate, 32 g fat (8 g saturated), 219 mg cholesterol, 613 mg sodium, 829 mg potassium.

Cracker A thin, dry, crisp-tender, baked product. Most of the crackers eaten today are baked commercially, although crackers can be made at home.

Types: Crackers come in a variety of sizes— from miniature to large—and shapes, including square, round, oblong, bite-size, and fish-shaped. An assortment of flavors— plain, salted, seeded, seasoned, and sweetened—also is available. There are crackers to use with dips and cheese, with soups and salads, and just for munching.

A Tip from Our Kitchen

If your crackers get soft, crush them, place them in an airtight container, and keep them on hand in your freezer to use as a crust for main dishes and desserts, a topping for casseroles, or a coating for fried and baked foods, such as chicken and fish.

Storing: After opening, store crackers in airtight containers. They'll stay fresh for up to 3 months.

Nutrition information: Two saltine crackers (2-inch squares) have about 25 calories. Two rich, round crackers have about 30 calories.

(See *Crumb* **for measuring information.)**

Crackling One of the crisp, browned pieces that are left after fresh pork fat is rendered into lard. Cracklings may be added to beans, other vegetables, or corn bread for extra flavor. They also are served as a snack. The commercial version of this snack is called pork rinds.

Cranberry

A small, round, piquant fruit that is cultivated in bogs or peat swamps in North America. This plump, firm member of the berry family has red skin and a tart flavor. Harvested in late fall, cranberries are a staple of fall and winter holiday meals.

Market forms: Besides fresh cranberries, you also can find dried sweetened berries. The berries are sold canned as whole or jellied cranberry sauce and as a relish. Cranberries also are processed to make fruit drinks, especially cranberry juice cocktail.

Selecting: Fresh cranberries generally are sold bagged, but you can check for good quality by looking for a plump, unblemished appearance on the berries. The red color will vary from light to dark; the deepness of the color does not affect quality. Discard soft or bruised berries.

Storing: Refrigerate bagged fresh cranberries for up to 4 weeks. Or, freeze them for up to 9 months; double-wrap the bag of cranberries with freezer wrap. (It is not necessary to thaw berries before using.)

Preparation hint: Since chopping cranberries by hand can be tedious, try chopping them—a few cups at a time—in your food processor. You'll get about 3 cups of chopped berries from a 12-ounce package.

How to cook: To make cranberrry sauce, in a saucepan combine 1 cup *sugar* and 1 cup *water*. Bring to boiling, stirring to dissolve sugar. Boil rapidly for 5 minutes. Add 2 cups *cranberries* (8 ounces). Return to boiling; reduce heat. Boil gently over medium-high heat for 3 to 4 minutes or till skins pop, stirring occasionally. Remove from heat. Serve warm or chilled with beef, pork, or poultry. Makes about 2 cups (about 108 calories per ¼-cup serving).

Nutrition information: One-half cup of unsweetened whole cranberries contains about 20 calories; a ¼-cup serving of canned, sweetened cranberry sauce contains about 105 calories; 1 cup of cranberry juice cocktail contains about 150 calories.

(See *Dried Fruit* for the Cooking Dried Fruit chart and storing and preparation hints.)

Cranberries

Crayfish/Crawfish

A freshwater shellfish that looks like a small lobster and tastes like shrimp, only sweeter. They're also called crawdads. You can buy whole crayfish live or boiled. Cooked, peeled tails also are available either fresh or frozen.

Cooking hints: Like lobster and crab, whole crayfish should be cooked live. All the meat is found in the tail. The raw peeled crayfish tails can be panfried or added to étouffé, a seafood stew (see recipe, page 70).

How to cook: See the Preparing and Cooking Shellfish chart under *Shellfish*. To eat cooked crayfish, see photos, right.

Nutrition information: Three ounces of crayfish meat has about 100 calories. Crayfish are lower in sodium than most other shellfish.

(See *Shellfish* for storing and other information.)

1. When eating cooked crayfish, remove the meat from the shell by gently twisting the tail away from the body.

2. Unwrap the first two or three sections of shell from the tail to expose more meat.

3. Pinch the end of the tail and with the other hand pull out the meat. If desired, carefully suck the flavorful juices from the head of the crayfish.

Cream (noun) A dairy product that is made from the fatty portion of fresh milk that rises to the surface when milk is left to stand. The high fat content gives cream a rich, buttery flavor and velvety texture.

Types: What makes one cream different from another is the milk-fat content. The ones with less milk fat are generally used in cooking or coffee, and the ones with a lot of milk fat are used for whipping. Here's what's available.

☐ **Half and Half:** A mixture of milk and cream. Half and half contains between 10½ and 18 percent milk fat. Half and half cannot be beaten into whipped cream.

☐ **Light:** Between 18 and 30 percent milk fat. Light cream may not be available in all areas and cannot be beaten into whipped cream. Light cream also is known as coffee cream and table cream.

☐ **Light Whipping:** Between 30 and 36 percent milk fat. Light whipping cream may not be available in smaller markets. It also is known as whipping cream.

☐ **Heavy Whipping:** Contains not less than 36 percent milk fat. Heavy whipping cream also is called heavy cream.

☐ **Cream in Aerosol Cans:** Whipping cream packed under pressure. It also may contain sweeteners, flavoring, and stabilizers.

Storing: Make cream one of your last purchases at the supermarket and refrigerate it as soon as you get home. It will stay fresh for about a week.

A Tip from Our Kitchen
When you're making a cooked product and come up a cup short of half and half, substitute 1 tablespoon melted butter plus enough whole milk to make 1 cup.

Q: **What's the best way to whip cream?**
A: First choose a bowl that's deep enough to allow the cream to double in volume. Then put the bowl and the beaters of an electric mixer (or a rotary beater) into the freezer for about 10 minutes before you begin to whip. (Cream whips better if it's very cold, and having the bowl and beaters cold will help, too.) Generally, beat cream till soft peaks form. If you're using an electric mixer, beat on medium speed to be sure you don't overbeat the cream. You'll know if you overbeat the cream, because it will turn to butter.

Whipping cream doubles in volume when it is whipped—so 1 cup of cream gives you about 2 cups whipped.

Freezing Whipped Cream
When you've whipped more cream than you need, freeze the extra. Just spoon the whipped cream into mounds on a baking sheet lined with waxed paper. Freeze till firm, then transfer the mounds to a freezer container. Store in the freezer for 2 to 3 days. To serve, let stand 5 minutes, then place on top of your dessert. Or, if using the mounds on hot beverages, use them directly from the freezer.

Cream Facts
The calories and fat in a tablespoon of cream can vary greatly depending on the type you buy. Here's a comparison.

Type of Cream	Fat	Calories
Half and half	2 grams	20
Light	3 grams	29
Light whipping	5 grams	44
Heavy whipping	6 grams	52

Cream (verb)

Cream (verb) To beat a fat, such as margarine, butter, or shortening, either alone or with sugar to a light and fluffy consistency. Creaming can be done by hand with a spoon or with an electric mixer. This technique incorporates air into the fat, which gives a lighter texture and better volume to baked products.

Cream Cheese

Cream Cheese A white, fresh cheese with a smooth, dense, and spreadable consistency, and a mild and slightly acidic flavor. This rich cheese is made from a mixture of cow's cream and milk.

Types: A variety of cream cheeses have emerged in the marketplace.
□ **Regular Cream Cheese:** Available in 3- and 8-ounce bricks or by the pound and used in cooking for recipes such as cheesecakes, frostings, dips, sauces, and baked foods.
□ **Soft and Whipped Cream Cheeses:** Cream cheeses that are blended during manufacturing to give them a softer texture. The softer consistency makes them easier to spread on bread, bagels, and other foods than regular cream cheese. There's no need to soften these cheeses to room temperature before using them.
□ **Flavored Cream Cheeses:** Regular, soft, and whipped cream cheeses with added ingredients, such as smoked salmon, olive and pimiento, chives and onion, and various fruit flavors.
□ **Neufchâtel Cheese:** A light style of cream cheese that contains fewer calories and less fat and is somewhat softer than regular cream cheese. It is available in brick form.
□ **Light Cream Cheese Product:** Contains fewer calories and less fat than regular cream cheese. It is available in tubs and may include cottage cheese as an ingredient.

Storing: Refrigerate cream cheese. Once the package is opened, use within 2 weeks. Discard cream cheese with mold on it.

Nutrition information: Regular and soft cream cheeses have the same nutritional content of about 100 calories, 10 grams of fat, and 31 milligrams of cholesterol per ounce. Neufchâtel cheese has 74 calories, 7 grams of fat, and 22 milligrams of cholesterol per ounce, and the light cream cheese product in tubs contains about 60 calories, 5 grams of fat, and 15 milligrams of cholesterol per ounce.

Cream cheese

Cream of Tartar

Cream of Tartar A white, powdery, natural fruit acid found in grape juice after fermentation. Cream of tartar reacts with baking soda to leaven certain baked products.

Cream of tartar often is beaten into egg whites because it makes them firmer and more stable, and it increases their tolerance of heat. Cream of tartar also gives candies and frostings a whiter color and creamier consistency.

Cream Pie

Cream Pie A single-crust pie with a sweet, rich, puddinglike filling that has a smooth, creamy texture. Either a pastry or a crumb crust is used. Cream pie is usually topped with meringue, but whipped cream or fresh fruit also can be used.

New Meringue Baking Time
Eating uncooked or slightly cooked eggs in recipes such as those with a meringue topping may be harmful because of possible bacterial contamination (see Using Eggs Safely under *Eggs*). Because of this concern, we altered our method of making a meringue-topped pie.

When you apply the meringue topping, *evenly* spread the meringue mixture over *hot* cream pie filling. Then bake the pie in a 350° oven for 15 minutes. This method makes meringue-topped pies safe for everyone to eat.

(See *Pie* for Pie-Making Hints and storing information.)

1. Using a wooden spoon, stir the flour into the water-butter mixture while it is over medium heat. Continue cooking and stirring over medium heat till the mixture forms a ball that doesn't separate.

2. After the dough has cooled 10 minutes, add the eggs, one at a time, beating 1 to 2 minutes after each. The mixture should be thick, smooth, and slightly sticky after the eggs are beaten in.

3. While the puffs are hot, carefully split each puff with a knife. Then, with a fork, gently remove any soft dough inside the puff, leaving a crisp shell.

Cream Puff
A crisp, hollow pastry shell made from a dough called chou paste that is a combination of flour, margarine or butter, water, and eggs. Cream puffs may be filled with sweetened whipped cream, ice cream, or a pudding and served as a dessert. They sometimes are sprinkled with powdered sugar or drizzled with a glaze. They also may be filled with a salad and served as a main dish or in a miniature size as an appetizer.

Cream Puff Tips
- See the how-to photos, left.
- Before adding the eggs to your cream puff dough mixture, remove the saucepan from the heat and let the dough cool 10 minutes. If the dough is too hot when the eggs are added, the eggs may overcook and the puffs may not be puffy and light.
- For round puffs, when dropping cream puff dough, push the dough off the spoon with a spatula or another spoon. Then don't go back and add to the original mound.
- Store baked cream puff shells in an airtight container or plastic bag to prevent them from drying out. Refrigerate the shells and use within 24 hours. Or, freeze them for up to 2 months. It takes the shells only 5 to 10 minutes to thaw at room temperature.
- To keep the shells from becoming soggy, fill cream puffs no more than 2 hours before serving. Refrigerate the filled cream puff shells.

Cream Puffs

  1 cup water
  ½ cup margarine *or* butter
  ⅛ teaspoon salt
  1 cup all-purpose flour
  4 eggs
    Pudding, whipped cream, ice cream, sherbet, *or* fresh fruit
    Powdered sugar (optional)

■ In a medium saucepan combine water, margarine or butter, and salt. Bring to boiling. Add flour all at once, stirring vigorously. Cook and stir till mixture forms a ball that doesn't separate. Remove from heat. Cool 10 minutes. Add eggs, one at a time, beating with a wooden spoon after each addition till the mixture is smooth.
■ Drop batter by heaping tablespoons, 3 inches apart, onto a greased baking sheet. Bake in a 400° oven for 30 to 35 minutes or till golden brown. Cool on a wire rack. Split puffs and remove any soft dough from inside. Fill puffs with pudding, whipped cream, ice cream, sherbet, or fruit. Replace tops. Lightly sift powdered sugar over tops, if desired. Makes 10.

Nutrition information per puff (without filling): 157 calories, 4 g protein, 10 g carbohydrate, 11 g fat (2 g saturated), 85 mg cholesterol, 158 mg sodium, 42 mg potassium.

Crème Brûlée   *(KREHM broo LAY)* A
custard topped with brown sugar that is then broiled to caramelize the sugar. Usually the custard is chilled before it is broiled with the topping so the custard won't overcook.

Tips from Our Kitchen
- Use a broilerproof dish when making the custard so the dish will be able to withstand the high temperatures needed to cook the topping.
- To get an even sprinkling of brown sugar on the custard, place the sugar in a sieve, hold the sieve over the custard, and push the sugar through the sieve with a spoon.

Crème Fraîche   *(krem FRESH)* A
dairy product made from whipping cream and a bacterial culture. The culture causes the whipping cream to thicken and develop a sharp, tangy flavor. Crème fraîche is similar to sour cream but is softer and has a milder flavor. Popular in French cooking, crème

fraîche often is spooned over fresh fruit or used in recipes as you would sour cream. It is available at specialty food stores.

A Tip from Our Kitchen
If you can't find crème fraîche in your area, make this substitute:

In a small saucepan heat 1 cup *whipping cream* over low heat till warm (90° to 100°). Pour the cream into a small bowl. Stir in 2 tablespoons *buttermilk.* Cover and let the mixture stand at room temperature for 24 to 30 hours or until the mixture is thickened. *Do not stir.* Store in a covered container in the refrigerator for up to a week. Stir before serving. Makes 1 cup.

Crenshaw
An oval-shaped melon with a mottled green and yellow, almost smooth rind. Its moist, juicy meat is salmon-colored and highly aromatic. A crenshaw has a rich, sweet, and spicy melon flavor. The center of the melon is filled with tiny, oval-shaped, inedible seeds.

(See *Melon* for the Selecting Melons chart and storing, preparation, nutrition, and other information.)

Crenshaws

Crepe
(kraype) A very thin, unleavened pancake. Crepes often are spread with a filling and rolled or folded. Depending on the type of filling, crepes can be served as appetizers, main dishes, or desserts.

You can purchase crepes that are already made or you can make crepes from a batter. Homemade crepes generally are cooked in a crepe pan or in a 6-inch skillet with sloping sides. Electric crepe pans and inverted crepe pans, which resemble upside-down skillets, also can be used to prepare crepes.

A Tip from Our Kitchen
Crepes can be cooked several days or months ahead of when they are to be used. Stack the cooked crepes with 2 pieces of waxed paper between the layers. Place the stack in an airtight container, label, and seal. Store the crepes in the refrigerator for up to 2 days or freeze for up to 4 months. Let frozen crepes thaw at room temperature about 1 hour before using them.

Cress
Green, glossy leaves from plants of the mustard family. They are used in salads, soups, and sandwiches. These pungent, peppery leaves include not only the well-known watercress, but also garden cress and peppergrass.

Q: What is the best way to store cress?
A: Cress should be rinsed and dried, then placed in the refrigerator in a plastic bag along with a damp paper towel. Stored properly, cress should keep up to a week.

Crimp
To pinch or press pastry or dough together using the fingers, a fork, or another utensil.

Fold a filled crepe in one of these ways (from left):
1. Fold the crepe in half, then fold it in half again.
2. Fold the two opposite edges of the crepe to overlap in the center over the filling.
3. Roll the crepe, jelly-roll style.

Crisp
A baked dessert, usually made with fruit, that has a crumbly topping. The term also is used to describe brittle or crusty foods.

Two-Fruit Crisp

½   cup quick-cooking rolled oats
⅓   cup packed brown sugar
¼   cup all-purpose flour
¾   teaspoon ground cinnamon, apple
     pie spice, *or* pumpkin pie spice
¼   cup margarine *or* butter
1   pound pears *or* apples, peeled, cored,
     and sliced
1   pound peaches, peeled, pitted, and
     sliced *or* nectarines, pitted and
     sliced
3   tablespoons sugar *or* ⅓ cup caramel
     ice-cream topping *or* ⅓ cup maple-
     flavored syrup
     Ice cream (optional)

■ In a medium mixing bowl combine oats, brown sugar, flour, and cinnamon or pie spice. Cut in margarine or butter till mixture resembles coarse crumbs; set aside.
■ Toss together pear or apple slices and peach or nectarine slices. Transfer to a 10x6x2-inch baking dish. Sprinkle with sugar or drizzle with caramel topping or maple-flavored syrup. Sprinkle crumb mixture over all.
■ Bake in a 350° oven for 35 to 40 minutes or till fruit is tender and topping is golden. Serve warm with ice cream, if desired. Serves 6.

Nutrition information per serving: 259 calories, 3 g protein, 47 g carbohydrate, 8 g fat (2 g saturated), 0 mg cholesterol, 96 mg sodium, 320 mg potassium.

Crisp-Tender
A term that describes vegetables that are cooked till just tender but are still somewhat crunchy.

To test for doneness, pierce the vegetable with a fork. When the fork goes into the vegetable with only slight pressure, it is crisp-tender.

Crockery Cooker
An electric cooking appliance in which foods cook slowly for several hours without requiring attention. These electric slow crockery cookers are available in small and large sizes. Some cookers have removable crockery liners for easy cleanup.

Crockery Cooking Tips
● As a rule of thumb, a food will take about twice as long to cook on the lower heat setting as it will on the high setting.
● Resist the temptation to lift the lid. Each time the cover is removed during cooking, heat and steam are lost, and it can take up to 30 minutes to regain them.
● Liquids don't boil away in the electric slow crockery cooker as they do on top of the range or in the oven. So, if you want to convert conventionally cooked recipes to use in a crockery cooker, you may need to decrease the liquid in soup and stew recipes.

Croissant
(kwah SAWN) A rich and flaky, crescent-shaped yeast roll. The flaky texture of this classic French roll is produced by folding and rolling the butter-layered dough. The layers of dough separate slightly as the rolls bake, producing a puffy texture. Ready-to-eat and frozen croissants also are available.

Tips from Our Kitchen
● For the lightest, flakiest dough, use butter, not margarine. With margarine, the layers of dough may not stay separated, which will produce a heavy, compact croissant.
● To freeze croissant dough, wrap it tightly in foil or freezer bags and freeze for up to 1 month. Let the dough thaw in the refrigerator, then shape and bake it. Or, freeze baked croissants in a freezer container for up to 2 months. To serve, heat the frozen croissants in foil in a 400° oven for 5 to 8 minutes.

Two-Fruit Crisp

Croquette *(crow KET)* A shaped ball, cone, or roll made from a mixture of ground or chopped meat, fish, or poultry and vegetables. The mixture is held together by a thick white sauce or by a mixture of egg and bread crumbs. Once shaped, croquettes are coated with bread crumbs and deep-fat fried for a crisp, golden crust.

Crouton A small toasted cube or piece of bread used as an accent for salads and soups or as a topping for casseroles. Whether homemade or commercially produced, croutons may be plain or flavored with herbs, grated cheese, or other seasonings.

Crudités *(CREW dee tay)* Assorted raw vegetables and fruit cut into small pieces and served as an appetizer. Crudités usually are served as finger food with a dip or sauce.

Q: Can crudités be made ahead of time?
A: Vegetable crudités can. Cut them up as desired. Then refrigerate them in a small amount of water in covered containers for up to 3 days.

Cruller *(KRUHL er)* A small, puffy, golden, sweet bread that is leavened with either baking powder or yeast. The dough is rolled out, cut into strips, twisted or braided, and deep-fat fried. Crullers usually are sprinkled with sugar.

Crumb A fine particle of food that has been broken off a larger piece. Bread, crackers, and cereal often are made into crumbs to be used as breading or coating, or as a thickener or binder (see also *Bread Crumbs*). Crumbs also can be mixed with melted margarine or butter and sprinkled on top of casseroles for a garnish. Cookie crumbs can be used as a crust for pies and desserts.
    The term also refers to the process of crushing, rolling, or grinding a food into fine particles.

When making cracker crumbs or dry bread crumbs, save cleanup by crushing food in a plastic bag. Leave one end open a bit so air can escape as the rolling pin is rolled over the bag.

Crumb Math
To make 1 cup of finely crushed crumbs, you'll need:
    28 saltine crackers
    24 rich, round crackers
    14 graham cracker squares
    15 gingersnaps
    22 vanilla wafers
    3 cups uncrushed cornflakes

Crumble To break a food into pieces of irregular size. The term also refers to a dessert, often fruit-based, that has a crumbly flour-sugar topping.

Crush To smash or otherwise break down a food in order to soften or crumble it or to free its juices, flavor, or aroma.

Crust The crisp, and usually browned, exterior of some baked, fried, and roasted foods. The term also refers to the shell of a pie (see also *Piecrust*).

Crystallize The process by which a sugar mixture forms crystals as it cools or dries out. Some foods, such as crystallized ginger and candied orange peel, are preserved by allowing sugar to crystallize on the outer surface of the food.

Cube To cut a food with a knife or cleaver into uniform pieces so that all sides of each piece are equal. If no specific size is given in a recipe, the pieces should be about ½ inch on all sides (see also *Chop* for how-to photograph).

Cucumber

A long, slender vegetable with deep green skin and edible seeds surrounded by a mild, creamy white, crisp flesh. It has a very mild flavor and can be enjoyed both raw and cooked.

Types: There are three common types.
☐ **Regular:** Fairly large (8 inches long and 1½ inches wide) slicing cucumber with dark green, slick skin.
☐ **English:** Long (12 to 15 inches), thin-skinned, and virtually seedless slicing cucumber. They're also known as European, burpless, greenhouse, hothouse, and seedless cucumbers.
☐ **Pickling:** Small (2 to 4 inches long) cucumber with pale to dark green, bumpy skin, used for making pickles. Pickling cucumbers sometimes are known as Kirbys.

Selecting: Cucumbers are available year-round. However, most pickling cucumbers are available only in the summer. Look for firm cucumbers without shriveled or soft spots. Smaller cucumbers of any type will be more tender.

Storing: Keep cucumbers in your refrigerator for up to 2 weeks. For best results, pickling cucumbers should be picked and used the same day.

Preparation hint: To give a decorative touch to cucumber slices, score the whole cucumber by running the tines of a fork lengthwise down the cucumber, pressing to break the skin. Repeat at regular intervals around the cucumber. Then slice or bias-slice.

Q. Do you need to peel cucumbers?
A: No. If you have garden-fresh cucumbers, there really is no need to peel them. However, supermarkets often wax their cucumbers to keep them fresh longer, so you may wish to peel them. The best way to tell if peeling is needed is to cut a slice off the cucumber and taste it. If it seems bitter, remove the skin.

Nutrition information: One regular cucumber has about 40 calories.

Cucumbers

Regular

English

Pickling

Cumin

(KUM uhn) The small, amber-colored seed of a plant in the parsley family. Cumin also is known by its Spanish name, "comino." The aromatic seed has a pungent, spicy, and slightly bitter flavor. Cumin is available either whole or ground.

Cumin is a mainstay in chili powders and curry powders. It also is a predominant flavor in many Mexican dishes. In Indian cuisine it goes into most curries and chutneys.

(See *Spice* for the Spice Alternative Guide and selecting, storing, and nutrition information.)

Cupcake

A small, individual cake usually baked in a paper bake cup set in a muffin tin. It can be made from most layer-type cake recipes and served plain or frosted.

Baking hints: To prevent cupcake batter from rising too high for the paper liners, fill
continued

the paper bake cups only half full with batter. If you're making cupcakes from a cake recipe that doesn't have cupcake directions, bake them at the same temperature called for in the cake recipe, but reduce baking time slightly. Expect to get about 24 cupcakes from a 2-layer-cake recipe.

Curdle To cause semisolid pieces of coagulated protein to develop in a dairy product. This process is undesirable in cooking. Curdling often occurs when foods such as milk, whipping cream, and sour cream are heated to too high a temperature or when they are combined with acid foods such as tomatoes, lemon juice, and wine.

Tips from Our Kitchen
To reduce the risk of curdling dairy products when cooking with them, use the following tips.
● For cream soups and sauces, wait until after you have thickened the mixture with flour or cornstarch before adding any acid ingredients, such as wine and tomatoes.
● Once you've stirred sour cream or yogurt into a hot mixture, don't boil it.

Cure To preserve a food by one of several processes. Meats and fish may be cured by soaking them in a brine solution, rubbing them with salt, or drying or smoking them. Cheese is cured by spraying or injecting it with a culture. Curing adds flavor and texture to food.

Currant A tiny, firm berry with brilliantly colored, shiny skin and a tart and tangy flavor. Currants are most often red, but they can be white or black. The latter types are more commonly found in Europe.

Currants

Market forms: Fresh currants are not widely available, but some are sold in markets from June through August. You also will find red currant jelly and sauces.

Black currants are used to make the liqueur cassis. You also will find black currant juice in larger supermarkets and gourmet shops.

(See *Berry* for the Selecting Berries chart, including calories, and for selecting and storing information.)

Currant, Dried A tiny, dried, Black Corinth grape. Dried currants taste sweet and tangy. With their dark brown, wrinkly skin, they are similar in appearance to raisins, but smaller. Dried currants are not related to the berries of the same name.

A Tip from Our Kitchen
When a recipe calls for chopped raisins, dried currants are a good substitute. Not only do you get the same flavor, you also eliminate the chopping.

Nutrition information: Two tablespoons of dried currants have about 50 calories.

(See *Dried Fruit* for storing information.)

Curry An Indian or Far Eastern dish that features foods seasoned with curry powder. A curry may be either a side dish or a main dish. A side-dish curry uses vegetables or fruits as major ingredients, and a main-dish curry features meats, fish, poultry, or eggs. A main-dish curry often is served with rice and assorted condiments, such as chutney, grated coconut, chopped nuts, and raisins.

Curry Powder
A blend of as many as 16 to 20 ground spices designed to give the flavor of Indian curry cookery. Typical ingredients include cumin, coriander, red pepper, fenugreek, and turmeric. Other spices sometimes used include cinnamon, allspice, fennel, ginger, and black or white pepper.

A Tip from Our Kitchen
Cook curry powder in a little butter or oil at the beginning of a recipe to avoid a harsh, raw flavor.

(See *Spice* for selecting, storing, and nutrition information.)

Custard
A sweetened egg and milk mixture that is served as a dessert. Baked custard is firm enough to hold its shape when unmolded. Stirred custard, which is cooked on top of the range, has a creamy, pourable consistency and often is used as a sauce over fruit or cake. Both have a delicate flavor and can be served warm or chilled.

Baked Custard

  3 **beaten eggs**
1½ **cups milk *or* light cream**
  ¼ **cup sugar**
  1 **teaspoon vanilla**
     Ground nutmeg (optional)

■ Combine eggs, milk, sugar, and vanilla. Beat till well combined but not foamy. Place four 6-ounce custard cups in a 9x9x2-inch baking pan. Place pan on oven rack. Pour egg mixture into custard cups. If desired, sprinkle with ground nutmeg. Pour hot tap water into pan around custard cups to a depth of 1 inch. Bake in a 325° oven for 30 to 45 minutes or till a knife inserted near the centers comes

out clean (see photo, top right). Serve custard warm or chilled. Makes 4 servings.

Nutrition information per serving: 150 calories, 8 g protein, 17 g carbohydrate, 6 g fat (2 g saturated), 168 mg cholesterol, 92 mg sodium, 187 mg potassium.

Stirred Custard

  3 **beaten eggs**
  2 **cups milk *or* light cream**
  ¼ **cup sugar**
  1 **teaspoon vanilla**
  2 **tablespoons amaretto *or* orange liqueur *or* coffee liqueur (optional)**

■ In a heavy medium saucepan, combine eggs, milk or cream, and sugar. Cook and stir over medium heat. Continue cooking egg mixture till it just coats a metal spoon (see photo, bottom right). Remove from heat. Stir in vanilla and, if desired, amaretto or other specified liqueur. Quickly cool by placing the saucepan in a sink or bowl of *ice* water for 1 to 2 minutes, stirring constantly. Pour custard mixture into a bowl. Cover surface with clear plastic wrap. Chill till serving time. If desired, serve custard mixture over cake slices or fruit. Makes 3 cups (6 servings).

Nutrition information per serving: 110 calories, 6 g protein, 13 g carbohydrate, 4 g fat (2 g saturated), 114 mg cholesterol, 71 mg sodium, 156 mg potassium.

Cut In
To work a solid fat, such as shortening, lard, margarine, or butter, into dry ingredients, usually with a pastry blender.

Q: Is a pastry blender the only way to cut in shortening?
A: No. You can use 2 table knives. Hold one knife in each hand and draw the knives across each other to cut through the shortening and dry ingredients mixture.

Cutlet
A thin, boneless slice of pork, veal, or lamb, cut from the leg or sirloin portion of the animal and cooked by broiling, frying, or braising. This term also refers to a mechanically tenderized slice of meat taken from a less tender part of the animal.

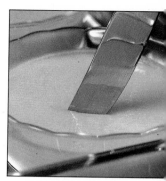

Test a baked custard for doneness by inserting a table knife near the center of the custard, about ½ inch deep. The knife should come out clean.

To determine if a stirred custard is cooked, dip a clean metal spoon into the custard. The custard should coat the spoon. Wipe your finger across the back of the spoon. The edges of the custard along the path of your finger should hold their shape.

D-F

Eggnog for a Crowd
(see recipe, page 153)

Divinity
(see recipe, page 145)

Fettuccine Alfredo
(see recipe, page 162)

Daikon *(DIE kuhn)* A long, carrot-shaped, white, Japanese radish. Daikons range from 6 to 15 inches in length with an average diameter of 2 to 3 inches. The daikon's flesh is juicy and white with a mildly spicy, radishlike flavor.

Selecting: Look for firm daikons with a smooth, white skin.

Storing: Refrigerate daikons in a plastic bag for up to 2 weeks.

Nutrition information: One-half cup raw, sliced daikon has about 10 calories.

(See *Radish* for an identification photo.)

Dandelion Green A dark green, thick, jagged-edged leaf from the dandelion plant. Dandelion greens have a slightly bitter flavor with a bite, which intensifies as the greens age. They can be used fresh or cooked.

Selecting: Purchase healthy-looking greens with dark green leaves and no brown spots. (If you pick your own, make sure they haven't been treated with chemicals.)

Storing: Discard bruised leaves. Wash fresh greens in cold water; pat dry. Place them in a plastic bag lined with a paper towel, and store in the refrigerator for up to 3 days.

How to cook: See Greens on the Cooking Fresh Vegetables chart under *Vegetable.*

Nutrition information: One-half cup cooked, chopped dandelion greens has about 15 calories.

Danish Pastry A flaky, rich, buttery yeast-bread dough that usually is shaped into sweet rolls or coffee cakes. A traditional favorite in Denmark, this pastry is made by spreading the dough with chilled butter, folding it, and rolling it out in much the same way as croissants are made. Jelly, cheese, chocolate, and fruit often are used as fillings. Danish is an informal name for such a sweet roll or coffee cake.

Dash A measure of dry or liquid ingredient that equals $1/16$ teaspoon. One way to measure a dash is to fill a ¼-teaspoon measuring spoon one-quarter full.

Date A small, oblong fruit with a pit and a golden brown to deep amber color. Dates are plump and lustrous and have a rich, sugary flavor and a slightly chewy texture.

Types: Dates often are classified as dry, semidry, semisoft, and soft. Semidry dates comprise a large percentage of the dates sold in the United States. Semidry varieties include the *Deglet Noor* and the *Zahidi.* Another popular date variety is the *Medjool,* a very large, premium, semisoft date.

Medjool

Deglet Noor

Zahidi

Dates

Market forms: You'll find dates available whole (with or without pits) and in chopped form. Dates also come stuffed with almonds or coated with finely chopped nuts or sugar for elegant snacks. In some areas, you may find other date products, such as extruded date pieces and date paste.

Storing: Keep dates in a tightly closed container in the refrigerator up to several months or in the freezer up to a year.

Q: **Once dates have lost moisture during storage, can they be softened as raisins can be for recipes?**
A: Yes, simply heat a cup or so of water or fruit juice to boiling, and pour it over the dates. Let stand 5 to 10 minutes, and your dates will soften nicely. Then drain the dates. Save the flavor-filled plumping liquid to substitute for some of the liquid in your recipe, if desired.

Tips from Our Kitchen
● Prechopped dates are coated with a light sprinkling of sugar to prevent the fruit from sticking together in the package. The additional sugar is such a small amount that recipes generally won't be affected.
● To make chopping whole dates easier, dip your knife in water frequently. The water will help keep the dates from sticking to the knife. Or, use kitchen shears, dipping them in water between snips.

Nutrition information: One date has about 20 calories.

Deglaze Adding a liquid, such as water, broth, or wine, to a pan that has just been used to cook meat. The liquid is poured into the pan with the pan juices after the meat is removed and is used to help loosen the browned bits left in the pan so they can be used to make a sauce or gravy.

Dehydration A process that removes water from food to slow growth of bacteria and minimize spoilage so foods can be stored longer. Foods such as fruits, vegetables, herbs, spices, soups, meats, and milk can be dehydrated. Foods can be left in the open air to dry naturally, or they can be dehydrated mechanically. Mechanical methods include using food dehydrators to circulate air over the food and using low-temperature ovens to dry the food. The moisture in foods can be reduced by anywhere from 15 to 98 percent. Reduction in moisture alters the appearance, flavor, weight, and volume of the food, and in most cases the food must be rehydrated before it is used.

Dessert A sweet food served at the end of the meal or as a refreshment. Desserts include everything from custards and puddings to cakes, cookies, pastries, pies, and refrigerated and frozen mixtures. Desserts may be as simple as a piece of fresh fruit or as elaborate as a three-layer torte.

Selecting desserts for a menu: When planning a dessert, consider the entire menu.

If the meal is heavy, choose a light dessert, such as a fruit compote. If the meal is light, you might consider serving a rich dessert, for instance a pie, shortcake, or cheesecake.

Try to avoid repeating an ingredient or flavor from the previous courses.

If a menu involves a lot of last-minute preparation, choose a dessert that can be made ahead.

continued

Health-Conscious Desserts
- Serve a tray of fresh fruit and low-fat cheese for an impressive, yet nutritious, dessert.
- Select desserts based on fruit, such as baked apples, poached pears, and fruit crisp, to get the nutrition of the fruit as well as a sweet flavor.
- In recipes, substitute low-fat dairy products, such as low-fat yogurt, for higher calorie sour cream.
- Serve small pieces of dessert. This will keep people from overeating just to clean their plates.

Dessert Topping   A fluffy, white product that resembles whipped cream. Dessert topping may or may not be made with dairy products.

Dessert topping is available whipped and frozen, unwhipped and frozen, in pressurized cans, and as a dry packaged mix.

Nutrition information: A 1-tablespoon portion of frozen, whipped, nondairy dessert topping has 15 calories and 1 gram of fat. One tablespoon of dessert topping prepared from a dry mix has 8 calories and less than a gram of fat.

Devein   To lift out and remove the black vein from the back of a shrimp.

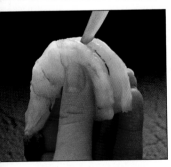

To devein a shrimp, use a sharp knife to make a shallow slit along the back of the shrimp. If the vein is visible, use the tip of the knife to remove it. Rinse the shrimp under cold water.

Deviled   A term that refers to a highly seasoned food, such as deviled eggs or crab. The spicy-hot flavor comes from ingredients such as black pepper, ground red pepper, bottled hot pepper sauce, mustard, chili powder, Worcestershire sauce, and horseradish.

Deviled Ham   A canned mixture of ground fully cooked ham and seasonings used as a sandwich filling and in main dishes and appetizers.

Devil's Food Cake   A light-textured, chocolate layer-type cake with a deep reddish brown color. Devil's food cake generally has more baking soda, a stronger flavor, and a darker color than regular chocolate cake.

Devil's Food Cake

> 2 cups all-purpose flour
> 2 cups sugar
> ½ cup unsweetened cocoa powder
> 1½ teaspoons baking soda
> ¼ teaspoon salt
> 1½ cups milk
> ½ cup shortening
> 1 teaspoon vanilla
> 2 eggs
>   Chocolate Butter Frosting

■ In a bowl combine flour, sugar, cocoa powder, baking soda, and salt. Add milk, shortening, and vanilla. Beat with an electric mixer on low speed till combined. Beat on medium speed for 2 minutes. Add eggs and beat 2 minutes more. Pour into 2 greased and floured 9x1½-inch round baking pans. Bake in a 350° oven for 30 to 35 minutes or till a toothpick comes out clean. Cool on wire racks for 10 minutes. Remove from pans. Cool thoroughly on racks. Frost with Chocolate Butter Frosting. Makes 12 servings.

Chocolate Butter Frosting: In a medium mixing bowl beat ⅓ cup *margarine or butter* till fluffy. Gradually add 2 cups sifted *powdered sugar,* beating well. Slowly beat in ¼ cup *milk;* 2 squares (2 ounces) *unsweetened chocolate,* melted and cooled; and 1½ teaspoons *vanilla.* Slowly beat in 2½ to 2¾ cups sifted *powdered sugar.* Beat in additional milk, if necessary, to make frosting of spreading consistency. Frosts tops and sides of two 8- or 9-inch layers.

Nutrition information per serving: 533 calories, 6 g protein, 91 g carbohydrate, 19 g fat (6 g saturated), 39 mg cholesterol, 237 mg sodium, 173 mg potassium.

Dice   To cut a food with a knife or cleaver into small cubes. The cubes should be ⅛ to ¼ inch on all sides (see also *Chop* for how-to photograph).

Diet   See *Nutrition.*

Dijon Mustard   See *Mustard.*

Dill   Refers to both dillweed, an herb, and dillseed, a spice. Dillweed comes from the feathery, bright green leaves, which are used fresh or dried. Dillweed has a delicate, somewhat refreshing flavor. Sprigs of fresh dill also may be found at the supermarket.

The small, hard, dried seeds, which are available whole, are called dillseed. The seeds have a more dominant flavor than dillweed and a sharp, warm, slightly bitter taste.

Q: Some pickle recipes call for a fresh dill head. What is that?

A: A dill head is the greenish yellow, umbrella-shaped seed head of a fresh dill plant. Dill heads are available (during the summer months) wherever you find other fresh herbs. Pickle recipes often call for a certain number of dill heads or so many tablespoons of dillseed. You can substitute 2 to 3 tablespoons of dillseed for 4 to 6 heads of fresh dill.

(See *Herb* for the Herb Alternative Guide and selecting, storing, preparation, cooking, nutrition, and other information. See also *Spice* for selecting, storing, and nutrition information.)

Dill

Dilute   To thin a food or weaken its flavor by adding a liquid, such as water.

Dip   To immerse food for a short time into a liquid or dry mixture in order to coat, cool, or moisten the food.

The term also refers to an appetizer that consists of a soft mixture into which items, such as chips or vegetables, are dunked. It can be savory or sweet, hot or cold, and is usually based on a creamy ingredient, such as sour cream, yogurt, cream cheese, or mayonnaise.

Dissolve   To stir a solid food and a liquid food together to form a mixture in which none of the solid remains. Sometimes heat is needed to form the mixture. For example, flavored gelatin is dissolved in boiling water.

Divan

Divan Originally the term referred only to a dish that contained chicken breasts, broccoli spears, and a rich cream sauce. Today the term often refers to any main dish that includes broccoli and a cream sauce.

Chicken Divan

- 2 **cups frozen chopped broccoli**
- 3 **tablespoons margarine** *or* **butter**
- 3 **tablespoons all-purpose flour**
- ⅛ **teaspoon pepper**
  Dash ground nutmeg
- ¾ **cup light cream** *or* **milk**
- ½ **cup chicken broth**
- ½ **cup shredded Swiss cheese**
- 2 **tablespoons dry white wine**
- 1½ **cups cubed cooked chicken** *or* **turkey**
- 3 **tablespoons grated Parmesan cheese**
  Paprika

■ Cook broccoli according to package directions; drain. Arrange in a 10x6x2-inch baking dish.
■ Meanwhile, for sauce, in a medium saucepan melt margarine or butter. Stir in flour, pepper, and nutmeg. Add cream or milk and chicken broth all at once. Cook and stir till thickened and bubbly. Add Swiss cheese and wine, stirring till cheese melts.
■ Pour *half* of the sauce over the broccoli. Top with the chicken or turkey, then the remaining sauce. Sprinkle with Parmesan cheese and paprika. Bake in a 350° oven about 20 minutes or till heated through. Makes 4 servings.

Nutrition information per serving: 354 calories, 27 g protein, 12 g carbohydrate, 22 g fat (9 g saturated), 77 mg cholesterol, 386 mg sodium, 417 mg potassium.

Divinity A delicate, soft-textured candy that is made by slowly beating a hot, cooked sugar syrup into beaten egg whites. Chopped nuts or candied fruit and food coloring can be added to divinity.

Q: Why is divinity so tricky to make?
A: Three factors are important when you're making divinity. First, check the humidity before making divinity. The candy may never set up if the humidity in the room is above 60 percent. Second, follow recipe directions precisely—timing is everything. Third, always use a sturdy, freestanding electric mixer (see tip box, opposite).

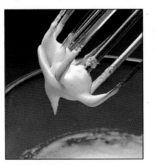

As soon as the sugar mixture has cooked to the recommended temperature, begin beating the egg whites with a sturdy, freestanding, electric mixer. Beat till stiff peaks form (tips stand straight).

Gradually pour the hot candy mixture over the beaten egg whites in a slow, steady stream (slightly less than ⅛-inch diameter) while beating on high speed. Scrape sides of bowl occasionally.

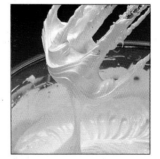

Continue beating just till the candy starts to lose its gloss. When the beaters are lifted, the mixture should fall in a ribbon, forming a mound but not disappearing into the remaining mixture.

Once the candy is beaten properly, work quickly so it doesn't get stiff. Use a second spoon to push the candy off the first one. If the candy does get too stiff, beat in a few drops of *hot water*.

Divinity-Making Tips

● Make divinity on a relatively dry day. Because sugar absorbs moisture, which makes the divinity too runny to set up, no amount of beating on a humid day will make this candy set up.

● Allow the egg whites to come to room temperature before beating so they'll whip up to their maximum volume.

● Use a sturdy, freestanding electric mixer when making divinity. It requires heavy beating, which puts a strain on mixer motors. Portable mixers and some lightweight, freestanding mixers don't have the power necessary for this chore.

(See *Candy* for Candy-Making Tips and equipment, storing, and other information.)

Divinity

    2½ cups sugar
    ½   cup light corn syrup
    ½   cup water
    2   egg whites
    1   teaspoon vanilla
    1 or 2 drops food coloring (optional)
    ½   cup chopped candied fruit *or* nuts
        (optional)

■ In a heavy, 2-quart saucepan, combine sugar, corn syrup, and water. Cook and stir over medium-high heat to boiling. Clip candy thermometer to pan. Cook over medium heat, without stirring, to 260°, hard-ball stage (10 to 15 minutes). Remove saucepan from heat. Remove candy thermometer.

■ In a large mixing bowl, beat egg whites with a sturdy, freestanding electric mixer on medium speed till stiff peaks form (tips stand straight). *Gradually* pour hot mixture in a thin stream over beaten egg whites, beating on high speed about 3 minutes; scrape bowl. Add vanilla and, if desired, food coloring. Continue beating on high just till candy starts to lose its gloss. When beaters are lifted, mixture should fall in a ribbon that mounds on itself. This final beating should take 5 to 6 minutes.

■ Drop a spoonful of candy mixture onto waxed paper. If it stays mounded, the mixture has been beaten sufficiently. *Immediately* stir in fruit or nuts, if desired. *Quickly* drop remaining mixture from a teaspoon onto waxed paper. If mixture flattens out, beat ½ to 1 minute more; check again. If mixture is too stiff to spoon, beat in a few drops *hot water* till candy is a softer consistency. Store tightly covered. Makes about 40 pieces.

Nutrition information per serving: 60 calories, 0 g protein, 16 g carbohydrate, 0 g fat, 0 mg cholesterol, 5 mg sodium, 4 mg potassium.

Dollop
To place a scoop or spoonful of a semiliquid food, such as whipped cream, on top of another food.

The term also refers to the scoop or spoonful of food itself, as in "a dollop of whipped cream."

Dough
A mixture of flour and liquid to which other ingredients, such as seasonings, sweeteners, shortening, margarine, butter, egg, or a leavening agent, may be added. A dough is thick and nonpourable; some doughs can be kneaded. Soft doughs have more liquid and generally are used for biscuits, breads, and drop cookies. Stiff doughs are firm enough to be rolled out easily and are used to make items such as piecrusts and cutout cookies.

Doughnut
Small, individual sweet breads, usually ring-shaped, leavened by baking powder or yeast, and deep-fat fried. Doughnuts are golden brown, uniform in shape, and have a tender crust and a slightly moist texture. Those leavened with baking powder (cake doughnuts) have a soft, cakelike texture. Yeast doughnuts are lighter and more breadlike than cake doughnuts. Doughnuts often are glazed with icing, dusted with sugar, or filled with jelly or pudding.

continued

Q: When deep-frying doughnuts, how can I keep them from becoming greasy?

A: Watch the oil closely to make sure it maintains the temperature that's specified in the recipe. Oil that's not hot enough soaks into doughnuts before the crust forms. (However, oil that's too hot cooks the outside of the doughnuts too fast, leaving the inside uncooked.)

Also, cook only two or three doughnuts at a time. Too many doughnuts in the pan lowers the temperature of the oil and makes turning them more difficult.

A Tip from Our Kitchen

When frying doughnuts, use either a 3-quart saucepan or a deep-fat fryer. Both pans have high sides that help prevent spattering. If using a 3-quart saucepan, put about 2 inches of oil in it for frying. If using a deep-fat fryer, follow the manufacturer's directions.

Nutrition information: One plain cake doughnut (3¼x1 inches) has about 210 calories. A yeast doughnut (3¾x1¼ inches) has about 240 calories.

Drain To allow the liquid or fat to run off a solid food before serving the food or adding other ingredients to it.

Drawn A term that refers to a whole fish, with or without scales, that has had its internal organs removed. The term also refers to melted butter.

Dredge To coat a food, either before or after cooking, with a dry ingredient, such as flour, cornmeal, or sugar. The coating helps increase browning, add flavor, and improve appearance.

Dress To remove the internal organs and heads from fish, poultry, and game. A dressed item also has been cleaned of feathers or scales for cooking. For fish, the cleaning may include the removal of fins and tail.

The term also refers to the process of tossing salad ingredients with salad dressing.

Dressing A flavorful liquid or semi-liquid seasoning for salads (see also *Salad Dressing*).

The term also refers to a seasoned stuffing mixture for poultry, fish, and meats that usually is based on bread, rice, or potatoes (see also *Stuffing*).

Dried Beef Beef, usually from the hindquarters of the animal, that is cured, smoked, and dried. Dried beef, also called chipped beef, has a smoky, salty taste and a dark red or deep brown color.

Dried beef is smoked and dried until most of the moisture is removed, then it is sliced paper thin and sealed in small jars or plastic bags or sold by the pound.

Q: Why does dried beef taste salty?

A: Smoking and drying concentrate the salt from the curing process. To remove some of the saltiness, rinse or soak the dried beef in hot water, then drain well.

Nutrition information: A 3-ounce serving of dried beef contains about 170 calories and 3,664 milligrams of sodium.

Dried Fruit
Fruit that has been depleted of more than half of its water content by exposure to the sun or by mechanical heating methods. Dried fruit has a chewy texture and a very sweet flavor, due to the concentration of sugars during the drying process.

Types: You can purchase any of the following dried fruits: apples, apricots, bananas, carambolas, cherries, cranberries, currants, figs, peaches, pears, persimmons, pineapples, prunes, and raisins. You also can purchase mixed dried fruit and fruit bits.

Storing: Dried fruits store exceptionally well in unopened packages. Once you have opened the package, wrap the fruit securely in airtight plastic wrap or bags and store in the refrigerator. Or, wrap for freezing and freeze for up to 6 months.

Preparation hints: To keep dried fruit from sticking to your knife when you're chopping and to make it easier to cut, use a sharp knife dipped frequently in hot water. Or, try kitchen shears dipped in water to make quick work of snipping dried fruit.

How to cook: See the Cooking Dried Fruit chart, right.

Nutrition information: A piece of dried fruit has the same number of calories as a fresh piece of the same fruit. However, it takes an average of 5 pounds of fresh fruit to make 1 pound of the dried. So, when the fruit is measured by volume or weight, dried fruits are higher in calories than fresh. Some dried fruits, such as prunes and raisins, are a source of iron and fiber. Calories range from 100 to 290 per ½-cup serving.

Cooking Dried Fruit*

Place dried fruit in a saucepan. Add water to fruit. Bring to boiling. Reduce heat. Cover and simmer for time specified in the chart, adding sugar, if desired, for last 5 minutes of cooking. This is enough dried fruit and syrup to make 4 servings.

Dried Fruit	Water	Sugar	Cooking Time
Apple chunks 6-ounce package (2½ cups)	2 cups	¼ cup	6 minutes
Apricot halves 6-ounce package (2 cups)	1½ cups	⅓ cup	13 minutes
Cherries 6-ounce package (1⅓ cups)	1⅓ cups	⅓ cup	7 minutes
Cranberries 6-ounce package (1½ cups)	1½ cups	½ cup	7 minutes
Figs 8-ounce package (1½ cups)	1½ cups	2 tablespoons	20 minutes
Mixed fruit 8-ounce package (2 cups)	1½ cups	¼ cup	12 minutes
Mixed fruit bits 6-ounce package (1½ cups)	1½ cups	¼ cup	6 minutes
Peach halves 7-ounce package (2 cups)	1½ cups	¼ cup	15 minutes
Pear halves 8-ounce package (1½ cups)	1 cup	¼ cup	17 minutes
Persimmons, halved, stems removed 8-ounce package (1½ cups)	1½ cups	⅓ cup	20 minutes
Prunes 12-ounce package (2 cups)	1¼ cups	2 tablespoons	12 minutes

To plump dried fruit for use as an ingredient, cover with water. Bring to boiling. Remove from heat; cover and let stand 5 minutes.

Drying See *Dehydration.*

Duchess Potatoes A light, fluffy mixture of mashed potatoes, egg yolk, margarine or butter, and seasonings. The mixture can be piped through a pastry tube into individual servings or used as a decorative edging for meats, poultry, fish, or casseroles.

Duck, Duckling A wild or domestic bird known for its distinctive flavor and moist dark meat. The flavor of duck and duckling meat is affected by the diet of the bird, as well as its age and weight. Generally, older and heavier birds are stronger flavored and less tender.

Types: There are hundreds of species of duck all over the world. Here are some of the most popular birds you'll find.
☐ **Domestic:** Commercially raised ducks fed a special regulated diet to produce sweet and tender meat. Most domestic birds have a dressed weight of 3 to 6 pounds. A domestic duckling is a young duck, 8 weeks old or younger. Roast these plump birds without stuffing.
☐ **Wild:** Mallard, wigeon, and teal are the most well-known species. Mallards weigh from 1¼ to 1¾ pounds (dressed), wigeons weigh about 1 pound (dressed), and teals weigh about ½ pound (dressed). Wild duck can be roasted, broiled, or braised.

Market forms: Duck is available frozen and fresh.

Q: How should duck be prepared so it doesn't taste greasy?
A: Greasiness is a problem only with domestic ducks, because they have a thick layer of fat under their skin. When roasting them, be sure you prick the skin to allow the fat to escape.

How to cook: For roasting directions, see the Roasting Poultry chart under *Poultry.* Grilling is not recommended. Plan on about 1 pound of duck per serving.

Nutrition information: A 3-ounce serving of cooked, domestic duck with skin has about 290 calories, 24 grams of fat, and 72 milligrams of cholesterol.

(See *Poultry* for selecting, refrigerating, freezing, thawing, cooking, and other information.)

Dumpling A light, tender ball or dollop of leavened batter or dough that is cooked atop a semiliquid mixture, such as a stew or a saucy dessert. (For a dumpling recipe, see page 150.)
This term also refers to a dessert made by wrapping a fruit, such as an apple or pear, in pastry or a rich biscuit dough, and baking it.
An Oriental food that's made by wrapping dough around a filling and then steaming it also is called a dumpling.

Tips from Our Kitchen
When cooking dumplings atop a mixture, keep these two points in mind.
● For light, fluffy dumplings that aren't doughy or soggy on the bottom, be sure the cooking liquid is bubbly hot before you add the batter or dough.
● When cooking dumplings on the range top, don't peek in the saucepan. Keep the cover on the pan until the cooking time is almost complete. Otherwise, the dumplings may deflate.

Chicken and Dumplings
(see recipe, page 150)

Chicken and Dumplings

> 2 **pounds meaty chicken pieces**
> ½ **cup chopped onion**
> 1 **teaspoon instant chicken bouillon granules**
> ½ **teaspoon poultry seasoning** *or* **dried sage, crushed**
> ¼ **teaspoon pepper**
> 2½ **cups water**
> 1 **cup coarsely shredded carrots**
> ½ **cup sliced celery**
> **Dumplings**
> ⅓ **cup cold water**
> 3 **tablespoons all-purpose flour**
> 2 **tablespoons snipped parsley**

■ Skin chicken, if desired. Rinse well. In a 4½-quart Dutch oven combine chicken, onion, chicken bouillon granules, poultry seasoning or sage, and pepper. Add the 2½ cups water. Bring to boiling; reduce heat. Cover and simmer for 25 minutes. Add carrots and celery. Simmer, covered, for 10 minutes more.
■ Meanwhile, prepare Dumplings. Drop into 4 mounds directly onto chicken. Cover and simmer about 12 minutes or till a toothpick inserted into dumplings comes out clean. Using a slotted spoon, transfer chicken and dumplings to soup plates. Cover; keep warm.
■ Skim fat from broth; discard fat. Measure 1½ cups broth into Dutch oven. Combine the ⅓ cup water and flour. Stir into broth. Cook and stir till thickened and bubbly. Cook and stir 1 minute more. Stir in parsley. Season to taste with salt and pepper. Spoon thickened broth onto each serving. Makes 4 servings.

Dumplings: In a medium mixing bowl stir together ⅔ cup *all-purpose flour,* 1 teaspoon *baking powder,* and ⅛ teaspoon *salt.* In a small bowl combine ¼ cup *milk* and 2 tablespoons *cooking oil.* Add to flour mixture. Stir with a fork just till combined.

Nutrition information per serving: 413 calories, 29 g protein, 27 g carbohydrate, 20 g fat (5 g saturated), 83 mg cholesterol, 472 mg sodium, 435 mg potassium.

Dust To lightly coat or sprinkle a food with a dry ingredient, such as flour or powdered sugar, either before or after cooking in order to improve the flavor or appearance of a food.

A Tip from Our Kitchen
To quickly decorate an unfrosted cake, lay a paper pattern or doily over the cake, and dust it with cocoa powder or powdered sugar. Then carefully remove the pattern or doily to reveal a design.

Éclair An oblong cream puff shell filled with pudding, pastry cream, or whipped cream and served as a dessert (see also *Cream Puff*). Éclairs usually are drizzled with a glaze.

To make éclairs, pipe Cream Puff dough (see recipe, page 130) onto a greased baking sheet using a pastry tube fitted with a round tip. Make strips 4½x1x¾ inches. Or, use spoons to drop and shape the dough into strips.

Edam Cheese *(EE duhm)* A mild, nutty, and sometimes salty cheese. Edam is made from cow's milk and can be semisoft to hard with a firm body and small holes. It is a creamy yellow cheese often coated in red wax. Edam's appearance and flavor are similar to Gouda, but Edam has a firmer texture and a tangier flavor.

Edam cheese

A Tip from Our Kitchen

Edam's red rind makes an ideal serving container for cheese spread. Cut off a top portion of the rind and spoon out the cheese, leaving a ¼- to ½-inch-thick shell. Prepare a dip or cheese spread with the scooped-out cheese and then spoon the mixture back into the cheese shell. Serve with crackers and fresh vegetables and fruit.

(See *Cheese* for the Selecting Cheese chart and selecting, storing, serving, nutrition, and other information.)

Egg A hard-shelled reproductive body made by birds. There are many different types of eggs, but chicken eggs are the ones that are used most commonly in cooking. Domestic chicken eggs have white or brown shells. The color of the shell does not affect the flavor or nutritional value of the egg.

Grades and sizes: Eggs are sold by both grade and size. Grade primarily measures an egg's appearance once it is broken out of the shell. Most eggs sold are Grade AA or A. Grade AA eggs spread less and have a slightly higher, firmer yolk and white than Grade A eggs. Grade B eggs spread more than the other two grades and usually are sold only for use by food manufacturers.

The sizes of eggs include jumbo, extra large, large, medium, small, and peewee. Price differences are based largely on egg size, with larger sizes costing more per dozen than smaller sizes. There is about a 3-ounce difference in weight per dozen between sizes.

Market forms: The majority of consumers buy eggs in the shell by the dozen. Of all the sizes sold, large and extra large are most readily available. (See Preparation Hints, page 152, for information on using large eggs in recipes.)

While frozen and dried plain eggs are mostly for commercial use, dried eggs often are sold in camping goods stores. Frozen omelets, frozen scrambled eggs, and other egg products also are available.

Egg substitutes also may be purchased. These products usually are manufactured using an egg white base. Because they contain no yolk, they contain little to no cholesterol. They're sold in the frozen or refrigerated sections of most supermarkets.

Using Eggs Safely

Wholesome egg dishes depend on eggs that are in top condition. Here are some egg-handling pointers to remember.
- Select clean, fresh eggs from refrigerated display cases. Don't use dirty, cracked, or leaking eggs. They may have become contaminated with harmful bacteria.
- When cracking eggs, avoid getting any eggshell in with the raw eggs. Also, when separating eggs, don't pass the yolk from shell half to shell half. Instead, use an egg separator so that if bacteria are present on the shell, it won't contaminate either the yolk or white.
- Be sure to wash your hands, utensils, and countertops after working with eggs.
- Serve hot egg dishes as soon as they're cooked. Refrigerate cold egg dishes immediately. Chill leftovers promptly and reheat thoroughly before serving.
- Eating uncooked or slightly cooked eggs may be harmful because of possible bacterial contamination. The individuals most susceptible include the elderly, infants, pregnant women, and those who are already ill. Check with your doctor to see if you are at risk. If you are, you probably should avoid eating foods that contain raw or partially cooked eggs. Healthy people should eat raw eggs with discretion.

continued

Storing: Eggs graded by the U.S. Department of Agriculture are washed and sprayed to seal the eggshell pores before selling. These eggs will stay fresh longer if they are not rewashed at home.

Remember to refrigerate eggs promptly after buying them. Store them in their cartons, because eggs absorb refrigerator odors easily.

Fresh eggs can be refrigerated for up to 5 weeks after the packing date (a number stamped on the carton from 1 to 365, with 1 representing January 1 and 365 representing December 31).

To store raw egg whites, refrigerate them in a tightly covered container for up to 4 days. Refrigerate raw yolks, covered with water, in a tightly covered container for up to 2 days. Refrigerate hard-cooked eggs in their shells in their cartons for up to 7 days.

Q: Can I freeze eggs at home?
A: Yes. Raw whole eggs, whites, and yolks can be frozen to use in recipes. Eggs cannot be frozen in their shells.

To freeze whole eggs, break them into a bowl and beat just till blended before freezing in a freezer container. If freezing several eggs in one container, indicate the number of eggs on the label.

To freeze raw egg yolks, add ⅛ teaspoon salt or 1½ teaspoons sugar or corn syrup per 4 yolks. The salt or sugar will help prevent gelling. Freeze the yolks in a freezer container.

When freezing raw egg whites, place each one in a different compartment of an ice-cube tray. Cover tightly with plastic wrap and freeze till solid. Transfer the egg white cubes to a freezer container and freeze.

Thaw the eggs in the refrigerator overnight and use yolks or whole eggs immediately after thawing. Egg whites can sit at room temperature for 30 minutes after thawing. Allowing them to stand will give them better volume when beating. Be sure to thoroughly cook eggs that have been frozen.

Preparation hints: Most recipes that call for eggs were developed using large eggs. For some recipes, especially baked products, using smaller or larger eggs may alter the end product. See *Meringue* for Egg White Pointers.

Cooking hints: When an egg is hard-cooked, a harmless but unattractive greenish ring can form around the yolk. To minimize the chances of a ring forming, time the cooking carefully. Also, cool the hard-cooked eggs in an ice-water bath.

Sometimes large batches of scrambled eggs can take on a greenish cast. To prevent this discoloration, cook the eggs in small batches and serve them as soon as possible.

How to cook: Here are some basic ways to cook eggs.

☐ **Hard-cooked:** Place *eggs* in a single layer in a saucepan. Add enough *cold* water to come 1 inch above the eggs. Bring them to boiling over high heat. Reduce the heat so the water is just below simmering; cover. Cook 15 minutes; drain. Run *cold* water over the eggs or place them in ice water till cool enough to handle. Drain. Gently tap each egg on the countertop. Roll the egg between the palms of your hands. Peel off the eggshell, starting at the large end. (About 75 calories per egg.)

☐ **Scrambled:** For 3 servings, in a bowl beat together 6 *eggs*, ⅓ cup *milk*, ¼ teaspoon *salt*, and a dash *pepper*. In a large skillet, melt 1 tablespoon *margarine or butter;* pour in egg mixture. Cook over medium heat, without stirring, until the mixture begins to set on the bottom and around the edge. Using a large spoon or spatula, lift and fold the partially cooked eggs so the uncooked portion flows underneath. Continue cooking over medium heat for 2 to 3 minutes or until the eggs are cooked throughout but are still glossy and moist. Remove from the heat immediately. (206 calories per serving.)

☐ **Fried:** For 2 servings, in a large skillet, melt 2 teaspoons *margarine or butter* over medium heat. (*Or,* spray a *cold* skillet with *nonstick spray coating,* then heat.) Break 4 *eggs* into the skillet. When the whites are set, add 1 to 2 teaspoons *water.* Cover the skillet; cook the eggs to desired doneness, 4 minutes for firm. (192 calories per serving.)

☐ **Poached:** For 2 servings, lightly grease a 2-quart saucepan, if desired. Add water to half-fill the pan; stir in 1 teaspoon *instant chicken bouillon granules,* if desired; bring to boiling. Reduce the heat to simmering (bubbles should begin to break the surface of the water). Carefully break 1 *egg* into a small dish or measuring cup. Carefully slide the egg into the simmering water, holding the lip of the dish or cup as close to the water as possible. Repeat with 3 more *eggs,* allowing each egg an equal amount of space. Simmer eggs, uncovered, about 5 minutes or till yolk is just set. Remove the poached eggs with a slotted spoon. Season them to taste. (159 calories per serving.)

A Tip from Our Kitchen

If you are on a cholesterol-restricted diet, try to replace whole eggs with egg whites whenever you can. The whites contain no cholesterol or fat. You can substitute 2 egg whites for 1 whole egg in many recipes. You'll need to do a little experimenting with recipes, especially those for baked goods.

For scrambled eggs, use 1 whole egg plus 2 whites for each serving, and cook them in a nonstick skillet or use nonstick spray coating on the skillet's cooking surface.

Nutrition information: One large egg has about 75 calories, 5 grams fat, and 213 milligrams cholesterol. The yolk contains all of the cholesterol and fat and about 59 calories. The white has about 17 calories.

Eggnog
A rich, creamy beverage traditionally made from eggs, milk, sugar, and flavorings and served during the Christmas season. Sometimes rum, whiskey, or other alcohol is added for flavor.

Using uncooked or slightly cooked eggs in recipes such as homemade eggnog may be harmful because of possible bacterial contamination (see Using Eggs Safely under *Eggs*). However, you can make homemade eggnog starting with a cooked custard base, such as the one used in the recipe below, or buy commercially prepared eggnog made with pasteurized eggs.

Cooked Eggnog

  6 **beaten eggs**
2½ **cups milk**
 ⅓ **cup sugar**
  1 **teaspoon vanilla**
  1 **cup whipping cream**
  2 **tablespoons sugar**

■ In a heavy, large saucepan combine eggs, milk, and the ⅓ cup sugar. Cook and stir over medium heat till mixture just coats a metal spoon. Remove from heat. Quickly cool by placing saucepan in a sink or bowl of *ice water* for 1 to 2 minutes, stirring constantly. Stir in vanilla. Chill for 4 to 24 hours.
■ To serve, whip cream and the 2 tablespoons sugar in a bowl till soft peaks form. Transfer chilled egg mixture to a punch bowl. Fold in whipped cream mixture. Serve at once. If desired, sprinkle each serving with ground nutmeg. Makes 10 (4-ounce) servings.

Eggnog for a Crowd: Double all ingredients for Cooked Eggnog. In a heavy, large saucepan mix eggs, *3 cups* of the milk, and sugar. Cook and stir over medium heat till mixture just coats a metal spoon. Remove from the heat. Stir in the remaining 2 cups milk, then quickly cool in ice water for 3 to 4 minutes, stirring constantly. Stir in vanilla. Chill 4 to 24 hours.

At serving time, whip cream and ¼ cup sugar in a bowl till soft peaks form. Continue as above. Makes 20 (4-ounce) servings.

Nutrition information per serving: 193 calories, 6 g protein, 13 g carbohydrate, 13 g fat (7 g saturated), 166 mg cholesterol, 76 mg sodium, 149 mg potassium.

Eggplant

Eggplant A large, typically pear-shaped or long and slender fruit (that is used as a vegetable) with a smooth, glossy, deep purple or white skin and bright green cap. Eggplant has yellowish white flesh with tiny edible seeds. The mild flavor combines well with lots of seasonings. The flesh of eggplant becomes soft and watery when cooked.

Eggplants

Western

Baby white

Japanese

Varieties: There are several kinds of eggplants available.

☐ **Western:** Large with a smooth, glossy, purple or white skin. This is the most common eggplant in the United States. It can be round, but is usually pear-shaped.
White: Smaller and firmer than Western eggplant. White eggplant's skin is tough and thick, and it requires peeling. The flesh is a little sweeter than the other varieties.
Japanese: Long, slender, and purple with a mild flavor.
Baby: Smaller versions of the other types. Baby eggplants can be purple or white. These small eggplants are tender and sweet.

Selecting: Fresh eggplant is available year-round. Look for plump, glossy, heavy eggplants. Skip any with scarred, bruised, or dull surfaces. The cap should be fresh-looking, tight, and free of mold.

Storing: Refrigerate whole eggplants for up to 2 days.

How to cook: See the Cooking Fresh Vegetables chart under *Vegetable.*

Nutrition information: A ½-cup serving of cooked cubed eggplant has about 20 calories.

Egg Roll

Egg Roll An Oriental appetizer featuring a mixture of chopped vegetables and sometimes meat, seafood, or poultry that is rolled and sealed in a thin wrapper of dough, then deep-fat fried. Traditionally, egg rolls are cut crosswise into thirds and served with sweet-and-sour sauce and hot Chinese-style mustard. (See recipe under *Wonton.*)

Eggs Benedict

Eggs Benedict A rich egg dish often served for breakfast or brunch. It is made by layering Canadian-style bacon slices, poached eggs, and hollandaise sauce atop toasted English muffin halves.

Eggs Benedict

    8 slices Canadian-style bacon
    4 eggs
       Hollandaise Sauce (see recipe, page 210)
    2 English muffins, split and toasted, *or* 4 rusks

■ In a 12-inch skillet lightly brown Canadian-style bacon over medium heat for 3 minutes on each side. Cover and keep warm.

■ Lightly grease a medium saucepan or skillet. Add water to half-fill the pan; bring to boiling. Reduce the heat to simmering. Break *1* egg into a small dish. Carefully slide egg into simmering water, holding the lip of the dish as close to the water as possible. Repeat with remaining eggs, allowing each egg an equal amount of space. Simmer eggs, uncovered, about 5 minutes or till yolk is just set. Remove with a slotted spoon. Place eggs in a large pan of warm water to keep warm while preparing Hollandaise Sauce.

■ If desired, butter the muffin halves. To serve, top each English muffin half or rusk with 2 slices of Canadian-style bacon and an egg; spoon Hollandaise Sauce over eggs. Makes 4 servings.

Nutrition information per serving: 480 calories, 22 g protein, 15 g carbohydrate, 36 g fat (9 g saturated), 400 mg cholesterol, 1,274 mg sodium, 435 mg potassium.

Eggs Benedict

Emulsion A mixture of two liquid or semiliquid ingredients that do not dissolve into each other. Instead, one ingredient, usually a fat such as oil, margarine, or butter, is suspended in the other ingredient in the form of tiny globules. Examples of common food emulsions are oil-and-vinegar salad dressing, mayonnaise, and hollandaise sauce.

Enchilada A classic Mexican recipe that features a corn or flour tortilla rolled around a meat, vegetable, or cheese filling. The roll is topped with a spicy chili-tomato sauce or more cheese. Traditionally in Mexico, enchiladas are served as soon as they are assembled, but in the United States, enchiladas often are placed in a baking dish, topped with sauce, and heated through. (See *Mexican Cooking* for a recipe.)

A Tip from Our Kitchen

If you wish to make enchiladas a few hours ahead of time, chill the filled tortillas and the sauce separately. Then pour the sauce over the filled tortillas just before baking and add a few minutes to the cooking time. Waiting to add the sauce helps prevent the enchiladas from becoming soggy.

Endive Any of several varieties of salad greens that grow in bunchy heads. Endive may have slender, whitish green leaves, frilly green leaves, or reddish leaves, depending on the variety. Endive is known for its mildly bitter taste.

Varieties: There are three main kinds of endive.
☐ **Belgian Endive:** A small, cone-shaped salad green with 5- to 6-inch-long, slender leaves that are tightly packed. The leaves are creamy white with pale yellow tips.
☐ **Curly Endive:** Heads of crisp, frilly, narrow, dark green leaves that curl at the edges. It has a prickly texture. Curly endive also is known as chicory. Radicchio is a red chicory variety.
☐ **Escarole:** Elongated heads with green, irregularly shaped leaves with slightly curled edges.

Selecting: Pick heads that have crisp, fresh texture; avoid those with discoloration.

Storing: Refrigerate curly endive and escarole, tightly wrapped, for up to 3 days.

Nutrition information: Fresh endive has about 10 calories per cup.

(See *Belgian Endive* and *Radicchio* for selecting and storing information. See *Belgian Endive, Chicory, Escarole,* and *Radicchio* for identification photos.)

English Muffin A round, flat, unsweetened yeast bread that's baked on a griddle. The coarse-textured, baked muffins usually are split and toasted, then spread with butter or jam. Whole wheat, sourdough, and raisin English muffins also are available.

A Tip from Our Kitchen
Don't cut English muffins with a knife or you will ruin their airy texture. Instead, pull them apart gently with your fingers or repeatedly insert a fork around the edge. Either method of splitting gives a porous surface with lots of pockets for butter and jam.

Nutrition information: One plain English muffin has about 140 calories.

Entrée *(ON tray)* A French term that originally referred to the first course of a meal or to food served between the soup and meat courses. Now, in the United States, entrée refers to the main dish of a meal.

Escarole

been opened, transfer any unused milk to another covered container. Store it in the refrigerator and use it within 3 days.

Q: Can evaporated milk be substituted for sweetened condensed milk?

A: No. Evaporated milk and sweetened condensed milk are two entirely different products. Sweetened condensed milk has sugar added to it, so don't use the two interchangeably in cooking.

Nutrition information: One cup of undiluted evaporated milk has about 340 calories and 20 grams of fat. One cup of undiluted evaporated skim milk has about 200 calories and less than 1 gram of fat.

Escarole *(ES kuh role)* A variety of endive with elongated and irregularly shaped, flat, green leaves with slightly curled edges. Escarole also is known as broadleaf endive. It has a firm, chewy texture, mildly bitter flavor, and can be eaten raw or cooked.

Q: How is escarole used?

A: Serve escarole raw in salads. Its slightly bitter flavor is best when it is mixed with mild lettuces. Or, serve escarole warm in wilted salads. Its firm leaves make it an excellent choice for wilting.

(See *Endive* for selecting, storing, and nutrition information.)

Evaporated Milk A concentrated milk made from whole milk from which 60 percent of the water has been removed. The milk is sealed in cans and heat-sterilized so no refrigeration is necessary until the can is opened. Evaporated skim milk and evaporated low-fat milk also are available.

Storing: Unopened cans of evaporated milk can be stored at room temperature for up to a year. To retain the best flavor once a can has

Extract and Oil Products based on the aromatic essential oils of plant materials that are distilled by various means. In extracts, the highly concentrated oils usually are suspended in alcohol to make them easier to combine with other foods in cooking and baking. Almond, anise, lemon, mint, orange, peppermint, and vanilla are some of the pure extracts sold. Some undiluted oils also are available, usually at pharmacies. These include oil of anise, oil of cinnamon, oil of cloves, oil of peppermint, and oil of wintergreen.

Storing: Because of their high alcohol content, extracts vaporize easily. Purchase them in small sizes, and screw the lids on tightly after each use to prevent evaporation. Extracts and oils lose some of their potency when exposed to heat, so store them in a cool place.

Q: What kinds of foods call for extracts and oils?

A: Extracts are commonly used in baking and dessert recipes. Sweet breads of all sorts, icings, fruit pies, ice cream, and beverages all use extracts in varying amounts. Oils often are used in candy.

continued

A Tip from Our Kitchen

Don't try to substitute oils for ground spices in recipes. Oils are so concentrated that they're measured in drops, not teaspoons. Oil of cinnamon, for example, is 50 times stronger than ground cinnamon. You can, however, substitute 1 or 2 drops of an oil for ½ teaspoon extract in frosting or candy recipes.

Fajita *(fah HEE tuh)* A Mexican or Tex-Mex dish consisting of thin, marinated beef strips that are cooked and wrapped in a flour tortilla with assorted accompaniments, such as cooked onion or sweet pepper, salsa, guacamole, shredded cheese, and sour cream. Fajitas originally were made with beef skirt or flank steak, but now other cuts of beef as well as chicken also are used.

Sizzling Beef Fajitas

    ¾ **pound boneless beef plate skirt steak,**
        flank steak, *or* round steak
    ¼ **cup Italian salad dressing**
    ¼ **cup salsa**
    1 **tablespoon soy sauce**
    8 **6- or 7-inch flour tortillas**
    1 **tablespoon cooking oil**
    1 **small onion, thinly sliced and**
        separated into rings
    1 **medium green pepper, cut into thin**
        strips
    ½ **cup frozen avocado dip, thawed**
    ½ **cup salsa**
    ½ **cup dairy sour cream**
    ½ **cup shredded cheddar cheese**

■ Partially freeze beef. Thinly slice across the grain into thin bite-size strips and set aside.
■ For marinade, in a large bowl stir together salad dressing, ¼ cup salsa, and soy sauce. Add beef, stirring to coat. Cover and marinate in the refrigerator for 6 hours or overnight, stirring occasionally. Drain beef well.
■ Stack tortillas and wrap in foil. Heat in a 350° oven for 10 minutes to soften.

■ Meanwhile, pour cooking oil into a large skillet. (Add more oil as necessary during cooking.) Preheat over medium-high heat. Cook and stir onion rings in hot oil for 1½ minutes. Add pepper strips. Cook and stir for 1½ minutes or till vegetables are crisp-tender. Remove vegetables from skillet; set aside.
■ Add beef to the hot skillet. Cook and stir for 2 to 3 minutes or till done. Drain well. Return vegetables to skillet. Cook and stir for 1 to 2 minutes more or till heated through.
■ To serve, immediately fill warmed tortillas with beef-vegetable mixture, then add avocado dip, salsa, sour cream, and cheese. Roll fajitas up. Makes 4 servings.

Nutrition information per serving: 645 calories, 28 g protein, 50 g carbohydrate, 40 g fat (15 g saturated), 73 mg cholesterol, 1,202 mg sodium, 559 mg potassium.

Farina Coarse, off-white granular particles made from grinding the endosperm of hard wheats. Mild-flavored farina is a prime ingredient in many breakfast cereals, baby foods, and inexpensive pastas. In cooking, it can be added to puddings, muffins, baked desserts, and dumplings. Farina is available in instant and malt- or cocoa-flavored forms.

Storing: Store farina in an airtight container in a cool, dry place for up to 1 year.

How to cook: See the Cooking Grains chart under *Grain.*

Nutrition information: A ¾-cup serving of cooked farina contains about 105 calories.

Fat Any of numerous fatty-acid-containing compounds found in food and used as a nutrient by the body. Fat is the most calorie-dense nutrient.

In the body, fat serves as a storage depot for energy, insulates against heat and cold, protects organs against shock and injury, and helps transport important fat-soluble vitamins. See Fat and Cholesterol Primer, opposite.

(See *Nutrition* for information on planning a balanced diet and lowering fat in the diet.)

Fat and Cholesterol Primer

There is much talk about fat and cholesterol and their roles in the diet. Since much of the information available on this subject can be confusing, here is a primer to help you sort out the facts.

● **Saturated fats:** Usually solid at room temperature, these fats are found primarily in animal products and tropical oils. Meats; chicken fat; meat fat, such as lard or suet; dairy products; and coconut and palm oils have saturated fats.

● **Unsaturated fats:** Soft or liquid at room temperature, these fats are found primarily in vegetables, nuts, and grains. Unsaturated fats can be monounsaturated or polyunsaturated. Vegetable oils, such as corn, safflower, and soybean, are all common polyunsaturated fats; foods with monounsaturated fats include olive oil, peanut butter, avocados, and cashews.

● **Cholesterol:** A substance present in foods of animal origin and also produced by the liver. It helps blanket nerve fibers and lends durability to cell walls. Although necessary in moderate amounts, the body manufactures an adequate supply. It is carried in the blood in units called lipoproteins, of which there are two types. Low-density lipoprotein (LDL), containing what is often called bad cholesterol, tends to clog arteries and may lead to heart disease and stroke. High-density lipoprotein (HDL), containing what is sometimes called good cholesterol, appears to clear fat and excess cholesterol from the blood.

● **The diet/disease connection:** Experts say that high levels of saturated fats and cholesterol in the diet raise the amount of cholesterol in the blood. Elevated blood cholesterol levels are associated with increased risk of heart attack and some forms of cancer. To lower the risk of these illnesses, watch the amount of total fat—especially saturated fat—and cholesterol in your diet. The total fat should be no more than 30 percent of your calorie intake.

To calculate the percentage of calories from fat in a food, you need to know how many calories and grams of fat are in the food and that 1 gram of fat contains 9 calories. Plug those numbers into these two equations: 1. Total fat in grams x 9 = total calories from fat; 2. (total fat calories ÷ total calories) x 100 = % calories from fat.

Fat and Oil Any of a group of energy-rich, slick-feeling substances made from animal or vegetable sources and used in cooking.

Types: The following fats and oils are used extensively in cooking.

☐ **Fats:** Solid at room temperature and can be either an animal or vegetable product, or a blend. Some common fats are *butter, margarine, vegetable shortening,* and *lard* (see also *Butter, Margarine,* and *Lard*). Margarine and vegetable shortening are processed from oils to be solid at room temperature.

☐ **Oils:** Generally liquid at room temperature and made from vegetables, nuts, or seeds. Some common vegetable oils are *corn, olive, soybean, peanut, canola, sunflower,* and *safflower.* Popular flavored oils include *walnut, hazelnut, almond,* and *sesame.* The tropical oils, used commercially in some packaged foods, include *coconut, palm,* and *palm kernel.*

Market forms: Most butters, margarines, and butter-margarine blends are available in the dairy case in stick form or as spreads.

continued

Lard comes in 1-pound blocks and often is sold on the shelf or in the refrigerated meat section at the supermarket.

Plain and butter-flavored vegetable shortenings are available in containers on grocery shelves.

Vegetable oil is sold in bottles and in a spray form. The nonstick spray coating is available plain or flavored with butter or olive oil.

Selecting: When deciding which fat or oil to use, consider what you are going to make. For baking, butter, margarine, and shortening are used more commonly than oil for flavor and texture. For shallow-fat or deep-fat frying, cooking oil or shortening works well. For salads, choose mild vegetable or flavored oils that complement the flavor of the salad ingredients.

Storing: Store all fats and oils in airtight containers, especially butter and margarine, which absorb off-odors easily.

Refrigerate butter, margarine, and lard for up to 1 month. Store oil and shortening at room temperature—oil for up to 9 months and shortening for up to 1 year. Olive oil can be stored at room temperature for up to 6 months or in the refrigerator for up to 1 year. (When olive oil is chilled, it gets too thick to pour, so let it stand at room temperature for a few minutes or run warm water over the bottle before using it.)

If you use butter or lard occasionally for special baked goods, you can freeze unused butter or lard, tightly wrapped in freezer wrap or containers.

Cooking hints: By combining different fats and oils, you can get the benefits of both foods. Here are some ideas.

When butter is melted with margarine or oil, there are several benefits. One advantage is that the butter can be heated to higher temperatures and will be less likely to burn. Also, you get the flavor of butter while using less of it.

For salad dressing, a mixture of olive oil and vegetable oil will be milder in flavor and less expensive than using all olive oil.

For stir-fries, peanut oil works well because it can be heated to a higher temperature than other oils without burning. For flavor, add a few drops of flavored oil, such as sesame oil.

Nutrition information: One tablespoon of butter, margarine, or lard has about 100 calories; shortening has about 110 calories; and oil has about 120 calories.

(See *Fat* for the Fat and Cholesterol Primer.)

Feijoa *(fay YOH uh)* An oval, tropical fruit about the size of an egg, with a green skin and pale yellow meat. Its flavor is sweet and tangy, reminiscent of pineapple, lemon, and mint. Feijoas sometimes are called pineapple guavas. Fresh feijoas are available most of the year.

Feijoas

Selecting: Feijoas in the supermarket sometimes are very firm and green. They're ripe when slightly soft, and their aroma is fragrant. If you buy unripe fruit, you can ripen it at home.

Storing: Keep unripened feijoas at room temperature for several days until ripened. Then refrigerate the ripe fruit for 1 or 2 days.

Preparation hints: Enjoy the raw fruit by peeling off the skin and slicing, chopping, or quartering the fruit. If the fruit is very ripe, spoon the meat out of the skin.

Nutrition information: Feijoas have about 50 calories per fruit.

Fennel

Fennel A vegetable with a creamy white or pale green, broad, bulbous base with celerylike stalks that are wide at the bottom, but narrow at the top. Fennel has feathery, bright green leaves that grow from the middle of the bulb. Raw fennel has a light, licoricelike flavor and a celerylike texture. When cooked, the flavor becomes more delicate and the texture softens. The feathery green tops of this vegetable have an even more delicate licorice flavor and are used for seasoning salads and soups.

Fennel also is known as Florence fennel and finocchio. Fennel seed comes from the fennel plant (see also *Fennel Seed*).

Selecting: Fennel usually is available September through April. Look for firm, smooth bulbs without cracks and brown spots. Stalks should be crisp, and the leaves should be bright green and fresh-looking.

Storing: Store fennel in a plastic bag in the refrigerator for up to 4 days.

How to cook: See the Cooking Fresh Vegetables chart under *Vegetable*.

Nutrition information: One-half cup cooked fennel has about 15 calories.

Fennel Seed The small, yellowish brown seeds of the vegetable, fennel. The seeds, which are sold whole or ground, have a mild licoricelike flavor and aroma. Fennel seed is traditionally one of the spices used in Italian sausage.

(See *Spice* for selecting, storing, and nutrition information.)

Feta Cheese *(FEHT uh)* A soft, white, crumbly cheese with a sharp, salty flavor. Feta is made from cow's, sheep's, or goat's milk, and is cured in salt brine. It is an important ingredient in Greek cooking.

Q: **What can be done with leftover feta cheese?**
A: Freeze it for future use. Because it's a crumbly cheese to begin with, the texture changes little when frozen. Wrap tightly in freezer wrap, and freeze quickly at 0° for up to 2 months. Thaw in the refrigerator before using.

(See *Cheese* for the Selecting Cheese chart and selecting, storing, serving, nutrition, and other information.)

Feta cheese

Fettuccine *(feht uh CHEE nee)* A flat, narrow, ribbon-shaped pasta. It is cooked in boiling water, drained, and usually served with a sauce. Fettuccine can be homemade but also is produced commercially. Commercial fettuccine comes in dried and refrigerated forms. Fettuccine Alfredo is a classic dish featuring this pasta favorite. (For a fettuccine Alfredo recipe, see page 162.)

(See *Pasta* for an identification photo and storing, how-to-cook, and other information.)

Fettuccine Alfredo

>   3 quarts water
>   1 teaspoon salt
>   1 tablespoon cooking oil (optional)
>   8 ounces packaged fettuccine
>   ½ cup grated Parmesan cheese
>   ⅓ cup light cream *or* whipping cream,
>   at room temperature
>   3 tablespoons margarine *or* butter, cut
>   up and at room temperature
>   Coarsely cracked black pepper

■ In a large kettle or Dutch oven, bring water and salt to a rolling boil. If desired, add oil to help keep pasta separated.

■ Add pasta a little at a time, so water does not stop boiling. Reduce the heat slightly and continue boiling, uncovered, for 8 to 10 minutes or till pasta is al dente (tender but still firm), stirring occasionally.

■ Immediately drain. Return pasta to the hot kettle or Dutch oven. Add Parmesan cheese, light cream or whipping cream, and margarine or butter. Toss gently till pasta is well coated. Transfer to a warm serving dish. Sprinkle with pepper. Serve immediately. Makes 4 servings.

Nutrition information per serving: 359 calories, 12 g protein, 44 g carbohydrate, 15 g fat (5 g saturated), 15 mg cholesterol, 367 mg sodium, 42 mg potassium.

Fiber The parts of plant foods that cannot be digested or are only partially digested by the body. High-fiber foods are important in the diet not only because they provide roughage to help keep the body regular, but also because some experts say that a diet high in fiber may reduce the risk of heart disease and certain forms of cancer.

Soluble and insoluble fiber: There are two types of fiber.

☐ **Insoluble:** Fibers that cannot be dissolved in water. They are found in dried beans, vegetables, and the skins of fruits as well as in the bran of grains, such as wheat. They act as sponges, absorbing water and adding bulk to food passing through the body. Insoluble fibers keep the digestive system working. Some experts say that when insoluble fiber is eaten as part of a low-fat diet, it helps reduce the risk of colon cancer.

☐ **Soluble:** Fibers that dissolve in water to form a gel-like mixture that slows down absorption of nutrients into the bloodstream. Fruits, vegetables, dried beans, brown rice, and certain grains (such as barley and oats) have good supplies of soluble fiber. Some experts say soluble fiber helps lower blood cholesterol levels. For diabetics, it is thought to help curb erratic swings in blood sugar levels by slowing down the flow of sugar from the digestive tract into the bloodstream.

Nutrition information: As a guide, try to eat between 20 and 30 grams of dietary fiber each day. Don't overdo it, though; too much fiber can interfere with the absorption of other nutrients. Because foods vary in the amounts and types of fiber they contain (some foods even contain both types of fiber), it is a good idea to get your dietary fiber from a variety of foods, rather than depending on just one or a few sources.

Q: **How can I get more fiber in my diet?**
A: Though it takes a conscious effort, you can get the fiber you need without drastic changes in what you eat. Start by eating whole foods, such as apples with their peels and potatoes with their skins. Choose high-fiber vegetables, such as corn, peas, or beans, more often. Eat whole grain bread and use high-fiber cereals at breakfast, or add high-fiber ingredients, such as wheat bran, to baked items.

Start increasing the fiber in your meals slowly, so your body has time to adapt. Each day try adding a food that has about 5 grams of dietary fiber. As you increase your fiber intake, drink plenty of water to offset the water that the fiber absorbs.

Here are some examples of foods that have 5 grams or more of fiber: 2 slices of whole wheat bread, 1 cup whole grain cereal, 1 baked potato with skin, 1 large apple or orange, and ½ cup cooked beans or lentils.

Fig **163**

Fiddlehead Fern

Fiddlehead Fern The young, edible, tightly curled, green shoot of any species of fern. Most commercially grown fiddlehead ferns are from the ostrich fern. Fiddlehead ferns are 2 to 5 inches long and 1½ inches in diameter. Their texture is similar to green beans, and their flavor is like a cross between asparagus and green beans. They can be eaten raw in salads, stir-fried in oil for about 1 minute, or steamed for about 1½ minutes.

Selecting: Fresh fiddlehead ferns are available occasionally from April through June in some stores that carry exotic produce. Select those that are firm, have closed leaves, and have bright color. Fiddlehead ferns that are found in the wild should only be used if a knowledgeable person has determined that they are an edible variety.

Storing: Refrigerate fiddlehead ferns, unwashed, in a plastic bag for up to 2 days. Wash fiddleheads thoroughly before using.

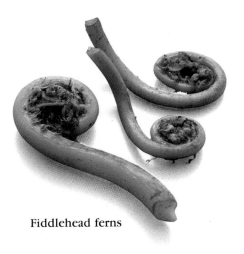

Fiddlehead ferns

Fig A soft, teardrop-shaped fruit with edible seeds inside. The skin may be purplish, reddish brown, green, or greenish yellow. Fig meat ranges from pale pink to purple and tastes delicate and sweet.

Varieties: Here are some fig varieties.
☐ **Black Mission:** A dark purple-skinned fig with a pink interior and a hearty flavor. This

Calimyrna (fresh)

Black Mission (fresh)

Black Mission (dried)

Calimyrna (dried)

Figs

is one of the most versatile varieties. It is available both fresh and dried.
☐ **Brown Turkey:** Known for its reddish brown skin and purple meat. This richly flavored, juicy fig is most often sold fresh.
☐ **Calimyrna:** A large fig with greenish yellow skin, a pale pink interior, and a nutlike flavor. It most commonly is found dried and rarely is available fresh.
☐ **Kadota:** A pale yellow-skinned fig when ripe, with pink to purple fruit inside. Most Kadota figs are sold canned.

Selecting: Available from June through October, fresh figs are extremely delicate. Look for good color for the variety. Figs should be somewhat firm to the touch with plump shapes. Avoid bruised, very soft, very hard, or split fruit. Sniff fresh figs before buying. A sour odor means that the fruit has begun to ferment and spoil.
When selecting dried figs, avoid hard, overly dry figs, and those with flattened sides, splits, or signs of mold.

Storing: Place fresh figs in a single layer in a paper-towel-lined container. Refrigerate them only 2 or 3 days. Store dried figs in an airtight container and refrigerate for up to 6 months or in the freezer for up to 1 year.

Preparation hints: To enjoy fresh or dried figs, trim off the stems with a sharp knife.
continued

Nutrition information: A dried, medium-size fig has about 50 calories, and ½ cup canned figs in heavy syrup has 115 calories.

(See *Dried Fruit* for the Cooking Dried Fruit chart and preparation hints.)

Filbert   See *Hazelnut.*

Filé Powder   *(fee LAY; fuh LAY)*
Ground sassafras leaves used by Cajun cooks to thicken and add a thymelike flavor to gumbos. Filé powder gets stringy when it's boiled, so add it just before serving or pass it at the table. Store filé powder in a cool, dry, dark place.

Filet, Fillet   Although there is some
confusion over the pronunciation and spelling of these words, generally filet *(fi LAY)* is a small, boneless piece of meat. For example, a slice of beef tenderloin is called filet mignon *(fi LAY mean YOHN)*.

A fillet *(FILL uht)* is a boneless piece of fish cut lengthwise from the side of the fish. A boneless piece of poultry breast also is called a fillet.

Fillet *(fi LAY)* also refers to the process of cutting the boneless piece of fish or poultry.

Fines Herbes   *(feen ZERB)* A French
phrase describing a combination of finely chopped fresh herbs, most generally including chervil, parsley, chives, and tarragon. Dried fines herbes are available at the supermarket.

(See *Herb* for selecting, storing, preparation, cooking, nutrition, and other information.)

Fish   A freshwater or saltwater animal with
backbones, fins, gills, and usually scales. Fish get their shape from their skeletons.

Types: Fish are divided into freshwater and saltwater types (see the Selecting Fish chart, opposite).
☐ **Freshwater:** Come from rivers, lakes, and streams. Some popular varieties include large- and smallmouth bass, catfish, pike, and trout (see also individual entries).
☐ **Saltwater:** Found in oceans, gulfs, and seas around the world. Some common varieties include sea bass, cod, flounder, pompano, red snapper, swordfish, and tuna (see also individual entries).

Market forms: See Common Market Forms, page 168.

Selecting: Choose fresh fish that has a mild smell, not a strong odor. When buying whole fish, look for eyes that are clear and bright, and not sunken. Select fish with bright red or pink gills. Check that the skin is shiny and elastic, with scales tightly in place. When choosing fresh fillets and steaks, select ones that appear moist and freshly cut.

For frozen fish of the best quality, select those with packaging intact and no evidence of ice or blood.

Fish Math
The amount of fish to buy depends on its form. Here's a general rule for how much fresh fish to buy for each serving.
- 8 ounces of drawn or dressed fish
- 4 to 5 ounces of steaks or fillets

Storing: Fresh fish is very perishable, so it's best to cook it the same day that you buy it. When that isn't possible, store fish in the coldest part of the refrigerator for up to 2 days. Be sure that it is properly wrapped in moisture- and vaporproof material.

continued on page 166

Selecting Fish

Check this guide to become acquainted with the various types of fish. Also, use the list of suggested substitutes, which can be tried in recipes. Note that the flesh colors range from white to darker, and the flavors range from delicate to pronounced.

Types	Color	Flavor	Suggested Substitutes
Freshwater Fish Bass*, Large- and Smallmouth	Light meat	Mild	Pike, Sole
Carp	Darker meat	Mild	Cod, Drum, Haddock, Redfish
Catfish*	White meat	Mild	Cusk, Red Snapper, Sea Trout
Lake Perch	White meat	Mild	Ocean Perch, Pike, Rainbow Trout
Pike*	Light meat	Mild to moderate	Cod, Orange Roughy, Whitefish
Trout*, Lake	Light meat	Mild	Pike, Sea Trout, Whitefish
Trout*, Rainbow	Light meat	Delicate	Coho Salmon, Pike, Sea Trout
Whitefish*	White meat	Delicate	Haddock, Lake Trout, Pike
Saltwater Fish Bluefish	Darker meat	Moderate	Lake Trout, Pike
Butterfish	White meat	Mild to moderate	Pompano, Porgy
Cod*	White meat	Delicate	Haddock, Halibut, Pike, Pollock
Flounder*	White meat	Delicate to mild	Pike, Sole, Whitefish, Whiting
Haddock*	White meat	Delicate	Cod, Halibut, Lake Trout, Sole, Whitefish
Halibut*	White meat	Delicate	Cod, Flounder, Sea Bass, Snapper, Sole
Mackerel*	Light meat	Pronounced	Swordfish, Tuna
Mahimahi*	Light meat	Mild to moderate	Cusk
Mullet	Light meat	Mild to moderate	Substitution not recommended
Ocean Perch	Light meat	Mild	Lake Perch, Rainbow Trout, Sea Bass
Orange Roughy*	White meat	Delicate	Cod, Flounder, Sea Bass, Sole
Pollock	Light meat	Mild to moderate	Cod, Flounder, Pike
Pompano*	Light meat	Mild to moderate	Butterfish, Ocean Perch, Sole
Redfish*	White meat	Mild	Carp, Croaker, Drum
Red Snapper*	White meat	Mild to moderate	Lake Trout, Rockfish, Whitefish
Rockfish	Light meat	Mild to moderate	Cod, Drum, Ocean Perch, Red Snapper
Salmon*, Chinook and Coho	Light meat	Mild to moderate	Swordfish, Tuna
Salmon*, Pink	Light meat	Mild to moderate	Swordfish, Tuna
Salmon*, Sockeye	Darker meat	Mild to moderate	Bluefish, Sea Bass, Tuna
Sea Bass	Light to darker meat	Delicate to mild	Cod, Orange Roughy, Sea Trout
Sea Trout	White meat	Mild to moderate	Cod, Haddock, Pike, Pollock
Shark*	Light meat	Mild to moderate	Salmon, Sea Bass, Swordfish, Tuna
Sole*	White meat	Delicate to mild	Flounder, Pike
Swordfish*	Light meat	Mild to moderate	Sea Bass, Shark, Tuna
Tuna*	Darker meat	Mild to moderate	Mackerel, Salmon, Swordfish
Whiting*	White meat	Delicate	Flounder, Pike, Pollock, Sole

See individual entries for additional information.

Fish Doneness Test: To test fish for proper degree of doneness, insert the fork tines into the fish. Then twist the fork gently.

Properly cooked fish
When the fish is opaque, begins to flake easily, and comes away from the bones readily, it is properly cooked. The juices should be a milky white.

Undercooked fish
If the fish resists flaking and is still translucent, and if the juices are clear and watery, the fish is underdone.

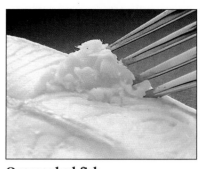

Overcooked fish
If the fish looks dry or mealy with little or no juices, and it falls apart easily into small pieces, it is overdone.

Store frozen fish in its original wrap and keep it solidly frozen in your freezer at 0° or lower. For best quality, keep fish in the freezer for no longer than 3 months.

Thawing: To thaw frozen fish, place the unopened package in a container in the refrigerator, allowing overnight thawing for about a 1-pound package. If necessary, you can place the wrapped package of fish under *cold* running water to hasten thawing. Thawing fish at room temperature or in warm water isn't recommended, since the fish won't thaw evenly and may spoil.

Fillets and steaks can be cooked from the frozen state, without thawing. If you do this, add extra minutes to the cooking time.

Q: Can frozen fish be thawed in the microwave oven?

A: Yes. To thaw fish in the microwave oven, place 1 pound frozen fillets or steaks in a microwave-safe baking dish. Cover with vented plastic wrap. Micro-cook on 30% power (medium-low) for 6 to 8 minutes, turning and separating fish after 3 minutes. Let fillets stand 10 minutes; steaks, 15 minutes. Fish should be pliable and cold on the outside but slightly icy in the center of thick areas. Rinse; pat dry.

How to cook: For cooking directions, see the Cooking Fish chart, opposite. Cook fish just till done, because it toughens and dries out when overcooked.

Nutrition information: Fish is generally quite low in both fat and calories. For example, one 3-ounce portion of baked flounder contains about 100 calories and 2 grams fat.

The fat in fish contains unique, highly polyunsaturated omega-3 fatty acids that might lower blood cholesterol levels. Some fish contain more omega-3 fatty acids than others. Mackerel, salmon, tuna, and swordfish are some of the best sources.

Fishing for Answers?
If you have questions about fish, call this toll-free fish hot line of the American Seafood Institute, Wakefield, Rhode Island, from 9 a.m. to 5 p.m. eastern time. The number is 1-800-EAT-FISH.

continued on page 168

Cooking Fish

Fish in most of its forms makes a quick-cooking main dish. Follow the times and directions below, cooking the fish until it just begins to flake easily when tested with a fork (see photos, opposite).

Season the cooked fish to taste with salt and pepper. If desired, serve lemon wedges with the fish. For grilling directions, see the Direct-Grilling Fish chart under *Barbecue*.

Cooking Method	Fresh (or Thawed Frozen) Fillets or Steaks	Frozen Fillets or Steaks	Dressed
Bake: Place in a single layer in a greased, shallow baking pan. For fillets, tuck under any thin edges. Brush with melted margarine or butter.	Bake, uncovered, in a 450° oven for 4 to 6 minutes per ½-inch thickness.	Bake, uncovered, in a 450° oven for 9 to 11 minutes per ½-inch thickness.	Bake, uncovered, in a 350° oven for 6 to 9 minutes per ½ pound.
Broil: Preheat broiler. Place fish on the greased unheated rack of a broiler pan. For fillets, tuck under any thin edges. Brush with melted margarine or butter.	Broil 4 inches from the heat for 4 to 6 minutes per ½-inch thickness. If fish is 1 inch or more thick, turn it over halfway through broiling.	Broil 4 inches from the heat for 6 to 9 minutes per ½-inch thickness. If fish is 1 inch or more thick, turn it over halfway through broiling.	Not recommended.
Poach: Add 1½ cups water, broth, or wine to a large skillet. Bring to boiling. Add fish. Return to boiling; reduce heat.	Simmer, covered, for 4 to 6 minutes per ½-inch thickness.	Simmer, covered, for 6 to 9 minutes per ½-inch thickness.	Simmer, covered, for 6 to 9 minutes per ½ pound.
Micro-cook: Remove head and tail from dressed fish, if present. Arrange fish in a single layer in a shallow, microwave-safe baking dish. For fillets, tuck under any thin edges. Cover with vented microwave-safe plastic wrap.	Micro-cook on 100% power (high). For ½ pound of ½-inch-thick fillets, allow 3 to 4 minutes; for 1 pound of ½-inch-thick fillets, allow 4 to 7 minutes. For 1 pound of ¾- to 1-inch-thick steaks, allow 7 to 9 minutes.	Thaw before micro-cooking. See question and answer, opposite, for timings.	Micro-cook on 100% power (high). For two 8- to 10-ounce fish, allow 5 to 7 minutes; for one 1- to 1½-pound fish, allow 10 to 12 minutes, giving dish a half-turn once. Let stand for 5 minutes.
Panfry: Heat ¼ inch of shortening or cooking oil in a skillet. Dip fish in a mixture of 1 beaten egg and ¼ cup water or milk. Coat fish with flour, cornmeal, or seasoned fine dry bread crumbs.	For 1 pound of fillets, panfry coated fillets in hot shortening or cooking oil, allowing 3 to 4 minutes on each side for ½-inch-thick fillets (5 to 6 minutes on each side for 1-inch-thick fillets) or till golden and crisp and fish tests done.	Not recommended.	For an 8- to 12-ounce fish, panfry coated fish in hot shortening or cooking oil, allowing 5 to 8 minutes on each side or till golden and crisp and fish tests done.

Common Market Forms

Besides the market forms listed, some fish are available canned, salted, pickled, or smoked.

- **Drawn** A whole fish with the internal organs removed. It may or may not be scaled. Once scaled, it is ready for poaching, baking, or grilling.

- **Dressed** A whole fish with the scales, internal organs, and fins removed; often the head and tail also are removed. It is ready for poaching, panfrying, baking, grilling, or micro-cooking.

- **Steak** A crosscut slice of a dressed fish. It contains bones and is ready for grilling, broiling, baking, poaching, or micro-cooking.

- **Fillet** The side of a dressed fish that is cut lengthwise away from the backbone. It's usually boneless. Large fillets from big fish often are cut into smaller pieces. Fillets are ready for baking, broiling, poaching, panfrying, micro-cooking, or grilling.

- **Frozen portion** A uniform block of filleted fish. It is ready for baking, poaching, or broiling.

- **Frozen breaded stick or portion** A fish stick is a piece cut from a block of frozen fish, then breaded or coated with batter. Follow package directions for cooking. A frozen portion is larger than a stick. It might be frozen raw or partially cooked, so it also should be cooked according to package directions.

Fish-and-Chips
A British term that refers to the combination of deep-fat-fried, batter-coated fish fillets served with deep-fat-fried potato pieces.

Five-Spice Powder
A mixture of ground spices used in Chinese cooking. Combinations may vary, but the fragrant powder usually includes cinnamon, aniseed or star anise, fennel, black or Szechwan pepper, and cloves.

Q: Is there a way to make five-spice powder at home?

A: Yes. In a blender container combine 3 tablespoons ground *cinnamon;* 2 teaspoons *aniseed or 6 star anise;* 1½ teaspoons *fennel seed;* 1½ teaspoons whole *Szechwan peppers or* whole *black peppers;* and ¾ teaspoon ground *cloves.* Cover and blend till powdery. Store mixture in a covered container. Makes about ⅓ cup.

(See *Spice* for selecting, storing, and nutrition information.)

Flake
To gently break a food into small, flat pieces. The term also refers to a form of commercial cereal sold in small thin pieces.

Flambé
(flahm BAY) The French term that refers to a food prepared or served with flaming alcohol.

Q: What type of alcohol is best for flaming?

A: Use a brandy or liqueur that is about 70 proof. *Do not use* 150-proof spirits, however, because they are too volatile and may explode as you ignite them. Carefully heat the alcohol in a small saucepan or skillet over low heat until the liquid almost simmers. Then carefully ignite it with a match.

To flame brandy or a liqueur, use a long match to ignite the warmed liquor. Then pour it carefully over the food in a flame-proof dish.

Flan A Spanish dessert made from a custard that is baked in a caramel-coated dish. When the baked custard is inverted, the caramel forms a layer on top. Flan also refers to a shallow pastry shell filled with custard and sometimes fruit. It also may be called a tart and usually is served as a dessert.

Flavor The special quality that a food has that affects the sense of taste. The four flavors most people can distinguish are sweet, sour, salty, and bitter. It also refers to seasoning a food to change how it tastes.

Flavoring An imitation extract made of chemical compounds (see also *Extract and Oil*). Unlike an extract or oil, a flavoring often does not contain any of the original food it resembles.

Some of the common imitation flavorings available are: banana, black walnut, brandy, cherry, chocolate, coconut, maple, pineapple, raspberry, rum, strawberry, and vanilla. Store all flavorings in a cool, dark place.

A Tip from Our Kitchen
Brandy and rum flavorings are used in cases where the amount of actual liquor required to give good flavor would change the consistency of a food. Frosting, pumpkin pie, and hard sauce are good examples.

Floating Island A dessert consisting of a chilled custard topped with poached meringue. The custard may contain fruit, and the meringue is sometimes drizzled with a thin stream of caramel syrup.

Florentine A term used for a dish that contains spinach. The term usually refers to eggs, fish, poultry, and meats that are served on a bed of spinach, often with a sauce.

Flounder A flatfish found in the Atlantic and Pacific oceans that swims on its side. It is sandy brown on top and white underneath and has white flesh. Flounder has a delicate to mild flavor and fine texture.

Types: Some common American types are *Winter* flounder (also called *Lemon Sole*), *Sanddab* (also marketed as *American Plaice*), *Gray Sole,* and *Summer* flounder (also called *Fluke*).

Market forms: Flounder most commonly is sold as fresh or frozen fillets.

How to cook: Flounder can be prepared a variety of ways. Cooking methods include poaching, baking, broiling, and micro-cooking. For cooking directions, see the Cooking Fish chart under *Fish*.

Nutrition information: Baked flounder has about 100 calories in a 3-ounce serving.

(See *Fish* for selecting, storing, thawing, and other information.)

Flour (noun) The very finely ground meal of an edible food, particularly a grain.

Types: When referring to flour, most people mean wheat flour unless they say otherwise. Flours made from other foods include amaranth, barley, buckwheat, millet, oats,

continued

quinoa, rice, rye, and triticale. (See also *Cornmeal* and other individual entries.)

Wheat flours are classified by the amount of protein they contain. Wheat flours made from soft wheats are relatively low in protein and generally are used for making cakes, cookies, pastries, and crackers. Those flours made from hard wheats are high in protein and generally are used for quick and yeast breads. Durum wheat, the hardest wheat of all, makes a flour very high in protein that's good for making pasta.

Market forms: By using different classes of wheat in the milling process, a variety of flours are produced.

□ **All-Purpose:** A white flour that generally is a combination of soft and hard wheats, or medium-protein wheats. It works well for all types of home-baked products, including yeast breads, cakes, and quick breads. Most all-purpose flours come presifted. You may find bleached and unbleached flour at the store.

All-purpose flours vary in protein content from brand to brand (see *Bread, Yeast* for additional information).

□ **Bread:** Made entirely from hard wheat. With its high gluten strength, bread flour is well-suited for making yeast breads.

□ **Cake:** A soft wheat blend. Its low protein and gluten content makes it especially suitable for baking fine-textured cakes.

□ **Instant:** A patented process used to produce a quick-mixing flour for use in thickening gravies and sauces.

□ **Pasta:** A durum wheat blend used for making pasta.

□ **Pastry:** A soft wheat blend, with less starch than cake flour, used for making pastry.

□ **Self-Rising:** An all-purpose flour with salt and a leavener such as baking powder added. It is used for baking non-yeast products.

□ **Whole Wheat:** A coarse-textured flour ground from the entire wheat kernel. Whole wheat flour, also called graham flour, is good in breads and some cookies, but generally is not the best choice for pastry or other delicate baked goods.

Q: **Can whole wheat flour be used interchangeably with all-purpose flour?**

A: You can replace part of the all-purpose flour with whole wheat flour. Use proportions of half all-purpose flour and half whole wheat flour in most baked goods. The end product will not look the same and may have less volume and a coarser texture.

Storing: Store all-purpose flour in an airtight container in a cool, dry place for 10 to 15 months; store whole grain flours for up to 5 months. For longer storage, refrigerate or freeze the flour in a moisture- and vaporproof container. Before using a refrigerated flour in yeast breads, warm it to room temperature so it does not slow the rising of the bread.

To Sift or Not to Sift

You usually can skip the sifting of all-purpose flour. Even though most all-purpose flour is presifted, the flour settles in the bag during shipping. So, it's a good idea to stir through the flour in the bag or canister before measuring to make it lighter. Then gently spoon the flour into a dry measuring cup and level it off with a spatula.

You will need to sift cake flour before measuring it.

Nutrition information: Most all-purpose flours are enriched with iron, thiamin, niacin, and riboflavin because those nutrients are greatly reduced during milling. Fortified flours have been enriched with a higher level of nutrients than the original grain.

Flour (verb) To coat or dust a food or utensil with flour. Food may be floured before cooking to add texture and improve browning. Baking utensils sometimes are floured to prevent sticking.

Flower, Edible Any item botanically considered a flower that is safe to eat. Like herbs, each variety of flower imparts a different flavor to food. For some flower suggestions, see the Edible Flowers chart, right. The more fragrant a flower, the more flavor it imparts. Flowers may be used as an ingredient in foods or as a colorful garnish. Before using, rinse flowers and gently pat dry.

Q: What's the best way to find out if a specific flower is safe to eat?
A: Contact the poison control center or the extension service in your area.

Selecting: Choose flowers that have been grown without the use of pesticides or other chemicals. They also should be fresh and free of bruises.
  Edible flowers are available in the produce section of some supermarkets or at a local herb garden, restaurant supplier, or produce supplier who specializes in edible flowers. Or, you might try getting flowers from mail-order flower and herb farms. The best flowers, however, are unsprayed blossoms from your own garden. (Do not use flowers from florist shops—they're usually treated with chemicals.)

Storing: Store flowers in an airtight container in the refrigerator for up to 1 day.

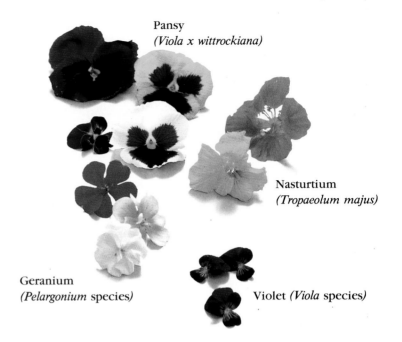

Pansy
(Viola x wittrockiana)

Nasturtium
(Tropaeolum majus)

Geranium
(Pelargonium species*)*

Violet *(Viola* species*)*

Edible Flowers

Flowers can add color and flavor to foods you prepare. Here are some familiar flowers to consider using as a garnish or in food preparation. If you are in doubt whether or not a flower is edible, contact your local poison control center or local extension service.

Common Name	Botanical Name	Color and Flavor
Borage	*Borago officinalis*	Blue; cucumberlike
Calendula (Pot Marigold)	*Calendula officinalis*	Yellow or golden; bland
Chive	*Allium schoenoprasum*	Pale lavender; onionlike
Geranium	*Pelargonium* species	Pink, red, white; flavor varies with variety—taste before using
Nasturtium	*Tropaeolum majus*	Bright orange and red; peppery
Pansy	*Viola x wittrockiana*	Wide color range; slightly spicy
Rose	*Rosa* species	Many colors; slightly sweet
Squash	*Cucurbita* species	Golden yellow; slightly squashlike
Viola, violet	*Viola* species	Many colors; sweet, sometimes tangy or spicy

Fluting Piecrust

Dressing up a pie with a decorative edge is a snap when you choose one of these simple fluting methods.

Scallop Flute

Place the thumb of one hand flat against the inside edge of the pie. Press the dough around your thumb, using the thumb and index finger of your other hand.

Rickrack Flute

First make the Scallop Flute. Then pinch the edge of each scallop into a point, as shown.

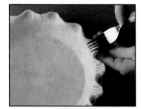

Flower Petal Flute

First make the Scallop Flute. Then press the tines of a fork lightly into the center of each scallop.

Flummery   A dessert, similar to a soft pudding or custard, that usually is served over berries or other fruit. A flummery also can be similar to a thickened fruit sauce.

Flute   A method of making a decorative pattern or impression in food. The term most often is applied to sealing the pastry edges of a pie (see how-to photographs, left).

Focaccia   *(foh COT see uh)* An Italian yeast bread, similar to deep-dish pizza crust with a breadlike texture. The bread usually is topped with onions, herbs, olives, and cheese and served warm as a snack or as a side dish. Ready-to-eat focaccia is available at the supermarket, and focaccia mixes are available at specialty stores.

Foie Gras   *(fwah GRAH)* A French term that refers to the liver of a goose or duck that has been force-fed for fattening. Pâté de foie gras is a seasoned appetizer spread made from these livers.

Fold   A method of gently mixing ingredients. It is used for delicate or whipped ingredients that cannot withstand stirring or beating. To fold, use a rubber spatula to cut down through the mixture, move across the bottom of the bowl, and come back up, folding some of the mixture from the bottom over close to the surface. Turn the bowl often so the ingredients are evenly distributed.

Fondant   A rich, creamy, melt-in-your-mouth candy that's made with sugar, water, and corn syrup or cream of tartar. Once a fondant mixture is cooked and cooled on a platter or marble slab, it is worked with a wooden spoon or paddle. The mixture changes in appearance from thick and translucent to creamy and opaque. Then the mixture is kneaded till it is smooth and free of lumps. Fondant often is used for mint patties or as the centers of dipped chocolates.

Q: **Most fondant recipes say to let the candy "ripen" for 24 hours. What does this mean?**
A: After it is kneaded, fondant should be wrapped and stored at room temperature. During this time, the candy becomes more creamy and pliable, much as a fruit or vegetable softens as it ripens.

(See *Candy* for Candy-Making Tips and equipment, storing, and other information.)

Fondue   A food cooked at the table using a ceramic or metal pot with its own heat source. There are three kinds of fondue. *Cheese* fondue is a melted cheese mixture into which chunks of crusty bread are dipped. *Meat* fondue involves cooking cubes of meat or poultry in hot oil. *Dessert* fondue is a heated dessert sauce, often chocolate, that is used to coat pieces of cake or fruit.
   The term also refers to a puffy baked casserole that is made with cubes of bread.

Food Additive   Any substance that becomes part of a food product. A food additive can be anything from a vitamin added to enrich foods to an artificial flavor added to make foods taste better. All food additives must be tested and proved safe by the manufacturer and then approved by the Food and Drug Administration.

Food Coloring   Either liquid or paste edible dyes that are used to tint foods made at home and commercially.

Food Groups   See *Nutrition.*

Food Safety

Protecting food from the growth of illness-causing organisms. The basic rules of food safety are: Keep cold foods cold; keep hot foods hot; and keep foods clean.

Food Safety Tips
- Maintain the refrigerator at 36° to 40° and the freezer at 0° or below.
- Thaw food in the refrigerator overnight or in the microwave oven. Do not thaw food at room temperature.
- Cook all foods thoroughly (see individual entries for doneness tests). Do not partially cook food, stop, and then finish cooking later.
- When serving hot foods, hold them for no longer than 2 hours and keep the food between 140° and 165°.
- Discard chilled food that has been at room temperature for more than 2 hours.
- Promptly place leftovers in the refrigerator or freezer. A large quantity of hot food should be cooled quickly before refrigerating or freezing it. To do this, place the container in a sink filled with ice water. Or, divide the food into smaller portions before refrigerating or freezing, so it will cool faster.
- When handling raw meat and poultry, wash hands, counters, and utensils with hot, soapy water between recipe steps. Never put cooked meat or poultry on the plate that held the uncooked food.
- Reheat leftovers thoroughly. Covering helps the food heat evenly. Gravy should come to a rolling boil.

Meat and Poultry Hot Line: For answers to questions about meat and poultry handling and safety, call the toll-free United States Department of Agriculture's Meat and Poultry Hot Line at 1-800-535-4555 between 10 a.m. and 4 p.m. eastern time. (In the Washington, D.C., area, call 447-3333.)

Food Storage

Placing edible products on a shelf, in the refrigerator, or in the freezer so they will keep for later use. Prepare the foods for storage following the information listed below. Whenever possible, select reusable containers with tight-fitting lids when products need to be tightly covered.

How to store: Store foods in the appropriate place. Follow product label directions, if present, for storage place, and heed the "use or sell by" dates.

☐ **Canned Foods:** Store canned goods in a cool (50° to 70°), dry, well-ventilated area away from sunlight up to about 1 year.

☐ **Cooked Foods:** Cool quickly, cover, and promptly refrigerate or freeze.

☐ **Meat and Poultry:** For short-term storage, leave items in the store's packaging and place in the coldest section of the refrigerator. For longer storage, wrap tightly in moisture- and vaporproof material and freeze. (See also *Meat* for the Storing Meat chart and *Poultry* for refrigerating and freezing information.)

☐ **Fish:** Wrap tightly in moisture- and vaporproof material before storing in the refrigerator or freezer. (See also *Fish* for storing information.)

☐ **Fresh Fruits and Vegetables:** See individual entries for storing information.

☐ **Dairy Products and Eggs:** See individual entries for storing information.

(See *Freezing* for additional information.)

Frankfurter

A cooked and smoked link sausage that goes by many names, including hot dog, coney, wiener, and frank. Sold skinless or in natural casings, frankfurters may be made of pork, beef, turkey, chicken, or a combination of meats. Some franks also include cheese.

Market forms: Frankfurters vary from tiny, bite-size cocktail franks to foot-long hot dogs. The most common length is 4 to 5 inches, with 10 frankfurters of this size per pound. Longer bun-length franks are sold eight links per pound, and oversize hot dogs come four or six to a pound. *continued*

Selecting: Whether you buy prepackaged franks or individual links, choose ones with even color and a moist surface.

Nutrition information: One 5-inch-long regular beef and pork frankfurter (8 per pound) has about 185 calories, 17 grams of fat, and about 640 milligrams of sodium.

(See *Sausage* for Cooking Sausages and storing information.)

Frappé *(fra PAY)* The French term for a beverage that consists of a liqueur poured over crushed ice. The term also refers to a dessert made by beating a partially frozen mixture until it is slushy.

Freeze-Dried A term used to describe a food that has been preserved by freezing it in a vacuum chamber and removing moisture. Although brittle and crumbly, freeze-dried foods maintain their color and shape better than other dried foods. Freeze-dried foods are light, compact, and can be stored at room temperature. Coffee is one of the most common freeze-dried foods. A variety of other freeze-dried foods also are available for camping or backpacking.

Freezing To preserve food by keeping it chilled at 0° or below.

Freezer containers and wrappings: Heavy foil, freezer wrap, plastic wrap for the freezer, and freezer bags are good for packaging solid or dry foods. Wide-top freezing or canning jars, rigid plastic freezer containers with tightly fitting lids, and freezer bags are good for packaging liquid or semiliquid foods.

If a casserole is to be frozen in a baking dish, wrap the dish with heavy foil and seal. When the recipe contains an acid ingredient, such as tomatoes, cover the food with plastic wrap before covering with foil. The plastic wrap will prevent a reaction between the foil and the food during storage. The foil can be used as a cover when heating the food, but the plastic wrap should be removed before cooking.

Sealing packages: If the food is liquid or semiliquid, leave enough headspace in the container for the food to expand as it freezes. (On wide-top containers leave ½ inch for pints and 1 inch for quarts; on narrow-top containers leave ¾ inch for pints and 1½ inches for quarts.) With other foods packaged in freezer wrap, foil, or bags, press out as much air as possible before sealing the package. Tightly seal bags and containers. Seal freezer wrap, plastic wrap for the freezer, and foil with a drugstore fold (fold long edges in a series of locked folds, then fold the short ends under), and secure with freezer tape.

Labeling: Always label packages with the contents, quantity or number of servings, date frozen, and any special instructions.

Freezing Tips
- Freeze foods at the peak of their flavor and texture, because freezing preserves the already-present quality of a food, but does not improve it. Also, freeze only top-quality baked goods and prepared dishes.
- Contact your county extension agent for information on freezing specific fruits, vegetables, and other foods.
- Don't skip the blanching step when it is recommended. Placing the items in boiling water for the specified time destroys enzymes that would reduce the quality of the food. Cool the food immediately in cold water, then drain and package.
- Some seasonings change when a prepared food is frozen. Put less seasoning in a recipe you plan to freeze, then adjust the seasoning when you serve it.

Storing: When adding foods to the freezer, add only 2 pounds of food per cubic foot of freezer space at any one time. Adding too much food at once delays the freezing and hurts the quality of the food. Also, place foods as close to the coils as possible, and spread the packages out so air can circulate around them. When the packages are frozen solid, they can be stacked.

Q: What is freezer burn?
A: Freezer burn is the discoloration and drying out that occur when a frozen food is exposed to the cold air. Foods that have freezer burn are safe to eat, but they may be tough and less flavorful. The way to prevent freezer burn is to wrap food tightly in freezer packaging material and immediately replace any torn packaging.

Freezing Prepared Food

Freeze extra portions of everything from breads to stews so you'll have food in reserve. Freeze most casseroles before baking. However, before freezing, cook those casseroles that contain raw rice, raw vegetables, or raw meat that has been frozen and thawed. See also the freezing information above and on the opposite page.

Food	Preparation for Freezing	How to Serve	Storage Time
Breads, rolls, biscuits	Bake and cool. Seal in a freezer bag or container.	Thaw in package 1 hour or reheat in foil in a 300° oven about 20 minutes.	3 months
Cakes, cupcakes	Bake, remove from pans, and cool. Freeze on a tray, then wrap.	Unwrap. Thaw at room temperature 1 to 2 hours.	6 months
Casseroles (fish, poultry, or meat with vegetables or pasta)	Use less seasoning (can intensify during freezing) and undercook slightly. Cool quickly. Pour into a freezer container, freezer bag, or freezer-to-oven casserole (overwrap or seal lid with freezer tape).	Bake in a 400° oven for 1¾ hours per quart. Cover for first half of the baking time, then uncover.	2 to 4 weeks
Cookies	*Unbaked:* Drop dough on a tray and freeze till firm; put into freezer bags. Or, shape into rolls; wrap individually; freeze.	Bake dropped dough without thawing. Thaw rolls of dough until just soft enough to slice; bake.	6 months
	Baked: Cool. Freeze in containers.	Thaw.	6 to 8 months
Leftovers (stews, meat with gravy)	Cool. Package in rigid freezer containers (leaving headspace) or freezer bags.	Thaw, covered, in the refrigerator. Reheat thoroughly.	1 to 3 months
Pies	*Unbaked:* Do not freeze pecan pie. Treat light-colored fruit with ascorbic acid color keeper. Prepare pie as usual, but do not cut slits in top crust. Use a metal or freezer-to-oven pie plate. Cover with inverted paper plate to protect crust. Place in a freezer bag.	Unwrap; cut slits in top. Cover edge with foil. Bake frozen pie in a 450° oven for 15 minutes, then in a 375° oven for 15 minutes. Uncover; bake about 30 minutes more or till done.	2 to 4 months
	Baked: Do not freeze cream, custard, or meringue-topped pies. Bake pie and cool. Package as directed for unbaked pies.	Thaw in package at room temperature. Reheat.	6 to 8 months
Sandwiches	Spread bread with margarine. Use cheese, meat, poultry, tuna, salmon, or peanut butter filling. Wrap individually. *Not recommended:* Lettuce, tomatoes, celery, jelly, cooked egg whites, mayonnaise, or salad dressing.	Thaw meat, poultry, or fish sandwiches in wrap in the refrigerator for 1 to 2 hours. Thaw other sandwiches at room temperature.	2 months
Stews, soups	Use vegetables that freeze well (not potatoes). Omit salt and thickening if storage will be longer than 2 months. Undercook vegetables. Cool quickly. Pour into freezer containers or bags, leaving some headspace.	Place frozen food in a heavy saucepan. Cook over low heat, separating often with a fork till thoroughly heated. Season and thicken.	1 to 3 months

French Bread

French Bread A long, cylindrical loaf of chewy, crusty yeast bread. French bread dough contains no fat and is made with water instead of milk and little, if any, sugar.

Q: What's the difference between French bread and Italian bread?
A: The shape is the only difference. French bread loaves are longer and narrower than Italian bread loaves.

Convenience products: Ready-to-eat, brown-and-serve, and frozen loaves of French bread are available.

A Tip from Our Kitchen

French bread does not store well, so wrap and freeze it for up to a month after baking and cooling if you're not going to eat it the same day it is baked.

French Bread

5½ to 6 cups all-purpose flour
2 packages active dry yeast
1½ teaspoons salt
2 cups warm water (120° to 130°)
  Cornmeal
1 slightly beaten egg white
1 tablespoon water

■ In a large mixing bowl combine *2 cups* of the flour, the yeast, and salt. Add warm water. Beat with an electric mixer on low speed for 30 seconds, scraping bowl constantly. Beat on high speed for 3 minutes. Using a spoon, stir in as much remaining flour as you can.
■ Turn out onto a lightly floured surface. Knead in enough remaining flour to make a stiff dough that is smooth and elastic (8 to 10 minutes total). Shape into a ball. Place in a greased bowl; turn once to grease surface. Cover; let rise in a warm place till double (about 1 hour).
■ Punch dough down. Turn out onto a lightly floured surface. Divide in half. Cover; let rest 10 minutes. Roll each half into a 15x10-inch rectangle. Roll up from long sides; seal well.

Pinch and pull ends slightly to taper. Place, seam side down, on a greased baking sheet sprinkled with cornmeal. Combine egg white and water; brush over loaves. Cover; let rise till nearly double (35 to 45 minutes). With a sharp knife, make 3 or 4 diagonal cuts about ¼ inch deep across the top of each loaf.
■ Bake in a 375° oven for 20 minutes. Brush again with egg white and water mixture. Continue baking for 15 to 20 minutes more or till bread tests done. Remove from baking sheet; cool. Makes 2 loaves (30 servings).

Nutrition information per serving: 85 calories, 3 g protein, 18 g carbohydrate, 0 g fat, 0 mg cholesterol, 109 mg sodium, 36 mg potassium.

Mini French Bread Loaves: Prepare French Bread as at left, *except* cut each half of dough into quarters, making 8 pieces total. Shape into balls. Cover; let rest 10 minutes. Shape each ball into a 6-inch loaf; taper ends. Place 2½ inches apart on a greased baking sheet sprinkled with cornmeal. Brush with egg white and water mixture. Cover; let rise till nearly double (35 to 45 minutes). With a very sharp knife, make 3 shallow diagonal cuts across the top of each loaf.
■ Bake in a 375° oven for 15 minutes. Brush again with egg white and water mixture. Bake for 10 to 15 minutes more or till bread tests done. Remove from baking sheet; cool. Makes 8 loaves (16 to 24 servings).

Nutrition information per serving: 160 calories, 5 g protein, 33 g carbohydrate, 0 g fat, 0 mg cholesterol, 205 mg sodium, 67 mg potassium.

French Cooking
The simple, country cooking of provincial France as well as the more elaborate haute cuisine developed by master chefs. France is considered by many to be the gastronomic capital of the world, and French cooks, whether they are chefs or homemakers, are noted for their ability to make the best of local ingredients.

Cuisine highlights: French cooks show the greatest genius in their use of sauces, which are based on homemade stocks. Beurre blanc (a creamy butter sauce), hollandaise, béchamel, and béarnaise are some of the

continued

French Bread

Beef Bourguignonne
(see recipe, page 178)

better known sauces (see also *Hollandaise Sauce, Béchamel Sauce,* and *Béarnaise Sauce*). Additional flavor often is added to stocks and sauces by means of a bouquet garni, mirepoix (a mixture of finely chopped vegetables), wine, onion, or garlic (see also *Bouquet Garni*).

Regional specialties: Each region of France is known for its distinctive flavors based on local ingredients.

On the *northern coast,* Normandy and Brittany have an enviable variety of fresh fish and seafood. Normandy is known for its apples and its dairy products, such as Camembert cheese and crème fraîche (see also *Camembert Cheese* and *Crème Fraîche*). Brittany is recognized for its fish dishes and crepes (see also *Crepe*).

The Bordeaux region in the *southwest* of France is known for its truffles (a vegetable delicacy) and pâté de foie gras (made from fattened-goose livers). It is also where cognac and Armagnac brandies are produced.

In *southern France,* cassoulets, mixtures of white beans and a variety of meats, are a favorite. Provence on the Italian border boasts the famous fish stew called bouillabaisse, as well as the Provençal sauce of tomatoes, garlic, shallots, and olive oil. In Burgundy, the famous wine is added to tender pieces of meat to make beef bourguignonne (recipe follows).

Paris specialties: Paris is world famous for its range of dining experiences, from the sophisticated dishes prepared by five-star chefs to the more simple fare served at neighborhood bistros. Bistro cuisine typically consists of long-simmered, home-style dishes, such as pot-au-feu (boiled beef); veal, beef, lamb, or rabbit stews; and bean and vegetable soups. Pears in wine, fruit tarts, and mousses are popular desserts. Paris also is known for long loaves of crusty French bread as well as its celebrated wine cellars. Parisians serve more champagne than citizens of any other city in the world.

Beef Bourguignonne

- 1 **pound boneless beef chuck roast, cut into ¾-inch cubes**
- 2 **tablespoons cooking oil**
- 1 **cup chopped onion**
- 1 **clove garlic, minced**
- 1½ **cups burgundy**
- ¾ **cup beef broth**
- 2 **bay leaves**
- 1 **teaspoon dried thyme, crushed**
- ¾ **teaspoon dried marjoram, crushed**
- ½ **teaspoon salt**
- ¼ **teaspoon pepper**
- 3 **cups fresh mushrooms**
- 4 **medium carrots, cut into ¾-inch pieces**
- ½ **pound pearl onions *or* 2 cups small frozen whole onions**
- ¼ **cup cold water**
- 2 **tablespoons all-purpose flour**
- 2 **slices bacon, crisp-cooked, drained, and crumbled**
- 3 **cups hot cooked noodles**
  Snipped parsley (optional)

■ In a large Dutch oven or kettle, cook *half* of the meat in *1 tablespoon* of the hot oil till meat is brown. Remove from pan and add remaining oil, remaining meat, the chopped onion, and garlic. Cook till meat is brown and onion is tender. Drain fat. Return all meat to Dutch oven.

■ Stir in burgundy, beef broth, bay leaves, thyme, marjoram, salt, and pepper. Bring to boiling; reduce heat. Cover and simmer for 45 minutes. Add mushrooms, carrots, and pearl onions. Return to boiling; reduce heat. Cover and cook for 25 to 30 minutes more or till tender. Combine water and flour. Stir into meat mixture. Cook and stir till thickened and bubbly. Cook and stir 1 minute more. Discard bay leaves. Stir in bacon. Serve with noodles and, if desired, garnish with parsley. Makes 6 servings.

Nutrition information per serving: 382 calories, 23 g protein, 35 g carbohydrate, 13 g fat (4 g saturated), 79 mg cholesterol, 375 mg sodium, 639 mg potassium.

French Fry
A term for a method of cooking a food in deep, hot fat until it is crisp. This method often is used to cook potato strips, but other foods, such as shrimp and onion rings, also are french fried. The term also refers to deep-fried potato strips.

French Toast
Sliced bread, dipped in an egg-milk mixture, and cooked on a griddle till crunchy on the outside but tender inside. French toast usually is served for breakfast or brunch with maple syrup, powdered sugar, or other toppings.

A Tip from Our Kitchen
Use 1-inch-thick slices of French bread if you like French toast with a custardlike center. Use regular slices of white bread if you prefer a crisp French toast.

Fricassee
(FRIC uh see) A French term for meat or poultry (often veal or chicken) cooked slowly in a cream sauce.

Fried Pie
A dessert made by wrapping a sweet dough around fruit and then deep-fat frying it. Usually eaten warm, these pies are often topped with icing or powdered sugar.

Frittata
An Italian dish made from beaten eggs that is similar to an omelet. For a frittata, additional ingredients, such as vegetables, meat, or cheese, often are used, and the mixture is cooked over low heat until it is set but still moist on top. The frittata is then put under a broiler, or allowed to stand in the covered skillet, for several minutes to finish cooking. The frittata is then served in wedges.

Frittata

- 6 **eggs**
- ⅛ **teaspoon pepper**
- ¼ **cup chopped onion**
- 1 **clove garlic, minced**
- 1 **tablespoon margarine** *or* **butter**
- ¾ **cup chopped cooked vegetables** *or* **meat**
- 2 **tablespoons grated Parmesan** *or* **Romano cheese**

■ In a bowl beat eggs and pepper; set aside. In a 10-inch broilerproof or regular skillet cook onion and garlic in margarine or butter till onion is tender. Stir in the chopped vegetables or meat.
■ Pour egg mixture into skillet over vegetables or meat. Cook over medium heat. As mixture sets, run a spatula around edge of skillet, lifting egg mixture to allow uncooked portions to flow underneath. Continue cooking and lifting edges till egg mixture is almost set (surface will be moist).
■ Place broilerproof skillet under the broiler 4 to 5 inches from the heat. Broil for 1 to 2 minutes or till top is just set. (*Or,* if using a regular skillet, remove skillet from the heat; cover and let stand 3 to 4 minutes or till top is set.) Sprinkle with Parmesan or Romano cheese. Cut into wedges. Makes 3 servings.

Oven Frittata: Prepare Frittata as above, *except* use an *ovenproof* skillet. After pouring egg mixture into the skillet, bake in a 350° oven about 15 minutes or till a knife inserted near the center comes out clean.

Nutrition information per serving: 233 calories, 16 g protein, 9 g carbohydrate, 15 g fat (5 g saturated), 429 mg cholesterol, 246 mg sodium, 229 mg potassium.

Greek Frittata: Prepare Frittata as above, *except* substitute 4 cups torn *fresh spinach* for the chopped cooked vegetables or meat. After adding spinach to onion and garlic in the skillet, cook for 2 to 3 minutes more or till spinach is limp. Substitute ½ cup crumbled *feta cheese* for Parmesan or Romano cheese.

Nutrition information per serving: 257 calories, 18 g protein, 6 g carbohydrate, 18 g fat (7 g saturated), 443 mg cholesterol, 436 mg sodium, 576 mg potassium.

Fritter Small portions of batter or dough that are deep-fat fried. Sometimes chopped foods are stirred into the batter.

The recipe title usually includes the name of the main ingredient used in the fritter, such as apple fritters or corn fritters.

Frog Leg A long hind leg of a large edible frog. Frog legs are similar in flavor to chicken. Frogs are farm-raised for their legs, which are skinned and usually sold frozen. Broiling and panfrying are popular ways to cook frog legs.

Frosting A sweet cooked or uncooked topping for cakes, cupcakes, and cookies that generally is soft enough to spread, but stiff enough to hold its shape. Frostings can be made from a recipe or a mix or purchased in ready-to-spread form.

Tips from Our Kitchen

Try these helpful hints to make frosting cakes go smoothly:
- Thoroughly cool cakes before frosting.
- For a smooth finish, use a pastry brush to sweep away crumbs before frosting.
- To keep the serving plate free of frosting, arrange narrow strips of waxed paper around the edges of the plate. Then position the cake on top. Once the cake is frosted, just pull out the waxed paper strips.
- For a cake with a flat top, stack the cake layers with the rounded tops together, adding a layer of frosting or filling between them.
- Once this cake is assembled, spread a thin layer of frosting on the sides of the cake to seal in any remaining crumbs. Once this frosting is set, decoratively frost the sides and then the top of the cake with a thicker frosting layer.

Types: Make your favorite cake, cupcake, or cookie special with one of these frostings.
☐ **Butter or Cream Cheese:** Frostings that are beaten together without cooking and are relatively failureproof because they can easily be thinned or thickened by adding more liquid or powdered sugar.
☐ **Fudge:** A cooked frosting that is really a soft fudge-candy mixture that is beaten only until it reaches a spreadable consistency.
☐ **Icing:** Usually refers to a thin, uncooked frosting that is used as a glaze.
☐ **Seven-Minute:** A light, cooked frosting named for the amount of time that the mixture of egg whites and sugar syrup is beaten while heating in a double boiler.
☐ **Boiled:** A cooked frosting in which a hot sugar syrup is beaten into stiffly beaten egg whites. A fluffy white frosting mix is available that produces a similar frosting.

Fruit The mature seed-bearing structure of a flowering plant. Nuts, cereal grains, olives, corn, tomatoes, and some spices are technically fruits just as bananas and peaches are. In the cooking sense, however, only foods that are succulent, pulpy, sometimes juicy, and either naturally sweet or sweetened before they are eaten are considered fruits. Most fruits are relatively low in calories and high in vitamins and fiber.

Some fruits grow on trees. Well-known tree fruits include apples, pears, cherries, dates, figs, and persimmons.

Market forms: Nearly all fruit is available fresh at the supermarket, although growing seasons may limit the supply. A variety of exotic fruits also are becoming more readily available. If you are unfamiliar with the flavors of some of these new fruits, ask the produce manager to cut you a tasting sample.

Besides fresh, fruit comes in many other forms, including dried, frozen, pickled, and canned. Canned fruits may be packed in water, in their own juice, or in light or heavy syrup. Fruits also are processed into a vast array of products including juices, jellies, jams, sauces, and relishes. (See individual fruit entries.)

Fruitcake

A rich, compact cake full of candied or dried fruit, nuts, and fruit peel. The batter usually contains margarine, butter, or shortening. The texture and flavor of this traditional holiday cake improve when it is stored for several weeks wrapped in cheesecloth soaked with brandy, rum, wine, or fruit juice.

Fruitcake

- 1½ cups all-purpose flour
- 1 teaspoon ground cinnamon
- ½ teaspoon baking powder
- ¼ teaspoon baking soda
- ¼ teaspoon ground nutmeg
- ¼ teaspoon ground allspice
- ¼ teaspoon ground cloves
- ¾ cup diced mixed candied fruits and peels, *or* snipped mixed dried fruit
- ½ cup raisins *or* snipped pitted dates
- ½ cup candied red *or* green cherries, quartered
- ½ cup chopped pecans, walnuts, *or* toasted slivered almonds
- 2 eggs
- ½ cup packed brown sugar
- ½ cup orange juice *or* apple juice
- ⅓ cup margarine *or* butter, melted
- 2 tablespoons light molasses
  Brandy *or* fruit juice

■ Grease an 8x4x2-inch loaf pan. Line bottom and sides of pan with brown paper to prevent overbrowning; grease paper. In a bowl combine flour, cinnamon, baking powder, baking soda, nutmeg, allspice, and cloves. Add fruits and peels, raisins or dates, cherries, and nuts; mix well.

■ In a mixing bowl beat eggs; stir in brown sugar, orange or apple juice, margarine or butter, and molasses till ingredients are combined. Stir egg mixture into fruit mixture. Pour batter into the prepared loaf pan.

■ Bake in a 300° oven for 1¼ to 1½ hours or till a toothpick inserted near the center comes out clean. (Cover pan loosely with foil after 1 hour of baking to prevent overbrowning.) Cool in pan on a wire rack. Remove fruitcake from pan. Wrap in brandy- or fruit-juice-moistened cheesecloth. Overwrap with foil. Store in the refrigerator for 2 to 8 weeks to mellow flavors. Remoisten cheesecloth about once a week, or as needed. Serves 16.

Nutrition information per serving: 207 calories, 3 g protein, 35 g carbohydrate, 7 g fat (1 g saturated), 27 mg cholesterol, 83 mg sodium, 141 mg potassium.

Light Fruitcake: Prepare Fruitcake as above, *except* omit nutmeg, allspice, and cloves. Substitute *light corn syrup* for the molasses. Add 1 teaspoon finely shredded *lemon peel* and 1 tablespoon *lemon juice* with the corn syrup to the egg mixture.

Nutrition information per serving: 209 calories, 3 g protein, 35 g carbohydrate, 7 g fat (1 g saturated), 27 mg cholesterol, 84 mg sodium, 119 mg potassium.

Fruit Cocktail

A chilled fruit mixture, served as a first course or dessert. Fruit cocktail can be made from any fresh fruit, or it can be purchased canned. The canned product often is used as an ingredient in recipes and usually consists of peaches, pears, green grapes, and maraschino cherries.

Fruit Juice

The liquid squeezed or pressed from fruit that is served as a beverage or used as an ingredient in cooking.

Fruit Soup   A slightly sweet soup made with fresh or dried fruit. Sometimes tapioca is added for thickening. Also, wine or liqueur often is added for flavor. Fruit soup can be served warm or chilled as either an appetizer or a dessert.

Fry   To cook a food in hot cooking oil or fat, usually giving food a crisp, brown crust.

Methods: Frying techniques vary depending mainly on the amount of melted shortening or cooking oil used. Here are some of the most common methods.
☐ **Panfry:** To cook a food in a skillet in a small amount of hot fat or oil. Often, panfried foods have a very light breading or coating.
☐ **Shallow-Fry:** To fry food in about 1 inch of hot fat or oil. Typically, shallow-fried foods are breaded or coated with batter.
☐ **Deep-Fat Fry:** To fry food in enough hot fat or oil to cover the food. The length of cooking time varies with each food. Usually, the fat temperature ranges from 365° to 375°, depending on the food. Deep-fat-fried foods often have a thicker coating.
☐ **Stir-Fry:** An Oriental method of quickly cooking small pieces of food in a small amount of hot cooking oil in a wok or skillet while stirring constantly. High heat is used in stir-frying.

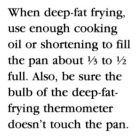

When deep-fat frying, use enough cooking oil or shortening to fill the pan about ⅓ to ½ full. Also, be sure the bulb of the deep-fat-frying thermometer doesn't touch the pan.

Deep-Fat-Frying Hints
● Don't heat the cooking oil or melted shortening to the point that it smokes. By that time, it is already breaking down. Instead, invest in a deep-fat-frying thermometer and heat the fat or oil to the temperature called for in the recipe.
● Fry in small batches. Adding too much food at one time cools the fat or cooking oil too much and makes fried foods soggy and greasy.
● For freshest flavor, use new cooking oil or shortening. However, you can reuse fat *once*. Cool the hot fat enough to handle safely. Strain through a paper drip coffee filter set in a metal strainer or through a double thickness of cheesecloth. Refrigerate in a covered jar or container; use within a few days.
  To reuse oil, add *equal amounts* of fresh oil to help avoid smoking and possible flare-ups. It is not necessary to add fresh shortening to old shortening.

Fudge   A soft, creamy candy made of sugar, milk or cream, butter, and often chocolate. After partially cooling, the candy mixture is beaten with a wooden spoon to the proper consistency.

Types: Fudge can be divided into three basic types according to the predominant flavor.
☐ **Chocolate:** Made with unsweetened chocolate squares, unsweetened cocoa powder, or chocolate pieces. Chopped nuts often are added to this type of fudge.
☐ **White or Blond:** Features vanilla instead of chocolate as the basic flavor. Nuts and candied fruit are popular additions.
☐ **Penuche:** Brown sugar gives this fudge a caramel-like flavor and golden brown color.

Fudge-Making Tips

● Be sure to completely dissolve the sugar in the boiling mixture. You shouldn't be able to feel sugar crystals when you rub the spoon against the side of the saucepan. Any undissolved sugar will give your fudge a grainy texture. If you see any crystals on the sides of the saucepan, cover the pan, and the steam will wash down any crystals that may be present.

● To get an accurate reading when cooling fudge, the candy mixture *must* cover the bulb of the candy thermometer. If it doesn't, carefully prop the saucepan with a folded hot pad so the bulb is covered. Do this immediately after removing the pan from the heat. Then leave the pan undisturbed till the mixture cools to the specified temperature.

● When you begin to beat fudge, it will be thin and very glossy. Beat vigorously with a wooden spoon till it just begins to thicken; stir in nuts or other ingredients. Continue beating till the fudge becomes very thick and *just starts* to lose its gloss. At this point, transfer the fudge to the prepared pan.

● If you beat the fudge too long, you won't be able to pour it from the saucepan. If this happens, scrape it out, knead it with your fingers, and shape it into logs or roll it into balls.

● While your fudge is warm and still in the prepared pan, use a knife to mark it into squares. When it is firm, lift it out of the pan. Place it on a cutting board, and, using a long, thin-bladed, sharp knife, cut the fudge into squares along the markings.

Fudge in a Hurry

Shortcut fudge can be made with marshmallow creme and evaporated milk. This version doesn't require the cooling and beating steps of traditional fudge and usually makes a larger batch than many fudge recipes. The texture is not quite as smooth.

Q: **Why do fudge recipes call for lining the pan with buttered foil?**

A: Lining the pan with buttered foil when making fudge allows you to lift the scored block of candy out of the pan in one piece. Cutting the candy outside the pan not only prevents you from scratching the pan, it also allows you to make firm, straight-down cuts for even pieces of candy. Buttering the foil keeps the candy from sticking to the foil. Perhaps the best part of lining the pan with foil is that it cuts down on panwashing.

Always line your pan with buttered foil *before* you start to make the fudge. If you stop to do it later, you probably won't get the fudge out of the saucepan.

(See *Candy* for Candy-Making Tips and equipment, storing, and other information.)

Funnel Cake   A spiral-shaped, deep-fat-fried pastry. The pastry is called funnel cake because the batter is poured through a funnel into the hot fat for frying. Funnel cakes are served warm and usually are sprinkled with powdered sugar or topped with jelly or syrup. Funnel cakes can be a dessert, snack, or breakfast pastry. Funnel cake mixes are available in the supermarket.

Hot Cross Buns
(see recipe, page 213)

Gazpacho
(see recipe, page 187)

Game

Game   A wild animal that's hunted for food. The flavor of game varies depending on the type of animal and its diet. Usually, game animals have a stronger flavor than farm-raised animals.

Types: Game covers a wide range of animals. Here are the three main categories of game.
☐ **Game birds:** Birds, such as ducks, geese, pheasant, quail, grouse, partridges, doves, and wild turkeys.
☐ **Small game:** Wild animals of lesser size, including rabbits, squirrels, raccoons, opossums, muskrats, and woodchucks.
☐ **Large game:** Wild animals of greater size, such as members of the deer family, bear, bison (American buffalo), and wild boar.

Common forms: In the United States, game hunting is tightly regulated. Game can be hunted only in season and only for personal use; it is against the law to sell it. Any game that's sold in supermarkets, specialty stores, or by mail order has been raised on a game farm. Rabbit, buffalo, venison, and duck are the most common farm-raised types.

Tips from Our Kitchen
● Trim as much fat as possible from all game. The fat from some game has a strong flavor.
● To enhance or mellow the flavor of wild game, before cooking, marinate the meat in a favorite meat or poultry marinade. Or, use a bottled vinegar-and-oil-type salad dressing for a quick marinade.
● To keep game birds that have been skinned moist, brush them with cooking oil or place bacon slices on the breast before cooking. Or, cook them in an oven cooking bag or in a covered baking pan.

Cooking hints: Proper cooking is important for good-tasting game. The cooking method affects the tenderness and the flavor. As a general rule, for large game and game birds, choose your cooking method by matching the game cut to a similar beef or poultry cut. For small game, moist-heat cooking methods (braising and stewing) generally result in the best product.

Use poultry or meat roasting, broiling, and grilling charts as timing guidelines for dry-heat methods, but check for doneness before the minimum times. The lean meat of game tends to dry out quickly if overcooked.

For moist-heat cooking, find a basic recipe for meat or poultry and use the timing as a guideline, again checking for doneness earlier than indicated.

(*Note:* It's important to cook bear and boar to 170°.)

Garlic   The strongly scented, pungent bulb of a plant related to the onion. Each bulb has a papery outer skin and is made up of several small segments called cloves. Each clove also has a papery skin.

Varieties: Two major varieties of garlic that are similar in flavor are available. One is a small white or off-white bulb; the other is a larger bulb with a pinkish color.

Elephant garlic

Garlic

Q: **What is elephant garlic, and how is it used?**

A: Elephant garlic looks like a giant bulb of garlic; however, it is related more to a leek. It may also be labeled great-headed or oriental garlic. Just look for a garlic bulb that's anywhere from the size of a peach to a large orange.

Elephant garlic's mild aroma and flavor make it perfect to bake whole in pot roasts or sauté as you would regular garlic. One mammoth clove has the same potency as about 10 cloves (almost a whole bulb) of regular-size garlic.

Market forms: Besides fresh garlic, you'll also find dried minced garlic, garlic juice, garlic powder, garlic salt, and bottled minced garlic. Dried minced garlic, garlic powder, and bottled minced garlic are pure garlic; garlic salt is garlic powder combined with salt.

Storing: Store firm, plump, fresh garlic in a cool, dry, dark place. Leave the bulbs whole because the individual cloves dry out quickly. Keep any of the dried garlic products in a cool, dry, dark place and use within 6 months. Store the bottled minced garlic in the refrigerator for up to 6 months.

Hint for using: For just a touch of garlic, swish a cut garlic clove around a salad bowl. As you toss the salad, the greens will pick up the garlic flavor.

Garlic Math

1 fresh clove = ⅛ teaspoon dried minced garlic *or* garlic powder
1 fresh clove = ½ teaspoon bottled minced garlic
1 teaspoon garlic salt = ⅛ teaspoon garlic powder plus ⅞ teaspoon salt

Garnish To add visual appeal to a finished dish by decorating it with small pieces of food or edible flowers. The term also refers to the items used for decoration.

Gazpacho *(guhz PAHCH oh)* A spicy soup made from tomatoes, cucumbers, green peppers, and onions. Gazpacho has its roots in Spanish cooking and often is flavored with garlic, olive oil, vinegar, and hot pepper sauce. Usually it is served chilled, although some recipes are heated.

Gazpacho

3 **medium tomatoes**
1 **small cucumber, chopped**
1 **medium green pepper, chopped**
2 **green onions, sliced**
1 **12-ounce can (1½ cups) vegetable juice cocktail**
2 **tablespoons vinegar**
1 **teaspoon olive oil** *or* **cooking oil**
1 **clove garlic, minced**
¼ **teaspoon salt**
¼ **teaspoon dried basil, crushed**
 Several dashes bottled hot pepper sauce
 Croutons (optional)

■ Peel tomatoes. Coarsely chop the tomatoes. In a large mixing bowl combine tomatoes, cucumber, green pepper, and green onions. Stir the vegetable juice cocktail, vinegar, olive oil or cooking oil, garlic, salt, basil, and hot pepper sauce into the tomato mixture.
■ Cover and refrigerate for several hours or till thoroughly chilled. Ladle into soup bowls. Garnish with croutons, if desired. Serves 4.

Nutrition information per serving: 63 calories, 2 g protein, 12 g carbohydrate, 2 g fat (0 g saturated), 0 mg cholesterol, 475 mg sodium, 525 mg potassium.

Gefilte Fish *(guh FILL tuh)* A traditional Jewish dish made from ground fish fillets, vegetables, egg, matzo meal, and seasonings. The mixture is formed into balls and poached in fish stock. It may be eaten warm or chilled.

Gelatin   A commercial product containing powdered natural animal protein that will thicken or set a liquid. Gelatin is available in unflavored and flavored forms and is used primarily for salads and desserts. Flavored gelatin is a mixture of gelatin, sugar or artificial sweetener, and flavorings.

Preparation hints: There are a few foods that shouldn't be used in gelatin mixtures because they contain an enzyme that prevents the gelatin from setting up. These include fresh pineapple, kiwi fruit, figs, guava, papaya, and gingerroot. After these foods have been cooked or canned, they can be combined successfully with gelatin.

Gelatin Stages

The secret to perfectly set gelatin mixtures is recognizing each of the stages gelatin goes through as it sets. Here are the stages most commonly referred to in recipes.
- **Partially set:** The gelatin mixture is the consistency of unbeaten egg whites. Solids, such as fruit pieces or nuts, may be stirred into the gelatin at this stage.
- **Almost firm:** The gelatin mixture appears set but tends to flow if tipped to one side. The gelatin mixture is sticky to the touch. Another layer of gelatin mixture may be added at this stage.
- **Firm:** The gelatin mixture holds an edge when cut and doesn't move when tilted in a mold. The gelatin mixture is ready to serve.

Q: What can I do if the gelatin mixture has chilled beyond the stage I want?

A: Place the bowl of gelatin mixture in hot water. Stir the gelatin frequently to melt it slightly. Return the mixture to the refrigerator to chill to the correct stage.

Gelato   (*jell AH toe*) A rich, smooth, frozen dessert made with milk, sweetener, and egg yolks. This Italian favorite is similar to ice cream, but is firmer and not as sweet. Sometimes gelato is called custard cream.

German Cooking   The cooking style of Germany, characterized by hearty meat and sausage dishes, sweet and sour flavor combinations, and a wide assortment of breads and pastries.

Cuisine highlights: Pork is the favored meat of Germany, followed by veal and beef. All three are used in the numerous sausages called "wursts," for which the Germans are famous. Sauerbraten (recipe follows) is one of the national dishes (see also *Sauerbraten*). Fish, game, and poultry, especially goose, also are well-liked.

Cabbage and potatoes are vegetable mainstays. Cabbage is likely to be made into sauerkraut or cooked with apples. Potatoes are used in potato pancakes, dumplings, soups, and hot and cold salads.

Regional specialties: The cooking of *northern Germany* is influenced by its proximity to the North and Baltic seas, as well as by its neighbors—Poland, the Netherlands, and Scandinavia. Hearty soups made with cabbage, bacon, lentils, or peas and thickened with sour cream are popular, as are smoked meats and fish.

Central Germany is most famous for its beer, rye bread, and ham, but its stews, fresh vegetables, and pastries are equally good.

Eastern Germany flavors its food in much the same way as the bordering countries of

Austria, Czechoslovakia, and Poland. Paprika, sour cream, caraway, poppy seeds, and dried mushrooms are common ingredients.

In *southern Germany,* a wide variety of noodle dishes are served, especially spaetzle (recipe follows) (see also *Spaetzle*). Fresh salmon is a specialty, and common meats are pork, veal, and venison. Veal, pounded into thin slices, is served as schnitzel in dozens of ways, including wiener schnitzel (see also *Wiener Schnitzel*). Bavarian strudel features savory mixtures as well as fruit fillings (see also *Strudel*).

Sauerbraten

> 2 cups water
> ½ cup dry red wine
> ½ cup red wine vinegar
> 1 medium onion, thinly sliced
> 4 whole cloves
> 4 whole black peppers
> 2 bay leaves
> 1 3-pound beef round rump roast
> 2 tablespoons cooking oil *or* shortening
> ½ teaspoon salt
> ⅓ cup finely crushed gingersnaps (5 to 6 cookies)
> Spaetzle (optional)

■ For marinade, in a saucepan combine water, red wine, wine vinegar, onion, cloves, black peppers, and bay leaves. Bring mixture to boiling. Reduce heat and simmer for 5 minutes. Cool to room temperature. Place roast in a large bowl; pour marinade over roast. Turn roast to coat all sides. Cover and refrigerate for 2 to 3 days, turning the roast at least twice a day.
■ Remove roast from marinade; pat dry with paper towels. Strain marinade to remove onion, cloves, peppers, and bay leaves. In a Dutch oven brown the rump roast in hot cooking oil or shortening. Drain off the fat. Add the strained marinade and salt. Simmer, covered, for 1½ to 1¾ hours or till the meat is tender. Add more water, if necessary.
■ Place roast on a serving platter. Pour the remaining marinade into a large measuring cup; skim off fat. Add enough *water* to the remaining marinade to make 2 cups liquid. Return marinade to Dutch oven and stir in crushed gingersnaps. Cook and stir for 5 to 10 minutes or till the crumbs dissolve and the marinade mixture thickens. Cut the roast into thin slices. Serve with the thickened marinade and Spaetzle, if desired. Makes 12 servings.

Nutrition information per serving: 239 calories, 23 g protein, 4 g carbohydrate, 14 g fat (5 g saturated), 62 mg cholesterol, 161 mg sodium, 349 mg potassium.

Spaetzle

> 1 cup all-purpose flour
> ⅛ teaspoon salt
> 1 egg
> ⅓ cup milk
> 1 tablespoon margarine *or* butter
> 3 tablespoons fine dry bread crumbs

■ In a large saucepan or Dutch oven, bring about 3 quarts *lightly salted water* to boiling.
■ Meanwhile, for spaetzle batter, in a bowl stir together flour and salt. In another bowl stir together egg and milk. Stir egg mixture into the flour mixture.
■ Set a colander that has large holes (at least ³⁄₁₆-inch diameter) on a large piece of waxed paper. (*Or,* use a spaetzle maker according to manufacturer's directions.)
■ Pour the spaetzle batter into the colander. Immediately hold the colander over the pan of boiling water; press the batter through the colander with a wooden spoon to form the spaetzle. Cook about 5 minutes or till done, stirring occasionally. Drain well.
■ Melt margarine or butter; toss with bread crumbs. Sprinkle crumb mixture over the hot spaetzle. Makes 4 servings.

Nutrition information per serving: 186 calories, 6 g protein, 28 g carbohydrate, 5 g fat (1 g saturated), 55 mg cholesterol, 161 mg sodium, 88 mg potassium.

Whole Wheat Spaetzle: Prepare Spaetzle as above, *except* reduce all-purpose flour to ½ cup and add ½ cup *whole wheat flour.*

Nutrition information per serving: 180 calories, 7 g protein, 27 g carbohydrate, 5 g fat (1 g saturated), 55 mg cholesterol, 161 mg sodium, 132 mg potassium.

Gherkin   *(GUR kuhn)* A dark green, miniature cucumber, about 2½ inches long, that is pickled and used as a condiment. One sweet gherkin has about 20 calories and 110 milligrams of sodium.

Giblets   The edible internal organs of poultry, such as the liver, heart, and gizzard. Sometimes giblets also include the neck and wing tips of poultry. Use giblets in preparing homemade stocks, or cook them and use the finely chopped meat in stuffings.

Nutrition information: Three ounces of cooked chicken giblets contain about 140 calories, 4 grams of fat, and 340 milligrams of cholesterol.

Ginger   A semitropical plant whose root is used as a pungent spice. Ginger has a slightly hot flavor and nippy aroma.

Market forms: Ginger is used both as a seasoning and as a confection.
☐ **Candied or Crystallized:** A confection rather than a spice. Bits of gingerroot are cooked in a sugar syrup, then coated with sugar. Candied ginger often is found in chutneys and preserves.
☐ **Gingerroot:** The fresh form of the root. Its flavor is hotter and more aromatic than ground ginger. Gingerroot is a staple for anyone who does a lot of Chinese cooking.
☐ **Ground:** Gingerroot dried and ground to a powder; used mostly in baked goods.
☐ **Pickled:** Gingerroot preserved in vinegar and often served as an accompaniment to sushi, a Japanese delicacy.
☐ **Preserved:** A confection, not a spice. Gingerroot is packed in a heavy sugar syrup. Preserved ginger is used in the same way as candied ginger.

Selecting: When choosing fresh gingerroot, select a piece that's firm and heavy; avoid shriveled stems. Purchase ground ginger as you do other spices.

To grate ginger, hold a piece of unpeeled gingerroot at a 45-degree angle and rub it across a fine grating surface. Or, use a ginger grater like the one shown on the cutting board.

Storing: For short-term storage of fresh gingerroot, wrap the root in a paper towel and refrigerate. For long-term storage, immerse peeled slices of gingerroot in dry sherry, wine, or oil and refrigerate in a covered container for up to 3 months. (The ginger-flavored sherry or oil can be used in cooking.) Or, place the root in a moisture- and vaporproof bag and freeze. Then, grate or cut off what you need from the unpeeled frozen root.

Store ground and candied ginger as you do other spices—in a cool, dry, dark place.

(See *Spice* for the Spice Alternative Guide and nutrition information.)

Gingerbread   A layer-type cake or a thin cookie seasoned with ginger and sweetened with molasses. This holiday specialty has been baked in various shapes for centuries.

The cake version is thick, moist, and aromatic (recipe follows). It often is served warm with whipped cream, vanilla ice cream, or fruit sauce. Gingerbread cookies are thinner and crisper than the cake version but are still spicy. Often they're cut in the shape of people and decorated with icing.

Gingerbread

1½	cups all-purpose flour
¼	cup packed brown sugar
¾	teaspoon ground cinnamon
¾	teaspoon ground ginger
½	teaspoon baking powder
½	teaspoon baking soda
½	cup shortening
½	cup light molasses
½	cup water
1	egg

■ In a bowl combine flour, brown sugar, cinnamon, ginger, baking powder, and baking soda. Add shortening, molasses, water, and egg. Beat with an electric mixer on low to medium speed till combined. Beat on high speed for 2 minutes. Pour into a greased and floured 8x8x2-inch baking pan. Bake in a 350° oven for 35 to 40 minutes or till a toothpick inserted near the center comes out clean. Cool on a wire rack for 10 minutes. Remove from pan; serve warm. Serves 9.

Nutrition information per serving: 247 calories, 3 g protein, 32 g carbohydrate, 12 g fat (3 g saturated), 24 mg cholesterol, 74 mg sodium, 216 mg potassium.

■ **Microwave directions:** Prepare Gingerbread batter as in recipe, opposite, *except* substitute *cooking oil* for shortening. Grease a 2-quart microwave-safe ring mold. Coat with 2 tablespoons toasted *wheat germ*. Pour batter into mold. Micro-cook, uncovered, on 50% power (medium) for 10 minutes, giving dish a quarter-turn every 3 minutes. If not done, cook on 100% power (high) for 30 seconds to 2 minutes more or till surface is nearly dry. Cool for 5 minutes.

Nutrition information per serving: 260 calories, 3 g protein, 33 g carbohydrate, 13 g fat (2 g saturated), 24 mg cholesterol, 75 mg sodium, 231 mg potassium.

Gingersnap
A crisp shaped cookie that is flavored with molasses and ginger. Gingersnaps often are crushed to make crusts for cheesecakes, pies, and other desserts.

(See *Cookie* for Cookie-Making Hints and preparation, baking, storing, and other information.)

Glacé
(gla SAY) A term used to describe a food with a glossy coating. Glacé fruits and nuts are coated with a sugar syrup that hardens into a shiny surface. Glacé cakes, such as petits fours, are coated with a thin icing for a smooth, glossy look. Sometimes frozen desserts or drinks are called glacé because they have a shiny appearance.

The term also refers to the act of applying a glossy coating to a food.

Glaze
A thin, glossy coating on a food. There are numerous types of glazes. A mixture of powdered sugar and milk can be drizzled on cookies, cakes, and breads for a glaze. A fruit sauce can serve as a glaze for ham; a mixture of brown sugar and butter makes a glaze for vegetables; and melted jelly can be used as a dessert glaze. Sometimes breads and pastries are brushed with a glaze of egg and water before baking to give them a shiny surface.

Gluten
An elastic protein present in flour, especially wheat flour, that provides most of the structure for baked products. It helps breads and cakes hold together. The amount and strength of gluten varies with different flours. For example, rye flour is low in gluten, but wheat bread flour contains a great deal of it.

Gnocchi
(NO key) An Italian dumpling made from potatoes, semolina flour, or puff pastry. These dumplings can be squares, strips, or balls and are either simmered in liquid or baked. Gnocchi are served as an appetizer or a side dish.

Goose
A wild or domestic waterfowl weighing from 6 to 14 pounds. The meat, which is mostly dark, tastes moist and rich.

Market forms: Goose is sold whole, either frozen or fresh.

How to cook: For roasting directions, see the Roasting Poultry chart under *Poultry*. Grilling is not recommended. Allow about 1 to 1½ pounds per serving.

Nutrition information: A 3-ounce serving of cooked goose with skin contains about 260 calories, 19 grams of fat, and 77 milligrams of cholesterol.

(See *Poultry* for selecting, refrigerating, freezing, thawing, cooking, and other information.)

Gooseberries

Gooseberry
A small, tart, firm berry that's usually green with light stripes, but can be white, yellow, or red. Gooseberries are so tart that they generally are cooked and sweetened. As they ripen, they become bland in flavor.

Market forms: Fresh domestic gooseberries are in peak supply in the summer months. New Zealand gooseberries are available October through December. Fresh gooseberries sometimes can be found at the supermarket or at local farmer's markets. They also are available canned.

Storing: If properly stored, gooseberries will keep for up to a week. For general storage information, see *Berry*.

A Tip from Our Kitchen
To clean fresh gooseberries, first remove the blossom part and the stem. Then wash and drain the berries before using.

(See *Berry* for the Selecting Berries chart, including calories, and selecting information.)

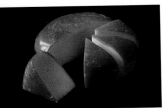

Gouda cheese

Gouda Cheese
(GOO duh) A semisoft to hard cow's-milk cheese that ranges in flavor from mild and nutty when young to sharp when aged. Gouda has a smooth yellow interior with small holes. It is shaped into a flattened round and is coated with a yellow or red wax rind. It is similar to Edam, except Gouda has a higher milk-fat content, a slightly softer texture, and a milder flavor.

(See *Cheese* for the Selecting Cheese chart and selecting, storing, serving, nutrition, and other information.)

Goulash
A Hungarian beef (or veal) and vegetable stew that's seasoned with paprika.

Beef Goulash

- 1 pound beef stew meat, cut into ¾-inch cubes
- 2 medium onions, cut into wedges
- 1 tablespoon cooking oil
- 2½ cups beef broth
- ¼ cup tomato paste
- 1 tablespoon sweet Hungarian paprika *or* paprika
- ¼ teaspoon caraway seed
- ¼ teaspoon pepper
- 3 medium potatoes (1 pound), cut into 1-inch pieces
- 2 tablespoons snipped parsley

■ In a large kettle or Dutch oven, cook meat and onion wedges in hot oil till meat is brown. Drain fat. Stir in broth, tomato paste, paprika, caraway seed, and pepper. Bring to boiling. Reduce heat and simmer, covered, for 1 hour. Add potatoes. Cover and cook for 25 to 35 minutes more or till meat and potatoes are tender. Uncover the last 10 minutes, if desired, to slightly thicken the mixture by evaporating some of the liquid. Stir in parsley just before serving. Makes 4 servings.

Nutrition information per serving: 381 calories, 29 g protein, 35 g carbohydrate, 14 g fat (5 g saturated), 79 mg cholesterol, 563 mg sodium, 1,053 mg potassium.

Graham Cracker
A flat, slightly sweet cracker made with whole wheat flour. Honey sometimes is used as part of the sweetener. The crackers often are crushed and used in desserts or for piecrusts.

A Tip from Our Kitchen
To easily serve a chilled piece of pie that has a graham cracker crust, try this: Wrap the bottom of the pie plate in a hot, damp towel for a few minutes. This softens the margarine or butter in the crust, making it less likely to stick to the pie plate. To prepare the towel, rinse it in very hot water, then wring it out.

Nutrition information: Two graham crackers (2½-inch squares) have about 60 calories.

(See *Crumb* for measuring information.)

Grain
The edible seed of members of the grass family. The most common grains (also called cereal grains) are wheat, barley, corn, sorghum, rice, oats, rye, and millet (see also *Cornmeal* and other individual entries).

continued

Cooking Grains

Use this chart as a guide when cooking grains. Measure the amount of water into a medium saucepan and bring to a full boil unless the chart indicates otherwise. If desired, add ¼ teaspoon salt to the water. Slowly add the grain and return to boiling. Cover and simmer for the time specified or till most of the water is absorbed and grain is tender. The serving size for the cooked grain can vary from ½ cup to about ¾ cup.

Grain and Amount	Amount Of Water	Cooking Directions	Yield (4 servings)
Barley, pearl ¾ cup	3 cups	Simmer about 45 minutes. Drain, if necessary.	3 cups
Barley, quick cooking 1¼ cups	2 cups	Simmer for 10 to 12 minutes.	3 cups
Buckwheat groats or kasha ⅔ cup	1½ cups	Add to *cold* water. Bring to boiling. Cover and simmer for 10 to 12 minutes.	2 cups
Bulgur 1 cup	2 cups	Add to *cold* water. Bring to boiling. Cover and simmer for 12 to 15 minutes.	3 cups
Cornmeal 1 cup	2¾ cups	Combine cornmeal and 1 cup *cold* water. Add to the 2¾ cups boiling water. Cover and simmer about 10 minutes.	3½ cups
Farina, quick cooking ¾ cup	3½ cups	Simmer for 2 to 3 minutes, stirring constantly.	3 cups
Hominy grits, quick cooking ¾ cup	3 cups	Simmer about 5 minutes.	3 cups
Millet ¾ cup	2 cups	Simmer for 15 to 20 minutes. Let stand, covered, for 5 minutes.	3 cups
Oats, rolled, quick cooking 1½ cups	3 cups	Simmer for 1 minute. Let stand, covered, for 3 minutes.	3 cups
Oats, rolled, regular 1⅔ cups	3 cups	Simmer for 5 to 7 minutes. Let stand, covered, for 3 minutes.	3 cups
Oats, steel cut 1 cup	2½ cups	Simmer for 20 to 25 minutes.	2½ cups
Quinoa ¾ cup	1½ cups	Rinse well. Simmer 12 to 15 minutes.	2¾ cups
Rye berries ¾ cup	2½ cups	Simmer about 1 hour. Drain. *Or,* for quicker cooking, soak berries in the 2½ cups water in the refrigerator for 6 to 24 hours. Do not drain. Bring to boiling; reduce heat. Cover and simmer for 30 minutes.	2 cups
Wheat, cracked ⅔ cup	1½ cups	Add to *cold* water. Bring to boiling. Cover and simmer for 12 to 15 minutes. Let stand, covered, for 5 minutes.	2 cups
Wheat berries ¾ cup	2½ cups	Simmer for 45 to 60 minutes. Drain. *Or,* for quicker cooking, soak and cook as for rye berries, above.	2 cups

How to cook: When cooking grains, choose a saucepan that is large enough to allow for expansion of the grain. Most grains expand to two to three times their original size when cooked. Millet and barley expand to four times their original size.

For cooking directions, see the Cooking Grains chart, page 193, and the Cooking Rice chart, page 352.

Granola

A cereal made of various grains (one of which usually is rolled oats), brown sugar or honey, nuts, oil, dried fruits, and coconut. Granola may be flavored with spices such as cinnamon and nutmeg. It is used as a snack, a breakfast food, and an ingredient in baked goods.

Storing: Store in an airtight container in a cool, dry place for up to 1 month or in the refrigerator for up to 3 months.

Nutrition information: A ½-cup serving of granola contains about 260 calories.

Grape

A small fruit that grows in clusters on vines. Skin color and interior meat can range from pale green to deep purple and black. Grapes taste sweet and may have tiny, inedible seeds.

There are thousands of varieties of grapes. Grapes can be used for eating out of hand and for making raisins, juice, and wine. So many varieties are harvested that it is possible to purchase fresh grapes in most supermarkets year-round.

Varieties: Green and red seedless grapes are usually the most common, although some of the seeded varieties are thought to have fuller flavor. Here are descriptions of several grape varieties you might find.

☐ **Black Corinth:** Also called *Zante Currants* or *Champagne* grapes. These tiny, purple grapes grow in small, tight clusters. The grapes are very sweet and rich. When dried, they are sold as currants.

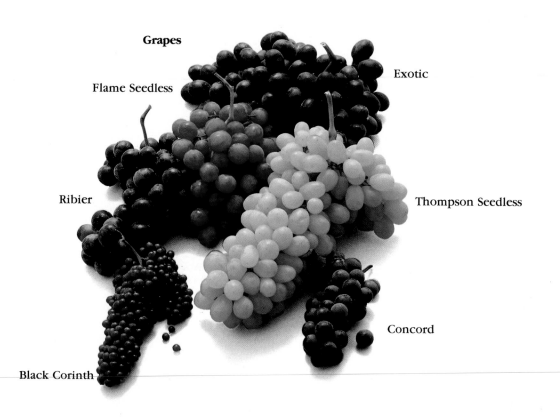

Grapes

Flame Seedless

Exotic

Ribier

Thompson Seedless

Concord

Black Corinth

□ **Concord:** Purplish blue grapes that are rich and mellow. Although mostly used for juice and jelly, Concords sometimes are eaten out of hand.

□ **Emperor:** Large, round, red to purplish black grapes with small seeds. The grapes have a mild cherry taste and grow in large full clusters.

□ **Exotic:** Beautiful, black grapes with shiny, plump skins. The grapes are crisp with a mild flavor.

□ **Flame Seedless:** Slender bunches of oval, purplish red grapes. They have a crunchy bite and taste mildly sweet with a touch of tartness.

□ **Muscat:** Very large, yellow-green grapes with a heady, winy flavor. Usually considered wine grapes, muscats also are a favorite for serving with cheese.

□ **Ribier:** Large, purple to blue-black grapes. These plump grapes have seeds and a mild flavor.

□ **Thompson Seedless:** Olive-shaped, green grapes. They are light, sweet, and seedless, and one of the most widely available varieties.

□ **Tokay:** Large, round, red grapes that grow in tightly packed bunches. Tokays have seeds and a mild flavor and crisp texture.

Market forms: You can purchase grapes fresh or canned. White, purple, and red grape juice comes canned, bottled, and in frozen concentrate form. Sparkling (carbonated) grape juice also is available. Dried grapes, in the form of light or dark raisins, are made from Thompson seedless or muscat grapes.

Selecting: Look for plump, fresh grapes without bruises, mold, or soft spots and with good color for the variety. Grapes often have a frosty white cast or bloom. The bloom is typical and does not affect quality.

Storing: Grapes are good keepers if stored in plastic bags in the crisper of your refrigerator. Store for up to 1 week.

Nutrition information: Ten grapes have between 15 and 36 calories, depending on the type of grape.

(See also *Raisin*.)

Grapefruit A somewhat round, yellow- to pink-skinned citrus fruit with sweet-tart, tangy meat that grows in even sections within the peel. Larger than an orange, a grapefruit is less sweet but is just as versatile.

Types: Most grapefruit is classified as either white or red. White grapefruit has honey-colored meat and bright yellow skin. Red grapefruit, also called ruby or pink grapefruit, has pink meat with a ruby blush to the skin. Red grapefruit tastes similar to white grapefruit. Either type can be seeded or seedless.

A *Pummelo*, also known as a Chinese grapefruit, is a different type of citrus fruit that looks like a jumbo version of yellow-skinned grapefruit. It has thick skin, yellow to red fruit, and a sweet-tart taste.

Here are some grapefruit varieties you might see at the supermarket.

□ **White:** *Duncan* is a large, juicy, yellow grapefruit often tinged with green or russet. The *Marsh* varies in size and has a yellow rind with yellow fruit that is usually seedless. It is the most popular variety. *Oro Blanco*, a new sweeter variety of grapefruit, has a thick, yellow rind and pale yellow fruit.

□ **Red:** *Ruby Red* grapefruit is juicy with deep pink flesh and yellow skin with a red blush. It comes with or without seeds. *Thompson*, also called Pink Marsh, has yellow skin with flesh that is pink, juicy, and sweet.

Market forms: Grapefruit is available fresh, canned, and refrigerated in jars. Grapefruit juice is available in cans, bottles, and frozen concentrate.

continued

Grapefruits

White

Red

Pummelo

Selecting: Juicy grapefruits will be heavy for their size, with full-colored skins and even, rounded shapes, usually with flattened ends. Avoid bruised or softened fruit.

A Tip from Our Kitchen
Use a grapefruit knife (a small, curved paring knife) to remove individual sections from the shell or to hollow out grapefruit so the shells can be used as serving containers.

(See *Citrus Fruit* for the Selecting Citrus Fruit chart and storing and nutrition information.)

Grate   To rub food across a grating surface to make very fine pieces. Spices such as nutmeg, vegetables, and hard cheeses are grated.

Q. **What's the difference between grating and shredding?**

A. The difference is the appearance of the product you get. If you want short or fine pieces, such as grated Parmesan cheese, use a grater. It has tiny punched holes and rough, irregular edges. However, if you want longer strips of food of varying widths, such as citrus peel or cheddar cheese, use a shredder. It has medium to large holes or slits with smooth edges.

Gravy   A sauce containing meat or poultry juices that is thickened with flour, cornstarch, or another thickening agent. Gravy is served over meats, poultry, or other foods, such as potatoes. Pan gravy is a type of gravy made by stirring the flour or cornstarch directly into the fat in the pan. Other gravies are made by combining the flour or cornstarch with a cold liquid, such as milk or water, before stirring it into the fat and juices.

A Tip from Our Kitchen

For a smoother gravy, be sure the flour or cornstarch is thoroughly mixed with the fat or with the cold liquid before cooking. Then cook and stir constantly until the gravy thickens.

Gravy

- 2 cups liquid (pan drippings from cooked meat *or* poultry, *or* chicken broth *or* beef broth)
- 3 tablespoons margarine, butter, *or* fat from drippings
- ¼ cup all-purpose flour *or* 2 tablespoons cornstarch
- ¼ teaspoon onion salt
- ¼ teaspoon dried thyme, basil, leaf sage, *or* marjoram, crushed (optional)
- ⅛ teaspoon garlic powder
- ⅛ teaspoon pepper

■ If using pan drippings, remove meat or poultry from the pan in which it was cooked. Pour pan drippings into a large measuring cup, scraping out the browned bits in the bottom of the pan. Skim fat, reserving 3 tablespoons, if desired. (To skim fat, tilt measuring cup, and spoon off the oily liquid that rises to the top.) Discard remaining fat. Measure drippings. If necessary, add to drippings enough *chicken broth, beef broth, water, or milk* to equal *2 cups* liquid.
■ In a medium saucepan melt the margarine or butter, or use reserved fat from drippings. Stir in flour or cornstarch; onion salt; herb, if desired; garlic powder; and pepper till combined. Add the 2 cups reserved liquid all at once. Cook and stir over medium heat till mixture is thickened and bubbly. Cook and stir for 1 to 2 minutes more. Makes 2 cups (8 to 10 servings).

Nutrition information per serving: 63 calories, 2 g protein, 3 g carbohydrate, 5 g fat (1 g saturated), 0 mg cholesterol, 294 mg sodium, 60 mg potassium.

Grease

To coat a utensil, such as a baking pan or skillet, with a thin layer of shortening, margarine, butter, cooking oil, or another fat to keep food from sticking.

The term also refers to the fat released from meat or poultry during cooking.

Grill

To cook food by direct or indirect heat either on a barbecue grill or on a griddle with little, if any, fat, producing food with a browned surface (see also *Barbecue*).

The word also refers to a piece of cooking equipment that consists of a rack or grid over a heat source. A grill can be heated by charcoal, gas, or electricity.

Grind

To mechanically cut a food into small pieces. Most grinding is done with a food grinder or food processor.

Ground Beef

A term used to describe types of meat ground from beef. Usually made by grinding less tender beef cuts with fat trimmings, ground beef is sometimes referred to as hamburger.

Ground beef is a popular meat because of its convenience, versatility, and relatively low cost. It is the main ingredient in a variety of popular dishes, including burgers, tacos, meat loaf, meatballs, and casseroles.

Types: The types of ground beef and the way it is sold vary from store to store. For years, ground beef has been categorized into ground round, ground sirloin, ground chuck, and hamburger or ground beef. When meat is labeled in this manner, it is meat ground from the corresponding cut of beef, with ground beef or hamburger being ground from a combination of cuts.

But because the taste of ground beef depends more on the amount of fat than on the cut used, much of the ground beef now is labeled according to the fat content. The label may state as a percentage either the amount of lean meat or the amount of fat in the meat.

continued

For instance, one store may label a package as 85 percent lean, while another may label the same meat as 15 percent fat. Some stores state both the origin of the beef and the fat content.

Market forms: Ground beef almost always is sold fresh, although some is sold frozen. Some frozen beef is sold preformed in patties for burgers.

Selecting: If the fat content isn't listed on the label, visually judge the fat content. Look for the amount of white fat mixed with the red meat. The lighter the color, the more fat the meat contains. Avoid ground beef that has gray or brown patches and any off-odors.

Storing: See the Storing Meat chart under *Meat*.

Preparation hints: Handle ground beef as little as possible before and during cooking. Use a light touch when shaping, and avoid pressing out juices when cooking.

When browning ground beef for skillet dishes or soups, break up the meat for even browning, then drain off fat before adding other ingredients.

How to cook: For broiling and panbroiling ground-meat patties, see the Broiling Meat and the Panbroiling and Panfrying Meat charts under *Meat*. For grilling directions, see the Direct-Grilling Meat chart under *Barbecue*.

Is It Done?

Ground-meat patties with no other ingredients added should be cooked at least till their centers are brownish pink (medium doneness). Ground-meat patties and meat loaves with additional ingredients, such as eggs, bread crumbs, onions, or liquid, should be cooked to 170° or till no pink remains. Check for doneness by cutting into a patty or the loaf to see that the inside color of the meat is brown, or check the temperature of baked loaf with a meat thermometer.

Q: What type of ground beef is best for making burgers?
A: Because shrinkage is greater when meat is fatty, choose a leaner ground beef, such as ground round or ground sirloin. Burgers and meat loaves are more attractive when shrinkage is minimal. Also, avoid overcooking the meat.

Nutrition hints: When you're trying to cut calories and reduce fat in your diet, select ground beef that's 85 percent to 90 percent lean. If you have to use meat with a little higher fat content, be sure to thoroughly drain off any fat that cooks out of the meat. You can drain crumbled, cooked ground beef in a colander, blotting the meat with a paper towel to absorb clinging grease.

Nutrition information: A 3-ounce serving of 85-percent lean ground beef, cooked, has about 205 calories and 12 grams of fat.

Gruyère Cheese *(groo YEHR)* An

ivory-colored, firm-bodied cheese with a mild nutty flavor that is similar to, but more sharp-flavored than, Swiss cheese (see also *Swiss Cheese*). Switzerland and France are the major producers of this cow's-milk cheese, but it also is manufactured in the United States.

Types: Gruyère is marketed in two forms.
☐ **Natural:** A firm, naturally ripened cheese with a more pronounced flavor than Swiss. It forms few, if any, holes during its long aging process.

Gruyère cheese

☐ **Process:** A blend of natural Gruyère and Emmentaler (a type of Swiss) cheeses that is processed, shaped, and wrapped in foil.

Q: Can Gruyere and Swiss cheese be used interchangeably?

A: Yes. In most instances, the cheeses can be substituted for each other. Gruyère and Swiss sometimes are combined in dishes for a blend of flavors. Both are good for cooking and are perfect for sauces, casseroles, quiches, soufflés, and Swiss fondue (see also *Fondue*).

(See *Cheese* for the Selecting Cheese chart and selecting, storing, serving, nutrition, and other information.)

Guavas

Guacamole *(gwahk uh MOH lee)*
A well-seasoned Mexican dish made from mashed avocado, lemon or lime juice, onion, and sometimes tomato and chili peppers. It can range from mild to fiery hot and is served as an appetizer with tortilla chips, as a salad on lettuce, or as a garnish for Mexican dishes.

Guava
An oval, tropical fruit with yellow to green skin and meat that ranges from off-white to red. Guavas have tiny edible seeds and a taste reminiscent of pineapple and lemon. Very similar to feijoas in taste and appearance, guavas are botanically different. Guavas range from 1 to 4 inches in diameter.

Guavas can be eaten fresh, but are more popular in the United States when made into a jelly.

Selecting: Guavas generally are available most of the year except in early spring. Left to ripen on trees until they fall, most guavas found in supermarkets will be ripe and ready to eat. Don't purchase any guava that is overly soft or has bruises.

Storing: If necessary, ripen guavas at room temperature until they are slightly soft and fragrant. Then refrigerate them for up to 1 week.

Nutrition information: There are about 45 calories in a medium guava.

Guinea Hen
A small domestic bird that has a dressed weight of about 2 to 3 pounds and is all dark meat.

Because the meat from a guinea hen is leaner than the meat from a chicken, guinea hen can dry out easily. So, don't overcook it. Guinea hen is best prepared by roasting, frying, or broiling. Allow about 1 to 1½ pounds per serving.

Nutrition information: A 3-ounce serving of roasted guinea hen without skin and bones has about 140 calories and 3 grams of fat.

(See *Poultry* for selecting, refrigerating, freezing, thawing, cooking, and other information.)

Gumbo
A thick Cajun stew made from a variety of ingredients that can include seafood, meat, sausage, and vegetables. Poultry often is added. Gumbo usually starts with a roux and has okra or filé powder added (see also *Filé Powder* and *Roux*). It frequently is served with rice. (For a gumbo recipe, see page 201.)

Gumbo

Gumbo

- 1 pound fresh *or* frozen fish fillets
- 1 pound fresh *or* frozen shrimp in shells
- ½ cup all-purpose flour
- ½ cup cooking oil
- 1 large onion, chopped (1 cup)
- 2 stalks celery, chopped (1 cup)
- 1 medium green pepper, chopped (¾ cup)
- 6 cloves garlic, minced
- 6 cups chicken broth
- 2 cups sliced okra *or* one 10-ounce package frozen cut okra
- 3 bay leaves
- 1 teaspoon dried oregano, crushed
- 1 teaspoon dried thyme, crushed
- 1 teaspoon dried basil, crushed
- ½ teaspoon salt
- ½ teaspoon ground red pepper
- ¼ teaspoon ground black pepper
- 1 pound andouille *or* smoked sausage, cut into ½-inch-thick slices
- 2 to 4 teaspoons filé powder (optional)
- 4 cups hot cooked rice

■ Thaw fish and shrimp, if frozen. Remove skin from fish, if present; cut fish into 1-inch pieces. Peel and devein shrimp. Rinse. Chill the fish and shrimp in the refrigerator till ready to use.

■ In a heavy Dutch oven stir together flour and oil till smooth. Cook over medium-low heat, *stirring constantly,* about 35 minutes or till a dark reddish brown roux forms. Add onion, celery, green pepper, and garlic. Cook and stir over medium heat for 10 to 15 minutes or till vegetables are very tender. Gradually stir in chicken broth. Stir in fresh or frozen okra, bay leaves, oregano, thyme, basil, salt, red pepper, and black pepper. Bring to boiling. Reduce heat and simmer, covered, about 1 hour.

■ Add sausage and simmer 10 minutes. Add fish and shrimp. Simmer about 5 minutes more or till fish flakes easily with a fork. Stir once. Discard bay leaves and spoon off fat. Season each serving to taste with filé powder, if desired. Serve with rice. Makes 8 servings.

Nutrition information per serving: 541 calories, 30 g protein, 44 g carbohydrate, 27 g fat (6 g saturated), 106 mg cholesterol, 1,181 mg sodium, 652 mg potassium.

Gumdrop A chewy, sugar-coated candy with a gelatinous texture. Commercial gumdrops are traditionally shaped like flat-nosed cones, but they are available in other shapes. Gumdrops can be made at home, using pectin for their chewy structure. Homemade gumdrops, which are cut into squares, have a more delicate texture than the commercial ones. They can be cinnamon-, mint-, orange-, or lemon-flavored.

Q: **What's the best way to store gumdrops so they don't get sticky?**
A: Store gumdrops loosely covered so their surfaces remain dry. Moisture makes the sugar coating soft and sticky.

A Tip from Our Kitchen
If a recipe calls for chopped gumdrops (in a cookie recipe, for instance), snip the gumdrops into small pieces with kitchen scissors. Dip the scissor blades into cold water if they get sticky.

Haddock A lean, saltwater fish belonging to the cod family and averaging 2 to 5 pounds. Haddock has delicately flavored, firm, white flesh that flakes easily.

Market forms: Haddock most commonly is marketed as fillets, either fresh, frozen, or smoked.

Haddock costs more than other cod family members, so be sure you're getting what
continued

you're paying for by looking for haddock's characteristic black stripe on the skin.

Depending on the size of the fish, haddock also can be sold by other names. For example, *Scrod* is the term for a young haddock (or cod) that weighs less than 2½ pounds. *Finnan Haddie* is the market name for split, salted, smoked haddock fillets.

How to cook: Try baking, broiling, poaching, or micro-cooking haddock. For cooking directions, see the Cooking Fish chart under *Fish*.

Nutrition information: A 3-ounce serving of baked haddock has about 95 calories.

(See *Fish* for selecting, storing, thawing, and other information.)

Halibut   A saltwater fish that is the largest member of the flatfish family. Halibut has a delicate flavor and firm, white flesh.

Market forms: Halibut steaks are sold fresh or frozen. The fillets of these fish are usually so large that they're cut into smaller pieces or chunks and sold fresh or frozen. The small pieces and strips of fish also are sold dried or smoked.

How to cook: Popular ways to prepare halibut include baking, grilling, poaching, and broiling. For baking, poaching, and broiling directions, see the Cooking Fish chart under *Fish*. For grilling directions, see the Direct-Grilling Fish chart under *Barbecue*.

Nutrition information: A 3-ounce serving of baked halibut has about 120 calories.

(See *Fish* for selecting, storing, thawing, and other information.)

Ham   Meat from the hind leg of a hog. It may be fresh but usually is cured and smoked. Cured ham is rosy pink to red, with a flavor that ranges from salty to slightly sweet.

Although other parts of the hog may be cured and smoked, they cannot be called ham. For example, the same cut from the front leg is called picnic or Callie. While picnics may look somewhat similar to ham, they are not the same; picnics have more bone. Check the label to see what you're buying.

Processing: The salty flavor of ham comes from the salt used to cure the meat. After curing, most hams are smoked. Hams are suspended in the smokehouse over hardwood fires that cook and impart a smoky flavor to the meat. Processing for most hams ends here, but a few are aged for several months to a year or more. Reserved for specialty regional and European hams, such as Westphalian and prosciutto, aging intensifies flavor but increases the cost.

Some hams labeled "water-added" weigh more than they did before curing. The added water cannot be more than 10 percent of the fresh uncured ham's weight. Water is added for moistness and juiciness.

Market forms: Before you head for the store to select your next ham, take a look at some of these types of ham you're likely to see.
☐ **Bone-In:** A traditional pear-shaped ham that has at least part of the shank bone present. Bone-in hams sometimes are sold whole, but they more commonly are available cut into halves or rump or shank portions, and as center-cut slices (sometimes called ham steaks). Whole hams weigh from 10 to 18 pounds.
☐ **Semi-Boneless:** A ham with the shank and hipbone removed, leaving only the round leg bone.
☐ **Boneless:** A ham with the bone, outside skin, and fat removed that is shaped by placing it into a casing or a can before processing.

☐ **Sectioned and Formed:** A ham that is shaped from whole boneless ham muscles of several cured hams, then packaged in a casing or can.

☐ **Canned:** A boneless piece of ham that is fully cooked during processing. Canned hams are sold with or without a glaze.

☐ **Boiled, Cooked, or Baked:** A boneless, formed ham that has been simmered, steamed, or slowly baked. Buy it prepackaged or sliced to order.

☐ **Country or Country-Style:** A dry-cured ham that often is smoked, then aged. Country hams usually are saltier and firmer than other hams and need to be cooked before eating. (See question and answer, below right.) Named for the city or locality where they are processed, some well-known country hams are Smithfield, Virginia, Kentucky, and Tennessee.

Ham cuts: See the ham identification photos under *Pork* for some of the various retail cuts.

Bone-in hams often are divided into rump and shank portions. Expect to pay a little more for the rump half because it is cut from the meatier upper leg. The shank or lower part of the leg has more bone and tendons.

Selecting: If the ham is packaged so you can see the meat, look for a finely grained texture and a rosy pink color. (Country hams vary from pale pink to wine red.) Press the ham; it should be firm not spongy. Iridescence on the meat's surface is usually a result of curing agents reacting with air and light and has no effect on quality.

Most hams are labeled "fully cooked." They have been cooked during processing and are ready to eat with or without further heating. Some hams are labeled "cook before eating." Before serving, these hams need to be cooked to an internal temperature of 160°.

Storing: A ham slice can be stored in the coldest part of the refrigerator for up to 4 days. For a ham half, see the Storing Meat chart under *Meat.*

Storing Canned Hams

Though they are fully cooked inside the vacuum-sealed cans, most canned hams are still perishable and require refrigeration. Some of the smallest hams and some imported hams may be stored safely on the shelf, but read the label to be sure. If in doubt, store the ham in the refrigerator. Read can labels for storage times.

How to cook: When it comes to ham, the terms baking and roasting are used interchangeably. To bake fully cooked ham, heat it to an internal temperature of 140°. A cook-before-eating ham should be roasted to 160°. Be sure to remove the paper casing, if present, before roasting.

For roasting (baking), broiling, and panbroiling directions, see the Roasting Meat, the Broiling Meat, and the Panbroiling and Panfrying Meat charts under *Meat*. For grilling directions, see the Direct-Grilling Meat and the Indirect-Grilling Meat charts under *Barbecue*.

Q: **Does country ham have to be prepared differently than other hams?**

A: Yes. For many cook-before-eating country hams, you need to allow up to a day to prepare them for baking. The ham must be scrubbed, soaked for several hours, simmered, and skinned before baking. For best results, follow the label directions that accompany the ham.

Nutrition information: A 3-ounce serving of roasted cured ham (trimmed) has about 135 calories and 1,130 milligrams sodium.

(See *Meat* for Using a Meat Thermometer and other information.)

Hamburger A flat, round patty made from ground meat, primarily beef, and served with assorted condiments on a flat, round bun. These meat patties also are referred to as burgers. It is also the name that's sometimes given to ground beef.

Hard Sauce A sweet, creamy mixture of margarine or butter, powdered sugar, and a flavoring, such as vanilla, rum, or brandy. It usually is served chilled over a warm dessert, such as plum pudding.

Hartshorn Powder A compound once used as a leavening agent. It also is known as baker's ammonia and most often is used in foreign recipes, especially Danish baking. Look for hartshorn powder at a pharmacy.

Harvard Beets A deep crimson, New England dish of sliced or diced cooked beets served in a vinegar-and-sugar sauce.

Harvard Beets

    4 medium beets *or* one 16-ounce can
        sliced *or* diced beets
    2 tablespoons sugar
    2 tablespoons vinegar
    2 teaspoons cornstarch
    1 tablespoon margarine *or* butter

■ In a medium saucepan cook fresh whole beets, covered, in boiling water for 40 to 50 minutes or till tender. Drain, reserving ⅓ *cup* liquid. Cool slightly. Slip off skins and slice or cut into ½-inch cubes. (*Or,* drain canned beets, reserving ⅓ *cup* liquid.)
■ In a medium saucepan combine reserved liquid, sugar, vinegar, and cornstarch. Cook and stir till thickened and bubbly. Cook and stir for 2 minutes more. Stir in beets and margarine. Heat through. Makes 4 servings.

Microwave directions: Prick fresh whole beets. In a 1½-quart microwave-safe casserole, micro-cook beets and 2 tablespoons *water,* covered, on 100% power (high) for 10 to 12 minutes or till tender, rearranging once. Drain, reserving ¼ *cup* liquid. Cool slightly. Slip off skins; slice or cut into ½-inch cubes. (*Or,* drain canned beets, reserving ¼ *cup* liquid.)
■ In the 1½-quart casserole, combine reserved liquid, sugar, vinegar, and cornstarch. Cook, uncovered, on high for 1 to 2 minutes or till thickened and bubbly, stirring every 30 seconds. Stir in beets and margarine. Cook on high for 2 to 3 minutes or till heated through.

Nutrition information per serving: 69 calories, 1 g protein, 11 g carbohydrate, 3 g fat (1 g saturated), 0 mg cholesterol, 58 mg sodium, 165 mg potassium.

Hash A mixture of meats, vegetables, and seasonings cooked slowly in a skillet till browned and crusty. Traditionally, hash was served as a way to use up leftover corned or roast beef and potatoes. Corned beef hash also is available canned.

Hazelnut The nut grown on the bushy hazel shrub or oriental hazel tree. Hazelnuts, also known as filberts, have a hard, helmet-shaped, reddish brown shell. This smooth shell has a light-colored cap. The small, round, pale gold nut, with its mild, sweet flavor, may be covered with a thin brown skin.

Hazelnuts (Filberts)

Storing: Unshelled hazelnuts will last for 6 months in a cool, dry place. Refrigerate shelled nuts in an airtight container for up to a month or freeze them for up to 6 months.

(See *Nut* for the Selecting Nuts chart and selecting, nutrition, and other information.)

Harvard Beets

Head Cheese

Head Cheese A type of sausage made from the meat from the head of a hog. It is chopped, cured, and seasoned; then the mixture is formed into a jellied loaf with a pink and white mosaic pattern. Head cheese usually is served cold as a luncheon meat.

Nutrition information: A 1-ounce slice of head cheese contains 60 calories.

Heart of Palm The cream-colored interior of a young palm tree that usually is grown in Florida and tropical countries. Sometimes called swamp cabbage, hearts of palm look like thick stalks of white asparagus. They have a silky texture and a delicate flavor reminiscent of artichokes. You can find them canned in supermarkets.

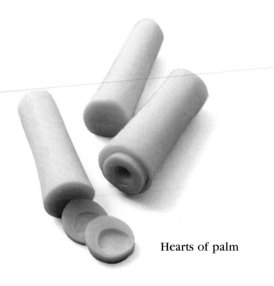

Hearts of palm

Herb *(urb)* The leaves of plants and shrubs with nonwoody stems. Herbs flavor, color, and give an appealing aroma to foods. Some plants, such as coriander and dill, give us both an herb and a spice (see also *Spice*).

Market forms: Parsley used to be the only fresh herb you would see in the supermarket, but today a great many herbs—either potted or cut—are available year-round. The majority of herbs used in cooking are dried—and sold in leaf or ground form.
☐ **Fresh:** Basil, chives, cilantro, marjoram, mint, oregano, parsley, sage, and thyme are some that can be purchased.
☐ **Dried Leaf:** Basil, bay leaf, chervil, chives, cilantro, dillweed, marjoram, mint, oregano, parsley, rosemary, sage, savory, tarragon, and thyme are available.
☐ **Ground:** Marjoram, oregano, sage, savory, and thyme are available.

Selecting: When purchasing fresh herbs, look for leaves that look fresh and have no brown spots. When buying dried herbs, select small containers so you can use up the herbs within a year.

Q: Is it possible to dry or freeze fresh herbs at home?
A: You can do either. First rinse and pat the herbs dry with paper towels.

To dry fresh herbs, hang them in bunches, upside down by the stem, in a dry, warm spot out of direct sunlight. Be sure air circulates freely around the bunches of herbs. Let the herbs dry till the leaves are brittle, usually a few days to a week, depending on the thickness of the leaves. Then pick off the leaves and discard the stems. Store the dried leaves in tightly covered containers.

To freeze fresh herbs, place them in plastic freezer containers or bags. (Remove the stems from herbs such as basil, sage, mint, oregano, and parsley before freezing the leaves.) Expect frozen herbs to discolor some. When you're ready to use them, there's no need to thaw them. Just add the frozen herbs to the food you are cooking.

Storing: Fresh herbs are highly perishable, so purchase them only as you need them. For short-term storage, immerse the freshly cut stems in water about 2 inches deep. Cover the leaves loosely and refrigerate for several days. A plastic bag or plastic wrap makes a good covering.

For dried herbs, mark each container with the date of purchase; after a year, discard any of the remaining herb. Keep dried herbs in tightly covered, lightproof containers in a cool, dry place—not above your range. Heat, moisture, and light all rob herbs of flavor.

One way to crush dried leaf herbs is to place them in the bottom of a mortar or small bowl. Use a pestle or the back of a spoon to crush the leaves.

Q: **Is there a way to tell if a dried herb is still fresh?**

A: If you're in doubt, just crush a small amount of the herb in the palm of your hand. The aroma should be full-bodied. If the aroma is weak, discard the herb and invest in a fresh supply. Also, if the herb looks faded and straw colored, the flavor may be weakened.

Preparation hints: When using fresh herbs, finely snip the leaves beforehand. When using a dried herb, measure it first, then crush it in the palm of your hand, between your fingers, or with a mortar and pestle to release the aromatic oils. (If you're using your own dried whole herbs, crush them slightly before measuring.)

Cooking hints: Fresh and dried herbs complement just about every dish in your recipe collection—from soups and salads to pickles and jellies. If you're experimenting with fresh herbs, start by adding about 1 teaspoon of the herb for each 4 servings. If you want a stronger flavor, add more of the herb gradually, tasting as you go, until you're satisfied. Add whole herbs such as bay leaves at the beginning of long, slow cooking periods to draw out more flavor.

Nutrition information: In today's health-conscious world, you can use herbs with abandon. They contain virtually no calories, sodium, or fat.

A Tip from Our Kitchen

You can have the wonderful fragrance and flavor of fresh herbs at your fingertips if you grow them at home. Just save a spot in your garden—or on your windowsill. Herbs thrive in most any well-drained soil and demand little more than sun and water. Fresh herbs make beautiful garnishes on everything from main dishes to desserts.

Herb Substitutions

When your herb garden is flourishing in midsummer, try substituting fresh herbs for dried—just triple the amount of dried leaf herb called for in the recipe. For example, if a recipe uses 1 teaspoon dried herb, add 1 tablespoon fresh.

Work in reverse when you're substituting a dried leaf herb for fresh because dried herbs have a more concentrated flavor. Use about one-third of the amount that the recipe suggests.

When you're substituting ground herbs for dried leaf herbs, use about half the amount called for.

For suggestions on replacing one herb with another, see the Herb Alternative Guide, page 208.

continued

Herb Alternative Guide

Whether you're making an emergency substitution or experimenting with a new flavor, follow these suggestions for herb alternatives. Some of the suggestions are similar flavors, and others are acceptable flavor alternatives. As a general rule, start with *half of the amount* the recipe calls for (unless directed otherwise), and add the herb till it suits your taste.

Basil: oregano *or* thyme
Chervil: tarragon *or* parsley
Chive: green onion; onion; *or* leek
Cilantro: parsley
Italian Seasoning: blend of any of these: basil, oregano, rosemary, and ground red pepper
Marjoram: basil; thyme; *or* savory
Mint: basil; marjoram; *or* rosemary
Oregano: thyme *or* basil
Parsley: chervil *or* cilantro
Poultry Seasoning: sage plus a blend of any of these: thyme, marjoram, savory, black pepper, and rosemary
Red Pepper: dash bottled hot pepper sauce *or* black pepper
Rosemary: thyme; tarragon; *or* savory
Sage: poultry seasoning; savory; marjoram; *or* rosemary
Savory: thyme; marjoram; *or* sage
Tarragon: chervil; dash fennel seed; *or* dash aniseed
Thyme: basil; marjoram; oregano; *or* savory

Hermit   A chewy, spicy cookie flavored with brown sugar, cinnamon, nutmeg, and cloves. Sometimes raisins and nuts are added. Hermits can be either drop or bar cookies.

Herring   A saltwater fish with a soft texture and flavorful dark meat that's high in fat. Herring is sometimes called sea herring; it is not related to lake herring.

Types: The two most important commercial types of herring are Atlantic and Pacific herring. Their average length is 9 to 11 inches. Small, young herring are sold as *Sardines* (see also *Sardine*). The largest member of the herring family is *Shad*, which has lighter, sweeter meat. The *Alewife*, or *Spring* herring, is sold pickled or smoked.

Market forms: Although herring is available fresh and frozen in the United States, there isn't much demand for these forms. The most popular forms are canned products. For example, pickled herring is chunks of herring in a vinegar mixture. Two cured products, bloater and kipper, also are available.

Nutrition information: Herring is higher in calories than most fish—about 170 calories, with 10 grams of fat, in 3 ounces cooked. Pickled herring has about 40 calories, with 3 grams of fat, in a small piece weighing about ½ ounce.

Hickory Nut   The fruit of an American tree that grows wild in woods and forests. Hickory nuts have a round, paneled, light tan shell. The nut itself looks like a miniature pecan and has a rich, oily flavor.

(See *Nut* for selecting, nutrition, and other information.)

Hickory nuts

High-Altitude Cooking   Methods

of food preparation that are necessary at altitudes of more than 3,000 feet above sea level. Because of lower atmospheric pressure at higher altitudes, foods react differently when cooked. For example, water boils at a lower temperature so foods cooked in water will take longer to cook. Foods also dry out more quickly. These differences require that adjustments be made to recipes.

Q: Where can I get more information on cooking at high altitudes?

A: Contact your county extension agent or write: Colorado State University, Bulletin Room, Fort Collins, CO 80523. You also can call 303/491-7334.

Cake Adjustments

If you live more than 3,000 feet above sea level, use this chart to adjust the cake ingredients listed. Try the smaller amounts first, then make any necessary adjustments on your next cake.

Ingredient	3,000 Feet	5,000 Feet	7,000 Feet
Liquid: Add for each cup	1 to 2 table-spoons	2 to 4 table-spoons	3 to 4 table-spoons
Baking powder: Decrease for each teaspoon	⅛ tea-spoon	⅛ to ¼ tea-spoon	¼ tea-spoon
Sugar: Decrease for each cup	0 to 1 table-spoon	0 to 2 table-spoons	1 to 3 table-spoons

High-Altitude Adjustments

For the best results, experiment with ingredient amounts and recipe timings to find the right balance for your location. Be sure to measure carefully and keep track of the amounts you use and results you achieve each time you cook.

General hints

- When cooking foods in boiling liquid on the range top or in the microwave oven, increase the cooking time. Also, you may need to increase the liquid.
- Deep-fat fry foods at a lower temperature for a longer time. Lower the temperature of the fat 3 degrees for each 1,000 feet above sea level you live.
- Dried beans and peas take much longer to cook than at sea level and usually require more cooking liquid.
- Items made by just adding boiling water, such as rice, potatoes, and cereals, may need a short cooking time in addition to boiling the water.

Baking or roasting

- Meat, poultry, fish, and game may need to be roasted longer than the times listed on sea level roasting charts. Use a thermometer to check for doneness.
- For cakes and cookies, increase the oven temperature 20° to 25° and decrease the baking time slightly.
- For cakes that contain a large amount of fat or chocolate, you may need to reduce the shortening by 1 to 2 tablespoons and add an egg to prevent the cake from falling.
- The liquid, leavening, and sugar in cakes may need adjustment. See the Cake Adjustments chart, above.
- Allow yeast doughs to rise according to recipe directions, checking rising time early. Then punch the dough down and let the dough rise one extra time before shaping the dough. If a yeast dough seems dry, add more liquid or reduce the amount of flour the next time you make the recipe.
- For angel food cakes, beat the egg whites only to *soft* peaks rather than stiff peaks.

Hollandaise Sauce *(HALL uhn dayz)* A rich, slightly lemony, golden yellow sauce made with margarine or butter, egg yolks, and lemon juice. This classic sauce is served warm with a variety of foods, including vegetables, poultry, fish, and eggs.

Because eating uncooked or slightly cooked eggs may be harmful due to possible bacterial contamination, we no longer recommend the blender or food processor method of making hollandaise sauce. With this method, hot melted margarine or butter is emulsified with raw egg yolks in a blender or food processor and the mixture is not heated after combining. Because this process does not thoroughly cook the yolks, the sauce made by this method may pose a risk to some people (see Using Eggs Safely under *Egg).* Instead, use the recipe below when preparing hollandaise sauce.

Hollandaise Sauce

    ½ cup margarine *or* butter
    3 beaten egg yolks
    1 tablespoon water
    1 tablespoon lemon juice
       Dash salt
       Dash white pepper

■ Cut margarine or butter into thirds and bring it to room temperature. In the top of a double boiler, combine egg yolks, water, lemon juice, salt, and pepper. Add *one piece* of the margarine or butter. Place over *boiling* water (upper pan should not touch water). Cook, stirring rapidly, till margarine melts and sauce begins to thicken. Add the remaining margarine or butter, a piece at a time, stirring constantly. Cook and stir till sauce thickens (1 to 2 minutes). Remove from heat at once. Serve immediately with vegetables, poultry, fish, or eggs. Makes ¾ cup (twelve 1-tablespoon servings).

Microwave directions: In a 2-cup microwave-safe measure, combine margarine or butter, water, lemon juice, salt, and pepper. Micro-cook, uncovered, on 100% power (high) for 1 to 1½ minutes or till margarine melts. Stir. Place egg yolks in a microwave-safe bowl. Gradually add margarine mixture to egg yolks, beating constantly with a wire whisk till smooth. Cook, uncovered, on high for 30 to 45 seconds or till thickened, stirring every 10 seconds.

Nutrition information per tablespoon: 83 calories, 1 g protein, 0 g carbohydrate, 9 g fat (2 g saturated), 53 mg cholesterol, 102 mg sodium, 10 mg potassium.

Q: Can a curdled hollandaise sauce be saved?

A: Yes. As soon as you notice your sauce starting to curdle, add 1 to 2 tablespoons hot water to about ¾ cup of the sauce and beat vigorously till smooth. Repeat with any remaining sauce.

Hominy Dried corn with the hull and germ removed. Hominy has a slightly sweet, cornlike flavor. It usually is available cooked and canned, and sometimes you'll find dried hominy in specialty stores. (The dried hominy has to be soaked as dried beans do and cooked before using.) Hominy can be served as a vegetable side dish or as an ingredient in casseroles, stews, and soups.

Hominy that is ground is called grits or hominy grits. The cooked grits often are served as a thick cereal mixture. Hominy grits are popular in the South where they often appear on the breakfast table. Hominy grits come in regular, quick-cooking, and instant forms, and in white and yellow varieties.

Storing: Store dry hominy in an airtight container and canned hominy in a cool, dry place for up to a year. Keep hominy grits in an airtight container in a cool, dry place for up to 6 months.

How to cook: See the Cooking Grains chart under *Grain* for quick-cooking hominy grits.

Nutrition information: One-half cup of canned hominy has about 60 calories, and a ¾-cup serving of cooked, quick-cooking hominy grits contains about 100 calories.

Honey

A sweet, sticky substance produced by bees from floral nectar and stored as food. The honey is deposited in the waxy network of cells known as a honeycomb.

The flavor of honey depends on the flowers from which it is made and, to some degree, on location and climate. Most honey is made from clover, which gives the honey a very mild flavor. Other types of honey come from acacia, alfalfa, buckwheat, heather, orange, rosemary, sage, tupelo, and other floral sources. The color of honey may vary from pale yellow to amber.

Market forms: Honey is processed into various products.

☐ **Liquid:** The most familiar form. The honey is removed from the comb using a centrifuge. In addition, honey may be pasteurized to destroy yeasts, strained to remove debris and wax, and filtered to remove finer particles. It generally is clear and free of crystals and is sold in jars and plastic bottles.

☐ **Whipped or Spun:** Honey that is finely crystallized. Although all honey will crystallize in time, the crystallization of whipped or spun honey is controlled during processing so that it is spreadable at room temperature. Spun honey can be combined with other ingredients or flavors.

☐ **Comb:** Honey contained in the beeswax comb. It comes in squares or rounds and both the honey and comb can be eaten.

☐ **Chunk:** Pieces of comb honey cut to fit inside a container that is then filled with liquid honey.

Selecting: Check the label for the source of the honey, and look at the color. In general, the paler the honey is, the milder the flavor.

Storing: Keep honey at room temperature in a dry place for up to 1 year. Store comb or chunk honey at room temperature for up to 6 months.

Q: Can honey be substituted for granulated sugar in recipes?

A: Although recipes specially formulated to use honey produce the best results, honey can be substituted for sugar in some recipes. When making the substitution you'll have to do some experimenting, and here are some guidelines.

Substitute honey for up to one-half of the sugar. In baked goods, reduce the amount of liquid in the recipe by 2 tablespoons for each ½ cup of honey used. Add ¼ teaspoon baking soda for each ½ cup of honey in baked goods. Reduce the oven temperature by 25 degrees to prevent overbrowning of baked goods.

As Smooth as Honey

Honey that has become crystallized or cloudy can be made clear and smooth again. Place the jar of honey in a container of warm water, and occasionally stir the honey till the crystals dissolve. Change the warm water as necessary.

Nutrition information: One tablespoon of honey contains about 65 calories.

Honeydew A pale, smooth, round melon, with mildly sweet fruit and slender, beige seeds. Varieties may be green, gold, orange, or pink inside, with pastel-colored, waxy rinds. The rind may have a green cast when unripe but will change to a creamy white to pale yellow when ripe. The meat is juicy. Honeydews average 6 to 9 inches in diameter. Their aroma is sweet like honey.

(See *Melon* for the Selecting Melons chart and storing, preparation, nutrition, and other information.)

Honeydew

Hors d'Oeuvre *(or DERV)* A French term for small, hot or cold portions of savory food served as an appetizer. These tidbits usually are eaten as finger food or are served with toothpicks or on small, wooden skewers. Hors d'oeuvres can be made from many ingredients including seafood, meat, poultry, and vegetables.

Q: **How many hors d'oeuvres do you need per person for a party?**
A: When planning hors d'oeuvres, consider whether they'll be followed by a meal, and if so, how closely. If a meal follows closely, allow four or five per guest. If a late meal is planned, figure on six or seven per guest. When no meal follows, allow 10 to 12 per guest.

Horseradish The root of a plant of the mustard family that has a hot and pungent flavor. It commonly is used grated to season soups, sauces, and spreads.

This term also refers to a prepared mixture of ground horseradish, white vinegar, and seasonings that is used as a condiment and a recipe ingredient.

Market forms: Fresh horseradish root is available from fall through spring.

Prepared horseradish can be purchased year-round and can be found in jars in the refrigerated dairy case at supermarkets. Besides plain prepared horseradish, other types include horseradish colored with beet juice and horseradish sauce.

Horseradish

A Tip from Our Kitchen

When grating fresh horseradish root, avoid breathing deeply as you work. The fumes from grated horseradish can burn your eyes and nose.

Storing: Refrigerate unused horseradish root in a plastic bag for up to 3 weeks, or freeze it in a plastic freezer bag for up to 6 months.

Once opened, prepared horseradish loses its hotness and pungency and develops a bitter flavor. If you have leftover prepared horseradish that won't be used within 3 weeks, wrap it in small portions in plastic wrap. Then place the portions in a freezer bag and freeze for up to 6 months.

Nutrition information: One teaspoon of prepared horseradish has about 2 calories.

Hot Cross Bun

A small, round, tender yeast roll with the shape of a cross snipped into or frosted on the top. Traditionally served at Easter time, hot cross buns usually contain currants or raisins or candied fruits and peels.

Hot Cross Buns

    4   to 4½ cups all-purpose flour
    1   package active dry yeast
    ¾   teaspoon ground cinnamon
    ¼   teaspoon ground nutmeg
        Dash ground cloves
    ¾   cup milk
    ½   cup margarine *or* butter
    ⅓   cup sugar
    ½   teaspoon salt
    3   eggs
    ⅔   cup currants *or* raisins
    ¼   cup diced candied orange peel
        (optional)
    1   beaten egg white
    1   tablespoon water
        Powdered Sugar Icing

■ In a large mixing bowl stir together *2 cups* of the flour, the yeast, cinnamon, nutmeg, and cloves. In a medium saucepan heat and stir the milk, margarine or butter, sugar, and salt till warm (120° to 130°) and margarine or butter almost melts. Add to flour mixture along with the eggs. Beat with an electric mixer on low speed for 30 seconds, scraping bowl. Beat on high speed for 3 minutes. Using a spoon, stir in the currants or raisins, candied orange peel, if desired, and as much of the remaining flour as you can.
■ Turn out onto a lightly floured surface. Knead in enough remaining flour to make a moderately soft dough (3 to 5 minutes total). Shape into a ball. Place in a greased bowl, turning once. Cover and let rise in a warm place till double (about 1½ hours).
■ Punch dough down. Turn out onto a floured surface. Cover and let rest 10 minutes. Divide dough into 20 portions. Shape each portion into a smooth ball. Place balls 1½ inches apart on a greased baking sheet. Cover; let rise till nearly double (45 to 60 minutes).
■ Using a sharp knife, make a crisscross slash across the top of each bun. In a small mixing bowl combine the beaten egg white and water. Brush a mixture of egg white and water over rolls. Bake in a 375° oven for 12 to 15 minutes or till golden brown. Cool slightly. Drizzle the Powdered Sugar Icing into criss-cross slashes atop each bun. Serve warm. Makes 20.

Powdered Sugar Icing: In a small mixing bowl combine 1 cup sifted *powdered sugar,* ¼ teaspoon *vanilla,* and enough *milk* to make of drizzling consistency (1 to 2 tablespoons).

Nutrition information per serving: 196 calories, 4 g protein, 32 g carbohydrate, 6 g fat (1 g saturated), 33 mg cholesterol, 125 mg sodium, 107 mg potassium.

Hot Dog   See *Frankfurter.*

Hot Pepper Sauce

Any of several pungent sauces commercially made with fresh or dried hot peppers and vinegar or sherry. A drop or two of these potent sauces is all that's needed to flavor cocktails, gumbos, barbecue sauces, and other dishes.

Hull   The outer layer of nuts, seeds, and grains, or the inedible leaves and stems of some fruits, such as strawberries. The term also refers to removing the hull.

Hummus   *(HUM us)* A Middle Eastern dish consisting of cooked garbanzo beans (chick-peas) that are mashed and mixed with sesame oil, lemon juice, garlic, parsley, and sometimes soy sauce or mint. Hummus is served as an appetizer, often with pita bread.

Hush Puppy   A deep-fat-fried fritter or dumpling made from a cornmeal batter that often is served with fried fish. Popular in the South, this fritter supposedly got its name because it was used to quiet the dogs that barked during fish fries.

Ice   A frozen dessert made with fruit, water, and sweetener that is similar to sorbet and sherbet. Ice also refers to frozen water that is used to cool drinks and other foods. The term also means to spread baked goods with a thin frosting.

Ice Cream   A sweet, creamy, frozen dessert made with cream, sugar or sweetener, flavoring, and sometimes eggs or gelatin.

Types: You can make ice cream at home or purchase a variety of commercial products.
☐ **Homemade:** Ice cream made from a mixture that may or may not be cooked before freezing. If the ice-cream mixture contains eggs, it should be cooked before freezing.
☐ **Commercial:** Ice cream and similar products that are available in many different forms and flavors. Ice cream comes in pint, quart, half-gallon, and larger containers. Supermarkets also carry ice-cream bars, sandwiches, cones, and other specialty items.
   Regular ice cream has from 8 to 10 percent milk fat, and *premium* ice creams may have up to 20 percent milk fat. *Ice milk* has between 2 and 7 percent milk fat. *Mellorine* is similar to ice cream but has a vegetable or other fat used for part of the milk fat. There also are dietetic ice creams and nondairy frozen desserts.

Storing: To store commercial ice cream for more than a few days, place the carton in an airtight container or freezer bag to prevent it from drying out and absorbing flavors from other foods. Store homemade ice cream in a freezer container with a tight-fitting lid. Keep for up to 2 months in the freezer.

Nutrition information: A ½-cup portion of commercial vanilla ice cream contains about 135 calories and 7 grams of fat. If chocolate, fruit, or other flavoring is added, the calories and fat will vary.

No-Cook Vanilla Ice Cream

   3 **cups light cream** *or* **half and half**
1½ **cups sugar**
   1 **tablespoon vanilla**
   3 **cups whipping cream**

■ Mix light cream, sugar, and vanilla. Stir till sugar dissolves. Stir in whipping cream. Freeze in a 4- or 5-quart ice-cream freezer according to the manufacturer's directions. Makes 2 quarts (16 to 20 servings).

Nutrition information per serving: 285 calories, 2 g protein, 22 g carbohydrate, 22 g fat (14 g saturated), 78 mg cholesterol, 36 mg sodium, 93 mg potassium.

No-Cook Chocolate Ice Cream: Prepare No-Cook Vanilla Ice Cream as above, *except* reduce sugar to *1 cup.* Stir in 1 cup *chocolate-flavored syrup* before freezing.

Nutrition information per serving: 304 calories, 3 g protein, 27 g carbohydrate, 22 g fat (14 g saturated), 78 mg cholesterol, 51 mg sodium, 135 mg potassium.

No-Cook Strawberry Ice Cream: Prepare No-Cook Vanilla Ice Cream as above, *except* thaw one 10-ounce package *frozen sliced strawberries.* Finely crush the berries. Stir into cream mixture before freezing.

Nutrition information per serving: 302 calories, 2 g protein, 26 g carbohydrate, 22 g fat (14 g saturated), 78 mg cholesterol, 36 mg sodium, 110 mg potassium.

Tips for Making Ice Cream

When making ice cream or sherbet in an ice-cream maker, follow these tips for delicious results. (Also check the directions that came with the maker.)

● Chill the ice-cream mixture in the refrigerator for several hours before starting the freezing process. This cuts the freezing time so the ice cream will be smoother and have more volume.

● Under-fill the canister to no more than two-thirds capacity. This allows room for the ice-cream mixture to expand as air is beaten into it. The ice cream will be creamier and fluffier.

● Add layers of crushed ice and rock salt to the outer container, using about 1 cup of salt to 6 cups of ice.

● For electric models, follow the manufacturer's directions. For hand-crank models, turn the handle till there's a slight pull, then turn it at a steady pace. Continue until turning becomes difficult. It's important to add ice and salt occasionally as the ice melts.

● When the ice cream is finished, remove the ice to below the level of the can lid so no salty water can seep into the ice cream. Wipe the lid and the top of the can. Remove the lid and dasher.

● To ripen the ice cream, cover the canister with waxed paper, plastic wrap, or foil, and replace the lid. Plug the hole in the lid with a cork. Push the can back down into the ice. Pack additional layers of ice and salt into the freezer to cover the top of the can. Use 1 cup salt to 4 cups of ice (the higher proportion of salt will make the ice cream colder and harder). Cover the freezer with newspapers or a heavy cloth to keep it cold. The ice cream needs to stand for 4 hours to develop flavor and texture. Or, transfer it to a freezer container with a tight-fitting lid; then ripen the ice cream in a home freezer at least 4 hours.

Ice Milk A sweet, smooth, frozen dessert similar to ice cream. Ice milk contains less milk fat and milk solids and usually more sweetener than ice cream. Ice milk has between 2 and 7 percent milk fat. It is sold in both hard-frozen and soft-serve forms.

Nutrition information: A ½-cup serving of hard-frozen vanilla ice milk (about 4 percent fat) contains about 90 calories and 3 grams of fat. A ½-cup portion of soft-serve ice milk contains about 110 calories and 2 grams of fat.

Imitation A food product made to resemble or substitute for another product.

A Tip from Our Kitchen

Some imitations don't work the same as the real thing in certain recipes. For example, imitation cheese and imitation chocolate may melt and set up differently from the products they are meant to replace. If you wish to use imitation products in cooking, do a little experimenting. This way you won't be surprised by visual and textural differences in your finished dish.

Indian Pudding A dessert made with cornmeal, milk, molasses, and spices. The pudding's flavor is similar to pumpkin pie. Sliced apples sometimes are added.

Irish Soda Bread A traditional Irish bread leavened with baking soda. The round loaves have a slightly coarse texture. Buttermilk or sour milk often is an ingredient, along with currants or raisins and sometimes caraway seed.

Irish Stew A hearty lamb or mutton stew that contains vegetables such as potatoes, onions, and carrots. Traditionally, Irish stew has been called a "white" stew because the meat is not browned before it is simmered with the vegetables.

Irish Stew

    ¾ **pound lean boneless lamb, cut into**
         1-inch cubes
    2 **cups beef broth**
    ¼ **teaspoon salt**
    ¼ **teaspoon pepper**
    1 **bay leaf**
    4 **medium carrots, sliced ½ inch**
         thick
    3 **medium potatoes (1 pound), peeled**
         and quartered
    2 **medium onions, cut into wedges**
    ½ **teaspoon dried thyme, crushed**
    ½ **teaspoon dried basil, crushed**
    ½ **cup cold water**
    2 **tablespoons all-purpose flour**
         Snipped parsley

■ In a large saucepan or Dutch oven, combine lamb cubes, beef broth, salt, pepper, and bay leaf. Bring meat mixture to boiling; reduce heat. Cover and simmer for 30 minutes.
■ Skim fat off the meat mixture. Add carrot slices, potato pieces, onion wedges, thyme, and basil to meat mixture. Cover and simmer for 30 minutes more or till vegetables are tender. Discard bay leaf.
■ In a small bowl combine water and flour. Stir into meat mixture. Cook and stir till mixture is thickened and bubbly. Cook and stir for 1 minute more.
■ To serve, season to taste with salt and pepper. Sprinkle each serving with snipped parsley. Makes 6 servings.

Nutrition information per serving: 184 calories, 14 g protein, 24 g carbohydrate, 4 g fat (1 g saturated), 35 mg cholesterol, 416 mg sodium, 563 mg potassium.

Italian Bread A long, cylindrical loaf of chewy, crusty yeast bread with blunt ends. It has the same flavor and texture as French bread, but an Italian bread loaf is a little shorter and slightly fatter.

Convenience products: Loaves of ready-to-eat and brown-and-serve Italian bread are available in bakeries and supermarkets.

Nutrition information: One slice of Italian bread (¾ inch thick) has about 85 calories.

Italian Cooking The diverse cooking styles of southern and northern Italy, well known for such foods as pizza, antipasto, salami, Parmesan and mozzarella cheeses, spaghetti, manicotti (recipe opposite), and lasagna (see also *Lasagna*).

Cuisine highlights: Much of the appeal of Italian cooking lies in the quality and variety of its ingredients. Veal is the preferred meat, along with a large variety of fish and seafood, including halibut, shrimp, mussels, and squid. Basic ingredients include fresh tomatoes; mushrooms; beans; sweet peppers; sausages; herbs, such as basil and oregano; pine nuts; almonds; and pistachios.
 Italy also has some outstanding desserts. Prime among them are flavored ice, gelato, and ice cream (see also *Gelato*). The frozen classics spumoni and tutti-frutti are known around the world (see also *Spumoni* and *Tutti-Frutti*). Other famous sweets include zabaglione, zuppa inglese, and panettone (a Christmas fruit bread) (see also *Zabaglione* and *Zuppa Inglese*).

Southern and northern cooking: *Southern Italian* cooking is what many people in the United States think of as Italian food. It's characterized by hearty food that is highly seasoned with olive oil, garlic, and herbs. Macaroni and spaghetti, blanketed in seafood and tomato sauces, are very popular. The pastas come in all shapes and sizes.

Northern Italian cooking uses butter more often than olive oil, and makes greater use of cheese and milk than southern Italian cooking. Polenta, risotto, and fresh egg noodles are preferred over the pastas used in southern Italy (see also *Polenta* and *Risotto*). Seasoning is delicate with little use of garlic.

The cuisine of *central Italy,* which includes Rome, is a blend of both these cooking styles.

Local specialties: Some cities and regions in Italy are famous for distinctive dishes.

Naples in southern Italy is known for its fresh tomato marinara sauce. But its most significant contribution is pizza.

The *Lombardy* region of northern Italy specializes in osso buco and vegetable soups (see also *Osso Buco*). The fresh basil sauce called pesto comes from the city of *Genoa,* as do many sausages.

The *Emilia-Romagna* area of central Italy is the birthplace of Bolognese sauce (a meaty tomato sauce), Parmesan cheese, egg noodles, and mortadella sausages.

Rome claims fettuccine Alfredo (see also *Fettuccine*) and fried baby artichokes with garlic among many other dishes.

Spicy Cheese Manicotti

    8 manicotti shells
    ½ pound bulk Italian sausage
    ½ cup chopped onion
    2 cloves garlic, minced
    1 16-ounce can tomatoes,
        cut up
    1 8-ounce can tomato sauce
    1 teaspoon dried Italian seasoning,
        crushed
    ¼ teaspoon salt
    ⅛ teaspoon pepper
    2 beaten eggs
    2 cups shredded provolone cheese *or*
        mozzarella cheese (8 ounces)

 1¼ cups ricotta cheese *or* cream-style
        cottage cheese
    ½ cup grated Parmesan cheese
        (2 ounces)
    ¼ cup snipped parsley
    ½ teaspoon dried Italian seasoning,
        crushed
    ⅛ teaspoon ground red pepper

■ Cook manicotti shells according to package directions; drain. Rinse manicotti shells with cold water.

■ Meanwhile, for sauce, in a large skillet crumble the Italian sausage. Stir in onion and garlic. Cook sausage mixture till meat is browned and onion is tender. Drain off fat. Stir in *undrained* tomatoes, tomato sauce, the 1 teaspoon Italian seasoning, salt, and pepper. Bring to boiling. Reduce heat and simmer, uncovered, about 15 minutes or till sauce is slightly thickened.

■ For filling, in a medium mixing bowl combine eggs, *half* of the provolone or mozzarella cheese, the ricotta or cottage cheese, Parmesan cheese, parsley, the ½ teaspoon Italian seasoning, and the ground red pepper.

■ Spoon the filling into manicotti shells. Pour *half* of the sauce into a 12x7½x2-inch baking dish. Arrange stuffed manicotti shells in baking dish. Pour remaining sauce over shells. Cover with foil.

■ Bake in a 350° oven for 30 to 35 minutes or till heated through. Remove foil; sprinkle with remaining provolone or mozzarella cheese. Bake for 2 to 3 minutes more or till cheese melts. Makes 4 servings.

Nutrition information per serving: 695 calories, 44 g protein, 34 g carbohydrate, 42 g fat (23 g saturated), 226 mg cholesterol, 1,834 mg sodium, 859 mg potassium.

Italian Seasoning   A blend of dried herbs and spices that gives a characteristic Italian flavor to dishes. The combination of seasonings usually includes oregano, basil, ground red pepper, rosemary, and sometimes garlic powder.

Cranberry Muffins
(see recipe, page 264)

Fruit Jelly Roll
(see recipe, page 221)

Chicken Jambalaya
(see recipe, page 220)

Jackfruit See *Breadfruit*.

Jam

A mixture of fruit and sugar that is cooked to a very thick consistency and is used as a spread for breads, a filling for pastries, a topping for desserts, and a glaze for meats and poultry. Jams usually have small pieces of crushed fruit suspended in them. In many jam recipes, commercial pectin products are added to create the desired consistency (see also *Pectin*). Other jam recipes use natural pectin found in fruits to give products the desired consistency.

Q: **What is the difference between jam, jelly, and preserves?**

A: Jam is made from whole fruit that is crushed or mashed and cooked with sugar. Jelly is made from fruit juice that has been sieved or strained to remove any fruit particles and then cooked with sugar. Jam usually is opaque and firm enough to softly hold its shape; jelly typically is translucent and somewhat firmer than jam. Preserves are made in much the same way as jams, but preserves usually have larger and more distinct pieces of fruit.

Jambalaya *(jum buh LIE uh)*

A Cajun stew that is the Louisiana version of Spanish paella. Although there are many variations, the dish usually contains rice, chicken, and/or seafood, as well as ham or sausage. A tomato-based sauce with green pepper and seasonings also is common.

Chicken Jambalaya

    1   cup long-grain rice
    1   large onion, chopped
    ½   cup chopped celery
    ½   cup chopped green pepper
    2   cloves garlic, minced
    ¼   cup margarine *or* butter
    1   16-ounce can tomatoes, cut up
    ½   of a 6-ounce can (⅓ cup)
          tomato paste

    ½   cup chopped smoked sausage
    1   teaspoon Creole seasoning *or*
          Three-Pepper Seasoning*
    2   whole large chicken breasts (about 2
          pounds total), skinned, boned, and
          cut into bite-size pieces
    ¼   teaspoon bottled hot pepper sauce

■ Cook rice according to package directions. Set aside. In a 3-quart saucepan cook onion, celery, green pepper, and garlic in margarine or butter till tender. Stir in *undrained* tomatoes, tomato paste, sausage, and Creole seasoning or Three-Pepper Seasoning. Bring to boiling. Reduce heat. Cover and simmer for 30 minutes. Stir in chicken pieces and hot pepper sauce. Simmer, covered, about 15 minutes more or till chicken is tender.
■ Stir in cooked rice. Cook, stirring occasionally, till heated through. Serve with okra, if desired. Makes 6 servings.

***Three-Pepper Seasoning:** In a tightly covered container combine 2 tablespoons *salt,* 1 tablespoon ground *red pepper,* 1 teaspoon ground *white pepper,* 1 teaspoon *garlic powder,* and 1 teaspoon ground *black pepper.* Store at room temperature; use to season meats, fish, vegetables, and soups. Makes about ¼ cup seasoning.

Nutrition information per serving: 362 calories, 23 g protein, 34 g carbohydrate, 15 g fat (4 g saturated), 57 mg cholesterol, 465 mg sodium, 587 mg potassium.

Jelly

A translucent mixture of fruit juice, sugar, and pectin that is used as a spread for breads, a filling for pastries, and as a glaze for meat or poultry (see also *Pectin*). In many jelly recipes, commercial pectin products are added for desired consistency. Other jelly recipes use the natural pectin found in certain fruits to give the products the desired consistency.

Q: **What do the expressions "full rolling boil" and "sheets off the spoon" mean in jelly recipes?**

A: A full rolling boil refers to the stage when the jelly mixture is boiling so rapidly that you can't stir the boil down with a spoon.

Sheets off the spoon is a test used to see when jelly has reached the jelling point. For the test, dip a metal spoon into the boiling jelly and hold it over the pan. When two drops of jelly hang off the edge of the spoon and then run together, the jelly has reached the sheets off the spoon stage and has cooked long enough.

Jelly-Making Tips

● Use the type of pectin called for in a recipe. It doesn't work to substitute liquid and powdered pectin for one another.

● Use a Dutch oven or kettle that is large enough to hold the jelly mixture when it boils vigorously. The pan should be no more than one-third full before the jelly mixture starts cooking.

● Follow the most recent recommendations from the United States Department of Agriculture for making jelly. Some changes in past years include sterilizing jelly jars, using canning lids and screw bands instead of paraffin, and processing in a boiling-water canner. Check with your county extension agent for current information.

Jelly Roll
A dessert made by spreading filling on sponge cake and rolling it up into a log shape. The cake is baked in a flat, rectangular pan to form a thin sheet. Jelly is the traditional filling, but pudding, ice cream, flavored whipped cream, and fruit mixtures also are used. Jelly rolls can be served plain, sprinkled with powdered sugar, or frosted.

A Tip from Our Kitchen
To avoid cracking a jelly roll cake, invert it onto a towel dusted with powdered sugar as soon as it comes out of the oven. Then immediately roll it up in the towel and let the cake cool. The towel prevents the cake from sticking together as it cools. Unroll the cake and fill.

Fruit Jelly Roll

 ½ **cup all-purpose flour**
 1 **teaspoon baking powder**
 4 **egg yolks**
 ½ **teaspoon vanilla**
 ⅓ **cup sugar**
 2 **tablespoons fruit-flavored brandy**
   (optional)
 4 **egg whites**
 ½ **cup sugar**
   Powdered sugar
 ½ **cup raspberry *or* apricot preserves***
   Fresh raspberries (optional)

■ In a mixing bowl combine flour and baking powder. Set aside.

■ In another mixing bowl beat egg yolks and vanilla with an electric mixer on high speed for 5 minutes or till thick and lemon colored. Gradually add the ⅓ cup sugar, beating on high speed till sugar is nearly dissolved. Stir in fruit-flavored brandy, if desired. Wash beaters thoroughly.

■ In another mixing bowl beat egg whites on medium speed till soft peaks form (tips curl). Gradually add the ½ cup sugar, beating till stiff peaks form (tips stand straight). Fold yolk mixture into beaten egg whites. Sprinkle flour mixture over egg mixture; fold in gently just till combined.

■ Spread batter into a greased and floured 15x10x1-inch jelly roll pan. Bake in a 375° oven for 12 to 15 minutes or till cake springs back when lightly touched near the center.

■ Immediately loosen the edges of the cake from the pan and turn cake out onto a towel sprinkled with powdered sugar. Roll up towel and cake, jelly roll style, starting from one of the cake's short sides. Cool on a wire rack. Unroll cake. Stir preserves; spread over cake to within ½ inch of edges. Roll up cake *without* towel. Sift powdered sugar over cake. Garnish with fresh raspberries, if desired. Makes 1 cake (10 servings).

Note: For another filling, try 2 cups sweetened *whipped cream* or thoroughly chilled *vanilla or chocolate pudding.* Store filled cake roll in the refrigerator.

Nutrition information per serving (with preserves): 162 calories, 3 g protein, 33 g carbohydrate, 2 g fat (1 g saturated), 85 mg cholesterol, 56 mg sodium, 48 mg potassium.

Jerky Thin strips of meat, usually beef, that is salted and then cured by either smoking or drying. Jerky was a staple for pioneers. Today it is served as a salty, chewy snack. Jerky can be stored at room temperature for several days, but it is best to refrigerate it for longer storage.

Jerusalem Artichoke The brown-skinned tuber of a sunflower. Jerusalem artichokes, often known as sunchokes, can be either round with fairly smooth skin or more elongated and lumpy. The tubers look a lot like fresh gingerroot. The raw, ivory-colored flesh has a crisp texture like a potato and a sweet, nutty flavor. It is eaten raw or cooked.

Selecting: Fresh Jerusalem artichokes are available year-round and are at their peak from fall through winter. Look for firm tubers with no soft spots, and avoid any tinged with green.

Jerusalem artichokes

Storing: Refrigerate Jerusalem artichokes in a plastic bag for up to 1 week. Wash thoroughly before using.

How to cook: See the Cooking Fresh Vegetables chart under *Vegetable.*

Nutrition information: One-half cup of sliced raw Jerusalem artichokes has about 60 calories.

Jicama *(HE kuh muh)* A large, tuberous root vegetable with pale brown, thin skin and crisp white meat. Jicama resembles a large, brown turnip. The skin peels off easily to reveal pure white, potatolike meat that has a clean, crisp bite and a mildly sweet flavor. It is peeled before using and is eaten raw or cooked.

Selecting: Fresh jicamas are available year-round in large supermarkets and Mexican specialty stores. Look for firm, heavy jicamas with unblemished skin.

Jicamas

Storing: Store whole jicamas in the refrigerator for up to 3 weeks. After cutting, wrap in plastic wrap and refrigerate for up to 1 week.

How to cook: See the Cooking Fresh Vegetables chart under *Vegetable.*

Nutrition information: One-half cup sliced raw jicama contains about 25 calories.

Johnnycake A thin, flat, round bread, usually baked on a griddle. Johnnycakes originally contained only cornmeal, water, milk, and salt. Today some recipes call for eggs, leavening, and shortening or butter.

Juice The natural liquid extracted from fruits, vegetables, meats, and poultry. Fruit and vegetable juices are used as beverages and as ingredients in cooking. Meat and poultry juices often are used in gravies and sauces.

Julienne To cut food into thin match-like sticks about 2 inches long. The term also is used to describe a food cut in thin sticks.

A Tip from Our Kitchen
To speed up cutting julienne strips, first cut the food into slices about 2 inches long and ¼ inch thick. Then stack the slices and cut them lengthwise into thinner strips, about ⅛ to ¼ inch wide.

Kabob/Kebab Pieces of food, often meat, poultry, fish, seafood, or vegetables, threaded on a skewer and broiled or grilled. The food pieces sometimes are marinated before cooking. Kabobs often are brushed during cooking with a marinade or sauce to prevent the food from drying. Dessert kabobs can be made with cubes of cake and pieces of fruit and may or may not be cooked.

Tips from Our Kitchen
- If you're using wooden skewers to cook food on, soak the skewers in water for a few minutes before you start threading the kabobs. This way the skewers won't burn as the food cooks.
- To make sure all items on a kabob are cooked evenly, thread the pieces loosely onto the skewers, leaving at least ¼ inch between pieces.

Kale   A member of the cabbage family that doesn't form a head. Kale has frilly, dark green leaves and a cabbagelike flavor. It is eaten either fresh or cooked and also is used as a garnish.

Selecting: Fresh kale is sold year-round but is most abundant during the winter. Choose small bunches with no yellow or limp leaves.

Storing: Wash fresh kale in cold water; pat dry. Place leaves in a plastic bag lined with a paper towel, and store in the refrigerator for up to 3 days. The greens may become bitter with longer storage.

How to cook: See Greens on the Cooking Fresh Vegetables chart under *Vegetable*.

Nutrition information: One-half cup of chopped kale has about 20 calories.

Kale

Kimchi   *(kim CHEE)* A pungent, pickled cabbage dish used as an accompaniment to most Korean meals. Kimchi is mild when served fresh but becomes stronger in flavor and odor as it ferments.

Kitchen Bouquet   A commercial product used to enrich the flavor and color of foods, such as gravies and stews. This dark brown liquid is made from spices, vegetables, and caramelized sugar. A spray-on version to add color to microwaved foods also is sold.

Kiwanos

Kiwano   *(key WAHN oh)* An oval, orange to yellow fruit covered with spikes and filled with a green, jellylike meat and edible seeds. Also called horned melon, kiwanos are about 5 inches long and have an inedible shell. They taste like a blend of lime, banana, and cucumber.

Selecting: Look for bright orange to bright yellow fruit with no blemishes or soft spots. The spikes should be intact.

Storing: Kiwanos keep exceptionally well. Store at room temperature for up to 6 months. Do not refrigerate.

Nutrition information: Kiwanos have about 25 calories per ½-cup serving.

Kiwi Fruits

Kiwi Fruit

Kiwi Fruit A fuzzy, brown-skinned, egg-shaped fruit with a green interior flecked with tiny black seeds. Also called the Chinese gooseberry, most kiwi fruits come from New Zealand and California. Their sweet, fresh flavor is reminiscent of a mingling of strawberries, melons, and peaches.

Selecting: Kiwi fruit should yield to gentle pressure and have no bruises or soft spots.

Storing: Ripen kiwi fruits at room temperature until they yield to gentle pressure, then keep them in the refrigerator up to 1 week if you do not plan to use them immediately.

Preparation hints: It is not necessary to peel kiwi fruit before eating it. However, if desired, rub the brown skin gently with a clean cloth to remove the excess fuzz. Kiwi fruit is best when eaten fresh.

A Tip from Our Kitchen

Do not add kiwi fruit to gelatin salads. It prevents the gelatin from setting up, just as fresh pineapple does.

Nutrition information: Kiwi fruit is a good source of vitamin C and contains about 50 calories per fruit.

Knead To work dough with the heels of the hands in a pressing and folding motion until it becomes smooth and elastic. Kneading is especially important in making a yeast dough because kneading develops the protein, called gluten, that helps the bread hold together (see also *Bread, Yeast*).

Q: **What's the best way to knead dough that's leavened with yeast?**

A: To knead dough, start by placing it on a lightly floured surface. Then push it down and away from you with the heels of your hands. Give the dough a quarter-turn; fold it over and push down again. Continue turning and kneading until the dough is smooth and elastic, adding flour as necessary to keep the dough from sticking to the surface.

Kohlrabi *(coal RAH bee)* A globe-shaped vegetable bulb that grows above the ground and is topped with dark green leaves. Kohlrabi usually is pale green, although purple varieties may be found. Both varieties have white flesh. The kohlrabi bulb has a sweet, mild, turniplike flavor, and the leaves taste like spinach.

Selecting: Kohlrabi is available mid-spring through mid-fall, and the peak season is June and July. Choose small, young bulbs with healthy-looking stems and leaves. Any kohlrabi larger than 3 inches in diameter is likely to have a woody texture.

Kohlrabies

Storing: Store kohlrabi in a plastic bag in the refrigerator for up to a week.

A Tip from Our Kitchen

Peel kohlrabi before cooking to remove the outer woody fibers. Use a sharp knife to pull off strips of the kohlrabi peel from top to bottom.

How to cook: See the Cooking Fresh Vegetables chart under *Vegetable*.

Nutrition information: One-half cup of cooked kohlrabi has about 25 calories.

Kolacky *(kuh LA chee)* A yeast bun made from a rich sweet dough, traditionally filled with a poppy seed filling. Cottage cheese, apricot, prune, and other fruit fillings also are common.

An Eastern European favorite, kolacky traditionally are shaped into circles with an indentation in the center for the filling. The circle is a symbol of good luck, prosperity, and eternity. Today you'll find kolacky shaped into squares and diamonds.

Kosher Food The food that is acceptable to eat according to the rules of Judaism. Commercial kosher food must be processed according to long-established laws. The contents and production must be supervised by a rabbi.

Kumquat A bright orange, miniature citrus fruit with edible, tangy skin. Oval-shaped, kumquats are no bigger than an inch or two in length, with smooth skins and tiny, edible seeds embedded in pale orange meat that has a sweet, tart flavor. Kumquats also are called Chinese oranges.

Market forms: Fresh kumquats generally are available November through May. Syrup-glazed kumquats are available canned.

Kumquats

Selecting: Choose plump brightly colored kumquats with perfect skin that are firm but not hard. Avoid fruit that is wrinkled, dull in appearance, or moldy.

Storing: Keep kumquats at room temperature for up to 1 week. Or, store them in a plastic bag in the refrigerator for up to 3 weeks.

(See *Citrus Fruit* for the Selecting Citrus Fruit chart and nutrition information.)

Labeling The information about ingredients and nutrition that is included on a food's packaging. Ingredient information is required by law on nearly every packaged food product. Ingredients are listed in descending order according to their weight in the package. Nutrition information also may be listed on the label, although it is not required on many products.

Label language: Sometimes reading a label can be a challenge. Knowing the terms you're likely to find, however, will make the job easier. The following terms have been defined by the Food and Drug Administration or the Department of Agriculture for use on labels.

☐ **Enriched:** A product in which nutrients that were lost in processing have been replaced. The most common examples are bread and other grain products that have had B vitamins and iron added to replace those lost in refining.

☐ **Fortified:** A product to which nutrients not originally present have been added. Examples are milk with vitamin D, salt with iodine, and cereals with additional vitamins and minerals.

☐ **Lean:** A product with no more than 10 percent fat by weight. (Note that 10 percent by *weight* is not the same as 10 percent of *calories*.)

☐ **Extra Lean:** A product that contains no more than 5 percent fat by weight.

continued

☐ **Low-Calorie:** A product that has no more than 40 calories per serving.
☐ **Reduced-Calorie:** A product that has at least one-third fewer calories than the product it most closely resembles.
☐ **Sodium-Free:** A product that has no more than 5 milligrams of sodium per serving.
☐ **Very Low-Sodium:** A product that contains no more than 35 milligrams of sodium per serving.
☐ **Low-Sodium:** A product that contains no more than 140 milligrams of sodium per serving.
☐ **No Salt Added:** A product to which no salt has been added during processing, but which may contain naturally occurring sodium.
☐ **Substitute:** A product that is nutritionally equal to the food it resembles.
☐ **Sugar-Free/Sugarless:** A product that contains no carbohydrate sweeteners or that contains sugar alcohols such as sorbitol or xylitol in place of sugar.

Lady Baltimore Cake   A white layer-type cake, usually in three layers, filled with a mixture of fluffy, white frosting, figs, raisins, pecans, and sometimes candied fruit. The cake is then frosted with more fluffy, white frosting.

Ladyfinger   A small single-serving-size sponge cake that's named for its long, narrow, oval shape (see also *Sponge Cake*). The batter is poured into a mold or piped onto a parchment-paper-lined baking sheet and baked. Ladyfingers often are sprinkled with powdered sugar or sandwiched together with a filling and served as a cookie. They also can be used to make desserts such as a trifle (see also *Trifle*).

Lamb   Meat from sheep less than a year old. Generally, lamb has a mild flavor. Quality lamb ranges in color from reddish pink to dark red, and the meat is finely grained.

Unlike the sheep bred years ago to produce wool and meat, sheep today are raised predominantly for just one product. This means that lamb raised for meat is leaner, tastier, and more tender.

Certification: Although quality grading, which is similar to beef grading, is still used in the United States, a certification program also is used to identify a superior lamb product. The amount of fat and the age of the animal are taken into consideration when the lamb is certified. Yearling and mutton are inspected but not graded. These two products are seldom sold in the United States, except in ethnic and specialty markets. Here is what each designation means.
☐ **Certified American Lamb:** Meat from a sheep that is less than 1 year old. This lamb must have a ¼-inch or less fat trim. Certified American lamb is the highest quality lamb available.
☐ **Yearling:** Meat from a sheep that is between 1 and 2 years old.
☐ **Mutton:** Meat from a sheep that is 2 years old or older. Mutton is stronger in flavor.

Market forms: Most lamb raised in the United States is marketed fresh, although a limited amount may be frozen. Deli-sliced, cooked lamb and sausages made with lamb also are available. In some areas of the country, you may find imported frozen lamb from New Zealand and Australia.

Imported or Domestic?
There are flavor and size differences between imported and domestic lamb. Domestic lamb is milder in flavor than imported lamb because the animal is grain-fed rather than grass-fed. Lamb cuts from domestic animals are meatier and up to twice the size of the same cuts taken from imported animals. Domestic lambs are bigger and meatier because of differences in genetics and breeding.

Retail Lamb Cuts: The number listed with each retail cut refers to the wholesale cut marked on the drawing below. Besides the name of the retail cut, you'll find the best ways to cook each meat cut.

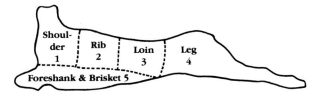

Lamb cuts: For the names and locations of the various retail cuts, see identification photos, right. Although cuts vary slightly, all lamb tends to be tender because it comes from such a young animal. However, as with beef, the most tender cuts come from the lightly used muscles along the upper back of the lamb (rib and loin), and the less tender cuts come from the more exercised muscles (shoulder, leg, foreshank, and brisket).

Selecting: Look for fresh lamb with a pinkish red color and a thin layer of firm, white fat surrounding it. A cross section of the bone should be red, moist, and porous. Meat from older lamb is darker in color, and the bones are drier and whiter.

Q: What is the "fell" on larger lamb cuts?
A: It is a thin parchmentlike membrane or skin that covers the fat of lamb. The fell is usually removed from chops before marketing, but it can be left on larger cuts to help the meat retain its shape and juiciness during cooking.

Storing: See the Storing Meat chart under *Meat*.

How to cook: Since lamb is from a very young animal, almost all cuts are tender and suitable for cooking with or without liquid.

continued

Arm chop (1)
Braise; broil; panbroil; panfry

Boneless shoulder roast (1)
Roast; braise

Blade chop (1)
Braise; broil; panbroil; panfry

Rib chop (2)
Broil; panbroil; panfry; roast

Rib roast (2)
Roast

Loin chop (3)
Broil; panbroil; panfry

Loin roast (3)
Roast

Sirloin chop (4)
Braise; broil; panbroil; panfry

Boneless leg roast (4)
Roast; broil (if butterflied)

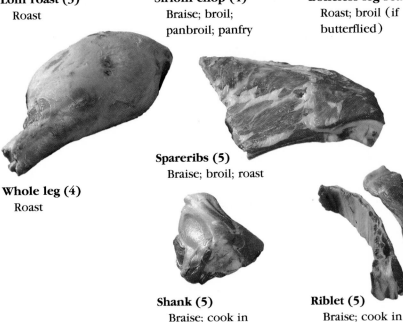

Whole leg (4)
Roast

Spareribs (5)
Braise; broil; roast

Shank (5)
Braise; cook in liquid

Riblet (5)
Braise; cook in liquid; broil

For suggested cooking methods of individual cuts, see the identification photos, page 227.

For roasting, broiling, panbroiling, and panfrying directions, see the Roasting Meat, the Broiling Meat, and the Panbroiling and Panfrying Meat charts under *Meat*. For grilling directions, see the Direct-Grilling Meat and Indirect-Grilling Meat charts under *Barbecue*.

Nutrition information: A 3-ounce serving of broiled lamb loin chop, lean only, has about 190 calories.

(See *Meat* for Using a Meat Thermometer and labeling, preparation, and other information.)

Lard A type of fat processed from pork. Lard sometimes is used in baking, especially to make piecrusts.

The term also refers to the process of inserting pieces of fat into or over a food, such as lean meat or game, in order to make the food taste more juicy or flavorful.

Lasagna/Lasagne *(luh ZAHN yuh)* A wide, ribbon-shaped pasta with straight or wavy edges that is made from noodle dough. Lasagna may be homemade or produced commercially. Packaged lasagna comes in dried and no-boil forms.

The term also refers to an Italian baked dish made with this noodle. Traditionally, the dish is prepared by alternating layers of cooked lasagna noodles, a tomato-based sauce, sometimes meat, ricotta or cottage cheese, and mozzarella cheese. Lasagna also can be made with a white sauce.

(See *Pasta* for an identification photo and storing, how-to-cook, and other information.)

Classic Lasagna

¼ pound bulk Italian sausage
⅓ cup chopped onion
1 clove garlic, minced
1 16-ounce can tomatoes, cut up
1 15-ounce can tomato sauce
1 4-ounce can sliced mushrooms, drained
1 teaspoon sugar
1 teaspoon dried basil, crushed
1 teaspoon dried oregano, crushed
½ teaspoon dried marjoram, crushed
1 beaten egg
1 cup ricotta *or* cream-style cottage cheese, well drained
¼ cup grated Parmesan cheese
6 packaged lasagna noodles
1 cup shredded mozzarella cheese
¼ cup grated Parmesan cheese

■ For sauce, in a saucepan cook sausage, onion, and garlic till sausage is brown and onion is tender. Drain off fat. Stir in *undrained* tomatoes, tomato sauce, mushrooms, sugar, basil, oregano, marjoram, and ⅛ teaspoon *pepper*. Bring to boiling. Reduce heat and simmer, uncovered, for 30 minutes or to desired consistency.
■ Meanwhile, in a small mixing bowl stir together egg, ricotta or cottage cheese, and ¼ cup Parmesan cheese. Set aside.
■ Cook lasagna noodles in boiling salted water for 8 to 9 minutes or till *almost* al dente (tender but still firm). Immediately drain. Rinse with cold water, then drain well.
■ Arrange *3* noodles in a greased 10x6x2-inch baking dish. Trim to fit. Spread with *half* of the ricotta cheese mixture. Spoon *half* of the sauce over top. Sprinkle with *half* of the mozzarella cheese. Repeat layers of noodles, cheese mixture, and sauce; reserve remaining mozzarella cheese. Sprinkle ¼ cup Parmesan cheese over all. Bake, covered, in a 350° oven for 35 minutes. Uncover; sprinkle remaining mozzarella cheese on top. Bake for 5 to 10 minutes more or till heated through. Let stand for 10 minutes before serving. Serves 6.

Nutrition information per serving: 341 calories, 21 g protein, 30 g carbohydrate, 16 g fat (8 g saturated), 83 mg cholesterol, 1,022 mg sodium, 645 mg potassium.

Classic Lasagna

Leavening Agent Any ingredient that causes a batter or dough to expand or rise and become light and porous. Yeast, hot air, and steam are natural leaveners. Baking powder and baking soda are chemical leavening agents.

Q: How do air and steam leaven baked products?

A: Leavening by air takes place whenever air is beaten into egg whites for such products as soufflés and angel food cakes. Leavening by steam happens when heat changes some of the water in a food into steam. Popovers and cream puffs are examples of foods leavened by steam.

Leek A member of the onion family that resembles an oversize green onion with overlapping, wide, green leaves; a fat, white stalk; and shaggy roots at the bulb end. Leeks have a subtle onion flavor. Use them as you would onions.

Selecting: Leeks are available year-round. Look for healthy-looking leeks with crisp, green leaves. Avoid leeks that are larger than 1½ inches in diameter because they'll be less tender.

Leeks

Storing: Refrigerate leeks in a plastic bag for up to 5 days.

How to cook: See the Cooking Fresh Vegetables chart under *Vegetable*.

Nutrition information: Cooked chopped leeks have about 15 calories per ½ cup.

Legume A term used for a variety of dried vegetable seeds, especially beans and peas. There are more than 25 legumes available, including kidney beans, navy beans, black-eyed peas, soybeans, garbanzo beans, pinto beans, flageolets (dried French green beans), lentils, and peanuts (see also *Bean, Dried; Black-Eyed Pea; Lentil;* and *Peanut*). Unless they're preprocessed, most legumes require soaking and long cooking. Legumes are a source of vegetable protein, and they are popular in a variety of recipes, such as soups, stews, casseroles, and ethnic dishes.

Lemons

Lemon An oval, bright yellow citrus fruit, with smooth skin and pale yellow, sour meat. Their sour taste makes lemons undesirable for eating out of hand, but the juice and peel are delightful enhancers for all kinds of sweet and savory dishes.

Market forms: Purchase lemons fresh or buy the dried peel or full-strength lemon juice in containers. Frozen lemon juice and sweetened lemonade concentrate are other available convenience products.

Selecting: Look for well-shaped lemons with smooth, evenly yellow skin. Bruised and wrinkled lemons probably are old.

Lemon Math

1 medium lemon = 3 tablespoons juice
= 2 teaspoons shredded peel

(See *Citrus Fruit* for the Selecting Citrus Fruit chart and storing and nutrition information.)

Lemon Curd

A tangy-sweet English favorite made with lemon juice, sugar, eggs, and margarine or butter. This thick, creamy mixture is used as a dessert filling for tarts and cakes or as a spread on bread.

A Tip from Our Kitchen

Lemon curd may be purchased at specialty shops. If you can't find it and need some for a tart or cake filling, substitute lemon pudding. If pudding is too thick, thin it with some milk.

Lemongrass

A lemon-flavored plant resembling a fibrous green onion. Used in Oriental cooking, it can be purchased in Oriental markets either fresh or dried.

A Tip from Our Kitchen

If you don't have lemongrass on hand, substitute a little lemon peel. For example, if recipe calls for 1 tablespoon finely chopped fresh lemongrass (about 2 stalks), you can substitute ½ teaspoon finely shredded lemon peel.

(See *Oriental Cooking* for an identification photo.)

Lemon-Pepper Seasoning

A mixture that's mainly salt, with black pepper and grated lemon peel added. This blend adds a delicate and subtle lemon flavor to foods.

Lentil

Typically, a tiny, brownish green, disk-shaped, dried seed that is a member of the legume family. Lentils are a source of vegetable protein. Cooked lentils have a beanlike texture and a mild, nutty flavor. Yellow varieties and red (actually orange in color) varieties of lentils also are available.

Selecting: Choose plump-looking lentils. Discard shriveled or spotted lentils.

Storing: Store lentils, tightly wrapped, in a cool, dry place for up to 1 year.

How to cook: For 4 servings (2 cups cooked lentils), start with ⅔ cup uncooked *lentils*. Rinse the lentils. Place them in a saucepan with 1⅓ cups *chicken broth or water*. Bring to boiling; reduce heat. Simmer, covered, for 15 to 20 minutes (for green and yellow varieties) or 3 to 5 minutes (for red varieties). Drain, if necessary.

If you are cooking lentils in a tomato mixture, you'll need to increase the cooking time by about half.

Nutrition information: A ½-cup serving of cooked lentils contains about 120 calories.

Lentils

Lettuce A term for any of a number of leafy salad greens. Lettuces are somewhat mild-flavored and range in color from red to deep green. Most are crisp in texture, but some are tender and buttery. Though chiefly used in salads, lettuces also can be used in cooked dishes.

Varieties: See the Selecting Lettuce chart.

Selecting: Choose fresh-looking heads according to variety. Avoid heads with leaves that are shriveled or brown. Head varieties should be firm but not hard.

Preparation hints: Clean lettuce before storing it. Before washing it, remove any outer leaves that are bruised, discolored, tough, or wilted.

To clean iceberg lettuce, remove the core. Wash the lettuce by placing it core side up under cold running water. Rinse well, then invert the head and let the water run out.

To clean butterhead, leaf, or romaine lettuce, cut the bottom core off. Then wash the leaves under cold running water.

To dry lettuce leaves, place them on paper towels or a clean kitchen towel. Place a

Lettuces

Butterhead

Iceberg

Leaf

Red-tip leaf

Romaine

Selecting Lettuce

Use this guide to compare the various types of lettuce. You'll find that they range in texture from crisp to soft and most have a mild flavor.

Type	Appearance	Texture/ Flavor
Butterhead (Bibb or Boston)	Small, round, loosely formed heads; bright to pale green outer leaves and pale yellow-green inner leaves	Soft, buttery; slightly sweet
Iceberg (or Head)	Round, tightly packed, solid heads with bright green leaves on the outside and pale green leaves inside	Crisp; rather bland
Leaf	Large, frilly-edged leaves that are bright green or green with reddish bronze tips and are loosely attached to a core	Tender; sweet, delicate
Romaine (or Cos)	Large, elongated, dark green leaves that branch out from a white base	Crisp; mild

second paper towel over them. Gently pat dry. A salad spinner also works well.

Storing: Refrigerate clean greens in a plastic bag or airtight container for up to 5 days.

Q: What's the easiest way to core iceberg lettuce?
A: Hit the stem end sharply on a countertop. Twist the core and lift it out.

Nutrition information: Lettuce is low in calories, averaging 5 to 10 calories per cup. One iceberg lettuce leaf has only 3 calories.

(For information on other salad greens, see *Arugula, Belgian Endive, Chicory, Escarole,* and *Radicchio.*)

Light
A term used on food labels to indicate a product that is low in calories, fat, or sodium. Food labels also may use the terms lite or leaner. Because there is no industry-wide agreed-upon definition of these terms, light, lite, and leaner can mean different things for different products. Also, these terms do not guarantee that a product is low in all three items—calories, fat, and sodium. It only signifies that the product has reduced amounts of at least one.

Limburger Cheese
A cow's-milk cheese that's famous for its pungent aroma and robust flavor. It has a pale yellow color with a soft, creamy texture. Wisconsin is the only state that produces this cheese.

A Tip from Our Kitchen
Serve limburger and other pungent cheeses on a glass or marble serving tray. Their strong flavor and aroma can be absorbed by wood and other porous materials.

(See *Cheese* for the Selecting Cheese chart and selecting, storing, serving, nutrition, and other information.)

Lime
An oval, green citrus fruit with tart, pale green meat. Most limes have seeds, but some types are seedless. Like lemons, limes are best used as a flavoring ingredient. Both the peel and juice have bold flavors.

Varieties: There are two main varieties of limes you can find in your supermarket year-round.
☐ **Persian:** Larger, oval, bright green limes with fine-grained, very tart meat. Persian limes are the most familiar and widely available limes.
☐ **Mexican:** Smaller oval limes with thin yellow-green skin that tend to be more tart than Persian limes. A well-known variety of the Mexican lime is the Key lime. Key limes are moderately seedy and highly aromatic. They are not grown commercially to any great extent in the United States, and outside of Florida are available only rarely in supermarkets or gourmet food stores.

Q: What is Key lime pie?
A: Key lime pie is a rich, creamy pie that is a specialty in Florida. There are many versions, but the main ingredients usually are lime juice, sweetened condensed milk, and eggs. Aficionados argue, however, that to be authentic, Key lime pie must be made using juice from Key limes.

Market forms: Purchase fresh limes or full-strength juice. Frozen sweetened limeade concentrate is another convenience product that is available.

Selecting: Persian limes should be deep green all over, have shiny skin, and feel heavy for their size. Yellowing skin means the fruit is aging and losing flavor. Mexican limes should be light yellow-green with very thin, fine-grained skin. Both varieties should be free from blemishes.

Limes
Persian
Key

continued

Lime Math

1 medium lime	= 2 tablespoons juice
	= 1½ teaspoons shredded peel

(See *Citrus Fruit* for the Selecting Citrus Fruit chart and storing and nutrition information.)

Limequat
A citrus fruit that's a cross between a lime and a kumquat and looks like a miniature lime. The small, oval fruit has a smooth, green peel, a pale green interior, and a tart lime flavor. A limequat can be used in the same way you would use a lime or lemon.

Selecting: Limequats usually are found in the winter months, mainly in larger produce markets. Look for shiny green skins and even shapes without bumps.

Nutrition information: Although high in vitamin C, such a small amount of limequat is used in recipes that the calories and vitamin content are negligible.

(See *Citrus Fruit* for the Selecting Citrus Fruit chart and storing information.)

Limequats

Limpa
(LIM puh) A Swedish, yeast-leavened rye bread. Limpa traditionally is shaped into a pudgy, round loaf. It is sweetened with molasses and flavored with grated orange peel.

Liqueur
A sweetened alcoholic beverage made from fruits or plants. Although usually served in a small glass or over ice as an after-dinner drink, a liqueur also can be used as an ingredient in cooking. Liqueurs come in a variety of flavors including orange, almond, cherry, chocolate, and mint.

Liquid Smoke
A commercial product made by diffusing smoke in liquid. It is used to add a hickory-smoke barbecue flavor to foods. Liquid smoke can be brushed on meats, poultry, or fish; added to marinades; or stirred into ground meat or poultry mixtures to add flavor.

Litchi/Lychee
(LEE chee) An Oriental fruit that resembles a large, white grape inside a thin, red, bumpy shell. Its flavor is sweeter and more fragrant than a grape, and the meat is soft and juicy. Litchis have a dark, inedible pit. When litchi fruits are dried, they're called litchi nuts.

Selecting: Litchis are most commonly available canned in syrup. The peak months for fresh litchis are June and July. Choose fresh litchis that are full and heavy and red to reddish brown in color. To enjoy them, simply peel off the shell.

Storing: Keep fresh litchis in an airtight container in the refrigerator for up to 2 weeks. Litchi nuts may be refrigerated for several months.

Litchis

Nutrition information: Ten litchis provide about 60 calories.

Liter/Litre
A metric measure of liquid volume. One liter is equal to a little more than 1 quart (4 cups).

Lobster
A large shellfish with 10 legs. When alive, lobsters are bluish green to reddish brown. After cooking, they turn bright red. The sweet, plump, white meat is succulent and firm-textured.

Types: Two major types of lobster live in the waters off the United States coasts. The *American* or *Maine* lobsters have claws and tails full of meat. Most are sold live. The *Spiny* or *Rock* lobsters have no claws, so almost all of the meat is found in the tail.

Market forms: Whole lobster is sold live or cooked. Lobster tails can be purchased several ways—cooked or uncooked and fresh or frozen. Cooked lobster meat is available fresh, frozen, and canned.

Selecting: When buying live lobsters, choose the most active ones. (Before picking one up, be sure its claws are plugged or banded.) Select lobsters that feel heavy for their size. Also, check that the tail curls under the body.

Cooked lobster that's sold in the shell should have a bright red, hard shell. The tail should curl under and spring back quickly when pulled out. Cooked lobster meat should be snow-white with red streaks on the surface. It should have a fresh sea smell.

Frozen tails should be in packaging that is intact, with no evidence of ice or juices. The meat should be free of dry or frosty areas.

Lobster Math

Use these guidelines to determine how much lobster to buy for each person.
- one 1- to 1½-pound whole lobster
- one 8-ounce lobster tail
- 3 to 4 ounces of cooked lobster meat

Storing: If possible, cook live lobsters on the same day you buy them. Otherwise, place them on a tray and refrigerate them covered with a damp towel, or place them on damp newspapers in an insulated cooler half-filled with ice. Cook them within 1 day. Before cooking, discard any lobsters that aren't alive. (Live lobsters will become docile under refrigeration, but if they are still alive they should move their legs slightly.)

Use freshly cooked lobster meat within 2 days, or freeze for up to 1 month. Once opened, canned lobster should be used within 2 days.

1. To split a cooked lobster, place it on its back on a cutting surface. Using kitchen shears, halve the body lengthwise up to the tail, cutting to, but not through, the back shell.

2. Using the shears, cut away the membrane on the tail to expose the meat. Discard the intestinal vein running through the tail and the small sand sac near the head of the lobster.

3. Along with lobster meat, serve the green tomalley (liver) and the coral-colored roe (roe are found only in female lobsters). They're considered delicacies. Or, use them in a sauce or lobster stuffing.

4. Twist the large claws away from the body of the lobster. Using a nutcracker, break open the claws.

Use a seafood fork to remove the meat from the claws, tails, and body.

continued

Cooking hints: Take care when cooking lobster—overcooking makes the meat stringy and chewy. As soon as the meat turns opaque, it's done.

How to cook: Whole lobster typically is boiled but also can be broiled. For boiling and broiling directions, see the Preparing and Cooking Shellfish chart under *Shellfish*.

To prepare lobster tails, thaw tails if frozen. Rinse them under cold running water. The tails generally are either boiled or broiled, but they also can be grilled or steamed. For grilling directions, see the Direct-Grilling Fish chart under *Barbecue*.

To boil 4 tails, in a 3-quart saucepan bring 6 cups *water* and 1½ teaspoons *salt* to boiling. Add tails; return to boiling. Simmer, uncovered, for 4 to 8 minutes for 3-ounce tails (6 to 10 minutes for 6-ounce tails; 8 to 12 minutes for 8-ounce tails) or till shells turn bright red and meat is opaque. Drain.

To broil lobster tails, use kitchen shears to cut the hard outer shell lengthwise down the center. Using fingers, press tails open, exposing meat. Devein, if necessary. Place tails, meat side up, on rack of a broiler pan. Brush with melted margarine or butter. Broil 6-ounce tails 4 to 6 inches from heat for 8 to 14 minutes or till meat is opaque.

A Tip from Our Kitchen

A popular way to eat lobster meat is to dip it in melted butter. When you are served a whole lobster, first remove the meat from the tail. Then twist off and crack open the large claws (see how-to photo 4, page 235); pick out the meat. Next break off the legs and carefully suck the meat and juices from them. Finally, remove and eat any meat plus tomalley (liver) and roe from the body.

Nutrition information: One 3-ounce serving of American lobster has only about 80 calories; spiny lobster has about 120. However, keep in mind that the tomalley and roe are loaded with cholesterol.

Lord Baltimore Cake A yellow layer-type cake, usually made in three layers and filled with a mixture of fluffy, white frosting, macaroons, maraschino cherries, and chopped nuts. The cake is then frosted with more fluffy, white frosting.

Low-Calorie A term that appears on the label of a food product and means that the item has 40 calories or fewer per serving.

Low-calorie recipes typically have fewer calories than their familiar counterparts. For example, 1 tablespoon of low-calorie white sauce has 8 calories, and the same amount of regular white sauce contains 18 calories.

Lox A version of smoked salmon that is a traditional food for many Jewish Americans. Nova Scotia lox is considered the best lox because it has the richest flavor. It also is usually the most expensive.

Lox is sold in delicatessens and specialty food shops and is very expensive. It is ready to eat and always is served cold. Sometimes whole fillets or smaller portions of smoked salmon can be found in the seafood section of supermarkets and in seafood stores.

Lox usually is sliced paper-thin and served on a bagel with cream cheese. Or, it's served on thin toast accompanied by capers, minced red onion, snipped fresh dillweed, and a squeeze of lemon. A 3-ounce serving of lox has about 100 calories.

Luau *(LOU ow)* A traditional Hawaiian feast that usually includes special decorations, music, and hula dancing. Typical foods served at a luau include a whole pig (roasted in an underground oven), poi (a paste made of taro root), haupia (coconut pudding), and tropical fruits, such as pineapple and papaya.

Luncheon Meat   A general term for ready-to-eat meat that most often is served thinly sliced. Luncheon meats include many combinations of meats and seasonings that are cooked or baked and shaped into loaves or sausages. Prepackaged or sliced to order from the deli case, luncheon meats are used in sandwiches, salads, and cold meat platters. They also are called cold cuts.

Some luncheon meats are canned. These luncheon meats usually are subtly spiced and contain other ingredients. Canned luncheon meats are fully cooked, but some people prefer to heat them.

Nutrition information: One ounce of canned luncheon meat contains 70 to 100 calories.

Lyonnaise   A term used for a food prepared with sautéed onions. This cooking style originated in Lyons, France, and often is used with vegetables, especially potatoes.

Macadamia Nut   The nut from the macadamia tree. The creamy beige, unevenly round nut is smooth, rich, sweet, and buttery. Because the brown shells are so hard and so difficult to remove, almost all of the macadamia nuts sold are shelled. These shelled nuts are roasted in oil or dry-roasted. Once opened, the jars or cans of nuts should be tightly re-covered and used within a month or frozen for longer storage.

Macadamia nuts

Q: **What are some of the best uses for macadamia nuts in cooking?**
A: Because of their sweet, buttery flavor, chopped macadamia nuts are wonderful as an ingredient in cookies and cakes or sprinkled over fish and vegetable dishes. Probably the most popular way to eat these nuts is right out of the jar.

(See *Nut* for the Selecting Nuts chart and selecting, nutrition, and other information.)

Macaroni   A type of commercially produced pasta that is made from flour and water. Macaroni is available in a variety of sizes and shapes, including curved tubes (elbows), shells, spirals, wagon wheels, and alphabet letters. Flavored macaroni also is available.

(See *Pasta* for identification photos and storing, how-to-cook, nutrition, and other information.)

Macaroon   A small, shaped or drop cookie usually made with egg whites, sugar, almond paste, and flavoring. Macaroons can range in texture from light and crisp to dense and chewy. Coconut often is added.

(See *Cookie* for Cookie-Making Hints and preparation, baking, storing, and other information.)

Mace   The fragile, lacy, red skin that surrounds the nutmeg seed (see also *Nutmeg*). The color of this spice changes to a tannish orange as it dries, and the skin becomes brittle. The flavor is more intense and pungent but less sweet than nutmeg. Ground mace is most readily available, but whole mace also is sold.

(See *Spice* for the Spice Alternative Guide and selecting, storing, and nutrition information.)

Mackerel A saltwater fish in the tuna family that has light-colored flesh and a firm texture. Most mackerel are strongly flavored and high in fat.

Types: Some common types include *Spanish, Atlantic, Pacific,* and *King* mackerel. Spanish mackerel is one of the best types for eating because it is milder than the others.

Market forms: You can buy fresh and frozen mackerel drawn or cut into fillets or steaks. You also can buy mackerel smoked, canned, and salted.

Storing: Fresh mackerel doesn't keep well because of its high fat content. If possible, cook it the day you purchase it.

How to cook: For baking, broiling, poaching, panfrying, and micro-cooking directions, see the Cooking Fish chart under *Fish.*

Nutrition information: A 3-ounce serving of baked Spanish mackerel has about 130 calories and 5 grams of fat; the same-size serving of Atlantic mackerel has about 220 calories and 15 grams of fat.

(See *Fish* for selecting, thawing, and other information.)

Mahimahi (*mah he MAH he*) The Hawaiian or Polynesian word for saltwater dolphin fish. (This is a fish and shouldn't be confused with the dolphin that is a mammal.) Mahimahi has a mild to moderate flavor, and its lean, white flesh has a firm texture. It most often is sold as fillets with the skin left on, but sometimes it is cut into steaks.

How to cook: Try this versatile fish baked, broiled, grilled, or poached. For baking, broiling, and poaching directions, see the Cooking Fish chart under *Fish.* For grilling directions, see the Direct-Grilling Fish chart under *Barbecue.*

Nutrition information: A 3-ounce serving of broiled mahimahi has about 90 calories.

(See *Fish* for selecting, storing, thawing, and other information.)

Malt A germinated grain used in brewing and distilling alcoholic beverages and as a flavoring for food. Although malt can be produced from any grain, barley malt is the most common type. Malt is used primarily in the beer industry, but it also is used to make malted milk powder and malt vinegar.

A soda fountain beverage made with milk, malted milk powder, and ice cream is sometimes referred to as a malt.

Mandarin Generally, a small, thin-skinned citrus fruit with segments that easily separate. Mandarins include tangerines and tangelos (see individual entries). Mandarins are sweet and juicy with easy-to-remove peels. Fresh mandarins often are sold under the name tangerines; however, you might see variety names such as *Kinnows* and *Satsumas* at the supermarket. Canned mandarins, labeled mandarin oranges, are commonly available packed in a syrup. A ½-cup serving of this canned fruit has about 80 calories.

Mango An oval, round, or kidney-shaped tropical fruit with green to yellow skin tinged with red, depending on the variety. Mangoes have a deep golden yellow meat, with a large, flat, oval, white seed. The fruit has a spicy peach flavor, but is more perfumy than a peach and very juicy.

Selecting: Mangoes are available in larger supermarkets in the United States from March through September. When ripe, mangoes should be fully colored, smell fruity, and feel fairly firm when pressed gently. Avoid extremely soft or very bruised fruit or fruit with blemishes.

Mangoes

a sauce and baked. Manicotti are distinctive in that they are rolled up diagonally from corner to corner.

Commercially made manicotti are sold as dried tubes that may be either smooth or ridged and are ready to cook and fill.

A Tip from Our Kitchen

Packaged manicotti shells are easier to stuff if you use a narrow spoon. A long-handled baby spoon or a narrow iced-tea spoon works best. Or, you can slit the cooked shells and wrap them around a filling.

(See *Pasta* for an identification photo and storing and how-to-cook information; see *Italian Cooking* for a recipe.)

Storing: Store mangoes at room temperature to ripen. Refrigerate them as soon as they are ripe and use them within 4 or 5 days.

Preparation hints: Since the meat from the mango holds tightly to the seed, an easy way to remove the meat is to make a cut through the mango, sliding a sharp knife next to the seed along one side of the mango. Repeat on other side of the seed, resulting in two large pieces. Then cut away all of the meat that remains around the seed. Remove the peel on all pieces and cut up or puree the meat.

Or, to remove the meat from the peel and cut it into pieces at the same time, work with one of the large pieces at a time. Make cuts in crosshatch fashion through the meat just to the peel (shown above). Bend the peel back and carefully slide the knife between the peel and the meat to separate. Discard the peel.

Nutrition information: Mangoes are a very good source of vitamin A. There are about 140 calories in a mango.

Manicotti *(man uh COT ee)* A pasta
made from a square or rectangle of noodle dough that is cooked in boiling water, drained, filled with a meat or cheese mixture, and rolled up. The rolls often are topped with

Maple A natural, sweet syrup or sugar
made with the sap from the sugar maple tree. The sap is concentrated through an evaporation process to make syrup or sugar. Maple products have a very distinctive flavor, ranging from very delicate maple to almost caramel-like. The color of maple syrup ranges from light amber to a deep, rich, dark amber.

Maple products: Here are some items available at the supermarket.
☐ **Maple Syrup:** A sweet, thick liquid. *Pure maple* syrup is made from maple sap that has been boiled down until it is the consistency of syrup. *Maple-flavored* syrup is a blend of pure maple syrup and corn syrup. Although maple syrup is used in baking, it is most popular as a topping for pancakes, waffles, and ice cream.
☐ **Maple Sugar:** Crystallized maple syrup. Used as a sweetener or as a candy, it may be sold loose or molded into decorative shapes, such as leaves. It has a grainy texture.
☐ **Maple Cream or Butter:** Cooked maple syrup that is cooled, then stirred until smooth and creamy. Maple cream is enjoyed as a frosting and as a spread for toast or waffles. It sometimes is blended with butter to make a spread.

continued

☐ **Other Products:** *Imitation maple* syrup is a blend of artificial maple flavoring and corn syrup.

Q: Does pure maple syrup differ in taste from other types of maple syrup?

A: Pure maple syrup has a more subtle maple flavor. If you're used to maple-flavored or imitation maple syrup, you'll probably notice that 100-percent maple syrup also is a little thinner and doesn't taste as sweet as either of those products.

Pure Maple Syrup

The United States government has strict ingredient standards for a product sold as pure maple syrup and requires quality grading for commercial sales. Some states and Canadian provinces have adopted their own strict grading standards. U.S. Grade A or Fancy is usually the highest quality grade for maple syrup. Generally, the lighter the color of the syrup, the higher the quality and the more delicate the taste.

Storing: Keep pure maple syrup for up to 1 year in a glass container in the refrigerator or indefinitely in the freezer. To store other syrups, see label directions.

Q: Can I use maple syrup that has crystallized or molded?

A: You can use maple syrup that has started to crystallize by simply pouring the maple syrup into a saucepan and heating it over low heat till the crystals dissolve. However, any syrup that has molded should be discarded.

Nutrition information: Pure maple syrup has about 50 calories per tablespoon. Maple-flavored and imitation maple syrups contain about 60 calories per tablespoon.

Margarine

A table spread of butterlike consistency and flavor. Most margarine is made with a single vegetable oil (cottonseed, corn, or soybean), but a combination of vegetable and animal oils sometimes is used. Like butter, regular margarine must be 80 percent fat, but margarine usually is vegetable fat, not animal fat.

Types: There are a number of margarine and margarinelike products.

☐ **Regular:** Available in stick form as a salted or an unsalted product.

☐ **Diet:** Contains half the fat of regular margarine and more water.

☐ **Liquid:** Specially blended to maintain a liquid state.

☐ **Soft:** A vegetable-oil-based margarine that is processed to make it spread easily.

☐ **Whipped:** Similar to soft margarine but whipped with air to make it spread even more easily.

☐ **Other Products:** A *butter-margarine blend* combines butter and margarine into one stick or soft product. *Vegetable oil spreads*, found in stick or tub form, contain more fat than diet margarine, but less fat than margarine.

Market forms: Margarine is available in foil- and paper-wrapped quarter-pound sticks or in plastic tubs. Liquid margarine comes in a squeeze container.

Q: Can margarine be substituted for butter in recipes?

A: In most recipes, margarine can be used instead of butter in equal amounts. Exceptions include French silk pie, croissant dough, Danish pastry dough, puff pastry dough, and toffee candy. In these recipes, butter is essential for satisfactory results. For information on using margarine in cookie recipes, see the tip under *Cookie*.

Storing: Keep margarine tightly wrapped in the refrigerator or freezer. You can store most margarine in the freezer for up to 6 months.

Preparation hints: Using whipped or diet margarine and vegetable oil spreads for cooking and baking generally is not recommended unless the recipe has been developed using these products. These products contain a lot of air and water and have a reduced fat content. Liquid margarine, however, can be used for a few cooking steps, such as for sautéing vegetables.

Nutrition hint: If you're concerned with saturated fat in your diet, it pays to know the differences between margarines. Generally, the softer the margarine, the less saturated fat it contains. This means liquid margarines are less saturated than soft tub margarines, which are less saturated than soft stick margarines, which are less saturated than hard stick margarines. But this is not a totally reliable guideline—be sure to look at the ingredient list on the label. For margarines lowest in saturated fat, the first ingredient listed should be *liquid* vegetable oil, such as corn, safflower, or soybean oil.

Nutrition information: One tablespoon of regular, soft, or liquid margarine has about 100 calories. The butter-margarine blends also have 100 calories per tablespoon. Whipped margarine has about 70 calories per tablespoon. Diet margarine has about 50 calories per tablespoon, and vegetable oil spreads contain anywhere from 50 to 75 calories per tablespoon.

Margarine made with only vegetable oils has no cholesterol, but it can vary in saturated fat. Read the label for more information.

Marinade
A liquid in which food is allowed to stand in order to flavor or tenderize it. The liquid usually contains an acid, such as wine, vinegar, or lemon juice, plus seasonings and sometimes cooking oil.

A dry mixture or paste of herbs and spices that is rubbed onto a food before cooking sometimes also is called a marinade.

A Tip from Our Kitchen
If a recipe for marinated meat, poultry, or fish calls for any leftover marinade to be served with the finished food, be sure to heat the marinade to boiling before you serve it. Boiling destroys any harmful bacteria that may have been transferred from the raw meat, poultry, or fish to the marinade. If desired, for a better appearance, you may wish to strain the liquid before serving it.

Nutrition hint: Use a low-calorie salad dressing for a quick marinade that will add a lot of flavor without a lot of extra calories.

Marinate
To allow a food to stand in a seasoned liquid mixture in order to flavor or tenderize the food.

Tips from Our Kitchen
● Avoid marinating in a metal container. The acid in the marinade may pit the container. The pitting not only ruins the container, but it also may add an off-flavor to the marinade.
● To reduce cleanup, use a plastic bag set in a bowl to hold the food you are marinating. When you use a plastic bag, you also may be able to use less marinade.
● If you are working with a small amount of marinade, use the plastic bag method. Seal the bag and turn it occasionally to distribute the mixture over the food.
● To be sure your marinated foods are safe to eat, don't marinate them at room temperature for more than 1 hour. If a recipe calls for a longer marinating time, refrigerate the marinating food.

Marjoram *(MAR juhr uhm)* An herb with light gray-green leaves and a spicy, sweet flavor. Marjoram sometimes is called sweet marjoram. In addition to fresh marjoram, dried leaves and ground marjoram are available.

Q: Is wild marjoram the same as marjoram?
A: Wild marjoram is another name for the herb oregano. The flavor differences are great, so do not use marjoram and oregano interchangeably.

(See *Herb* for the Herb Alternative Guide and selecting, storing, preparation, cooking, nutrition, and other information.)

Marjoram

Marmalade A mixture of fruit, fruit peel, and sugar that is cooked to a jamlike consistency and used as a spread for breads, a filling for pastries, a topping for desserts, and a glaze for meats or poultry. A marmalade can be made from one or more fruits, but typically contains at least one citrus fruit. It differs from a jam in that it is slightly softer and contains small pieces of fruit peel.

Marrow A fatty tissue found in the center of animal bones. Smooth in texture, marrow is light colored and has a delicate meaty flavor. Marrow is scooped out of the center of larger beef and veal bones. Raw marrow sometimes is chopped and added to stuffings, ground meat, and dumplings. It also can be cooked and used as a garnish or a spread.

Marshmallow A soft, springy candy made of sugar, corn syrup, gelatin, and egg whites. Commercial marshmallows come large and small, white and colored. Marshmallow creme is a thick, creamy commercial product that looks like melted marshmallows. It's often used as an ice-cream topping or in making shortcut fudge.

People seldom realize that marshmallows can be made at home. The preparation method—a hot syrup is added very slowly to a beaten egg white—is similar to divinity.

Marzipan *(MAR zuh pan)* A confection made of almond paste, sugar, and sometimes egg whites. Marzipan traditionally is molded into flowers, small fruits, leaves, and other fancy shapes or rolled into sheets to decorate cakes and pastries. Marzipan, which usually is tinted bright colors, can be made at home or purchased in bakeries or gourmet shops.

Mash To press or beat a food to remove lumps and make a smooth mixture. Utensils such as a fork, potato masher, food mill, food ricer, or electric mixer can be used.

Matzo/Matzoh *(MAHT suh)* A large, flat sheet of unleavened bread, usually made only with flour and water. It traditionally is eaten during the Jewish Passover.

Mayonnaise A spoonable, uncooked dressing made using egg and salad oil. The eggs and oil emulsify as they are whisked together when making the mayonnaise. Mayonnaise often is flavored with lemon juice and seasonings.

Eating uncooked or slightly cooked eggs in homemade mayonnaise may be harmful because of possible bacterial contamination (see Using Eggs Safely under *Eggs*). However, you can make homemade mayonnaise with commercial egg substitutes, which are based mostly on egg whites that have been pasteurized. Or, you can purchase commercial forms of mayonnaise, which contain pasteurized eggs.

Types: In addition to regular mayonnaise, reduced-calorie mayonnaise is sold. It contains less oil as well as fewer calories.

Nutrition information: One tablespoon of mayonnaise contains about 100 calories and 11 to 12 grams of fat. Reduced-calorie mayonnaise has about 50 calories and 4 to 5 grams of fat.

Meal The granular product made from grinding cereals or grains, such as corn.

The term also refers to several foods eaten at one sitting.

Mealy A term used to describe a food with a crumbly texture and an appearance similar to coarsely ground meal.

Measure To determine the quantity or size of a food or utensil. To measure volume, use the appropriate measuring cups or spoons. Use a ruler to determine dimensions.

Using the right utensil to correctly measure recipe ingredients is important for consistent results. For liquid ingredients, there are special measuring cups featuring a pour spout plus a rim above the last mark that guards against spilling. Another type of cup is used to measure dry ingredients; it allows any excess to be leveled off with the straight edge of a metal spatula or knife. Measuring spoons are used for small amounts of dry or liquid ingredients.

Measuring techniques: Follow these directions for accurately measuring ingredients and volume of containers.

☐ **Liquid:** Use a glass or clear plastic liquid measuring cup placed on a level surface. Bend down so your eye is level with the marking on the cup that you wish to read (see Photo 1). When liquid is measured in a measuring spoon, fill the spoon to the top, without letting it spill over. Don't pour liquid ingredients over the bowl of your other ingredients.

☐ **Flour:** Stir the flour in the canister to lighten it. (Sifting isn't necessary except for cake flour.) Then gently spoon the flour into a dry measuring cup and level off the top with a straight edge of a metal spatula or knife (see Photo 2).

☐ **Sugar:** Granulated or powdered sugar should be spooned into a dry measuring cup and leveled off. Brown sugar, on the other hand, is pressed firmly into a dry measure so it holds the shape of the cup when it is turned out (see Photo 3).

☐ **Dry Ingredients:** When using measuring spoons for small amounts of dry ingredients, level off the spoon with the straight edge of a metal spatula or knife (see Photo 4). Remember not to level ingredients over the bowl of other ingredients.

☐ **Shortening and Cooking Oil:** Solid shortening is measured by pressing it firmly into a dry measuring cup or spoon with a rubber scraper, then leveling the excess off with the straight edge.

Oil, being a liquid, requires the same kind of measuring cup and technique used for measuring liquids.

continued

Photo 1

Photo 2

Photo 3

Photo 4

☐**Margarine and Butter:** Margarine and butter often are packaged in stick form, with markings on the paper or foil wrapper indicating tablespoon and cup measures. Use a sharp knife to cut off the amount needed. If margarine or butter is not marked on the wrapper, measure it as you would shortening.

☐**Dried Herbs:** Lightly fill a measuring spoon just to the top with the dried herb (leveling with a spatula or knife is not necessary). Then empty the spoon into your hand. Crush the herb with the fingers of your other hand. This breaks the leaves and releases their flavor. (Some of the harder dried herbs, such as rosemary and thyme, are best crushed with a mortar and pestle.)

☐**Containers:** To measure volume, count the number of cups of water it takes to completely fill the container. To measure container sizes, see the question and answer under *Baking Pan*.

Meat

Meat Flesh of animals used as food. The most familiar meats are from cattle, hogs, and sheep. These animals give us beef, veal, pork, sausage, lamb, and variety meats (see also individual entries). The flesh of small and large game animals also is considered meat.

Inspection and grading: To ensure that the meat in the United States is safe and free of disease, all meat must be inspected before being sold.

Grading is a measure of meat quality and is voluntary. Some packing plants and retail stores rely on the United States Department of Agriculture to grade meat, but others have their own grading system that is identified by brand names.

USDA grading is based on the amount of marbling (the small flecks of fat in the meat). It is an indicator of tenderness, juiciness, and flavor. The age of the animal and the amount of marbling determine the grade.

Beef is the meat you'll most often find graded in the supermarket. If USDA grades are used, the ones you are most likely to see in the store on beef are prime, choice, and select (see also *Beef*). If a leaner beef product is what you are looking for, choose select grade meat, available in some supermarkets.

Only two grades of veal—prime and choice—are available at the supermarket. Pork is not graded in the supermarket because there is little variation in quality. The lamb industry uses a certification program along with grades (see also *Lamb*).

Labeling: To ease the task of selecting meats, many supermarkets use a voluntary meat labeling system set up by the meat industry.

Labels give you three kinds of information: 1) the kind of meat—beef, lamb, pork, or veal; 2) the wholesale cut—chuck or shoulder, rib, loin, round, or leg; and 3) the retail cut—blade steak, round roast, rib chop, or other cut.

Market forms: Although most meat is sold fresh, you also can purchase cured, canned, frozen, precooked, freeze-dried, shelf-stable, and vacuum-sealed packaged meat.

Meat Servings

The greater the amount of bone and fat in a meat cut, the fewer the servings per pound. To estimate how much meat to buy, allow four or five servings per pound for boneless, such as ground meat, boneless roasts, and variety meats, such as liver or tongue. For meat cuts with a moderate amount of bone, such as chops and steaks, allow two or three servings per pound. For bony meat cuts, such as spareribs, allow one or two servings per pound.

If you want to calculate the cost per serving, divide the cost per pound by the number of servings you expect to get from each pound of meat.

Selecting and storing: For selecting information, see individual entries.

To keep meat at its best, see the Storing Meat chart, opposite.

Q: **What is the best way to thaw meat?**
A: Thaw frozen meat in the refrigerator overnight. For faster thawing, use a microwave oven following oven manufacturer's directions. *Do not thaw meat at room temperature.*

Preparation hints: There are several ways to prepare less tender meat cuts. Marinating, pounding with a meat mallet, moist-heat cooking, and sprinkling with a commercial meat tenderizer are all ways of making meat less tough. Some cuts, such as cubed steaks, are pretenderized by machine.

For better penetration of flavor from marinades and herb rubs, score the meat by making shallow slits or slashes in the outer surface of the meat or fat.

To prevent steaks from curling as they cook, trim most of the fat from the meat, then score any of the remaining fat around the edge of the meat before cooking.

Frozen beef steaks can be broiled without thawing. For 1-inch-thick steaks, broil 5 inches from the heat (instead of 3 inches) and increase the cooking time.

Tips from Our Kitchen

When your recipe calls for cubed meat, and you can't buy meat that's already cubed, buy larger cuts of beef (round or chuck roasts), veal (shoulder roasts), lamb (leg or shoulder roasts), or pork (shoulder or loin roasts). Trim and discard fat and remove any bones. Then cut the meat into cubes of uniform size.

How to cook: For roasting, broiling, panbroiling, and panfrying directions, see the Roasting Meat, the Broiling Meat, and the Panbroiling and Panfrying Meat charts, pages 246–248. For grilling directions, see the Direct-Grilling Meat and the Indirect-Grilling Meat charts under *Barbecue.*

Please note that if you cook beef and lamb to an internal temperature of 140° (rare), be aware that some organisms that cause food poisoning may survive at this temperature.

continued

Storing Meat

To maintain the quality of fresh meats, store them properly. Uncooked meat should be refrigerated in the store's packaging at 36° to 40° for short-term storage; the length of time it will remain fresh depends upon the type of meat as well as the storage temperature and the state of freshness when purchased. Refer to the chart below for maximum storage guidelines. Refrigerate meat in the store's plastic-wrapped package, unless the wrapping is torn. If the wrapping is damaged, or if the meat was wrapped in wrapping paper, rewrap the meat in plastic wrap or foil.

For longer storage, meat should be frozen at 0° or below. Prepackaged meat should be overwrapped or rewrapped to prevent freezer burn (drying of the surface that causes meat to discolor). Package the meat in freezer wrap, freezer bags, or plastic wrap for the freezer, and wrap tightly, eliminating all air if possible. Remember to label the packages with the contents and date.

	Refrigerator	Freezer
Beef Cuts		
Roasts, steaks	3 to 5 days	6 to 12 months
Stew meat	1 to 2 days	3 to 4 months
Ground beef	1 to 2 days	3 months
Variety meats	1 to 2 days	3 to 4 months
Corned beef	7 days	2 to 3 months
Cooked beef	3 to 4 days	2 to 3 months
Veal Cuts		
Roasts	1 to 2 days	4 to 8 months
Steaks, chops, cutlets, ground veal	1 to 2 days	3 to 4 months
Cooked veal	3 to 4 days	2 to 3 months
Lamb Cuts		
Roasts, chops	3 to 5 days	6 to 9 months
Ground lamb, stew meat	1 to 2 days	3 to 4 months
Cooked lamb	3 to 4 days	2 to 3 months
Pork Cuts		
Fresh		
Roasts	3 to 5 days	4 to 8 months
Chops	3 to 5 days	3 to 4 months
Ground pork	1 to 2 days	3 to 4 months
Sausage	1 to 2 days	1 to 2 months
Processed		
Bacon	7 days*	1 month
Bacon bits	7 days	3 months
Frankfurters	7 days*	1 to 2 months
Ham (half)	3 to 5 days	1 to 2 months
Luncheon meats	3 to 5 days*	1 to 2 months
Sausage (smoked)	7 days	1 to 2 months
Cooked		
Cooked pork	3 to 4 days	2 to 3 months

*Once a vacuum-sealed package is opened. Unopened vacuum-sealed packages can be stored in the refrigerator for up to 2 weeks.

Using a Meat Thermometer

Use a meat thermometer so you don't have to peek and poke to see if the meat is roasted the way you like it. To get an accurate reading, insert the thermometer into the center of the largest muscle or thickest portion of the meat. Do not allow the bulb of the thermometer to touch any fat or bone, or the bottom of the pan.

When the meat reaches the desired doneness (consult the meat temperatures for desired doneness on the Roasting Meat chart), push the thermometer into the meat a little farther. If the temperature drops, continue cooking. If the temperature stays the same, remove the roast from the oven.

For easier slicing, let the meat stand about 15 minutes before carving (cover the meat to help keep it warm). The meat will continue to cook slightly.

Broiling Meat

Place meat on the unheated rack of a broiler pan. For cuts less than 1¼ inches thick, broil 3 inches from the heat (see how-to photo, page 60). For cuts 1¼ inches thick or thicker, broil 4 to 5 inches from the heat. Broil the meat for the time given in the chart or till desired doneness, turning the meat over after half of the broiling time.

Cut	Thickness (Inches)	Doneness	Time (Minutes)
Beef			
Flank steak	¾	Medium	12 to 14
Steak (chuck, blade, top round)	1	Rare	16 to 20
		Medium	22 to 24
		Well-done	26 to 28
	1½	Rare	18 to 25
		Medium	26 to 30
		Well-done	31 to 36
Steak (top loin, tenderloin, T-bone, porterhouse, sirloin, rib, rib eye)	1	Rare	8 to 12
		Medium	13 to 17
		Well-done	18 to 22
	1½	Rare	14 to 18
		Medium	19 to 22
		Well-done	23 to 28
Veal			
Chop	1	Medium to well-done	12 to 15
Lamb			
Chop	1	Rare	8 to 10
		Medium	10 to 12

Cut	Thickness (Inches)	Doneness	Time (Minutes)
Pork*			
Blade steak	½	Well-done	12 to 14
Canadian-style bacon	¼	Heated	3 to 5
Chop	¾	Medium to well-done	8 to 14
	1¼ to 1½	Medium to well-done	18 to 25
Ham slice	1	Heated	14 to 18
Miscellaneous			
Frankfurters		Heated	3 to 5
Ground-meat patties (beef, lamb, pork*)	¾ (4 to a pound)	Medium to well-done	14 to 18

Pork should be cooked till the juices run clear.

Roasting Meat

Place meat, fat side up, on a rack in a shallow roasting pan. (Roasts with a bone do not need a rack.) For ham, if desired, score the top in a diamond pattern. Insert a meat thermometer.

Do not add water or liquid, and do not cover. Roast in a 325° oven, unless chart or recipe says otherwise, for the time given and till the thermometer registers the specified temperature.

Cut	Weight (Pounds)	Doneness	Roasting Time (Hours)
Beef			
Boneless rolled rump roast	4 to 6	150° to 170°	1½ to 3
Boneless sirloin roast	4 to 6	140° rare 160° medium 170° well-done	2¼ to 2¾ 2¾ to 3¼ 3¼ to 3¾
Eye round roast	2 to 3	140° rare 160° medium 170° well-done	1¼ to 1¾ 1¾ to 2¼ 2¼ to 2¾
Rib eye roast (roast at 350°)	4 to 6	140° rare 160° medium 170° well-done	1¼ to 2 1¼ to 2¼ 1½ to 2½
Rib roast	4 to 6	140° rare 160° medium 170° well-done	1¾ to 3 2¼ to 3¾ 2¾ to 4¼

Tenderloin roast
  Half
  Whole
(roast at 425°)
	2 to 3
	4 to 6
		140° rare
		140° rare
			¾ to 1
			¾ to 1

Round tip roast	3 to 5 6 to 8	140° to 170° 140° to 170°	1¾ to 3¼ 3 to 4½
Top round roast	4 to 6	140° to 170°	1½ to 3
Veal			
Boneless rolled breast roast	2½ to 3½	170° well-done	1¾ to 2¼
Boneless rolled shoulder roast	3 to 5	170° well-done	2¾ to 3¼
Loin roast	3 to 5	160° to 170°	1¾ to 3
Rib roast	3 to 5	160° to 170°	1¼ to 2½
Lamb			
Boneless rolled leg roast	4 to 7	160° medium-well	2 to 4
Boneless rolled shoulder roast	2 to 3	160° medium-well	1¼ to 2
Rib roast	1¾ to 2½	140° rare 160° medium-well	¾ to 1 1 to 1½

Cut	Weight (Pounds)	Doneness	Roasting Time (Hours)
Lamb			
Whole leg roast	5 to 7	140° rare 160° medium-well	1½ to 2½ 2 to 3
Pork*			

Boneless top loin roast
  Single loin
  Double loin, tied
	2 to 4
	3 to 5
		160° to 170°
		160° to 170°
			1 to 1¼
			1¾ to 2½

Loin back ribs, spareribs	2 to 4	Well-done	1½ to 1¾
Country-style ribs (roast at 350°)	2 to 4	Well-done	1½ to 2
Loin blade or sirloin roast	3 to 4	170° well-done	1¾ to 2½
Loin center rib roast (backbone loosened)	3 to 5	160° to 170°	1½ to 2½
Rib crown roast	6 to 8	160° to 170°	2 to 3½
Tenderloin (roast at 425°)	¾ to 1	160° to 170°	25 to 35 minutes
Ham (fully cooked)			
Boneless half	4 to 6	140°	1¼ to 2½
Boneless portion	3 to 4	140°	1½ to 2¼
Smoked picnic	5 to 8	140°	2 to 4
Ham (cook-before-eating)			
Bone-in half	7 to 8	160°	2½ to 3¼
Bone-in portion	3 to 5	160°	1¾ to 3¼

*Pork should be cooked till the juices run clear.

Panbroiling and Panfrying Meat

To panbroil these meats, preheat a heavy skillet over high heat till very hot. Do not add water or fat. (For beef steaks and veal, brush skillet lightly with cooking oil.) Add meat. Do not cover. Reduce heat to medium and cook for the time given or till done, turning meat over after half of the cooking time. If meat browns too quickly, reduce heat to medium-low. Spoon off fat and juices as they accumulate during cooking.

To panfry these meats, in a heavy skillet melt 1 to 2 tablespoons margarine or butter over medium-high heat. Add meat. Do not cover. Reduce heat to medium and cook for time given or till done, turning meat over after half of the cooking time.

Cut	Thickness (Inches)	Doneness	Panbroiling Time (Minutes)	Panfrying Time (Minutes)
Beef Cubed steak	½	Well-done	5 to 8	6 to 8
Steak (sirloin, top loin, tenderloin, rib eye, top round)	1	Rare Medium Well-done	6 to 8 9 to 12 14 to 18	8 to 11 12 to 14 15 to 17
Veal Cutlet	¼	Medium to well-done	3 to 5	4 to 6
Lamb Chop	1	Medium	8 to 10	7 to 9
Pork* Chop	¾	Medium to well-done	7 to 10	7 to 10

To panbroil these meats, place meat in a cool skillet. (If using an electric range, preheat the burner for 2 to 4 minutes.) Turn heat to medium. Turn meat halfway through cooking time (for bacon, turn occasionally). If meat browns too quickly, reduce heat slightly.

Cut	Thickness (Inches)	Doneness	Panbroiling Time (Minutes)
Pork Bacon	Slices	Well-done	8 to 10
Canadian-style bacon	¼	Heated	3 to 5
Ham slice	1	Heated	16 to 18
Miscellaneous Ground-meat patties (beef, lamb, pork*)	¾ (4 to a pound)	Medium to well-done	10 to 12

Pork should be cooked till the juices run clear.

Meatball
A seasoned ground meat mixture that's shaped into balls before cooking. Meatballs can range from bite-size to 2 or more inches in diameter. They are served as a main dish or as an appetizer.

Q: What's an easy way to shape meatballs?
A: Here are a couple of ways to shape meatballs quickly.

For 1-inch meatballs, pat the meatball mixture into a 1-inch-thick square on waxed paper; then cut the square into 1-inch cubes. Dip your hands in water and gently roll the cubes into balls. Similarly, for 1½-inch meatballs, make a 1½-inch-thick square and cut 1½-inch cubes.

Another easy method is to shape the meatball mixture into a log the same diameter as the size meatball you need. For 1-inch meatballs, work with a 1-inch-diameter log. Then slice the roll into even pieces and round them into balls.

German-Style Meatballs

 1 **egg, slightly beaten**
 ¼ **cup beer**
 ¼ **cup fine dry bread crumbs**
 ½ **teaspoon salt**
  Dash pepper
 1 **pound ground beef**
 2 **medium onions, sliced and separated**
   into rings
 2 **tablespoons cooking oil**
 3 **tablespoons all-purpose flour**
 1 **teaspoon instant beef bouillon**
   granules
 1 **teaspoon brown sugar**
 ¼ **teaspoon dried thyme, crushed**
 1 **cup beer**
 ¼ **cup water**
 1 **teaspoon vinegar**
 2 **tablespoons snipped parsley**
  Hot cooked fettuccine (optional)
 3 **slices bacon, crisp-cooked, drained,**
   and crumbled (optional)

■ In large bowl combine egg, the ¼ cup beer, bread crumbs, salt, and pepper. Add ground beef; mix well. Shape into twenty-four 1½-inch meatballs. Place meatballs in a single

German-Style Meatballs

layer in a 15x10x1-inch baking pan. Bake in a 350° oven for 15 to 20 minutes or till done. Drain off fat.

■ Meanwhile, in a large saucepan cook onion in hot oil till tender but not brown. Stir in flour, beef bouillon granules, brown sugar, and thyme. Add the 1 cup beer, water, and vinegar all at once. Cook and stir till thickened and bubbly. Cook and stir 1 minute more. Stir in parsley and drained meatballs; heat through.

■ Serve over hot cooked fettuccine and sprinkle with bacon, if desired. Serves 4.

Nutrition information per serving: 403 calories, 25 g protein, 16 g carbohydrate, 25 g fat (8 g saturated), 128 mg cholesterol, 632 mg sodium, 367 mg potassium.

Meat Loaf A seasoned ground meat mixture that's shaped into a rectangular or round loaf or into a ring, then baked.

A Tip from Our Kitchen

Because ground meat is handled more than other meats during processing, cook meat loaves till well-done to ensure maximum food safety. To check doneness, cut into loaf—inside meat color should be brown. Or, use a meat thermometer at end of cooking; it should register 170°.

Meat Tenderizer A commercial product containing an enzyme, such as papain, that breaks down the connective tissue of meat to make it easier to cut and chew. Meat also may be tenderized by pounding it or by marinating it.

Melba Toast A very thin bread slice slowly heated in the oven till crisp and brown. Melba toast is used as a base for appetizers and spreads, as well as for a snack. It is available in supermarkets as small rounds or rectangles and comes in rye, whole wheat, onion, and garlic flavors.

Nutrition information: One melba toast round (about 1¾-inch diameter) has about 10 calories.

Melon A large, oval to round fruit with a thick rind and soft, juicy meat. Grown on trailing vines, melons are descendants of both the squash family and the cucumber family.

Selecting Melons

Melons differ in appearance—shape, size, and interior and exterior color—as well as in flavor and texture. Look for melons with characteristics that match those listed here for each type.

Melon	Appearance	Interior Color	Flavor and Texture
Cantaloupe*	Round; cream-colored netting over a yellowish green rind	Orange	Sweet; moist and juicy
Casaba*	Globe-shaped with one pointed end; golden yellow rind with wrinkled appearance	Creamy white	Sweet; moist and juicy
Crenshaw*	Oval-shaped; mottled green and yellow rind that is mostly smooth	Salmon-colored	Rich, sweet and spicy taste; highly aromatic; moist and juicy
Galia	Round; heavily netted, green to golden rind	Pale green	Medium-sweet; highly fragrant; moist and juicy
Honeydew*	Round; smooth, waxy rind that is creamy white with a green to pale yellow cast	Pale green (sometimes pink, green, gold, or orange)	Sweet; honey aroma; moist and juicy
Juan Canary (Jaune Canari)	Football-shaped; bright yellow, usually smooth rind	Creamy white tinged with pink	Very sweet; moist and juicy
Persian*	Round; fine netting over a green to golden yellow rind	Salmon-colored	Tastes like a mildly sweet cantaloupe; firm with buttery texture
Santa Claus or Christmas	Football-shaped; green or gold (or yellow) stripes over a mottled, hard rind	Creamy white to pale green	Mildly sweet with a fruit tang; crisp and juicy
Watermelon*	Oblong, oval, or round; hard, smooth rind that is solid, striped, or mottled green	Deep pink to red (sometimes yellow)	Sweet; crisp and juicy

*See individual entries for additional information.

Cantaloupe

Casaba

Crenshaw

Galia melon

Honeydew

Juan Canary melon

Persian melon

Santa Claus melon

Market forms: Melon varieties are becoming available fresh nearly year-round. Melons usually are sold whole, but many supermarkets sell cut melons as well. You'll also find melon balls, either plain or in syrup, in the supermarket freezer section.

Varieties: See the Selecting Melons chart, opposite.

Selecting: See the Selecting Melons chart, opposite, for information on appearance, interior color, flavor, and texture of individual varieties. For all varieties, however, note that melons should feel heavy for their size and be well-shaped. Avoid fruit that is wet, dented, bruised, or cracked.

Storing: Most melons, except watermelons, continue to ripen after picking. If a melon seems underripe, store it at room temperature

Watermelons

continued

for a few days. Then refrigerate it and use it within 3 to 4 days. Wrap cut melons and refrigerate for 2 to 3 days.

Preparation hints: To serve most melons, halve or quarter the melon and scoop out or remove the seeds. Use a grapefruit knife or other knife to cut the fruit from the rind. Slice, cut up, or puree the fruit.

Nutrition information: One cup of melon cubes generally has between 45 and 60 calories. Cantaloupe is an excellent source of vitamins A and C, and honeydew is an excellent source of vitamin C.

Melt To heat a solid food, such as chocolate, sugar, butter, or cheese, until it becomes liquid or semiliquid.

A Tip from Our Kitchen
A microwave oven can help with many melting tasks, especially melting margarine or butter. Use a microwave-safe dish. For 2 tablespoons, allow 40 to 50 seconds on 100% power (high). For ¼ cup, allow 45 to 60 seconds, and for ½ cup, 1 to 2 minutes. (Low-wattage microwave ovens may take a little longer.)

Meringue Sweetened, stiffly beaten egg whites that are used for desserts. There are two basic types of meringues. Soft meringues are moist and tender and are used for topping pies and other desserts. Hard meringues are sweeter than soft meringues and are baked to form crisp, dry dessert shells or cookies, such as macaroons. Meringue shells often are filled with fresh fruit or puddings.

Preparation hints: Start adding the sugar to the meringue mixture as soon as the egg whites are foamy and form soft peaks (tips curl). Add 1 to 2 tablespoons of sugar at a time, beating until stiff peaks form (tips stand straight).

Underbeating will cause low volume and shrinkage and can result in undissolved sugar, which gives meringues a gritty texture. Underbeating also can produce meringues that don't hold their shape and that spread too much. Overbeating may result in a meringue with low volume.

Egg White Pointers
Properly beaten egg whites are the secret to high, light meringues, soufflés, puffy omelets, and other dishes. Follow these tips for stiffly beaten egg whites with good volume.
● Be sure to use the size bowl called for in the recipe. A copper, stainless steel, or glass bowl works best. Avoid wooden or plastic bowls because they can absorb fat, which isn't easily washed out. This fat will keep the egg whites from beating properly. Also make sure the electric mixer beaters are very clean.
● When separating eggs, use an egg separator and be careful not to get any yolk in the whites. The fat in the egg yolk will keep the egg whites from beating properly.
● Eggs separate most easily when they're cold, but egg whites beat to the highest volume when they're at room temperature. So, after separating, refrigerate the yolks till needed and let the whites stand at room temperature for 30 minutes before beating.
● For more stable egg whites, add ⅛ teaspoon cream of tartar for each 2 egg whites when adding them to the bowl.

Q: **What causes meringue on a cream pie to shrink or leak?**

A: The soft meringue on a pie will shrink if the meringue isn't well-sealed to the piecrust. To seal the meringue on a cream pie filling, spread the meringue so it touches the edges of the piecrust all the way around. A pie will leak or "weep" if the meringue is not spread on the pie while the filling is hot.

Meringue Shells

3 egg whites
1 tablespoon vanilla
¼ teaspoon cream of tartar
1 cup sugar

■ Bring egg whites to room temperature. Meanwhile, cover a baking sheet with plain brown paper. Draw one 9-inch circle *or* eight 3-inch circles on paper. In a large mixing bowl combine egg whites, vanilla, and cream of tartar. Beat with an electric mixer on medium speed about 1 minute or till soft peaks form (tips curl). Gradually add sugar, *1 tablespoon* at a time, beating on high speed till very stiff peaks form (tips stand straight) and sugar is almost dissolved (about 7 minutes).

■ Pipe meringue through a pastry tube onto the circle or circles on the brown paper, building the sides up to form a shell or shells. *Or,* use the back of a spoon to spread the meringue over the circle or circles, building the sides up.

■ Bake in a 300° oven for 45 minutes for the large shell (35 minutes for small shells). Turn off oven. Let shell or shells dry in oven, with door closed, for at least 1 hour. Remove from paper. Store in an airtight container. If desired, fill shell or shells with ice cream or pudding and top with whipped cream. Makes 8 servings.

Nutrition information per serving: 103 calories, 1 g protein, 25 g carbohydrate, 0 g fat, 0 mg cholesterol, 28 mg sodium, 22 mg potassium.

Meringue for Pie

3 egg whites
½ teaspoon vanilla
¼ teaspoon cream of tartar
6 tablespoons sugar

■ Bring egg whites to room temperature. In a large mixing bowl combine egg whites, vanilla, and cream of tartar. Beat with an electric mixer on medium speed about 1 minute or till soft peaks form (tips curl). Gradually add sugar, *1 tablespoon* at a time, beating on high speed about 4 minutes more or till mixture forms stiff, glossy peaks and sugar dissolves. Immediately spread meringue over the *hot* cream pie filling, carefully spreading to edge of pastry to seal and prevent shrinkage. Bake the pie in a 350° oven for 15 minutes. (For additional information on safe meringue baking times, see tip under *Cream Pie.*)

Nutrition information for ⅛ of recipe: 43 calories, 1 g protein, 9 g carbohydrate, 0 g fat, 0 mg cholesterol, 27 mg sodium, 22 mg potassium.

1. For a meringue, start beating egg whites and cream of tartar with an electric mixer on medium to high speed, stopping the mixer occasionally and lifting the beaters to check for soft peaks. When the peaks are foamy and bend over slightly, as shown, they are at the soft-peak stage.

2. Continue beating the egg whites, slowly adding sugar, on high speed until the mixture looks glossy and peaks stand straight when the beaters are lifted. The mixture should not slide when the bowl is tipped.

3. To find out if the sugar is dissolved, rub some meringue between your fingers. It should feel smooth for a soft meringue and almost smooth with just a few grains for hard meringue. If the meringue feels very grainy, beat longer.

Mexican Cooking

Mexican Cooking The cuisine of Mexico, which combines Aztec and Mayan Indian traditions with Spanish influences. The cooking often is characterized by spicy foods, such as enchiladas, tacos, and tamales (see also individual entries), but it also features many mildly seasoned dishes.

Cuisine highlights: Mexican cooking makes full use of foods native to Central and South America, especially corn, tomatoes, chili peppers, beans, sweet potatoes, avocados, and squashes. Beans come in several varieties, and they're commonly mashed and cooked with lard to make frijoles refritos (refried beans).

The most characteristic feature of Mexican cooking is the widespread use of chili peppers. About a dozen varieties are commonly used, ranging from mild to very hot. Chili peppers are an ingredient in most Mexican sauces.

Pork, beef, and chicken are the most frequently used meats and poultry. Fish and shellfish are abundant in some areas, particularly along the coasts. The basis of many Mexican dishes is the tortilla, made of cornmeal in the south and wheat flour in the north (see also *Tortilla*).

Mexico is known for several desserts, especially the flan (see also *Flan*). Another favorite is the sopaipilla (a biscuit puff sprinkled with cinnamon and sugar).

Sauce specialties: There are a number of sauces that add spicy flavor to Mexican dishes. Some sauces are used in cooking, and other sauces are added at the table.

Red mole *(MO lay)* sauce contains red chilies and ripe tomatoes, and green mole has green chilies, green tomatoes, and cilantro. The most exotic mole is mole poblano, a sauce containing unsweetened chocolate. Mole sauces are cooked with food.

Salsa verde and salsa cruda are two sauces often kept on the table to be added to food as desired. Salsa verde is a mixture including tomatillos, chili peppers, and cilantro, and salsa cruda is an uncooked mixture including tomatoes, chili peppers, and cilantro.

Pork Enchiladas

1 16-ounce can tomatoes
1 8-ounce can tomato sauce
1 4-ounce can green chili peppers, rinsed and seeded
1 small green pepper, cut up
1 clove garlic
1 teaspoon sugar
½ teaspoon coriander seed
2 cups finely chopped cooked pork
¾ cup shredded Monterey Jack *or* cheddar cheese (3 ounces)
¼ cup finely chopped onion
¼ teaspoon salt
2 tablespoons cooking oil
12 6-inch flour *or* corn tortillas
¾ cup shredded Monterey Jack *or* cheddar cheese (3 ounces)

■ In a blender container or food processor bowl, combine the *undrained* tomatoes, tomato sauce, chili peppers, green pepper, garlic, sugar, and coriander. Cover; blend or process till smooth. Set the mixture aside.

■ In a bowl combine cooked pork, ¾ cup Monterey Jack or cheddar cheese, the onion, and salt. Set aside.

■ In a skillet heat the cooking oil. Dip tortillas, one at a time, into hot oil for 10 seconds or just till limp. Drain on paper towels. Spoon about ¼ *cup* pork mixture on *each* tortilla; roll up. Place filled tortillas, seam side down, in a 13x9x2-inch baking dish. Pour tomato mixture over tortillas. Cover with foil.

■ Bake in a 350° oven about 30 minutes or till heated through. Remove foil. Sprinkle ¾ cup shredded Monterey Jack or cheddar cheese atop. Makes 6 servings.

Nutrition information per serving: 456 calories, 25 g protein, 38 g carbohydrate, 24 g fat (9 g saturated), 68 mg cholesterol, 997 mg sodium, 618 mg potassium.

Microwave Cooking

A method of cooking or warming food using electromagnetic waves generated by a special appliance. The waves cause the molecules in food to move and produce friction, which provides the heat necessary to cook the food. Microwave ovens are available as full-size models, ranging in cooking power from about 600 to 700 watts, and as lower wattage models, having about 400 to 500 watts of cooking power. In addition to a full-power setting, most microwave ovens have variable power settings that allow the ovens to be used at less than full power for such cooking chores as defrosting and reheating.

Q: What kinds of cookware work best in microwave ovens?

A: Cookware that's labeled "microwave safe" is best for cooking in your microwave oven. Other dishes, however, can be used. To find out if a dish is microwave safe, pour ½ cup of cold water into a glass measure. Set the measure in the microwave oven, inside or beside the dish you wish to test. Micro-cook on 100% power (high) for 1 minute. If the water is warm but the dish remains cool, you can use the dish for micro-cooking. If the water is warm and the dish feels lukewarm, the dish is suitable for heating or reheating food in the microwave, but probably not for micro-cooking food. If the water stays cool and the dish becomes hot, *do not use the dish in the microwave.*

Also, *do not use a dish or plate that has gold or silver trim or markings.* The metal in the trim or markings may overheat and blacken or crack the dish.

White paper towels and paper plates that are labeled microwave safe also may be used in your microwave oven, if the food is moist and the total cooking time is less than 10 minutes on high power. Don't use them for more than 10 minutes or if the amount of food is less than ¼ cup, because the paper could catch fire.

Microwave Cooking Tips

● Use the dish lid or microwave-safe plastic wrap to cover containers when cooking foods, such as casseroles, fish, poultry, and meat. Covering the food helps retain steam, prevent drying, and cook the food faster. Use waxed paper as a cover when heating foods that spatter.

● When using plastic wrap as a cover, vent it by turning back one corner to allow excess steam to escape.

● Because microwave energy tends to penetrate the edges of food first, stir food often. This way, the hotter portion on the outside will be mixed into the cooler center.

If the food can't be stirred (such as chicken pieces or fish fillets), rearrange it to ensure even cooking. Move the less-cooked food from the center to the edges of the baking dish. For foods in individual dishes, rearrange the dishes from the center of the oven to the edges.

If the food can't be stirred or rearranged, the dish or the food should be turned. When a recipe says to turn a food, rotate the dish halfway, unless it specifies otherwise. Turn over large pieces of food, checking for uneven cooking.

● Always test food after the minimum cooking time given in a recipe, using the doneness test given. Some micro-cooked foods may look as if they need more cooking when they actually are done. Finished cakes and muffins, for example, may look wet on the surface but may be cooked underneath.

Milk

Milk A white, opaque liquid secreted by female mammals. In the United States, milk from cows is by far the most popular kind of milk used. Outside the U.S., goats, sheep, and camels are popular sources of milk.

Types: Here are the most common types of milk available.

☐ **Whole:** Contains at least 3.5 percent milk fat, although standards vary slightly from state to state. *Chocolate* milk is made by adding chocolate or cocoa and sweeteners to whole milk.

☐ **Low-Fat:** Contains from 0.5 percent to 2 percent milk fat. The law requires the percentage of milk fat to be clearly stated on labels. *Low-fat chocolate* milk, sometimes labeled chocolate dairy drink, also is available.

☐ **Skim:** Must contain less than 0.5 percent milk fat. Skim milk also is known as *nonfat* milk.

☐ **Buttermilk:** Milk, usually skim, to which special bacterial cultures are added. Buttermilk is tangier and thicker than other fluid milk products. *Dry buttermilk powder* also is available.

☐ **Acidophilus** *(as uh DOF lus):* Skim or low-fat milk that's made similarly to buttermilk, but with a different type of bacterial culture. Once the milk is drunk, the bacteria become active at body temperature, and doctors say that helps maintain the balance of beneficial microorganisms in the body's intestinal tract.

☐ **Nonfat Dry:** Skim milk that has the water removed. This powdered form of milk reconstitutes easily in water. Nonfat dry milk also is known as *powdered* milk.

☐ **Evaporated:** Whole milk from which 60 percent of the water has been removed. Evaporated low-fat (2 percent) and evaporated skim milk also are available.

☐ **Sweetened Condensed:** Whole milk to which sugar is added and from which more than half the water is removed.

Q: What is pasteurization?
A: Pasteurization is a process that destroys any harmful bacteria present in milk without affecting the milk's flavor and nutritional value. During pasteurization, milk is heated, then rapidly cooled. In recent years, new technology has led to the development of ultrapasteurized milk. This product is heated to very high temperatures, which extends the refrigerated shelf life even further. Ultrahigh-temperature-processed milk (called UHT-processed milk) also is available. It is treated as ultrapasteurized milk, then packaged into sterilized containers and aseptically sealed. It can be kept unrefrigerated for at least 3 months, but must be refrigerated and used within a few days once it is opened.

Storing: Make the dairy case your last stop in the supermarket, and refrigerate fluid milk as soon as you get home. Keep opened milk containers closed so the milk doesn't absorb odors in the refrigerator. If milk is kept at room temperature for more than 30 minutes (in a milk pitcher, for example), don't pour it back into the original container. Refrigerate it in a separate container because its storage life has been reduced. Because freezing changes milk's consistency, it is not a recommended way to store milk.

You can store unopened cans of evaporated milk at room temperature for up to 1 year and sweetened condensed milk for up to 6 months. To retain the best flavor, once either type of milk is opened, transfer any unused milk to another covered container. Store it in the refrigerator and use it within 2 to 3 days.

Dry milk will keep up to a year in a cool, dry place. Once you've opened the container, transfer the powdered milk to an airtight container so it doesn't get lumpy and stale. Refrigerate reconstituted dry milk and use it within 2 to 3 days.

Milk Facts

The calories and fat in 1 cup of milk can vary greatly depending on the type of milk you buy. Here's a comparison.

Type of Milk	Fat	Calories
Whole	8 grams	150
Chocolate (made from whole milk)	8 grams	210
Low-fat (2%)	5 grams	120
Low-fat (2%) chocolate	5 grams	180
Low-fat (1%)	3 grams	100
Skim	less than 1 gram	86
Buttermilk	2 grams	100
Acidophilus	5 grams	120
Instant nonfat dry (reconstituted)	less than 1 gram	85
Evaporated, undiluted	20 grams	340
Evaporated low-fat (2%), undiluted	6 grams	220
Evaporated skim, undiluted	1 gram	200
Sweetened condensed, undiluted	27 grams	982

A Tip from Our Kitchen

Most milk products are marked with a "sell by" date. This date indicates when the product should be taken off the supermarket shelves. It does not mean the product is no longer safe to use past this date. The product will, in fact, stay good if properly refrigerated several days after the date on the container.

Q: What is homogenized milk?
A: After milk is pasteurized, it goes through a mechanical process that breaks the milk fat into small particles. These particles are too small to stick together, so they stay mixed throughout the milk instead of rising to the top as a layer of cream.

A Tip from Our Kitchen

If you get caught without a cup of milk, substitute ½ cup evaporated milk plus ½ cup water. Or, reconstitute ⅓ cup nonfat dry milk powder in 1 cup water.

Nutrition hint: If you're really trying to cut calories and fat, skim milk is the way to go. See the Milk Facts chart, left, for a comparison of the fat and calorie content of various milk products.

Milk Fat   A term used to describe the fat found in milk and cream. It is sometimes incorrectly called butterfat.

Millet   *(MILL uht)* A cereal grain with tiny, round, yellow kernels. Millet was one of the first grains used by man and is still an important food in Asia and northern Africa. Millet tastes slightly nutty and has a chewy texture. It can be cooked and eaten by itself, served with sauces, vegetables, and beans, and used in soups and casseroles. Millet also is ground into flour.

Storing: When millet is stored in a cool, dry place in an airtight container, it will keep for up to 2 years.

How to cook: See the Cooking Grains chart under *Grain*.

Nutrition information: A ¾-cup serving of cooked millet contains about 80 calories.

Mince To cut a food with a knife, cleaver, or other utensil, such as a garlic press, into tiny, irregular pieces (see also *Chop* for how-to photograph).

Mincemeat A fruit filling for pies or tarts made with chopped apples and raisins. Originally, mincemeat also contained ground meat and suet, but many mincemeat recipes now omit these ingredients. Often spices and rum or brandy are included as well as candied fruit. Canned or dried versions of mincemeat are available.

Mineral See *Vitamin and Mineral*.

Minestrone *(min uh STROH nee)* A hearty Italian vegetable soup commonly made with beans; small pasta, such as macaroni or broken spaghetti; seasonings; tomatoes; and other vegetables. Sometimes rice is used in place of the pasta. Minestrone often is served with Parmesan or Romano cheese or is topped with pesto (see also *Pesto*). Canned versions of this soup also are available.

Minestrone

      6 cups beef broth
      1 15-ounce can great northern beans
      1 14-ounce can peeled Italian-style
          tomatoes, cut up
      1 cup shredded cabbage
      1 medium potato, peeled and cut into
          julienne strips
      1 medium carrot, bias-sliced ¼ inch
          thick
      1 medium onion, chopped (½ cup)
      2 cloves garlic, minced
      ¾ teaspoon dried chervil *or* basil,
          crushed
      ¾ teaspoon dried oregano, crushed
      2 ounces thin spaghetti, broken
      1 small zucchini, halved lengthwise
          and sliced
      1 9-ounce package frozen Italian green
          beans *or* cut green beans
        Grated Parmesan cheese (optional)

■ In a Dutch oven combine beef broth, *undrained* great northern beans, *undrained* tomatoes, cabbage, potato, carrot, onion, garlic, chervil or basil, oregano, and ¼ teaspoon *pepper*. Bring to boiling.
■ Stir spaghetti, zucchini, and green beans into vegetable mixture in Dutch oven. Return to boiling. Reduce heat and simmer, covered, for 5 to 10 minutes or till vegetables and pasta are done.
■ Season to taste with salt. Ladle into soup bowls. Sprinkle each serving with Parmesan cheese, if desired. Makes 8 servings.

Nutrition information per serving: 132 calories, 8 g protein, 25 g carbohydrate, 1 g fat (0 g saturated), 0 mg cholesterol, 763 mg sodium, 603 mg potassium.

Mint (candy) A candy flavored with peppermint or spearmint. Many kinds of mints are available commercially. Hard, red-and-white-striped mints shaped in canes, sticks, or pieces are traditional at Christmastime. Small, creamy mints are frequently served as a refreshment at receptions. Chocolate-covered mint patties, butter mints, and after-dinner mints often are served as a taste refresher after a meal.

   Homemade mints can be made with fondant and flavored with oil of peppermint.

Mint (herb) A large family of herbs with many varieties. All the mints have a strong aroma, with a refreshing, sweet flavor and cool aftertaste. Mint is available fresh, dried, and as mint extract and oil of mint.

Varieties: *Spearmint* and *peppermint* are the two most widely used mints; lesser known varieties include *pineapple*, *lemon*, and *apple*. Peppermint has a sharp, pungent flavor;

continued

Minestrone

spearmint is more delicate. The others, such as the apple and orange mints, have fruity overtones.

(See *Herb* for the Herb Alternative Guide and selecting, storing, preparation, cooking, nutrition, and other information.)

Peppermint

Spearmint

Miso *(ME so)* A fermented soybean paste that also contains rice, barley, or wheat. Miso is used in Japanese cooking.

Mix To stir or beat two or more foods together until they are thoroughly combined.

Mixed Grill A main dish that consists of an assortment of meats, such as lamb chops, kidney, liver, and sausage, plus vegetables, such as tomatoes and mushrooms. The assortment is cooked on a grill or broiled.

Mixture A combination of two or more foods.

Mocha The term used to describe a dish, usually a dessert or beverage, that is flavored with coffee, or both chocolate and coffee. The term also refers to a variety of Arabian coffee.

Moisten To add enough of a liquid ingredient to a dry ingredient to dampen it but not make it runny.

Molasses A thick, dark brown syrup generally made from the juices pressed from sugarcane during refining. Molasses has a rich, heavy, sweet flavor that is concentrated by boiling. Primarily used for flavoring, molasses is an ingredient in foods, such as gingersnaps, gingerbread, baked beans, and some other baked goods.

Types: During processing, the juices from sugarcane are boiled. In the first boiling, *light* molasses is produced. Light molasses has a mild flavor and sometimes is used as a table syrup. In the second boiling, *dark* molasses is made. Dark molasses is not as sweet as light molasses, but has a more distinctive, robust flavor that is ideal for baking and cooking. The final by-product is *blackstrap* molasses. It has slightly bitter overtones and almost no sweetness. It rarely is used in cooking, but it sometimes is sold in health food stores.

Q: Should I use light or dark molasses in recipes?
A: These two forms of molasses are interchangeable, so use them according to your flavor preferences. Dark molasses is less sweet and has a bolder molasses flavor. As you'd expect, foods sweetened with dark molasses take on a darker color.

Nutrition information: Molasses contains 40 to 50 calories per tablespoon.

(See *Syrup* for storing information.)

Mold   A hollow form that holds a food in a shape until the food sets and is ready to be turned out. The finished product then retains the shape of the mold.

As a verb, the term refers to shaping a food either with the hands or with a form.

The term also refers to a woolly or fuzzy fungus that grows on damp food or on dry food stored in a damp place. Usually molds cause undesirable flavor changes and may also be a health threat. Some molds, however, are desirable and are used to give cheeses, such as blue cheese, their distinctive flavors.

Mole   (MO lay) A Mexican sauce made with chili peppers and tomatoes, which may or may not be spicy, depending upon the chilies used. Although there are many types of mole, one of the most popular is mole poblano, a spicy red sauce that includes unsweetened chocolate and often is served over turkey. Another type, green mole, contains green chilies and cilantro.

Turkey and Chorizo Mole

   4   **ounces chorizo sausage *or* bulk pork sausage, crumbled *or* sliced (optional)**
   1   **tablespoon cooking oil (optional)**
   ¾   **cup whole almonds**
   1   **small onion, chopped (¼ cup)**
   1   **6-inch flour tortilla, torn, *or* 1 slice dry bread, torn**
   1   **clove garlic, minced**
   ¼   **teaspoon ground cinnamon**
   ⅛   **teaspoon ground cloves**
   1   **10-ounce can tomatoes with green chili peppers**
   ¾   **cup chicken broth**
   1   **square (1 ounce) unsweetened chocolate, cut up**
   ⅛   **teaspoon salt**
   6   **turkey breast tenderloin steaks (1 to 1½ pounds total)**
   ½   **cup shredded Monterey Jack cheese**

■ In a 12-inch skillet cook chorizo or pork sausage till brown. Remove with a slotted spoon, reserving *1 tablespoon* drippings in

pan; set sausage aside. If not using sausage, heat cooking oil in skillet. Add almonds, onion, tortilla or bread, garlic, cinnamon, and cloves to skillet. Cook, uncovered, over medium heat, stirring often, about 5 minutes.
■ In a blender container or food processor bowl, place almond mixture, *undrained* tomatoes, broth, chocolate, and salt. Cover; blend or process till nearly smooth.
■ Pour tomato mixture into skillet. Bring to boiling; reduce heat. Add cooked sausage (if using) and turkey steaks. Return to boiling. Cover, reduce heat, and simmer for 15 to 20 minutes or till turkey is no longer pink, stirring once or twice. To serve, remove turkey. Transfer sauce to dinner plates. Slice turkey into 1-inch-thick slices and arrange atop sauce, fanning turkey, if desired. Sprinkle with cheese. Makes 6 servings.

Nutrition information per serving: 289 calories, 25 g protein, 10 g carbohydrate, 18 g fat (5 g saturated), 56 mg cholesterol, 430 mg sodium, 436 mg potassium.

Monosodium Glutamate   A white, crystalline powder that's used to enhance or "wake up" the flavor of foods. Monosodium glutamate, also known as MSG, comes from a naturally occurring glutamic acid in plants. You'll find MSG in the herb and spice section of most supermarkets. It keeps indefinitely in a cool, dark, dry place.

MSG, which is widely used in Oriental cooking, sometimes causes negative reactions, such as headaches and facial tightness.

Monterey Jack Cheese   A creamy white cow's-milk cheese with a mild to mellow flavor. Monterey Jack is semisoft to hard, with a smooth, slightly chewy texture.

Market forms: Monterey Jack cheese comes in two forms.
☐ **Semisoft:** Made from whole milk and sometimes called Monterey cheese, this is the most common form of this variety. Because of its mild flavor, it often is combined with flavors, such as jalepeño and green peppers, onion, herbs, bacon, salami, taco seasonings, caraway seed, and assorted garden vegetables.

Monterey Jack cheese

continued

□ **Hard:** Made from skim or low-fat milk and used mainly as a grating cheese. This cheese also is called dry Monterey or dry Jack.

(See *Cheese* for the Selecting Cheese chart and selecting, storing, serving, nutrition, and other information.)

Mornay Sauce *(more NAY)* A rich,
white sauce made with margarine or butter, flour, and milk to which cheese, usually Swiss, Gruyère, or Parmesan, is added. This classic French sauce is served with chicken, fish, eggs, and vegetables.

Mortar and Pestle A utensil, usually
made from porcelain, metal, or wood, that is used to crush or grind such foods as herbs or spices. Usually sold as a set, the mortar is a small bowl and the pestle is a small cylinder with a club-shaped end.

Moussaka *(moo suh KAH)* A Middle
Eastern baked main dish, made by layering slices of eggplant with a seasoned ground lamb or beef mixture. It also may be topped with a white sauce and cheese.

Moussaka

       1 large eggplant (1½ pounds), peeled
          and cut into ½-inch-thick slices
       2 tablespoons cooking oil *or* olive oil
       1 pound ground lamb
       ½ cup chopped onion
       1 clove garlic, minced
       1 8-ounce can tomato sauce
       2 tablespoons snipped parsley
       ¼ teaspoon salt
       ¼ teaspoon ground cinnamon
       1 bay leaf
       2 tablespoons margarine *or* butter
       2 tablespoons all-purpose flour
          Dash pepper
    1½ cups milk
       1 beaten egg
       3 tablespoons grated Romano *or*
          Parmesan cheese
       1 tablespoon snipped parsley

■ Brush eggplant slices lightly with oil. Place on the unheated rack of a broiler pan. Broil 3 to 4 inches from heat about 5 minutes on each side or till brown. Place *half* the eggplant slices in the bottom of an 8x8x2-inch baking dish; set aside.

■ Meanwhile, in a 10-inch skillet cook lamb, onion, and garlic till meat is brown and onion is tender. Drain off fat. Stir in the tomato sauce, the 2 tablespoons parsley, salt, cinnamon, and bay leaf. Bring to boiling. Reduce heat and simmer, covered, for 10 minutes. Remove the bay leaf.

■ For sauce, in a saucepan melt the margarine or butter. Stir in the flour and pepper. Add milk all at once. Cook and stir till mixture is thickened and bubbly. Slowly stir *half* of the hot mixture into the beaten egg; return all to saucepan. Cook and stir over low heat for 2 minutes. Stir in 2 *tablespoons* of the grated Romano or Parmesan cheese. Set sauce aside.

■ Spoon all of the meat mixture over eggplant layer in baking dish. Arrange remaining eggplant slices atop. Pour the sauce over all. Sprinkle with the remaining Romano or Parmesan cheese. Bake, uncovered, in a 350° oven for 40 minutes. Sprinkle with the 1 tablespoon parsley. Let stand 10 minutes before serving. Makes 4 servings.

Nutrition information per serving: 418 calories, 30 g protein, 21 g carbohydrate, 24 g fat (7 g saturated), 135 mg cholesterol, 727 mg sodium, 926 mg potassium.

Mousse A light, airy, creamy dessert or
main dish. A mousse is made by folding beaten egg whites or whipped cream into a custard or gelatin mixture to create a light, airy texture (see Using Eggs Safely under *Eggs*). A dessert mousse often is flavored with pureed fruit, chocolate, or coffee. It may be chilled or frozen.

A main-dish mousse is made with fish, meat, poultry, or vegetables. It usually is molded and can be served either hot or cold. When cut in smaller portions, a main-dish mousse is sometimes served as an appetizer.

Apricot Mousse

- 1 8¾-ounce can unpeeled apricot halves
- ¼ cup sugar
- 1 envelope unflavored gelatin
- 1 12-ounce can apricot nectar
- 1 cup whipping cream
  Chocolate curls (optional)

■ Drain apricots, reserving ¼ *cup* syrup. Finely chop the apricots. Set aside.

■ In a saucepan combine sugar and gelatin. Stir in about *half* of the apricot nectar. Heat and stir till gelatin dissolves. Remove from heat; stir in remaining nectar and reserved syrup. Chill till partially set (consistency of unbeaten egg whites).

■ Whip cream to soft peaks; fold into partially set gelatin. Fold in chopped apricots. Transfer to dessert glasses or a serving bowl. Refrigerate for 6 to 24 hours. Garnish with chocolate curls, if desired. Makes 6 servings.

Nutrition information per serving: 239 calories, 2 g protein, 26 g carbohydrate, 15 g fat (9 g saturated), 54 mg cholesterol, 20 mg sodium, 153 mg potassium.

Mozzarella Cheese *(maht suh REHL uh)*

A mild-flavored, unripened cheese that has a semisoft and chewy consistency. This creamy white cheese was originally made in Italy with buffalo's milk, but is now made extensively in the United States with whole or part-skim cow's milk. When the cheese is made, the warm curds are blended and stretched until they develop their smooth appearance and elastic texture. This cheese usually is brine cured.

Types: There are two types of mozzarella. The most common type is produced commercially on a large scale and is readily available in the dairy case. It is found in chunks or shredded in packages of various sizes. Generally, this type is firm with a very elastic texture.

Another type of mozzarella typically is made by small cheese makers, so supplies are limited in most areas. This type has a soft texture with a mild, sweet flavor. It usually is sold in balls and sometimes is packed in whey or brine. It's best uncooked and used in salads and antipasto.

Q: **Why are some mozzarellas stringy?**
A: Most mozzarellas are stringy to a certain degree when heated because of the way they are manufactured. But, mozzarella may become extra stringy and tough if heated at too high a temperature or melted too quickly.

(See *Cheese* for the Selecting Cheese chart and selecting, storing, serving, nutrition, and other information.)

Mozzarella cheese

Muddle

To stir or crush a semiliquid or nonliquid food, such as ice cream or sugar cubes, in the bottom of a cup or glass before mixing in a liquid.

Muenster Cheese *(MUHN ster)*

A cow's-milk cheese that varies in flavor from mild to pungent; it can be smooth with a waxy texture or dry and crumbly. Muenster (also spelled Munster) made in the United States is typically the mild variety with small holes and an edible orange-red exterior. Its French or German counterpart is usually a drier, more pungent cheese.

(See *Cheese* for the Selecting Cheese chart and selecting, storing, serving, nutrition, and other information.)

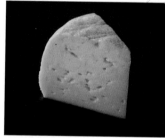
Muenster cheese

Muesli *(MEWS lee)*

A European variation of granola. Muesli basically is rolled oats combined with other cereals or grains, fresh or dried fruit, and nuts. It usually is served with plain yogurt or milk. Muesli also is eaten as a snack food or made into a cooked cereal.

Storing: Store muesli in a cool, dry place for up to 1 month. Or, transfer it to an airtight container and refrigerate for up to 3 months.

Muffin A small, individual, savory or sweet bread made from a batter and leavened with baking powder or baking soda. Muffins have a slightly rounded top that is pebbly rather than smooth. The crust is tender and golden brown, and the crumb is light, moist, and breadlike. Sweeter muffins have a crumb that's more fine-grained and cakelike.

Most muffins are made in a pan with cups that measure about 2½ inches wide at the top and about 1½ inches deep, but some muffins are as large as 4 inches across and 2 inches high or as small as 1¾ inches across and ¾ inch high.

Q: Why do muffin recipes caution against overmixing?
A: Muffins that have been stirred till all the lumps are out have pointed tops and tunnels (elongated cells) throughout them. Although muffins with these undesirable characteristics don't taste bad, they're usually tough.

Storing: Place muffins in a plastic bag and store at room temperature for up to 3 days.

To freeze, wrap baked muffins tightly in heavy foil or place them in freezer bags and freeze for up to 3 months. To reheat, wrap frozen muffins in heavy foil. Heat in a 300° oven for 15 to 18 minutes.

A Tip from Our Kitchen
"Ledges on the edges" are those unwanted rims around the edges of your muffins. To get nicely rounded products without ledges, grease the muffin cups on the bottoms and only *halfway* up the sides, or use paper bake cups. Don't use nonstick spray coating in muffin cups because it will coat the sides of the cups too high up.

Q: What is the doneness test for muffins?
A: Check muffins after the minimum baking time given in the recipe. Muffins are done when their tops are golden brown and a wooden toothpick inserted near centers comes out clean. Remove muffins from pans immediately to avoid soggy bottoms.

Muffins

   1¾ **cups all-purpose flour**
   ⅓   **cup sugar**
   2   **teaspoons baking powder**
   ¼   **teaspoon salt**
   1   **beaten egg**
   ¾   **cup milk**
   ¼   **cup cooking oil**

■ In a mixing bowl combine flour, sugar, baking powder, and salt. Make a well in the center. Combine egg, milk, and oil; add all at once to flour mixture. Stir just till moistened (batter should be lumpy). Lightly grease muffin cups (see tip, below left) or line with paper bake cups; fill ⅔ full. Bake in a 400° oven about 20 minutes or till golden. Remove from pans; serve warm. Makes 10 to 12.

Nutrition information per serving: 171 calories, 3 g protein, 24 g carbohydrate, 7 g fat (1 g saturated), 23 mg cholesterol, 127 mg sodium, 59 mg potassium.

Blueberry Muffins: Prepare Muffins as above, *except* fold ¾ cup fresh or frozen *blueberries* and, if desired, 1 teaspoon finely shredded *lemon peel* into muffin batter.

Nutrition information per serving: 177 calories, 4 g protein, 26 g carbohydrate, 7 g fat (1 g saturated), 23 mg cholesterol, 128 mg sodium, 69 mg potassium.

Cranberry Muffins: Prepare Muffins as above, *except* combine 1 cup coarsely chopped *cranberries* and 2 tablespoons additional *sugar*. Fold the sweetened berries into muffin batter.

Nutrition information per serving: 185 calories, 4 g protein, 28 g carbohydrate, 7 g fat (1 g saturated), 23 mg cholesterol, 127 mg sodium, 66 mg potassium.

Oat or Wheat Bran Muffins: Prepare Muffins as above, *except* reduce flour to *1¼ cups* and add 1 cup *oat or unprocessed wheat bran (miller's bran)* to the flour mixture.

Nutrition information per serving: 171 calories, 4 g protein, 26 g carbohydrate, 7 g fat (1 g saturated), 23 mg cholesterol, 127 mg sodium, 105 mg potassium.

Mull To slowly heat a beverage, such as red wine or cider, with spices and sugar.

Mulligan Stew A term for a meat and vegetable stew prepared with whatever is on hand at the moment.

Mulligatawny A highly seasoned soup that originated in India. It usually has a rich chicken or meat broth accented with curry powder, which is known as "pepper water."

Mush A cooked mixture of cornmeal and water or milk. It can be served as a thick porridge or molded, sliced, and fried till golden brown.

Mushroom A plant in the fungus family that's available in many colors and shapes. Mushrooms range in flavor from mild and nutty to meaty.

Varieties: You'll find edible mushrooms available in numerous varieties. Here are some that you may find at the store. (Mushrooms that are found in the wild should only be used if a knowledgeable mushroom hunter has determined they are edible.)
□ **Common:** Varieties, such as white, cream, and brown, used for commercial production and sometimes referred to as button mushrooms. They have a mild flavor and the familiar umbrella shape with caps that range from ½ inch to 3 inches in diameter. These mushrooms vary in color from white to brown.
□ **Chanterelle** *(shant uh REL):* Looks like a trumpet, with a large, flowerlike cap. This variety has a golden to yellow-orange color and a delicate meaty flavor.
□ **Enoki** *(ee KNOCK ee):* An Oriental variety with a long, slender stem and a tiny cap. The stems are attached to a central base. Enoki mushrooms have a very mild flavor.

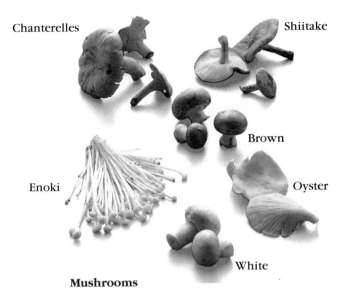

Mushrooms

□ **Morel:** A golden brown mushroom that looks like an irregularly shaped sponge without a stem. Rarely available fresh in stores, it is prized for its hearty flavor and tender texture.
□ **Oyster:** An Oriental variety with a pale cream to gray color that has a large, flowerlike cap and a very short, fat stem. It has a mild flavor.
□ **Shiitake** *(shih TOCK ee):* A brown Oriental mushroom with a large, floppy cap; a tough, slender stem; and a rich, meaty flavor. Only the caps are used.
□ **Straw:** An Oriental variety grown on straw made from rice plants. These brown, umbrella-shaped mushrooms have a mild flavor and a meaty texture.
□ **Other:** A less commonly available mushroom variety is the *Cèpes,* or *Porcini.*

Market forms: Mushrooms most often are available fresh, but many varieties also are sold dried. Common mushrooms are the varieties used most often for canned mushrooms. These come whole, sliced, chopped, and in stems and pieces. Small, whole button mushrooms also are available frozen in butter sauce.

continued

Selecting: Fresh mushrooms should be firm, fresh, and plump and have no bruises or moistness. Size is a matter of preference, not quality. Avoid spotted or slimy mushrooms.

Storing: Store fresh mushrooms, unwashed, in the refrigerator for up to 2 days. Store prepackaged mushrooms in the package. Loose mushrooms or those in an open package should be stored in a paper bag or in a damp cloth bag in the refrigerator. This allows them to breathe so they stay firmer longer. Do not store mushrooms in plastic bags because this causes mushrooms to deteriorate more quickly.

Dried mushrooms will keep up to 6 months in a cool spot.

Mushroom Math

| 1 pound | = 6 cups sliced |
| | = 2 cups sliced and cooked |

Preparation hints: Wipe fresh mushrooms with a clean, damp cloth or rinse them lightly, then dry them gently with paper towels. (Rinsing is especially important for mushrooms you have found in the wild, to remove any bugs that may be in the mushrooms. You may wish to cut wild mushrooms in half before rinsing.) Never soak fresh mushrooms. Soaking ruins their texture.

Slice ¼ inch from the stem of common mushrooms. Trim ½ to 1 inch off base of enoki mushrooms to separate them. Remove and discard stems from the shiitake variety.

Q: How are dried mushrooms prepared for use?
A: To rehydrate dried mushrooms, soak them for about 30 minutes in enough warm water to cover. Then rinse them well and squeeze to drain thoroughly. Remove and discard the tough stems.

How to cook: Most mushrooms should be cooked before eating—common button and enoki mushrooms also can be eaten raw. To cook fresh mushrooms, see the Cooking Fresh Vegetables chart under *Vegetable*. Dried mushrooms are used most often in Oriental stir-fries and soups.

Nutrition information: On the average, common fresh mushrooms have about 10 calories per ½ cup of slices.

Mussel A shellfish most commonly enclosed in a bluish black, hinged, oblong shell, measuring 2 to 4 inches in length. The cooked meat ranges in color from orange to tan and is mildly to moderately flavored. New Zealand exports mussels with green shells.

Types: Mussels live in fresh and salt water, but only saltwater varieties are eaten. The most common mussels are blue mussels.

In the United States, most of the mussels are farm raised. Farm-raised mussels tend to be plumper and milder tasting than wild ones.

Market forms: Mussels are sold live in the shell or fresh shucked. They're also available canned in many forms, such as cooked, smoked, pickled, and in sauces.

Selecting: When buying live mussels, look for tightly closed shells that are moist, intact, and not chipped. If any of the shells are open, tap them lightly. If the mussels are alive, the shells should close. Mussels should smell like the sea and should not have a strong odor. When buying fresh shucked mussels, select plump ones in clear liquid.

Storing: Refrigerate live mussels, covered with a moist cloth in an open container, for up to 5 days. Before cooking, discard any mussels that aren't alive.

Refrigerate shucked mussels covered in their liquor (juice) for up to 3 days. If more liquor is needed to keep them covered, make a homemade brine by mixing ½ teaspoon salt with 1 cup water. Or freeze shucked mussels, covered in their liquor, for up to 3 months.

How to cook: Mussels sometimes are served steamed and dipped in melted butter. For cooking directions, see the Preparing and Cooking Shellfish chart under *Shellfish*.

Nutrition information: A 3-ounce serving of cooked mussels has about 150 calories.

To clean mussels, scrub shells with a stiff brush under cold water. Pull off the beard visible between the two shells. (Remove the beards just before cooking because the mussels will die once they are debearded.)

Mustard A white, brown, or black seed that is ground to make a powder for use as a seasoning or that is used whole as a pickling spice. When dry, mustard is rather bland, but when mixed with water and allowed to stand, the strength increases.

This term also refers to the prepared mustard paste made from mustard powder and other ingredients. Prepared mustard is used as a condiment and as a recipe ingredient.

Market forms: Mustard seeds and dry mustard powder are sold in containers in the spice section of supermarkets. Brown and black mustard seeds may be available only in specialty stores. Prepared mustard is sold in jars or containers alongside other condiments on the supermarket shelf.

Prepared mustards: There are many different kinds of prepared mustard. They range in color from yellow to brown and in flavor from mild to spicy. Here are some of the most common types.

☐ **American or Yellow:** A bright yellow blend made from white (also called yellow) mustard seeds, vinegar, turmeric, and seasonings. This mustard is characterized by a mild, slightly sweet flavor and a smooth texture. It can be used when a recipe calls for prepared mustard.

☐ **Bordeaux:** A dark and rough-textured mustard. Its sweet-sour tarragon flavor complements hearty fare, such as sausage.

☐ **Chinese:** A very hot mustard. It can scorch the mouth and clear the sinuses unlike any other mustard. It is often used as an Oriental dipping sauce.

☐ **Dijon:** A light grayish lemon-colored mustard with a velvety texture that is made with brown or black mustard seeds, white wine, and a blend of spices. Its clean, sharp flavor is ideal for mild dishes in which the flavor of the food must not be covered up.

☐ **English:** A blend of brown or black and white mustard seeds plus other ingredients. It can have a sharp flavor.

☐ **Flavored:** Any of numerous seasoned mustards including honey mustard and horseradish mustard.

☐ **German:** A dark-colored mustard with either a smooth or rough texture. Its sweet-sour flavor and spiciness make it perfect for cured meats and sausage. *Dusseldorf* is the most popular German mustard.

Preparation hints: To make dry mustard easier to mix with foods, mix it with a tiny amount of water. Also, letting it stand for 10 minutes after mixing develops the full flavor of the dry mustard powder.

Nutrition information: One tablespoon of American or yellow prepared mustard has about 10 calories and 196 milligrams sodium.

Mustard Green A young, dark green leaf of certain mustard plants that can be cooked or used raw in salads. The frilly-edged leaves add a peppery bite to salads, so use torn fresh mustard greens in small amounts.

continued

Selecting: Choose young leaves with bright color and no brown spots. Avoid wilted, yellow leaves.

Storing: Wash fresh greens in cold water; pat dry. Place them in a plastic bag lined with a paper towel, and store in the refrigerator for up to 3 days.

How to cook: See Greens on the Cooking Fresh Vegetables chart under *Vegetable*.

Nutrition information: One cup of chopped fresh mustard greens has about 15 calories; ½ cup of cooked chopped mustard greens has about 10 calories.

Mustard greens

Napoleon

Napoleon An elegant dessert made with puff pastry, a rich filling, and a glaze.

Napoleons are made by cutting puff pastry into small rectangles before baking. After baking, the rectangles are separated into three horizontal layers. A puddinglike filling is spread on two of the layers and the layers are reassembled with the filling inbetween. The top is glazed with a vanilla icing and drizzled with melted chocolate.

Nectar A sweet, thick, pulpy juice extracted from fruit. Nectars are much thicker than other fruit juices. Some popular types are apricot, peach, and pear nectars.

Nectarine A fruit with a smooth, yellow and red skin. Inside, the fruit is golden with tinges of red surrounding a brown pit. Nectarines have a rich, sweet, peachlike flavor.

Varieties: There are more than 100 varieties of nectarines available, with new varieties being developed every year. Nectarines can be either freestone or cling (cling means that the fruit adheres to the stone). Popular varieties include *Fantasia*, *Flamekist*, *May Grand*, and *Fairlane*.

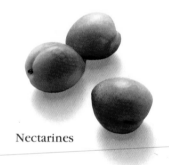

Nectarines

Selecting: Nectarines are usually at their peak between June and September. The lovely red blush on nectarine skins is related to variety not ripeness. It is better to look for fruit with a healthy golden yellow skin without tinges of green. Ripe nectarines should yield slightly to gentle pressure. Don't buy bruised or misshapen fruit.

Nectarine Math

1 pound nectarines	=	3 medium or 4 small
	=	3 cups sliced
	=	2¼ cups chopped

Storing: Nectarines are picked mature but firm for packing and shipping. Complete the ripening at home by placing them in a loosely closed paper bag for several days at room temperature. Keep ripe nectarines in the refrigerator for 3 to 5 days.

Preparation hints: As with peaches, it is your choice as to whether to peel nectarines. Slice, chop, or puree them as you would peaches. Also note that nectarines will discolor after being cut, so treat cut surfaces with ascorbic acid color keeper or a mixture of lemon juice and water to preserve their color.

Nutrition information: One medium nectarine has about 70 calories.

Neufchâtel Cheese (new shuh TEL)
A soft, creamy, white, unripened cheese with a mild and delicate flavor. This cow's-milk cheese is sold in brick form and has a taste and appearance similar to cream cheese, but Neufchâtel has less milk fat and more moisture. It also is a little softer than cream cheese.

(See *Cream Cheese* for storing, nutrition, and other information.)

Newburg A term to describe a food,
such as lobster or shrimp, served in a rich sauce of cream, egg yolks, and sherry.

Nonpareil (non puh REL) A tiny sugar
candy used to decorate cakes, cookies, and other desserts. Nonpareils come in assorted shapes and colors. The term also refers to a small, flat disk of chocolate covered with tiny, white sugar candies.

Noodle Generally, a pasta made from a
dough that includes flour; a liquid, usually water; and eggs. In some homemade recipes a small amount of oil is included. Some Oriental noodles are made with ground mung beans or rice flour in place of wheat flour (see also *Chinese Noodles*).

Noodles can be homemade or produced commercially in dozens of shapes, including wide, medium, and fine ribbons (in long and short lengths), as well as in squares, rectangles, and fine pieces or shreds. Noodles can be naturally flavored by adding vegetables, herbs, or seeds to the dough. Noodle dough also can be filled to form such pastas as ravioli and tortellini. Most homemade pasta is made from noodle dough.

Market forms: Noodles are available dried, frozen, and refrigerated. Naturally flavored noodles also are sold.

(See *Pasta* for identification photos and storing, how-to-cook, nutrition, and other information.)

Nougat (NEW gut) A dense, chewy
candy made with sugar, corn syrup, and egg whites, with almonds and/or candied cherries added. Traditionally, nougat is cut into squares or oblong shapes.

Q: What is the difference between nougat and divinity?
A: Nougat and divinity are like first cousins. Although divinity has a light, soft texture and nougat has a chewier texture, they're related because they use similar ingredients, have similar flavors, and require beating a sugar syrup into beaten egg whites. Nougat is cooked to a higher temperature than divinity, which gives it a chewier texture.

(See *Candy* for Candy-Making Tips and equipment, storing, and other information.)

Nouvelle Cuisine A style of French cooking that emphasizes lighter and leaner foods and simpler preparation methods than the heavier, richer style of classic French cooking. Nouvelle cuisine incorporates more fresh fruits and vegetables, quicker cooking methods to retain nutrients, and less use of fats and starches.

Nut A dry seed or fruit with an internal, edible kernel surrounded by a hard, removable shell or rind.

Market forms: There is a huge selection of nuts available in a variety of forms. Depending on the particular variety of nut you want, you can buy nuts shelled and unshelled, oil- and dry-roasted, salted and unsalted, sugared, and spiced. They come halved, sliced, slivered, chopped, ground, blanched, whole, and in pieces, and with and without skins. At stores, you'll find nuts loose in barrels and packaged in cans, jars, and transparent bags.

Selecting: When buying nuts in the shell, look for clean, unbroken shells without any

Selecting Nuts

Use this chart for a quick comparison of nut flavors, market forms, and calories. The last column of measures will come in handy as a guideline when you're ready to purchase nuts for recipes.

Nut*	Flavor	Market Forms	Approximate Calories (½ cup)	Approximate Yields
Almond	Rich, mild	Shelled and in the shell; whole (blanched and unblanched); chopped; sliced; slivered; dry-roasted; smoke-flavored; sugared or spiced	420 (whole)	1 lb. in the shell = 1¼ cups shelled = 5½ oz. whole
Brazil Nut	Rich, oily	Shelled and in the shell; whole	460 (whole)	1 lb. in the shell = 1½ cups shelled = 7 oz. whole
Cashew	Rich, buttery	Shelled only; raw or roasted; dry-roasted	374 (whole or halves, oil-roasted)	1 lb. shelled = 3¼ cups
Chestnut	Sweet, starchy	In the shell; canned (whole or pureed); candied; dried	175 (whole, roasted)	1 lb. in the shell = 2½ cups shelled = 12 oz. whole
Hazelnut (Filbert)	Mild, sweet	Shelled and in the shell; whole; chopped	364 (chopped)	1 lb. in the shell = 1½ cups shelled = 7 oz. whole
Macadamia Nut	Rich, sweet, buttery	Shelled and in the shell; roasted; dry-roasted	481 (whole, oil-roasted)	1 lb. in the shell = 1¼ cups shelled = 5½ oz. whole
Pecan	Rich, buttery	Shelled and in the shell; halves; pieces; chopped	361 (halves)	1 lb. in the shell = 2 cups shelled = 7 oz. halves
Pine Nut	Sweet, faint pine	Shelled; whole	408 (whole)	1½ oz. shelled = ¼ cup
Pistachio Nut	Mild, sweet	In the shell, raw or roasted; shelled available in some areas	370 (whole)	4 oz. in the shell = 1 cup shelled = 4 oz. whole
Walnut, Black	Rich, intense	Shelled; pieces	380 (chopped)	1¼ lbs. in the shell = 1 cup shelled = 4 oz. chopped
Walnut, English	Mild	Shelled and in the shell; halves and pieces; chopped	385 (chopped)	1 lb. in the shell = 2 cups shelled = 8 oz. chopped

See individual entries for additional information.

splits, cracks, stains, or holes. The nuts should feel heavy for their size—if they feel light, the nuts inside may be old and shriveled. Although nuts in the shell are plentiful at Christmastime, many are not readily available the rest of the year.

Shelled nuts should be plump and somewhat uniform in color and size. They also should be firm, not limp or rubbery. Shelled nuts are sold year-round in a variety of forms. Because of the oils they contain, shelled nuts tend to go rancid quickly.

Q: **If I don't have the particular nut called for in a recipe, what can I substitute?**
A: In most recipes, nuts are selected for their flavor as well as appearance. Walnuts and pecans are versatile enough in flavor that they are good substitutes for most any nut in some recipes. Almonds and hazelnuts (filberts) also can be interchanged in most recipes.

However, some recipes, such as tortes, are formulated using a specific nut, so you have to be more selective in your substitutions. Limit your substituting to walnuts for pecans and almonds for hazelnuts (filberts), and vice versa; any other exchanges are not recommended.

A Tip from Our Kitchen
Some flourless cakes (tortes) use nuts in place of all or some of the all-purpose flour. For these recipes, it is important to use *very fine* and *dry* ground nuts. Grinding nuts to the right stage can be tricky because nuts will form a paste if ground too much. To prevent this, grind the nuts in small batches with a food grinder, blender, or food processor. If using a blender or food processor, try adding 1 tablespoon of the sugar from the recipe for each cup of nuts when processing, then quickly start and stop the appliance for better control over the fineness of the ground nuts.

Storing: Heat, light, and moisture cause nuts, especially shelled nuts, to go rancid quickly. Store nuts, shelled or unshelled, in a cool, dry place. After opening a package of shelled nuts, refrigerate or freeze them in a tightly covered container. (See individual nut entries for specific storage information.)

Q: **Why do some recipes call for toasted nuts?**
A: Toasting nuts brings out their full flavor and aroma. Toasting also helps keep nuts crisp when they're used in liquid or moist mixtures, such as salad dressings, sauces, and fruit salads. (See the how-to photo under *Almond*.)

Nutrition hints: Nuts are a good source of protein for anyone on a meatless diet, but they should be used in moderation because they're high in calories and fat.

Nutmeg   The seed of the fruit of the nutmeg tree. When the fruit is ripe, it splits open and reveals a seed that's covered with what looks like red lace. This fragile, red skin (mace) is removed before the nutmeg is dried (see also *Mace*). The brown, oval nutmegs are usually about an inch in length and have wrinkled surfaces. When grated, a slightly sweet and spicy aroma is released.

Most nutmeg is sold ground, but whole nutmeg is available for grating.

(See *Spice* for the Spice Alternative Guide and selecting, storing, and nutrition information.)

Nutrition   All of the processes involved in how the body uses food. Most often this term refers to the scientific study of how diet promotes good health.

Food contains the nutrients that are necessary to good health. Those nutrients are carbohydrates, fats, proteins, vitamins and minerals, and water (see also individual entries). They allow your body to grow, maintain, and repair body tissues; to perform activities such as walking, breathing, and many other actions; and to balance body chemistry.

Planning a balanced diet: Because no single food supplies all the nutrients your body needs, good nutrition depends on eating a variety of foods. To help translate nutrients into food on the plate, nutritionists have suggested a plan that organizes food into groups. Eating a variety of foods from each of these food groups will prevent nutrient deficiencies and help keep you healthy. For a description of the food groups, see The Basic Food Groups chart, below.

Steps to help plan daily menus: As you plan your menus, think of all the meals for the day. Make sure the sum of the foods you choose includes the recommended amounts from each of the Basic Food Groups. Keep in mind, too, that some dishes, such as casseroles, combine foods from the groups.

Finally, double-check your food choices by comparing them to the daily nutrient recommendations listed in the box, opposite below. If your choices meet these guidelines, you're on the right track.

The Basic Food Groups

	Foods in Group	Number of Daily Servings	Serving Size	Major Nutrients
Vegetables And Fruits	All vegetables and fruits (fresh, canned, frozen, or dried) and their juices.	4 servings. (For vitamin C, serve foods such as citrus fruits, melons, berries, tomatoes, or dark green vegetables daily. For vitamin A, serve dark green or deep yellow vegetables or fruits.)	½ cup or a typical portion, such as 1 medium orange, ½ of a medium grapefruit, 1 medium potato, or 1 wedge of lettuce.	Carbohydrates, fiber, and vitamins A and C. Dark green vegetables are good sources of riboflavin, folacin, iron, and magnesium. Some greens contain useful amounts of calcium.
Breads and Cereals	All foods based on whole grains or enriched flour or meal. Includes breads, biscuits, muffins, waffles, pancakes, pasta, rice, and cereals.	4 servings. (For fiber, include some whole grain bread or cereal every day.)	1 slice bread; 1 biscuit or muffin; 1 pancake or waffle; ½ to ¾ cup cooked pasta, rice, bulgur, or cereal; or 1 ounce ready-to-eat cereal.	Carbohydrates, protein, thiamin, riboflavin, niacin, B vitamins, and iron. Whole grain products provide magnesium, fiber, and folacin.
Milk and Milk Products	All types of milk, yogurt, cheese, ice milk, ice cream, and foods prepared with milk (milk shakes, puddings, and creamed soups).	Children under 9, 2 to 3 servings. Children 9 to 12, 3 servings. Teens, 4 servings. Adults, 2 servings. Pregnant women, 3 servings. Nursing mothers, 4 servings.	1 cup milk or yogurt, 1⅓ cups cottage cheese, 1½ ounces cheese, 2 ounces process cheese food or spread, ¼ cup Parmesan cheese, or 1½ cups ice cream.	Protein, calcium, riboflavin, and vitamins A, B_6, and B_{12}. When fortified, these products also provide vitamin D.
Meats and Meat Alternates	Beef, veal, lamb, pork, poultry, fish, shellfish, variety meats, dry beans or peas, soybeans, lentils, eggs, peanuts and other nuts, peanut butter, and seeds.	2 servings.	2 to 3 ounces lean cooked meat, poultry, or fish; 1 to 1½ cups cooked dry beans, peas, or lentils; 2 eggs; ½ to 1 cup nuts or seeds; or ¼ cup peanut butter.	Protein, phosphorus, and vitamin B_6. Foods of animal origin provide vitamin B_{12}. Meats, dry beans, and dry peas provide iron. Liver and egg yolks provide vitamin A.
Fats, Sweets, And Alcohol	All fats and oils; mayonnaise and salad dressings; all concentrated sweets; highly sugared beverages; alcoholic beverages; unenriched, refined flour products; bacon and salt pork.	No serving number is recommended. In moderation, these foods can be included to round out your meals, as long as recommendations from the other categories are satisfied.	No specific serving size is recommended.	These foods provide few nutrients in proportion to the number of calories they contain. Vegetable oils provide vitamin E and essential fatty acids.

Planning delicious, attractive, and healthful menus is easy when you use the Basic Food Groups and this handy menu-planning checklist for each meal.

☐ Start with a selection from the meat and meat alternates group.

☐ Add a bread or cereal, such as rolls or rice, if one is not a part of a main dish.

☐ Choose a hot or cold vegetable and/or select a fruit or vegetable salad.

☐ Choose a beverage. This is an excellent place for a serving from the milk group.

☐ If desired, add a dessert. Fruit and milk-based desserts, such as pudding, can help you meet your quotas from the Basic Food Groups; desserts such as cake or candy mostly just add calories.

☐ After you've met the Basic Food Group recommendations, add extras, if you like, from the fifth group—fats and sweets. Remember to use these foods in moderation and only to the extent that they meet the recommendations listed below.

Daily Recommendations

Nutritionists suggest that for good health adults follow these daily recommendations. To use these guidelines, you'll need to know your daily calorie needs. To help you estimate the number of calories you need for weight maintenance, see the question and answer under *Calorie*.

Protein: about 15% of calories

Fat: no more than 30% of calories

Carbohydrate: about 55% of calories

Cholesterol: no more than 300 milligrams

Sodium: 500 to 3,000 milligrams

Dietary Fiber: 20 to 30 grams

You'll also need to know that 1 gram of fat contains 9 calories and 1 gram of protein and carbohydrate each contains 4 calories. For example, to calculate your recommended maximum grams of fat per day, multiply your daily calorie needs by 0.3 (30%) and divide by 9. This gives you the maximum grams of fat you can have.

Q: How can I lower the fat in my diet?

A: First take a look at the type and amount of high-protein foods you are eating. Replace fatty meat cuts with lean ones. Substitute poultry (without skin) and fish for some of the meat.

Next look at how you prepare foods. Here are some suggestions that can make a big difference.

Avoid deep-fat and shallow-fat frying. Instead, stir-fry or oven-fry. Or, broil, bake, steam, poach, or boil.

Broil meats, fish, and poultry on a rack and let the fat drip away.

Cut all visible fat from meats and poultry before cooking.

Cook soups a day ahead and chill them. Then skim off fat that rises to the top and reheat the soup before serving.

Substitute skim (or at least reduced-fat) milk for whole milk; yogurt for sour cream; and low-fat cottage cheese for regular cottage cheese.

Season vegetables with herbs, lemon juice, or reduced-calorie salad dressings instead of margarine or butter.

Hints for losing weight: If you have been thinking about losing weight, consult with your doctor. Then, if you start a weight-loss program, plan to lose 1 or 2 pounds per week. (To lose 1 pound a week, you need to cut your daily intake by only 500 calories.) Also, keep these dos and don'ts in mind.

☐ Do include a variety of foods, such as breads, cereals, fruits, vegetables, meats, fish, poultry, and dairy products.

☐ Do drink plenty of liquids. You should drink 6 to 8 glasses a day.

☐ Do get regular exercise. You'll lose more weight than by just dieting. Even a gradual increase in activity makes a difference.

☐ Don't skip meals. Meal skippers often overeat later in the day.

☐ Don't use appetite suppressants or diuretics.

☐ Don't believe promises that a product or a plan will help you lose weight rapidly and easily. Choose a plan that has been developed by a registered dietitian or a nutritionist with a degree from an accredited university.

O-Q

Classic Quiche Lorraine
(see recipe, page 342)

Sour Cream Pound Cake
(see recipe, page 335)

Oysters Rockefeller
(see recipe, page 288)

Oat The edible cereal grain produced by the cereal grass of the same name. Oats are light tan in color. They have a nutty flavor and a chewy texture and must be hulled before they can be eaten. Whole oats minus the hulls are called groats.

Market forms: There are several forms of oats. Here are the most popular.

☐ **Rolled:** Oat groats that have been steamed then flattened by steel rollers into flakes. They also are known as old-fashioned oats.

☐ **Quick-Cooking:** Oat groats that are cut into several pieces before rolling to shorten the cooking time. Quick-cooking and rolled oats can be used interchangeably in most recipes.

☐ **Instant Oatmeal:** Oat groats that are cut into very small pieces and specially processed so that they need no cooking, just the addition of boiling water. Some brands of instant oatmeal are flavored with sugar, spices, or fruit, and usually salt.

☐ **Steel-Cut:** Oat groats that have been sliced by steel blades. Also known as Scottish or Irish oatmeal, steel-cut oats have a firm texture when cooked. Find steel-cut oats at specialty markets.

☐ **Oat Flour:** The finely ground grain. Usually found at health food stores, oat flour sometimes is used in baked goods.

☐ **Oat Bran:** The ground outer layer of the oat. Used in cooking and as a hot cooked breakfast cereal, oat bran is considered a good source of fiber (see also *Bran* for information on 100-percent oat bran).

Making Oat Bran Substitute

Your blender or food processor can double as a grain mill to make this handy substitute for oat bran. To make enough mixture to replace ½ cup oat bran, process ⅔ cup rolled oats in a covered blender container or food processor bowl till the oats are ground.

Storing: Store oats in an airtight container in a cool, dry place for up to 6 months. Freeze in a moisture- and vaporproof container for up to 1 year.

How to cook: See the Cooking Grains chart under *Grain.*

Nutrition information: A ¾-cup serving of hot cooked oatmeal made from rolled oats contains about 110 calories.

Octopus An eight-armed saltwater mollusk with firm and delicately flavored white meat. Octopus is popular in Italian, Greek, Spanish, Portuguese, and Oriental cuisines. More octopus is eaten in Japan than in any other country.

Market forms: Octopus is sold fresh, frozen, or precooked. Some seafood stores and delicatessens sell marinated octopus salad. Other octopus products include imported sun-dried, smoked, and canned items.

Nutrition information: Poached octopus has about 80 calories in a 3-ounce serving.

Oil See *Fat and Oil.*

Okra A small, green or purple, edible pod with a fuzzy, ridged skin and tapered, oblong shape. Inside the pod are lots of small white seeds. Okra has a mild asparaguslike flavor and, when cooked, develops a slippery quality (called ropy) that thickens any liquid in which it is cooked.

Market forms: Fresh okra, frozen whole or cut okra, and canned cut okra all are available.

Okra

Selecting: Fresh okra is available in the South throughout the year, and is most plentiful in other parts of the country July through September. Look for small, crisp, bright colored pods without brown spots or blemishes. Avoid shriveled pods.

Storing: Keep okra tightly wrapped in the refrigerator for up to 3 days.

How to cook: See the Cooking Fresh Vegetables chart under *Vegetable*.

Nutrition information: One-half cup of cooked sliced frozen okra has about 35 calories.

Olive

The small, oval fruit of the olive tree. When first picked, olives have a bitter taste. A curing process removes the bitterness and produces their characteristic flavor and shiny appearance. Olives range in size from small to supercolossal, depending on the variety. They are served plain as a relish and are used as recipe ingredients.

Types: *Spanish-style* or *green* olives are underripe olives. They have a salty, tart taste. They're sold in jars and come pitted, unpitted, and stuffed. Green olives can be stuffed with pimiento; anchovies; whole, blanched almonds; or tiny, whole onions.

Black olives are ripe olives. They have a smooth, mellow taste. They're sold in cans and come pitted, unpitted, sliced, and chopped.

Specialty olives include small, shriveled, Italian-style ripe olives that are salt-cured and oil-coated, as well as large, plump, marinated green or black olives. These can be found in the specialty sections of some supermarkets, delicatessens, and specialty food stores.

Nutrition information: The calories and sodium content of olives vary depending on the type. For instance, 5 pimiento-stuffed green olives have about 25 calories and 469 milligrams sodium, 5 pitted black olives have about 25 calories and 196 milligrams sodium, and 5 Italian-style black olives have about 35 calories and 315 milligrams sodium.

Omelet

Beaten eggs that are cooked in a skillet and served open-faced or folded in half or thirds. Most typically, omelets contain savory fillings and are served for breakfast or brunch. But they also can be filled with sweet fillings, such as fruit, and served for dessert.

Types: There are two basic kinds of omelets.
☐ **Puffy:** A light, airy omelet that's made by folding stiffly beaten egg whites into beaten egg yolks. A puffy omelet is cooked on the range top till puffed and set on the bottom, then transferred to the oven until it is browned and set on the top. This omelet is served open-faced or folded in half, often with a filling or topped with a sauce.
☐ **Plain or French:** A flat omelet made by beating whole eggs together. It is commonly cooked over moderate heat on top of the range. The egg mixture usually is allowed to cook and set around the edges. Then the edges are lifted so the uncooked portion can run underneath to cook. This type of omelet usually is folded over a filling.

Preparation hints: To make puffy omelets, see *Meringue* for Egg White Pointers.

continued

1. To serve a plain or French omelet, use a spatula to carefully lift one-third of the omelet over the filling, as shown. Repeat with the remaining one-third of the omelet.

2. Slide the omelet to the side of the skillet. Tilt the skillet and slide the omelet out onto a warm plate. If necessary, cover the omelet with foil to keep it warm while preparing any other omelets.

(continued from below left)

A Tip from Our Kitchen

You can create new and delicious omelets just by varying the filling. Use whatever ingredients you have on hand. You can mix and match items, such as heated diced ham or cooked sausage; sautéed sliced mushrooms, chopped onion, or chopped green pepper; or shredded cheese. For dessert omelets, choose ingredients such as sliced fruit, fruit-flavored yogurt, and jellies or jams.

Cooking hints: Use a well-seasoned skillet or omelet pan, or one with a nonstick surface, to keep omelets from sticking.

Cook plain omelets just until the egg portion is cooked through and set. Over-cooking the eggs makes an omelet tough.

French Omelet

    2 eggs
    1 tablespoon water
   ⅛ teaspoon salt
       Dash pepper
    1 tablespoon margarine *or* butter

■ In a mixing bowl combine eggs, water, salt, and pepper. Using a fork, beat till combined but not frothy. In an 8- or 10-inch skillet with flared sides, heat margarine or butter till a drop of water sizzles. Lift and tilt the pan to coat the sides.
■ Add egg mixture to skillet; cook over medium heat. As eggs set, run a spatula around the edge of the skillet, lifting eggs and letting the uncooked portion flow underneath. When eggs are set but still shiny, remove from heat. Fold unfilled omelet in half. Transfer onto a warm plate. Serves 1.

Microwave directions: In a mixing bowl combine *3* eggs, *2 tablespoons* water, salt, and pepper. In a 9-inch microwave-safe pie plate, micro-cook *1 teaspoon* margarine or butter on 100% power (high) for 30 to 40 seconds or till melted. Spread margarine to coat pie plate.

Add egg mixture. Cook, uncovered, on high for 2½ to 3½ minutes or till eggs are set but still shiny, pushing cooked portions toward center every 30 seconds. Fold and serve as below left. Makes 1 or 2 servings.

Nutrition information per serving: 252 calories, 13 g protein, 1 g carbohydrate, 21 g fat (5 g saturated), 426 mg cholesterol, 522 mg sodium, 128 mg potassium.

Mushroom French Omelet: Prepare French Omelet as below left, *except,* for filling, cook ⅓ cup sliced fresh *mushrooms* in 1 tablespoon *margarine or butter* till tender. Spoon across center of omelet. Fold sides over.

Nutrition information per serving: 360 calories, 13 g protein, 3 g carbohydrate, 33 g fat (8 g saturated), 426 mg cholesterol, 657 mg sodium, 219 mg potassium.

Cheese French Omelet: Prepare French Omelet as below left, *except* omit salt. For filling, sprinkle ¼ cup shredded *cheddar, Swiss, Monterey Jack, or American cheese* across center of omelet. Fold sides over. Top with additional shredded *cheese* and snipped *parsley.*

Nutrition information per serving: 395 calories, 22 g protein, 2 g carbohydrate, 33 g fat (13 g saturated), 463 mg cholesterol, 475 mg sodium, 169 mg potassium.

Puffy Omelet

    4 egg whites
    4 egg yolks, beaten
    1 tablespoon margarine *or* butter

■ In a mixing bowl beat egg whites till frothy. Add 2 tablespoons *water;* continue beating about 1½ minutes or till stiff peaks form (tips stand straight). Fold egg yolks into egg whites.
■ In a large ovenproof skillet heat margarine or butter till a drop of water sizzles. Pour in egg mixture, mounding it slightly higher at the sides. Cook over low heat for 8 to 10 minutes or till puffed, set, and golden brown on the bottom. Then bake in a 325° oven for 8 to 10 minutes or till a knife inserted near the center comes out clean. Loosen sides of

omelet with a metal spatula. Make a shallow cut slightly off center across the omelet. Fold smaller side over the larger side. Serves 2.

Nutrition information per serving: 203 calories, 13 g protein, 1 g carbohydrate, 16 g fat (4 g saturated), 426 mg cholesterol, 191 mg sodium, 131 mg potassium.

Cheese-Herb Puffy Omelet: Prepare Puffy Omelet as in recipe opposite, *except,* while omelet is baking, melt 1 tablespoon *margarine or butter* in a saucepan. Stir in 1 tablespoon all-purpose *flour,* 1 teaspoon snipped *chives,* and ¼ teaspoon dried *fines herbes,* crushed. Add ⅔ cup *milk.* Cook and stir till thickened and bubbly. Cook and stir 1 minute more. Stir in ⅓ cup shredded *cheddar or Swiss cheese* till melted. Pour over folded omelet.

Nutrition information per serving: 384 calories, 21 g protein, 9 g carbohydrate, 30 g fat (10 g saturated), 453 mg cholesterol, 414 mg sodium, 286 mg potassium.

Ham-and-Cheese Puffy Omelet: Prepare Puffy Omelet as in recipe opposite, *except,* while omelet is baking, melt 1 tablespoon *margarine or butter* in a saucepan. Stir in 1 tablespoon *all-purpose flour.* Add ⅔ cup *milk.* Cook and stir till thickened and bubbly. Cook and stir 1 minute more. Stir in ⅓ cup shredded *cheddar or Swiss cheese* till melted. Stir in ¼ cup diced fully cooked *ham* and one 2-ounce jar sliced *mushrooms,* drained. Heat through. Pour over folded omelet.

Nutrition information per serving: 416 calories, 26 g protein, 10 g carbohydrate, 31 g fat (11 g saturated), 463 mg cholesterol, 737 mg sodium, 368 mg potassium.

One-Bowl Cake   A layer-type cake
made by mixing the batter in only one bowl and omitting the step of creaming the shortening, margarine, or butter and the sugar. In this method, shortening, margarine, or butter, the liquid, and the flavoring are added to the dry ingredients and beaten. The eggs are added, and the batter is beaten again. Since recipe ingredients are balanced for a particular mixing method, stick to the method given in a recipe. (See *Devil's Food Cake* for a one-bowl cake recipe example.)

Tips from Our Kitchen
Here are two hints to make one-bowl mixing easy.
- Use room-temperature shortening, margarine, or butter so that it combines quickly and easily with the other cake batter ingredients.
- Prevent ingredients from spattering by starting the beating on low to medium speed for 30 seconds. Then increase to medium and high speeds.

(See *Cake* for How to Solve Cake Problems, Cake-Making Hints, and baking, storing, and other information.)

One-Dish Meal   A recipe that
combines several foods and is served as a complete meal. Casseroles, stews, and hearty salads are considered one-dish meals because they combine meats, poultry, eggs, or fish with vegetables and sometimes pasta or rice.

Onion   A bulb vegetable of the lily family
that has a sharp flavor when raw and is mellow and aromatic when cooked.

Types: Although there are numerous kinds of onions, they can be grouped by the time of year you'll find them in the supermarket. (See also *Chive, Leek,* and *Shallot.*)

Some descriptive onion names refer to the size. For example, boiling (or boiler) onions are ⅞ to 1½ inches in diameter and pearl (or creamer) onions are about ½ inch in diameter.

☐ **Spring/Summer Onions:** Dry, bulb onions with a milder, sweeter, and less pungent flavor than fall/winter onions. They can be white, yellow, or red and sometimes are referred to as fresh onions. These onions have thin, light outer skins, a high water and sugar content, bruise easily, and are fragile, so they have a fairly short storage life. They're generally available from April through August.

continued

Onions

White

Yellow

Red

Green

Boiling

Pearl

batter-coated onion rings also are sold. French fried onions also are available canned. Other products you'll find are dried minced onion, onion powder, and onion salt.

Selecting: Dry onions range in size from ½ inch to 4 inches and larger in diameter. Select dry onions that are firm, have short necks and papery outer skins, and are free of blemishes and soft spots. Avoid onions that have begun to sprout. Choose green onions with fresh-looking tops and clean white ends.

Storing: Store fall/winter onions in a cool, dry, well-ventilated place for up to several months. Keep spring/summer onions in the refrigerator for up to several weeks, depending on the variety. Green onions should be wrapped then refrigerated for up to 5 days.

For longer storage, freeze sliced or chopped onions in freezer containers for up to 1 year.

Preparation hints: To peel small pearl and boiling onions, immerse the whole onions in boiling water for 3 minutes; drain. Trim off the root ends and gently press to slip off the skins.

To chop an onion quickly, halve it from top to root end. Placing the onion halves flat side down, make parallel vertical slices. Then cut across the slices, as shown.

In this group are the special sweet onion varieties, including *Vidalia, Walla Walla, Maui, Texas Spring Sweet, Imperial Sweet,* and *Carzalia Sweet* onions.

Fall/Winter Onions: Dry, bulb onions that have thicker, darker outer skins than spring/summer onions and can be white, yellow, or red onions. These firm onions are excellent for storage and sometimes are referred to as storage onions. They generally are available from late August through March or April. These onions have a lower water content and a more pungent flavor than the spring/summer onions.

Green Onions or Scallions: Fresh, immature onions with a mildly pungent flavor. They have a white end with long green shoots or tops.

Q: Can the tops of green onions be used?
A: Yes, they add a delicious mild onion flavor to dishes. Slice off as much of the shoot as you want. Just remove any wilted, brown, or damaged tops.

Market forms: Onions are available fresh, canned, pickled, and frozen. In addition to frozen chopped and small, whole onions, frozen onions in cream sauce and frozen

Onion Math

1 small	=	⅓ cup chopped
1 medium	=	½ cup chopped
1 large	=	1 cup chopped
1 green onion	=	2 tablespoons sliced

How to cook: See the Cooking Fresh Vegetables chart under *Vegetable*.

Nutrition information: Chopped raw onions contain about 30 calories per ½ cup. One tablespoon of chopped green onion, including bulb and top, has only 2 calories.

Onion Soup A soup that features onion as the main ingredient. Onion soup can be clear or creamy. French onion soup is the
continued

French Onion Soup
(see recipe, page 282)

most common clear type. It usually is made by simmering onions in beef broth. A slice of toasted French bread topped with one or more kinds of cheese usually is baked on the soup as a garnish.

Cream of onion soup is a creamy version. It combines onions with a thickened milk or cream base and is served plain.

Commercially prepared onion soups are available in both dried and condensed forms.

French Onion Soup

3 large onions, thinly sliced
   (about 4 cups)
¼ cup margarine *or* butter
2 cloves garlic, minced
2 14½-ounce cans beef broth
1 tablespoon Worcestershire sauce
¼ teaspoon pepper
4 ½-inch-thick slices French bread,
   toasted and cut into quarters
1 cup shredded Swiss *or* Gruyère
   cheese (4 ounces)
2 tablespoons grated Parmesan cheese

■ In a large saucepan combine onions, margarine or butter, and garlic. Cover and cook over low heat, stirring occasionally, for 20 to 25 minutes or till onions are tender.
■ Stir in beef broth, Worcestershire sauce, and pepper. Bring to boiling; reduce heat. Cover and simmer for 15 minutes.
■ Ladle soup into 4 ovenproof soup bowls.* Top each serving with 4 pieces of toasted bread. Sprinkle each serving with *one-fourth* of the shredded Swiss or Gruyère cheese, then *one-fourth* of the Parmesan cheese. Bake in a 500° oven for 1 to 3 minutes or till cheese melts. Makes 4 servings.

   Note: If you don't have ovenproof soup bowls, do not quarter the toasted bread slices. Instead, place the 4 slices on a baking sheet. Sprinkle each with *one-fourth* of the cheeses. Broil 3 inches from heat for 45 to 60 seconds or till cheese melts and turns golden. Ladle soup into bowls and float bread atop.

Nutrition information per serving: 384 calories, 16 g protein, 30 g carbohydrate, 22 g fat (8 g saturated), 28 mg cholesterol, 1,173 mg sodium, 372 mg potassium.

Oranges

Navel

Valencia

Blood

Orange
A citrus fruit characterized by a round to oval shape and bright orange skin surrounding juicy, segmented, orange-colored meat. Oranges are sweet enough to enjoy without adding sugar.

Varieties: There are a number of special orange varieties to enjoy. See the Selecting Oranges chart, opposite, for information.

Market forms: Purchase oranges fresh and also as freshly squeezed juice, juice products made from concentrate, juice drinks, punches, and frozen juice concentrate. You'll also find oranges canned and refrigerated with other fruits, dried orange peel in jars, candied orange peel, and orange marmalade, liqueurs, and flavorings.

Orange Math

1 medium orange = ⅓ cup sections
= ¼ to ⅓ cup juice
= 4 teaspoons shredded peel

Selecting: Look for well-formed fruit that's heavy for its size and has healthy color. Brown speckling and a slight greenish tinge found on the surface of some oranges don't affect the eating quality. Choose fresh oranges according to the characteristics for the individual variety. See the Selecting Oranges chart for information.

Preparation hints: Wash oranges thoroughly before cutting or slicing. To remove peel and white membrane, cut a thin slice off each end of the orange. Set fruit on one end, then cut a strip of peel from top to bottom. Continue cutting from top to bottom until peel is removed.

(See *Citrus Fruit* for the Selecting Citrus Fruit chart and storing and nutrition information.)

Orange Roughy   A saltwater fish from New Zealand waters with a rough, bright orange skin. It sometimes is called deep sea perch and Australian sole. The meat is white and firm with a sweet, delicate flavor. Orange roughy is currently a very popular fish in the United States.

Selecting Oranges

Oranges differ in skin and meat color, size, shape, flavor, and juiciness. These characteristics make certain types more desirable for eating out of hand, using in salads or compotes, or for cooking or baking.

Variety	Characteristics	Uses	Season
Blood	Small; round; blushing orange-red skin; reddish orange meat; intense orange flavor; some seeds	Salads; compotes; eating out of hand	December-July (supply is limited)
Navel	Large; round to oval; orange skin; very juicy, sweet meat; seedless; very easy to peel	Salads; compotes; eating out of hand; cooking/baking	November-June
Temple	Large; oval; hybrid of the orange and tangerine; orange skin; juicy, sweet meat; many seeds; fairly easy to peel	Eating out of hand	January-May
Valencia	Large; oval; smooth, thin, deep orange skin; sweet, golden juice; few seeds	Juice; beverages; sauces; cooking/baking	February-June

Market forms: You'll find orange roughy sold as skinless fillets.

How to cook: Orange roughy is great grilled, baked, poached, or panfried. For baking, poaching, and panfrying directions, see the Cooking Fish chart under *Fish*. For grilling directions, see the Direct-Grilling Fish chart under *Barbecue*.

Nutrition information: Orange roughy has about 140 calories in a 3-ounce serving.

(See *Fish* for selecting, storing, thawing, and other information.)

Oregano *(uh REG uh no)* A robust herb with small, green leaves. Oregano has a strong spicy flavor and bitter undertones. It is sometimes called wild marjoram, but the flavor differences are great, so do not use oregano and marjoram interchangeably.

Oregano is available fresh and dried. Dried oregano is packaged as whole leaves and as a ground herb.

(See *Herb* for the Herb Alternative Guide and selecting, storing, preparation, cooking, nutrition, and other information.)

Oregano

Oriental Cooking
The cooking of Asia in general, but usually referring to that of China, Japan, Korea, Thailand, Vietnam, and other countries in Southeast Asia.

Cuisine highlights: Because of the vast geographic differences, there is much diversity within Oriental cooking. Rice is about the only staple food common to all of the cuisines. There also is heavy use of grains, vegetables, and fruits, with less attention paid to meats. People in island countries and coastal lands rely on fish and seafood, and those in inland regions use more chicken,
continued on page 286

Oriental Ingredients

Here's a selection of specialty ingredients frequently called for in Oriental recipes. Use this guide to help you become familiar with these ingredients.

Bamboo shoots: Ivory-colored shoots from certain bamboo plants. They add texture to stir-fry dishes. They are available canned, both whole (cone-shaped) and sliced. Fresh shoots are rarely sold.

Dried lily buds: Pale golden brown, delicately flavored buds. They also are called tiger lily buds and golden needles. Soak the dried buds in hot water before using in stir-fries.

Fish sauce: A thin, brown liquid made from salted fish. Its bold, salty flavor is used to season foods during cooking and at the table.

Shrimp paste: A strong-flavored, thick mixture of fermented shrimp, chili peppers, and curry. Dilute it with water and use sparingly in meat mixtures. Anchovy paste is a good substitute.

Bean threads: Thin, almost transparent, dry noodles made from mung bean flour. They also are called bean noodles or cellophane noodles. Soak them in water or deep-fry. Serve instead of rice.

Chili paste: A fiery condiment; its strength varies depending on the country where it is made. It takes only ¼ to ½ teaspoon chili paste to season a 4-serving stir-fry dish.

Cloud ears and wood ears: Dried, edible mushroom-type fungi. Wood ears (also called tree ears) are larger and coarser than cloud ears. To use, soak ears in hot water, rinse, and remove tough stems.

Coriander: An herb with leaves resembling parsley. The leaves are also called cilantro or Chinese parsley. The leaves, roots, and crushed seeds give hearty flavor to soups, stews, and sauces.

Dashi-No-Moto: Powdered form of dashi, the basic Japanese fish stock. Mix it with water to rehydrate, and use in soups.

Laos: A mild-flavored cousin of ginger. Laos also is known as galangal root. Use it to enhance the flavor of curries. Laos comes dried or ground.

Lemongrass: A grass that resembles a fibrous green onion. Its strong lemon flavor is good for seasoning main dishes. It is available fresh or dried. Lemon peel may be substituted for it.

Loquat: An orange-colored, slightly tart fruit. Loquats usually are served for dessert. They are sold canned and dried.

Lotus root: The pink root of aquatic lotus plants. Use it raw for crunch, or pickled and cooked in soups, or in stir-fries. Lotus root is available fresh, canned, or dried.

Rice vinegar: A mild, slightly sweet vinegar made from rice. Chinese rice vinegars are stronger than Japanese ones. White or cider vinegar may be substituted for rice vinegar.

Sweet soy sauce: A thick, heavy sauce. Sweet soy is flavored with molasses so it is sweeter and darker than traditional soy sauce. It is used to flavor many foods, especially grilled meats.

Tofu: A cream-colored, mild-flavored food with a custardlike texture. It is made from soybeans and also is called fresh bean curd and soybean curd.

duck, and pork. Most Oriental cuisines use some type of soy sauce as well as ginger and garlic for seasoning.

The techniques of Oriental cooking were developed in China long ago and were adopted by other countries in the Orient. To save precious fuel, quick-cooking methods, such as stir-frying, were devised (see also *Stir-Fry*). Other methods of Oriental cooking include steaming, stewing, grilling, roasting, boiling, poaching, and frying.

Chinese cooking: Each region has its own nuances. In the north, noodles, millet, and barley are staples. In the west in Szechwan, food is hot and spicy. Hunan cooking is spicy, and sweet and sour; Fukien, on the coast, features excellent clear soups and seafood dishes. The Chinese foods that Westerners know best are from Canton in the south. This is the home of egg rolls, fried rice, and various steamed dumplings (see also *Egg Roll*). Some often-used flavorings in Chinese cooking are five-spice powder, dried mushrooms, hoisin sauce, oyster sauce, star anise, toasted sesame oil, and chili oil. Moo Goo Gai Pan (see recipe at right) is a typical stir-fried main dish.

Japanese cooking: The Japanese emphasize freshness, flavor, and serving foods in season. They also place great importance on aesthetics in food presentation. Seafood and tofu are main-dish basics. Miso, shoyu (a slightly sweeter soy sauce), and seaweed are some of the flavorings used (see also *Miso*). Familiar Japanese dishes include sukiyaki, tempura, sushi, and teriyaki (see also individual entries).

Korean cooking: Koreans like their food strongly flavored and use garlic, ginger, black pepper, green onions, soy sauce, and sesame seed. Beef is their favorite meat, and they sometimes combine it with fish and seafood. The most well-known dish is kimchi, which appears at every meal (see also *Kimchi*).

Thai cooking: Thailand's basic cooking style is Chinese, but its people's love of spices, especially curries, and pungent condiments comes from India. Saucy mixtures known as kaeng usually contain chicken, fish, seafood, or beef, and spicy seasoning. Curries commonly include coconut milk and cream. Thai cooks rely on shrimp paste for flavoring, as well as peanuts, fish sauce, curry powder, lemongrass, tamarind (a flavorful pod that imparts a sweet-sour flavor), coriander, and chili peppers.

Vietnamese cooking: Vietnamese food has a flavor and character all its own. Chili peppers, coriander, garlic, lemongrass, and several varieties of mint are frequent seasonings. Nuoc mam (a fish sauce), which is the staple table condiment, is used in place of soy sauce. It is served alone or is mixed with chili peppers, garlic, sugar, and lime in a pungent sauce called nuoc cham. The national dish, pho (a brothy beef and noodle soup mixed with raw vegetables), is typically eaten for breakfast.

Moo Goo Gai Pan

    4 medium boneless, skinless chicken
        breast halves (12 ounces total)
    ½ cup chicken broth
    2 tablespoons soy sauce
    2 tablespoons rice wine *or*
        dry white wine
    4 teaspoons cornstarch
    ½ teaspoon sugar
    1 tablespoon cooking oil
    3 cloves garlic, minced
    2 medium carrots, thinly sliced into
        carrot flowers or bias-sliced
    8 ounces small whole mushrooms *or*
        large mushrooms, halved
    2 cups fresh pea pods, tips and strings
        removed, *or* one 6-ounce package
        frozen pea pods, thawed
    ½ of an 8-ounce can sliced water
        chestnuts, drained
    2 cups hot cooked rice

■ Partially freeze chicken. Thinly slice into bite-size strips; set aside.
■ For sauce, in a small bowl stir together the chicken broth, soy sauce, rice wine or white wine, cornstarch, and sugar. Set aside.

■ Pour cooking oil into a wok or large skillet. (Add more oil as necessary during cooking.) Preheat over medium-high heat. Stir-fry garlic in hot oil for 15 seconds. Add carrots; stir-fry for 3 minutes. Add mushrooms and, if using, fresh pea pods; stir-fry about 1 minute or till carrots and pea pods are crisp-tender. Remove the vegetables from the wok; set aside.

■ Add the chicken to the hot wok or skillet. Stir-fry for 2 to 3 minutes or till chicken is no longer pink. Push chicken from the center of wok. Stir sauce. Add sauce to the center of the wok or skillet. Cook and stir till thickened and bubbly. Return vegetables to the wok or skillet. Add water chestnuts and, if using, thawed frozen pea pods. Stir ingredients together to coat with sauce. Cook and stir about 1 minute more or till heated through. Serve immediately over hot cooked rice. Makes 4 servings.

Nutrition information per serving: 371 calories, 28 g protein, 47 g carbohydrate, 7 g fat (1 g saturated), 54 mg cholesterol, 683 mg sodium, 755 mg potassium.

Orzo *(OR zoh)* A tiny, commercially produced, dried pasta, shaped like long grains of rice. It also is called rosamarina. Orzo can be added to soups and stews or cooked and served as a side dish in place of rice.

(See *Pasta* for an identification photo and storing and how-to-cook information.)

Osso Buco *(OH so BOO ko)* An Italian dish made with veal marrow bones (usually knuckles or shanks) that are cooked with vegetables in a tomato-wine sauce. Osso buco often is served on saffron rice and is sprinkled with a mixture of lemon peel, garlic, and parsley.

Oven-Fry To cook a food in a hot oven so that it has the flavor and appearance of a fried food, but uses less fat. The food, sometimes brushed with margarine or butter, usually is coated with a seasoned flour or crumb mixture before baking.

Oyster A shellfish with rough, hinged shells and a soft, edible body. Oysters grow in brackish and salt water. The color and taste of an oyster vary depending on where it is grown. The color can be tan, cream, or gray.

Small oysters usually are cooked in the shell; large ones usually are fried. Other uses include oyster stew and poultry stuffing.

Q: Is it safe to eat raw oysters on the half shell?

A: Although they are a traditional favorite, recent concerns over shellfish that contain harmful organisms have made eating oysters on the half shell or any raw fish or shellfish risky. It is recommended that high-risk individuals cook seafood thoroughly. This is especially important for people with serious medical conditions, including those with liver problems, iron imbalances, and weakened immune systems, as well as the elderly, infants, and pregnant women. Check with your doctor to see if you are at risk.

If you decide that you want to eat oysters that are raw or undercooked, lessen the risk by buying them from reputable dealers and making sure that they come from growing waters that have been certified as safe. Then keep the oysters refrigerated and handle them properly.

Types: In the United States, oysters are found on both the east and west coasts. Sometimes they are named for their harvesting areas, such as Chesapeake or Blue Point. Many of the oysters are farm raised.

continued

1. To shuck an oyster, with one hand in a heavy oven mitt, hold the oyster, flat side up, firmly against a cutting board or surface. Using a strong-bladed oyster knife with a hand guard, insert the knife tip between the shells near the hinge. *Be careful that the knife blade doesn't slip.*

2. Twist the blade and push it into the opening, prying the oyster open. Move the blade along the inside of the upper shell to free the muscle from the shell. Remove and discard the top shell of the oyster. Slide the knife under the oyster to sever the muscle from the bottom shell. Discard any bits of shell.

Before cooking, a raw oyster looks very soft and milky (top spoon). When properly cooked, the edges start to curl, and the oyster becomes plump and opaque (bottom spoon).

Market forms: Oysters are marketed live in the shell by the dozen. Shucked oysters also are available and are sold fresh or frozen. When shucked, they're usually sold by the pint or half-pint. Oysters also can be purchased canned, either plain or smoked.

Selecting: Live oysters should have shells that are tightly closed, moist, and intact. Be sure to ask your grocer when the oysters arrived at the store. Choose live oysters that are no more than 2 days old. Shucked oysters should have clear, not cloudy, liquid around them. Whether live or shucked, they should have no off-odor.

Storing: Refrigerate live oysters, covered with a moist cloth in an open container, for up to 5 days. If shells have opened during storage, tap them; discard any oysters that don't close quickly.

Refrigerate shucked oysters, covered in their liquor (juice), for up to 5 days. Or, freeze shucked oysters, covered in their liquor, for up to 3 months.

How to cook: See the Preparing and Cooking Shellfish chart under *Shellfish.*

Nutrition information: Cooked oysters have about 120 calories in a 3-ounce serving.

Oyster Cracker
A tiny, round, slightly puffy cracker usually served with soups and stews, especially oyster stew.

Oysters Rockefeller
Oysters that are topped with a mixture of spinach and bread crumbs, baked or broiled till the oysters are cooked, and served on half of a shell. Food lore says the recipe was first served at Antoine's, a New Orleans restaurant. It was so rich it was named after one of America's richest men.

A Tip from Our Kitchen
Oysters Rockefeller traditionally are placed on a bed of rock salt in a shallow pan to balance them and keep their juices from spilling as they bake or broil. If you don't have rock salt, simply crumple a large piece of foil to help balance them.

Oysters Rockefeller

  2 **cups chopped fresh spinach**
  ¼ **cup finely chopped onion**
 24 **oysters in shells**
  3 **tablespoons margarine *or* butter, melted**
  2 **tablespoons snipped parsley**
  1 **clove garlic, minced**
    Several drops bottled hot pepper sauce
    Dash pepper
  ¼ **cup fine dry seasoned bread crumbs**
    Rock salt

■ In a saucepan cook spinach and onion in a small amount of boiling water for 2 to 3 minutes or till tender. Drain; press out excess moisture.

■ Thoroughly wash oysters. Open shells with an oyster knife (see photos, page 287). Remove oysters and dry. Discard flat top shells; wash deep bottom shells. Place each oyster in a shell.

■ Combine spinach mixture, *2 tablespoons* of the margarine or butter, parsley, garlic, hot pepper sauce, and pepper. Spoon *1 teaspoon* atop *each* oyster.

■ Toss together crumbs and remaining margarine or butter. Sprinkle over spinach-topped oysters.

■ Line a shallow baking pan with rock salt to about ½-inch depth (see tip, above). Arrange oysters atop. Bake in a 425° oven 10 to 12 minutes or till oysters are done. Serves 8.

Nutrition information per serving: 85 calories, 4 g protein, 5 g carbohydrate, 6 g fat (1 g saturated), 23 mg cholesterol, 151 mg sodium, 196 mg potassium.

Paella

Paella A traditional main dish from Spain containing chicken, seafood, rice, and vegetables. Its characteristic yellow color and distinctive flavor come from saffron. The term also refers to a large, round, covered baking pan with handles that's used to cook this dish.

A Tip from Our Kitchen

If you don't own a paella pan, use a very large skillet with a cover instead.

Paella

2 **pounds meaty chicken pieces**
¼ **teaspoon salt**
⅛ **teaspoon pepper**
1 **tablespoon olive oil *or* cooking oil**
2 **cups chicken broth**
1 **cup long grain rice**
1 **medium onion, cut into thin wedges**
½ **cup chopped celery**
1 **2-ounce jar sliced pimiento**
2 **cloves garlic, minced**
½ **teaspoon dried oregano, crushed**
⅛ **teaspoon powdered saffron**
1 **9-ounce package frozen artichoke hearts**
4 **ounces fresh *or* frozen shelled shrimp**
8 **small fresh clams *or* mussels in shells, washed**

■ Remove skin from chicken. Rinse chicken and pat dry. Season with the salt and pepper.
■ In a 12-inch skillet or 4-quart Dutch oven, cook chicken pieces in hot oil, uncovered, for 10 to 15 minutes or till light brown, turning to brown evenly. Remove chicken from pan; drain off fat.
■ In skillet or Dutch oven combine chicken broth, *uncooked* rice, onion, celery, pimiento, garlic, oregano, and saffron. Return chicken to pan. Bring to boiling. Reduce heat and simmer, covered, for 15 minutes.

■ Meanwhile, run warm water over frozen artichoke hearts to separate. Add artichokes, shrimp, and clams or mussels to pan. Cover and cook for 10 to 15 minutes more or till chicken and rice are tender, shrimp turn pink, and clams or mussels are cooked. Makes 4 servings.

Nutrition information per serving: 432 calories, 36 g protein, 47 g carbohydrate, 10 g fat (2 g saturated), 111 mg cholesterol, 683 mg sodium, 654 mg potassium.

Panbroil To cook a food, especially a meat, in a skillet without added fat, removing any fat as it accumulates.

Pancake A flat, round, tender quick bread made from a batter and cooked on a griddle or in a skillet. Pancakes most often are made with all-purpose flour, but they can have grains, such as buckwheat or cornmeal, in the batter, or they can be made with buttermilk or a sourdough starter.

Q: How can I keep my pancakes from being cooked around the edges yet doughy in the center?

A: Even though pancakes cook quickly, it is important not to rush them. For perfect pancakes, always preheat your griddle or skillet over medium-high heat before pouring on the batter. Test for readiness by sprinkling a few drops of water on the hot surface. If the water jumps or dances and sizzles, the griddle is ready.

Cook the pancakes till about half of the bubbles that form have broken and the edges are slightly dry. Turn the pancakes over and cook about 1 minute more. Lift the pancakes slightly and peek underneath. If the bottoms are brown, your pancakes are done.

Preparation hints: As with other quick breads, a light hand and only a little stirring are the keys to perfect pancakes. Stir the liquid and dry ingredients together only till combined—don't overmix.

continued

Q: How can I make evenly shaped pancakes that are the same size?

A: To make pancakes that are uniform in size and shape, pour the batter from a measuring cup, making sure you keep pouring the stream of batter into the center of the pancake. (To make 4-inch-diameter pancakes, use about 1/4 cup of batter.) Also remember to leave plenty of room for expansion between pancakes.

A Tip from Our Kitchen

To keep cooked pancakes warm till serving time, put them on an ovenproof plate in a 300° oven.

Q: What are potato pancakes?

A: Potato pancakes aren't actually pancakes at all. They're patties made from shredded potatoes mixed with eggs and sometimes onion. They're fried till golden and usually served with applesauce. The Jewish name for a potato pancake is latke (*LOT kuh*); latkes traditionally are served at Hanukkah.

Convenience products: For extra-easy pancakes, pancake mixes—plain, buckwheat, and buttermilk—are available, as are frozen pancakes that just need heating in the toaster or microwave oven.

Nutrition information: One plain pancake (4-inch diameter) has about 60 calories.

Pandowdy   A deep-dish baked apple or fruit dessert with a pastrylike, biscuit topping. Similar to fruit cobbler, pandowdy usually is served warm with light cream or a sauce. Traditionally the crust is broken up with a serving spoon and stirred into the filling before serving. This serving technique, called dowdying, gives the dessert its name.

Panfry   To cook a food in a skillet using a small amount of fat or oil.

Papain   *(puh PAY uhn)* An enzyme found in papaya that prevents gelatin mixtures from setting up. Papain also is an ingredient used in meat tenderizers.

Papaw   *(PAH pah)* A creamy, yellow fruit about 6 inches long with greenish yellow skin and many seeds. Shaped like papayas but unrelated, papaws have a custardlike texture and a very rich flavor similar to a mixture of bananas and lemons. Their aroma is heavy and fragrant.

Selecting: Select a fruit that is just beginning to soften. Avoid bruised or overly soft fruit.

Storing: Keep papaws in the refrigerator for 2 or 3 weeks.

Preparation hints: Papaws can be eaten and served in the same ways you would papayas or melons. When the fruit is soft, it can be sliced or spooned from the skin. Scoop out the seeds and discard them.

Papaya   *(puh PIE uh)* A melonlike, pear-shaped fruit (sometimes confusingly called papaw). Papayas have from greenish yellow to yellow-orange skin and golden orange meat. The seed cavity has tiny black seeds. Papayas taste like a cross between peaches and melons. They are fragrant and very sweet with a creamy, spoonable consistency. Papayas weigh about 1 pound each.

Selecting: Choose fruit that is at least half yellow and feels somewhat soft when pressed. The skin should be smooth and free from bruises or soft spots.

Storing: A firm papaya can be ripened at room temperature for 3 to 5 days until mostly yellow to yellowish orange. Store a ripe papaya in a paper or plastic bag in the refrigerator for up to 1 week.

Papayas

Preparation hints: Peel papayas, then halve and scoop out the seeds. Slice, chop, or puree papayas, or use the hollowed-out fruit shells as serving containers.

Because papaya contains the enzyme papain, the fruit must be cooked before using it in a gelatin mixture. Cooking deactivates that enzyme, which would prevent gelatin from setting up.

Nutrition information: A 1-cup serving of cubed papaya has about 60 calories and is rich in vitamin C.

Paper Bake Cup A paper liner with fluted sides that is placed in a muffin pan. The cups are used to hold cake or muffin batter for baking, and salad or dessert mixtures for chilling or freezing. These liners allow the food to be easily removed from the pan. Paper bake cups come in sizes ranging from tiny to jumbo. Some liners have a foil coating and can be used without muffin pans.

Papillote *(pop ee YOTE)* A French term meaning curled paper. The phrase "en papillote" refers to a cooking technique in which foods, such as meat, fish, poultry, and/or vegetables, are placed in heavy parchment paper (often cut into a heart shape). The paper is folded to form a packet that helps retain flavor and aroma as the food cooks. Usually the food is served in its packet with a crisscross cut in the top so the food can be removed.

Pompano en Papillote

> 4 **fresh** *or* **frozen skinless pompano** *or*
>   **sole fillets (¾ to 1 pound)**
>   **Parchment paper** *or* **brown paper**
> 2 **teaspoons lemon juice**
> 1 **tablespoon margarine** *or* **butter**
> 1½ **cups sliced mushrooms**
> ¼ **cup sliced green onion**
> 1 **tablespoon cornstarch**
> ½ **teaspoon instant chicken bouillon**
>   **granules**
>   **Dash ground red pepper**
> ¾ **cup light cream**
> 1 **tablespoon dry sherry (optional)**

■ Thaw fish, if frozen. Cut 4 pieces of parchment paper or brown paper into heart shapes, 12 inches wide and 9 inches long.
■ Season fish with ¼ teaspoon *salt,* dash *pepper,* and lemon juice. Fold fish fillets in half. Set aside.
■ For sauce, in a medium saucepan melt margarine or butter. Add mushrooms and green onion. Cook and stir till tender. Stir in cornstarch, bouillon granules, and red pepper. Add cream all at once. Cook and stir over medium heat till bubbly. Cook and stir 2 minutes more. Stir in sherry, if desired.
■ To assemble *each* packet, place *1 tablespoon* sauce in center of half of *each* parchment heart. Top with a folded fish fillet. Divide remaining sauce mixture atop the fillets. Fold the other half of the heart over the fillet. Starting at the top, seal tightly by turning up edges of heart and folding in twice. At the bottom, twist the tip of the heart to seal. Place packets in a shallow baking pan. Bake in a 450° oven about 10 minutes or till slightly puffed. Transfer to plates. To serve, cut an X in top of each. Pull back the paper. Serves 4.

Nutrition information per serving: 240 calories, 19 g protein, 5 g carbohydrate, 16 g fat (7 g saturated), 60 mg cholesterol, 355 mg sodium, 503 mg potassium.

Paprika

Paprika   The ground, red spice derived from the flesh of a dried, mild pepper. The intensity of both the color and flavor of paprika depends on the peppers used to make it. Most of the bright red paprika used today is the mild Spanish type, which is slightly sweet. This paprika, often used more for its color than flavor, gives French dressing its vibrant color.

Q: What is Hungarian paprika?
A: Hungarian paprika is lighter in color than other paprikas, but more pungent. Hungarian paprika is imported and can be labeled as sweet (mild) or hot. Look for it in specialty food stores.

(See *Spice* for selecting, storing, and nutrition information.)

Paraffin   A waxy material that traditionally has been melted and spooned over homemade jellies or jams in jars to form an airtight seal and prevent spoilage. Now, however, because paraffin allows the growth of possibly harmful surface mold, its use is no longer recommended. Homemade jellies and jams should be processed in a water bath, using two-piece canning lids.

(See *Canning* for information on boiling-water canning.)

Parboil   To boil a food until it is partially cooked. Cooking usually is completed by another method, as in the case of vegetable pieces that are parboiled before being added to a stir-fry.

Pare   To cut off the skin or outer covering of a fruit or vegetable, using a small knife or a vegetable peeler.

Parfait   A chilled or frozen dessert that is served in a tall, slender glass. Often the dessert is assembled in layers.

The term also refers to a rich frozen pudding made with cream and eggs.

A Tip from Our Kitchen

To minimize the mess when assembling parfaits, use a long-handled spoon, such as an iced-tea spoon, to neatly add ingredient layers to the parfait glasses. Be sure to use a separate spoon for each mixture to keep from mixing layers.

Parmesan Cheese   A pale yellow, hard cheese that is made from cow's milk and tastes sharp and salty.

Parmesan cheese

Market forms: Parmesan cheese is available in many forms, including imported and domestic versions in chunks and shredded and freshly grated pieces. Parmesan cheeses vary in flavor from mild to robust depending on how long they have been aged. You'll need to taste several types to decide which flavor level you prefer.

A mild, domestic Parmesan cheese in a drier, grated form also is available in shakers in the grocery section. A blend of grated Parmesan and Romano cheeses is another product that's available. Close the shakers after each use and store in a cool, dry place.

(See *Cheese* for the Selecting Cheese chart and selecting, storing, serving, nutrition, and other information.)

Parsley   A decorative herb with bright green leaves used as a seasoning and a garnish. In addition to cut fresh parsley, dehydrated leaves, called parsley flakes, also are available.

Types: There are two main types of parsley: curly-leaf and Italian. *Curly-leaf* parsley is the most commonly available type. It has ruffled leaves and a fresh, slightly peppery flavor. *Italian* parsley has flat, dark green leaves and a milder flavor.

Selecting and storing: When selecting fresh parsley, look for bright green, unwilted leaves. Wash the parsley leaves and shake off the excess moisture. Wrap in paper towels and refrigerate in a plastic bag for up to 1 week.

Q: Is there a way to save wilted parsley?
A: Revitalize parsley by cutting the stems and standing the parsley in cold water for about an hour.

(See *Herb* for the Herb Alternative Guide and preparation, nutrition, and other information.)

Parsley

Parsnip   A winter root vegetable shaped like a large carrot with a thin, beige skin and creamy white meat. Parsnips have a sweet, nutty flavor.

Selecting: Fresh parsnips are available year-round, with peak season during January, February, and March. Look for small to medium parsnips that are firm with fairly smooth skin and few rootlets. Avoid shriveled, limp, or cracked parsnips.

Storing: Refrigerate parsnips in a plastic bag for up to 10 days.

How to cook: See the Cooking Fresh Vegetables chart under *Vegetable*.

Nutrition information: One-half cup of sliced cooked parsnips has about 65 calories.

Parsnips

Partially Set   A phrase that describes a gelatin mixture that is chilled until it is the consistency of unbeaten egg whites. Gelatin is chilled to this stage before items such as fruit and vegetables pieces and nuts are added. At this stage, the pieces stay evenly distributed throughout and don't settle to the bottom or float to the top. (See tips under *Chill.*)

Passion Fruit

A purple or pink fruit with a hard shell that encases a yellowish green meat and seeds that are edible. It's larger than a golf ball. When ripe, the fruit has shriveled, deeply dented skin. Passion fruit, also called granadilla, tastes tangy yet sweet. One variety of passion fruit found in Hawaii has a yellow shell and pinkish meat.

Passion fruit
Yellow
Pink
Red

Selecting: Choose a fruit that is firm. If the fruit is wrinkled, it is ripe and ready to use.

Storing: If fruit is smooth skinned, ripen at room temperature until it looks shriveled. After the fruit is ripe, keep it in the refrigerator for up to 1 week.

Nutrition information: One passion fruit has about 20 calories.

Pasta

A dough or paste that is made from flour, a liquid, and sometimes eggs and is formed into any one of numerous shapes (shown opposite). Pasta can be homemade or produced commercially.

Types: Pasta products are classified according to the ingredients that are used to make them. Here are some of the basic kinds.
☐ **Non-Egg Pasta (macaroni products):** Pasta that usually is made with just flour and water. Some well-known shapes include spaghetti, elbow macaroni, and shell macaroni.
☐ **Egg Pasta:** Pasta made from flour; a liquid, usually water; and eggs. Most homemade pasta, including spaetzle, as well as most commercial products that are labeled noodles are made from egg-based doughs. Most flavored pasta is made from an egg-based dough with an added vegetable, herb, or seed. Some popular flavors are spinach, tomato, red pepper, parsley, and sesame.

continued on page 297

Common Pasta Shapes

Acini di pepe

Ditalini (thimbles)

Fettuccine

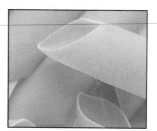
Manicotti

Mostaccioli

Rigatoni

Rings (anelli)

Spaghetti

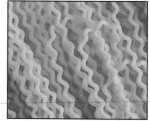
Spaghetti, twisted (fusilli)

Alphabets

Bow ties, tiny

Bow ties, large

Capellini

Cavatelli

Gemelli

Lasagna

Linguine

Macaroni, elbow

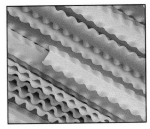

Mafalda

Noodles, fine

Noodles, medium

Noodles, wide

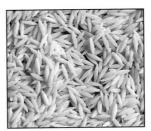

Orzo (rosamarina)

Ravioli

Rotini (corkscrew noodles)

Shells, jumbo

Shells, large

Shells, small

Spaetzle

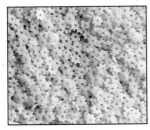

Stars

Tortellini

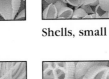

Vermicelli, nested

Wagon wheels (ruote)

Ziti

Cooking Pasta

For packaged dried pasta, follow the manufacturer's directions. Or, in a large saucepan or Dutch oven, bring water (about 3 quarts of water for 4 to 8 ounces of pasta) to boiling. If desired, add 1 teaspoon salt and 1 tablespoon olive oil or cooking oil to help keep the pasta separated. Add the pasta a little at a time so the water does not stop boiling. Hold long pasta, such as spaghetti, at one end and dip the other end into the water. As the pasta softens, gently curl it around the pan and down into the water. Reduce the heat slightly and boil, uncovered, for the time specified or till the pasta is al dente (tender but still firm). Stir occasionally. Test often for doneness near the end of the cooking time. Drain in a colander.

Homemade Pasta	Cooking Time*	Homemade Pasta	Cooking Time*
Bow ties, tiny	2 to 3 minutes	Noodles	1½ to 2 minutes
Bow ties, large	2 to 3 minutes	Ravioli	7 to 9 minutes
Fettuccine	1½ to 2 minutes	Spaetzle	5 to 10 minutes
Lasagna	2 to 3 minutes	Tagliatelle	1½ to 2 minutes
Linguine	1½ to 2 minutes	Tortellini	7 to 9 minutes
Manicotti	2 to 3 minutes	Tripolini	2 to 3 minutes

Packaged Pasta (Dried)	Cooking Time	Packaged Pasta (Dried)	Cooking Time
Acini di pepe	5 to 6 minutes	Orzo (rosamarina)	5 to 8 minutes
Alphabets	5 to 8 minutes	Rigatoni	15 minutes
Bow ties, tiny	5 to 6 minutes	Rings (anelli)	9 to 10 minutes
Bow ties, large	10 minutes	Rotini (corkscrew noodles)	8 to 10 minutes
Capellini	5 to 6 minutes	Shells, jumbo	18 minutes
Cavatelli	12 minutes	Shells, large	12 to 14 minutes
Ditalini (thimbles)	7 to 9 minutes	Shells, small	8 to 9 minutes
Fettuccine	8 to 10 minutes	Spaetzle	10 to 12 minutes
Gemelli	10 minutes	Spaghetti	10 to 12 minutes
Lasagna	10 to 12 minutes	Spaghetti, thin	8 to 10 minutes
Linguine	8 to 10 minutes	Spaghetti, twisted (fusilli)	15 minutes
Macaroni, elbow	10 minutes	Stars	5 to 8 minutes
Mafalda	10 to 12 minutes	Tortellini	15 minutes
Manicotti	18 minutes	Vermicelli	5 to 7 minutes
Mostaccioli	14 minutes	Wagon wheels (ruote)	12 minutes
Noodles	6 to 8 minutes	Ziti	14 to 15 minutes

*If homemade pasta is dried or frozen, allow a few more minutes.

(Some flavored commercial pastas don't have egg in the dough.)

Filled pasta is made from a noodle dough that is wrapped around a filling, usually meat or cheese. Ravioli and tortellini are two popular filled pastas.

Market forms: Commercially prepared pasta is available in dried, refrigerated, and frozen forms. Each of these forms comes in a variety of shapes and sizes. Special pastas for the microwave oven and no-boil dried forms also are available. For some of the most common shapes, see the pasta identification photos, pages 294-295.

What's in a Shape?

The shape and size of pasta often dictate how it is used.
- Long strands, small tubes, small shells, and spirals are cooked in boiling water, drained, and often served with a sauce. Spaghetti, fettuccine, linguine, rotini, and rigatoni are some examples.
- Very wide and flat pastas, as well as large, hollow pastas are cooked in boiling water, drained, and often stuffed or layered with cheese and a sauce before they're baked. Lasagna, manicotti, and jumbo shells are common types.
- Small or tiny pasta shapes are added to soups. These include alphabets, rings, tiny bow ties, and small shells.
- Filled pastas, such as ravioli, are cooked in boiling water, drained, and usually served with a sauce. Once cooked, they also can be layered with a sauce, topped with cheese, and baked.

Storing: Store dried pasta indefinitely in a closed package in a cool, dry area.

Store fresh or refrigerated pasta in an airtight container in the refrigerator for up to 5 days or in the freezer for up to 8 months. Keep frozen pasta in the freezer for up to 8 months.

Pasta Math
- To make 2½ cups of cooked elbow or shell macaroni, use 1 cup (about 3½ ounces) of uncooked packaged elbow or small shell macaroni.
- To make 3 cups of cooked medium noodles, use 3 cups (4 ounces) of uncooked packaged medium noodles.
- To make 2 cups cooked spaghetti, use 4 ounces of uncooked packaged spaghetti. (Held together in a bunch, 4 ounces of 10-inch-long spaghetti has about a 1-inch diameter.)

Preparation hints: When cooking homemade or refrigerated pasta, plan on 4 ounces for each main-dish serving and 2 ounces for each side-dish serving. When cooking packaged dried pasta, use 2 ounces for each main-dish serving and 1 ounce for each side-dish serving.

How to cook: Follow the manufacturer's cooking instructions printed on the package of dried pasta, or see the Cooking Pasta chart, opposite. For commercially prepared frozen or refrigerated pastas, follow the manufacturer's cooking directions.

Nutrition information: A ¾-cup serving of plain cooked spaghetti, macaroni, or noodles has between 145 and 160 calories.

Paste   A soft, smooth, pliable food mixture. The term can refer to a dough, as in the case of puff paste, or to a food that has been processed, such as almond paste.

Pastrami   Beef that is cured, rubbed with spices, coated with cracked pepper, smoked, and cooked. Pastrami is prepared from beef chuck, flank, or plate. It is similar to corned beef in appearance but spicier in flavor.

Nutrition information: One ounce of pastrami contains about 100 calories.

Pastry

Pastry A rich, unleavened dough usually made with flour, water, and either shortening, lard, margarine, or butter. It commonly is used to make a tender, flaky piecrust, and it also can be used for encasing foods, such as meats, poultry, game, and seafood (see also *Piecrust*).

Puff pastry is made from an extra rich pastry dough with butter layered or worked into it. When baked, this pastry puffs into many paper-thin layers that are crisp on the outside and tender on the inside. Puff pastry is used to make croissants and other light pastries with a flaky texture.

Pastry also is a general name used for sweet baked items such as tarts, cream puffs, and sweet rolls.

Pasty *(PASS tee)* A British pie or turnover usually containing chopped cooked beef, potatoes, and seasonings.

Pâté *(pah TAY)* A rich, well-seasoned ground mixture that's made from meat, liver, game, fish, vegetables, or a combination of these, and usually is baked. Pâté can be soft enough to spread or firm enough to slice. It can be served hot or cold as an appetizer, and usually is served on toast, crackers, or bread.

Pâté can be shaped, molded, or encased in pastry. The texture of pâté can vary from a fine, smooth liver pâté to a coarse, chunky pâté that is more like meat loaf. Sometimes the texture and appearance of a pâté are varied by adding one or more layers of another ingredient, such as vegetable strips.

Q: What is a terrine?

A: A terrine is a deep, straight-sided dish with a cover, in which a pâté can be cooked. The pâté made in this dish also is called a terrine. For a typical meat terrine, the baking dish is lined with strips of bacon before the pâté mixture is added. Then a layer of lard is placed on top, and the terrine is cooked.

Herbed Pork Pâté

12 ounces ground pork
½ cup chopped onion
2 cloves garlic, minced
4 ounces beef liver, cut up, *or* chicken livers, halved
¾ cup milk
2 eggs
2 tablespoons fine dry bread crumbs
1 tablespoon cornstarch
1 teaspoon dried basil, crushed
½ teaspoon dried rosemary *or* thyme, crushed
½ teaspoon salt
¼ teaspoon pepper
6 thin asparagus spears *or* thin carrot sticks (about 3½ inches long), cooked
  Parsley (optional)
  Hard-cooked egg (optional)
  Chopped walnuts (optional)
  Assorted crackers and sliced party bread

■ Grease the bottom and sides of a 7½x3½x2-inch loaf pan. Line bottom with foil. Grease foil. Set aside.

■ In a large skillet cook pork, onion, and garlic till meat is just brown. Add liver; cook and stir over medium-high heat for 3 to 4 minutes or till liver is no longer pink. Drain well. Cool slightly.

■ In a blender container or food processor bowl, place liver mixture and milk. Cover and blend or process till smooth. Add eggs, bread crumbs, cornstarch, basil, rosemary or thyme, salt, and pepper. Cover and blend or process thoroughly. Pour about *half* of the mixture into the prepared pan. Arrange asparagus spears or carrot sticks atop. Spread remaining mixture over the asparagus or carrots. Cover pan with additional foil. Place in a larger baking pan in the oven; pour hot water around loaf pan to a depth of 1 inch.

■ Bake in a 325° oven for 1 to 1¼ hours or till a knife inserted off center comes out clean and a meat thermometer inserted in mixture registers 170°. Remove foil. Cool in pan. Cover and chill.

■ To serve, loosen edges and invert pan. Remove pan and foil. If desired, garnish with parsley sprigs, hard-cooked egg white cut into wedges, sieved hard-cooked egg yolk, and chopped nuts. Slice and serve with crackers and party bread. Makes about 2 cups (16 to 20 servings).

Nutrition information per serving (without crackers or bread): 70 calories, 8 g protein, 3 g carbohydrate, 3 g fat (1 g saturated), 69 mg cholesterol, 106 mg sodium, 133 mg potassium.

Patty Shell   Puff pastry formed into an individual, cup-shaped, crisp shell in which a saucy main dish, side dish, or creamy dessert can be served. Patty shells can be made at home, but frozen ones are available in the supermarket.

Pea   A round seed of the legume family that grows in pods and is eaten as a vegetable. Peas have a sweet, mild flavor and tender texture when cooked.

Dry split yellow

Dry whole green

Dry split green

Peas   Fresh green

Varieties: There are several kinds of peas available in the marketplace.

☐ **Green Peas:** Grown to be eaten fresh, not dried, they are served removed from their pods. Green peas also are called English peas or garden peas. They are known for their sweet flavor and emerald color.

☐ **Edible Pods:** Grown to be eaten pod and all (see also *Pea Pod*).

☐ **Field Peas:** Yellow or green peas grown specifically for drying. They may be processed in whole or split forms, in which case they're known as split peas.

☐ **Southern Peas:** Any of several varieties that are more closely related to beans than peas. The black-eyed pea is the only variety that is readily available in supermarkets. This cream-colored pea, also known as the cowpea, has a black "eye." (See *Black-Eyed Pea* for an identification photo and selecting, storing, nutrition, and other information.)

Market forms: Fresh green peas are available almost year-round. Canned and frozen green peas also are available. Dried field peas and black-eyed peas are available in plastic bags or are sold in bulk. Certain varieties of cooked southern peas are available canned and frozen.

Selecting: When selecting green peas, choose small, plump, bright green, shiny pods that are filled with medium-size peas. When purchasing dried peas in bulk, avoid shriveled peas with brown spots.

Storing: Refrigerate green peas in their pods, unwashed, in a plastic bag for up to 2 days. Shell just before using. Store dried peas at room temperature for up to 1 year.

How to cook: For green peas, see the Cooking Fresh Vegetables chart under *Vegetable*. For black-eyed peas, see the Selecting and Cooking Dried Beans chart under *Bean, Dried*.

Nutrition information: One-half cup of cooked green peas has about 70 calories. One-half cup of cooked, dried split peas has about 120 calories.

Peach   A golden yellow, round fruit with yellow or white meat surrounding a brown pit. The fuzz, or tiny hairs, on the skin sometimes is removed from peaches before they're sold. The fruit is sweet, juicy, and tastes like a blend of rich melon, mild apricot, and nectarine.

Peaches

Varieties: There are many varieties of peaches, and they are classified in two ways: by the color of the fruit (white or yellow) and by the way the meat holds to the stone.

Cling peaches have meat that holds to the pit. These varieties are canned by food processors and seldom are sold fresh.

Semifreestone and *freestone* varieties are later-season peaches, with meat that comes away more easily from the pit. They are easiest to use for eating fresh and baking.

Market forms: Fresh peaches are at their peak between June and September. Peaches also are available year-round frozen, dried, and canned. You'll also find peach nectar, liqueur, and preserves.

Selecting: Choose fresh peaches that are firm to slightly soft when pressed. Skin color varies from golden yellow to dark reddish brown, but the peaches should have no tinges of green. Look for well-shaped fruit without blemishes or soft spots.

Peach Math

1 pound peaches	=	3 medium or 4 small
	=	3 cups sliced
	=	2¼ cups chopped

Storing: Ripen firm, fresh peaches at room temperature until they're slightly soft, then refrigerate the ripe fruit for up to 5 days.

Preparation hints: Peaches may be peeled, if desired, then sliced, chopped, pureed, or eaten whole. Like apricots and nectarines, peaches discolor when cut, so treat cut surfaces with ascorbic acid color keeper or lemon juice mixed with water.

To easily remove the peel from peaches, insert a fork into the end of a peach. Then dip the peach into boiling water for 20 seconds and remove. While the peach is still on the fork, peel off the skin with a paring knife, working from the stem end to the bottom of the peach. If the skin doesn't peel off easily, dip it into the boiling water for a few more seconds.

Nutrition information: One medium peach has about 40 calories.

(See *Dried Fruit* for the Cooking Dried Fruit chart and storing and preparation hints.)

Peanut   A legume from a plant that bears seeds in pods that grow underground (see also *Legume*). Peanuts often are thought of as a nut. The oval, ivory-colored seeds are covered with a papery skin and encased in a fragile, tan pod. Peanuts have a buttery, nutty flavor when roasted.

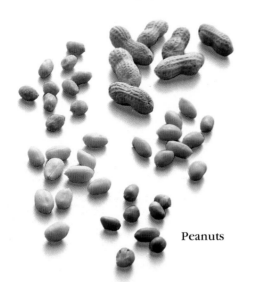

Peanuts

Q: What's the difference between cocktail peanuts and dry-roasted peanuts?
A: The main difference is that cocktail peanuts are roasted in oil and dry-roasted peanuts are roasted by a dry-heat method. Cocktail peanuts are available red-skinned and skinless and salted and unsalted. Dry-roasted peanuts come salted and unsalted.

Market forms: Peanuts are available in many forms. Peanuts in the shell can be found raw and roasted. Shelled peanuts come raw, roasted in oil, and dry-roasted, and salted and unsalted. About half of the peanut crop grown for use in the United States is used for peanut butter, and a small portion is used to make peanut oil (see also *Peanut Butter*).

Q: How are raw peanuts used in cooking?
A: The most typical use is in peanut brittle, where the raw peanuts are cooked in hot candy syrup. (If you use roasted peanuts in brittle, there is a chance the nuts will develop a slightly burned flavor and get darker during cooking.) Raw peanuts sometimes are deep-fried, salted, and eaten as a snack.

Selecting: Choose peanuts in the shell with clean shells that are free of blemishes. Look for shelled peanuts that are free of blemishes and not overly darkened from roasting.

Storing: Raw peanuts in the shell keep about 9 months in the refrigerator and indefinitely if frozen. Raw, shelled peanuts keep 3 to 6 months in the refrigerator and indefinitely if frozen. Roasted peanuts will keep on the shelf for about a month. Once opened, they're best if kept in an airtight container in the refrigerator for up to 6 months or the freezer for up to 1 year. Keep unopened, vacuum-packed peanuts for a year. Once opened, refrigerate or freeze in an airtight container the same as roasted peanuts.

Nutrition information: One-half cup of oil-roasted or dry-roasted peanuts has about 420 calories.

A Tip from Our Kitchen
Roast raw peanuts in the shell by spreading them in a single layer in a shallow baking pan. Bake in a 350° oven for 25 to 30 minutes, stirring occasionally.
   Raw, shelled peanuts, both with and without skins, can be roasted the same way. Just reduce the baking time to 15 to 20 minutes or till the peanuts are golden brown.

Peanut Butter   A spread made from ground, roasted peanuts. By law, peanut butter must be at least 90 percent peanuts; no artificial flavor, colors, or preservatives are allowed. Additives are limited to salt, sweeteners, and stabilizers. Also available are 100-percent peanut butters. Chunky peanut butter has chopped peanuts added to the creamy spread.

continued

Storing: An unopened jar of regular peanut butter will stay fresh in a cool, dry place for 2 years. Once the jar is opened, the flavor deteriorates after 3 months; however, refrigeration slows down the deterioration so you can keep peanut butter up to 6 months in the refrigerator. Peanut butters that are 100 percent peanuts should be refrigerated after opening and will keep up to 6 months. These peanut butters need to be stirred before using.

Nutrition information: Peanut butter is low in saturated fat. One tablespoon has 95 calories and 8 grams of fat.

Snow peas

Sugar snap peas

To remove strings from pea pods, use your finger or a knife to pull off the tip of the pod without breaking the string. Then pull the string down the entire length of the pod and discard the string.

Pea Pod
A slender, bright green, edible casing that holds peas. Pea pods are used most often in Oriental cooking.

Varieties: There are two types of edible-pod peas.
☐ **Snow Peas:** Thin, crisp, bright green pods that are almost translucent. Snow peas, also known as Chinese pea pods, are tender and sweet and have a crisp, firm texture. The tiny peas inside are small and flat.
☐ **Sugar Snap Peas:** Sweet, tender pods that have fully developed plump, rounded peas inside. Sugar snap peas also are called sugar peas.

Market forms: Pea pods are available both fresh and frozen.

Selecting: Fresh pea pods are available year-round. For both varieties, choose crisp, brightly colored pods. Avoid broken, shriveled, or spotted pods. Snow peas should be small and flat, with immature seeds. Sugar snap peas should be plump, but not bursting.

Storing: Refrigerate fresh pea pods in a plastic bag for up to 3 days.

How to cook: See the Cooking Fresh Vegetables chart under *Vegetable.*

Nutrition information: One-half cup of pea pods has about 35 calories.

Pear
A tree fruit that has a core, tapers at one end, and has a rich, sweet flavor.

Varieties: Here are some of the most common pear varieties available.
☐ **Anjou:** An egg-shaped, winter pear with a pale green, yellow-green, or red skin. Because it is a sweet and juicy pear, it is good for salads and snacks.
☐ **Bartlett:** Both yellow and red versions are bell-shaped and available in the summer and fall. This variety is good for canning and cooking because it holds its shape. It also is an excellent pear for eating fresh.
☐ **Bosc:** A winter variety, with golden brown skin that has russeting and a long neck. It has a creamy texture and is full-flavored. It holds its shape well during cooking so is good for baking, poaching, and broiling.
☐ **Comice:** A chubby, green or greenish yellow winter pear with a thick, short stem and sometimes a red blush on one side. This variety is not recommended for cooking or baking, but it is fine fresh, especially with cheese, because it is very sweet and juicy.
☐ **Forelle:** A small, golden pear with a freckled skin and red blush. It is slightly larger than a Seckel pear with more of a bell shape. This sweet and juicy pear is good for eating out of hand.
☐ **Nelis:** An egg-shaped winter variety with russet-colored skin. It is a good choice for salads and snacks.
☐ **Seckel:** A small pear. It is available in late summer and fall. It is egg-shaped and can vary in color from dark green with a red blush to dark red all over. It is one of the sweetest types of pears and is great for snacks and for pickling and canning whole.

Market forms: Pears are available fresh and dried. Pear nectar also is available.

Pear Math
1 pound pears	=	3 medium
	=	3½ cups sliced
	=	3 cups chopped

Selecting: Look for fresh pears without bruises or cuts. Also, remember that skin color is not a good indicator of ripeness because the color of some pear varieties does not change much as the pears ripen.

For baking, a pear should be fairly firm when you pick it up. If you're planning to eat pears out of hand, look for ones that yield to gentle pressure at the stem end.

Q: What's the best way to ripen pears?
A: Place the firm pears in a paper bag or a loosely covered bowl. Let them stand at room temperature for a few days. You can tell most varieties are ripe when they yield to gentle pressure at the stem end. Yellow Bartlett pears, however, become a bright yellow, and red Bartletts become a brillant red when ripe.

Storing: Once ripened, you can keep fresh pears in the refrigerator for several days. Pears do not freeze well.

Preparation hints: If you cut up pears, treat the cut surfaces with ascorbic acid color keeper or lemon juice mixed with water to keep them from darkening.

To Peel or Not to Peel

Knowing when to peel pears can be confusing. Follow these rules of thumb.
- Leave the peel on for eating out of hand or cutting up for salads.
- When cooking pears, in sauces, for example, remove the peel, because the skin toughens and darkens as it cooks.
- Planning to fix baked pears? Take your choice of with or without peel. If you leave the peel on, cut away a strip of peel to add a decorative touch.

Nutrition information: A medium pear has about 100 calories.

(See _Dried Fruit_ for the Cooking Dried Fruit chart and storing and preparation hints.)

Pears

Yellow Bartlett

Red Bartlett

Anjou

Bosc

Comice

Forelle

Nelis

Seckel

Pearl Barley The most readily available form of the cereal grain barley. It has the outer hull removed and has been polished (also called pearled). Light gray to white in color, pearl barley is used primarily in soups and stews, such as Scotch broth. It also is served as a side dish instead of pasta or rice. When cooked, pearl barley has a nutty flavor and a slightly chewy texture.

Market forms: Pearl barley is available in regular and quick-cooking forms.

Storing: Store pearl barley in a cool, dry place in an airtight container for up to 1 year.

How to cook: See the Cooking Grains chart under *Grain.*

Nutrition information: A ¾-cup serving of cooked pearl barley contains about 150 calories.

Pecans

Pecan A nut from the pecan tree. Pecans have a smooth, oval, pale brown shell that is very hard. The shell, which is usually about an inch long, often has black markings on it and is sometimes dyed red to hide blemishes. The ridged, irregular, golden brown shelled nut (that is flat on one side) has a delicate, rich, buttery flavor.

Storing: Pecans in the shell stay fresh in a cool, dry place for 6 months or in the freezer indefinitely. Shelled nuts will keep in an airtight container in the refrigerator for up to 1 year and in the freezer at least 2 years, often longer.

(See *Nut* for the Selecting Nut chart and selecting, nutrition, and other information.)

Pectin A natural substance found in some fruits that makes fruit-and-sugar mixtures used in jelly- or jam-making set up. How much pectin a fruit contains depends upon the kind and variety of fruit, its ripeness, and seasonal conditions. If the fruit used in a jam

or jelly does not have enough natural pectin to set up, commercial pectin must be added. Commercial pectin is available in powdered, liquid, and light forms. Light pectin is a product designed to be used when making reduced-sugar jellies and jams.

Q: Can liquid, powdered, and light pectins be used interchangeably?
A: No. Be sure to use the type of pectin called for in a recipe, because methods and proportion of ingredients needed may differ with each type of pectin.

Peel The skin or outer covering of a fruit or vegetable, sometimes called the rind. In the case of citrus fruits, the peel often is grated or finely shredded to use as a flavoring.
   The term also refers to removing the skin or outer covering of a food.

Penuche *(puh NEW chee)* A fudge made with brown sugar (see also *Fudge*). The brown sugar gives penuche a golden brown color and caramel-like flavor.

(See *Candy* for Candy-Making Tips and equipment, storing, and other information.)

Pepper (spice) The tiny red berries of a tropical vine that grow in clusters like grapes. Pepper is the most commonly used spice in the world.

Market forms: Black, white, and green pepper come from the same berry, or peppercorn, but are harvested at different stages of maturity.
☐ **Black:** Dried, immature pepper berries. As they dry, the berries turn dark and wrinkled, producing the familiar whole black peppercorn. Inside the dark pepper hull is a light-colored core—that's why ground black pepper is a mixture of dark and light particles. Black pepper has a warm, pungent fragrance and flavor. It comes whole, cracked (peppercorns that are crushed but not

ground), and ground. Ground pepper comes in fine, medium, and coarse grinds.

☐ **Green:** Tender, immature pepper berries. Green peppercorns come packed in brine or water, dried, and freeze-dried. They're milder in flavor and bite than black pepper and are noticeably different from white pepper. They also are easy to crush.

☐ **White:** Mature pepper berries that are hulled, exposing a creamy white core. White pepper has a pungent flavor, but lacks the bouquet of black pepper. White pepper comes whole and ground.

Q: Are ground red pepper and Szechwan pepper related to black pepper?

A: No. Ground red pepper, which is sometimes called cayenne, comes from a variety of dried red chili peppers. It is orange-red to deep red in color and has a hot, pungent flavor.

Szechwan pepper, which is used primarily in Oriental cooking, comes from the reddish brown berries of a tree that is not in the pepper family at all. The pepper lends a distinctive fragrance and tongue-tingling spiciness to foods.

Storing: Store pepper in a cool, dry, dark place to avoid flavor loss. You can keep whole peppercorns almost indefinitely, but replace ground pepper every 3 months.

Once green peppercorns in brine have been opened, they will last about a month in an airtight container in the refrigerator; green peppercorns in water will last only for a week. Keep freeze-dried peppercorns in a cool, dry, dark place for up to 6 months.

A Tip from Our Kitchen

Since it's less conspicuous, use white pepper in any recipe where you want to avoid seeing black specks.

(See *Spice* for selecting and nutrition information.)

Pepper (vegetable)

A fruit, shaped like a thick pod, that is produced by a plant of the capsicum family. It grows in various shades of green, yellow, red, and purplish black. Peppers, though classified botanically as a fruit, are enjoyed as a vegetable and a seasoning. Some may be rounded and have thick walls; others may be long and slender. Most are filled with tiny seeds. Peppers can vary in flavor from mild and sweet to pungent and burning.

Varieties: See the Selecting Peppers chart, page 306.

Market forms: The sweet varieties often can be found fresh, prechopped and frozen, and as dehydrated flakes.

Hot varieties of peppers can be purchased fresh and dried in whole and flake forms. They also can be purchased canned and pickled in whole and sliced forms. Mild green chili peppers and pimientos are available in cans, either whole or chopped. Cayenne peppers are available ground and in flakes. These peppers usually are sold as ground or crushed red chili peppers.

Selecting: Fresh peppers, whether hot or sweet, should have bright colors and good shapes for the variety. Avoid shriveled, bruised, or broken peppers.

Storing: Cover and store fresh peppers in your refrigerator for up to 5 days. You can freeze sliced or chopped fresh peppers in freezer bags or containers for up to 6 months.

Store dried peppers in a cool, dark place for up to 1 year.

Preparation hints: To use sweet or hot peppers, slice off the stem end, then remove the seeds. *(See the how-to photo, right, for precautions to take when handling hot peppers.)* If you want a milder flavor from the hot peppers, also remove the membranes. To peel peppers, you will need to roast them (see the question and answer on page 307).

continued on page 307

Because hot peppers contain oils that can burn your eyes, lips, and skin, protect yourself when working with the peppers by covering one or both hands with plastic bags (or wear plastic gloves). Be sure to wash your hands thoroughly before touching your eyes or face.

Selecting Peppers

Use this guide to become familiar with some of the fresh and dried peppers that are available. Note that the appearance and the hotness of the peppers vary with the type of pepper.

Type	Appearance	Hotness
Fresh, Sweet: Chocolate	Brown bell pepper with a green stem and interior; turns green when cooked	Mild
Golden or Orange	Red-orange bell pepper with a green stem and orange interior	Mild
Green	Traditional green bell pepper with a green stem and interior	Mild
Purple	Purple bell pepper with a green stem and interior; turns green when cooked	Mild
Red	Vine-ripened green bell pepper that turns red and has a green stem and a red interior	Mild
Yellow	Yellow bell pepper with a green stem and yellow interior	Mild
Fresh, Hot: Anaheim or Green Chili	Slender, elongated shape; light green color	Mild
Fresno	Small, slender shape; green to greenish red color	Very, very hot
Jalapeño (hall uh PAIN yo)	Short, fat oval shape; green to reddish green color	Hot to very hot

Type	Appearance	Hotness
Poblano (po BLAH no)	Long, irregular bell-pepper shape; deep green color	Mild to medium-hot
Serrano (suh RAH no)	Tiny, slender shape; deep green color, sometimes ripening to bright red	Very, very hot
Yellow Banana	Short, fat, oval shape; pale yellow color	Very hot
Dried, Hot: Ancho	A dried poblano; dark reddish brown color	Mild to medium-hot
Cascabel (CAHS kuh bell)	Small, round shape with a fairly smooth skin; dark red color	Medium-hot to hot
Cayenne (KIY en) (Ground Red Pepper)	Tiny, narrow shape; red color; usually sold ground	Very hot
Chipotle (chi POHT lay)	A smoked and dried jalapeño with wrinkled skin; dull reddish brown color	Hot
Pasilla (paw SEE yuh)	Long, slender shape with wrinkled skin; brownish black color	Very hot
Pequin (pay KEEN) or Tepin	Tiny, round or oval shape with slightly wrinkled skin; orange-red color; sometimes available fresh	Very, very hot

Peppers

Green

Golden

Red

Purple

Yellow

Anaheim

Cayenne

Chipotle

Ancho

Jalapeño

Cascabel

Pasilla

Serrano

Poblano

Pequin (dried) Pequin (fresh)

For dried peppers, remove the stems and seeds, then chop the peppers. Soak them in hot water for 30 minutes to 1 hour.

Q: Why and how are peppers roasted?
A: Fresh peppers are roasted to soften the peppers and make the skin easier to remove. When your recipe specifies roasted peppers, try the following method.

Use small peppers, or quarter or halve larger peppers. Remove stems, membranes, and seeds. Place peppers, cut side down, on a foil-lined baking sheet. Bake in a 425° oven for 20 to 25 minutes or till skin is bubbly and browned. Place the peppers in a *new* brown paper bag; seal and let stand for 20 to 30 minutes or till cool enough to handle. Pull the skin off gently and slowly using a paring knife.

How to cook: To cook fresh sweet peppers, see the Cooking Fresh Vegetables chart under *Vegetable.* Most hot fresh or dried peppers are added in small amounts to dishes as a seasoning, rather than being cooked as a vegetable.

Nutrition information: One-half cup of chopped fresh bell peppers or chopped canned chili peppers has about 15 calories.

Pepper Steak Any of three popular meat dishes. In Italian cuisine, pepper steak refers to a dish prepared with beef, green pepper strips, and tomatoes; it is cooked slowly in a flavorful sauce. (For a pepper steak recipe, see page 309.)

In Oriental cooking, pepper steak is a highly seasoned Chinese stir-fry made with beef. And in French cooking, steak au poivre or pepper steak is beef that is quickly cooked in a skillet and seasoned with crushed black peppercorns.

Pepper Steak

Pepper Steak

- 1   14½-ounce can tomato wedges
- 1   pound beef top round steak, cut ½ inch thick
- 1   tablespoon cooking oil
- 1   small onion, thinly sliced
- ¼   cup water
- 1   clove garlic, minced
- 2   teaspoons Worcestershire sauce
- 1   teaspoon instant beef bouillon granules
- ½   teaspoon sugar
- ¼   teaspoon pepper
- 2   medium green peppers, cut into 2-inch strips
- ¼   cup cold water
- 1   tablespoon all-purpose flour
- 4   baking potatoes, baked and cut into wedges (optional)

■ Drain tomatoes, reserving liquid (you should have about ½ cup). Trim excess fat from round steak; cut meat into 2x¼-inch-thick strips.

■ In a 10-inch skillet brown meat, half at a time, in hot oil. Drain off excess fat. Return all meat to pan. Add onion, ¼ cup water, garlic, Worcestershire sauce, bouillon granules, sugar, pepper, and reserved tomato liquid. Bring to boiling. Reduce heat and simmer, covered, for 20 minutes. Add green pepper strips. Cover and simmer for 5 minutes more.

■ Combine ¼ cup cold water and flour. Stir into mixture in skillet. Cook and stir till thickened and bubbly. Cook and stir 1 minute more. Add tomato wedges and heat through. Serve over baked potato wedges, if desired. Makes 4 servings.

Nutrition information per serving: 242 calories, 26 g protein, 11 g carbohydrate, 10 g fat (3 g saturated), 69 mg cholesterol, 483 mg sodium, 650 mg potassium.

Persian melon

Persian Melon
A fruit that resembles an oversize cantaloupe, with a green to golden yellow, finely netted rind, and brilliant salmon-colored meat. Persian melon is aromatic, especially at the stem end, and has a mildly sweet flavor and firm, buttery texture.

(See *Melon* for the Selecting Melons chart and storing, preparation, nutrition, and other information.)

Persimmon
A soft-textured winter fruit with shiny, brilliant orange skin and red-orange meat. It's sometimes called the "apple of the Orient." Depending on the variety, a persimmon can have an astringent quality when unripe, but develops a spicy-sweet flavor when ripe.

Persimmons

Varieties: The more common *Hachiya* persimmon is large, acorn-shaped, soft when ripe, and very sweet. The *Fuyu* tends to be smaller than a hachiya, rounded, and crisp like an apple.

continued

Market forms: Fresh persimmons are sold mainly from October through December. Dried persimmons also are available.

Selecting: Choose brilliant, smooth-skinned persimmons that have green caps. Hachiya persimmons can be soft, but the fuyu persimmons are firm.

Storing: Allow fresh hachiya persimmons to ripen at room temperature. They will become soft to the touch when ripe. The fuyu persimmon will remain firm. Refrigerate persimmons. Or, you can wrap ripe persimmons in freezer wrap and freeze them for up to 3 months.

How to eat: Eat a persimmon out of hand as you would an apple, or slice or puree it for recipes.

Nutrition information: A medium persimmon has about 120 calories.

(See *Dried Fruit* for the Cooking Dried Fruit chart and storing and preparation hints.)

Pesto   A mixture of crushed fresh basil leaves, garlic, grated cheese, and olive oil that usually is served with pasta, but also may be used to top soups and stews or as an ingredient in appetizers and main dishes. Often pine nuts or walnuts are added to the mixture.

A Tip from Our Kitchen
A little pesto can go a long way. So, if you have some left over and you plan to use it in a day or two, store it in a covered jar in the refrigerator, with a thin layer of oil poured over the top. For longer storage, spoon the pesto into ice cube trays and freeze. Then pop the blocks of pesto out and place them in a freezer bag. Store them in the freezer up to 1 month. This lets you use only as many blocks as needed.

Pesto

    1 cup firmly packed fresh basil leaves
    ½ cup firmly packed parsley sprigs with stems removed
    ½ cup grated Parmesan *or* Romano cheese
    ¼ cup pine nuts or walnuts
    1 large clove garlic, quartered
    ¼ teaspoon salt
    ¼ cup olive oil *or* cooking oil

■ In a blender container or food processor bowl, combine basil leaves, parsley, Parmesan or Romano cheese, nuts, garlic, and salt. Cover and blend or process with several on-off turns till a paste forms, stopping the machine several times and scraping the sides. With the machine running slowly, gradually add oil and blend or process to the consistency of soft butter. To serve, dollop some of the pesto atop hot soups or toss with hot cooked pasta. Makes about ¾ cup.

Nutrition information per tablespoon: 76 calories, 2 g protein, 1 g carbohydrate, 7 g fat (2 g saturated), 3 mg cholesterol, 110 mg sodium, 66 mg potassium.

Petit Four   A bite-size cake cut in the shape of a square, diamond, or circle. Made from a sponge or layer-type cake, the shape is glazed with several layers of white or pale pastel icing, then is decorated with icings of contrasting colors, melted chocolate, or candy flowers.

Pheasant   A large, long-tailed game bird that is related to quail and partridge. Its flavor is heartier than chicken.

Market forms: Wild pheasant can be hunted in season, or farm-raised pheasant can be purchased dressed and frozen in specialty stores and some large supermarkets.

Storing: Store pheasant as you would chicken (see *Chicken*).

Cooking hints: Broiling, roasting, and baking are common ways of cooking young, tender pheasant. A pheasant has very little fat, so it can dry out quickly. Covering the breast with strips of bacon and frequent basting with margarine or butter will keep the meat moist and tender during roasting.

Older, larger birds may be slightly less tender than younger ones. For older pheasants, moist-heat cooking methods, such as braising, simmering, or steaming, may be more suitable. Or, tenderize the meat before cooking by marinating it for 2 to 3 hours in the refrigerator.

How to cook: For roasting directions, see the Roasting Poultry chart under *Poultry.* For grilling directions, see the Indirect-Grilling Poultry chart under *Barbecue.*

Nutrition information: A 3-ounce serving of roasted pheasant without bones and skin has about 170 calories.

Phyllo *(FEE low)* A Greek pastry made from a flour and water mixture that is stretched until paper thin then cut into sheets. Although phyllo can be made at home, a frozen commercial product is available. The pastry is used in layers to make desserts, appetizers, and main dishes.

A Tip from Our Kitchen
Allow frozen phyllo dough to thaw while it is still wrapped. Once unwrapped, sheets of phyllo dough quickly dry out and become unusable. To preserve the phyllo sheets, keep the opened stack of dough covered with a slightly moistened cloth while you're preparing your recipe. Rewrap any remaining sheets of the dough and return them to the freezer.

Piccalilli A spicy relish that is made from chopped vegetables, such as green tomatoes, peppers, and onions, packed in a sugar-vinegar solution, and seasoned with mustard, celery seed, cinnamon, and allspice. Piccalilli often is used as a condiment with cold meats, such as ham and roast pork.

Pickle A vegetable or fruit preserved in a solution of salt or vinegar and pickling spices. The most commonly preserved food is the cucumber. Pickled foods often are served as condiments.

Pickle also refers to the process of preserving food in a salt or vinegar solution.

Types and market forms: There are several kinds of homemade vegetable pickles, including dill, bread and butter, mustard, and sweet and sour pickles. There also are fruit specialties, such as watermelon pickles. Pickles also are made commercially and include the following groups.

☐ **Fresh-Pack:** Foods, especially fresh cucumbers, that are covered with a seasoned vinegar solution and pasteurized. These pickles have a crisp texture and a lighter flavor than most other pickles. They may be dill or kosher dill pickles, either whole or cut into slices or strips. (The term "kosher" with regard to pickles means garlic flavored.) Bread and butter pickles also are fresh-pack. They are sweet in flavor and may be cut into slices or strips. Look for fresh-pack pickles on the grocery shelf of the supermarket.

☐ **Processed:** Made from fully fermented cucumbers that have been soaked in a salt brine for several months. After the cucumbers have fermented, most of the salt is rinsed out of them, and they are made into a variety of different products. Look for these products in the grocery sections of the supermarket. Following are the most common kinds.

Dill: Cucumbers prepared in brine with dill added. Kosher dill pickles are similar to dill pickles but also have garlic added to the pickling solution. These often are spicier than plain dill pickles.

continued

Sour: Cucumbers prepared in a brine with seasonings other than dill added.

Sweet: Cucumbers prepared in a sweet mixture of vinegar, sugar, and spices. Gherkins are miniature sweet pickles. Sweet mixed pickles are cucumber chunks mixed with other vegetables and sold as a combination. Candied dill pickles are sticks, strips, or slices of dill pickles packed in a very sweet solution.

Relish: Small pieces of cucumber usually mixed with other vegetables and prepared in a vinegar solution. The solution may be dill or sweet. Although there are numerous types of relishes, perhaps the most common is sweet pickle relish. It is made from finely chopped sweet pickles that usually are mixed with finely chopped pickled red peppers. Salad cubes are a variation of relish and are larger pieces; they may be sweet or dill.

☐ **Refrigerated:** Foods, especially fresh cucumbers, that are covered with a seasoned vinegar solution and refrigerated. These pickles generally are more highly seasoned. You'll find them in the refrigerated dairy or cold-cuts case at the supermarket. Plain dill pickles and kosher deli dills may be whole or halved. Some dill pickles also are available at delicatessens.

Nutrition information: One dill pickle (about 3¾ inches long) has 12 calories and 833 milligrams of sodium. One sweet pickle (about 2½ inches long) has about 40 calories and 329 milligrams of sodium. One tablespoon of sweet pickle relish has about 20 calories and 107 milligrams of sodium.

Pickling Spice
A pungent mixture of whole and broken spices, herbs, and seeds used for making pickles and relishes and for preserving meats. Blends vary, but the seasoning usually includes allspice, bay leaves, cardamom, cloves, red pepper, black pepper, coriander seed, ginger, mace, and mustard seed.

Pie
A sweet or savory baked good made with a crust and filling. Pies can have a single or a double crust (see also *Piecrust*).

Types: Savory pies include potpies and quiches of all types (see individual entries). Sweet dessert pies also are popular. Here are the common types of dessert pies.

☐ **Chiffon:** A single-crust pie with a fluffy filling that is made with dissolved gelatin, stiffly beaten egg whites, flavoring, and sometimes whipped cream. The filling is moderately sweet with an airy texture. Either a pastry piecrust or a crumb crust commonly is used.

Because chiffon pies include uncooked egg whites, eating them may be harmful to some people due to possible bacterial contamination (see Using Eggs Safely tip under *Egg*).

☐ **Cream:** A single-crust pie with a sweet, rich puddinglike filling that has a smooth, creamy texture. Either a pastry piecrust or a crumb crust commonly is used. Cream pie is usually topped with meringue, but whipped cream or fresh fruit also can be used.

☐ **Custard:** A single-crust pie with a sweet, rich filling made from eggs and milk. Custard pie has a smooth texture that's firmer than cream pie filling. Pastry most often is used for the crust. Custard pie sometimes is topped with whipped cream. Pumpkin and pecan pies are types of custard pies.

☐ **Frozen:** A single-crust pie made with an ice-cream or a chiffon-type filling and either a pastry or a crumb crust. Sometimes a whipped-cream topping is added.

☐ **Fruit:** A double- or single-crust pie with a fresh, canned, frozen, or dried fruit filling. For a double-crust fruit pie, the crust is made from pastry with a solid or lattice top. For a single-crust pie, either a pastry or a crumb crust can be used. Single-crust fruit pies can be decorated with pastry cutouts or sprinkled with a crumb topping.

Storing: Always refrigerate pies with fillings that contain eggs or dairy products. Examples are chiffon, cream, and custard pies. Store fruit pie at room temperature for up to 1 day. After that, refrigerate the pie.

Q: Can pies be frozen?
A: Yes, especially fruit pies and ice-cream pies. However, freezing cream or custard pies is not recommended.

To freeze an unbaked fruit pie, treat light-colored fruit with ascorbic acid color keeper. Then prepare the pie as usual, but don't cut slits in the top crust. Use a metal or freezer-to-oven pie plate. Cover with an inverted pie plate to protect the crust. Seal pie in a freezer bag and freeze it for up to 4 months.

To bake the frozen fruit pie, unwrap the pie, remove the inverted pie plate, and cut slits in the top of the pie. Cover edges of pie with foil. Bake in a preheated 450° oven for 15 minutes, then in a 375° oven for 15 minutes. Uncover and bake about 30 minutes more or until done.

To freeze a baked fruit pie, wrap it as you would an unbaked pie and freeze it for up to 8 months. To serve, thaw wrapped pie. Then unwrap pie. Remove the inverted pie plate; reheat pie.

Frozen ice-cream pies in freezer bags can be kept frozen for up to 2 weeks.

Pie-Making Hints

Chiffon, cream, custard, frozen, and fruit pies are all very different. Here are some preparation tips for each type.

Chiffon
● Before preparing a chiffon pie with uncooked egg whites, see Using Eggs Safely tip under *Egg*.
● For perfect chiffon pie, chill the dissolved gelatin mixture until it is as thick as corn syrup. Let the gelatin stand at room temperature while you stiffly beat the egg whites. By the time you finish beating the whites, the gelatin should have thickened to the consistency of unbeaten egg whites. Then you can fold the stiffly beaten egg whites into the gelatin mixture.
● When chiffon pies contain both stiffly beaten egg whites and whipped cream, first fold the egg whites into the gelatin mixture, then fold in the whipped cream. This way, you'll avoid overmixing the whipped cream.
● Chill chiffon pies for at least 6 hours before serving.

Cream
● To add a meringue to a cream pie, see *Meringue* for Egg White Pointers and information on what causes the meringue on a cream pie to shrink or leak. See *Cream Pie* for meringue baking times.
● Refrigerate meringue-topped cream pies after 1 hour of cooling. Chill for 3 to 6 hours before serving. Cover and refrigerate any leftover pie.
● For perfect slices of a meringue-topped pie, dip the knife in water before cutting each slice. Also, wipe knife clean between slices.
● To protect a meringue- or whipped-cream-topped pie when covering it with plastic wrap for storage, insert toothpicks halfway into the pie to keep the wrap from touching the top. Remove the picks before serving.

Custard
● To avoid messy spills, position the pie shell on the oven rack before pouring in the filling.
● To tell if a custard pie is done, insert a knife slightly off-center. If the knife comes out clean, the pie is done. (It is typical for a crack to form in the filling as a result of this test.) Or, gently wiggle the pie. If the custard is firm except for a spot in the center about the size of a quarter, the pie is done. (The center will firm up as it cools.)

● Don't overcook custard pies. When overcooked, custard fillings become tough and can get watery. To prevent overcooking, check for doneness a little before the minimum baking time.

Frozen
● For easy slicing, let frozen pies soften at room temperature about 15 minutes.
● To make slices easy to remove and serve, wrap the bottom of the plate in a hot, damp towel for a few minutes before cutting the pie.
● For perfect slices, dip the knife in water between each cut.

Fruit
● For double-crust pies, cut slits in the top crust before baking to release steam during cooking.
● To catch messy spills from a pie filling that may bubble over, bake your pie on a baking sheet or pizza pan.
● For pretty pies, brush unbaked pie tops with milk or water. Or, sprinkle with sugar or a cinnamon-sugar mixture, then bake.
● For an extra-festive look, reroll pastry trimmings and make cutouts. Add cutouts to top of a double-crust pie, lightly brush with milk, and bake according to recipe.

1. Use a pastry blender (or 2 table knives, holding one in each hand and drawing the knives across each other) to cut in shortening till the pieces are the size of small peas.

2. On a lightly floured surface, flatten the ball of pastry dough into a circle, smoothing the edges and keeping pastry in a circle.

3. Using a lightly floured rolling pin, roll dough from the center out to the edges into a 12-inch circle. (For a tender crust, roll dough using just enough flour to keep the dough from sticking to the surface and rolling pin.)

4. Keep edges from overbrowning by covering them with a foil ring. To make a foil ring, fold a 12-inch square of foil into quarters. Cut out the center, leaving a 7½-inch hole in foil. Unfold and loosely mold foil rim over the pie edges.

Piecrust The mixture used to form the shell or foundation of a pie. Piecrust usually is made with tender, flaky pastry, but crusts made with cookie and cracker crumbs also are popular.

Some pies are made with one crust and others have two. In a single-crust pie, pastry or a crumb mixture forms a shell to hold a filling. The top can be decorated with pastry cutouts or a crumb topping. A deep-dish pie is a type of single-crust pie made in a casserole dish or deep pie plate, but its crust is usually on the top, instead of the bottom.

A double-crust pie has two crusts, usually made of pastry, enclosing a filling. A lattice-top pie is a type of double-crust pie that has a top crust made from loosely woven strips of pastry instead of a solid piece of pastry.

Market forms: Pastry piecrust can be purchased in many forms, including piecrust mixes, piecrust sticks, refrigerated piecrust dough, and frozen ready-to-use pie shells. Ready-to-use crumb crusts also can be found on the grocery shelf.

Tips from Our Kitchen

● When rolling out pastry for a piecrust, repair any tears by moistening the edges with water and using small pieces of the trimmings to patch the tears.

● It's easy to make a mock lattice pie top by using a miniature cookie or biscuit cutter. Roll out the top crust of a double-crust pie as usual. Then make a cutout in the center of the pastry. Working from the center of the pastry out to the edges, repeat the cutouts in a pattern, making them equal distances apart. Take care not to make the cutouts too close together or the pastry may rip when it is transferred to the pie.

Pastry Piecrust-Making Hints

With practice and these helpful tips, even an inexperienced cook can make tender, flaky piecrust.

● For tender piecrust, add just enough cold water to moisten the flour mixture, tossing it gently with a fork. Once the mixture is moistened, stop mixing.

● Handle the dough as little as possible so piecrust stays tender.

● To minimize sticking, roll the pastry out on a lightly floured pastry cloth, using a lightly floured stockinette cover on your rolling pin.

● For crisp piecrust, use glass or metal pie plates with a dull finish. (If using a shiny pie pan, you may need to bake piecrust a little longer to get it brown.)

● To easily transfer rolled-out pastry to a pie plate, loosely roll the dough around the rolling pin. Then, starting at one side of the pie plate, unroll the dough over it. Another way to transfer the dough is to gently fold the rolled-out dough into quarters. Then center the point of the folded dough in the pie plate and unfold the dough.

● To keep crusts from shrinking, ease the rolled-out pastry dough into the pie plate without stretching it.

● For prebaked single-crust pie shells, avoid large bubbles by pricking the crust all over with a fork before baking.

● For pies that have the filling and piecrust baked together, do not prick the bottom crust or the filling will leak out and make the crust soggy.

● After baking, cool the piecrust or pie on a wire rack. Allowing air to circulate under the pie plate during cooling helps it cool faster.

Pike

A lean freshwater fish with a long, narrow body and light-colored, firm flesh. It is sweet and mild to moderate in flavor.

Types: Two important species are the *Muskellunge*, sometimes called muskie, and the *Northern* pike. The muskellunge generally grows to be a larger fish than the northern pike, and it is one of the largest freshwater fish in North America. (Despite its name, the walleye or yellow pike is actually in the perch family.)

Market forms: Fresh pike is sold drawn, dressed, and cut into fillets and steaks. Frozen pike is available as fillets and steaks.

Q: What's the best way to remove scales from pike (or other fish)?

A: To remove the scales from a whole or drawn pike (or any other fish), first wet the fish. Then firmly grasp the tail with one hand. With the other hand, use a scaler or dull knife to scrape the fish from tail to head. Use short, swift strokes until you've removed all the scales. Rinse the scaled fish under cold running water.

How to cook: Pike can be panfried, baked, poached, grilled, and broiled. For panfrying, baking, poaching, and broiling directions, see the Cooking Fish chart under *Fish*. For grilling directions, see the Direct-Grilling Fish chart under *Barbecue*.

Nutrition information: One 3-ounce serving of baked pike has about 100 calories.

(See *Fish* for selecting, storing, thawing, and other information.)

Pilaf

A Middle Eastern dish containing rice or sometimes cracked wheat that is cooked with seasonings and broth. Sometimes vegetables are added. Pilaf usually is served as a side dish, but it can be combined with meat, poultry, or fish to make a main dish. (For a pilaf recipe, see page 316.)

Rice Pilaf

- ½ **cup chopped onion**
- ¼ **cup sliced celery**
- 1 **tablespoon margarine** *or* **butter**
- 1½ **cups water**
- ⅔ **cup long grain rice**
- 2 **tablespoons snipped parsley**
- 1½ **teaspoons instant chicken bouillon granules**
- ¼ **teaspoon dried thyme, crushed**
- ¼ **teaspoon salt**
- ⅛ **teaspoon pepper**
- ½ **cup finely chopped, cooked, desired vegetable** *or* **chicken**

■ In a medium saucepan cook onion and celery in margarine or butter till tender but not brown. Stir in water, *uncooked* rice, parsley, bouillon granules, thyme, salt, and pepper. Bring to boiling; reduce heat. Cover and simmer about 15 minutes or till rice is tender and liquid is absorbed. Stir in vegetable or chicken. Cover and cook for 3 minutes more. Makes 4 servings.

Nutrition information per serving: 160 calories, 3 g protein, 29 g carbohydrate, 3 g fat (1 g saturated), 0 mg cholesterol, 527 mg sodium, 146 mg potassium.

Indian Pilaf: Prepare Rice Pilaf as above, *except* omit thyme and add ½ teaspoon *curry powder* and ⅛ teaspoon ground *allspice* with the onion. Omit the vegetable or chicken and stir in ½ cup *raisins* and ¼ cup chopped *peanuts.*

Nutrition information per serving: 266 calories, 6 g protein, 46 g carbohydrate, 8 g fat (1 g saturated), 0 mg cholesterol, 555 mg sodium, 322 mg potassium.

Pimiento *(puh MENT oh)* A roasted, sweet red pepper with the skin removed. It is used as a colorful garnish. Pimiento is packed in oil, sold in jars, and is available whole, chopped, or cut into strips.

Pineapple A tropical fruit with an elongated oval shape, a thick skin with a diamond pattern studded with "eyes," and yellow meat. Pineapples have green leaves at their tops and seedless meat that grows around a core. They are sweet and juicy, and the texture is slightly stringy. Once they are picked, they do not become sweeter.

Market forms: Look for fresh whole pineapples, pineapple halves, and peeled pineapples in the produce department of your supermarket. You can buy canned pineapple in a variety of forms—slices, spears, chunks, tidbits, and crushed—packed in syrup or its own juice. In addition, pineapple preserves, sauce, and dried and candied products are available. Canned pineapple juice and frozen juice concentrate are other products.

Pineapples

Selecting: Picking a ripe, fresh pineapple can be tricky. Look for a pineapple with a plump shape. Smell the stem end—it should be sweet and aromatic, not heavy or fermented. The pineapple should be slightly soft to the touch, heavy for its size, and have deep green leaves. Avoid those with mold or bruises and dark, watery eyes.

Storing: Refrigerate ripe, fresh pineapple for up to 2 days. Do not store it at room temperature. Cut pineapple lasts another couple of days if placed in a tightly covered container and chilled. Pineapple also can be cut up and frozen in a freezer container.

Preparation hints: To cut up a pineapple, use a large, sharp knife. Slice off the bottom stem end and the green top. Stand the pineapple on one cut end and slice off the skin in wide strips, from top to bottom. To remove the eyes, cut diagonally around the fruit, following the pattern of the eyes and making narrow wedge-shaped grooves into the pineapple (see photo). Cut away as little of the meat as possible. Then slice or chop it away from the core; discard the core.

For pineapple "boats," leave both ends on the pineapple and halve or quarter the pineapple lengthwise. Use a thin paring knife or grapefruit knife to hollow out the boats. Fill the shells with fruit, ice cream, or a main-dish salad mixture.

Nutrition information: A ½-cup serving of fresh cut pineapple provides about 40 calories. A ½-cup serving of pineapple chunks canned in juice contains about 75 calories, and chunks in heavy syrup have about 100 calories. A ½-cup serving of pineapple juice contains 70 calories.

Pine Nut   The small seed from one of several pine tree varieties. The pine nut, which has a sweet, faint pine flavor, also is known as pignolia and piñon. The small, creamy white nut can be slender and pellet-shaped or more triangular.

Pine nuts turn rancid quickly, so refrigerate them in an airtight container for up to 2 months or freeze them for up to 6 months.

Q: How are pine nuts used in cooking?
A: Pine nuts frequently are used in Italian cuisine—pasta sauces, pesto, rice dishes, and cookies. Greek recipes sometimes call for pine nuts in stuffed grape leaves.

(See *Nut* for the Selecting Nuts chart and selecting, nutrition, and other information.)

Pine nuts

Pinwheel   A food that is shaped so it has the spiral appearance of a spinning wheel. Sandwiches, cookies, and meat rolls often are shaped this way. A pinwheel is made by spreading bread, dough, or meat with a filling and rolling it up. Then the roll usually is cut into thin slices.

Pipe   To force a semisoft food, such as frosting or mashed potatoes, through a pastry tip in order to form attractive shapes for decorating or garnishing.

Piquant   *(PEA kahnt)* A term used to describe a food that stimulates the appetite and has a pungent or pleasantly sharp flavor.

Piquant Sauce   A spicy variation of the classic brown sauce with shallots, wine or vinegar, capers, chopped pickles, and herbs added (see also *Brown Sauce*). Piquant sauce often is served with sliced meats. It should not be confused with picante sauce *(pih KAHN tay)*, which is a type of Mexican salsa.

Pistachios

Pistachio Nut *(puh STASH ee oh)* The
seed of the fruit of a small evergreen tree.
Two colors—red and green—usually are
associated with pistachio nuts. The thin, oval
shell, which is split at one end, is naturally
beige, but often is dyed bright red. Inside, the
pistachio, which is usually about ½ inch
long, has a paper-thin brown skin and a
distinctive green to yellow flesh. Pistachios
have a mildly sweet flavor similar to almonds.

Store pistachios in an airtight container in
the refrigerator or freezer for up to 1 year.

Q: Why are pistachio nuts dyed red?
A: In the 1930s, the United States began
dying pistachios red to disguise their
blemished shells. Many pistachios are still
dyed red, but only because consumers
expect it—undyed nuts also are available.

**(See *Nut* for the Selecting Nuts chart and
selecting, nutrition, and other information.)**

Pit The single seed inside a piece of fruit.
The term also refers to removing this seed.

Pita A round, flat, Middle Eastern,
unleavened bread that typically forms a
pocket when it is cut crosswise. Pita bread,
sometimes called pocket bread, can be filled
with hot or cold sandwich fillings. Plain and
whole wheat pita bread is available in
supermarkets in small and large sizes.

A Tip from Our Kitchen
For a simple snack, make crisps out of
pita bread. Split 2 pita rounds in half
horizontally. Quarter halves to form a
total of 16 triangles. Place on a baking
sheet. Bake in a 325° oven for 12 to 15
minutes or till crisp.

Nutrition information: One pita round
(6½-inch diameter) has about 170 calories.

Pizza An Italian favorite that features
either a thin or thick yeast-dough crust that is
baked with a topping of a flavorful sauce and
a variety of ingredients, such as cooked meats,
vegetables, and cheeses. The thin-crust
version of pizza is called Neapolitan pizza,
and the thick-crust version (pan pizza) is
referred to as Sicilian pizza.

Pizza

2¾ to 3¼ cups all-purpose flour
1 package active dry yeast
¼ teaspoon salt
1 cup warm water (120° to 130°)
2 tablespoons cooking oil
1 15-ounce can pizza sauce
1 pound bulk Italian sausage, ground
    beef, *or* ground pork, cooked and
    drained; 6 ounces sliced pepperoni;
    or 1 cup cubed fully cooked ham
    or Canadian-style bacon
½ cup sliced green onion *or* pitted ripe
    olives
1 cup sliced fresh mushrooms *or*
    chopped green pepper
2 to 3 cups shredded mozzarella cheese

■ In a large bowl combine *1¼ cups* of the
flour, the yeast, and salt. Add warm water and
oil. Beat with an electric mixer on low speed
for 30 seconds, scraping bowl constantly. Beat
on high speed for 3 minutes. Using a spoon,
stir in as much of the remaining flour as you
can. Turn out onto a lightly floured surface.
Knead in enough remaining flour to make a
moderately stiff dough that is smooth and
elastic (6 to 8 minutes total). Divide dough
in half. Cover and let rest 10 minutes.

Thin Pizzas: Grease two 12-inch pizza pans
or baking sheets. If desired, sprinkle with
cornmeal. On a lightly floured surface, roll
each half of dough into a 13-inch circle.
Transfer to pans. Build up edges slightly. *Do
not let rise.* Bake in a 425° oven about 12
minutes or till browned. Spread pizza sauce
over hot crust. Sprinkle meat, vegetables, and
cheese atop. Bake 10 to 15 minutes more or
till bubbly. Makes 6 servings.

Pan Pizzas: Grease two 11x7x1½-inch or 9x9x2-inch baking pans. If desired, sprinkle with cornmeal. With greased fingers, pat dough into bottoms and halfway up sides of prepared pans. Cover;* let rise in a warm place till nearly double (30 to 45 minutes). Bake in a 375° oven for 20 to 25 minutes or till lightly browned. Spread pizza sauce over hot crust. Sprinkle meat, vegetables, and cheese atop. Bake for 15 to 20 minutes more or till bubbly. Makes 6 servings.

  Note: If desired, cover and refrigerate 2 to 24 hours. Bake as directed, omitting rising.

Nutrition information per serving: 575 calories, 29 g protein, 52 g carbohydrate, 27 g fat (10 g saturated), 65 mg cholesterol, 1,088 mg sodium, 356 mg potassium.

Plantain *(PLAN tin)* A tropical fruit that resembles a banana with thick, green skin and a longer, more squared-off shape. Unlike bananas, plantains must be cooked as you would a vegetable to be enjoyed. They can be cooked when they are in various stages of ripeness. The flavor of plantains is very mild, and they often are served in place of potatoes.

Selecting: Look for plump, undamaged plantains, but don't be too concerned about slight bruises. The skin is tough enough to absorb most bumps.

Plantains

Storing: Ripen plantains at room temperature. It takes 1 week for them to turn from totally green to yellow-brown and another week or two until the plantains are black and fully ripe.

Nutrition information: A ½-cup serving of cooked, sliced plantains has about 90 calories.

Plum A small, round, tree fruit that is a bit larger than an apricot. Plums have smooth skin and come in a variety of colors from green, yellow, and purple to red, blue, and black. They have soft, sweet to tart meat. A few types of plums are dried to make prunes (see also *Prune*).

Plums

Friar
Queen Ann
Kelsey
French Prune
Ace

Varieties: Plums are grown in numerous varieties. Here are some plum varieties you might find at the supermarket.

☐ **Ace:** Medium-size with deep reddish purple skin and sweet, reddish-colored meat. Use for fruit compotes and snacks.

☐ **Casselman:** Medium-size with red skin and firm, deep yellow meat. It has a tangy-sweet flavor. Use for jams, jellies, and salads.

☐ **French Prune:** Small, oval to pear-shaped with greenish red skin and greenish golden, sweet meat. Use for snacks.

☐ **Friar:** Very large with deep black skin and very juicy, sweet, amber-colored meat. Use for sauces, fruit compotes, and snacks.

continued

☐ **Italian Prune:** Small with dark blue to purple skin and golden meat. Sweet and rich-tasting, this variety is used mainly for prunes.
☐ **Kelsey:** Large, oblong-shaped with a pointed tip. Its thick, green skin turns to yellow tinged with red. The inside of the plum is yellow, firm, crisp, sweet, and juicy. Use for desserts.
☐ **Queen Ann:** Large, dark reddish purple skin with rich, sweet, golden meat inside. Use for fruit compotes and snacks.
☐ **Red Beaut:** Small to medium-size with bright red skin and firm, yellow meat that's mildly sweet. A good eating plum.
☐ **Santa Rosa:** Small to medium-size with purple-crimson skin and juicy, yellow meat that is dark red around the pit. Its rich, tart flavor makes it great for canning, freezing, and making jellies and jams.

Market forms: Fresh plums are mainly available June through September. They also are sold canned and in jams and jellies year-round.

Selecting: Look for firm, plump, well-shaped fresh plums with good color for the variety. Press a plum gently; it should give slightly. The bloom (light gray cast) on the skin is natural protection and doesn't affect quality. Avoid overly soft, bruised, or exceptionally hard fruit.

Plum Math

1 pound plums	= 6 (2-inch) whole
	= 3 cups sliced
	= 2½ cups chopped

Storing: Ripen plums at room temperature, then refrigerate them for up to 5 days. To freeze plums, halve and pit fruit. Then treat them with ascorbic acid color keeper; drain

well. Place in freezer containers, leaving a ½-inch headspace. Freeze for up to 10 months.

Nutrition information: Plums have about 40 calories per fruit.

Plump

To allow a food to soak in a liquid, such as water, juice, or wine, in order to rehydrate and soften the food.

The term also is used to describe any fruit that has a full, rounded shape.

Plum Pudding

A cakelike dessert with a dense, moist texture. Plum pudding is made from a batter to which dried fruits, suet, and spices have been added. Despite its name, plum pudding does not contain plums. It usually is steamed in a mold and served warm with a hard sauce. Plum pudding is a traditional holiday dessert and sometimes is called Christmas pudding.

Poach

To cook a food by partially or completely submerging it in a simmering liquid.

A Tip from Our Kitchen

For best results, poach such delicate foods as eggs and fish in a liquid that is simmering and not boiling. If the liquid is boiling, it may overcook the food.

To poach an egg, break it into a small dish. Slowly slide the egg into the simmering liquid, holding the lip of the dish as close to the liquid as possible. Cook until the yolk is just set, not runny.

Polenta

(poh LEN tuh) Italian-style mush made by boiling a mixture of cornmeal or farina and water. Polenta usually is served with Parmesan cheese and sometimes a tomato sauce as a vegetable dish or as a bread substitute. It is eaten as a thick porridge, or it can be molded, sliced, fried, or broiled.

Polenta

- **2 cups water**
- **⅔ cup yellow cornmeal**
- **⅔ cup cold water**
- **¼ teaspoon salt**

■ In a medium saucepan bring the 2 cups water to a rolling boil. Meanwhile, combine cornmeal, the ⅔ cup cold water, and salt. Slowly pour cornmeal mixture into boiling water, stirring constantly. Return just to boiling; reduce heat to low. Cook, uncovered, about 5 minutes or till thick, stirring frequently. Serve immediately. If desired, serve with margarine or butter, grated Parmesan cheese, or desired sauce. Serves 6.

Baked Polenta: Prepare Polenta as above. Transfer hot mixture to a 9-inch pie plate. Cover with foil. Chill at least 45 minutes or overnight till firm. Bake, covered, in a 350° oven about 30 minutes or till heated through. Cut into wedges.

Nutrition information per serving: 56 calories, 1 g protein, 12 g carbohydrate, 0 g fat, 0 mg cholesterol, 89 mg sodium, 25 mg potassium.

Fried Polenta: Prepare Polenta as above. Transfer hot mixture to an 8x4x2-inch loaf pan. Cover and chill at least 45 minutes or overnight till firm. Turn out and cut into ½-inch-thick slices. Fry slowly in hot *butter or cooking oil* for 10 to 12 minutes on each side or till browned and crisp.

Nutrition information per serving: 90 calories, 1 g protein, 12 g carbohydrate, 4 g fat (1 g saturated), 0 mg cholesterol, 134 mg sodium, 27 mg potassium.

Broiled Polenta: Prepare Polenta as at left. Transfer hot mixture to an 8x4x2-inch loaf pan. Cover and chill at least 45 minutes or overnight till firm. Turn out and cut into ½-inch-thick slices. Place on the unheated rack of a broiler pan. Brush with melted *margarine or butter.* Broil 4 inches from heat about 8 minutes on each side or till browned and crisp, brushing with melted margarine after turning slices.

Nutrition information per serving: 90 calories, 1 g protein, 12 g carbohydrate, 4 g fat (1 g saturated), 0 mg cholesterol, 134 mg sodium, 27 mg potassium.

Pomegranate

A hard-shelled, tomato-shaped tree fruit with bright red, leathery skin and hundreds of crunchy, red seeds embedded in white membranes. Pomegranates have a lightly sweet flavor and a deep red juice when the seeds are cut into. The seeds can be used as you would nuts to sprinkle over salads.

Pomegranates

Market forms: Purchase fresh pomegranates September through December. Or look for canned sweetened pomegranate juice (grenadine syrup) year-round.

Selecting: Pomegranates should have a shiny, bright red skin with no signs of shriveling. Buy the largest fruits you can find. Pomegranates should feel heavy for their size.

continued

Storing: Pomegranates found in the supermarket should be ready to eat. Because they keep well, you can store them in the refrigerator for several weeks. Or, you can freeze the pomegranate seeds in freezer containers or bags for up to 1 year.

How to Eat a Pomegranate
Cut the pomegranate in half through the skin. Remove the peel and break the fruit into sections. Then separate the seeds from the membrane; discard the membrane and eat the seeds. If desired, transfer the seeds and any juice to a blender or food processor container; cover and process until pulverized. Strain and use the juice.

Nutrition information: A medium pomegranate has about 100 calories.

Pompano *(POM puh no)* A saltwater fish with a firm texture and light color. It has a mild to moderate flavor that's somewhat sweet. It is one of the tastiest catches of the Florida and Gulf coasts, and because supplies are limited, it is very expensive. The average pompano weighs 1½ to 2 pounds.

Market forms: Pompano is sold dressed, drawn, or as fillets when fresh. It is commonly sold as fillets when frozen.

How to cook: Broiling, baking, panfrying, and grilling are recommended ways to cook pompano. For broiling, baking, and panfrying directions, see the Cooking Fish chart under *Fish.* For grilling directions, see the Direct-Grilling Fish chart under *Barbecue.*

Nutrition information: A 3-ounce serving of baked pompano has about 180 calories.

(See *Fish* for selecting, storing, thawing, and other information.)

Popcorn A type of corn that bursts open into white or yellow, fluffy balls when heated. Popcorn is bland and faintly cornlike in flavor with a crunchy texture. Popcorn is enjoyed as a snack and often is seasoned with butter and salt.

Types: Although there are hundreds of varieties of popcorn, nearly all popcorn is sold as either yellow or white. Yellow popcorn is popular because of its large kernels, and white popcorn is favored for its tenderness and flavor.

Market forms: Unpopped popcorn is sold in nearly all supermarkets. Special popcorn for popping in a microwave also is available as well as already popped and flavored popcorns.

Q: **What makes popcorn "pop"?**
A: As the kernel is heated, the moisture inside changes to steam. The hard outer surface resists the building pressure until it finally bursts. The soft starch inside pops out as the steam inside the kernel is released and the kernel turns inside out.

Storing: Because the moisture inside the kernel is what makes the corn pop, store popcorn in an airtight container in a cool, dry place for up to 1 year. Refrigeration is not recommended, because it dries the popcorn.

Nutrition information: One cup of plain, air-popped popcorn has about 30 calories; buttered popcorn has 90 to 120 calories.

Popover A big, puffy, steam-raised quick bread made from an egg-rich batter. Popovers have a hollow, crusty, yet tender, shell that's deep golden brown. The lining of the shell is tender and moist and usually has a few thin filaments of dough inside.

Popover batter sometimes is used to make another quick bread. Baked in a large pan with roast beef drippings, it becomes Yorkshire pudding.

continued

Herb Popovers
(see recipe, page 324)

A Tip from Our Kitchen

Popovers are quick to make; it takes just minutes to stir the batter together. After baking, serve the crispy, hollow puffs in a variety of ways. Hot from the oven accompanied with butter is just one possibility. Another is to fill the hollows of plain popovers with a seafood or poultry salad, fruit mixture, or pudding.

Q: **Why do popovers sometimes collapse?**
A: Sometimes popovers collapse after they're removed from the oven because they've been underbaked. So, always bake popovers for the time the recipe indicates or till very firm. Also, don't peek at popovers while they're baking; opening the oven door lets in cool air, which can cause the popovers to fall. Another reason popovers fall is that small eggs instead of large eggs were used to make the batter.

Baking hints: Pans used for baking popovers must be well greased so the popovers will be easy to remove. Use ½ teaspoon of shortening for each cup of a popover pan or generously spray each cup with nonstick spray coating.

After removing popovers from the oven, prick each one with a fork to let steam escape. This keeps popovers from becoming soggy. For even crisper popovers, turn off the oven and return the popovers to the oven for 5 to 10 minutes. Then remove popovers from pans while still warm.

Q: **Can popovers be made without special popover pans?**
A: Yes. You can make popovers in 6-ounce custard cups or 2½-inch muffin pans. Just remember to grease the cups or pans completely and fill them half full of batter. If the recipe you use calls for preheating the pans and you are using custard cups, don't preheat the cups.

Storing: Popovers are best when served hot from the oven. But if you have any left over, put them in a sealed freezer bag and freeze for up to 3 months. To reheat, place frozen popovers on a shallow baking pan and heat in a 400° oven for 10 to 15 minutes.

Herb Popovers

> 1 tablespoon shortening *or* nonstick spray coating
> 2 eggs
> 1 cup milk
> 1 tablespoon cooking oil
> 1 cup all-purpose flour
> ¼ teaspoon salt
> 1 tablespoon finely chopped fresh dillweed *or* basil *or* ¾ teaspoon dried dillweed *or* basil, crushed

■ Using *½ teaspoon* of shortening for *each* cup, grease the bottom and sides of the cups of a popover pan or six 6-ounce custard cups. *Or,* spray pan or cups with the nonstick coating. (If using custard cups, place them in a 15x10x1-inch baking pan.) Set pan or cups aside.

■ In a medium mixing bowl use a wire whisk or rotary beater to beat eggs, milk, and oil together till combined. Add flour and salt. Beat till smooth. Stir fresh or dried dillweed or basil into batter.

■ Fill the prepared pans or cups *half* full with batter. Bake in a 400° oven about 40 minutes or till very firm.

■ *Immediately* after removing popovers from oven, prick each popover with a fork to let the steam escape. Turn off oven.

■ For crisper popovers, return the popovers to the oven for 5 to 10 minutes or till desired crispness. Remove popovers from pans or cups; serve immediately. Makes 6 popovers.

Nutrition information per serving: 160 calories, 6 g protein, 18 g carbohydrate, 7 g fat (2 g saturated), 75 mg cholesterol, 130 mg sodium, 110 mg potassium.

Parmesan Popovers: Prepare Herb Popovers as above, *except* stir 3 tablespoons grated *Parmesan cheese* in with the flour. Omit the salt and the dillweed or basil.

Nutrition information per serving: 171 calories, 7 g protein, 18 g carbohydrate, 8 g fat (2 g saturated), 77 mg cholesterol, 88 mg sodium, 108 mg potassium.

Poppy Seed
Tiny, slate blue seeds from an annual poppy plant. The seeds have a slightly sweet, nutlike flavor that is enhanced when heated. In addition to the whole seeds, prepared poppy-seed fillings also are available. These sweetened mixtures are ready to use in cakes, breads, and pastries.

Storing: Because of their high oil content, poppy seeds turn rancid quickly. Store them in the refrigerator or freezer.

Pork
A meat from hogs raised for food. Light pink in color with a finely grained texture, fresh pork has a full flavor.

Market forms: Pork is marketed either fresh or processed. Only about one-third of the hog is marketed as fresh; the rest is processed before it is sold. Here's what you'll find in the stores.

☐ **Fresh:** Pork that has not been processed before marketing. Chops and roasts are the most popular fresh pork cuts.

☐ **Cured:** Pork that has been treated with a pickling solution or brine. The solution is a preservative and adds a special flavor to the meat. Salt pork, pickled pigs' feet, and some hams are sold as cured pork.

☐ **Cured and Smoked:** Pork that has been cured and then smoked to add flavor, aroma, and color. Cured and smoked pork either is fully cooked or requires cooking before eating. Bacon, Canadian-style bacon, smoked pork chops, smoked ham, smoked pork shoulder, country-style ham, and some sausages are examples of cured and smoked pork products (see also *Bacon, Canadian-Style Bacon,* and *Ham*).

Selecting: Fresh pork is light pink in color, and cured pork is rosy pink.

Pork cuts: For the names and locations of various retail cuts, see the identification photos, pages 326–327.

Tips from Our Kitchen
● Pork (and other meat) that is cooked with certain ingredients sometimes remains pink, even when it is well-done. These ingredients include bacon and other smoked meats, spinach, eggplant, and tomatoes. So, when cooking pork mixtures or stuffed roasts that contain these ingredients, the best way to check the meat for doneness is to use a meat thermometer.

● When you want to prepare stuffed pork chops, select loin or rib chops that are cut about 1¼ inches thick. Then, to make a pocket in each chop, cut from the fat side of the chop nearly to the bone. After adding the stuffing, you may need to hold the pockets closed with wooden toothpicks.

Storing: See the Storing Meat chart under *Meat.*

How to cook: For suggested cooking methods, see identification photos, pages 326–327. For roasting, broiling, panbroiling, and panfrying pork, see the Roasting Meat, the Broiling Meat, and the Panbroiling and Panfrying Meat charts under *Meat.* For grilling directions, see the Direct-Grilling Meat and Indirect-Grilling Meat charts under *Barbecue.*

Pork doneness: Roasts from the loin and rib sections can be cooked to an internal temperature of 160° (medium well) or 170° (well-done). The meat will be slightly pink at the 160° internal temperature, but when a small cut is made in the meat, the juices of the meat cooked to either the 160° or 170° temperature should run clear.

Chops from the loin and rib sections also can be cooked till they are slightly pink, but
continued on page 327

Retail Pork Cuts:
The number listed with each retail cut refers to the wholesale cut marked on the drawing at right. Besides the name of the retail cut, you'll find the best ways to cook each meat cut.

Blade steak (1)
Braise; broil; panbroil; panfry

Blade roast (1)
Roast; braise

Boneless blade roast (1)
Roast; braise

Smoked picnic (1)
Roast; cook in liquid

Smoked hock (1)
Braise; cook in liquid

Smoked shoulder roll (1)
Roast; cook in liquid

Boneless loin roast (2)
Roast

Top loin roast (double) (2)
Roast

Tenderloin (2)
Roast

Butterfly chop (2)
Broil; panbroil; panfry; braise

Top loin chop (2)
Broil; panbroil; panfry; braise

Loin chop (2)
Broil; panbroil; panfry; braise

Boneless blade roast (2)
Roast; braise

Top loin roast (2)
Roast

Rib crown roast (2)
Roast

Rib chop (2)
Broil; panbroil; panfry; braise

Sirloin cutlet (2)
Braise; broil; panbroil; panfry

Sirloin chop (2)
Braise; broil; panbroil; panfry

Spareribs (3)
Roast; broil; cook in liquid; braise

Country-style ribs (2)
Roast; braise; broil; cook in liquid

Back ribs (2)
Roast; broil; braise; cook in liquid

Boneless smoked ham (whole muscle) (4)
Roast

Ham shank/center slice (4)
  Shank: roast
  Slice: broil; panbroil; roast

Boneless smoked ham (sectioned and formed) (4)
  Roast

Country ham (4)
  Roast

Canadian-style bacon (2)
  Roast; broil; panfry

Smoked loin chop (2)
  Roast; broil; panbroil; panfry

Bacon (3)
  Panfry; broil; bake

be sure the juices run clear. Less tender sirloin or loin blade roasts and chops should be cooked to 170° (well-done) for best flavor and texture. Ground pork also should be cooked till well-done with no pink remaining.

Nutrition information: Today's pork comes from a leaner hog than in the past, and the fresh meat is trimmed closer by meat processors and retailers. A 3-ounce serving of cooked pork loin chop (trimmed) contains about 170 calories and about 7 grams of fat. A

3-ounce serving of cooked pork tenderloin has about 130 calories and 4 grams of fat.

For those watching calories, note that lean cuts include boneless pork loin roast and pork tenderloin.

(See *Meat* for Using a Meat Thermometer and inspection and grading, labeling, preparation, and other information.)

Potato A tuberous vegetable with a relatively smooth skin that can be brown, yellow, red, or purple and a crisp meat that is usually white or yellow. Potatoes may be round, elongated, or oval. They sometimes have buds (eyes) that need to be removed. New potatoes are those that haven't been stored and usually are thought of as small.

Types: Here are some kinds of potatoes found in supermarkets.
☐ **Long White:** A thin-skinned, all-purpose potato with a firm and waxy texture.
☐ **Round White:** A thin-skinned potato with a firm and waxy texture that is best for boiling and frying.

Potatoes

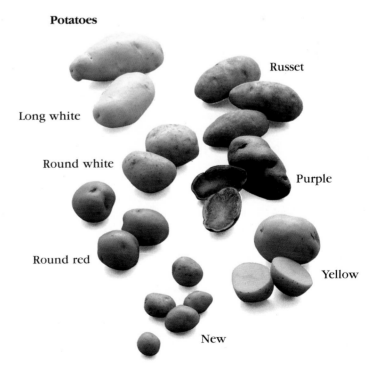

Long white

Russet

Round white

Purple

Round red

Yellow

New

Before baking or micro-cooking a whole potato, prick the potato several times with a fork. This gives the steam a place to escape, preventing the potato from bursting during cooking.

☐ **Round Red:** A thin-skinned potato with a firm and waxy texture that is good for boiling.

☐ **Russet:** A thick-skinned potato with a dry, mealy texture that is good for baking and frying.

☐ **Purple:** A violet-purple potato with purple meat. It has a dry, mealy texture and retains its color when it is cooked. Purple potatoes are good for baking and frying.

☐ **Yellow:** Any of several varieties of golden, thin-skinned potatoes with creamy yellow meat and a smooth texture. These potatoes have a mildly buttery flavor and are good for boiling and frying. Some varieties are good for baking. These potatoes are sold under the names Finnish Yellow, Yellow-Rose, and Yukon Gold.

Market forms: In addition to fresh potatoes, there is a wide variety of canned, frozen, refrigerated, and dehydrated potato products. Whole and sliced canned potatoes as well as shoestring potatoes and mayonnaise-style or German-style potato salads also are sold. Frozen products include stuffed baked potatoes, hash brown potatoes and patties, cottage fried potatoes, and french fried potatoes. Refrigerated potatoes include shredded and mashed potatoes. Dried products include instant mashed potatoes and numerous sliced and shredded potato mixes. Potato chips also are popular and come in a number of flavors and styles.

Selecting: Choose fresh potatoes with clean, smooth skins, a firm texture, and good shape for the variety. Avoid potatoes with green spots, soft or moldy areas, or wilted skins.

Storing: Store fresh potatoes in a well-ventilated, dark place that's cool and humid, but not wet. Potatoes should keep for several weeks. Lengthy exposure to light will cause greening of the skin, resulting in a bitter flavor. Avoid refrigerating potatoes because they become overly sweet and may darken when cooked. Home freezing of potatoes is not recommended.

Preparation hints: To use potatoes, scrub the skins well under running water. Whether or not to remove the skin will depend on the recipe you use. The fastest way to peel potatoes is with a vegetable peeler, removing any eyes as you peel. If the potatoes have any green parts, cut them away.

To keep cut or sliced potatoes from darkening before cooking, keep them immersed in water. For shredded potatoes, rinse and drain them after shredding, then pat them dry before using.

How to cook: See the Cooking Fresh Vegetables chart under *Vegetable*.

Nutrition information: One large, unpeeled baked potato (about 7 ounces) has about 220 calories.

Potato Salad
A cold or hot side-dish salad made with sliced, cubed, or mashed cooked potatoes, a flavorful dressing, and seasonings.

Types: The most familiar version of potato salad is served cold and may have celery, green peppers, hard-cooked eggs, and pickles added. The dressing may be based on mayonnaise or salad dressing, sour cream, or oil and vinegar. Often seasonings, such as prepared mustard or dillweed, also are added. Another well-known version of potato salad is German potato salad. It typically consists of potatoes, bacon pieces, and onions dressed with a warm mixture of vinegar, bacon drippings, and sugar.

Market forms: Commercially prepared potato salads are available in supermarket delicatessens. Canned potato salads in both creamy and German styles also are available.

Creamy Potato Salad

  4 **medium potatoes (about 1¼ pounds)**
  ¾ **cup thinly sliced celery**
  ¼ **cup finely chopped onion**
  3 **tablespoons chopped sweet pickle**
  1 **cup mayonnaise *or* salad dressing**
  2 **teaspoons prepared mustard**
1½ **teaspoons sugar**
1½ **teaspoons vinegar**
  1 **teaspoon celery seed**
  ½ **teaspoon salt**
  2 **hard-cooked eggs, coarsely chopped**

■ In a covered saucepan cook potatoes in boiling salted water for 20 to 25 minutes or till just tender. Drain well. Cool slightly. Peel and cube potatoes.

■ In a large bowl combine potatoes, celery, onion, and sweet pickle. For dressing, in a small bowl combine mayonnaise or salad dressing, mustard, sugar, vinegar, celery seed, and salt. Pour dressing over potato mixture. Toss to coat. Carefully fold in chopped eggs. Cover and chill for 6 to 24 hours.

■ Before serving, garnish with sliced sweet red or green pepper rings and parsley sprigs, if desired. Makes 6 servings.

Nutrition information per serving: 393 calories, 5 g protein, 26 g carbohydrate, 31 g fat (5 g saturated), 93 mg cholesterol, 556 mg sodium, 443 mg potassium.

German-Style Potato Salad

  4 **medium potatoes (about 1¼ pounds)**
  4 **slices bacon**
  ½ **cup chopped onion**
  1 **tablespoon all-purpose flour**
  1 **tablespoon sugar**
  ¾ **teaspoon salt**
  ½ **teaspoon celery seed**
  ⅛ **teaspoon pepper**
  ½ **cup water**
  ¼ **cup vinegar**
  1 **hard-cooked egg, chopped;**
      2 tablespoons snipped parsley; *or*
      2 slices bacon, cooked, drained, and crumbled (optional)

■ In a covered saucepan cook potatoes in boiling salted water for 20 to 25 minutes or till just tender. Drain well. Cool slightly. Peel and slice potatoes. Set aside while preparing dressing.

■ For dressing, in a large skillet cook 4 slices bacon till crisp. Drain and crumble, reserving *2 tablespoons* drippings. Set the bacon aside. Add chopped onion to reserved drippings. Cook till tender. Stir in flour, sugar, salt, celery seed, and pepper. Stir in water and vinegar. Cook and stir till thickened and bubbly. Stir in potatoes and bacon. Cook for 2 to 3 minutes more or till heated through, stirring gently. Season to taste.

■ Transfer to a serving bowl. Garnish with hard-cooked egg, parsley, or additional bacon, if desired. Makes 4 servings.

Microwave directions: Peel and slice *uncooked* potatoes ¼ inch thick. In a 1½-quart microwave-safe casserole, combine potatoes and ½ cup *water*. Micro-cook, covered, on 100% power (high) for 8 to 10 minutes or till the potatoes are just tender, stirring twice. Let stand, covered, while preparing the dressing.

■ For dressing, place 4 slices bacon in a 2-quart microwave-safe casserole. Cover with white paper towels. Cook on high for 3 to 5 minutes or till crisp, stirring once. Drain and crumble, reserving *2 tablespoons* drippings. Set bacon aside. Add onion to reserved drippings. Cover and cook on high for 2 to 3 minutes or till tender. Stir in flour, sugar, salt, celery seed, and pepper. Stir in ½ cup water and the vinegar. Cook, uncovered, on high for 2 to 3 minutes or till thickened and bubbly, stirring every 30 seconds. Drain the potatoes. Stir potatoes and bacon into dressing. Cook, covered, on high for 1 to 2 minutes or till heated through, stirring once. Serve as above.

Nutrition information per serving: 267 calories, 7 g protein, 35 g carbohydrate, 12 g fat (4 g saturated), 72 mg cholesterol, 594 mg sodium, 615 mg potassium.

Potpie   A savory main-dish pie. Potpies have either a single or double crust and include a filling of meat or poultry plus vegetables and a thickened gravy. Usually the crust is made from pastry, but sometimes a filling is baked in a casserole and topped with a biscuitlike crust. Commercially prepared potpies are available frozen.

Pot Roast   A large piece of meat, generally beef, that is covered and cooked in a small amount of liquid either on top of the range or in the oven. This moist-heat cooking method generally is used for less tender cuts of meat, such as shoulder and arm pot roasts. Vegetables often are added, and the cooking juices are thickened for gravy.

The term also refers to the technique of slowly cooking meats in a small amount of liquid in a covered pot.

Beef Pot Roast

  1 **2½- to 3-pound beef chuck pot roast**
  2 **tablespoons cooking oil**
  ¾ **cup water, dry wine, *or* tomato juice**
  1 **tablespoon Worcestershire sauce**
  1 **teaspoon instant beef bouillon granules**
  1 **teaspoon dried basil, crushed**
  12 **ounces whole tiny new potatoes, 2 medium potatoes, *or* 2 medium sweet potatoes**
  8 **small carrots *or* parsnips**
  2 **small onions, cut into wedges**
  2 **stalks celery, bias-sliced into 1-inch pieces**
  ¼ **cup all-purpose flour**

■ Trim fat from roast. In a Dutch oven brown roast on all sides in hot oil. Drain fat. Combine water, wine, or tomato juice; Worcestershire sauce; bouillon granules; and basil. Pour over roast. Bring to boiling; reduce heat. Cover and simmer for 1 hour.
■ Remove a narrow strip of peel from the center of each new potato, or peel and quarter each medium potato. Add potatoes, carrots or parsnips, onions, and celery to meat. Cover; simmer 45 to 60 minutes or till tender, adding additional water if necessary. Remove meat and vegetables from pan.
■ For gravy, measure pan juices; skim fat. If necessary, add water to equal *1½ cups.* Combine flour and ½ cup *cold water.* Stir into juices; return to pan. Cook and stir till thickened and bubbly. Cook and stir 1 minute more. Season to taste. Makes 8 to 10 servings.

Crockery-cooker directions: Trim the fat from roast and brown as at left. *Thinly* slice vegetables and place in the bottom of a 3½- or 4-quart electric slow crockery cooker. Cut roast to fit cooker; place atop vegetables. Combine water, wine, or tomato juice; Worcestershire sauce; bouillon granules; and basil. Pour over meat and vegetables. Cover; cook on low-heat setting for 10 to 12 hours. Prepare gravy as above, using a saucepan.

Oven directions: Trim fat from roast and brown meat as at left. Combine water, wine, or tomato juice; Worcestershire sauce; bouillon granules; and basil. Pour over roast. Bake, covered, in a 325° oven for 1 hour. Prepare potatoes as at left. Add vegetables. Bake for 45 to 60 minutes more or till tender. Prepare gravy as above.

Nutrition information per serving: 339 calories, 27 g protein, 20 g carbohydrate, 16 g fat (6 g saturated), 86 mg cholesterol, 226 mg sodium, 613 mg potassium.

Pots de Crème   *(poh duh KREM)* A very rich puddinglike dessert served cold in individual cups. Pots de crème can be chocolate, vanilla, or caramel. Tiny cups with lids that are used to serve this dessert are called pots de crème cups.

Chocolate Pots de Crème

    1 **cup light cream**
    1 **4-ounce package sweet chocolate,**
         coarsely chopped
    2 **teaspoons sugar**
    3 **beaten egg yolks**
    ½ **teaspoon vanilla**
       Whipped cream (optional)

■ In a heavy small saucepan combine light cream, chocolate, and sugar. Cook and stir over medium heat about 10 minutes or till mixture comes to a full boil and thickens. Gradually stir about *half* of the hot mixture into beaten egg yolks; return yolk mixture to saucepan. Cook and stir over low heat for 2 minutes more. Remove from heat. Stir in vanilla. Pour into 4 or 6 pots de crème cups or small dessert dishes. Cover and chill for 2 to 24 hours. Serve with whipped cream, if desired. Makes 4 or 6 servings.

Nutrition information per serving: 272 calories, 6 g protein, 21 g carbohydrate, 21 g fat (11 g saturated), 182 mg cholesterol, 32 mg sodium, 219 mg potassium.

Poultry
Domestic birds that are raised for their meat or eggs. Chicken, Cornish game hen, duck and duckling, goose, guinea hen, and turkey all qualify as poultry.

Market forms: Poultry comes in all shapes and sizes. For a specific kind of poultry, see individual entry. Here is a list of some of the general market forms available.
□ **Fresh:** Poultry that comes cleaned and ready to take home from the supermarket. Fresh poultry has not been frozen or cooked but may feel icy. Choose from whole birds, pieces (some are boneless and may be marinated or semiprepared), and ground poultry.
□ **Frozen:** Poultry that has been cleaned and frozen before arriving at your supermarket. Look for whole birds, pieces, cubed meat, and prepared poultry entrées in the supermarket freezer case.
□ **Canned:** Poultry that has been cooked and sealed in cans. Ready-to-use whole birds and boneless chopped or chunk poultry are available.
□ **Cooked:** Some supermarkets feature cooked, refrigerated whole birds, pieces, or slices. Find them at the deli or in the meat case.

Selecting: Choose plump, meaty birds with smooth, clean skin that is free of pinfeathers and bruises. Make sure that the package is not broken or leaking, and that there are no off-odors. In addition to your own inspection, look for the government inspection mark and a grade mark on the label.

The inspection mark tells you that the poultry has been inspected by the United States Department of Agriculture (USDA) and is safe, wholesome, and accurately labeled. Some poultry also may carry a state inspection mark.

The USDA grade mark, the use of which is voluntary by the poultry producer, gives the consumer another measure of quality. The top grade for poultry is U.S. Grade A, which means the poultry has a good shape and appearance, is full-fleshed, and is practically free from defects. Most poultry products in your supermarket are Grade A. Lower-grade poultry products commonly are used in processed products, such as luncheon meats and frankfurters.

Refrigerating: Always store fresh and cooked poultry at cold temperatures. Store poultry as soon as you get it home from the store. Place poultry in the coldest part of your refrigerator. Plan to use fresh poultry within 1 or 2 days. Poultry that is packaged in supermarket trays can be refrigerated in its original wrapping.

If stuffing a whole bird, don't stuff the poultry ahead of time and then store it. Instead, add the stuffing just before cooking. Also, once the poultry is cooked, refrigerate or freeze leftover poultry and stuffing separately as soon as possible.

Freezing: For longer storage, freeze fresh poultry at 0° or below. First rinse the poultry with cold water and pat dry with paper towels. Then repackage poultry and giblets separately in freezer wrap or freezer bags. Seal tightly, pressing out as much air as possible. Label, date, and freeze.

continued

For individual poultry pieces or cubed poultry, spread the meat on a tray and freeze till firm. Then transfer meat to freezer bags. Press out air, and seal, label, and freeze.

For the best flavor and texture, keep frozen uncooked whole turkeys or chickens no longer than a year, chicken pieces up to 9 months, and frozen uncooked turkey pieces and whole goose or duck no longer than 6 months. Keep frozen cooked poultry, not in broth or gravy, no longer than 1 month and frozen giblets up to 3 months.

Thawing: There's more to thawing poultry than simply removing it from the freezer. Here are some guidelines to follow.

Refrigerator thawing is the best way to thaw poultry. Place poultry in freezer wrapping on a tray in your refrigerator. Allow 5 hours of thawing time for every pound of poultry. For instance, a 5-pound chicken thaws in about 25 hours and a 12-pound turkey will thaw in about 2½ days.

Cold-water thawing is another safe way to thaw poultry. Place poultry in its freezer wrapping in a sink or large bowl of cold water. Allow about 30 minutes of thawing time for every pound of poultry, changing the water every 30 minutes. For example, a 5-pound chicken will thaw in about 2½ hours and a 12-pound turkey takes about 6 hours.

Room-temperature thawing is not recommended for poultry or other meats because bacteria that can cause food poisoning thrive at these warm temperatures. Also, do not thaw commercially frozen stuffed turkeys before roasting.

continued on page 334

Talking Poultry

Get the answers to poultry questions by calling the U.S. Department of Agriculture's Meat and Poultry Hot Line. The toll-free number is 1-800-535-4555. (In the Washington, D.C., area, call 447-3333.) Calls are taken from 10 a.m. to 4 p.m. eastern time (the hours usually are extended around Thanksgiving).

Broiling Poultry

Remove the skin from the poultry, if desired. Rinse and pat dry with paper towels. If desired, sprinkle with salt and pepper

Remove the broiler pan and preheat the broiler for 5 to 10 minutes. Arrange the poultry on the unheated rack of the broiler pan with the bone side up. If desired, brush with cooking oil. Place the pan under the broiler so the surface of the poultry is 4 to 5 inches from the heat. (Chicken and Cornish game hen halves should be 5 to 6 inches from the heat.) Turn the pieces over when browned on one side, usually after half of the broiling time. Chicken halves and meaty pieces should be turned after 20 minutes. Brush again with oil. The poultry is done when the meat is no longer pink and the juices run clear. Brush with a sauce the last 5 minutes of cooking, if desired.

Type of Bird	Weight	Broiling Time
Chicken, broiler-fryer, half	1¼ to 1½ pounds	28 to 32 minutes
Chicken breast, skinned and boned	4 to 5 ounces	12 to 15 minutes
Chicken breast halves, thighs, and drumsticks	2 to 2½ pounds total	25 to 35 minutes
Chicken kabobs (boneless breast, cut into 2x½-inch strips and threaded loosely onto skewers)	1 pound	8 to 10 minutes
Cornish game hen half	½ to ¾ pound	30 to 40 minutes
Turkey breast steak or slice	2 ounces	6 to 8 minutes
Turkey breast tenderloin steak	4 to 6 ounces	8 to 10 minutes
Turkey patties (ground raw turkey)	¾ inch thick	10 to 12 minutes

Roasting Poultry

To prepare a bird for roasting, follow the steps below. Since birds vary in size, shape, and tenderness, use the times as general guides.

• Rinse whole bird well on outside as well as inside body and neck cavities. Pat dry. Rub salt inside body cavity, if desired.

• For an *unstuffed bird,* place quartered onions and celery in body cavity, if desired. Pull the neck skin to the back and fasten with a skewer. If a band of skin crosses the tail, tuck the drumsticks under the band. If there is no band, tie the drumsticks to the tail. Twist the wing tips under the back.

For a *stuffed bird*, do not stuff until just before cooking. To stuff, spoon some stuffing loosely into the neck cavity; fasten neck skin as for an unstuffed bird. Lightly spoon stuffing into the body cavity. Secure drumsticks and wings as above.

• Place the bird, breast side up, on a rack in a shallow roasting pan. Brush the bird with cooking oil. (When cooking a domestic duckling or goose, prick the skin well all over and omit the cooking oil.) If desired, for large birds, insert a meat thermometer into the center of one of the inside thigh muscles. The bulb should not touch the bone.

• Cover Cornish game hen, quail, squab, and turkey with foil, leaving an air space between the bird and the foil. Press the foil lightly at the ends of the drumsticks and the neck. Leave all other types of poultry uncovered.

• Roast in an uncovered pan. Baste occasionally with pan drippings. When the bird is two-thirds done, cut the band of skin or string between the drumsticks. Uncover the bird for last 45 minutes of cooking (leave quail covered for entire cooking time).

Continue roasting until the meat thermometer registers 180° to 185°, or till drumsticks move easily in their sockets and juices run clear. (In a whole or half turkey breast, thermometer should register 170°.) Remove bird from the oven and cover it with foil. Let large birds stand for 15 to 20 minutes before carving.

Type of Bird	Weight	Oven Temp.	Roasting Time
Capon	5 to 7 pounds	325°	1¾ to 2½ hours
Chicken, whole*	2½ to 3 pounds	375°	1 to 1¼ hours
	3½ to 4 pounds	375°	1¼ to 1¾ hours
	4½ to 5 pounds	375°	1½ to 2 hours
	5 to 6 pounds	325°	1¾ to 2½ hours
Cornish game hen	1 to 1½ pounds	375°	1 to 1¼ hours
Duckling, domestic	3 to 5 pounds	375°	1¾ to 2¼ hours
Goose, domestic	7 to 8 pounds	350°	2 to 2½ hours
	8 to 10 pounds	350°	2½ to 3 hours
	10 to 12 pounds	350°	3 to 3½ hours
Pheasant	2 to 3 pounds	350°	1½ to 1¾ hours
Quail	4 to 6 ounces	375°	30 to 50 minutes

Type of Bird	Weight	Oven Temp.	Roasting Time
Squab	12 to 14 ounces	375°	45 to 60 minutes
Turkey, boneless, whole	2½ to 3½ pounds	325°	2 to 2½ hours
	4 to 6 pounds	325°	2½ to 3½ hours
Turkey, unstuffed**	6 to 8 pounds	325°	3 to 3½ hours
	8 to 12 pounds	325°	3 to 4 hours
	12 to 16 pounds	325°	4 to 5 hours
	16 to 20 pounds	325°	4¼ to 5 hours
	20 to 24 pounds	325°	5 to 6 hours
Turkey breast, whole	4 to 6 pounds	325°	1½ to 2¼ hours
	6 to 8 pounds	325°	2¼ to 3¼ hours
Turkey drumstick	1 to 1½ pounds	325°	1¼ to 1¾ hours
Turkey thigh	1½ to 1¾ pounds	325°	1½ to 1¾ hours

Choose broiler-fryer or roasting chickens.
**Stuffed birds generally require 30 to 45 minutes more roasting time than unstuffed birds.*

Cooking hints: Always cook poultry thoroughly. Poultry is done when the thickest part of the meat near the bone is no longer pink, the juices run clear, and the drumsticks twist easily in their sockets. For larger whole birds, a meat thermometer inserted in the thickest part of the thigh not touching bone should register 180° to 185°.

How to cook: See the Broiling Poultry and Roasting Poultry charts, pages 332–333. For grilling directions, see the Direct-Grilling Poultry and Indirect-Grilling Poultry charts under *Barbecue.*

Tips from Our Kitchen
When handling poultry, keep these points in mind.
● Always wash your hands, countertops, and utensils in hot soapy water *between each step of food preparation*. Bacteria on raw poultry, meat, or fish can contaminate other food that is exposed to the same surfaces.
● Never leave poultry out at room temperature for more than 2 hours. Cooked poultry that is not eaten immediately should be kept hot (140° to 165°) or chilled at 40° or less.
● Always thoroughly reheat leftover cooked poultry and gravy before eating (till bubbly, about 185°) for best taste and maximum food safety. Cover the food to retain as much moisture as possible and to thoroughly heat.

Poultry Seasoning   A blend of
thyme, sage, pepper, marjoram, sometimes rosemary, and other herbs and spices. This ground mixture is used mainly to season poultry stuffings and other poultry dishes.

Pound   To strike a food with a heavy
utensil to crush it or, in the case of meat, to break up connective tissue in order to tenderize or flatten it.

A Tip from Our Kitchen
Avoid messy splatters when pounding meat by first covering it with heavy-duty plastic wrap. Lightweight plastic wrap or waxed paper is likely to tear as you pound.

Cover the meat or poultry with clear plastic wrap. Then, working from the center outward, pound the meat or poultry until it is flattened to the thickness you want.

Pound Cake   A rich, fine-textured cake
named for the fact that the original recipe combined a pound each of butter, sugar, eggs, and flour. Today, recipes frequently include baking powder, sour cream, fruits, or nuts and often are baked in a loaf pan.

Preparation hints: To ensure that a wet layer does not form on the bottom of a pound cake, cream the butter and sugar thoroughly and beat well as each egg is added.

A Tip from Our Kitchen
Don't worry if a slight crack forms along the top of a pound cake during baking. This is typical of pound cakes. To make sure the pound cake is done, check the cracked area. If it is still moist, bake the cake a little longer and test again.

(See *Cake* for How to Solve Cake Problems, Cake-Making Hints, and baking, storing, and other information.)

Sour Cream Pound Cake

- ½ **cup butter**
- 3 **eggs**
- ½ **cup dairy sour cream**
- 1½ **cups all-purpose flour**
- ¼ **teaspoon baking powder**
- ⅛ **teaspoon baking soda**
- 1 **cup sugar**
- ½ **teaspoon vanilla**

■ Bring butter, eggs, and sour cream to room temperature. Meanwhile, in a mixing bowl combine flour, baking powder, and baking soda.

■ In another bowl beat butter with an electric mixer on medium to high speed for 30 seconds. Gradually add sugar, beating about 10 minutes or till very light. Add vanilla. Add eggs, one at a time, beating 1 minute after each and scraping bowl often.

■ Add flour mixture and sour cream to egg mixture alternately, beating on low to medium speed after each addition just till combined. Pour into a greased and floured 8x4x2- or 9x5x3-inch loaf pan. Bake in a 325° oven for 60 to 75 minutes or till a toothpick comes out clean. Cool on a rack 10 minutes. Remove from pan. Cool. Serves 10.

Nutrition information per serving: 274 calories, 4 g protein, 35 g carbohydrate, 13 g fat (8 g saturated), 94 mg cholesterol, 120 mg sodium, 58 mg potassium.

Blueberry Sour Cream Pound Cake: Prepare Sour Cream Pound Cake as above, *except* gently fold ½ cup fresh or frozen *blueberries* into the batter.

Nutrition information per serving: 278 calories, 4 g protein, 36 g carbohydrate, 13 g fat (8 g saturated), 94 mg cholesterol, 121 mg sodium, 65 mg potassium.

Lemon-Poppy-Seed Pound Cake: Prepare Sour Cream Pound Cake as above, *except* substitute ½ cup *lemon yogurt* for sour cream. Add 1 teaspoon finely shredded *lemon peel,* 2 tablespoons *lemon juice,* and 2 tablespoons *poppy seed* to batter.

Nutrition information per serving: 271 calories, 5 g protein, 37 g carbohydrate, 12 g fat (6 g saturated), 89 mg cholesterol, 121 mg sodium, 81 mg potassium.

Praline A rich, patty-shaped candy made with sugar, cream, butter, and pecans. After cooling, the candy is beaten with a wooden spoon just till the mixture begins to thicken.

A Tip from Our Kitchen
Bring the pecans to room temperature before stirring them into the cooled praline mixture. If the pecans are cold, they'll cool the candy, and it may set up too quickly.

Q: If pralines get too stiff to drop easily, can anything be done to save them?
A: Stir a few drops of *hot water* into the candy mixture, then work quickly.

(See *Candy* for Candy-Making Tips and equipment, storing, and other information.)

Prawn A 10-legged shellfish similar to a shrimp. Prawns are popular in Hawaii, where they're raised.

How to cook: Prepare prawns as you would shrimp. See the Preparing and Cooking Shellfish chart under *Shellfish.*

Q: How do prawns and shrimp differ?
A: Although the name "prawn" often is used to mean large shrimp, prawns are not shrimp. Prawns are a large, freshwater shellfish. Prawns also have longer legs and a more slender body than shrimp. Shrimp live in salt water.

(See *Shellfish* for storing and other information.)

Precook To partially cook (blanch) or completely cook a food before using it as an ingredient in a recipe.

Preheat To heat an oven or a utensil to a specific temperature before using it.

Q: Is preheating an oven always necessary?

A: Not always. Preheating the oven is important for some foods, such as baked products. They depend upon just the right amount of heat to cause foods to rise and bake properly.

Preheating is less critical for other foods. For an item that is only being warmed, such as a casserole, preheating generally isn't necessary. However, you may want to add a few minutes to the heating time to make sure the casserole is completely warm.

Preserve A mixture of whole or large pieces of fruit and sugar that is cooked to a jamlike consistency and used as a spread for breads, a filling for pastries, and in dessert recipes. Sometimes pectin is used in the preserve to help it set up. Although similar to jam, a preserve usually contains larger and more distinct pieces of fruit.

The term also refers to any of several processes that help slow the rate of spoilage in food and lengthen the amount of time the food can be stored. Preservation methods include canning, freezing, pickling, salting, and dehydrating.

Pressure Cooking A method of steam cooking in a specially designed pan called a pressure saucepan or canner. This utensil is similar to a saucepan but has a locking cover and special features that allow steam, under pressure, to reach temperatures much higher than the boiling point of water.

A Tip from Our Kitchen
After each use, wash all the parts of your pressure pan, making sure the vent isn't clogged. When storing the cooker, turn the cover upside down over the pan. Don't fasten it onto the pan.

Pretzel A snack that may be breadlike or crackerlike and usually is shaped into a loose knot, a stick, or a circle. Homemade soft pretzels are breadlike and have a tough but chewy texture. Commercial pretzels often are crisp and brittle, but they can be soft, too.

Nutrition hint: To reduce sodium, make homemade pretzels and sprinkle them with sesame or poppy seed instead of coarse salt. Other sodium-reducing tips are to buy unsalted crisp pretzels and to omit sprinkling on the salt after heating frozen soft pretzels.

A Tip from Our Kitchen
When making homemade pretzels, moisten the ends of the shaped pretzels before sealing them. The water will help keep the ends in place and prevent them from "popping up."

Prickly Pear The egg-shaped fruit of the nopal cactus that is covered with a thick, spiny sheath that encases the juicy, mildly sweet meat. Prickly pears, also called cactus pears, contain small seeds, some of which are tiny enough to be edible. Prickly pears have green, orange, purple, or red skin with bright red fruit inside. The orange variety is the sweetest.

Prickly pears

Selecting: Prickly pears are available September through May. Most have had the spines removed, but handle them carefully. Look for fairly firm fruit without soft spots.

Storing: Ripen prickly pears at room temperature until slightly softened; then refrigerate and use them within a few days.

Preparation hints: Using tongs to hold the pear, slice off the ends. Then halve the fruit and scoop out the soft meat inside. Discard the skin. Enjoy as is, sliced, or chopped. Or, puree the pear and strain out the seeds.

A Tip from Our Kitchen

If the small hairlike prickles on the skin of the prickly pear become embedded in your fingers, remove the prickles with the sticky side of masking or transparent tape.

Nutrition information: One prickly pear has about 40 calories.

Process To preserve food at home by canning it in covered heatproof jars either in boiling water or under pressure (see also *Canning*). Foods are processed in order to destroy microorganisms and lengthen the amount of time the food can be stored.

The term also refers to preparing food in a food processor.

Profiterole *(pruh FIT uh role)* A tiny cream puff filled with a sweet or savory mixture. A chocolate or caramel sauce often is ladled over sweet profiteroles.

Proof A term that indicates the amount of alcohol in a distilled liquor. In the United States, half of the proof equals the percentage of alcohol. For example, a liquor that is labeled 70 proof contains 35 percent alcohol.

This term also refers to the process of allowing a yeast dough to rise before baking.

Prosciutto A spicy ham, originally made in Italy, that is rubbed with dry seasonings and aged for several months. Prosciutto is rose-colored with a slight gloss and usually is served very thinly sliced. It can be served cold as a luncheon meat or heated as part of a recipe.

Protein Any of numerous complex biochemical substances consisting of amino acids linked together to form long chains. Proteins obtained from foods perform many important functions in the body. They help build, maintain, and repair cells, produce antibodies that ward off disease, and contribute to the production of enzymes and hormones that regulate the body.

Although most foods contain at least some proteins, they are especially abundant in animal foods, such as beef, veal, lamb, pork, poultry, fish, dairy products, and eggs, and in certain plant foods, such as peanuts and peanut butter, dried peas and beans, and many nuts.

A protein is considered of high biological value when it can supply the body's need for protein all on its own (complete). It is considered of low biological value when it needs protein from another source to meet the need (incomplete). Most animal proteins are complete, and most plant proteins are incomplete. That is why it is important when serving meatless dishes to combine two or

continued

more plant foods that are equivalent to a complete protein. Dried beans or peas served with rice or corn is an example of combining plant foods that complement each other; the amino acids lacking in each food are present in the other. Some nutritionists say that complementary proteins must be eaten at the same meal, and others say the proteins can be eaten either at the same meal or within several hours of each other.

(See *Nutrition* for information on planning a balanced diet.)

For homemade pudding, to add eggs to the hot pudding mixture, remove the saucepan from the heat. Stir half of the hot pudding mixture into the beaten eggs to warm them. Then stir the egg mixture into the remaining pudding in the saucepan.

Prune Commonly, a dried plum. Only certain varieties of plums can be converted to prunes. In the fresh, fully ripe state, the plums used to make prunes are dark blue to purple and oblong or oval; they have firm flesh and are high in sugar. When dried, pit and all, the meat does not ferment or spoil as do other types of plums. Prunes have a very sweet, rich flavor that is more intense than that of fresh plums.

The Italian prune plum is the best known type of plum that is dried, but other varieties also are used. Sometimes these varieties of fresh plums are called prunes.

Market forms: Most prunes are sold in bags, boxes, and vacuum-pack cans, and they come pitted or unpitted. Also look for prune juice, cooked or stewed prunes in jars, and diced prunes.

Nutrition information: Five uncooked prunes have about 100 calories. A ½ cup of prune juice has about 90 calories.

(See *Dried Fruit* for the Cooking Dried Fruit chart and storing and preparation hints.)

Pudding Most commonly, a soft, creamy, sweet dessert made with milk, sugar, eggs, and a thickener, such as cornstarch, flour, or tapioca. This type of pudding is cooked by boiling. There also are baked and steamed

puddings, which may be either sweet or savory. Some of the most familiar ones are bread pudding, Indian pudding, and plum pudding (see individual entries).

Market forms: Puddings come ready to eat in canned and refrigerated forms. Pudding mixes also are available in regular or instant versions and in a variety of flavors. Artificially sweetened pudding mixes also are sold.

Tips from Our Kitchen
● For homemade pudding, stir the sugar and cornstarch or flour together well before adding the milk. This will make it easier to mix the ingredients together and will prevent lumps.
● Cover the surface of the pudding with plastic wrap while it is cooling or chilling. This helps prevent a film from forming on the surface.

Q: What are some quick dessert fix-ups that use pudding?
A: For a quick pie, prepare pudding and pour into a baked pastry pie shell or crumb crust. Top with whipped cream.

For a dessert parfait, alternate layers of pudding and fresh or canned fruit in tall glasses. Or, alternate layers of different pudding flavors.

For a torte, slice a pound cake or loaf cake into three horizontal layers. Spread chilled pudding between the layers.

For a marbled dessert, gently swirl chocolate syrup, ice-cream topping, or whipped topping into the pudding.

For a frozen pudding treat, pour prepared instant pudding into small flat-bottomed paper cups. Cover with foil and insert a wooden skewer for a handle. Freeze till firm. Tear off paper cup and eat as you would a frozen dessert on a stick.

Vanilla Pudding

- ½ to ⅔ cup sugar
- 2 tablespoons cornstarch *or* ¼ cup all-purpose flour
- 2 cups milk
- 2 beaten egg yolks *or* 1 beaten egg
- 1 tablespoon margarine *or* butter
- 1½ teaspoons vanilla

■ In a heavy medium saucepan combine sugar and cornstarch or flour. Stir in milk. Cook and stir over medium heat till mixture is thickened and bubbly. Cook and stir for 2 minutes more. Remove from heat. Gradually stir about *1 cup* of the hot mixture into beaten egg yolks or egg.

■ Return all of the egg mixture to the saucepan. If using egg yolks, bring to a gentle boil; if using a whole egg, cook till nearly bubbly, but *do not boil.* Reduce heat. Cook and stir for 2 minutes more. Remove from heat. Stir in margarine or butter and vanilla. Pour pudding into a bowl. Cover the surface with plastic wrap. Chill. *Do not stir.* Serves 4.

Nutrition information per serving: 222 calories, 5 g protein, 33 g carbohydrate, 8 g fat (3 g saturated), 117 mg cholesterol, 99 mg sodium, 199 mg potassium.

Chocolate Pudding: Prepare Vanilla Pudding as below left, *except* add 3 tablespoons *unsweetened cocoa powder* to sugar. Use *2¼ cups* milk and egg yolks (not whole egg).

Nutrition information per serving: 240 calories, 7 g protein, 36 g carbohydrate, 9 g fat (3 g saturated), 119 mg cholesterol, 107 mg sodium, 269 mg potassium.

Puff Pastry
A delicate, crisp, flaky baked product with numerous layers.

Puff pastry dough typically is made of flour, butter, and ice water. A thin layer of butter is placed between two layers of dough. Then it is rolled, folded several times, and chilled. This procedure is repeated numerous times to develop as many as 700 layers. (A quicker method for making puff pastry is to gently knead butter chunks with the flour instead of making a separate butter layer.) When baked, steam puffs the pastry to four or five times its original height. The final result is a golden pastry with a melt-in-your-mouth quality.

Puff pastry is used in making patty shells that are usually filled with main-dish mixtures. It also is used for appetizers and in classic desserts, such as napoleons.

Commercial puff pastry is sold frozen in sheets and as patty shells.

A Tip from Our Kitchen
When cutting the dough for puff pastry, use a very sharp knife and cut straight down. Do not pull the knife through the dough or cut at a slant. Either of these will cause the edges to puff unevenly when the pastry bakes.

Pumpernickel
A dark, heavy, rye yeast bread. Dark molasses, caraway seeds, and rye flour give this European-style bread its characteristic flavor. Pumpernickel can be medium-dark, dark, or very dark; usually, the darker the bread is, the chewier its texture and more tangy the taste.

Pumpkin A large, round, hard-shelled, orange squash. Pumpkins have sweet, slightly stringy flesh that often can be used in recipes calling for winter squash. Whole pumpkins can be purchased from September through early winter, but canned pumpkin, available year-round, is the form usually used for cooking.

Pumpkin

A Tip from Our Kitchen
If you'd like to make your own pumpkin pulp, here's how to do it. Cut a medium pumpkin (about 6 pounds) into 5-inch-square pieces. Remove the seeds and fibrous strings. Arrange the pieces in a single layer, skin side up, in a large, shallow baking pan. Cover with foil. Bake in a 375° oven for 1 to 1½ hours or till tender. Scoop the pulp from the rind. Working with part of the pulp at a time, place pulp in a blender container or food processor bowl. Cover and blend or process till smooth. Place the pumpkin in a cheesecloth-lined strainer, and press out any liquid. Makes about 2 cups.

Nutrition information: One-half cup of canned pumpkin has about 40 calories.

Pumpkin Pie Spice A blend of ground ginger, cinnamon, nutmeg, and cloves or allspice. The combination is just right for flavoring pumpkin pie, and it is excellent in sweet potatoes, gingerbread, and cookies.

(See *Spice* for selecting, storing, and nutrition information.)

Punch A cold or hot beverage mixture that may contain alcohol. Punch can be made with a variety of beverages, including carbonated beverages, fruit juice, wine, and liquor. Sherbet, ice cream, and fruit are popular additions. Usually, punch is ladled from a large bowl into small cups or glasses.

Puree To change a solid food into a liquid or heavy paste, usually by means of a blender, food processor, or food mill.
The term also refers to the mixture that results when a solid food is changed to a liquid or heavy paste.

Quail A small game bird that is mildly flavored. Quail can be hunted in the wild or raised on farms. Farm-raised quail usually is sold dressed and frozen in specialty stores.

How to cook: For roasting directions, see the Roasting Poultry chart under *Poultry*. For grilling directions, see the Indirect-Grilling Poultry chart under *Barbecue*.

Nutrition information: One 3-ounce portion of cooked meat without skin has about 150 calories.

Quantity Cooking The cooking methods necessary when preparing food for a
continued

Shopping for a Crowd

Use this guide when planning the amount of food to buy for a large group. The size for one serving is listed, but plan about 1½ servings for hearty eaters.

Food	Servings	Serving Size	Total Amount Needed
Beverages			
Coffee	25	¾ cup	½ to ¾ pound ground
Milk	24	1 cup	1½ gallons
Soft drinks	24	1 cup	3 2-liter bottles
Tea, hot	25	¾ cup	5 quarts (20 to 25 tea bags)
Tea, iced	25	1 cup	1½ gallons (24 to 30 tea bags)
Desserts			
Cake	24	1/12 cake	2 13x9-inch cakes
	24	2½-inch square	1 15x10x1-inch sheet
Ice cream or frozen yogurt	24	½ cup	3 quarts
Pie	24	⅛ pie	3 9-inch pies
Fruit			
Canned	24	½ cup	1 6½- to 7¼-pound can
Miscellaneous			
Butter or margarine	32	1 pat (1 teaspoon)	½ pound
Pizza	24	⅓ of a 12-inch pizza	8 12-inch pizzas
Potato or corn chips	25	¾ to 1 ounce (1½ cups)	1 to 1½ pounds
Relishes			
Carrot sticks	25	2 to 3 sticks (2 to 3 inches)	1 to 1¼ pounds
Cauliflower or broccoli flowerets	25	½ cup	4 1-pound heads
Celery	25	2 to 3 pieces (2 to 3 inches)	2 to 3 bunches
Olives	25	3 to 4	1¼ quarts (5 cups)
Pickles,			
sliced	25	3 to 4 slices	1 quart
spears	25	1 spear	1 to 1¼ quarts
Rice and pasta			
Elbow macaroni	25	1 cup cooked	2¼ pounds, uncooked
Rice, long-grain	24	¾ cup cooked	2¾ pounds (6 cups), uncooked
Spaghetti	24	1 cup cooked	3 pounds, uncooked
Salads			
Side-dish			
Fruit, fresh, cut up	24	½ cup	3 quarts
Gelatin	24	½ cup	3 6-ounce packages, flavored
Lettuce	24	1 cup	6 quarts, torn (4 heads)
Potato or pasta	24	½ cup	3 quarts
Main-dish	24	1½ cups	9 quarts
Soup	25	1½ cups	3 50-ounce cans, condensed
Vegetables			
Canned	25	½ cup	1 6½- to 7¼-pound can
Fresh potatoes, mashed or scalloped	25	½ cup	7 pounds
Frozen beans, carrots, peas, corn, or mixed	24	½ cup	3 16-ounce packages

large number of people. Cooking for restaurants and other eating establishments as well as cooking for church groups, clubs, or large family gatherings is included in this type of food planning and preparation.

Cooking hints: Most cooks and chefs for commercial establishments and volunteer groups use oversize cooking equipment and large recipes that often are not practical for home use. If you're planning to cook for a large group, you'll need to improvise with some of your own small-size recipes. For the basic amounts you'll need to put a meal together, see the Shopping for a Crowd chart, page 341.

Q: Can I double or triple my recipes to get more servings?
A: It is best to make several batches of the same recipe. Some recipes, especially ones for baked goods, don't work well when they are increased.

Quenelle *(kuh NELL)* A delicate, round or oval dumpling made from very finely chopped fish, meat, or poultry and a flour-thickened egg mixture. The dumplings usually are poached and served with a rich sauce as an appetizer, main dish, or side dish.

Quiche A rich baked pie or tart with a pastry crust and a savory custard filling containing small pieces of vegetables, meat, cheese, seafood, or a combination of these. A quiche typically is served as a main dish, although miniature versions or thin slices are popular as appetizers.

Q: How much meat, seafood, or vegetables can be added to a quiche?
A: A recipe for a 9-inch quiche that uses 3 eggs, 1½ cups milk, and 1½ cups shredded cheese should accommodate up to 1 cup cooked meat, poultry, seafood, or vegetables.

Classic Quiche Lorraine

    Pastry Shell
 6 slices bacon
 1 medium onion, thinly sliced
 3 beaten eggs
 1½ cups half and half, light cream,
        or milk
 ¼ teaspoon salt
    Dash ground nutmeg
 1½ cups shredded Swiss cheese
        (6 ounces)
 1 tablespoon all-purpose flour

■ Prepare Pastry Shell. Line the unpricked pastry shell with a double thickness of foil. Bake in a 450° oven for 8 minutes. Remove foil. Bake 4 to 6 minutes more or till pastry is golden. Remove from the oven. Reduce oven temperature to 325°.

■ Meanwhile, in a large skillet cook the bacon till crisp; drain, reserving *2 tablespoons* drippings. Crumble bacon; set aside. Cook sliced onion in reserved drippings till tender but not brown; drain.

■ In a medium mixing bowl stir together the eggs, cream or milk, salt, and nutmeg. Stir in the crumbled bacon and onion. Toss together shredded cheese and flour. Add to egg mixture; mix well.

■ Pour egg mixture into *hot* pastry shell. Bake in a 325° oven for 35 to 40 minutes or till a knife inserted near the center comes out clean. If necessary, cover edge of crust with foil to prevent overbrowning. Let stand for 10 minutes before serving. Makes 6 servings.

Pastry Shell: In a mixing bowl combine 1¼ cups *all-purpose flour* and ¼ teaspoon *salt*. Cut in ⅓ cup *shortening or lard* till pieces are the size of small peas. Sprinkle 1 tablespoon *water* over part of the mixture; gently toss with a fork. Push to side of bowl. Repeat with 2 to 3 tablespoons additional *water* till all is moistened. Form dough into a ball.

On a lightly floured surface, flatten dough with hands. Roll dough from center to edges, forming a circle about 12 inches in diameter. Wrap pastry around rolling pin. Unroll onto a 9-inch pie plate. Ease pastry into pie plate, being careful not to stretch pastry.

Trim pastry to ½ inch beyond edge of pie plate; fold under the extra ½ inch of pastry. Make a fluted edge. *Do not prick the pastry.*

Nutrition information per serving: 504 calories, 18 g protein, 26 g carbohydrate, 37 g fat (16 g saturated), 169 mg cholesterol, 455 mg sodium, 215 mg potassium.

Quince A hard, round or oval to pear-shaped tree fruit that resembles a large green to yellow apple with a knob on one end. Quinces can have a woolly surface on their skins, or they can have smooth skin. Not good eaten raw, quinces are best cooked and sweetened in such recipes as jams, sauces, and pies. Cooked quinces taste like mild, sweet apples, and have the texture of cooked apples.

Selecting: Quinces generally are available August through January. Look for firm quinces that are pale yellow all over without blemishes.

Storing: Ripen quinces at room temperature until they are pale yellow all over. Then refrigerate and use them within 2 weeks.

Nutrition information: One quince has about 50 calories.

Quinces

Quinoa *(kih NO uh)* A tiny, high-protein, calcium-rich grain. This pale yellow grain, which is cooked in the same way as rice, has a crunchy texture and a subtle nutty taste. Use it in salads, casseroles, stews, pilafs, stuffings, and even desserts. Quinoa also may be ground into a flour or made into pasta.

Storing: Store in an airtight container in a cool, dry place for up to 6 months.

How to cook: See the Cooking Grains chart under *Grain*.

Nutrition information: A ¾-cup serving of cooked quinoa contains 150 calories.

R-S

Strawberry Shortcake
(see recipe, page 374)

Swiss Steak
(see recipe, page 398)

Risotto
(see recipe, page 354)

Rabbit A small game animal that's related to the hare. Cooked rabbit is similar in flavor to chicken. Rabbits can be hunted in the wild or raised on farms. Farm-raised rabbit is sold dressed, cut up, and ready to cook. Rabbits can be cooked in the same ways you would chicken. One 3-ounce serving of roasted, farm-raised rabbit has about 130 calories.

Raclette *(raa CLET)* A Swiss snack or supper favorite made by placing a large piece of cheese near a heat source. As the cheese begins to melt, it is scraped off and spread on bread or boiled potatoes.

Radicchio *(raa DICK ee oh)* An Italian red chicory that's used as a salad green. The most widely available variety in the United States is the red Verona. Its brilliant ruby-red leaves have thick, white veins. The leaves form small, round, compact heads. Eaten alone, the fresh leaves are quite bitter and peppery tasting, but when mixed with other greens, radicchio adds a nice accent to salads.

Radicchio

Selecting: Radicchio is available year-round. Choose heads with fresh, crisp leaves. The white core at the base should be firm and unblemished.

Storing: Refrigerate radicchio in a plastic bag for up to a week.

Preparation hints: Cut out and discard the white core. Separate the leaves; rinse and dry well. Tear into bite-size pieces and use fresh in salads.

Radish A small, crunchy, peppery-flavored root vegetable that can be round, oval, or elongated. Radishes can be white, red, or black. Most often, radishes are eaten raw, but they can be used in cooked dishes.

Radishes

Japanese or Oriental (Daikon)

French Breakfast

Black

Icicle

Red

Types: These are some of the radishes you might find at the supermarket.

☐ **Black:** Can be round or elongated. Black radishes have a black skin with a crisp, white meat. They have a strong, pungent flavor.

☐ **French Breakfast:** Elongated, red-skinned radishes with a mildly pungent flavor.

☐ **Icicle:** Slender, white-skinned radishes with a mild flavor.

☐ **Japanese or Oriental:** Also known as daikon (See *Daikon*).

☐ **Red:** Small and round with a flavor that can vary from mild to peppery. Red radishes also are called button radishes. They have a bright cherry-red skin and white flesh.

Selecting: Some radishes are sold trimmed of their tops, and others are sold with their tops and roots attached. Buy firm, crisp radishes. Avoid those with cracks.

Storing: Store radishes tightly wrapped in the refrigerator for up to 1 week. Remove tops before storing.

Preparation hints: Rinse radishes well. Cut off the roots and discard.

Nutrition information: There is only 1 calorie in a red radish, about 2 calories in an icicle radish, and 13 calories in a ½ cup of cooked sliced Oriental radishes.

Ragout *(raa GOO)* The French term for stew that refers to a well-seasoned main dish containing meat, poultry, or fish, and sometimes vegetables in a thickened broth.

Country Pork Ragout

- ¾ pound boneless pork
- 1 large leek, thinly sliced
- 1 clove garlic, minced
- 1 tablespoon cooking oil
- 1 14½-ounce can chicken broth
- ¾ teaspoon dried basil, crushed
- ¼ teaspoon dried marjoram, crushed
- ⅛ teaspoon pepper
- 1 medium zucchini *or* yellow summer squash, halved lengthwise and cut into ½-inch-thick slices
- 2 cups small whole mushrooms
- ¼ cup cold water
- 2 tablespoons all-purpose flour

■ Trim fat from meat. Cut meat into ¾-inch cubes. In a 4-quart Dutch oven cook meat, leek, and garlic in hot oil till meat is brown and leeks are tender. Spoon off fat. Stir in chicken broth, basil, marjoram, and pepper.

Bring to boiling; reduce heat. Simmer, covered, about 40 minutes or till meat is tender. Stir in zucchini and mushrooms. Return mixture to boiling; reduce heat. Simmer, covered, for 3 minutes. Skim off fat.
■ Combine cold water and flour; stir into ragout. Cook and stir till thickened and bubbly. Cook and stir 1 minute more. Makes 3 servings.

Nutrition information per serving: 332 calories, 29 g protein, 14 g carbohydrate, 18 g fat (5 g saturated), 78 mg cholesterol, 506 mg sodium, 877 mg potassium.

Raisin A grape that has been dried either naturally by the sun or by artificial methods. Like other dried fruits, raisins are very sweet.

Varieties: You'll find several varieties of raisins available.
☐ **Dark Seedless:** Usually made from Thompson seedless grapes. These have a sweet flavor and are used for recipes or snacks. About 90 percent of all raisins produced are made from dark seedless grapes.
☐ **Golden Seedless:** Thompson grapes that have been dried under special conditions to retain the light golden color of the grapes. They have a tangy fruit flavor and are good for recipes and snacks.
☐ **Muscat:** Sun-dried muscat grapes that are large, dark, and very sweet. They have a very fruity flavor and are excellent in recipes.
☐ **Sultana:** Sun-dried sultana grapes. They closely resemble dark seedless raisins, but are softer and sweeter. They are used mainly for commercial purposes.
☐ **Zante Currants:** Tiny seedless raisins from sun-dried black corinth grapes. These raisins are sold as dried currants but are not related to the currant berry. Their sweet flavor is best used in recipes.

Nutrition information: A snack-size serving of 2 tablespoons seedless raisins has about 60 calories.

(See *Dried Fruit* for storing and preparation hints.)

Ramekin *(RAM ih kuhn)* A mixture, usually containing cheese, that is baked in individual dishes.

The term also refers to the dish used in this recipe. It usually has straight sides and resembles a small soufflé dish; it is used as an individual casserole.

Rarebit A dish consisting of cheese, usually cheddar, that is melted with liquid (often beer) and seasonings, such as mustard and Worcestershire sauce. The melted cheese mixture, also called Welsh rabbit, usually is served over toast or crackers.

Raspberry A small, round to oval shrub fruit with a very soft texture and mildly sweet flavor. Raspberries grow in various shades of yellow, red, and black and contain many tiny, edible seeds. Raspberries are sold without caps and stems. They are sweet enough to enjoy as is and in recipes.

Varieties: Most often you'll find the familiar red raspberry at markets, but occasionally other types, such as golden raspberries, which are yellow, and black raspberries, which are large and oval-shaped, also can be found.

Raspberries

Market forms: Fresh raspberries are plentiful in some parts of the United States in the summer. The forms that are available year-round are canned and frozen. Raspberry juice products, jams, and jellies also are available.

(See *Berry* for the Selecting Berries chart, including calories, and selecting and storing information.)

Ratatouille *(raa taa TOO ee)* A savory vegetable stew or casserole that typically includes eggplant, tomatoes, summer squash, onions, and green peppers.

Ratatouille

½ cup finely chopped onion
1 clove garlic, minced
1 tablespoon olive oil *or* cooking oil
2 cups cubed, peeled eggplant
1 small zucchini *or* yellow summer squash, halved lengthwise and cut into ¼-inch-thick slices (1 cup)
2 medium tomatoes, peeled and chopped, *or* one 7½-ounce can tomatoes, cut up
½ cup chopped green pepper
2 tablespoons water
½ teaspoon dried basil, crushed
⅛ teaspoon salt
⅛ teaspoon pepper
½ cup shredded Swiss cheese (optional)

■ In a large skillet cook onion and garlic in hot oil till onion is tender but not brown. Stir in eggplant, zucchini, tomatoes, green pepper, water, basil, salt, and pepper. Bring to boiling; reduce heat. Simmer, covered, about 20 minutes or till tender. Cook, uncovered, for 5 to 10 minutes more or till thickened, stirring occasionally. Sprinkle with cheese, if desired. Makes 4 servings.

Nutrition information per serving: 73 calories, 2 g protein, 10 g carbohydrate, 4 g fat (1 g saturated), 0 mg cholesterol, 76 mg sodium, 396 mg potassium.

Ratatouille

Ravigote Sauce *(raa vee GOT)* The name for two different herb-flavored sauces—one served cold and one hot. The cold sauce can be based on an oil and vinegar mixture, with herbs, onion, mustard, and hard-cooked egg yolks. Or, it can be based on mayonnaise, with herbs, lemon juice, and wine vinegar. Cold ravigote sauce usually is served with fish or shellfish.

The hot sauce is made with wine, vinegar, green onion, white sauce, and herbs. This version usually is served with poultry or fish.

Ravioli *(rav ee OH lee)* A filled pasta dumpling made by enclosing small spoonfuls of filling, usually meat or cheese, between two sheets of noodle dough. The dough is cut or folded into squares with the filling sealed inside. The dumplings are cooked in boiling water and may be served as an appetizer, main dish, or dessert, usually with a sauce. Ravioli also can be deep-fat fried and served as an appetizer.

Ravioli can be homemade or produced commercially. Commercial ravioli are available and come in dried, canned, refrigerated, and frozen forms.

(See *Pasta* for an identification photo and storing, how-to-cook, and other information.)

Reconstitute To bring a concentrated or condensed food, such as frozen fruit juice concentrate or condensed soup, to its original strength by adding water.

Redfish A saltwater fish with firm, white meat and a mild flavor. Cajun chef Paul Prudhomme made this fish, which also is called red drum, popular with his blackened fish recipe. So much redfish was taken from the Gulf of Mexico by the mid-1980s that authorities banned the commercial fishing of it. Black drum is a good substitute for redfish.

One 3-ounce portion of baked redfish has about 100 calories.

Red Snapper A bright red saltwater fish. Red snapper has firm, lean, white flesh that's mild to moderately flavored.

Market forms: Red snapper is available in fillets as well as whole in dressed or drawn forms. Since red snapper typically is sold with the skin on, beware of fish labeled red snapper that has no skin—it may not be the real thing.

How to cook: Red snapper can be cooked by a variety of methods. One way is to bake a stuffed, dressed fish. Other methods include poaching, broiling, and grilling. For baking, poaching, and broiling directions, see the Cooking Fish chart under *Fish*. For grilling directions, see the Direct-Grilling Fish chart under *Barbecue*.

Nutrition information: Baked red snapper has about 110 calories in a 3-ounce serving.

(See *Fish* for selecting, storing, thawing, and other information.)

Reduce To rapidly boil liquids, such as pan juices or sauces, so that some of the liquid evaporates, thickening the mixture.

Refried Beans A Mexican dish, called "frijoles refritos" *(free HOE lees reh FREE toes),* in which dried beans, such as pink or pinto beans, are cooked with seasonings. The mixture is then mashed and fried in fat. Refried beans are served as an appetizer with tortilla chips, as a side dish, or as a filling for tortillas.

Rehydrate To add water or other liquid to a dried or dehydrated food in order to replace fluid that has been removed.

Relish A food served with a meal for added flavor and color. A relish can be crisp, raw items, such as celery and carrot sticks, or pickled or spiced items, such as pickles, olives, and spiced crab apples.

The term also refers to a mixture of small pieces of vegetables or fruit in a sweet-sour flavored sauce that is used primarily as a condiment. Sweet pickle relish is one of the most commonly used relishes and is especially popular on hamburgers and hot dogs. One tablespoon of sweet pickle relish has about 20 calories and 110 milligrams of sodium.

Remoulade Sauce *(ray muh LAHD)*
A sharp-flavored sauce made with mayonnaise, anchovies, capers, pickles, mustard, and herbs. It is served cold as an accompaniment to cold fish and meat.

Rennet A natural enzyme, obtained from the lining of the fourth stomach of calves, that causes milk to coagulate. Available at supermarkets in tablet and powdered form, it is used in preparing delicate milk desserts and ice cream, and in making cheese.

Rhubarb A slender stalk vegetable that is served as a fruit. The stalks may be green with red overtones or light pink to cherry red in color with green overtones. Also known as pie plant because it is so popular in pies, rhubarb is too tart to be enjoyed raw. Cooked and sweetened, rhubarb has a sweet-sour fruity taste reminiscent of apricot, strawberry, and lemon. If you grow your own rhubarb, note that its large green leaves are poisonous; *do not eat them.*

Selecting: Look for crisp, young rhubarb stalks that are tender and firm. If the rhubarb is wilted-looking or has very thick stalks, don't buy it.

Storing: To preserve the crisp texture of raw rhubarb, wrap it tightly and refrigerate it. Store the rhubarb up to 1 week.

Rhubarb

Or, freeze rhubarb. Wash and slice. Blanch in boiling water for 1 minute. Cool quickly in cold water. Drain and place rhubarb into freezer containers, leaving ½-inch headspace, or into freezer bags. Freeze up to 6 months.

Preparation hints: Wash rhubarb and trim off the dry ends of the stalks, then slice or chop it according to your recipe. One pound raw rhubarb yields 3 cups sliced fruit.

How to cook: For rhubarb sauce, in a saucepan mix ½ to ⅔ cup *sugar,* ¼ cup *water,* and, if desired, 1 strip *orange peel.* Bring to boiling. Add 3 cups of ½-inch *rhubarb* slices. Reduce heat. Cover and simmer about 5 minutes or till rhubarb is tender. Remove peel. Serve as you would applesauce. Makes 2 cups (about 116 calories per ½-cup serving).

Nutrition information: Unsweetened raw rhubarb has about 30 calories per cup. Rhubarb is a source of calcium.

Rice   A semiaquatic member of the grass family. Its edible seed is the staple cereal grain for more than half of the world's population. Rice's flavor and aroma can range from very mild to distinctively nutty.

Those rices that are known for their fragrance, such as basmati rice, are classified as aromatic rices.

From long to short: Common types of rice come in several lengths. *Long Grain* rice is four or five times as long as it is wide. When cooked, the grains tend to remain separate and are light and fluffy. *Medium Grain* rice is plump but not round. When cooked, it is moister and more tender than long grain rice. *Short Grain* rice is almost round. It tends to cling together when cooked.

Cooking Rice

Use this chart as a guide when cooking rice. Measure the amount of water into a medium saucepan and bring to a full boil. If desired, add ¼ teaspoon salt to the water. Slowly add the rice and return to boiling. Cover and simmer for the time specified or till rice is tender (see photo opposite, bottom left) and most of the water is absorbed. (See also *Wild Rice* for other cooking directions.)

Rice and Amount	Amount Of Water	Cooking Directions	Yield (4 servings)
Brown 1 cup	2 cups	Simmer about 35 minutes. Remove from heat. Let stand, covered, for 5 minutes.	3 cups
White, long grain 1 cup	2 cups	Simmer about 15 minutes. Remove from heat. Let stand, covered, for 5 minutes.	3 cups
Precooked (quick cooking) 1½ cups	1½ cups	Follow package directions.	3 cups

Market forms: Look for these rice products at the supermarket.

☐ **Brown:** The least processed form of rice. Only the hull is removed from the grain. Its natural tan color comes from the bran layers left on the grain. Cooked brown rice has a nutty flavor and slightly chewy texture.

☐ **White:** Rice that is milled to completely remove the hull and bran layers. It also is called polished rice. This rice is mild and delicately flavored. Read the label to see if the rice is enriched. When white rice has been enriched (usually with a dusting of thiamin, niacin, and iron), you should not rinse it before cooking.

☐ **Precooked (quick cooking):** Cooked, dehydrated rice. Both white and brown rices are available in this form. They take only a few minutes to prepare.

☐ **Parboiled:** Rice treated in a steam-pressure process before milling to make the cooked grain extra fluffy without sacrificing nutrients. This rice takes a little longer to cook than regular white rice. Check package directions.

☐ **Rice Bran:** The ground outer layer of the rice kernel. Used in cooking and as a breakfast cereal, rice bran is considered a source of fiber (see also *Bran*).

☐ **Rice Flour:** Finely ground white or brown rice. It can be used as a thickener.

Storing: White rice can be kept indefinitely in an airtight container in a cool, dry place. Brown rice can be stored for up to 6 months.

A Tip from Our Kitchen
To save time later, cook up some extra rice and save it. Simply store the cooked rice in an airtight container in the refrigerator for up to 1 week or in the freezer for up to 6 months.

To reheat chilled or frozen rice, in a saucepan add 2 tablespoons liquid for each cup of rice. Cover and heat on top of the range about 5 minutes or till the rice is heated through.

Brown rice

Precooked white rice

Long grain white rice

How to cook: See Cooking Rice chart, opposite.

Q: Why is cooked rice sometimes sticky?
A: One reason is that rices vary in their tendency to become sticky. For example, long grain will be the most separate, medium grain will be less separate, and short grain rice will be the stickiest. Also, the amount of water you use to cook the rice is important. If you use too much water, the rice will tend to stick together. If you use less water, the rice will be drier and less sticky.

Nutrition information: Cooked long grain, white rice contains about 200 calories per ¾-cup serving, ¾ cup precooked white rice has about 120 calories, and ¾ cup cooked medium grain brown rice has about 160 calories.

Test the rice for doneness by squeezing a grain of rice between your fingers, as shown. If you can't feel a hard core, the rice is cooked.

Rice Stick An almost transparent, flavorless noodle. An ingredient in Oriental recipes, these noodles are made from rice flour and also are called rice noodles or rice vermicelli. They are served cooked in liquid or deep-fat fried. If fried, they puff to many times their original volume.

A Tip from Our Kitchen
Uncooked rice sticks should be stored in a tightly closed plastic bag or container and used within a few days after opening. Once the original packaging is opened, the rice sticks can absorb moisture, which reduces their ability to puff up when they are deep-fat fried.

Ricotta Cheese *(rih KOT uh)* A fresh, moist, white cheese that is very mild and semisweet. It has a soft and slightly grainy texture.

Whey, with or without cow's milk added, is used to make ricotta cheese. Or, sometimes ricotta is made entirely from cow's milk. It is available in whole milk or part-skim milk varieties with the whole milk cheese having a creamier consistency and fuller flavor.

Ricotta cheese

continued

Nutrition information: One-half cup of whole milk ricotta contains 214 calories, 16 grams of fat, and 62 milligrams of cholesterol. Part-skim milk ricotta contains 170 calories, 10 grams of fat, and 38 milligrams of cholesterol.

(See *Cheese* for storing and other information.)

Rind The skin or outer coating, usually rather thick, of foods such as citrus fruit, bacon, and cheese. It usually is peeled off or cut away before the food is eaten. In the case of citrus fruits, the outer part of the rind can be finely shredded to add flavor to recipes.

Ripen To allow food, especially fruits, to come to maturity in order to obtain the best flavor, texture, color, and aroma.

Risotto *(rih ZOT oh)* Rice cooked by an Italian method in which it is first browned in margarine, butter, or cooking oil, then cooked in broth. The cooked rice has a creamy, but not runny or sticky, consistency and a tender but slightly firm texture. Although risotto can be made with many kinds of rice, Arborio, an Italian rice that is available in specialty stores, is the traditional variety used because it cooks up to a very creamy consistency.

Risotto

> ½ cup finely chopped onion
>   2 tablespoons finely chopped
>   prosciutto *or* fully cooked ham
>   1 tablespoon margarine *or* butter
> ⅔ cup short, medium, *or* long grain
>   rice
>   2 cups water
> ½ teaspoon instant chicken *or* beef
>   bouillon granules
>   Dash pepper
>   3 tablespoons grated Parmesan *or*
>   Romano cheese

■ In a medium saucepan cook onion and prosciutto or ham in margarine or butter till onion is tender but not brown. Stir in rice; cook and stir 2 minutes more. Carefully stir in water, bouillon granules, and pepper. Bring to a full rolling boil; reduce heat to low. Cover with a tight-fitting lid. Continue cooking for 20 minutes (*do not lift cover*). Remove from heat. Let stand, covered, for 5 minutes. Rice should be tender but still slightly firm, and the mixture should be creamy. (If necessary, stir in a little water to reach desired consistency.) Stir in Parmesan or Romano cheese. Serve at once. Makes 4 servings.

Nutrition information per serving: 171 calories, 5 g protein, 27 g carbohydrate, 5 g fat (1 g saturated), 5 mg cholesterol, 277 mg sodium, 87 mg potassium.

Roast (noun) A large piece of meat or poultry that generally is cooked by a dry-heat method called roasting.

Roast (verb) A dry-heat method of cooking usually used for larger cuts of meat and poultry. Food may be roasted either in an oven in an uncovered pan or over a fire. Roasted meat or poultry usually has a crusty, browned exterior and a juicy interior. Roasting frequently is called baking when referring to ham and fish.

For roasting directions, see the Roasting Meat chart under *Meat* and the Roasting Poultry chart under *Poultry*.

In addition to meat and poultry, some vegetables, such as corn, potatoes, and peppers, can be roasted.

Roe The eggs of female fish and shellfish and the milt (sperm or reproductive glands filled wth sperm) of male fish. Fish roe are considered a delicacy. Male fish roe are called white roe or soft roe. Shellfish roe are taken from crustaceans, such as lobsters. Their roe are sometimes called the coral.

Edible varieties of roe include sturgeon, lumpfish, shad, herring, salmon, cod, mullet, and whitefish. Sturgeon roe are made into the highest quality caviar (see also *Caviar*).

Market forms: Roe are marketed fresh, smoked, and canned. Special products are made by salting, pickling, and pressing.

Selecting: Fresh roe should be moist, clean, and intact. They should smell fresh, not fishy, and should be uniformly colored, not cloudy.

Roll (noun) A small portion of yeast bread. Rolls can be plain or sweet, soft or hard, and seeded or sugared. They can be formed into many shapes. Some of the common shapes are Parker House, cloverleaf, bowknot, and butterhorn.

The basic yeast bread techniques apply to making rolls. After the dough is kneaded and has risen, it is shaped and allowed to rise again before baking.

Baking hints: To test for doneness, don't tap rolls as you would loaves of yeast breads. Instead, when the tops of the rolls are golden brown, peek at the sides and bottom of a roll. It should be lightly browned. If it is, remove the rolls from the oven.

Convenience products: The supermarket shelves have a wide array of substitutes for homemade rolls. There are brown-and-serve rolls, ready-to-serve rolls, hot-roll mixes, and refrigerated rolls. They come in a variety of styles including crescent, Parker House, butterhorn, French, and pan and dinner rolls.

A Tip from Our Kitchen

To achieve just the right type of crust on your next batch of homemade yeast rolls, try one of these techniques. For a soft, shiny crust, brush rolls with margarine or butter after baking. For a crisp, glossy crust, brush before baking with milk, water, or a beaten egg.

Roll (verb) To repeatedly turn a food in a fine coating, such as chopped nuts or fine dry bread crumbs, in order to coat the food.

The term also refers to forming a food into a shape. For example, a meat mixture can be rolled into balls or a dough rolled into ropes. Pieces of meat, fish, or poultry can be rolled into coils.

The phrase "roll out" refers to mechanically flattening a food, usually a dough or pastry, with a rolling pin.

Q: **What does the phrase "roll up jelly-roll style" mean?**

A: A jelly roll is a thin layer of cake that is spread with jelly or another filling and rolled up tightly so that when it is sliced, a spiral or coil design is seen. The phrase "roll up jelly-roll style" refers to the technique of rolling something just as you would a jelly roll so that it has the same coiled appearance.

Romaine A type of lettuce with large, elongated, dark green leaves that branch from a white base. Romaine is crisp with a slightly sharp flavor. Also called cos lettuce, romaine sometimes can be found in baby varieties.

Nutrition information: One cup of shredded romaine has about 10 calories, and each leaf has about 2 calories.

(See *Lettuce* for an identification photo and selecting, preparation, and storing information.)

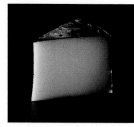

Romano cheese

Romano Cheese
A hard, dry, light yellow cheese that is similar to Parmesan, but has a slightly stronger flavor and aroma. Romano cheese is made with cow's and sometimes sheep's or goat's milk. Romano is available grated, or whole, or in pieces with a waxy, dark rind.

Q: Can Romano be substituted for Parmesan in recipes?
A: Yes. Both Romano and Parmesan are of the same family of cheeses and generally can be used interchangeably.

(See *Cheese* for the Selecting Cheese chart and selecting, storing, serving, nutrition, and other information.)

Rosemary
An aromatic herb with dark green leaves that look like curved pine needles. Rosemary's bold flavor often is described as pungent and piny, with a sweet scent. Fresh rosemary is available year-round as are dried rosemary leaves.

Preparation hints: Because of rosemary's strong flavor, you need to substitute just twice as much fresh herb for dried, not the usual three times as much.

Rosemary

A Tip from Our Kitchen
Dried rosemary's needlelike leaves are too sharp to crush between your fingers, so use a mortar and pestle to crush them or chop them on a cutting board.

(See *Herb* for the Herb Alternative Guide and selecting, storing, cooking, nutrition, and other information.)

Rosette
A thin, crisp pastry made by dipping a rose-shaped iron into an egg batter then deep-fat frying the batter. Rosettes can be used as the base for a creamy main dish or can be sprinkled with powdered sugar and served as a dessert. The term also refers to any food that is shaped to resemble a rose, such as a radish rose.

Roulade
(roo LAHD) A slice of meat, poultry, or fish that is topped with a filling and rolled up. The roll is then browned in a skillet and simmered in broth or wine.

Roux
(ROO) A French term that refers to a mixture of flour and a fat, such as cooking oil, margarine, or butter, that is cooked and used for thickening in sauces and gravies. Roux can be cooked to three different stages. If cooked just a few minutes, the mixture, sometimes referred to as a white roux, does not change color and is used to thicken white sauces. Heating the roux a few minutes more gives a golden color. This blond roux is used in lightly colored sauces. A brown roux is formed when the mixture is cooked slowly to a rich brown color. When properly browned, the roux also will have a nutty aroma. A brown roux is used, especially in French and Cajun cooking, to flavor, thicken, and color soups, stews, sauces, and gumbos.

1. To make a roux, use a wooden spoon to combine the flour and cooking oil, margarine, or butter. Make sure the mixture is smooth.

2. During cooking, a brown roux mixture will take on a toasty aroma and a dark reddish brown color, as shown. The coppery color often is compared to that of a tarnished penny.

Tips from Our Kitchen

Here are some tips to use when you're preparing a roux.
- Choose the right equipment. You'll need a heavy saucepan or skillet. Lightweight or thin metal pans increase the chance that the roux will burn. Also be sure to use a wooden spoon for stirring. Plastic utensils may melt in the hot fat, and metal ones may get too hot to hold.
- When making a brown roux, be patient. A brown roux needs to cook a long time over medium to medium-low heat, with constant stirring so it doesn't scorch or burn. Sometimes this can take as long as 20 to 30 minutes.

Rusk
A crisp, dry slice of bread that is used as a cracker. Rusks are made from sweet or plain bread. The baked bread is sliced (thick or thin) and baked again to dry it out and brown it. Packages of rusks, plain or flavored, are available at the supermarket.

Nutrition information: One rusk (3⅜-inch diameter) has about 40 calories.

Rutabaga
A large, round, root vegetable with tan, green, or purple skin and firm yellow or white meat. Often mistaken for turnips, and sometimes referred to as yellow turnips, rutabagas have a sweet flavor that is mild yet somewhat stronger than that of turnips.

Selecting: Rutabagas are available year-round, with peak seasons being fall and winter. Choose small (3 to 4 inches in diameter), smooth-skinned rutabagas that feel firm and heavy for their size.

Storing: Refrigerate rutabagas in a plastic bag for up to 1 month.

How to cook: See the Cooking Fresh Vegetables chart under *Vegetable.*

Nutrition information: One-half cup of cooked cubed rutabaga has about 30 calories.

Rutabagas

Rye
A cereal grain with dark brown kernels and a distinctive, robust flavor.

Market forms: Rye flour is the most popular form. The availability of other types is limited.
- **Rye Flour:** Finely ground rye. *Light* rye flour is sifted (also called bolted) and contains less bran than *Dark* rye flour. Rye flour often is used in baking bread.
- **Cracked Rye:** Coarsely ground unpolished rye kernels. Serve cracked rye as a cooked breakfast cereal and in pilafs.
- **Rye Berries:** Unpolished whole rye kernels. Cooked rye berries are suitable for using in casseroles, soups, and stuffings.

Storing: Store all forms of rye in an airtight container in a cool, dry place for up to 1 month. Rye flour and cracked rye keep for up to 3 months in the refrigerator or freezer. Keep rye berries for up to 5 months in the refrigerator or freezer.

How to cook: See the Cooking Grains chart under *Grain.*

Saffron comes in thin threads. To release saffron's wonderful flavor, crush it by rubbing the threads between your fingers.

Saffron
(SAF ruhn) The dried reddish orange, threadlike filaments, called stigmas, of a special variety of purple crocus. Saffron threads are used as a spice, and they impart a bright yellow color, bittersweet flavor, and exotic aroma to classic dishes, including arroz con pollo, bouillabaisse, and paella (see also individual entries).

Because the delicate filaments must be carefully picked by hand, saffron is the world's most expensive spice. There are only three filaments per flower, and it takes at least 225,000 filaments to make a pound of saffron. Saffron is sold in tiny strands called threads and as a powder.

Q: What's the best way to get the most flavor from saffron threads?

A: If the threads are not cooked in boiling liquid during recipe preparation, heat some of the liquid from the recipe and add crushed saffron threads. Let threads stand about 5 minutes to soften before returning them and the liquid to the dish.

(See *Spice* for the Spice Alternative Guide and selecting, storing, and nutrition information.)

Sage
A fragrant herb, with grayish green leaves, that has a pungent, slightly bitter flavor. Sage is easily recognized as the predominant flavor in the traditional Thanksgiving and Christmas Day turkey stuffings. It is also a mainstay as a sausage seasoning. Fresh sage is available year-round. Dried sage comes whole, rubbed, and ground. The dried form tends to lose flavor quickly. Store it in a cool, dry, dark place and replace it every 3 months.

Q: Can rubbed sage and ground sage be used interchangeably?

A: Although rubbed sage has a fluffier texture than the fine powder of ground sage, you can substitute one for the other.

Sage

(See *Herb* for the Herb Alternative Guide and selecting, preparation, cooking, nutrition, and other information.)

Salad
A savory or sweet mixture of foods, such as vegetables or salad greens, fruits, meats, poultry, fish, shellfish, grains, pastas, cheese, and eggs, that usually is served cold with a dressing. Salads are served as appetizers, side dishes, and main dishes. Depending on its function, a salad can be as casual as a bowl of leafy greens tossed with a vinaigrette or as elaborate as an artistically arranged main-dish salad.

Types: Salads can be divided into the following types.

☐ **Fruit:** A mixture of fresh, canned, dried, or frozen fruits served with or without a dressing. One type of fruit salad is a frozen fruit salad. For this type of salad, fruit is mixed with a creamy base, such as mayonnaise, salad dressing, sour cream, yogurt, or whipped cream, then it is frozen.

☐ **Gelatin:** A molded salad using flavored or unflavored gelatin often combined with fruits, vegetables, meats, poultry, shellfish, or cheese. Whipped cream, ice cream, cream cheese, or mayonnaise also can be added to give gelatin salads a rich flavor and a creamy appearance. Gelatin salads may be savory or sweet.

☐ **Pasta, Rice, Grain:** A mixture of cooked pasta, rice, or grain tossed with a vinaigrette or creamy dressing. Fruits and vegetables also can be added to the mixture.

☐ **Tossed:** A combination of leafy salad greens or only one type of green, often with tomatoes, cucumbers, green peppers, carrots, and/or onions added, that is tossed with salad dressing. It may contain additional ingredients, such as bacon bits, shredded or cubed cheese, croutons, herbs, nuts, and seasonings.

☐ **Vegetable:** A combination of raw or cooked vegetables mixed or marinated with a dressing. Salads such as coleslaw, bean salads, potato salads, and pea salads are served cold. German potato salad and wilted spinach salad generally are served with a hot dressing.

☐ **Whole Meal:** A mixture that includes meat, poultry, fish, eggs, cheese, or legumes so that it has enough protein to be considered a main dish. Sometimes these mixtures are used as sandwich spreads.

Salad Greens Math

When a salad recipe calls for a cup measure of greens, use this guide to figure out how much to buy. Measurements are for loosely packed torn greens.

Butterhead lettuce
    1 medium head (12 oz.) = 4 cups
Curly endive
    1 medium head (12 oz.) = 10 cups
Escarole
    1 medium head (8 oz.) = 7 cups
Iceberg lettuce
    1 medium head (18 oz.) = 10 cups
Leaf lettuce
    1 medium head (9 oz.) = 8 cups
Romaine
    1 medium head (16 oz.) = 6 cups
    (ribs removed)
Spinach
    16 oz. = 12 cups (stems removed)
Spinach
    10 oz. (prewashed) = 12 cups (large stems removed)

Market forms: You can purchase ready-to-eat salads at the delicatessen counter or at salad bars in many supermarkets. Some salads, such as potato salads and three-bean salads, are sold in cans or jars. You sometimes also can find fruit salads in refrigerated form.

Hints for Great-Tasting Salads

- Clean and chill ingredients ahead of time. Also chill salad plates and bowls.
- If a salad includes tomatoes, add them just before tossing to keep them from watering out and diluting the dressing.
- Mix a tossed salad with its dressing at the last minute to prevent the dressing from wilting the greens.
- Accent salads with simple trims, such as onion or green pepper rings, radish roses, pimiento strips, olives, small whole fruits, cherry tomatoes, and nuts.

Nutrition hint: If you are trying to cut calories, watch out for salads that contain lots of dressing and high-calorie ingredients, such as whipping cream and nuts. Instead, select an assortment of fresh vegetables and add reduced-calorie dressings sparingly. Go easy on the avocado, nut, and cheese toppings.

Salad Dressing

A flavored liquid or semiliquid blend of ingredients that adds sweet to tangy flavor to salads. Dressings range from vinaigrettes, which are thin and clear, to mayonnaise-type dressings, which are opaque and creamy. Although usually used on salads, creamy salad dressings also make tasty spreads for sandwiches and binders for sandwich fillings; vinaigrette-type dressings make good marinades for meats, poultry, and seafood.

Types: There are cooked, dairy, oil-based, and mayonnaise-based salad dressings. Cooked dressings, often called boiled dressings, generally are low in fat and require refrigeration. Dairy dressings are made with a dairy product, such as buttermilk, cottage cheese, sour cream, or yogurt, as a main ingredient. Oil-based dressings are made by combining salad oil with an acid, such as vinegar or lemon juice. Mayonnaise-based dressings combine mayonnaise with other ingredients for various flavors.

Market forms: There's a huge assortment of commercial bottled salad dressings and salad dressing mixes in the supermarket. Most bottled dressings are shelf stable, but a few are sold refrigerated. Dry salad dressing mixes are sold in packets. Reduced-calorie and oil-free dressings also are available.

Storing: Plain homemade oil and vinegar dressings keep up to several weeks in the refrigerator. If you add other ingredients, store the dressing up to 1 week. For commercial dressings, follow the storage information given on the label.

Salisbury Steak

A ground beef mixture, which may contain egg, bread or cracker crumbs, onion, and seasonings, that is shaped into a patty and broiled or cooked in a skillet. It often is served with a flavorful gravy or sauce.

Sally Lunn

A slightly sweet, coffee-cake-type bread. It usually is leavened with yeast, but can be made with baking powder. The bread can be baked in a variety of pans, including a Turk's head mold, a tube pan, loaf pan, square pan, and muffin pan.

Salmon

A fish that usually lives in salt water but spawns in fresh water. The flesh color ranges from orange to pink and deep red, depending on the type of salmon, and the flavor ranges from mild to rich.

Pull apart the sections of canned salmon. Then, if desired, remove the bones and skin, being careful to keep the fish in chunks. The chunks will make finished dishes more attractive.

Types: In the United States, several kinds of salmon are marketed.

☐ **Atlantic:** Flesh has a somewhat high oil content and is pink to red or orange.

☐ **Chinook or King:** The finest and most expensive of salmon from the Pacific Ocean. Its flesh is deep pinkish orange to white.

☐ **Chum, Keta, or Dog:** Salmon with the palest flesh and the least fat.

☐ **Coho or Silver:** Firmer, lighter in color, and lower in fat content than chinook.

☐ **Pink or Humpback:** A pink-fleshed, low-fat type of salmon. Most pink salmon is canned.

☐ **Sockeye or Red:** Familiar to most in the canned form. The deep red flesh is firm and sweet and has a moderate fat content.

Market forms: Fresh salmon is marketed dressed or as steaks, fillets, or roasts. It's also sold frozen, usually as fillets or steaks. It also can be found smoked, salted, and canned. The canned form is available with or without bones and skin. The bones of canned salmon, if present, are fairly soft.

How to cook: Fresh salmon can be poached, baked, broiled, micro-cooked, and grilled. For poaching, baking, broiling, and micro-cooking directions, see the Cooking Fish chart under *Fish*. For grilling directions, see the Direct-Grilling Fish chart under *Barbecue*.

Nutrition information: A 3-ounce serving of broiled or baked salmon has about 180 calories, depending on the variety. Canned sockeye salmon with bones has about 130 calories in a 3-ounce portion and is a good source of calcium if you eat the bones.

(See *Fish* for selecting, storing, thawing, and other information.)

Salsa

The general term for any of a variety of highly seasoned sauces, uncooked or cooked, that are especially popular in Mexican and Tex-Mex cooking.

Salsas generally are chunky in texture and almost always contain chili peppers. They can be used as a dipping sauce for tortilla chips or spooned over main dishes.

Although made of similar ingredients, picante sauce is usually smoother in texture and milder in flavor than salsa.

Types: *Salsa cruda* is an uncooked mixture that includes tomatoes, chili peppers, and cilantro. *Salsa verde* is a mixture of tomatillos, chili peppers, and cilantro.

Market forms: A variety of salsas and picante sauces are available at the supermarket. They range in flavor from mild to very hot.

Salsify *(SAL suh fye)* A long, slender root vegetable. Salsify also is known as oyster plant because of its delicate oysterlike flavor. The most common salsify has light brown skin with off-white flesh. Another variety, called scorzonera or black salsify, has muddy brown to black skin with cream-colored flesh.

Selecting: Salsify can be found in supermarkets from late fall to early spring. Look for medium-size, firm roots.

Storing: Refrigerate salsify in a plastic bag for up to 1 week.

How to cook: Rinse salsify well and peel. Slice or chop it and put it into a lemon juice and water mixture to prevent darkening (about 1 teaspoon lemon juice per cup of water). Boil or steam salsify till tender. Eat salsify as a vegetable or add it to soups and stews.

Nutrition information: One-half cup of cooked sliced salsify has about 45 calories.

Salsify

Salt The household name for sodium chloride. Salt is probably the most frequently used seasoning in the world. It intensifies the natural flavors of foods, making foods taste good. But salt doesn't just flavor food. In yeast breads, for instance, salt controls yeast growth so the dough doesn't rise too fast or too much. Salt also is used to preserve foods such as ham and fish. In pickle making, it helps keep vegetables crisp.

Market forms: The most common form of salt is table salt, but you'll find three other salts in most supermarkets.

☐ **Table:** Common household salt. It contains additives to keep it from clumping and to maintain its pure white color. Most table salt today is *iodized* (treated with potassium iodide) to help provide iodine, an essential dietary mineral.

☐ **Kosher:** Coarser ground than table salt. Kosher salt contains no additives and sometimes is sprinkled over pretzels or bread sticks before baking.

☐ **Pickling or Canning:** Finer ground than table salt. This salt is free of additives so it won't cloud pickling liquids.

☐ **Rock:** Nonedible, unrefined salt. Rock salt is used for freezing homemade ice cream and to keep shells from tipping when baking oysters on the half shell.

Storing: Salt stored in a covered container will keep indefinitely.

Nutrition information: Our bodies need salt to aid digestion and to regulate the water and nutrients that pass in and out of the body tissues. However, medical authorities say that eating too much salt may raise blood pressure. If you have been advised by your doctor to cut back on your salt intake, learn to use herbs and spices, vinegars, and lemon juice as flavor enhancers.

Veal Saltimbocca

Saltimbocca *(saul tuhm BAHK uh)* An
Italian dish made with thin slices of veal that
are topped with thin slices of ham or
prosciutto and flavored with sage. The slices
may be left flat or rolled up with cheese in
the center, then they're cooked in a skillet.

Veal Saltimbocca

    12 ounces boneless veal leg top round
          steak
     4 slices prosciutto (2 to 3 ounces)
     4 fresh sage leaves *or* ½ teaspoon dried
          sage, crushed
     2 tablespoons margarine *or* butter
          Pepper
     ⅓ cup dry white wine

■ Cut veal into 4 pieces. Pound each piece
between 2 pieces of plastic wrap to ⅛-inch
thickness. Remove the plastic wrap. Place a
slice of prosciutto atop each piece of veal.
Add a sage leaf and secure with a wooden
toothpick. (If using dried sage, crumble over
veal and top with prosciutto; secure with a
wooden toothpick.)
■ In a 12-inch skillet melt margarine or
butter. Cook meat over medium-high heat for
1 to 2 minutes on each side or till done.
Season lightly with pepper. Remove from
skillet; cover and keep warm.
■ Remove skillet from heat. Carefully add
wine. Return to heat and cook for 2 to 3
minutes or till wine is reduced slightly,
scraping up browned bits in skillet. Remove
wooden toothpicks and pour wine over veal.
If desired, serve with parslied rice and
asparagus spears. Makes 4 servings.

Nutrition information per serving: 182 calories,
22 g protein, 0 g carbohydrate, 9 g fat (2 g saturated),
74 mg cholesterol, 299 mg sodium, 311 mg potassium.

Chicken Saltimbocca: Prepare Veal
Saltimbocca as above, *except* use 4 medium
boneless, skinless *chicken breast halves* (12
ounces total). Pound, prepare, and cook as
above till no pink remains.

Nutrition information per serving: 197 calories,
23 g protein, 0 g carbohydrate, 9 g fat (2 g saturated),
62 mg cholesterol, 305 mg sodium, 218 mg potassium.

Sandwich   Bread, buns, or rolls filled or
topped with a number of different
ingredients. The essential ingredients of a
sandwich are the bread product (which can
range from plain white to dark rye), a filling,
and condiments, such as butter or margarine,
mayonnaise or salad dressing, or mustard.
Ingredients such as lettuce, tomatoes, and
pickles also can be added for flavor and
texture.

Nutrition hints: An open-face sandwich is
good to fix when counting calories. By
eliminating the extra slice of bread, you trim
some calories. You also can use thin-sliced
bread and low-calorie spreads, such as
mustard, diet margarine, and reduced-calorie
mayonnaise, to help keep the calorie count
down.

Sapodilla *(sap uh DILL uh)* A small,
round, applelike fruit with a custardlike
texture and thin, leathery yellow to red skin
that sometimes has a brownish tinge. The
sapodilla grows on the same tropical tree that
produces chicle, an ingredient used in
making chewing gum. Sapodillas contain a
few large, black inedible seeds around the
center. The fruit is aromatic and sweet.

Storing: Allow firm sapodillas to ripen at
room temperature until soft. Keep ripe
sapodillas in the refrigerator for up to 5 days.

Nutrition information: Sapodillas have
about 140 calories per fruit.

Sapote   See *White Sapote.*

Sardine Small, saltwater fish in the herring family with a strong flavor and soft bones. Sardines are suitable for canning whole without heads. They got their name from the island of Sardinia in the Mediterranean, where the canning industry began.

Types: Sardines are not one particular fish. Instead, they include *Pacific, Atlantic,* and *Blueback Herring* as well as *Sprat* and *Pilchards.* Sprat from Norway are sold as *Brisling* sardines.

Market forms: In some Mediterranean countries, sardines are sold fresh and lightly salted. Elsewhere, most are canned, usually in oil, mustard sauce, or tomato sauce.

Nutrition information: Sardines canned in oil have about 180 calories in 3 ounces, drained, and they are high in calcium.

Sashimi *(sah SHE me)* A Japanese delicacy of raw fish or seafood, artfully sliced and presented on a plate with beautiful garnishes and flavorful condiments.

Sassafras A tree of the laurel family. The ground leaves are used to make filé powder (see also *Filé Powder*).

Sate/Satay *(saa TAY)* An Indonesian dish of lamb, pork, chicken, or shrimp marinated and threaded on wooden skewers. These kabobs are grilled or broiled and served with a well-seasoned peanut sauce and accompanied by cooked rice.

Sauce A flavored liquid blend of ingredients that not only adds flavor but also enhances the appearance of foods.

Sauces are used on appetizers, main dishes, vegetables, and desserts. They can be thick or thin and hot or cold. Some types of salad dressings, such as mayonnaise and vinaigrette, are technically sauces.

Types: There are six major kinds of sauces. Each of these types can have numerous variations.
☐ **Brown:** A roux-based sauce made with margarine or butter, flour, and brown stock.
☐ **Butter:** A sauce made from melted butter or margarine to which seasonings are added.
☐ **Hollandaise-/Mayonnaise-Type:** A sauce made by forming an emulsion with fat, such as margarine, butter, or salad oil, and egg. Some sauces such as hollandaise and béarnaise are heated to form the emulsion; mayonnaise is made without heat. (See also *Béarnaise Sauce, Emulsion, Hollandaise Sauce,* and *Mayonnaise.*)
☐ **Tomato:** A sauce made with tomatoes and seasoned with spices and herbs.
☐ **Vinaigrette:** A sauce made from a blend of salad oil, vinegar, and seasonings.
☐ **White:** A roux-based sauce made with margarine or butter, flour, and milk, cream, or light stock. (See also *Roux.*)

Market forms: There is a large assortment of commercial sauces and sauce mixes in the supermarket. Dry sauce mixes, sold in packets, come in a variety of flavors and types. Most of these mixes simply require the addition of water or milk (some call for sour cream, margarine, or butter) and a few minutes of cooking.

Prepared sauces for pasta and meats as well as gravies and dessert sauces also are available.

Q. What sauces go with what foods?
A: Combining sauces and foods is mostly a matter of personal taste. But here are some tips for winning combinations.

Think of sauces as contrasting with and complementing the food on which or beside which they are served. For example, hollandaise sauce contrasts with the color and texture of vegetables such as broccoli and asparagus but complements their flavors.

In terms of flavor, some sauces go better with some types of food than with others. Some examples: Mint and dill are naturals with lamb; mustard, cheese, or cherries can be a good partner to ham; poultry and fruit sauces go together as do steak and mushroom sauces and seafood and butter sauces.

Tips from Our Kitchen

● Cook sauces over low to medium heat unless the recipe says otherwise, and cook sauces no longer than the time specified. High heat and lengthy cooking cause some sauces to curdle or break down.

● If lumps do form, quickly beat the sauce with a wire whisk or a rotary beater until it is smooth.

Sauerbraten　A German dish made with a less-tender cut of meat, often beef rump roast, that is marinated (for 1 to 3 days) in a spiced vinegar mixture then cooked slowly in the marinade. To finish off the dish, the marinade usually is thickened with gingersnaps and served with the meat slices. (See *German Cooking* for a recipe.)

Sauerkraut　A vegetable dish or condiment made from shredded cabbage that is allowed to ferment for several weeks in a brine of cabbage juice and salt until it develops a piquant flavor. Sauerkraut can be served plain as a vegetable or as a flavor accent to meats, sausages, and sandwiches. One-half cup of sauerkraut has about 20 calories.

Q: **Can anything be done to make sauerkraut less salty and strong?**

A: To reduce the salty, strong flavor sauerkraut sometimes has, place it in a sieve. Then rinse it well by running cold water over it for several seconds. Drain the sauerkraut well before using.

Sausage　Chopped or ground meat combined with seasonings and usually stuffed into a casing. Sausages were created by Old World "wurstmachers" to use every morsel of meat on a carcass.

Sausage is made from pork, beef, veal, lamb, poultry, game, or a combination of these meats. It is the unique seasoning blend that gives the sausage its personality. The flavor can range from mild to hot and spicy. During sausage making, sausage may be cooked, cured, smoked, and dried. Or, it can be left uncooked and sold fresh.

Types: Sausages are grouped by the processing method used. Following are descriptions. (For specific variety names of some sausages, see the Storing Sausage chart, page 366, and the photos on page 367.)

☐ **Fresh (Uncooked):** Sausage made from fresh meat. Since fresh sausage is neither cooked nor cured, cook it thoroughly before eating.

☐ **Uncooked and Smoked:** Sausage made with fresh or cured meat. This sausage is smoked but not cooked. It must be cooked thoroughly before serving.

☐ **Cooked:** Sausage usually made from fresh meat that is cured during processing and fully cooked. Although these sausages are ready to eat, some are heated before serving.

☐ **Cooked and Smoked:** Sausage made from fresh meat that is cured, smoked, and fully cooked. Serve these ready-to-eat sausages cold or hot.

☐ **Dry and Semidry:** Sausage made from fresh meat that is cured and dried during processing and is ready to eat. Sometimes dry and semidry sausages are smoked. The use of a bacterial fermentation during processing concentrates the flavor and acts as a

continued

preservative. Most dry sausages are salamis (a category of highly seasoned sausages having a characteristic fermented flavor); most semidry sausages are of the summer sausage type (mildly seasoned sausage with good storage qualities).

Market forms: Sausage is available in a variety of forms. Fresh sausage is available in bulk, link, or patty shape. Other sausage types come in links, rings, chunks, or slices. Brown-and-serve sausage comes in link or patty form.

Selecting: When selecting unwrapped sausage, make sure there are no off-odors and that the casing is dry and free of mold.

If you buy sausage in vacuum-sealed packages, check for meat that is fresh and moist. Look for a freshness date on the package and buy accordingly.

See the identification photos, opposite, for a selection of sausage varieties.

Storing: Place sausage in airtight wrap in the refrigerator. Although some dry sausages don't need refrigeration, they should be kept in a cool place. Be sure to check labels for storing directions. Once a dry sausage is cut, refrigerate it.

Freezing sausage may cause flavor changes; however, if necessary, you can freeze the sausage for only a short period of time, following the guidelines below.

For recommended storage time guidelines, see the Storing Sausage chart, below.

Storing Sausage

Storing sausage properly will maintain its quality. Refer to the chart below for guidelines for maximum storage times. Prepackaged sausage may be refrigerated in its original wrapping according to package directions. Opened prepackaged sausage and sausage that isn't prewrapped should be tightly wrapped in plastic wrap or foil, then refrigerated. For longer storage, freeze sausage at 0° or below. Package the sausage in freezer wrap, freezer bags, or plastic wrap for the freezer. Wrap it tightly, eliminating all air in the package, if possible. Label the packages with the contents and date.

Type	Refrigerator Storage (36° to 40°)	Freezer Storage (0° or lower)	Variety Names (Note that some sausage varieties, such as kielbasa and bratwurst, come in several types.)
Fresh	1 to 2 days	1 to 2 months	Bockwurst; Bratwurst; Chorizo (link or bulk); Italian; Kielbasa (Polish); Pork Sausage (bulk, link, patty, or country-style)
Uncooked, Smoked	7 days	1 to 2 months	Kielbasa; Mettwurst; Smoked Country-Style; Smoked Pork Sausage
Cooked	4 to 6 days	1 to 2 months	Blood Sausage; Bockwurst (precooked); Bratwurst (precooked); Braunschweiger; Kiszka; Liver Loaf; Liver Sausage; Yachtwurst
Cooked, Smoked	7 days*	1 to 2 months	Beef Salami; Bologna; Cotto Salami; Frankfurters (Wieners); German-Style Mortadella; Kielbasa; Knockwurst; Krakow; Mettwurst; New England Sausage (Berliner); Prasky; Smoked Thuringer Links; Teawurst; Vienna Sausage
Dry and Semidry	2 to 3 weeks	Not recommended	Cervelat; Chorizo; Frizzes; Genoa; German (hard); Kosher; Lebanon Bologna; Lyons; Medwurst (Swedish); Metz; Milano; Mortadella; Pepperoni; Salami; Summer Sausage; Thuringer

*After a vacuum-sealed package is opened. Unopened vacuum-sealed packages can be stored in the refrigerator for up to 2 weeks.

Cooking Sausages

Different market forms of sausage require different preparation methods. Here are some suggestions.

- *Uncooked Patties:* Place ½-inch-thick sausage patties in an unheated skillet and cook over medium-low heat for 10 to 12 minutes or till juices run clear, turning once. Drain well. Or, arrange the patties on a rack in a shallow baking pan. Bake in a 400° oven about 15 minutes or till juices run clear.
- *Uncooked Links:* Place 1- to 1¼-inch-diameter sausage links in an unheated skillet. Add ½ inch water. Bring to boiling; reduce heat. Cover and simmer about 15 minutes or till juices run clear. Drain. Cook for 1 to 2 minutes more or till browned, turning often.
- *Fully Cooked Links:* Place sausage links in a saucepan. Cover with *cold* water. Bring to boiling; reduce heat. Simmer for 5 to 10 minutes or till heated through.

Nutrition information: One pork sausage link (16 per 1-pound package) has about 50 calories.

If you enjoy eating sausage but need to cut back on calories, look for reduced-fat products, such as reduced-fat kielbasa, hot dogs, and luncheon meats.

Sauté *(saw TAY)* To cook or brown a food in a small amount of hot fat.

Savory *(SAY vuh ree)* An herb belonging to the mint family. It is well known in two varieties: *Winter* savory and *Summer* savory (the names have nothing to do with the times when the herbs are planted or harvested). Both savories have a warm, peppery flavor and grassy fragrance. Summer

continued

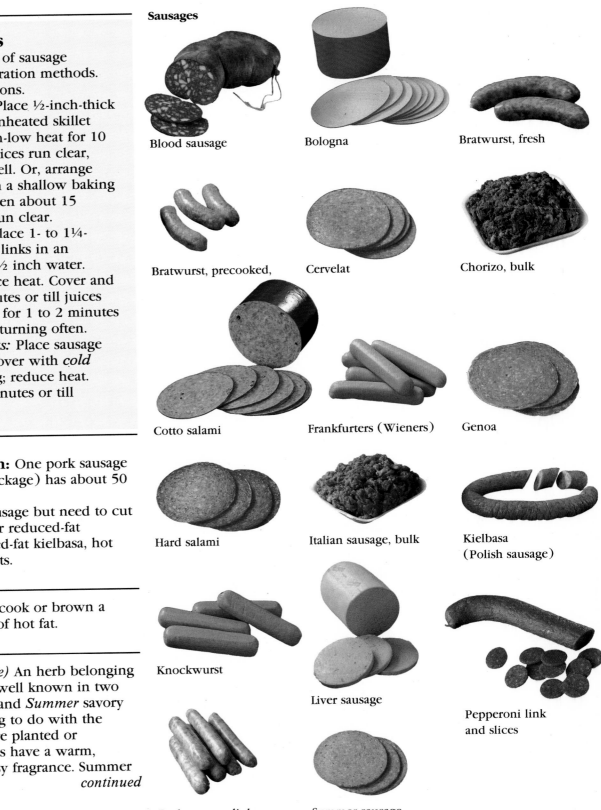

Sausages

Blood sausage

Bologna

Bratwurst, fresh

Bratwurst, precooked,

Cervelat

Chorizo, bulk

Cotto salami

Frankfurters (Wieners)

Genoa

Hard salami

Italian sausage, bulk

Kielbasa (Polish sausage)

Knockwurst

Liver sausage

Pepperoni link and slices

Pork sausage links

Summer sausage

Winter savory

savory has a sweeter, more delicate flavor. Savory leaves are used either fresh or dried—as whole leaves or ground.

(See *Herb* for the Herb Alternative Guide and selecting, storing, preparation, cooking, nutrition, and other information.)

Scald
To heat a liquid such as milk to a temperature just below boiling, when tiny bubbles just begin to appear around the edge of the liquid.

Scale
A device used to measure the weight of food. The term also refers to the small, flat, rigid plates that cover the outer surface of some fish. It also means the process of removing these plates by scraping the surface of the fish with a special utensil called a scaler or with a dull knife.

Scallop
A shellfish with hinged shells similar to the oyster and clam. Scallops propel themselves through the water with a large muscle that opens and closes their shells. This muscle, which is firm, sweet, and low in fat, usually is the only portion of the shellfish that is eaten.

Types: In the United States, there are usually three types of scallops available. *Sea* scallops are the largest, followed by *Bay* scallops and *Calico* scallops. The meat of these scallops can be creamy white, tan, or creamy pink.

Market forms: Scallops usually are shucked right after they're harvested. Most are sold fresh, but some are frozen. Scallops also are breaded and frozen.

Selecting and storing: Scallops should be firm and free of excess cloudy liquid. They should be sweet smelling; spoiled scallops have a strong sulfur odor. Refrigerate fresh shucked scallops covered with their own liquid in a closed container for up to 2 days.

How to cook: The tender, sweet scallop can be broiled, panfried, deep-fried, poached, grilled, or stir-fried. For poaching and panfrying directions, see the Preparing and Cooking Shellfish chart under *Shellfish.*

Nutrition information: Calories for a 3-ounce serving of scallops vary from about 100 calories for poached scallops to 180 calories for breaded, fried scallops.

Scalloped
A term used to describe a food that is combined with a saucelike mixture, often containing cracker or bread crumbs, and usually baked. Potatoes, corn, and oysters often are prepared this way.

The term also refers to a wavy border that sometimes is used in cooking. For example, a cookie cutter can have scalloped edges. Also, fruit, such as cantaloupe, can be cut into bowl-like shapes with scalloped edges.

Scaloppine
(skahl uh PEA nee) A term that refers to very thin boneless slices of meat, usually cut from veal top round.

The term also refers to an Italian dish that features these thin meat slices. Sometimes the slices are pounded extra thin, then coated with flour, browned, and served with a tomato or wine sauce.

Scampi
(SCAM pea) The Italian name for a shellfish that is similar to a large prawn or shrimp. In the United States, it is sometimes used to refer to large shrimp. Shrimp scampi, listed on restaurant menus, is shrimp cooked in garlic, butter, white wine, and herbs.

Scone
A plain or sweet biscuitlike quick bread. Scones are richer than biscuits because the dough frequently contains eggs, cream, and butter. Some versions contain dried fruit, currants or raisins, or nuts. Usually triangle-shaped, the scone dough also can be cut into diamonds, circles, or squares. To serve, split scones in half and serve with butter or preserves. (For a scone recipe, see page 370.)

Country Scones
(see recipe, page 370)

Country Scones

- ½ cup dried currants
- 2 cups all-purpose flour
- 3 tablespoons brown sugar
- 2 teaspoons baking powder
- ½ teaspoon baking soda
- ½ teaspoon salt
- ⅓ cup margarine *or* butter
- 1 8-ounce carton dairy sour cream
- 1 beaten egg yolk
- 1 slightly beaten egg white
- 1 tablespoon water
- 1 tablespoon brown sugar
- ⅛ teaspoon ground cinnamon

■ In a small bowl pour enough *hot water* over currants to cover. Let stand for 5 minutes. Drain well and set aside. In a large bowl stir together flour, 3 tablespoons brown sugar, baking powder, baking soda, and salt. Using a pastry blender, cut in margarine or butter till mixture resembles coarse crumbs. Add currants, then toss till mixed. Make a well in the center of the dry mixture. In a small bowl stir together sour cream and egg yolk. Add sour cream mixture all at once to dry mixture. Using a fork, stir *just till moistened.*
■ Turn the dough out onto a lightly floured surface. Quickly knead dough by gently folding and pressing dough for 10 to 12 strokes or till *nearly* smooth. Divide dough into 6 equal portions. Lightly shape each into a ball and pat or lightly roll each to a 4-inch round, about ½ inch thick.
■ Place scones 1 inch apart on an ungreased baking sheet. Using a sharp knife, cut *each* scone into 4 wedges. *Do not separate wedges.* Brush tops of scones with a mixture of egg white and water. Combine the 1 tablespoon brown sugar and cinnamon, then sprinkle mixture over tops of scones. Bake in a 425° oven for 12 to 15 minutes or till golden. Remove scones from baking sheet. Cool on wire rack for 5 minutes. Break scone circles apart into wedges and serve warm with jam, if desired. Makes 24 wedges.

Nutrition information per wedge: 101 calories, 2 g protein, 13 g carbohydrate, 5 g fat (2 g saturated), 13 mg cholesterol, 124 mg sodium, 64 mg potassium.

Score To cut narrow grooves or slits partway through the outer surface of a food in order to tenderize it or to form a decorative pattern.

Scrape To use an instrument, either sharp or blunt, to rub the surface of a food in order to remove its outer coating. Vegetables such as carrots often are scraped.

Nutrition hint: Health-conscious cooks often prefer to scrape vegetables rather than peel them, because scraping generally removes less of the outer surface and thus fewer of the nutrients.

Scrapple A seasoned mixture of ground meat or sausage, broth, and cornmeal that is cooked to a mushlike stage. The mixture is pressed into loaf pans and chilled. The chilled scrapple usually is sliced and fried to serve for breakfast or brunch.

Scrod A popular name for a young cod or haddock that weighs less that 2½ pounds. It can be prepared in a variety of ways. In New England, broiled scrod is a specialty.

Seafood Any edible saltwater fish or shellfish.

Sear To brown a food, usually meat, quickly on all sides using high heat to seal in the juices. Searing can be done either in an oven or on top of the range.

Season To use herbs, spices, or salt to enhance the basic flavor of a dish. When a recipe's directions say "season to taste," add enough of the herb, spice, salt, or pepper called for in the recipe to suit your taste.

Seasoning An ingredient, such as a condiment, herb, spice, or salt, that is added to food to improve the taste and aroma.

Seaweed A variety of sea plants used in cooking and in commercial food products. *Nori* is a common Japanese seaweed that is used as a wrapper for sushi. *Kelp,* also called *konbue,* is used to make a base for soups. *Carrageenan* or *Irish moss* is used commercially to help frozen desserts stay smooth, and *agar* is used for thickening.

Section A pulpy segment of a citrus fruit that has had the membrane removed.

The term also refers to the process of separating the segments of a citrus fruit from its membrane with a knife.

To section a citrus fruit, use a sharp paring knife to remove the peel and white rind. Working over a bowl to catch the juices, cut into the center of the fruit between one section and the membrane. Turn the knife and slide it along the other side of the section, next to the membrane, as shown, cutting outward.

Sesame Seed A tiny, pearly white seed from a tropical herb plant. Sesame seeds have a mildly sweet, nutty flavor that is enhanced by toasting. Sesame seeds also are known as benne seeds.

Storing: Sesame seeds tend to go rancid because of the high amount of oil they contain; therefore, it is best to store the seeds in the refrigerator or freezer.

A Tip from Our Kitchen
Toast sesame seeds by spreading a thin layer of the seeds in a shallow, ungreased pan. Heat in a 350° oven for 10 to 15 minutes, stirring once or twice.

Shallot A petite member of the onion family. Shallots are formed in the same way as garlic, with a head made up of several cloves. A thin, papery skin of reddish brown to yellow-brown covers off-white meat that is tinged with green or purple. Shallots have a mild, delicate flavor and tender texture. They can be eaten raw or cooked.

Selecting: Look for firm, well-shaped shallots that are not sprouting. Avoid wrinkled or shriveled shallots.

Storing: Store shallots in a cool, dry place for up to 1 month.

How to cook: Peel and chop or slice. Cook 2 tablespoons chopped shallots in 2 teaspoons margarine or butter over medium heat till tender but not brown, stirring often.

Nutrition information: Chopped shallots have about 10 calories per tablespoon.

Shallots

Shark Any of several species of predatory saltwater fish with dense flesh. Taste, color, and texture of the meat vary with the kind of shark. Some, such as *Blue, Blacktip,* and *Dogfish,* have white, mild-tasting meat. Others, such as *Mako,* are firm and meaty, with a stronger flavor. Mako is similar to swordfish. Most shark is sold as fresh steaks.

How to cook: Shark is good grilled, broiled, or baked. Since it has a firm flesh, it is good for cutting into cubes for cooking on kabobs. For baking and broiling directions, see the Cooking Fish chart under *Fish.* For grilling directions, see the Direct-Grilling Fish chart under *Barbecue.*

Nutrition information: A 3-ounce serving of broiled shark has about 150 calories.

(See *Fish* for selecting, storing, thawing, and other information.)

Shelf Stable A term used to describe a food that has been sterilized and sealed in special paper, foil, or plastic containers. This type of preservation also is referred to as aseptic packaging. Foods that are shelf stable require no refrigeration or freezing. Products such as milk, juice, soup, pudding, sauce, and dip are sold in shelf-stable form.

Shellfish A saltwater animal with a shell, but no fins, skull, or backbone.

Types: The two basic kinds of shellfish are crustaceans and mollusks. *Crustaceans,* recognizable by their pincers and antennae, include crab, crayfish, lobster, and shrimp. *Mollusks,* on the other hand, usually have hinged shells and include clams, mussels, oysters, and scallops. Squid and octopus are exceptions to the rule. They're considered mollusks but don't have hinged shells. (See also individual entries.)

Market forms: Shellfish are sold in several forms—live, fresh shucked, fresh cooked, frozen (raw and cooked), and canned.

Storing: Shellfish are very perishable. If you're cooking live crustacean shellfish, try to cook them on the day they're purchased. Molluscan shellfish have a longer shelf life (see individual entries).

How to cook: Most shellfish can be simply prepared and served with melted butter for dipping. For cooking directions, see the Preparing and Cooking Shellfish chart, opposite.

Nutrition information: Like fish, shellfish are excellent sources of protein and are low in total fat. Shellfish are low in saturated fat.

Shepherd's Pie A main dish that is a mixture of cubed cooked meat (usually lamb or beef), vegetables, and a gravy or tomato sauce. The mixture is placed in a casserole, topped with mashed potatoes, and baked.

Sherbet A sweet, smooth, frozen dessert. Sherbet is made with milk, sweetener, and sometimes gelatin or egg whites. It usually has a citrus or other fruit flavor.

Sherbet is similar to ice cream, but it is softer and not as rich. Sherbet is made with less milk fat than ice cream and ice milk so it is lower in fat. Sherbet has more sweetening than ice cream, so it contains about the same number of calories as vanilla ice cream.

Commercial sherbet is available in supermarkets in many flavors. Sherbet also can be made at home in an ice-cream maker, or the mixture may be frozen in a freezer tray then beaten to whip in air.

(For a sherbet recipe, see page 374.)

Nutrition information: A ½-cup serving of sherbet contains about 135 calories and 2 grams fat.

Preparing and Cooking Shellfish

Shellfish	Preparation Directions	Cooking Directions
Clam	Scrub live clams under cold running water. For 24 clams, in an 8-quart Dutch oven combine 4 quarts of cold water and ⅓ cup salt. Add clams and soak for 15 minutes. Drain and rinse. Discard water. Repeat twice.	To *steam* 24 clams in shells, add water to an 8-quart Dutch oven to ½-inch depth; bring to boiling. Place clams in a steamer basket. Steam, covered, for 5 to 7 minutes or till shells open and clams are thoroughly cooked. Discard any that do not open.
Crab, hard-shell blue	Grasp live crabs from behind, firmly holding the back two legs on each side. Rinse them under cold running water.	To *boil* 3 pounds live crabs, in a 12- to 16-quart kettle bring 8 quarts water and 2 teaspoons salt to boiling. Add crabs; return to boiling. Reduce heat. Simmer, covered, about 15 minutes. Drain and chill, *or* rinse crabs under cold running water until cool enough to handle. Crack and remove meat (see how-to photos under *Crab*).
Crayfish	Rinse live crayfish under cold running water. For 4 pounds live crayfish, in a 12- to 16-quart kettle combine 8 quarts cold water and ⅓ cup salt. Add crayfish and soak for 15 minutes; rinse. Drain.	To *boil* 4 pounds live crayfish, in a 12- to 16-quart kettle bring 8 quarts water and 2 teaspoons salt to boiling. Add crayfish; return to boiling. Reduce heat and simmer, covered, 5 minutes or till shells turn bright red. Drain. (To remove meat, see how-to photos under *Crayfish*.)
Lobster, whole	Grasp live lobster just behind the eyes; rinse lobster under cold running water. To prepare a 1- to 1½-pound whole lobster for *broiling*, plunge live lobster headfirst into enough boiling, salted water to cover. Cook 5 minutes. Remove. Place lobster on its back on a cutting board. With kitchen shears, open the body lengthwise from head to tail, cutting to, but not through, the back shell. Discard all organs in body section except red coral roe (in females only) and brownish green liver. (For cooking lobster tails, see How to Cook information under *Lobster*.)	To *boil* two 1- to 1½-pound live lobsters, in a 12- to 16-quart kettle bring 8 quarts water and 2 teaspoons salt to boiling. Add lobsters headfirst; return to boiling. Reduce heat. Simmer, covered, for 20 minutes. Drain. Remove bands on claws. When meat is removed, it should be opaque. To *broil* whole lobster, place prepared lobster (see directions, left) on its back on broiler pan. Snip off shell membrane from underside of tail section. Devein, if necessary. Using both hands, bend tail, cracking shell lengthwise so the tail lies flat on pan. Brush with melted margarine or butter. Broil about 4 inches from the heat for 5 to 7 minutes or until tail meat turns opaque.
Mussel	Scrub live mussels under cold running water. Using your fingers, pull out the beards that are visible between the shells (see how-to photo under *Mussel*). Soak as directed for Clam (see above).	To *steam* 24 mussels, add water to an 8-quart Dutch oven to ½-inch depth; bring to boiling. Place mussels in a steamer basket. Steam, covered, for 5 to 7 minutes or till shells open and mussels are thoroughly cooked. Discard any that do not open.
Oyster	Scrub live oysters under cold running water. For easier shucking, chill them before opening. Shuck, reserving bottom shells, if desired.	To *poach* 24 shucked oysters, in a saucepan bring 2 cups water and ½ teaspoon salt to boiling. Add oysters; return to boiling. Reduce heat and simmer about 5 minutes or till oysters are plump and opaque. Drain.
Scallop	Thaw shelled scallops, if frozen. Rinse scallops and cut large ones in half. If panfrying, pat dry with paper towels.	To *poach* 1 pound scallops, in a saucepan bring 4 cups water and 1 teaspoon salt to boiling. Add scallops; return to boiling. Reduce heat and simmer for 1 to 3 minutes or till opaque and firm, stirring occasionally. Drain. Use as cooked scallops in a recipe or chill and serve with a sauce. To *panfry* 12 ounces scallops, in a skillet cook and stir scallops about 1½ to 3 minutes in 1 tablespoon hot margarine or butter till scallops are opaque.
Shrimp (in shells or peeled and deveined)	Rinse shrimp in shells or peeled shrimp under cold running water and drain. Store in the refrigerator for up to 2 days if not to be used immediately.	To *boil* 1 pound shrimp, simmer, uncovered, in 4 cups water and 1 teaspoon salt for 1 to 3 minutes or till pink, stirring occasionally. Rinse under cold running water. Drain. Use as cooked shrimp in a recipe or chill and serve with a sauce.

Berry Sherbet

> 2 10-ounce packages frozen raspberries
> *or* strawberries, thawed
> ¾ cup sugar
> 1 envelope unflavored gelatin
> ½ cup water
> 1½ cups whole milk

■ In a blender container puree berries in syrup. If using raspberries, press mixture through a sieve to remove seeds.

■ In a medium saucepan combine ¼ *cup* of the sugar and gelatin; add water. Cook and stir till sugar and gelatin dissolve. Remove from heat. Stir in remaining sugar. Add milk (do not use skim or low-fat milk) and berry puree. (Mixture may appear curdled.)

■ Pour mixture into a 9x9x2-inch baking pan. Cover and freeze for 5 to 6 hours or till almost firm. (*Or,* after combining ingredients, freeze in a 4-quart ice-cream freezer according to manufacturer's directions. Omit remaining steps.)

■ Break frozen mixture into small chunks. Transfer to a large chilled bowl. Beat with an electric mixer till smooth but not melted. Return to pan. Cover and freeze till firm. Makes 8 to 10 servings.

Nutrition information per serving: 176 calories, 3 g protein, 39 g carbohydrate, 2 g fat (1 g saturated), 6 mg cholesterol, 25 mg sodium, 151 mg potassium.

Short
A term that is used to describe a food, such as pastry, that contains a high proportion of shortening, margarine, butter, or cooking oil to flour. A food that is called short is rich, flaky, and easily broken apart.

Shortbread
A rich, buttery, shaped cookie that's made from only three ingredients: flour, sugar, and butter. Because the dough contains a lot of butter, this Scottish favorite is very tender and crumbly.

(See *Cookie* for Cookie-Making Hints and preparation, baking, storing, and other information.)

Shortcake
A dessert with layers of rich, flaky biscuit, fruit, and whipped cream. The biscuit used in making the dessert also is called shortcake.

Sponge cake or pound cake sometimes is used for shortcakes instead of the biscuit. Fresh strawberries are popular for shortcakes although other fresh or frozen fruits, such as peaches and blueberries, also make delicious shortcakes. Shortcakes can be made as a large round that is served in wedges or in small single-serving-size rounds.

Strawberry Shortcake

> 6 cups sliced strawberries
> ¼ cup sugar
> 2 cups all-purpose flour
> ¼ cup sugar
> 2 teaspoons baking powder
> ½ cup margarine *or* butter
> 1 beaten egg
> ⅔ cup milk
> 1 cup whipping cream
> 2 tablespoons sugar
> ½ teaspoon vanilla

■ Stir together the berries and ¼ cup sugar; set aside. In a large bowl stir together the flour, ¼ cup sugar, and baking powder. Cut in margarine or butter till mixture resembles coarse crumbs. In a bowl combine egg and milk; add all at once to dry ingredients. Stir just to moisten.

■ Spread into a greased 8x1½-inch round baking pan, building up edge slightly. Bake in a 450° oven for 15 to 18 minutes or till toothpick inserted near center comes out clean. Cool in pan 10 minutes.

■ In a chilled bowl combine cream, 2 tablespoons sugar, and vanilla. Beat with the chilled beaters of an electric mixer on medium speed till soft peaks form. Remove shortcake from pan. Split into 2 layers. Spoon the fruit and whipped cream between layers and over top. Serve immediately. Serves 8.

Nutrition information per serving: 433 calories, 6 g protein, 50 g carbohydrate, 24 g fat (10 g saturated), 69 mg cholesterol, 238 mg sodium, 288 mg potassium.

Shortening Most commonly a vegetable oil that's been processed to be solid at room temperature (see also *Fat and Oil*). Some shortenings may contain animal fat. Shortening is used in cooking, mostly for baking and frying.

Shred To rub a food, usually vegetables, citrus peel, or cheese, across a shredding surface to make long, narrow strips. Vegetables such as lettuce and cabbage also can be shredded by thinly slicing them.

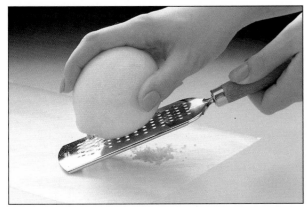

Food may be shredded finely, as shown, or coarsely, depending on the size of the holes of the shredding utensil that is used.

Tips from Our Kitchen

● Citrus peel and cheeses are two foods that often are shredded. Generally, citrus peel and other potent seasonings are finely shredded using a utensil with small holes. Cheeses and vegetables frequently are shredded with a utensil that has larger holes, making longer and wider strips.

● Save preparation time later by shredding more cheese or citrus peel than is needed for immediate use. Store the extra in the freezer, making sure it is properly wrapped and labeled with contents and date.

Shrimp A small shellfish with a long tail and 10 legs. Its tender white meat has a sweet flavor. Shrimp is the most popular shellfish in the United States.

Types: There are many species of shrimp. They can be divided into groups such as tropical, cold water, and freshwater shrimp. Tropical shrimp, sometimes categorized according to shell color, include the *white, brown, pink,* and *striped* or *tiger* shrimp. Cold water shrimp include the *pink* and *sidestripe* shrimp. Large freshwater shrimp are called *prawns* (see also *Prawn*). Shrimp farming in countries around the world is becoming an increasingly important source of shrimp.

Market forms: Raw shrimp (sometimes called green shrimp) in the shell are available fresh or frozen. They can be found whole or headless. Raw shrimp also are peeled, deveined, and frozen for sale.

Besides being sold raw, shrimp also are sold cooked. Cooked shrimp can be fresh or frozen, and in the shell or peeled. Peeled shrimp usually are deveined. Shrimp also come canned, breaded and frozen, and dried.

Selecting: Shrimp are sold by the pound. The price per pound usually is determined by the size—the bigger the shrimp, the higher the price and the fewer per pound. Fresh shrimp should be moist and firm, have translucent flesh, and smell fresh. Signs of poor quality are an ammonia smell and blackened edges or spots on the shells.

Shrimp Math

Allow 3 to 4 ounces of shelled shrimp per serving.

12 ounces of raw shrimp in the shell	=	8 ounces raw, shelled
	=	one 4½-ounce can
	=	1 cup cooked and shelled

continued

 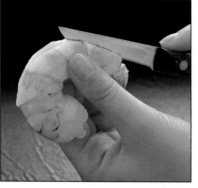 

1. To peel the shrimp, use your fingers to open the shell lengthwise down the body. Starting at the head end, peel back the shell. Gently pull on the tail portion of the shell and remove it.

2. To devein shrimp, use a sharp knife to make a shallow slit along its back from the head end to the tail. Rinse under cold running water to remove the vein, using the tip of a knife, if necessary.

3. To butterfly the shrimp, make a deeper slit along its back. *Do not cut all the way through the shrimp.* Lay the shrimp on a flat surface so the sides open to resemble a butterfly.

Storing: To store fresh shrimp, rinse them under cold running water. Drain them well. Then store the shrimp in a covered container in the refrigerator for up to 2 days. Store purchased frozen shrimp in the freezer for up to 6 months.

Cooking hints: Cook shrimp quickly; overcooking toughens them. Cook shrimp just till they curl, the shells turn pink, and their flesh turns opaque.

How to cook: Shrimp are delicious boiled, steamed, fried, broiled, grilled, panfried, or stir-fried. For boiling directions, see the Preparing and Cooking Shellfish chart under *Shellfish.*

Nutrition information: A 3-ounce serving of cooked shrimp, without fat and breading, has about 80 calories. Shrimp are higher in cholesterol than other shellfish, with the exception of squid.

Shuck To remove the shells or husks from such foods as oysters, clams, mussels, and corn.

Sieve A circular utensil with wire mesh or tiny holes through which food is passed. Foods are put through a sieve to separate small particles from large ones, to separate liquid from solids, and to puree a food.

The term also refers to the process of passing a food through such a utensil.

A Tip from Our Kitchen
When a recipe calls for sifted flour or powdered sugar, reach for your sieve. It makes a great substitute for a sifter. Just push the flour or powdered sugar through the sieve with a wooden spoon, stirring, if necessary, to break up any lumps.

Sift To put one or more dry ingredients, such as flour, through a sifter or sieve to incorporate air and break up any lumps.

Q: Do all flours need to be sifted before measuring?

A: No. Today's modern milling techniques produce all-purpose flours that are so uniform that simply stirring them with a spoon is all that's needed to break up any lumps. The flour is then ready to be gently spooned into the measuring cup. Cake flour, however, has a tendency to pack, so sift it before measuring.

Simmer To cook a food in liquid that is kept just below the boiling point. A liquid is simmering when a few bubbles form slowly and burst before they reach the surface.

Skewer A sharp piece of metal or wood used to hold food. Short skewers generally are used to secure meat, poultry, or fish around a filling while it cooks. Longer skewers are used to hold pieces of food, such as meats, poultry, fish, seafood, vegetables, and fruits, for kabobs.

A Tip from Our Kitchen
When threading meats, poultry, fish, and seafood onto skewers, leave at least ¼ inch of space between the pieces. This ensures even cooking and eliminates the raw areas that can occur when foods are crowded together.

Skim To remove a substance from the surface of a liquid. This includes spooning melted fat or grease from meat dishes, removing cream from the surface of nonhomogenized milk, and discarding the foam from boiling jelly and jam.

Slice A flat, usually thin piece of food cut from a larger piece. The term also refers to the process of cutting a food into flat, thin pieces.

Slit A small narrow cut or opening made in a food. Slits may be made in a variety of foods including the top crust of a pie (to allow steam to escape during baking) and a piece of meat (so that flavorful seasonings or a stuffing can be inserted).

Sliver A long, thin piece of food. The term also refers to the process of cutting food into such pieces.

Smorgasbord *(SMOR gus board)* A Swedish term that refers to a buffet that offers a variety of foods and dishes, such as hot and cold meats, hors d'oeuvres, salads, vegetables, breads, and desserts.

The traditional Swedish smorgasbord, or "bread and butter table," includes an assortment of foods that are good eaten with or on buttered bread. Typical selections of a Swedish smorgasbord include pickled herring, herring salad with potatoes and beets, smoked herring with sliced onion, lingonberries, stuffed eggs with fish roe, smoked tongue, Swedish meatballs, liver pâté, fruit salad, and a potato and anchovy dish. Several varieties of bread and cheese also are offered.

Snail A small, soft-bodied mollusk with a spiral shell. Snails also are known by their French name, "escargot." Some types of snails are highly prized in culinary circles. One of these is the tiny *periwinkle*. Snails are sold fresh, canned, and frozen. They often are served in garlic butter and eaten from the shells.

Snickerdoodle A round shaped cookie similar in flavor to a sugar cookie, with a texture that's crisp on the outside and chewy on the inside. The balls of dough are rolled in a mixture of sugar and cinnamon before baking.

(See *Cookie* for Cookie-Making Hints and preparation, baking, storing, and other information.)

Snip To cut a food with kitchen shears or scissors into very small uniform pieces using quick, short strokes.

Soda Another name for the chemical leavening agent baking soda (see also *Baking Soda*).

The term also refers to fruit or cola beverages with carbonation added. These beverages may be called by any of these names—soda, carbonated beverage, soda pop, and pop.

A soda fountain beverage made with ice cream and carbonated water also is referred to as a soda.

It is easy to snip parsley or other fresh herbs in a measuring cup, using kitchen shears, as shown. The markings on the side of the cup give a good indication of the amount chopped.

Sole A flat saltwater fish with a thick, oval body. The lean flesh is fine, white, and delicate to mild in flavor. Authentic sole is imported to the United States from Europe and often is referred to on menus in fancy restaurants as imported Dover sole. In the United States, *lemon* sole, *gray* sole, and *rex* sole, which are actually varieties of flounder, are sold. These fish make good substitutes for sole.

Market forms: Sole fillets and whole fish are sold fresh and frozen. Some also are available breaded and stuffed.

How to cook: See the Cooking Fish chart under *Fish*.

Nutrition information: Baked sole has about 100 calories in one 3-ounce serving.

(See *Fish* for selecting, storing, thawing, and other information.)

Sorbet *(sore BAY)* A frozen dessert similar to sherbet, except that sorbet is made with water, and sherbet is made with milk. This gives sorbet a softer, more icy texture than sherbet. Sugar, fruit, and sometimes gelatin also are ingredients in a sorbet. A small scoop of sorbet occasionally is served as a meat accompaniment or between courses to refresh the palate.

Sorghum A dark, sugary syrup made by boiling down the sweet juice from the canelike stalks of the tall, leafy sorghum (also called sorgo) plant. Often used as a molasses substitute, this thick, sweet, pungent syrup is served as a table syrup. It also is used to sweeten and flavor baked goods. Buy sorghum in some larger supermarkets or in health food stores. Sorghum is most popular in the southeastern part of the United States.

Nutrition information: One tablespoon of sorghum has about 50 calories.

(See *Syrup* for storing information.)

Sorrel *(SOR uhl)* A delicate salad green with smooth, arrow-shaped, bright green leaves. Sorrel has a sharp, lemonlike tang and

Sorrel

can be used raw in salads or cooked as flavoring for soups.

Selecting: Sorrel is available year-round. Look for crisp, bright green leaves with no signs of yellowing.

Storing: Wash fresh sorrel in cold water and pat dry. Place the leaves in a plastic bag lined with a paper towel and store in the refrigerator for up to 3 days.

Nutrition information: One cup of chopped fresh sorrel has about 30 calories.

Soufflé
A light, airy baked egg dish that is made from a thickened sauce combined with stiffly beaten egg whites and such ingredients as cheese and chocolate. A soufflé can be served as a main dish or a dessert.

Q: What is a chilled soufflé?
A: It is an unbaked egg dish with a gelatin base that is chilled and served as a dessert. Sometimes these soufflés are served frozen. (See Using Eggs Safely under *Eggs*.)

Preparation hints: Because overmixing can prevent a soufflé from fully rising, first lighten the sauce with a little of the beaten egg whites. Then gently fold the stiffly beaten egg whites with the other soufflé ingredients only until just mixed. See also *Meringue* for Egg White Pointers.

Use a collar on a soufflé dish when the dish is three-fourths full or more. For collar-making directions, see photo, above right.

Baking hints: For best volume, preheat the oven before starting a soufflé. Once prepared, the soufflé should go right into the oven.

Don't open the oven door to peek while a soufflé is baking—the soufflé could collapse.

Serve a soufflé straight from the oven since it will fall soon after being removed.

Q: What's the best way to serve a soufflé?
A: Using two forks, insert them back to back into the soufflé and gently pull the soufflé apart into serving-size portions. Serve the portions with a large spoon.

Soup
A liquid food that can be served either hot or cold as a first course, main dish, or dessert. There are many different types of soups, from thin and clear to thick and creamy. Soups can be made from meat, poultry, vegetables, seafood, a combination of these, and sometimes fruit.

Selecting soups for a menu: When choosing a soup to serve with a meal, consider the rest of the menu.
☐ If the main dish is rich and filling, serve a light soup, such as a consommé or other clear soup, or a light pureed vegetable soup.
☐ If the main dish is light, serve a hearty soup that will enrich the meal, for instance, a bisque, chowder, or cream soup.
☐ Avoid repeating ingredients or flavors in the soup that are used in other courses.
☐ If a menu has many complicated recipes, choose a simple soup.
☐ If you're planning to serve soup as a main dish, round out the meal with a crisp salad and rolls or crackers.

Health-Conscious Soup Tips
To reduce fat and calories in homemade soup, try these tips.
● Instead of thickening soups with a fat and flour roux or flour and water mixture, puree one or more of the vegetables and return the puree to the soup. Instant mashed potato flakes also work well.
● To remove excess fat from soup, cover and chill it overnight or until the fat solidifies on the surface of the soup. Then lift off the fat and discard it.

When a collar is needed for a soufflé dish, measure the circumference of the top of the dish and add 6 inches. Fold a 12-inch-wide piece of foil lengthwise into thirds.

For a sweet soufflé, lightly butter and sugar (except 3 inches on each end) one side of the foil. For a savory soufflé, sprinkle the buttered foil lightly with grated Parmesan cheese or fine dry bread crumbs.

Attach foil, buttered side in, around the outside of the dish so that the foil extends about 2 inches above the dish. Make a series of locked folds until the foil fits snugly on the dish.

Sour Cream

A thick, smooth dairy product made by the action of a bacterial culture on cream. Most of the sour cream available is made from sweet, light cream and in recipes is referred to as dairy sour cream. In some markets, sour half and half (a comparable product with less fat) is available. Canned imitation sour cream and packaged sour cream sauce mixes are also available.

Q: Is sour cream with a couple of little dots of mold on it OK to use?

A: No—throw it away. In cartons of soft dairy foods, such as sour cream, yogurt, and cottage cheese, little spots of mold on the top usually mean there is mold present throughout the food.

Storing: Keep sour cream tightly covered in the refrigerator for up to 4 weeks. Freezing is not recommended because the sour cream will separate as it thaws.

A Tip from Our Kitchen

To add sour cream to hot sauces or gravies, add it slowly (near the end of cooking if possible) and cook it over low heat to prevent scorching or separating. Unless your recipe calls for some flour to be mixed into the sour cream, do not allow sour cream mixtures to boil.

Nutrition information: One-half cup of dairy sour cream has about 250 calories and 24 grams of fat. One tablespoon has about 30 calories and 3 grams of fat.

Sourdough

Fermented dough originally used instead of yeast in making bread. Today, yeast, flour, water, and sugar are combined in a large bowl to make a sourdough starter. The starter bowl is covered with cheesecloth, and the starter stays at room temperature and ferments till a pleasantly sour flavor develops. The starter then is refrigerated or used with additional leavening in breads, biscuits, coffee cakes, and pancakes to give these foods a tangy flavor.

Tips from Our Kitchen

Follow these tips if you're making a sourdough starter.
- Do not use quick-rising yeast.
- Store the starter in the refrigerator in a glass jar covered with cheesecloth. *Do not cover jar tightly with a metal lid.* The pressure from the bubbling gases could cause the jar to explode.
- Always bring the starter to room temperature before adding it to recipes.

Soy Sauce

A salty, brown liquid commercially made from fermented soybeans, wheat, water, and salt. It is used as a seasoning, most commonly in Oriental cooking.

Varieties: A number of varieties are available, including Chinese and Japanese soy sauces. They range in color from light to dark, in taste from sweet to extremely salty, and in texture from thin to very thick. Low-sodium and sodium-reduced soy sauces also are available.

Nutrition information: Regular soy sauce has about 340 milligrams of sodium per teaspoon. Reduced-sodium soy sauces have about 170 milligrams of sodium per teaspoon. Soy sauce has about 3 calories per teaspoon.

Spaetzle

(SHPET sluh) A small German dumpling or noodle made from a batter that is pressed through a colander into boiling water. The dumplings cook in the water, then they are used in ways similar to noodles. (See *German Cooking* for a recipe.)

Spaghetti A rod-shaped, commercially produced macaroni that is made by pressing a flour and water dough through openings in a metal plate to form long strands. Spaghetti comes in regular, thin, and twisted variations and is available in dried, refrigerated, and frozen forms.

(See *Pasta* for identification photos and storing, how-to-cook, nutrition, and other information.)

Spice The seeds, bark, roots, fruit, or flowers of plants. Spices add flavor and color to sweet and savory dishes. Some plants, such as coriander and dill, actually give us both a spice and an herb (see also *Herb*). Spices vary in flavor and can be hot, sweet, or spicy.

Market forms: Spices are almost always dried and come whole as well as ground.
□ **Whole:** Allspice, aniseed, caraway, cardamom, celery seed, cinnamon, cloves, coriander, cumin, dillseed, fennel seed, gingerroot, mustard seed, nutmeg, pepper (black, green, and white), and saffron are available.
□ **Ground:** Allspice, cardamom, cayenne (red pepper), cinnamon, cloves, coriander, cumin, ginger, mace, mustard, nutmeg, paprika, pepper (black and white), saffron, and turmeric are available.

Selecting: To guarantee that you are using fresh spices, buy them in small quantities and date them. Replace old spices once a year. For suggestions on how to substitute spices, see the Spice Alternative Guide at right.

Q: How can you tell if a spice is fresh?
A: Judge the freshness by the color and aroma. When fresh, most spices have a bright, rich color and a strong aroma when you open the container. If either the color or the aroma seems weak, replace the spice.

Storing: Spices will keep their flavor longer if they're stored in a cool, dry place. Keep them tightly covered because exposure to the air accelerates flavor loss. Generally, whole spices have a longer shelf life than ground spices—whole spices stay fresh up to 2 years and ground spices about 6 months. It's also a good idea to store red spices, such as paprika and red pepper, in the refrigerator; they'll hold their color and keep their flavor longer.

Nutrition information: Like herbs, spices contain virtually no calories, sodium, or fat.

Spice Alternative Guide

Whether you're making an emergency substitution or experimenting with a new flavor, follow these suggestions for spice alternatives. Some of the suggestions are similar flavors, and others are acceptable flavor alternatives. As a general rule, start with *half of the amount* the recipe calls for (unless directed otherwise), and add the spice till it suits your taste.

Allspice: cinnamon; dash nutmeg; or dash cloves
Aniseed: fennel seed *or* a few drops anise extract
Cardamom: ginger
Chili Powder: dash bottled hot pepper sauce plus a combination of oregano and cumin
Cinnamon: nutmeg *or* allspice (use only ¼ of the amount)
Cloves: allspice; cinnamon; *or* nutmeg
Cumin: chili powder
Ginger: allspice; cinnamon; mace; *or* nutmeg
Mace: allspice; cinnamon; ginger; *or* nutmeg
Nutmeg: cinnamon; ginger; *or* mace
Saffron: dash turmeric (for color)

To package spices so they can easily be removed from cooked mixtures, bundle them together in several thicknesses of 100-percent cotton cheesecloth. Then tie them with a string to form a spice bag.

Spinach

Spinach A long-stemmed, dark green vegetable with oval to round leaves. Spinach has a mildly hearty flavor and is equally versatile raw or cooked.

Market forms: You can buy fresh spinach as well as canned spinach and frozen spinach in whole leaf and chopped forms. You also can find prewashed spinach at the supermarket.

Selecting: Fresh spinach should have dark green leaves that are crisp and free of moisture and mold. Avoid spinach with broken or bruised leaves.

Storing: Wash fresh spinach in cold water and pat dry. Place the leaves in a plastic bag lined with a paper towel and store in the refrigerator for up to 3 days.

Preparation hints: If fresh spinach is not already washed, rinse it thoroughly before using because it is very sandy. You may need to rinse it several times.

How to cook: See the Cooking Fresh Vegetables chart under *Vegetable.*

Spinach

Nutrition information: One cup of chopped fresh spinach contains about 10 calories; ½ cup of cooked frozen spinach has about 25 calories.

Sponge Cake A light cake similar to angel food cake in that it depends on beaten egg whites for its airy texture. It's richer and sturdier than angel food cake, however, because it includes egg yolks and sometimes baking powder. Plain sponge cake typically is golden yellow inside with a slightly sweet flavor, but the flavor can be varied with citrus peel, chocolate, or bottled flavorings.

Nutrition information: A 2½-inch slice of plain sponge cake has about 190 calories.

(See *Cake* for How to Solve Cake Problems, Cake-Making Hints, and baking, storing, and other information.)

Spoon Bread A soft, fluffy, baked product, usually based on cornmeal, that's baked in a casserole dish and served with a spoon. Spoon bread usually is served in place of bread, potatoes, or rice.

Spoon Bread

      1½ cups milk
       ½ cup cornmeal
       1 tablespoon margarine *or* butter
       ½ teaspoon baking powder
       ¼ teaspoon salt
       1 beaten egg yolk
       1 stiffly beaten egg white
          Margarine *or* butter (optional)

■ In a medium saucepan stir *1 cup* of the milk into cornmeal. Cook, stirring constantly, till mixture is very thick and pulls away from the sides of the pan. Remove from the heat. Stir in remaining milk, 1 tablespoon margarine or butter, the baking powder, and salt. Stir *1 cup* of the hot mixture into egg yolk; return all to saucepan. Gently fold in beaten egg white. Pour into a greased 1-quart casserole. Bake in a 325° oven for 35 to 40 minutes or till a knife inserted near the center comes out clean. Serve immediately with margarine or butter, if desired. Makes 4 servings.

Nutrition information per serving: 154 calories, 6 g protein, 18 g carbohydrate, 6 g fat (2 g saturated), 62 mg cholesterol, 265 mg sodium, 187 mg potassium.

Parmesan Spoon Bread: Prepare Spoon Bread as in recipe, opposite, *except* omit salt and stir ¼ cup grated *Parmesan cheese* into cooked cornmeal mixture.

Nutrition information per serving: 177 calories, 8 g protein, 18 g carbohydrate, 8 g fat (3 g saturated), 65 mg cholesterol, 226 mg sodium, 193 mg potassium.

Cheesy Corn Spoon Bread: Prepare Spoon Bread as in recipe, opposite, *except* add one 8-ounce can whole kernel *corn,* drained; ½ cup shredded *cheddar cheese* (2 ounces); and 2 tablespoons diced *green chili peppers,* drained, to the cooked cornmeal mixture. Bake for 40 to 45 minutes or till done.

Nutrition information per serving: 234 calories, 11 g protein, 24 g carbohydrate, 11 g fat (5 g saturated), 76 mg cholesterol, 460 mg sodium, 251 mg potassium.

Spread

A food or food mixture that has a consistency soft enough to allow it to be applied over the surface of another food, usually with a knife or spatula. Butter, margarine, sandwich filling, jam, and jelly are all examples of spreads.

The term also refers to the process of applying this food or mixture to another food.

Sprig

A small, leafy shoot from a plant, such as a fresh herb, that is used to flavor or decorate a food.

Sprinkle

To scatter fine particles of a solid food or droplets of a liquid over the surface of another food or a utensil (as when coating baking pans with flour).

Spritz

A rich cookie that's shaped by pressing the dough through a cookie press. These Scandinavian cookies are very tender and have a buttery flavor. Sometimes spritz cookie dough is tinted with food coloring or sprinkled with colored sugar before baking.

(See *Cookie* for Cookie-Making Hints and preparation, baking, storing, and other information.)

Sprout

A seed or bean that buds into an edible shoot. Fresh sprouts make a crunchy addition to sandwiches and salads.

Varieties: Look for these types of fresh sprouts in supermarkets.
☐ **Alfalfa:** Mildly nutty, tiny green and white shoots that come from alfalfa seeds.
☐ **Bean:** Pale, creamy white, crunchy shoots with a nutty flavor from the mung bean (see also *Bean Sprout*).
☐ **Lentil:** A mild, tender, nutty, brown and green sprout from a lentil.
☐ **Radish:** A tender, peppery sprout with a leafy green top that comes from a radish seed.
☐ **Wheat:** A tender, sweet and nutty, brown and green sprout from wheat berries.

Selecting: Fresh sprouts are available year-round. Look for small, tender, healthy shoots with a bright color and crisp texture for the variety.

Storing: Refrigerate sprouts in a plastic bag for up to 4 days.

Sprouts

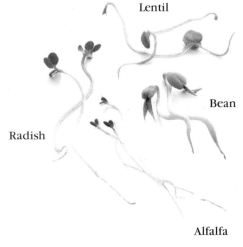

Lentil

Bean

Radish

Alfalfa

Spumoni A multilayered ice cream. Spumoni usually has a chocolate layer, a green layer, and a pink layer. Pistachio ice cream may be used for the green layer and strawberry or raspberry ice cream for the pink layer. Spumoni often is flavored with rum and may contain candied fruits or nuts.

Spumoni is available in supermarkets or Italian specialty stores. To make spumoni, use several different flavors of ice cream and assemble them in layers in a mold; freeze.

Squab A young pigeon, about 4 weeks old, that weighs about 1 pound and has tender, fairly dark meat and a mild flavor.

How to cook: For roasting directions, see the Roasting Poultry chart under *Poultry*. For grilling directions, see the Indirect-Grilling Poultry chart under *Barbecue*.

Nutrition information: A 3-ounce serving of roasted squab without skin and bones has about 180 calories and 10 grams of fat.

(See *Poultry* for selecting, refrigerating, freezing, thawing, cooking, and other information.)

Squash A general term for a group of vegetables that includes hard-shelled, edible gourds and soft-skinned vegetables that grow on vines. Squashes come in round, bulbous, turbanlike, and elongated shapes, and some have brilliantly colored rinds and skins.

Varieties: Traditionally, squashes are classified as summer and winter types. However, these classifications have blurred, because many squashes now are available year-round. Summer squashes generally mature in the summer months, are soft-skinned, and slice easily. Many are delicious raw or cooked. Winter squashes are hard-shelled, generally mature in the fall, and can be stored for winter use. These squashes must be cooked before eating. For the specific varieties, see the Selecting Squash chart, page 386. (See also *Chayote* and *Zucchini*.)

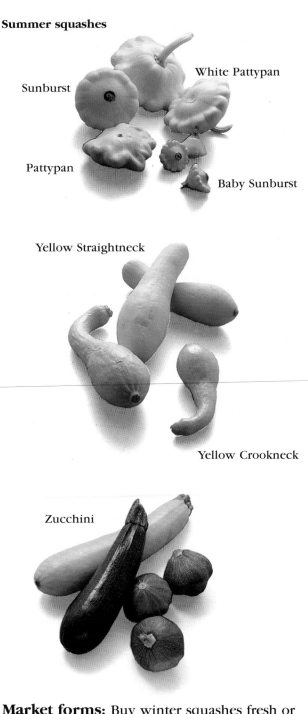

Summer squashes

Sunburst

White Pattypan

Pattypan

Baby Sunburst

Yellow Straightneck

Yellow Crookneck

Zucchini

Market forms: Buy winter squashes fresh or frozen in mashed form. Summer squashes are available fresh, frozen, and canned.

Selecting: Choose a well-shaped squash with good color for the variety. It should be heavy for its size, dry, and free from heavy bruising or cracks.

continued on page 386

Winter squashes

Acorn

Buttercup

Banana

Butternut

Hubbard

Spaghetti

Delicata

Turban

Selecting Squash

The various types of squash differ in flavor, shape, size, and color. Use this guide to become familiar with some of the varieties of winter and summer squashes that are available.

Type	Appearance	Flavor
Winter: Acorn	A medium-size, acorn-shaped squash with a deeply furrowed shell. It may be deep green, gold, or white with bright orange to off-white meat.	Sweet, slightly dry
Banana	A very large squash that usually is sold in pieces. Its shell may be pale orange or creamy white, and its meat is golden yellow.	Hearty, slightly dry
Buttercup	A round squash with a flattened bottom and a small dome shape on top. Its shell is deep green with gray stripes. It has pale yellow meat.	Sweet, slightly dry
Butternut	A long, tan-colored squash with a bulbous end and deep orange meat.	Sweet, rich
Delicata	A long, slender squash with a pale orange shell that has green or sometimes orange streaks. It resembles a miniature watermelon. Its meat is yellow.	Mild, cornlike
Hubbard	A large, irregularly shaped squash with a pale gray to greenish gray shell and orange meat.	Rich, flavorful
Turban	A round squash with a flattened bottom and small knobs on top. Its shell is usually bright orange with green or white streaks. Its meat is bright orange.	Sweet, very rich
Summer: Pattypan	A small scalloped squash with a flattened round shape, pale green to white skin, and off-white meat.	Mildly sweet
Sunburst	A medium to small scalloped squash shaped like a plump pattypan with very bright yellow skin and off-white meat.	Mildly sweet
Yellow	Available in crookneck and straightneck varieties. This squash has bright yellow skin and off-white meat.	Mild, zucchinilike
Zucchini	Usually a slender, elongated squash with green skin and off-white meat. However, globe-shaped and golden or yellow zucchini also are available.	Mildly sweet

Storing: Store winter squashes in a cool, dry place for up to 2 months. Summer squashes and tightly wrapped cut winter squashes can be stored for up to 4 days in the refrigerator.

Preparation hints: Trim off the stems of summer varieties. Unless the skin is bitter, summer squash varieties generally do not have to be peeled.

How to cook: See the Cooking Fresh Vegetables chart under *Vegetable.*

Nutrition information: In general, baked cubed winter squash has about 40 calories in a ½-cup serving; cooked sliced summer squash has about 15 calories per ½ cup.

Q. What is spaghetti squash and how is it served?

A. Spaghetti squash is a bright yellow, football-shaped vegetable with pale yellow, stringy meat that resembles spaghetti when it is cooked. It has a mildly sweet flavor and can be served in a variety of ways. Cook it following the directions in the Cooking Fresh Vegetables chart under *Vegetable.* Then remove the pulp as shown below. If desired, toss the strands with margarine or butter, and sprinkle with grated Parmesan cheese. Or, top it with spaghetti sauce or another sauce.

To serve spaghetti squash, use a fork to rake the stringy pulp from the shell. Hold on to the hot squash half with a hot pad.

Squid A saltwater shellfish that has 10 tentacles and is related to the octopus. The firm, white meat is mild and generally takes on the flavor of ingredients with which it's cooked. Squid also is known by its Italian name, calamari.

Fresh squid is available whole or processed into tubes, rings, or strips. Frozen squid is sold cleaned. Squid also can be found smoked and dried. If the squid you buy is not already cleaned, follow the how-to directions, far right, for cleaning.

Nutrition information: Squid has the highest cholesterol content of any shellfish; however, it is low in saturated fat. One 3-ounce serving of poached squid has about 200 milligrams of cholesterol and about 90 calories. Three ounces of fried squid has about 220 milligrams of cholesterol and 150 calories.

Stale A term used to describe food, especially a bread or cereal product, that is no longer fresh but has not yet become spoiled.

Starch Any food that is used as a thickening agent for liquid mixtures. The most common starches include flour, cornstarch, tapioca, and arrowroot. They are used in such foods as sauces, gravies, pie fillings, puddings, soups, and stews.

The term also is used to refer to a digestible carbohydrate of many types of plants, especially vegetables and grains, that is colorless, odorless, and tasteless. Starches and starchy foods, such as breads, cereals, pasta, rice, corn, potatoes, peas, and beans, are essential to a healthy diet. They provide energy, fiber, vitamins, and minerals.

Steak au Poivre *(oh PWAV ruh)* A main dish featuring beefsteak that is coated generously with crushed black peppercorns, then quickly cooked in a skillet. It may be flamed with brandy.

Steak au Poivre

2 **beef top loin steaks, cut 1 inch thick (1¼ to 1½ pounds total)**
1 **to 2 teaspoons whole black peppers**
1 **tablespoon margarine** *or* **butter**
1 **tablespoon cooking oil**
2 **tablespoons cognac** *or* **other brandy**
2 **tablespoons water**
¼ **teaspoon instant beef bouillon granules**

■ Cut each steak into 2 equal pieces; slash fat on edges of steaks at 1-inch intervals. Coarsely crack the peppers with mortar and pestle. Sprinkle both sides of steaks with pepper, pressing into surface. Let steaks stand at room temperature for 30 minutes.
■ In a large skillet or blazer pan of chafing dish, heat margarine or butter with oil. Cook steaks over medium-high heat to desired doneness, turning once. (Allow 12 to 14 minutes total cooking time for medium doneness.) Season steaks with salt, if desired. Remove skillet from heat. Remove steaks and keep them warm. Cool pan 1 minute.
■ Combine cognac or brandy, water, and bouillon granules and gradually add to meat juices in skillet. Bring to boiling; cook 1 minute, stirring to scrape up browned bits in pan. Pour over steaks. Makes 4 servings.

Nutrition information per serving: 290 calories, 31 g protein, 3 g carbohydrate, 16 g fat (5 g saturated), 81 mg cholesterol, 163 mg sodium, 429 mg potassium.

Steak Diane A main dish for which beefsteak is thinly pounded and sometimes seasoned with dry mustard. Then the meat is cooked, usually in a chafing dish, at the table. A mixture of pan drippings, lemon juice, chives or shallots, and Worcestershire sauce is poured over the finished meat.

1. To clean squid, firmly grasp the head. Then pull the head, tentacles, and entrails out of the body (pouch). Discard any entrails that remain in the body.

2. Pull out and discard the clear cartilage pen (quill) that serves as a backbone. With your fingers, peel the skin off the outside of the body, leaving body whole. Rinse body and pat dry.

3. Using a sharp knife, cut the head away from the tentacles. Discard the head and rinse tentacles; pat dry.

Steak Sauce   A liquid mixture of sweet, sour, and salty ingredients, usually in a tomato base, that is served on such meats as steaks, burgers, and chops. Ingredients in commercially prepared sauces vary from one brand to the next, but can include corn syrup or molasses, raisins, vinegar, soy sauce, and spices.

Steak Tartare   *(tar TAR)* A mixture of lean raw ground beef, onion, seasonings, and sometimes egg or egg yolk. The mixture is served as an appetizer spread on bread or crackers, or as a main dish in individual mounds. Because of possible bacterial contamination in raw ground meat and eggs, serving this dish is no longer recommended.

Steam   To cook a food in the vapor given off by boiling water. The food usually is placed in a pan on a rack just above, but not touching, the water. The pan then is covered to retain the steam. Foods may be steamed in a variety of utensils—everything from metal steamer baskets and other special steamers to a colander set into a saucepan.

Steep   To allow a food, such as tea, to stand in water that is just below the boiling point in order to extract flavor or color.

Sterilize   To destroy microorganisms that can cause spoilage and disease in food by applying heat to the food. Foods usually are sterilized to prevent food-borne illnesses and to prolong storage. Unlike some of the methods of food preservation in which the microorganisms remain present but their growth and activity are slowed, sterilization destroys the organism itself.

Stew   A mixture of foods—commonly meat, poultry, or fish plus vegetables and seasonings—that is cooked in liquid for a long time till the meat and vegetables are tender. A stew may be made either on top of the range or in the oven, usually in a covered pot. It differs from a soup in that the pieces of food are larger and the liquid often is thickened slightly before serving.

The term also refers to the process of cooking a food in liquid for a long time, usually in a covered pot.

Stir   To mix ingredients with a spoon or other utensil to combine them. Foods also are stirred during cooking to prevent sticking and to help them cook evenly.

A Tip from Our Kitchen
A *heat-resistant* rubber scraper is an excellent stirring utensil, especially when making a thickened sauce. With a scraper, you can clean all of the mixture from the bottom and sides of the saucepan so that the mixture stays in motion and cooks evenly without sticking or scorching.

Stir-Fry   An Oriental cooking technique in which pieces of meat, poultry, seafood, and/or vegetables are cooked quickly over high heat with constant stirring. Traditionally, a large, deep, slope-sided pan called a wok is used. The term stir-fry also is used to describe a finished dish prepared using the method of stir-frying.

Stir-frying hints: Here are some cooking techniques to try when preparing food by stir-frying.
☐ If you don't have a wok, use a large, deep skillet. The high sides on the skillet make it easy to stir and toss foods without making a mess.

continued

Vegetable-Stick Stir-Fry
(see recipe, page 390)

☐ Prepare all the ingredients and have them ready for the stir-fry. Some vegetables, such as fresh green beans or thick slices of carrot, take longer to cook than others. You may want to precook these vegetables in boiling water for a short time before adding the drained vegetables to a stir-fry mixture.

☐ Add the measured amount of cooking oil to the wok, lifting and tilting the pan to distribute the oil evenly over the bottom. Then preheat the pan over medium-high heat about 1 minute. To test the oil's hotness, add a vegetable piece; if it sizzles, proceed with the recipe.

☐ Don't overload your wok or skillet. If too much of any one item, especially meat, poultry, or seafood, is added at one time, the wok cools and the food stews rather than fries. Add no more than 12 ounces of meat, poultry, or seafood at a time. If your recipe calls for more meat than this, stir-fry half of the meat at a time.

☐ Stir-fry vegetables before the meat, poultry, or seafood so you use less cooking oil.

Vegetable-Stick Stir-Fry

  6 ounces fresh green beans, bias-sliced into 1-inch pieces (1½ cups)
  3 tablespoons cold water
  1 tablespoon soy sauce
  1 teaspoon sugar
  1 teaspoon cornstarch
    Dash ground ginger
    Dash pepper
  1 tablespoon cooking oil
  2 medium carrots, cut into julienne strips (1 cup)
  1 medium zucchini, cut into julienne strips (1½ cups)
  6 green onions, bias-sliced into 1-inch pieces (1¼ cups)

■ Cook green beans, covered, in a small amount of boiling salted water for 5 minutes; drain. For sauce, stir together cold water, soy sauce, sugar, cornstarch, ginger, and pepper. Set sauce aside.

■ Pour cooking oil into a wok or large skillet. (Add more oil as necessary during cooking.) Preheat over medium-high heat. Stir-fry carrots and beans in hot oil for 2 minutes. Add zucchini and onion; stir-fry for 2 to 3 minutes or till vegetables are crisp-tender. Push vegetables from center of the wok or skillet.

■ Stir sauce. Add sauce to center of the wok or skillet. Cook and stir till thickened and bubbly. Cook and stir for 30 seconds more. Stir in the vegetables to coat with the sauce. Serve immediately. Makes 4 servings.

Nutrition information per serving: 85 calories, 3 g protein, 12 g carbohydrate, 4 g fat (0 g saturated), 0 mg cholesterol, 278 mg sodium, 438 mg potassium.

Stock The thin, clear liquid in which the bones of meat, poultry, or fish are simmered with vegetables and herbs. Stock typically is richer and more concentrated than broth and gels when it is chilled. Stock can be used as a base for soups, stews, and sauces.

A popular type of stock is brown stock. For this stock, the bones and vegetables are browned before they're simmered to develop a richer flavor and color.

A Tip from Our Kitchen
To clarify homemade stock, first separate an egg. (Save the yolk for another use.) In a small bowl combine the egg white and ¼ cup cold water. In a Dutch oven or kettle, stir the egg white mixture into hot, strained stock. Bring to boiling. Remove from the heat and let stand 5 minutes. Place a large sieve or colander lined with several layers of damp 100-percent cotton cheesecloth over a large bowl. Pour the stock mixture through the cloth to strain out any particles.

Strain
To filter a food or beverage, usually by using a cloth or fine wire sieve.

Strata
A baked casserole made by layering ingredients, commonly bread and cheese, and often adding meat, poultry, fish, or vegetables. An egg-milk mixture then is poured over the layers.

A Tip from Our Kitchen
Strata is a great make-ahead meal because the assembled dish often needs to stand several hours or overnight in the refrigerator before baking to completely moisten the bread.

Curried Shrimp Strata

        1   6-ounce package frozen peeled,
              cooked shrimp
        ½   of a 1-pound loaf of French bread,
              cubed (about 6 cups)
      1½   cups shredded Swiss cheese
              (6 ounces)
        4   beaten eggs
      2¼   cups milk
        1   tablespoon curry powder
        2   green onions, sliced
        ½   teaspoon salt
              Dash pepper

■ Thaw shrimp. Drain well. In an 8x8x2-inch baking dish, layer *half* of the bread cubes. Top with cheese and shrimp. Arrange remaining bread cubes on top.
■ In a medium mixing bowl combine eggs, milk, curry powder, green onions, salt, and pepper. Pour mixture over layers in baking dish. Cover and refrigerate at least 1 hour or overnight.
■ Bake, uncovered, in a 325° oven for 50 to 55 minutes or till a knife inserted near the center comes out clean. Let stand 5 minutes before serving. Makes 6 servings.

Nutrition information per serving: 289 calories, 21 g protein, 25 g carbohydrate, 11 g fat (5 g saturated), 219 mg cholesterol, 584 mg sodium, 305 mg potassium.

Strawberry
A soft, heart-shaped, mildly sweet berry that's bright red with a green cap. Strawberries have tiny, edible, yellow seeds embedded throughout.

Market forms: Peak months for fresh strawberries are March through August. In addition to fresh berries, you'll find frozen whole and sliced berries, unsweetened as well as in syrup. Strawberry jams and preserves also are sold.

Strawberries

Selecting: Look for plump, fresh-looking berries with bright green caps and a healthy red color. Choose fully-ripened berries because strawberries do not ripen after picking. Size does not indicate quality; the largest berries aren't necessarily the most flavorful. Avoid bruised, wet, or mushy-looking berries.
    If you harvest berries at a pick-your-own patch, pick berries leaving the caps on.

Preparation hints: Do not wash or hull berries until you're ready to use them. A strawberry huller or small sharp knife is handy for removing the green caps.

(See *Berry* for the Selecting Berries chart, including calories, and storing information.)

Streusel
A crumbly mixture of flour, sugar, margarine or butter, and often spices, nuts, rolled oats, or granola. The mixture is sprinkled on top of coffee cakes, muffins, fruit crisps, and pies before baking.

String Cheese
Cheese that is pulled into long ropes during its manufacture. It is made using a variety of methods that usually involve soaking in a salty brine or vinegar.
    String cheese is a form of mozzarella and can be made with mozzarella only or combined with other cheeses. The flavor and nutrition content are similar to the cheese from which it's made.

String cheese

continued

Another type of string cheese, often called Syrian-style cheese, is sold at some ethnic food stores or gourmet markets. This type comes in longer ropes and usually is soaked in water before serving to rid it of excess salt from processing.

(See *Cheese* for selecting, storing, serving, nutrition, and other information.)

Stroganoff *(STROW guh noff)* A term that is used to describe a main dish that features pieces of meat (usually beef) in a thickened sauce made with sour cream. The dish also may contain mushrooms and onions. It often is served over noodles.

Nutrition hint: Save calories by substituting plain low-fat yogurt for the dairy sour cream.

Beef Stroganoff

- 1 **pound beef tenderloin steak *or* sirloin steak**
- 2 **tablespoons all-purpose flour**
- 1 **8-ounce carton dairy sour cream**
- ½ **cup water**
- 2 **teaspoons instant beef bouillon granules**
- ¼ **teaspoon pepper**
- 2 **tablespoons margarine *or* butter**
- 1½ **cups sliced fresh mushrooms**
- ½ **cup chopped onion**
- 1 **clove garlic, minced**
- 2 **cups hot cooked noodles**

■ Partially freeze beef. Thinly slice across the grain into bite-size strips. Combine flour and sour cream. Stir in water, bouillon granules, and pepper. Set aside. In a large skillet cook and stir *half* of the meat in the margarine or butter over high heat till done. Remove.
■ Add remaining meat, mushrooms, onion, and garlic. Cook and stir till meat is done and onion is tender. Return all meat to skillet. Add sour cream mixture. Cook and stir over medium heat till bubbly. Cook and stir 1 minute more. Serve over hot cooked noodles. Makes 4 servings.

Nutrition information per serving: 486 calories, 31 g protein, 29 g carbohydrate, 27 g fat (12 g saturated), 122 mg cholesterol, 624 mg sodium, 601 mg potassium.

Strudel A dessert made from layers of tissue-thin dough that surround a fruit or cheese filling. The name comes from the German word for whirlpool, which describes the look of the many spirals in a slice of strudel.

Strudel dough is a simple flour, water, egg, and margarine or butter mixture. The dough generally is stretched on a large, floured, cloth-covered surface until it is so thin you can see through it. The stretching task is accomplished by using the palms of your hands, working underneath the dough, and gently stretching from the middle, working to the edges from one corner to the next. The thinly stretched dough makes for a very flaky pastry when baked.

After stretching, the filling is spread near one edge of the dough. Then it is rolled up as you would a jelly roll. Traditionally, the roll is bent into a crescent or horseshoe shape before baking. Strudels are best when eaten warm just after baking.

A Tip from Our Kitchen
To save some work when making strudel, you can substitute frozen phyllo dough sheets that have been thawed for the strudel dough. Stack two sheets of phyllo on a large pastry cloth (do not brush butter between the sheets). Arrange another stack of two sheets on the cloth, overlapping the stacks 2 inches. Repeat with additional stacks of two phyllo sheets, making a rectangle the size called for in your strudel recipe.

Stuffing

A seasoned mixture, based on bread cubes or crumbs, rice, crumbled corn bread, or potatoes, that is used to fill the body cavities of whole fish or poultry; pockets made in meats; meat, fish, or poultry rolls; or hollows in vegetables. Stuffings often contain other ingredients, such as vegetables, meats, or seafood.

Q: **What can I do with the extra stuffing that doesn't fit in a turkey or chicken?**
A: Place the extra stuffing in a casserole and bake it in the oven with the bird during the last 30 to 45 minutes of cooking. The stuffing cooked inside the bird usually will be more moist because it absorbs juices during cooking. So, if you like moist stuffing, add a little liquid to the stuffing in the casserole before heating.

A Tip from Our Kitchen

Don't stuff foods until just before you're ready to cook them. If a stuffed item, especially a whole chicken or turkey, is refrigerated or allowed to stand, harmful bacteria may develop that might not be destroyed during cooking. You can prepare the stuffing ahead, but refrigerate it separately, then add it before cooking.

1. To stuff a turkey, begin by spooning some of the stuffing mixture into the neck cavity. Skewer the opening closed. Loosely spoon additional stuffing into the body cavity.

2. To finish preparing the turkey, tuck the legs under the band of skin across the tail. If the band is not present, tie the legs and tail together with string.

Substitution

See *Emergency Substitutions* chart, page 446.

Succotash

A vegetable dish made by cooking whole kernel corn and lima beans together. Green beans sometimes are substituted for the lima beans.

Suet

(SUE uht) The hard, white fat found in the loin and kidney regions of meat animals. Beef suet is the type usually called for in recipes, such as mincemeat.

Sugar

A crystalline, usually white sweetener that technically is a carbohydrate and is known as sucrose. It is made primarily from sugar beets and sugarcane. A small proportion of sugar also comes from the maple tree, sorghum plant, and certain palms, such as wild date palms.

Sugar generally is used as a flavoring and sometimes as a preservative. It also has properties that are essential to the structure, texture, and appearance of recipes, especially baked goods.

Q: **How much difference is there between cane sugar and beet sugar?**
A: There is no noticeable difference in taste and cooking properties. Some brands that are cane sugar indicate that on the package.

Market forms: The forms of sugar differ in the way they dissolve, their degree of sweetness, and the rate at which they are fermented by yeast. Because of these differences, recipes generally are developed using a specific form of sugar.
☐ **Brown:** A processed mixture of granulated sugar and molasses that is moist when fresh. Light brown sugar has less molasses flavor, and dark brown sugar has more. Brown sugar tends to produce dense, chewy cookies and cakes. Brown sugar also is sold in liquid form. The liquid brown sugar cannot be used in recipes interchangeably with regular brown sugar. Check label for specific uses.

continued

□ **Granulated:** A white, granular, crystalline sugar. There are several kinds of granulated sugar on the market. The most commonly available granulated sugar is known as fine. Superfine (also called ultrafine or caster sugar) is a finer grind of sugar that dissolves readily, making it ideal for frostings, meringues, and drinks. Granulated sugar is sold in loose, cube, and packet forms.

Granulated fructose is another type of granulated sweetener that sometimes is found at the supermarket. Equal to beet or cane sugar in calories, fructose can be up to twice as sweet, depending on temperature and other conditions. Some cooks use it in baking because less is needed; however, the texture of foods made with it may suffer unless the recipes followed have been specifically formulated for its use.

□ **Powdered or Confectioners':** Refined white granulated sugar that has been pulverized. Manufacturers usually add a small amount of cornstarch to prevent caking. Packages may or may not specify the grind, but they usually contain either very fine or ultrafine grade sugar. Powdered sugar often is used in uncooked dishes such as frostings and coatings because it doesn't produce a grainy texture.

□ **Raw:** Unprocessed sugar that typically contains impurities. It is illegal to sell raw sugar in the United States because it has so many impurities. Anything labeled raw sugar in the U.S. has been processed in some way to make it clean. *Turbinado sugar* is partially refined and is available in many health food stores and some supermarkets.

□ **Other:** Sugar mixtures, such as colored sugar and cinnamon sugar, also are sold. Fresh sugarcane is another specialty item that may be found in larger supermarkets or in some specialty markets. It comes in stick form and is eaten like candy.

A Tip from Our Kitchen
Take the edge off the acidity of the tomatoes in chili and spaghetti sauce by adding ½ teaspoon or so of sugar.

Q: **If the word sugar is absent from the ingredients list on a label, can the food still contain sugar?**

A: Yes. Keep an eye out for the suffix "ose." Dextrose, fructose, lactose, maltose, and sucrose, for instance, are all forms of sugar. Syrups, such as corn syrup and molasses, are another form of sugar.

Storing: If you store them in an airtight container in a cool, dry place, all sugars will keep indefinitely. Transfer brown sugar that comes in a box to a heavy plastic bag or a rustproof, airtight container and seal well. Keep powdered sugar dry in an airtight plastic bag or container.

Q: **What can I do with brown sugar that has hardened or has formed lumps?**

A: Empty the hardened brown sugar into a rustproof container and place a piece of plastic wrap or foil on top of the sugar then a damp paper towel. Cover the container tightly. The sugar will absorb the moisture and become soft in 8 to 12 hours. After the sugar has softened, remove the paper towel, then keep the container tightly closed.

If you need to quickly soften brown sugar for use in a recipe, try this microwave oven technique. In a 1-cup microwave-safe measure, micro-cook ½ cup water, uncovered, on 100% power (high) for 1 to 2 minutes or till boiling. Place the brown sugar in a microwave-safe container near the water. Heat, uncovered, on high till softened. Allow 1½ to 2½ minutes for ½ pound brown sugar, and 2 to 3 minutes for 1 pound.

Nutrition information: Packed brown sugar and granulated sugar each contain about 50 calories per tablespoon; sifted powdered sugar has about 25 calories per tablespoon.

Sugar Substitute
An ingredient sold as a powder, liquid, or tablet that simulates the sweetness of natural sugar. Also known as low-calorie sweeteners, sugar substitutes may

have calories, but their calorie counts generally are so low they're negligible.

Types: There are several low-calorie sweeteners you can look for on sugar substitute labels. Common ones are *aspartame, saccharin,* and *acesulfame-K.* Aspartame is made from amino acids and has about 180 times the sweetening power of sugar. Because it loses sweetness with prolonged exposure to high heat, it should be added to recipes after cooking. Saccharin has about 300 times the sweetening power of sugar and, to some people, leaves a slightly bitter aftertaste. Acesulfame-K is 200 times sweeter than sugar, and it works well in heated products.

Substituting Sweeteners

When replacing sugar with sugar substitutes, read labels carefully. For best results, look for recipes formulated with your brand of sweetener. Here are some tips for cooking with sugar substitutes.
● Sugar substitutes generally have more sweetening power than sugar, so a little goes a long way. Check the product label to determine its sugar equivalent. In recipes, you may find you need less than the exact sugar equivalent.
● When you need the bulk that sugar provides, as in baked goods, use saccharin-based sweeteners for up to half (but not all) of the sugar. Note that the baked item won't have the same volume it would have if made with all sugar. (Aspartame is not recommended because it can lose sweetness when heated.)
● To mask the slight aftertaste saccharin can sometimes leave, add a little fruit or fruit juice.

Sukiyaki *(ski YAHK ee)* A Japanese stew of thinly sliced meat, assorted vegetables, and other Oriental foods in a broth flavored with soy sauce. Beef usually is used, but sometimes chicken, pork, or seafood is featured. Vegetables often include green onion, celery, and mushrooms, plus other ingredients, such as tofu, bok choy, or bamboo shoots.

Sunchoke See *Jerusalem Artichoke.*

Sundae A festive dessert or snack made from scoops of ice cream with an ice-cream topping, such as hot fudge or caramel sauce. A sundae also may be topped with whipped cream, nuts, fruit, or candies.

Sunflower Seed The seed of certain varieties of the sunflower plant. The small, oval, tan kernel is encased in a thin, black and white outer shell. Sunflower seeds without the shells sometimes are referred to as sunflower kernels or nuts.

Keep in-the-shell and sunflower seeds without shells in an airtight container in the refrigerator or freezer. Store in-the-shell seeds and raw kernels for up to 1 year and roasted kernels for up to 4 months.

Market forms: The majority of sunflower seeds are pressed into oil. Besides sunflower oil, supermarkets carry shelled sunflower seeds in raw and roasted forms with roasted seeds being available salted and unsalted. These products can be used in baking as well as for sprinkling on salads or eating as a snack. Salted and unsalted in-the-shell sunflower seeds also are available for snacking.

A Tip from Our Kitchen

When baking with shelled sunflower seeds, avoid using recipes that call for baking soda. A chemical reaction between the sunflower seeds and the soda sometimes causes the baked product to take on a blue or green tint. There is no danger from the reaction, but the appearance is unattractive.

Surimi Seafood (suh REE me)

Processed fish that is flavored and re-formed to make restructured seafood products. It's typically made from Alaskan pollock, a lean, mild, saltwater fish. The seafood product often is shaped into sticks, chunks, flakes, or nuggets that resemble shellfish. Imitation crabmeat is the most popular product, but simulated lobster, shrimp, and scallops also are made. Surimi seafood has about 80 calories in a 3-ounce serving.

A Tip from Our Kitchen

Surimi seafood products are already cooked, so they can be used in cold dishes, such as salads, without further cooking. When used in hot dishes, a thorough heating is all that's needed.

Sushi (SUE she) A Japanese delicacy

featuring vinegared cooked rice that is wrapped in fish (either raw, cooked, or smoked) or seaweed. *Maki* refers to sushi that is rolled in seaweed, often with thin strips of vegetables and a layer of cooked egg in addition to the rice and fish. *Nigiri* is vinegared rice that is shaped by hand, rather than rolled, into small oval portions and wrapped or topped with fish or seafood.

Sweet-and-Sour Sauce A sauce

made by combining sweet and tart ingredients, such as sugar and vinegar. Homemade sweet-and-sour sauce usually is thickened slightly with cornstarch and may contain soy sauce and fruit juices. Sometimes pineapple chunks and bell peppers are added.

Jars of sweet-and-sour sauce are available at the supermarket.

Sweetened Condensed Milk

A concentrated milk made from whole milk to which sugar is added and from which more than half the water is removed. It is sealed in cans.

Sweetened condensed milk is cream-colored, smooth, thick, and sticky and is usually used in candies and desserts. Do not substitute sweetened condensed milk for evaporated milk in recipes.

Storing: Store unopened cans of sweetened condensed milk at room temperature for up to 6 months. To retain the best flavor once a can has been opened, transfer any unused milk to another covered container. Store in refrigerator and use it within 3 days.

Nutrition information: One cup of undiluted sweetened condensed milk has about 980 calories and 27 grams of fat.

Sweetener A substance added to food

and beverages to make them taste sweet. Sweeteners can be dry or liquid and can contain few or many calories. The caloric ones, which are used by the body to produce energy, include natural sugars, such as granulated and brown sugars, honey, maple products, molasses, sorghum, and other syrups. Low-calorie sweeteners, such as aspartame and saccharin, are not used by the body and contribute only a few calories to the diet (see also *Sugar Substitute*).

Sweet Potato A large root vegetable

that often is confused with a yam (see *Yam*). Sweet potatoes can be round, elongated with bulbous centers and tapered ends, or slim and tapering.

Sweet potatoes fall into two categories: moist and dry. The skin of the dry type is usually yellowish tan or brown. Its cream-colored to yellow meat is dry and crumbly after being cooked, much like a white baking

Sweet potatoes

potato, and its flavor is not sweet. The skin color of most moist types ranges from copper to dark orange. This type's sweet, bright orange flesh cooks to a much moister texture. The moist sweet potato often is erroneously labeled a yam in many supermarkets.

Market forms: Fresh sweet potatoes are available year-round, with peak seasons being the fall and winter. You also can buy canned and frozen sweet potatoes in syrup and vacuum-packed sweet potatoes.

Selecting: Look for small to medium, smooth-skinned potatoes that are firm and free of soft spots and blemishes.

Storing: Sweet potatoes are not good keepers. Store them in a cool, dry, dark place for up to 1 week.

How to cook: See the Cooking Fresh Vegetables chart under *Vegetable.*

Nutrition information: One baked sweet potato has about 120 calories, and it also contains vitamin A.

Swiss Chard A mild salad green that's actually a member of the beet family. Swiss chard is sometimes referred to as chard.

One variety has crinkly green leaves attached to an enlarged white stem. Another variety, known as rhubarb chard, has dark green leaves and a scarlet stem. The stems of both varieties have a delicate celerylike taste, and the leaves have a hearty spinach flavor.

Selecting: Fresh Swiss chard is available all year, but peak time is summer through early fall. Choose crisp and unblemished leaves. Yellow leaves indicate overmaturity.

Storing: Wash fresh Swiss chard in cold water; pat dry. Place it in a plastic bag lined with a paper towel and store in the refrigerator for up to 3 days.

Preparation hints: Cut the leaves from the stems. Use the large leaves to line salad bowls or mix them with other torn greens in a salad. The sliced stalks can be added to soups and stews, and the leaves and stems can be cut up and used in stir-fries or cooked and eaten as a side dish.

Nutrition information: One cup of fresh chopped Swiss chard has 6 calories; ½ cup of cooked Swiss chard has about 20 calories.

Swiss chard

Swiss cheese

Jarlsberg cheese

Swiss Cheese

A creamy, pale yellow cow's-milk cheese with a firm, smooth texture and mellow or mild, nutty taste. Swiss cheese is easily recognized by its holes or "eyes" that are scattered throughout the cheese. Holes are caused by the expansion of gas within the cheese during ripening.

Types: There are many domestic and imported Swiss cheeses available in your supermarkets. Here's a summary.

□ **Domestic:** A smooth-textured cheese with a mild flavor and large holes.

□ **Emmentaler** *(EM uhn tall er):* A firm-textured cheese with a sweet, nutlike flavor. It also is called Switzerland Swiss.

□ **Gruyère:** A firm-bodied cheese with a mild, nutty flavor that is sharper than Swiss cheese. It has few, if any, holes (see also *Gruyère Cheese*).

□ **Jarlsberg** *(YARLS berg):* A smooth, firm-textured, Norwegian Swiss cheese with small holes and a very mild flavor. Jarlsberg is white to light yellow and has a thick natural rind covered with a yellow wax.

(See *Cheese* for the Selecting Cheese chart and selecting, storing, serving, nutrition, and other information.)

Swiss Steak

A main dish traditionally made with pounded beef round steak, either left whole or cut into serving-size pieces. The meat is browned then cooked slowly in liquid (usually tomatoes or beef broth). Often celery, onion, carrot, and green pepper are added. Swiss steak can be made either on top of the range or in the oven.

Swiss Steak

- 1 pound beef round steak, cut ¾ inch thick
- 2 tablespoons all-purpose flour
- ¼ teaspoon salt
- ¼ teaspoon pepper
- 1 tablespoon cooking oil
- 1 16-ounce can tomatoes, cut up
- 1 small onion, sliced and separated into rings
- ½ cup sliced celery
- ½ cup sliced carrot
- ½ teaspoon dried thyme, crushed
- 2 cups hot cooked rice *or* noodles

■ Cut meat into 4 serving-size pieces. Trim fat. Combine the flour, salt, and pepper. With a meat mallet, pound flour mixture into meat. In a large skillet brown meat on both sides in hot oil. Drain fat.

■ Add *undrained* tomatoes, onion, celery, carrot, and thyme. Cover and cook over low heat about 1¼ hours or till meat is tender. Skim fat. Serve with hot cooked rice or noodles. Makes 4 servings.

Oven directions: Cut meat for Swiss Steak into 4 serving-size pieces. Trim fat, pound, and brown in the skillet as above. Transfer meat to an 8x8x2-inch baking dish. In the same skillet combine *undrained* tomatoes, onion, celery, carrot, and thyme. Bring to boiling, scraping up any browned bits in the pan. Pour over meat. Cover and bake in a 350° oven about 1 hour or till tender. Skim fat. Serve with rice or noodles.

Nutrition information per serving: 364 calories, 27 g protein, 40 g carbohydrate, 10 g fat (3 g saturated), 63 mg cholesterol, 397 mg sodium, 707 mg potassium.

Crockery cooker directions for Swiss Steak: Cut meat into 4 serving-size pieces and trim fat as in recipe, opposite. Omit flouring and pounding meat. Brown meat in hot oil. In a 3½- or 4-quart electric slow crockery cooker, place onion, celery, and carrot. Sprinkle with thyme, 2 tablespoons *quick-cooking tapioca,* ¼ teaspoon *salt,* and ¼ teaspoon *pepper.* Pour *undrained* tomatoes over vegetables. Add meat. Cover and cook on low-heat setting for 10 to 12 hours. Skim fat. Serve with rice or noodles.

Nutrition information per serving: 366 calories, 27 g protein, 42 g carbohydrate, 10 g fat (3 g saturated), 63 mg cholesterol, 397 mg sodium, 704 mg potassium.

Swordfish A large saltwater fish with an upper jawbone that extends to a bladelike point. Found worldwide, swordfish weigh several hundred pounds and are very difficult to catch, making them a prized game fish and one of the more expensive fish on the market.

The meat varies in color. It can be off-white, tan, pink, or orange. The meat is very firm and dense with a distinctive flavor.

Market forms: Swordfish is sold fresh or frozen and is cut into steaks or sometimes chunks.

How to cook: Methods of cooking swordfish steaks include broiling, baking, and grilling. For baking and broiling directions, see the Cooking Fish chart under *Fish.* For grilling directions, see the Direct-Grilling Fish chart under *Barbecue.*

Nutrition information: One 3-ounce serving of broiled swordfish has about 130 calories.

(See *Fish* for selecting, storing, thawing, and other information.)

Syrup A sweet, pourable, and often sticky liquid used for sweetening. A syrup usually is a solution of sugar and liquid, and may be flavored. Syrups often are used as toppings.

Types: Besides maple, molasses, and sorghum (see individual entries), one of the most common types of syrup you'll find at the supermarket is *corn syrup.* It is the liquid form of sugar refined from corn, and it comes in light and dark forms. Light corn syrup is bland and is less sweet than sugar. Dark corn syrup has caramel coloring and flavoring added and tastes similar to molasses. Corn syrup often is used in candy and frosting recipes because it keeps other sugars from crystallizing and thus produces a smooth, creamy texture.

Fruit-flavored syrups are used as pancake and waffle toppings as well as flavorings. One of the most common fruit-flavored syrups is grenadine, a sweet, deep red syrup made from fruits. It often is used to add sweetness and color to cocktails.

Chocolate-flavored syrup, another familiar syrup, is used as a topping for ice cream and dessert recipes.

Q: **What are simple sugar syrups and how are they commonly used?**
A: They are mixtures of sugar and water that often are heated to dissolve the sugar. Sugar syrups are used primarily in canning and freezing fruit.

Storing: An unopened bottle of syrup keeps for up to 1 year on the shelf in a cool, dry place. After you open a bottle, check the label for storing directions.

Be on the lookout for mold or bubbles on the surface of the syrup. These are signs of spoilage. If they're present, discard the syrup.

Preparation hints: When measuring syrup, use a glass or clear plastic measuring cup placed on a level surface. Then bend down so that your eye is level with the marking you want to read on the cup.

To keep the bottle caps from sticking on and making the bottle difficult to open, wipe the outside of the bottle, especially the lip, with a damp cloth after each use.

Nutrition information: One tablespoon of corn syrup or grenadine has about 60 calories. One tablespoon of chocolate-flavored syrup has about 45 calories.

Fruit Trifle
(see recipe, page 414)

T-Z

Tempura
(see recipe, page 406)

Wontons with Pork and Shrimp
Filling *(see recipe, page 442)*

Taco A Mexican food made with crisp corn tortilla shells or soft flour ones. The tortillas are filled with (or wrapped around a filling of) seasoned cooked meat or poultry. Refried beans, taco sauce, shredded cheese, chopped tomato, shredded lettuce, and sliced green onion also may be added.

Taffy A chewy candy made by boiling a sugar syrup. After it is cooked and cooled, the thick candy mixture is pulled, folded, and twisted by hand till it is light and creamy. Then it is pulled into long strands, cut into bite-size pieces, and individually wrapped so it doesn't get soft and sticky during storage.

Q: Does saltwater taffy really have salt water in it?
A: Saltwater taffy was introduced at New Jersey seashore resorts and got its name from its oceanside location. It doesn't contain salt water, although it does contain salt.

A Tip from Our Kitchen
After *a lot* of pulling, folding, and twisting, test a taffy mixture to see if it is ready to snip by tapping it on a work surface. If it cracks, it is ready.

(See *Candy* for Candy-Making Tips and equipment, storing, and other information.)

Tahini *(tuh HEE nee)* A smooth paste made from sesame seeds used as an ingredient to flavor Middle Eastern dishes and as a spread for bread.

Tamale *(tuh MAL ee)* A filled and steamed breadlike dish popular in Mexico. A tamale is made by spreading a cornmeal dough, called masa, on a corn husk, a piece of foil, or a piece of parchment, then topping the dough with either a spicy meat or sweet dessert filling. The dough is rolled around the filling and enclosed in the corn husk, foil, or parchment before it is steamed.

A Tip from Our Kitchen
When making tamales, it usually is convenient to make several at one time because of the quantities in which the ingredients are packaged. Freeze extra homemade tamales in freezer wrap and resteam them another time.

Tamarillo *(tam uh RILL oh)* A small, oval fruit with shiny red or yellow skin, a long green stem, and soft meat that contains small black seeds arranged like tomato seeds. The fruit has a pleasantly tart flavor and benefits from cooking and added sugar. The yellow variety is the sweetest.

Selecting: Tamarillos are imported from New Zealand and usually are available throughout the year, although there is a gap in the growing season in late winter. Look for firm, heavy fruit with no bruises or soft spots.

Storing: Let tamarillos ripen at room temperature until they yield slightly to

Tamarillos

pressure and become fragrant. Keep ripe tamarillos in the refrigerator for up to 1 week.

Preparation hints: Before eating a tamarillo, remove the bitter skin. The quickest way to do this is to plunge the fruit into boiling water for 30 seconds. Rinse it in cold water, then pull off the skin using a knife. Slice, chop, or quarter the fruit and sweeten it, if you like, with sugar or honey.

Nutrition information: Tamarillos have about 40 calories per fruit.

Tangelo

A citrus fruit in the mandarin family that is a hybrid created by crossing a tangerine and a grapefruit. Oval to round in shape, tangelos have light to deep orange skin that peels easily and a pale yellow to deep orange interior. Tangelos are juicy with a tangy-sweet orange flavor and few seeds.

Varieties: *Orlando* tangelos are light to deep orange in color with a pebbly peel. *Minneola* tangelos have a distinctive knob at one end and a deep orange to red-orange color.

(See *Citrus Fruit* for the Selecting Citrus Fruit chart and storing and nutrition information.)

Minneola tangelos

Tangerines

Sunburst

Fairchild

Robinson

Tangerine

A small, round variety of citrus fruit with bright orange, pebbly peel, and orange-colored meat with seeds. Tangerines are in the mandarin family. They are sweet and have a thin skin—often referred to as a "zipper" peel—that's exceptionally easy to peel.

Varieties: There are a number of tangerine varieties. One common variety you may find is the the sweet-tasting *Dancy* tangerine, a deep red-orange fruit. Other varieties include the *Robinson*, a larger tangerine with a richer, sweeter taste. The *Fairchild* is similar in size and flavor to the Dancy, but is a deeper orange in color. The *Honey* (also known as *Murcott)* tangerine has yellow-orange skin with reddish pulp and a honey-sweet flavor. *Sunburst* is a bright orange, smooth-skinned fruit with juicy, sweet pulp.

Selecting: Tangerines are sold from October through April. Look for well-shaped, brightly colored fruit without bruises or soft spots.

(See *Citrus Fruit* for the Selecting Citrus Fruit chart and storing and nutrition information.)

Tannin A natural plant substance that gives an astringent or puckery taste to foods. Tannins are especially noticeable in underripe fruits such as bananas and persimmons and in coffee, tea, or red wine.

Tapa *(TAH puh)* A Spanish word for a hot or cold hors d'oeuvre served with cocktails at bars and restaurants. Tapas are served in a large assortment and often take the place of a meal. They can be eaten as finger food, with toothpicks or from wooden skewers. Tapas are varied and can include pickled, stuffed, or grilled vegetables, sliced cured meats, grilled meat kabobs, and sausages.

Tapioca A starch extracted from the roots of the tropical cassava plant, used to thicken various cooked dishes. When cooked, most forms of tapioca don't dissolve completely; instead, the tiny particles become clear. Tapioca is an excellent thickener for foods that are going to be frozen, because unlike flour- and cornstarch-thickened mixtures, tapioca mixtures retain their thickness when reheated.

Store tapioca in a cool, dry place and it will keep for up to 2 years.

Market forms: Tapioca can be purchased in the following three forms.
☐ **Quick-Cooking:** Used as a thickener in puddings, fruit pies, desserts, and occasionally soups. When cooked, the small granules become clear.
☐ **Pearl:** Lesser-known type of tapioca that's usually made into a cooked pudding similar to rice pudding. The small, pearl-like balls must be soaked before using.
☐ **Tapioca Flour:** Finely ground form of tapioca that can be used as quick-cooking tapioca. The flour also is known as tapioca starch. Usually found at Oriental specialty shops, tapioca flour dissolves completely when used to thicken mixtures.

At the end of the cooking time, quick-cooking tapioca should be clear (spoon on the right). If it's not (spoon on the left), continue cooking for a few more minutes.

Tips from Our Kitchen
● Quick-cooking tapioca is perfect for using in your crockery cooker to thicken soups and stews and to make gravy for pot roasts. It is better than flour and cornstarch for two reasons. First, it doesn't need to be stirred during cooking to prevent it from settling. Second, it can withstand long cooking times without breaking down.
● If you find some small pieces of quick-cooking tapicoa objectionable in cooked products, you may want to grind the dry tapioca in a blender or food processor till it resembles the texture of cornmeal. It will be less noticeable in a cooked dish.

Taro Root *(TAHR oh)* The potatolike root of a tropical plant that has dark, hairy skin and firm, light-colored flesh. Used in Oriental and Polynesian cooking, the starchy root can be baked or boiled. It usually is served as a vegetable, but it also can be used to make puddings. Taro root is used in preparing poi, a famous dish served at Hawaiian luaus.

Tarragon *(TARE uh gun)* An herb with slender, green leaves, that is spicy, sharp, and aromatic with licoricelike overtones. Fresh tarragon is most plentiful in the summer; dried tarragon is available in whole leaf form.

Tarragon

Tarragon also is a popular flavor of vinegar that is excellent on salad greens. The jars of vinegar often come with a sprig of tarragon in them.

(See *Herb* for the Herb Alternative Guide and selecting, storing, preparation, cooking, nutrition, and other information.)

Tart

A single-serving-size pie that can be either sweet or savory and usually is prepared without a top crust. The bottom crust can be made from either plain or rich pastry or from cookie or cracker crumbs.

The term also refers to a full-size pie that is prepared in a special pan with straight sides and a removable bottom. Tarts with sweet fillings are served as desserts, and savory tarts can be main dishes or appetizers.

Tart also refers to a sharp or sour taste in foods.

Tartar Sauce

A mayonnaise-based sauce that contains finely chopped ingredients, such as pickles, onions, parsley, and lemon juice or vinegar. Tartar sauce traditionally is served with fried fish.

Commercially prepared tartar sauce is available at the supermarket, or it can be prepared easily at home, starting with purchased mayonnaise or salad dressing.

Tartar Sauce

- 1 **cup mayonnaise *or* salad dressing**
- ¼ **cup finely chopped sweet *or* dill pickle *or* sweet *or* dill pickle relish, drained**
- 1 **tablespoon finely chopped onion**
- 1 **tablespoon snipped parsley**
- 1 **tablespoon diced pimiento**
- 1 **teaspoon lemon juice**

■ In a mixing bowl combine mayonnaise or salad dressing, pickle or pickle relish, onion, parsley, pimiento, and lemon juice. Cover and chill for at least 2 hours before serving. Store in the refrigerator up to 2 weeks. Serve with fish or seafood. Makes 1¼ cups (twenty 1-tablespoon servings).

Nutrition information per tablespoon: 83 calories, 0 g protein, 1 g carbohydrate, 9 g fat (1 g saturated), 7 mg cholesterol, 84 mg sodium, 13 mg potassium.

Low-Fat Tartar Sauce: Prepare Tartar Sauce as left, *except* substitute ⅔ cup *reduced-calorie mayonnaise or salad dressing* and ⅓ cup plain *yogurt* for the mayonnaise. Omit lemon juice.

Nutrition information per tablespoon: 34 calories, 0 g protein, 2 g carbohydrate, 3 g fat (1 g saturated), 3 mg cholesterol, 75 mg sodium, 18 mg potassium.

Tea (beverage)

A beverage made from tea leaves of the *Camellia sinensis* plant that is served hot or iced.

Types: Here are the basic kinds of tea.
□ **Black:** A fermented tea. Black tea is extensively fermented, making it the strongest, richest, and most mellow of teas. Despite the name, black tea in many cases is dark brown in color. Darjeeling is an example of an unblended black tea.
□ **Blends:** Most commercial brands are made from a blend of black teas. Some popular gourmet blends include English Breakfast and Irish Breakfast teas.
□ **Green:** A nonfermented tea. Green tea has a pungent flavor with a slightly astringent bite. It is milder than black or oolong teas. Dragon Well is the name of a high-quality unblended green tea.
□ **Oolong:** A semifermented tea. Oolong tea is processed in the same way as black tea but isn't fermented as long. This gives oolong a richer, mellower flavor than green tea, but not as strong and rich as black tea. Formosa Oolong is an unblended oolong tea.

Q: What are herbal "teas"?
A: Although they may look like tea, herbals have no biological relationship to tea. In fact, they should be called tisanes, which is a general name for tealike beverages made with ingredients such as herbs. Some well-known herbs used in making these tealike beverages include chamomile, lemon verbena, and mint.

continued

Market forms: Teas are packaged as loose leaves or in individual tea bags and are sold in regular and decaffeinated forms. Instant iced tea powder also is a popular and convenient form of tea. It comes both regular and decaffeinated in many varieties including plain, flavored, and presweetened.

Q: What's a good way to brew loose tea?
A: There are a couple of ways to brew loose tea. One is to add boiling water directly onto the tea. This method requires you to strain the tea before you serve it.

Another way is to steep tea in an infuser. An infuser is a small ball- or spoon-shaped container with tiny holes that lets the water in, but doesn't let the tea leaves out. An infuser allows easy and quick removal of tea leaves so the tea doesn't become too strong. It also eliminates the need for straining.

Storing: You can store tea at room temperature for up to 2 years, as long as it's kept in an airtight container. Be sure to store different teas separately so they maintain their own distinct flavors.

Nutrition information: The amount of caffeine in tea varies with each type. When compared cup for cup, tea usually contains less caffeine than instant and brewed coffees.

Tea (occasion)   A semiformal or informal party, usually held in the late afternoon, at which people gather for a light snack and a beverage. Tea is offered, but other beverages also may be served. The foods often include dainty sandwiches, cakes, pastries, fancy cookies, nuts, and mints.

Tempura   *(tem PURE uh)* A Japanese dish in which seafood (usually shrimp or scallops), vegetables, and parsley sprigs are dipped in a light batter and deep-fat fried. The foods are served with a soy sauce for dipping.

Tips from Our Kitchen
- To minimize spattering when making tempura, make sure that seafood, vegetable, and parsley pieces are thoroughly dried before coating with batter and frying.
- Choose a pan that is large enough to allow space for the cooking oil to bubble high when food is added.
- Fry only a few pieces of food at a time to keep them from sticking together as they cook and to keep the cooking oil from foaming over the edge of the pan.
- Use a deep-fat frying thermometer to check the temperature of the cooking oil. Maintaining the proper temperature will help ensure that the food pieces cook evenly and have a crisp coating.

Tempura

12 ounces fresh *or* frozen shelled medium shrimp *or* scallops
 1 small sweet potato, peeled and sliced ¼ inch thick
 1 cup halved fresh mushrooms *or* eggplant cut into 1-inch cubes
 3 ounces fresh green beans *or* fresh asparagus, cut into 2-inch pieces
 3 green onions, cut into 2-inch pieces
 ¾ cup parsley sprigs
   Tempura Dipping Sauce
   Tempura condiments (optional)
     Grated gingerroot
     Grated daikon
     Lemon *or* lime wedges
   Cooking oil for deep-fat frying
 1 slightly beaten egg yolk
 1 cup ice water
 1 cup all-purpose flour

■ Thaw shrimp or scallops, if frozen; rinse. Using paper towels, thoroughly dry the shrimp or scallops, vegetables, and parsley. Prepare Tempura Dipping Sauce and, if desired, Tempura condiments. In a wok, deep-fat fryer, or 2-quart saucepan, heat 1½ to 2 inches oil to 365°.

■ Just before frying, prepare batter. In a medium mixing bowl mix egg yolk and ice water. Add flour; stir just till combined.

■ To serve, give each person a small bowl of dipping sauce. Pass condiments; add to sauce, as desired. Dip seafood, vegetables, and parsley into batter. Fry, a few pieces at a time, for 2 to 3 minutes or till light golden, turning once. Remove from oil; drain well. Dip into sauce mixture. Makes 6 servings.

Tempura Dipping Sauce: In a saucepan combine 1 cup *Dashi (fish stock) or chicken broth,* ¼ cup *sake or dry sherry,* ¼ cup *soy sauce,* and 1 teaspoon *sugar.* Bring to boiling, stirring till sugar dissolves. Serve warm with batter-coated seafood and vegetables. Makes 1½ cups.

Nutrition information per serving (with sauce): 397 calories, 13 g protein, 25 g carbohydrate, 26 g fat (4 g saturated), 109 mg cholesterol, 910 mg sodium, 317 mg potassium.

Tenderize
One of several methods by which the tough fibers of meat are made shorter so the meat is easier to eat. Meat can be tenderized chemically by using a marinade or a commercial meat tenderizer. It can be tenderized mechanically by grinding it, scoring it with a knife, or pounding it with a mallet. Also, long, slow cooking with moist heat will tenderize meat.

Q: My meat mallet has a coarse-toothed side, a fine-toothed side, and flat sides. How do I know which side to use?

A: Use the coarse-toothed side to break up tough fibers in large or less tender pieces of beef or pork. Use the fine-toothed side for more tender, thinly sliced meat, such as veal. This side breaks up fibers without tearing the meat. Use a flat side when you want to flatten already tender meat or boneless poultry, such as pork tenderloin slices or chicken breast halves.

Teriyaki
(tare ee YAHK ee) A Japanese dish in which meat, poultry, fish, or seafood is marinated in a sweetened soy sauce and wine mixture, then broiled or barbecued, usually on skewers. During cooking, the food is basted with the reserved marinade.

A Tip from Our Kitchen
The wine in teriyaki marinade not only adds flavor but also helps tenderize the food. Japanese wines, such as mirin or sake, usually are used, but you can substitute dry sherry, if you like.

Tetrazzini
(teh truh ZEE nee) A main dish that includes cooked chicken or turkey, pasta, mushrooms, almonds, and a rich cream sauce flavored with sherry. Often the mixture is sprinkled with Parmesan cheese.

Chicken Tetrazzini

      6 ounces spaghetti, broken
      3 tablespoons margarine *or* butter
  1½ cups sliced fresh mushrooms
      ¼ cup chopped green pepper
      ¼ cup all-purpose flour
      ¼ teaspoon salt
  1½ cups light cream *or* milk
      1 cup chicken broth
  2½ cups chopped cooked chicken *or* turkey
      2 tablespoons dry sherry (optional)
      ¼ cup grated Parmesan cheese
      ¼ cup sliced almonds

■ Cook spaghetti according to package directions. Drain; set aside. Meanwhile, in a large saucepan melt margarine. Add mushrooms and pepper. Cook till tender.

■ Stir flour and salt into mushroom mixture. Add light cream or milk and broth all at once. Cook and stir till thickened and bubbly. Stir in chicken or turkey and, if desired, sherry. Add spaghetti; toss to coat.

■ Turn into a 12x7½x2-inch baking dish. Sprinkle with Parmesan cheese and sliced almonds. Bake in a 350° oven for 20 to 25 minutes or till hot. Makes 5 or 6 servings.

Nutrition information per serving: 486 calories, 33 g protein, 36 g carbohydrate, 23 g fat (9 g saturated), 89 mg cholesterol, 505 mg sodium, 445 mg potassium.

Thermometer
An instrument for measuring cooking temperature.

A Tip from Our Kitchen
A candy thermometer can be checked for accuracy by submerging the tip in boiling water. It should read 212°. When you cook, adjust your cooking temperatures according to how much the thermometer reading varies from 212°. For example, if it reads 210° when the water boils, cook the food to a temperature 2 degrees lower than your recipe specifies. If it reads 214°, cook to 2 degrees higher.

Types: There are several kinds of thermometers used in cooking.

☐ **Candy/Deep-Fat Frying:** Used when making candy, some frostings, and sugar syrups and when frying foods in a large quantity of cooking oil or shortening. This thermometer is marked with the stages of candy making, such as thread, soft-ball, and hard-crack. Most candy thermometers also have markings for deep-fat frying temperatures.

☐ **Meat:** A pointed thermometer used to check the internal temperature of meat and poultry. This thermometer usually is marked with the stages of doneness, such as rare, medium, and well, and with the internal temperatures that match these stages.

☐ **Microwave:** A thermometer manufactured with less metal so it can be left in foods during cooking in the microwave oven.

☐ **Oven:** Used to verify that an oven is heating correctly, it is calibrated to match oven temperatures. To check the accuracy of your oven, set the oven control to 350° and preheat oven with the oven thermometer in place. The thermometer should also read 350° after preheating. If the temperatures don't match, have the oven control adjusted by a service technician.

☐ **Refrigerator:** Used to verify that a refrigerator or freezer is chilling correctly. If the temperatures don't match, have the controls adjusted.

Q: Can I use my regular meat thermometer in the microwave oven?
A: No. The metal in some thermometers can cause arcing (sparking). Select a thermometer that has been especially designed for use in microwave ovens.

Thickening Agent
A food substance used to give a thicker consistency to a mixture, such as sauces, gravies, puddings, and soups. The most common agents are cornstarch, egg yolk, flour, and tapioca.

There are two ways to prepare flour and cornstarch thickeners before they are stirred into another mixture. Either gradually stir cold liquid into the flour or cornstarch, or combine the starch and cold liquid in a screw-top jar and shake till thoroughly combined. Then stir into the mixture that needs thickening and keep stirring to prevent lumps from forming.

Thyme
(time) A strong-flavored herb with small, oval, grayish green leaves. Thyme has a heavy, spicy aroma and pungent clove-

Thyme

Lemon thyme

like taste. Another variety that may not be as familiar is *lemon* thyme, which has a delicate, lemon fragrance. Thyme leaves are available fresh, dried, and ground.

Q: What kinds of foods does thyme go with?

A: Thyme is a versatile, all-purpose herb that works well with other herbs such as basil and oregano, especially in tomato mixtures. Try lemon thyme in veal, poultry, and seafood dishes.

(See *Herb* for the Herb Alternative Guide and selecting, storing, preparation, cooking, nutrition, and other information.)

Tilapia *(tuh LAHP ee uh)* A lean freshwater fish with white, firm flesh. It has a mild, subtly sweet flavor. In some areas this fish is called American redfin. Where available, it usually is sold as fillets.

Timbale *(TIM bull)* A custard or creamed mixture that includes meat, vegetables, or fish and is baked in individual molds. The term also refers to the mold itself, which usually is round.

A timbale also can be a deep, round, edible cup or shell that is filled with a creamed mixture. The edible shell can be cooked pasta, rice, or potato. Or, it can be a pastry shell made by dipping a specially shaped iron into a batter then deep-fat frying it.

Toast A slice of bread that is exposed to heat so it becomes browner, crisper, and drier. The term also refers to browning, crisping, or drying a food by exposing it to heat. Coconut, nuts, and seeds sometimes are toasted to develop a fuller flavor and color.

Toffee A crunchy candy similar to brittle, but not as hard, that is made with a large amount of butter, giving it a very rich flavor (see also *Brittle*). Toffee often is spread with melted chocolate and topped with nuts.

A Tip from Our Kitchen

It is important to use butter when making toffee. When margarine is used, the fat separates out onto the surface of the candy.

(See *Candy* for Candy-Making Tips and equipment, storing, and other information.)

Tofu *(TOH foo)* Soybean curd that is made from soybean milk by a process similar to the one used for making cheese. It is sold in blocks or cakes. Tofu also is known as bean curd and is white or cream-colored and has a custardlike texture. Although it is almost tasteless by itself, tofu easily absorbs other flavors. Especially popular in Oriental cooking, tofu is fully cooked and may be cubed for use in stir-fries and casseroles, or pureed for dips and dressings.

Tofu

Market forms: Tofu may be purchased fresh or in an aseptic package. Fresh tofu generally is packed in water and sold in containers. This fresh product is found in the store's refrigerated case where it should be kept below 45°.

Aseptically packaged tofu is shelf stable and should be kept in a cool place. Because of the sterile packaging methods it undergoes, this type of tofu needs no refrigeration until it is opened.

Tofu is available in soft, firm, and extra-firm style. The soft type is good for whipping, blending, and crumbling. Use firm tofu for slicing and cubing. Extra-firm tofu is good for stir-fried dishes.

continued

Storing: Fresh tofu should be refrigerated, covered with water, in an airtight container. It can be stored this way for up to 1 week. Change the water daily to keep the tofu fresh and moist. It may be frozen up to 3 months, but freezing causes the texture to become less tender.

For shelf-stable tofu, follow label directions for place and length of storage.

Nutrition information: A ½-cup portion of regular tofu contains about 95 calories, 10 grams of protein, 6 grams of fat, and no cholesterol. (This information varies by brand and type of tofu, so the figures are only a guide. Soft tofu, for example, is usually a little lower in calories, but it's also lower in protein than firm tofu.)

Tomatillo *(toe muh TEE yo)* A small, olive green fruit that's covered with a thin, papery, brown husk, which is removed before using. Despite the name and appearance, tomatillos are not related to tomatoes. Their texture is like that of a firm tomato (with lots of seeds), and their flavor is rather acidic with hints of lemon and apple.

Tomatillos are popular in Mexican and Tex-Mex cooking. They're also called Mexican green tomatoes.

Tomatillos

Selecting: Fresh tomatillos are available year-round. Look for firm tomatillos with tight-fitting, dry husks. Avoid shriveled and bruised ones. Canned, husked tomatillos also are available.

Storing: Cover and refrigerate fresh tomatillos for up to 10 days.

Nutrition information: One-half cup of cooked tomatillos has about 50 calories.

Tomato A juicy, smooth-skinned, seed-filled fruit. Tomatoes, however, typically are used as vegetables in savory rather than sweet dishes. They have a juicy texture and mildly sweet, rich flavor.

Types: There are numerous varieties of tomatoes available. Here are some of the types most frequently found in supermarkets.
☐ **Common:** A rounded or slightly oval tomato that comes in all sizes and can be red, orange, or yellow. It has a firm, juicy texture.
☐ **Plum-Shaped:** A medium to small, oval-shaped tomato. Sometimes called Italian or Roma tomatoes, these red or yellow tomatoes are thick and meaty with small seeds, little juice, and a mild, rich flavor. They are especially good for canning and using in sauces.
☐ **Cherry:** A bite-size tomato about 1 inch in diameter with bright red or yellow skin and a sweet flavor.
☐ **Pear-Shaped:** A bite-size tomato that resembles a miniature pear. It has red or yellow skin and a mild, sweet flavor.

Market forms: In addition to fresh tomatoes, you'll find canned tomato juice, tomato paste, sauce, and puree, as well as canned whole, cut-up, and stewed tomatoes. You'll also find sun-dried whole and sliced tomatoes.

Selecting: Look for plump, well-shaped fresh tomatoes that are fairly firm-textured and bright-colored for the variety. Avoid bruised, cracked, or soft tomatoes.

Tomatoes

Plum-shaped

Common

Yellow cherry

Red cherry

Storing: If fresh tomatoes need to ripen, store them at room temperature in a brown paper bag or in a fruit ripening bowl with other fruits. Don't stand them in the sun to ripen or they will become mushy. When ripe, tomatoes will yield slightly to gentle pressure. Freezing tomatoes is not recommended if you plan to use them fresh because they soften when thawed. Frozen tomatoes can be used, however, in soups, stews, and casseroles.

Preparation hints: Before using, wash tomatoes thoroughly. Then remove and discard the stem end, core, and bruised areas, if any. If desired, scoop out the seeds before using tomatoes for recipes. You also can strain the seeds after pureeing.

Serve fresh tomatoes as soon as possible after slicing. They begin to juice out several minutes after being sliced. For tossed salads, add tomato pieces after tossing the salad with its dressing. This way the tomatoes won't thin the dressing.

Q: **Should tomatoes always be peeled?**
A: No. When eating tomatoes uncooked in salads or sandwiches, the skin helps the tomatoes hold their shape, so leave the skin on. Peel fresh tomatoes when you use them cooked in recipes where the skins would be difficult to eat—for example, in chili or spaghetti sauce.

To peel tomatoes, plunge them into boiling water for ½ minute, then rinse them in cold water. Remove the skins with a paring knife.

Nutrition information: A fresh medium-size tomato or ½ cup canned tomatoes has about 25 calories and is an excellent source of vitamin C.

Torte A rich dessert made of layers of cake, a tender pastry, or hard meringue; a filling, such as custard, fruit, or whipped cream; and a frosting or whipped cream topping. Frequently, in tortes made with cake layers, ground nuts or bread crumbs are substituted for all or part of the flour in the cake, and the only leavening in some is the air that is incorporated into the eggs.

Torte Favorites
Here are descriptions of some classics.
● **Black Forest Torte:** Made with chocolate cake, cherry filling, chocolate frosting, and whipped cream.
● **Blitz Torte:** Made with cake layers covered with a meringue then browned.
● **Dobos Torte:** Made with six or seven layers of cake, a chocolate buttercream filling, and a caramel glaze.
● **Linzer Torte:** Made with a pastry that includes ground almonds and spice and a raspberry jam filling; it is topped with the pastry in a lattice pattern.
● **Sacher Torte:** Made with chocolate cake, apricot filling, and chocolate icing.
● **Schaum Torte:** Made with layers of hard meringue, fruit, and whipped cream.

Tortilla *(tor TEE yuh)* A small, thin, flat round Mexican bread that is baked (but not browned) on a griddle or skillet. Tortillas can be made from corn or wheat flour.

To store homemade tortillas, stack them between sheets of waxed paper, wrap them in freezer bags, and freeze for up to 6 months.

Refrigerated corn and flour tortillas are available and should be stored according to their package directions. Canned corn tortillas also are available.

Q: What's the difference between corn and flour tortillas?

A: Corn tortillas, made from very finely ground, specially prepared corn, have a coarse texture and are usually about 6 inches in diameter. These off-white or yellow tortillas traditionally are used in such dishes as enchiladas, tacos, and tostadas. Flour tortillas, made from wheat flour, have a smoother texture than corn tortillas and are rolled very thin; they are usually 8 to 10 inches in diameter. White flour tortillas usually are used in dishes such as burritos and chimichangas.

Nutrition information: Depending on the recipe or brand, corn tortillas have anywhere from 45 to 70 calories. Flour tortillas have anywhere from 80 to 160 calories.

Tortoni A frozen dessert made of ice cream or whipped cream and almonds or macaroons. Tortoni also may include maraschino cherries and may be flavored with rum, sherry, or liqueur.

Toss To mix ingredients lightly by lifting and dropping them using two utensils, such as spoons or forks. Foods are tossed to evenly distribute the ingredients, but not completely combine them, as in the case of a lettuce salad that is tossed with salad dressing.

Tostada *(toe STAHD uh)* A flat, fried tortilla topped with assorted foods. This Mexican dish usually uses corn tortillas. The layered toppings often include refried beans or bean dip; seasoned ground, shredded, or chopped cooked meat or poultry; mashed avocado or guacamole; shredded lettuce; chopped tomato; olives; and shredded cheese. For ease in making tostadas, you can purchase flat, fried tortillas called tostada shells.

Chicken Tostadas

    2 cups shredded lettuce
    2 tablespoons salad oil
    1 tablespoon lemon juice
    1 tablespoon vinegar
    1 10½-ounce can jalapeño bean dip
    ¼ cup salsa *or* taco sauce
    1 small ripe avocado, seeded and
         peeled
    1 tablespoon lemon juice
    4 tostada shells
    1¾ cups cubed *or* shredded cooked
         chicken
    1 medium tomato, chopped
    ½ cup shredded cheddar *or* Monterey
         Jack cheese (2 ounces)
    ¼ cup sliced pitted ripe olives

■ In a medium bowl combine lettuce, salad oil, 1 tablespoon lemon juice, and vinegar. Toss to mix well. In another bowl stir together the bean dip and salsa or taco sauce; set aside. In a small bowl use a fork to mash avocado. Stir in 1 tablespoon lemon juice; set aside.

■ To serve, place a tostada shell on each of 4 dinner plates. Divide ingredients equally among tostadas, layering in the following order: bean dip mixture, avocado mixture, chicken, and lettuce mixture. Drizzle with any remaining liquid from the lettuce mixture. Top with tomato, cheese, and olives. Makes 4 servings.

Nutrition information per serving: 447 calories, 28 g protein, 28 g carbohydrate, 26 g fat (6 g saturated), 67 mg cholesterol, 809 mg sodium, 904 mg potassium.

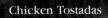
Chicken Tostadas

Trifle
A layered dessert of English origin. A trifle starts with sponge cake, ladyfingers, or macaroons that are sprinkled with sherry, wine, or brandy. Layers of fruit or fruit jam and pudding or custard are added. The trifle is topped with whipped cream and decorations of fruit, candied fruit, or nuts.

Fruit Trifle

  ¼   cup sugar
  3   tablespoons all-purpose flour
  2   cups milk
  3   beaten egg yolks
  1   teaspoon lemon peel
  1   teaspoon vanilla
  1   3-ounce package (12) ladyfingers, split
  2   tablespoons cream sherry
  2   small peaches, peeled, pitted, and chopped (1 cup)
  1   cup sliced fresh strawberries
  1   cup whipping cream
  2   tablespoons sugar
  1   teaspoon vanilla
  ⅓   cup currant jelly
  1½ cups whole fresh strawberries

■ For pudding, in a medium saucepan combine the ¼ cup sugar and the flour. Stir in milk. Cook and stir over medium heat till thickened and bubbly. Cook and stir for 2 minutes more. Remove from heat. Gradually stir about *half* of the hot mixture into beaten egg yolks. Return all of the egg mixture to the saucepan. Bring to a gentle boil. Reduce heat. Cook and stir for 2 minutes more. Remove from heat; stir in lemon peel and 1 teaspoon vanilla. Pour pudding into a bowl. Cover the surface with plastic wrap. Cool about 30 minutes.

■ In a 1½-quart soufflé dish or serving bowl, arrange *half* of the split ladyfingers on bottom and sides. Sprinkle with *half* of the sherry. Top with peaches. Spoon *half* of the pudding atop. Arrange remaining ladyfingers atop; sprinkle with remaining sherry. Spoon sliced strawberries over ladyfingers. Top with remaining pudding. Chill at least 4 hours.

■ One hour before serving, whip cream with the 2 tablespoons sugar and 1 teaspoon vanilla to soft peaks. Spread about *half* of the whipped cream atop pudding. Use pastry tube and tip to pipe remaining whipped cream around edge. Melt jelly. Toss the whole strawberries with jelly; place atop whipped cream layer. Makes 8 servings.

Nutrition information per serving: 301 calories, 5 g protein, 37 g carbohydrate, 15 g fat (9 g saturated), 164 mg cholesterol, 60 mg sodium, 272 mg potassium.

Triticale
(triht uh KAY lee) A hybrid cereal grain developed by crossing wheat and rye. Triticale kernels are gray-brown, oval-shaped, and longer and thinner than wheat. Triticale has a nutty, wheatlike taste. It is sold toasted and flattened into flakes and ground into flour. Use the flour in breads.

Storing: Store triticale flour in an airtight container in a cool, dry place for up to 1 month, or freeze for up to 1 year. Keep other forms of triticale in an airtight container in a cool, dry place for up to 6 months.

Q: How can I use triticale flour?
A: Add triticale flour to muffins, drop biscuits, cookies, and pancakes. When making yeast bread, combine triticale flour (which is low in gluten) with wheat flour just as you would other flours that are low in gluten.

Trout
A fish of the salmon family found mostly in freshwater lakes and streams. Trout vary in color, texture, and flavor depending on the trout's diet and species. The meat can be white, pale yellow, orange, pink, or red.

Types: Many different species of trout live in the lakes and streams of the United States. Some of the common trout species include *Rainbow, Steelhead, Brook,* and *Lake.* Other species of culinary interest include *Brown, Dolly Varden, Cutthroat,* and *Golden* trout.

Market forms: Most of the trout you'll see are rainbow trout. Fresh rainbow trout are sold dressed, dressed and boned, and butterflied. These forms, as well as breaded trout, also are marketed frozen. In addition, trout can be found smoked, and in some stores, sold live in tanks as lobsters are.

How to cook: Small dressed trout often are panfried. The steaks from larger trout are good broiled. Trout also can be baked and poached. Whole trout can be stuffed. For cooking directions, see the Cooking Fish chart under *Fish.*

Nutrition information: A 7- to 8-ounce baked rainbow trout with head and tail has about 165 calories.

(See *Fish* for selecting, storing, thawing, and other information.)

Truffle *(TRUFF uhl)* A rich, French candy made with melted chocolate, butter, cream, and sometimes eggs, and often flavored with liquor. The candy mixture is cooled, then dropped from a spoon or shaped into balls and rolled in cocoa powder or chopped nuts, or dipped in chocolate.

A truffle also is an edible fungus that grows underground near oak trees and is valued for its aroma and delicate flavor. A truffle is round, with a wrinkled surface, and is anywhere from the size of a walnut to that of an orange. Because truffles cannot be cultivated, they are extremely rare and expensive. Two highly prized varieties are the dark brown or black truffle of France and the white truffle of Italy. Truffles are sold fresh and canned in some gourmet specialty stores.

Chocolate Truffles

- ⅔ **cup whipping cream**
- 3 **tablespoons unsalted butter**
- 1 **tablespoon sugar**
- 6 **squares (6 ounces) semisweet chocolate, chopped**
- 2 **tablespoons desired liquor (optional) (choose brandy, amaretto, coffee liqueur, rum, whiskey, *or* currant liqueur)**
- ¼ **cup unsweetened cocoa powder**
- ¼ **cup sifted powdered sugar**

■ In a 1-quart saucepan combine the whipping cream, unsalted butter, and sugar. Cook and stir till butter is melted and mixture is very hot (180°). Remove from heat. Stir in the semisweet chocolate till melted and well mixed. Stir in liquor, if desired. Transfer mixture to a chilled bowl. Cover and chill 1 hour or till mixture is completely cool, stirring often.

■ Drop mixture from a level tablespoon onto a baking sheet lined with waxed paper. Chill 30 minutes or till firm. (If chocolate mixture is too soft to shape, quick-chill the mixture in the freezer for 5 to 10 minutes.) Working with a few at a time, shape drops into balls. Keep chilled. Roll the chilled chocolate balls in a mixture of cocoa powder and powdered sugar (*or* omit powdered sugar and increase cocoa powder to ½ cup). Store candy in the refrigerator. Makes 24.

Nutrition information per serving: 80 calories, 1 g protein, 6 g carbohydrate, 7 g fat (4 g saturated), 13 mg cholesterol, 4 mg sodium, 41 mg potassium.

Nutty Truffles: Prepare Chocolate Truffles as above, *except* omit coating the chocolate balls with cocoa powder and sugar. Instead, roll the chilled chocolate balls in 1 cup *finely chopped walnuts.* Store in the refrigerator.

Nutrition information per serving: 106 calories, 1 g protein, 6 g carbohydrate, 10 g fat (4 g saturated), 13 mg cholesterol, 4 mg sodium, 55 mg potassium.

Truss To secure the legs, wings, and front and back openings of poultry, using white kitchen string and small skewers. Poultry is trussed to keep it in an attractive, compact shape during roasting, to prevent overcooking and drying out of the wings and legs, and to keep any stuffing inside the cavity.

A Tip from Our Kitchen
Instead of tying the wings of poultry with string to hold them in place, twist the wing tips under the back of the bird. This technique also can help hold the neck skin in place without a skewer.

Tuna A large saltwater fish of the mackerel family. All but a small amount of the tuna eaten in the United States is canned. In recent years, however, the demand for fresh tuna has grown, especially for use in restaurants.

Fresh tuna has compact meat that ranges in color from light to darker, depending on the kind of tuna.

Types: *Albacore* tuna is the mildest tuna. It is the only type of tuna that can be canned and labeled "white meat tuna." *Yellowfin* tuna has light meat. *Bluefin* tuna has darker flesh and a stronger flavor. Another tuna on the market is *Skipjack*.

Market forms: You can find fresh and frozen tuna, usually sold as boneless steaks.

Canned tuna is packed in oil or water and comes three ways. Solid-pack canned tuna is the most expensive, and flaked or grated is the least expensive. Chunk-style is priced between the two and is most common.

How to cook: You can grill, broil, bake, or poach fresh tuna. For broiling, baking, and poaching directions, see the Cooking Fish chart under *Fish*. For grilling directions, see the Direct-Grilling Fish chart under *Barbecue*.

Nutrition information: A 3-ounce serving of baked fresh bluefin tuna has about 155 calories. The calorie count of a 3-ounce serving of canned tuna, drained, depends mostly on whether it's packed in water or oil. Tuna in water has about 110 calories. Tuna in oil has about 170 calories.

(See *Fish* for selecting, storing, thawing, and other information.)

Turkey A heavy-bodied, wild or domestic bird known for its large amount of white meat and smaller amount of dark meat. Turkeys are native to the United States and are noted for their mild flavor and versatility.

Types: The American wild turkey still exists, but bears little resemblance to its domestic, broad-breasted cousin. Here are the differences between these two types of birds.
☐ **Domestic:** Farm-raised birds that are bred to be very plump, juicy, and flavorful. Most domestic birds weigh 6 to 24 pounds, dressed. Look for domestic turkey in your supermarket's meat or freezer case.
☐ **Wild:** A native American bird that roams the countryside and weighs anywhere from 10 to 20 pounds. Wild turkey has a stronger flavor than domestic turkey.

Market forms: Turkeys used to be sold only as whole birds. But today many domestic turkey products are available. Most are available fresh and frozen. Luncheon meats are available fresh.
☐ **Whole:** The entire turkey, purchased unbasted or prebasted, and weighing from 6 to 24 pounds.
☐ **Boneless Roasts:** All-white meat, all-dark meat, or a combination of white and dark turkey meat. They are boneless and weigh from 2½ to 6 pounds.
☐ **Thighs:** All-dark-meat pieces with bone that weigh ½ pound to 1½ pounds each.
☐ **Hindquarters:** Units consisting of a turkey thigh and drumstick. Hindquarters are all dark meat and weigh 2 to 5 pounds each.
☐ **Drumsticks:** All-dark-meat pieces with bone that weigh ½ pound to 1½ pounds each.

☐ **Wings:** All-white-meat pieces with bone that weigh ¾ pound to 1½ pounds each.

☐ **Boneless and Bone-in Breasts:** Uncooked, white turkey meat that's sold fresh or frozen. Half portions may contain some bone. Roasted boneless breasts also are available; they come plain, smoked, or barbecued.

☐ **Breast Steaks:** Crosswise cuts from the turkey breast that are ½ to 1 inch thick.

☐ **Breast Slices or Cutlets:** Crosswise cuts from the turkey breast that are ¼ to ⅜ inch thick.

☐ **Tenderloin:** The whole muscle on the inside of the turkey breast.

☐ **Tenderloin Steaks:** Half-inch-thick lengthwise cuts from the turkey tenderloin. Half of a tenderloin steak is referred to as a turkey chop.

☐ **Sausages:** Made of ground turkey that is processed to give it traditional sausage flavor. Turkey sausage is available ground or in links. Turkey franks, which are flavored to taste like meat frankfurters, are a popular turkey sausage variety. Some sausage is smoked.

☐ **Ground:** A mixture of white and dark turkey meat or all dark turkey meat. It may contain some skin.

☐ **Luncheon Meats:** Boneless white and/or dark turkey meat that is smoked, cured, and spiced to taste like traditional cold cuts, such as bologna, salami, ham, and pastrami.

Selecting: The younger the turkey, the more tender the meat is. All domestic turkeys on the market are young and will be labeled "young turkey" (usually 4 to 6 months old at butchering time). Some turkeys are labeled "hen" or "tom," which indicates the sex. Buy a hen if you want more white meat, a tom if you want more dark meat.

In the store, look for the "sell by" date on the label of fresh turkey. This date is the last day the turkey should be sold by the retailer. The unopened turkey will maintain its optimal quality and safety for 1 or 2 days after the "sell by" date.

For frozen turkey products, look for packaging that isn't damaged and for other indications that the turkey didn't start to thaw and was refrozen.

continued

Whole turkey

Boneless turkey roast

Turkey thigh

Turkey hindquarter

Turkey drumstick

Turkey wing

Boneless turkey breast

Bone-in turkey breast (half)

Turkey breast steak

Turkey breast slice (cutlet)

Turkey breast tenderloin

Turkey breast tenderloin steak

Ground turkey sausage

Smoked turkey sausage

Ground turkey

Luncheon Meats

Turkey pastrami

Turkey bologna

Turkey ham

Turkey salami

Turkey Math

Not sure how much turkey to buy? Use this guide to figure how much to allow for each serving, depending on the size of the bird or the cut. (Remember to allow extra servings if you want seconds and leftovers.)

Turkey Product	Allow per Serving
Whole (6 to 12 pounds)	= ¾ to 1 pound
Whole (over 12 pounds)	= ½ to ¾ pound
Breast (bone-in)	= ⅓ pound
Drumstick or thigh (bone-in)	= ½ pound
Parts (boneless)	= ¼ to ⅓ pound

Storing: At home, fresh turkeys should be stored in the coldest part of your refrigerator for up to 2 days.

Frozen whole turkeys can be stored for up to 1 year in your freezer. Turkeys that have been purchased as frozen birds do not need to be rewrapped for freezer storage unless the packaging is damaged. Fresh and frozen turkey pieces can be stored in your freezer for up to 6 months. However, be sure to rewrap the fresh pieces in freezer wrap or place them in freezer bags before freezing.

Preparation hints: For thawing information, see *Poultry*. (Do not thaw commercially frozen stuffed turkeys before roasting; follow label directions for cooking.) Once the whole bird is thawed, remove neck and giblets from neck and body cavities. Cook thawed turkey as soon as possible.

How to cook: For roasting and broiling directions, see the Roasting Poultry and Broiling Poultry charts under *Poultry*. For grilling directions, see the Direct-Grilling Poultry and Indirect-Grilling Poultry charts under *Barbecue*.

Q: How can I tell when turkey pieces are done?

A: There's more than one way to tell when your turkey is done. Test white meat, small cuts, and ground turkey by making a small cut into the thickest part. The meat is done when the thickest part has turned from pink to white. Bone-in parts are done when juices run clear when the meat is pierced in the deepest part with a long-tined fork.

For larger cuts, such as boneless breasts and roasts, use a meat thermometer. Place the thermometer in the deepest part of the meat, not touching any bone for bone-in cuts. (You'll find that some of the larger cuts of turkey have a device that will pop up when the turkey is done. If you have a meat thermometer, you might want to check the cooking progress of the turkey with the thermometer.) The turkey is done when the thermometer registers 170° for breast meat and 180° for dark meat.

Nutrition information: The calories, fat, and cholesterol vary depending on whether the serving is white or dark meat. A cooked 3-ounce serving of turkey without skin contains about 135 calories, 3 grams fat, and 59 milligrams cholesterol for white meat and about 160 calories, 6 grams fat, and 72 milligrams cholesterol for dark meat.

Q: Can a turkey be stuffed the day before it's going to be roasted?

A: Definitely not! It may seem like a timesaving idea to stuff a turkey in advance, but harmful bacteria can multiply in the stuffing and cause food poisoning. Stuff the turkey right before roasting. Then, as soon as the bird is cooked, remove the stuffing. Harmful bacteria can grow in the stuffing if it sits in the bird after cooking.

(See also *Poultry*.)

Turmeric *(TUR muh rik)* The root of a tropical plant belonging to the ginger family. This spice looks like ginger on the outside, but that's where the resemblance ends. When dried and ground, turmeric's powder is bright yellow-orange, its flavor is bittersweet, and its aroma slightly musty. Turmeric is a major ingredient in curry powder, and it's also used to flavor and color prepared mustard. Ground turmeric is widely available.

(See *Spice* for selecting, storing, and nutrition information.)

Turnip A globe-shaped root vegetable with a thin, white and purple skin and creamy white meat. Young turnips have a mild, crisp, and sweet flavor that's compatible with other vegetables. As they age, though, they become stronger flavored and develop a woody texture. Turnip greens also are available and generally are sold separately. They have a slightly bitter flavor that's somewhat sharper than spinach.

Selecting: Fresh turnips are available year-round. Look for small turnips with unblemished skins that are heavy for their

Turnip greens

size. Select turnip greens that are tender, fresh looking, and without bruises.

Storing: Refrigerate turnips in a plastic bag for up to a week. Wash fresh greens in cold water; pat dry. Place them in a plastic bag lined with a paper towel, and store in the refrigerator for up to 3 days.

How to cook: See Greens and Turnips on the Cooking Fresh Vegetables chart under *Vegetable.*

Nutrition information: Cooked cubed turnips or cooked turnip greens each have about 15 calories per ½-cup serving.

Turnips

Turtle Any of a variety of reptiles that has a shell and lives in fresh or salt water. Turtle meat is similar in flavor to veal and is considered a delicacy. It is sold frozen or canned in some supermarkets and specialty stores. Chopped turtle meat often is added to soups, stews, and sauces. Canned snapper soup is a well-known turtle product.

Tutti-Frutti *(toòt ih FROOT ee)* A term used to describe either a dessert or ice cream containing several diced fruits or fruit flavors. The term also is applied to candy and gum.

Twice-Baked Potato A potato that is baked two separate times. First it is baked until tender. Then a slice is cut from the top and the pulp is removed, leaving a thin potato shell. The pulp is mashed, seasoned, and piled into the shell to bake a second time until heated through.

A Tip from Our Kitchen
Twice-baked potatoes make great make-ahead vegetables. Prepare them up to the point before the final baking time. Then securely wrap and freeze the potatoes up to 2 months. To reheat the frozen potatoes, unwrap and place them on a baking sheet. Bake them in a 375° oven about 45 minutes.

Twice-Baked Potatoes

    4 medium baking potatoes
        (6 to 8 ounces each)
    ½ cup dairy sour cream *or* plain yogurt
    ¼ teaspoon garlic salt
    ⅛ teaspoon pepper
    2 slices American cheese, halved
        diagonally (optional)

■ Scrub potatoes thoroughly with a brush. Pat dry. If desired, for soft skins, rub with shortening, margarine, or butter; prick potatoes with a fork. (*Or,* if desired, skip rubbing skins. Prick potatoes; wrap each in foil.) Bake in a 425° oven for 40 to 60 minutes or till tender. When the potatoes are done, roll each one gently under your hand.
■ Cut a lengthwise slice from the top of *each* potato; discard skin from slice and place pulp in a bowl. Gently scoop out each potato, leaving a thin shell. Add pulp to the bowl.
■ With an electric mixer on low speed or a potato masher, beat or mash potato pulp. Add

sour cream or yogurt, garlic salt, and pepper; beat till smooth. (If necessary, stir in 1 to 2 tablespoons *milk* to make of desired consistency.) Season to taste. Pile mashed potato mixture into potato shells. Place in a 10x6x2-inch baking dish.
■ Bake in a 425° oven for 20 to 25 minutes or till lightly browned. If desired, place cheese atop potatoes. Bake for 2 to 3 minutes more or till cheese melts. Makes 4 servings.

Microwave directions: Scrub potatoes, pat dry, and prick. *Do not rub* with shortening, margarine, or butter. On a microwave-safe plate, arrange potatoes spoke fashion. Micro-cook, uncovered, on 100% power (high) for 13 to 16 minutes or till tender, rearranging and turning potatoes over once. Let stand 5 minutes. Assemble potato shells as at left and above. In a 10x6x2-inch microwave-safe baking dish, micro-cook stuffed shells, uncovered, on 100% power (high) 4 to 5 minutes or till heated through, rearranging potatoes once. If desired, place cheese atop potatoes. Cook, uncovered, on high 30 to 60 seconds more or till cheese melts.

Nutrition information per serving: 282 calories, 6 g protein, 52 g carbohydrate, 6 g fat (4 g saturated), 13 mg cholesterol, 138 mg sodium, 886 mg potassium.

Vacuum-Packed A term used to describe a food that has been preserved by packaging it in a container from which the oxygen is removed. The airless environment inhibits the growth of microorganisms and extends the time a food can be stored. Some foods can be stored at room temperature, and others must be frozen or refrigerated. Vacuum-packed corn and boil-in-the-bag main dishes are examples of these foods.

Vanilla A liquid extract made from the seed of an orchid. The seed is a slender pod that is called a vanilla bean.

Market forms: Several different forms of vanilla are available.
☐ **Pure Vanilla Extract:** Made by repeatedly circulating diluted alcohol through finely chopped vanilla beans.

□**Vanilla Bean:** The pod of an orchid plant that is dried and cured. During curing, the pod turns a dark chocolate color and shrivels to the size of a pencil.

□**Imitation:** An artificial flavoring made of coloring and synthetic flavors, it is an inexpensive substitute for pure vanilla extract. Some brands may also contain some vanilla extract. Although some brands of imitation vanilla are slightly stronger, for most uses, measure the same amount of imitation vanilla as you would pure vanilla extract.

Storing: Store vanilla extract and imitation vanilla in a cool, dark place for up to a year. A vanilla bean can be stored in a tightly covered jar for several months.

Q: **What can be done with those long, skinny vanilla beans?**

A: Make your own vanilla sugar. Split a vanilla bean open lengthwise and put it in a jar with 1 to 2 cups of sugar or powdered sugar. Cover and let stand at least 1 month. Stir in more sugar as needed. Use the sugar in desserts and beverages and over cereal to add a hint of vanilla.

Variety Meat   An organ or nonfleshy part of an animal used for food. Although not as popular as in the past, variety meats are used in such classic dishes as liver and onions.

Types: Variety meats can be beef, lamb, pork, veal, or poultry. Following are the most common types available.

□**Brain:** A soft meat with a glossy, pale pink surface and a delicate flavor.

□**Chitterlings:** The intestines of a hog. Pinkish beige in color, chitterlings have a moist, clean surface and a subtle flavor. A regional specialty of the southern United States, chitterlings also are called chitlins.

□**Heart:** A firm muscle meat with a dense texture. Beef, lamb, and pork hearts are bright red in color; veal and chicken hearts are lighter in color. Beef heart is most popular because of its mild flavor.

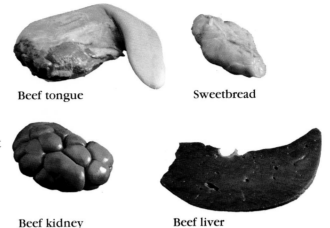

Beef tongue   Sweetbread

Beef kidney   Beef liver

□**Kidney:** A bean-shaped organ meat. The reddish brown meat is plump and firm, and covered with a thin, glossy membrane.

□**Liver:** An organ that is the most familiar variety meat. Liver's reddish brown meat is soft and smooth with a glossy surface. It is sold whole or in slices. Most of the liver sold comes from either beef calves or chickens. Calf liver has a full but not overpowering flavor. Pork and lamb livers rarely are sold in supermarkets because their stronger taste does not appeal to most consumers.

□**Sweetbread:** The thymus gland from the neck or throat of calves or lambs. Sweetbreads are light pink in color. The plump meat is covered with a shiny membrane and is delicate in flavor.

□**Tongue:** Usually beef. Tongue is grayish pink and has a fine, rough surface. Before eating, the outer skin should be removed from the cooked tongue. Cooked beef tongue is fine-grained and has a mild flavor and texture similar to beef.

□**Tripe:** The stomach lining of an animal. Usually beef or veal, tripe is yellow-beige in color and has a rubbery texture. Tripe generally is parboiled before it is sold. Tripe is light-tasting and chewy. The most desirable tripe comes from beef and has a honeycombed texture.

Nutrition information: Variety meats generally are high in dietary cholesterol, with brains having the highest amount in a serving. Liver is a good source of iron.

Veal Meat from a young beef or dairy calf. Creamy pink in color, veal has a delicate flavor and a finer texture than beef. The subtle flavor of veal blends well with a myriad of flavors.

Market forms: Veal is sold either fresh or frozen in the supermarket.

Q: What is the difference between milk-fed veal and grain-fed veal?

A: The most expensive veal comes from animals that have been raised on milk or special milk formula. Sold as milk-fed veal, the meat has a creamy pink, almost white, velvety appearance. When grain or grass has been added to the calves' diet, the calves are marketed as grain-fed veal. The meat of grain-fed veal is rosier in color with a slightly stronger flavor and coarser texture.

Retail Veal Cuts: The number listed with each retail cut refers to the wholesale cut marked on the drawing at right. Besides the name of the retail cut, you'll find the best ways to cook each meat cut.

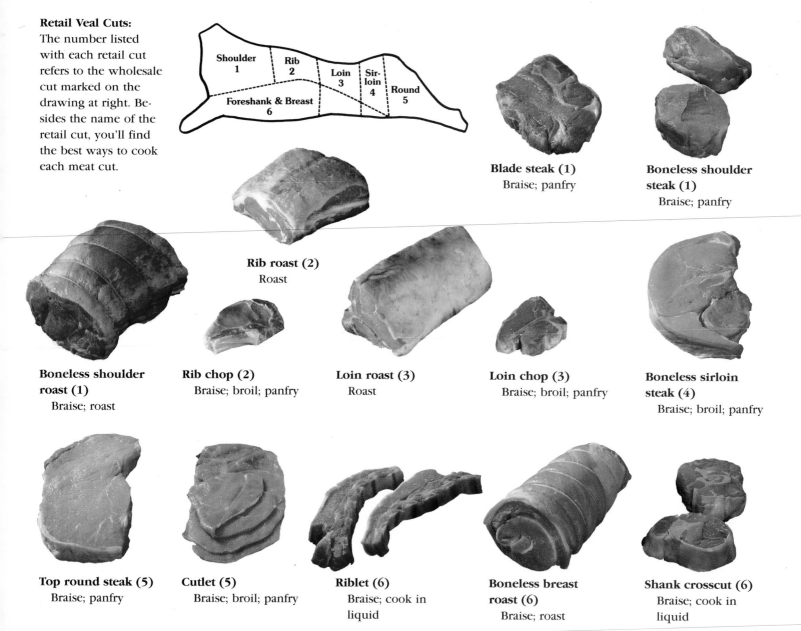

Shoulder 1 | Rib 2 | Loin 3 | Sir-loin 4 | Round 5 | Foreshank & Breast 6

Blade steak (1)
Braise; panfry

Boneless shoulder steak (1)
Braise; panfry

Rib roast (2)
Roast

Boneless shoulder roast (1)
Braise; roast

Rib chop (2)
Braise; broil; panfry

Loin roast (3)
Roast

Loin chop (3)
Braise; broil; panfry

Boneless sirloin steak (4)
Braise; broil; panfry

Top round steak (5)
Braise; panfry

Cutlet (5)
Braise; broil; panfry

Riblet (6)
Braise; cook in liquid

Boneless breast roast (6)
Braise; roast

Shank crosscut (6)
Braise; cook in liquid

Selecting: When buying veal, look for meat that is creamy pink and fine-textured. The bones of milk-fed veal should have reddish marrow. If fat is present, it should be white. When buying older veal and grain-fed veal, expect the bones to appear whiter and the fat to be more visible.

You may find prime and choice veal at the supermarket. Prime veal, the highest quality, is usually milk-fed veal. Choice veal is usually from larger or grain-fed animals and is of slightly lower quality.

Veal cuts: Veal cuts closely resemble those of beef, but they're smaller in scale. For the names and locations of various retail cuts, see the identification photos, opposite. Nearly all veal cuts are naturally tender since they come from young animals.

Storing: See the Storing Meat chart under *Meat.*

How to cook: For suggested cooking methods of individual cuts, see the veal identification photos, opposite. For roasting, broiling, panbroiling, and panfrying directions, see the Roasting Meat, the Broiling Meat, and the Panbroiling and Panfrying Meat charts under *Meat.* For grilling directions, see the Direct-Grilling Meat and the Indirect-Grilling Meat charts under *Barbecue.*

Nutrition information: A 3-ounce serving of braised or broiled veal round steak has about 130 calories.

(See *Meat* for Using a Meat Thermometer and labeling, preparation, and other information.)

Vegetable
Any edible portion of a plant that is used primarily as a side dish or in a main dish or salad. It may be a leaf, bud, root, stem, flower, pod, or seed of the plant.

Q: What are "baby" vegetables?
A: Some of these are regular varieties that are harvested early, but others are mature varieties bred to be small.

Market forms: Most vegetables are available fresh at the supermarket, although growing seasons may limit availability.

For year-round use, cans of single vegetables and mixtures are available as well as frozen vegetables and vegetable mixtures in plain, buttered, and specially sauced forms. Frozen vegetables also are available combined with rice or pasta. For extra convenience, packages of frozen chopped vegetables, such as onion and green pepper, are available, too.

How to cook: See the Cooking Fresh Vegetables chart, pages 424–427, for preparation and cooking directions. Cook frozen vegetables according to package directions. Heat commercially canned vegetables in their own liquid till heated through. Drain, if desired.

Nutrition hints: Vegetables are an important part of the daily diet. Considered as a group, vegetables are naturally low in calories, and they supply many essential nutrients, including carbohydrates, vitamins A and C, minerals, and fiber.

Q: What are cruciferous vegetables and what health value do they have?
A: Cruciferous *(crew SIF uh rus)* is the scientific name for the vegetable family that includes cabbage, broccoli, brussels sprouts, cauliflower, kale, Swiss chard, mustard greens, rutabagas, and turnips. The vegetables are loaded with vitamins, minerals, and fiber, and most experts say they exert a special protective effect against certain kinds of cancer.

continued

Cooking Fresh Vegetables

There are several ways to cook fresh vegetables, including on the range top, in the oven, and in the microwave.

Keep in mind that cooking and steaming times may vary depending on the particular vegetable. Also, the amounts given on the chart yield enough cooked vegetables for 4 servings, except where noted.

To steam vegetables, place the steamer basket in a saucepan. Add water to just below the bottom of the steamer basket. Bring to boiling. Add vegetables. Cover and reduce heat. Steam for time specified in the chart or till desired doneness.

To micro-cook vegetables, use a microwave-safe baking dish or casserole and follow directions in the chart.

Vegetable and Amount	Preparation	Conventional Cooking Directions	Microwave Cooking Directions
Artichokes Two 10-ounce (2 servings)	Wash; trim stems. Cut off 1 inch from tops, and snip off sharp leaf tips. Brush cut edges with lemon juice.	Cook, covered, in a large amount of boiling salted water for 20 to 30 minutes or till a leaf pulls out easily. (*Or,* steam for 20 to 25 minutes.) Invert to drain.	Place in a casserole with 2 tablespoons water. Micro-cook, covered, on 100% power (high) for 7 to 9 minutes or till a leaf pulls out easily, rearranging artichokes once. Invert to drain.
Asparagus 1 pound (1½ cups pieces)	Wash; scrape off scales. Break off woody bases where spears snap easily. Leave spears whole or cut spears into 1-inch pieces.	Cook spears or pieces, covered, in a small amount of boiling salted water for 4 to 8 minutes or till crisp-tender. (*Or,* steam spears or pieces for 4 to 8 minutes.)	Place in a baking dish or casserole with 2 tablespoons water. Micro-cook spears or pieces, covered, on 100% power (high) for 7 to 10 minutes or till crisp-tender, rearranging or stirring once.
Beans: green, Italian green, purple, and yellow wax ¾ pound (2¼ cups pieces)	Wash; remove ends and strings. Leave whole or cut into 1-inch pieces. For French-style beans, slice lengthwise.	Cook, covered, in a small amount of boiling salted water for 20 to 25 minutes for whole or cut beans (10 to 15 minutes for French-style beans) or till tender. (*Or,* steam whole, cut, or French-style beans for 18 to 22 minutes.)	Place in a casserole with 2 tablespoons water. Micro-cook, covered, on 100% power (high) for 13 to 15 minutes for whole or cut beans (12 to 14 minutes for French-style beans) or till tender, stirring once.
Beets 1 pound (2¾ cups cubes)	For whole beets, cut off all but 1 inch of stems and roots; wash. Do not peel. (For micro-cooking, prick the skins of whole beets.) *Or,* peel beets; cube or slice.	Cook, covered, in boiling salted water for 40 to 50 minutes for whole beets (about 20 minutes for cubed or sliced beets) or till crisp-tender. Slip skins off whole beets.	Place in a casserole with 2 tablespoons water. Micro-cook whole, cubed, or sliced beets, covered, on 100% power (high) for 9 to 12 minutes or till crisp-tender, rearranging or stirring once. Slip skins off whole beets.
Broccoli ¾ pound (3 cups flowerets)	Wash; remove outer leaves and tough parts of stalks. Cut lengthwise into spears or cut into ½-inch flowerets.	Cook, covered, in a small amount of boiling salted water for 8 to 12 minutes or till crisp-tender. (*Or,* steam for 8 to 12 minutes.)	Place in a baking dish with 2 tablespoons water. Micro-cook, covered, on 100% power (high) for 4 to 7 minutes or till crisp-tender, rearranging or stirring once.
Brussels sprouts ¾ pound (3 cups)	Trim stems and remove any wilted outer leaves; wash. Cut large sprouts in half lengthwise.	Cook, covered, in a small amount of boiling salted water for 10 to 12 minutes or till crisp-tender. (*Or,* steam for 10 to 15 minutes.)	Place in a casserole with 2 tablespoons water. Micro-cook, covered, on 100% power (high) for 4 to 6 minutes or till crisp-tender, stirring once.
Cabbage Half of a 1- to 1¼-pound head (4 cups pieces)	Remove wilted outer leaves; wash. Cut into 4 wedges or cut into 1-inch pieces.	Cook, uncovered, in a small amount of boiling water for 2 minutes. Cover; cook for 6 to 8 minutes for wedges (3 to 5 minutes for pieces) or till crisp-tender. (*Or,* steam wedges for 10 to 12 minutes.)	Place in a baking dish or casserole with 2 tablespoons water. Micro-cook, covered, on 100% power (high) for 9 to 11 minutes for wedges (4 to 6 minutes for pieces) or till crisp-tender; rearrange or stir once.

Vegetable and Amount	Preparation	Conventional Cooking Directions	Microwave Cooking Directions
Carrots 1 pound (3 cups slices)	Wash, trim, and peel or scrub. Cut into ¼-inch-thick slices or julienne strips.	Cook, covered, in small amount of boiling salted water for 7 to 9 minutes for slices (5 to 7 minutes for julienne strips) or till crisp-tender. (*Or,* steam slices for 8 to 10 minutes or strips for 6 to 8 minutes.)	Place in a casserole with 2 tablespoons water. Micro-cook, covered, on 100% power (high) for 7 to 10 minutes for slices (5 to 7 minutes for julienne strips) or till crisp-tender, stirring once.
Cauliflower One 1½-pound head (3 cups flowerets)	Wash; remove leaves and woody stem. Leave whole or break into flowerets.	Cook, covered, in a small amount of boiling salted water for 10 to 15 minutes for head (8 to 10 minutes for flowerets) or till tender. (*Or,* steam head or flowerets for 8 to 12 minutes.)	Place in a casserole with 2 tablespoons water. Micro-cook, covered, on 100% power (high) for 9 to 11 minutes for head (7 to 10 minutes for flowerets) or till tender; turn, rearrange, or stir once.
Celeriac 1 pound (2½ cups julienne strips)	Wash; trim off the leaves and ends; peel off hairy brown skin. Cut into julienne strips.	Cook, covered, in a small amount of boiling salted water for 5 to 6 minutes or till crisp-tender. (*Or,* steam julienne strips for 5 minutes.)	Place in a casserole with 2 tablespoons water. Micro-cook, covered, on 100% power (high) for 3 to 4 minutes or till crisp-tender, stirring once.
Celery 5 stalks (2½ cups slices)	Remove leaves; wash stalks. Cut into ½-inch slices.	Cook, covered, in a small amount of boiling salted water for 6 to 9 minutes or till tender. (*Or,* steam for 7 to 10 minutes.)	Place in a casserole with 2 tablespoons water. Micro-cook, covered, on 100% power (high) for 6 to 10 minutes or till tender, stirring once.
Chayote 1½ medium (15 ounces) (2 cups cubes)	Wash, peel, and halve lengthwise; remove seed; cube.	Cook, covered, in a small amount of boiling salted water about 5 minutes or till tender. (*Or,* steam about 8 minutes.)	Place in a casserole with 2 tablespoons water. Micro-cook, covered, on 100% power (high) for 5 to 6 minutes or till tender, stirring once.
Corn 2 cups	Remove husks from fresh ears of corn; scrub with a stiff brush to remove silks. Rinse. Cut kernels from cob.	Cook, covered, in a small amount of boiling salted water for 4 minutes. (*Or,* steam for 4 to 5 minutes.)	Place in a casserole with 2 tablespoons water. Micro-cook, covered, on 100% power (high) for 5 to 6 minutes, stirring once.
Corn on the Cob (1 ear equals 1 serving)	Remove the husks from fresh ears of corn; scrub with a stiff brush to remove silks. Rinse.	Cook, covered, in a small amount of lightly salted boiling water (or in enough boiling water to cover) for 5 to 7 minutes or till tender.	Wrap each ear in waxed paper; place on microwave-safe paper towels in the microwave. Micro-cook on 100% power (high) for 3 to 5 minutes for 1 ear, 5 to 7 minutes for 2 ears, or 9 to 12 minutes for 4 ears; rearrange once.
Eggplant 1 medium (1 pound) (5 cups cubes)	Wash and peel. Cut into ¾-inch cubes.	Cook, covered, in a small amount of boiling water for 4 to 5 minutes or till tender. (*Or,* steam for 4 to 5 minutes.)	Place in a casserole with 2 tablespoons water. Micro-cook, covered, on 100% power (high) for 6 to 8 minutes or till tender, stirring once.
Fennel 2 heads (2½ cups quarters)	Cut off and discard upper stalks, including feathery leaves (reserve leaves for garnish, if desired). Remove wilted outer layer of stalks; cut off a thin slice from base. Wash. Cut fennel into quarters lengthwise.	Cook, covered, in a small amount of boiling water for 6 to 10 minutes or till tender.	Place in a casserole with ¼ cup water. Micro-cook, covered, on 100% power (high) for 4 to 6 minutes or till tender, rearranging once.
Greens: beet, collard, dandelion, kale, mustard, and turnip ¾ pound (12 cups torn)	Wash thoroughly in cold water; drain well. Remove stems; trim bruised leaves. (See question and answer under *Collard Green.*)	Cook, covered, in a small amount of boiling salted water for 9 to 12 minutes or till tender.	

Cooking Fresh Vegetables
continued

Vegetable and Amount	Preparation	Conventional Cooking Directions	Microwave Cooking Directions
Jerusalem Artichokes 1 pound (2 cups slices)	Wash, trim, and peel or scrub. Cut into ¼-inch-thick slices.	Cook, covered, in a small amount of boiling salted water for 8 to 10 minutes or till tender. (*Or,* steam for 10 to 12 minutes.)	Place in a casserole with 2 tablespoons water. Micro-cook, covered, on 100% power (high) for 5 to 7 minutes or till tender, stirring once.
Jicama 10 ounces (2 cups cubes)	Wash, trim, and peel. Cut into ½-inch cubes.	Cook, covered, in a small amount of boiling salted water about 5 minutes or till hot and crisp-tender. (*Or,* steam about 5 minutes.)	Place in a casserole with 2 tablespoons water. Micro-cook, covered, on 100% power (high) for 5 minutes or till hot and crisp-tender, stirring once.
Kohlrabi 1 pound (3 cups julienne strips)	Cut off leaves; wash. Peel; chop or cut into julienne strips.	Cook, covered, in a small amount of boiling salted water for 6 to 8 minutes or till tender. (*Or,* steam about 8 minutes.)	Place in a casserole with 2 tablespoons water. Micro-cook, covered, on 100% power (high) for 6 to 8 minutes or till tender, stirring once.
Leeks 1½ pounds (3 cups slices)	Wash well; remove any tough outer leaves. Trim roots from base. Slit lengthwise and wash well. Cut into ½-inch-thick slices.	Cook, covered, in a small amount of boiling salted water for 5 minutes or till tender. (*Or,* steam slices about 5 minutes.)	Place in a casserole with 2 tablespoons water. Micro-cook, covered, on 100% power (high) for 4 to 5 minutes or till tender, stirring once.
Mushrooms 1 pound (6 cups slices)	Wash mushrooms with a damp towel or paper towel. Leave whole or cut into slices.	Cook sliced mushrooms, covered, in 2 tablespoons margarine or butter about 5 minutes. (*Or,* steam whole mushrooms for 10 to 12 minutes.)	Place sliced mushrooms in a casserole with 2 tablespoons margarine or butter. Micro-cook, covered, on 100% power (high) about 5 minutes, stirring twice.
Okra ½ pound	Wash; cut off stems. Leave whole or cut into ½-inch-thick slices.	Cook, covered, in a small amount of boiling salted water for 8 to 15 minutes or till tender.	Place in a casserole with 2 tablespoons water. Micro-cook, covered, on 100% power (high) for 4 to 6 minutes or till tender, stirring once.
Onions 1 large (1 cup chopped)	Peel and chop.	Cook in 2 tablespoons margarine or butter over medium heat till tender but not brown, stirring often.	Place in a casserole with 2 tablespoons water, margarine, or butter. Micro-cook, covered, on 100% power (high) for 3 to 4 minutes or till tender, stirring once.
Parsnips ¾ pound (2 cups slices)	Wash, trim, and peel or scrub. Cut into ¼-inch-thick slices.	Cook, covered, in a small amount of boiling salted water for 7 to 9 minutes or till tender. (*Or,* steam for 8 to 10 minutes.)	Place in a casserole with 2 tablespoons water. Micro-cook, covered, on 100% power (high) for 4 to 6 minutes or till tender, stirring once.
Pea pods ½ pound (2 cups)	Remove tips and strings; wash.	Cook, covered, in a small amount of boiling salted water for 2 to 4 minutes or till crisp-tender. (*Or,* steam for 2 to 4 minutes.)	Place in a casserole with 2 tablespoons water. Micro-cook, covered, on 100% power (high) for 3 to 5 minutes or till crisp-tender, stirring once.
Peas, green 2 pounds (3 cups shelled)	Shell and wash.	Cook, covered, in a small amount of boiling salted water for 10 to 12 minutes or till crisp-tender. (*Or,* steam for 12 to 15 minutes.)	Place in a casserole with 2 tablespoons water. Micro-cook, covered, on 100% power (high) for 6 to 8 minutes or till crisp-tender, stirring once.

Vegetable and Amount	Preparation	Conventional Cooking Directions	Microwave Cooking Directions
Peppers: green, sweet red, and yellow 2 large (2½ cups rings or strips)	Remove stems. Wash and remove seeds and ribs. Cut into rings or strips.	Cook, covered, in a small amount of boiling salted water for 6 to 7 minutes or till crisp-tender. (*Or,* steam for 6 to 7 minutes.)	Place strips or rings in a casserole with 2 tablespoons water. Micro-cook, covered, on 100% power (high) for 5 to 6 minutes or till crisp-tender, stirring once.
Potatoes 1 pound (2¾ cups cubes)	Wash and peel. Remove eyes, sprouts, or green areas. Cut into quarters or cube.	Cook, covered, in a small amount of boiling salted water for 20 to 25 minutes or till tender. (*Or,* steam about 20 minutes.) (To bake 4 whole potatoes, see directions on page 420.)	Place in a casserole with 2 tablespoons water. Micro-cook, covered, on 100% power (high) for 8 to 10 minutes or till tender, stirring once. (To cook 4 potatoes, see Microwave directions on page 420.)
Rutabagas 1 pound (2¾ cups cubes)	Wash and peel. Cut into ½-inch cubes.	Cook, covered, in a small amount of boiling salted water for 18 to 20 minutes or till tender. (*Or,* steam for 18 to 20 minutes.)	Place in a casserole with 2 tablespoons water. Micro-cook, covered, on 100% power (high) for 11 to 13 minutes or till tender, stirring 3 times.
Spinach 1 pound (12 cups torn)	Wash and drain; remove stems.	Cook, covered, in a small amount of boiling salted water for 3 to 5 minutes or till tender, beginning timing when steam forms. (*Or,* steam for 3 to 5 minutes.)	Place in a casserole with 2 tablespoons water. Micro-cook, covered, on 100% power (high) for 4 to 6 minutes or till tender, stirring once.
Squash: acorn, delicata, golden nugget, and sweet dumpling 1 pound (2 servings)	Wash, halve, and remove seeds.	Place halves, cut side down, in a baking dish. Bake in a 350° oven for 30 minutes. Turn cut side up. Bake, covered, for 20 to 25 minutes more or till tender.	Place squash halves, cut side down, in a baking dish with 2 tablespoons water. Micro-cook, covered, on 100% power (high) for 6 to 9 minutes or till tender, rearranging once. Let stand, covered, 5 minutes.
Squash: banana, buttercup, butternut, Hubbard, and turban One 1½-pound or a 1½-pound piece	Wash, halve whole squash lengthwise, and remove seeds.	Place squash, cut side down, in a baking dish. Bake in a 350° oven for 30 minutes. Turn cut side up. Bake, covered, for 20 to 25 minutes more or till tender.	Place squash, cut side down, in a baking dish with 2 tablespoons water. Micro-cook, covered, on 100% power (high) for 9 to 12 minutes or till tender, rearranging once.
Squash: pattypan, sunburst, yellow, and zucchini ¾ pound (2½ cups slices)	Wash; do not peel. Cut off ends. Cut into ¼-inch-thick slices.	Cook, covered, in a small amount of boiling salted water for 3 to 5 minutes or till crisp-tender. (*Or,* steam for 4 to 6 minutes.)	Place in a casserole with 2 tablespoons water. Micro-cook, covered, on 100% power (high) for 4 to 5 minutes or till tender, stirring twice.
Squash, spaghetti One 2½- to 3-pound	Wash, halve lengthwise, and remove seeds.	Place halves, cut side down, in a baking dish. Bake in a 350° oven for 30 to 40 minutes or till tender.	Place halves, cut side down, in a baking dish with ¼ cup water. Micro-cook, covered, on 100% power (high) for 15 to 20 minutes or till tender, rearranging once.
Sweet potatoes 1 pound	Wash and peel. Cut off woody portions and ends. Cut into quarters or cube. (For micro-cooking, cut into quarters.)	Cook, covered, in enough boiling salted water to cover for 25 to 35 minutes or till tender.	Place in a casserole with ½ cup water. Micro-cook, covered, on 100% power (high) for 10 to 13 minutes or till tender, stirring once.
Turnips 1 pound (2½ cups cubes)	Wash and peel. Cut into ½-inch cubes or julienne strips.	Cook, covered, in a small amount of boiling salted water for 10 to 12 minutes or till tender. (*Or,* steam for 10 to 15 minutes.)	Place in a casserole with 2 tablespoons water. Micro-cook, covered, on 100% power (high) for 12 to 14 minutes or till tender, stirring once.

Velouté Sauce *(vuh loo TAY)* The
French word for a basic white sauce made with margarine or butter, flour, and white stock. The white stock can be chicken, fish, or veal broth.

Venison
The meat from any large animal of the deer family including deer, elk, reindeer, moose, and antelope. Deer is by far the most common type.

Venison has a fine texture. Its flavor is similar to beef, but generally, venison is leaner.

Market forms: Wild deer can be hunted in season. And, the meat from farm-raised deer can be purchased in frozen portions from specialty stores, some supermarkets, and venison farms.

Venison cuts are similar to beef. Some popular cuts include roasts, steaks, and chops. Ground venison as well as venison luncheon meats and deer jerky sticks also is available.

Preparation hints: Freshly killed deer should be cleaned, skinned, and chilled immediately. Then, aging the meat tenderizes it and improves its flavor. Meat lockers are ideal places to age venison. Many meat lockers will age, butcher, and freeze the venison for you.

Because the fat carries most of the strong flavor, trim away as much fat as possible, while leaving a thin covering to keep the meat from drying out during cooking.

To ensure that your venison will be tender, check that all sinew has been removed and that the meat has been boned carefully. Also be sure to remove the silvery membrane from around the meat muscles.

For older or larger portions of venison, a brief marinating (up to 4 hours) can make the meat more tender, juicy, and flavorful.

Storing: Store venison as you would beef (see *Beef*).

Cooking hints: Cook venison as you would beef but keep in mind that venison is leaner than beef and needs less cooking time. Venison should be cooked until it is rare or medium-rare to keep it from drying out and becoming tough.

Nutrition information: A 3-ounce portion of roasted, farm-raised venison has about 130 calories.

Véronique *(vay rah NEEK)* A dish
prepared or garnished with seedless green grapes.

Vichyssoise *(vish ee SWAHZ)* A
pureed soup usually made from potatoes and leeks cooked in chicken broth. Vichyssoise generally is served chilled with cream added and snipped chives sprinkled on top for garnish. Commercially prepared vichyssoise is sold in cans.

Vichyssoise

½ cup sliced leeks *or* chopped onion
1 tablespoon margarine *or* butter
1½ cups sliced, peeled potatoes
1 cup chicken broth
⅛ teaspoon salt
  Dash white pepper *or* pepper
¾ cup milk
½ cup whipping cream

■ In a medium saucepan cook leeks or onion in margarine or butter till tender but not brown. Stir in potatoes, chicken broth, salt, and pepper. Bring to boiling; reduce heat. Cover and simmer 20 to 25 minutes or till potatoes are tender. Cool slightly.
■ Place potato mixture in a blender container or food processor bowl. Cover; blend or process till smooth. Pour into a bowl. Stir in milk and cream. If necessary, add additional milk to make desired consistency. Cover; chill well before serving. If desired, top with snipped chives. Makes 4 side-dish servings.

Microwave directions: Place leeks and margarine or butter in a 1½-quart microwave-safe casserole. Micro-cook, covered, on 100% power (high) for 2 to 3 minutes or till tender. Add potatoes, chicken broth, salt, and pepper. Cook, covered, on high for 8 to 10 minutes or till potatoes are tender, stirring once. Continue as in recipe, opposite.

Nutrition information per serving: 258 calories, 6 g protein, 26 g carbohydrate, 15 g fat (8 g saturated), 45 mg cholesterol, 335 mg sodium, 557 mg potassium.

Vienna Bread
A long, oval loaf of yeast bread with an especially crisp shiny crust. The crispy crust is achieved by baking the bread with steam in a special oven.

Vinaigrette
(vihn ih GRET) A thin, clear, oil-and-vinegar salad dressing or sauce, often containing herbs, spices, onion, and mustard. A vinaigrette also may serve as a marinade for meats, poultry, and fish.

Vinaigrette

- ½ **cup salad oil**
- ⅓ **cup white wine vinegar *or* vinegar**
- 1 **tablespoon sugar**
- 2 **teaspoons snipped fresh thyme, oregano, *or* basil; *or* ½ teaspoon dried thyme, oregano, *or* basil, crushed**
- ½ **teaspoon paprika**
- ¼ **teaspoon dry mustard *or* 1 teaspoon Dijon-style mustard (optional)**
- ⅛ **teaspoon pepper**

■ In a screw-top jar mix oil; vinegar; sugar; herb; paprika; mustard, if desired; and pepper. Cover; shake well. Store in the refrigerator for up to 2 weeks. Shake before serving. Makes ¾ cup (twelve 1-tablespoon servings).

Nutrition information per tablespoon: 86 calories, 0 g protein, 1 g carbohydrate, 9 g fat (1 g saturated), 0 mg cholesterol, 2 mg sodium, 8 mg potassium.

French Vinaigrette: Prepare Vinaigrette as below left, *except* omit herb. Use mustard and add a dash ground *red pepper.*

Nutrition information per tablespoon: 86 calories, 0 g protein, 2 g carbohydrate, 9 g fat (1 g saturated), 0 mg cholesterol, 15 mg sodium, 7 mg potassium.

Italian Vinaigrette: Prepare Vinaigrette as below left, *except* use oregano for herb and use mustard. Add 2 tablespoons grated *Parmesan cheese,* ¼ teaspoon *celery seed,* and 1 clove *garlic,* minced.

Nutrition information per tablespoon: 93 calories, 1 g protein, 2 g carbohydrate, 9 g fat (1 g saturated), 1 mg cholesterol, 19 mg sodium, 20 mg potassium.

Red Wine Vinaigrette: Prepare Vinaigrette as below left, *except* reduce vinegar to *3 tablespoons.* Use *half* thyme and *half* oregano for the herb. Add 2 tablespoons *dry red wine* and 1 clove *garlic,* minced.

Nutrition information per tablespoon: 87 calories, 0 g protein, 1 g carbohydrate, 9 g fat (1 g saturated), 0 mg cholesterol, 2 mg sodium, 11 mg potassium.

Garlic Vinaigrette: Prepare Vinaigrette as at left, *except* omit herb and paprika. Add 2 large cloves *garlic,* minced.

Nutrition information per tablespoon: 86 calories, 0 g protein, 1 g carbohydrate, 9 g fat (1 g saturated), 0 mg cholesterol, 2 mg sodium, 7 mg potassium.

Vinegar
A sour liquid that is a by-product of fermentation. Through fermentation, the alcohol from grapes, grains, apples, and other sources is changed to acetic acid to create vinegar.

Types: Vinegar, once a plain-Jane ingredient, has gone fancy. You can find it in dozens of varieties, colors, and flavors.

☐ **Balsamic:** Made from the juice of a very sweet white grape. It is dark brown with a delicate, sweet flavor. This vinegar is aged in wooden barrels for at least 10 years, making it more expensive than other types.

☐ **Cider:** Made from the juice of apples. This is the most popular form of vinegar. Cider vinegar is a pale, golden brown with a strong bite and faint apple flavor.

continued

☐ **Distilled or White:** Made from grain alcohol. It is colorless and the very strongest and sharpest flavored vinegar.

☐ **Flavored:** Has the added taste of herbs or fruits, such as garlic, basil, tarragon, and raspberry.

☐ **Rice:** Used in Chinese and Japanese cooking. These vinegars are made from rice wine or sake and have a subtle tang and slightly sweet taste. They are usually clear to pale gold in color.

☐ **Wine:** Made from white, red, or rosé wine, champagne, or sherry. The color and flavor of these vinegars depend on the type of wine used. Red wine vinegar, for example, is more full-bodied than white wine vinegar.

Storing: Vinegar does not need refrigeration, and because of its acidic nature, its shelf life is almost indefinite. You may notice some changes, such as a color change or the development of a sediment, but they don't affect the flavor.

Vitamin and Mineral

Substances found in food that are essential for good health and are needed in relatively small amounts. For a brief rundown of selected vitamins and minerals that are important to the body, see the Some Common Vitamins and Minerals chart, below. Do keep in mind, however, that almost all of your cells need almost all of the vitamins and minerals, at least in minute amounts.

Some Common Vitamins and Minerals

Vitamin or Mineral	Examples of Function	Useful Sources
Vitamin A	Keeps skin, hair, and body membranes healthy; aids in resistance to infection; is the basis for eye pigments necessary for vision	Yellow, orange, and green leafy vegetables and fruits (carrots, cantaloupe, broccoli, spinach, etc.); liver; eggs; cheese; and milk
Vitamin B₁ (Thiamin)	Helps release energy from food; aids in muscle coordination	Whole grain and enriched grain products, dried beans, dairy products, pork, and poultry
Vitamin B₂ (Riboflavin)	Helps release energy from food; builds and maintains body tissues	Milk, dark green vegetables, enriched and whole grain products, and nuts
Niacin	Maintains normal function of skin, nerves, and digestive system; involved in releasing energy from food	Meats, fish, whole grain and enriched products, and milk
Vitamin C	Promotes healthy gums and teeth; aids iron absorption; important in healing wounds	Citrus fruits, tomatoes, potatoes, strawberries, dark green vegetables, and many other fruits and vegetables
Vitamin D	Forms and maintains bones and teeth	Made when sun shines on your skin; also found in egg yolks and fortified milk
Calcium	Necessary for healthy bones and teeth	Dairy products, bones (as in sardines or canned salmon), and many fruits and vegetables
Iodine	Essential for the healthy functioning of the thyroid gland and for normal growth and development	Iodized salt; fish, shellfish, and seaweed; foods grown on iodine-rich soils
Iron	Important part of the hemoglobin of red blood cells	Meat, poultry, fish, enriched and whole grain products, some vegetables and fruits
Phosphorus	Necessary for healthy bones and teeth	Widely distributed in most foods
Potassium, Sodium, Chloride	Regulate body fluids	Readily available in many foods

Q: **Are vitamin supplements a good idea?**

A: Experts say that a balanced diet provides all the vitamins and minerals most people need, so vitamin pills aren't necessary. Exceptions include people on very low-calorie weight-loss diets, pregnant women, and some postmenopausal women. Breast-fed infants may need extra vitamin D. Before you decide to take vitamin supplements, check with a doctor.

(See *Nutrition* for information on planning a balanced diet.)

Wafer A thin, disk-shaped cookie, cracker, or piece of candy.

Waffle A quick bread with a honeycomb appearance that's made from a batter and cooked in a special appliance called a waffle iron or baker. Waffles have an even golden brown color with a tender, crisp crust and a light and slightly moist interior.

Q: **How is waffle batter different from pancake batter?**

A: Waffle batter usually is higher in fat than pancake batter. Also, waffle batter often has beaten egg whites folded into it.

A Tip from Our Kitchen

To keep cooked waffles warm till serving time, arrange them in a single layer on a wire rack. Set the rack atop a baking sheet and place it in a 300° oven. If you stack freshly baked waffles, they'll get soggy.

Waffle bakers: The grids on waffle bakers come in round, square, rectangular, and even heart shapes. Waffle bakers can be electric or designed for use on top of the range with regular or nonstick surfaces.

Electric waffle bakers have a built-in thermostat that heats the unit to a predetermined temperature then signals you when it is ready to use. Electric waffle bakers cook both sides of the waffle at once. Waffle bakers heated on top of the range must be turned over once to cook the second side.

The grids on any waffle bakers need to be seasoned well. Follow the manufacturer's directions for use and care.

Convenience products: Frozen waffles are available in many sizes and flavors. To reheat most of them, just pop them into a toaster; others can be heated in the microwave oven.

Q: **What are Belgian waffles?**

A: Belgian waffles are thick waffles with extra-deep indentations. A common way to serve them is with strawberries and ice cream or whipped cream.

Belgian waffle bakers, both electric and stove-top, are available. Some manufacturers recommend using only their recipe for Belgian waffles; others say any waffle recipe will work. Be sure to follow your manufacturer's directions.

Nutrition hint: Cut calories by topping your waffles (or pancakes) with fresh fruit or unsweetened applesauce instead of butter or margarine and syrup.

Nutrition information: One waffle (4½x4½x⅝ inches) has about 100 calories.

Waldorf Salad A chopped mixture of apples, celery, and walnuts or pecans that is combined with mayonnaise or salad dressing. It usually is served on lettuce as a side-dish salad. Grapes, dates, or raisins sometimes are added, and occasionally whipped cream is folded into the mixture. (For a Waldorf salad recipe, see page 433.)

Waldorf Salad

Waldorf Salad

> 2 cups chopped apple
> 1½ teaspoons lemon juice
> ¼ cup chopped celery
> ¼ cup chopped walnuts *or* pecans
> ¼ cup raisins *or* snipped pitted whole
>   dates
> ¼ cup seedless green grapes, halved
>   (optional)
> ⅓ cup whipping cream *or* ⅔ cup frozen
>   whipped dessert topping, thawed
> ¼ cup mayonnaise *or* salad dressing
>   Ground nutmeg

■ In a bowl toss chopped apple with lemon juice. Stir in celery, nuts, raisins or dates, and, if desired, grapes.
■ For dressing, if using whipping cream, in a chilled mixing bowl whip cream to soft peaks. Fold mayonnaise into the whipped cream or dessert topping. Fold dressing into the apple mixture. Sprinkle with a little nutmeg. Cover and chill for 2 to 24 hours. To serve, if desired, spoon onto lettuce-lined plates and garnish with nut halves. Makes 4 to 6 servings.

Nutrition information per serving: 186 calories, 1 g protein, 13 g carbohydrate, 15 g fat (4 g saturated), 23 mg cholesterol, 63 mg sodium, 147 mg potassium.

Walnut The seed of a walnut tree. The most popular walnut varieties are the *English* or *Persian* walnut and the *black* walnut.

The English walnut is encased in a brown outer shell that covers a large, round, golden shell that is slightly rough and has two distinct halves. The mildly flavored nut inside is actually a pair of irregular, ridged, brown nuts that are connected near the middle.

Black walnuts

English walnuts

The native North American black walnut has a very hard, thick, rough, black shell. The nut itself is smaller than the English walnut and has a darker skin and richer, much more intense flavor. Black walnuts are difficult to hull and shell, and they are not as widely available as English walnuts.

Storing: Unshelled walnuts will keep indefinitely in a cool, dry place. Store shelled nuts in an airtight container in the refrigerator and they'll stay fresh for 6 months. For long-term storage, freeze shelled walnuts for up to a year.

Q: **Is there a way to crack English walnut shells so the nut doesn't break?**
A: There are no guarantees, but try this method. Hold the shell by the seam so it stands on its flat end. Tap the pointed end of the shell with a hammer and it should break open, leaving the walnut halves intact.

(See *Nut* for the Selecting Nuts chart and selecting, nutrition, and other information.)

Wasabi *(WAH suh bee)* The pale green flesh of an Asian root that is sold in powder or paste form. Known as Japanese horseradish, this condiment for sushi and sashimi is botanically unrelated to Western horseradish but has a similar taste.

Wassail *(WAHS uhl)* A hot, spiced punch, sometimes containing alcohol, that is usually served at Christmastime.

Water A colorless, usually flavorless liquid with many uses as a beverage and in cooking.

Water as a nutrient: Your body is nearly two-thirds water. Maintaining that proportion is just as important as eating the right foods. Because water bathes tissues, lubricates joints, carries nutrients to the cells, and takes wastes away, it's important to drink 6 to 8 glasses of water a day.

Types: Many different bottled waters are sold. Here are some common ones.
☐ **Club Soda:** An artificially carbonated water with added minerals and mineral salts, which often is mixed with alcohol to make cocktails. Club soda is interchangeable with plain seltzer or sparkling water, although club soda is slightly saltier tasting and contains more sodium.
☐ **Distilled:** Pure bottled water with a flat flavor.
☐ **Mineral:** Carbonated or noncarbonated water with a high mineral content and a slightly metallic taste. The carbonated variety can be naturally or artificially carbonated and is called sparkling mineral water.
☐ **Seltzer or Soda:** An artificially carbonated water usually without added minerals or mineral salts. Flavored seltzer has a natural or artificial flavor added. Seltzer also may be sweetened.
☐ **Sparkling:** A naturally or artificially carbonated water. Flavored sparkling water has a natural or artificial flavor added. Sparkling water also may be sweetened.
☐ **Tonic:** A carbonated beverage flavored with quinine that has a bittersweet flavor. Although tonic water is sweetened, the quinine flavor masks the sweetness.

Comparing Calories
The calorie content of 6 ounces of a specialty water product varies greatly. Here are some examples:
● Distilled water; mineral water; unsweetened, plain or flavored seltzer or sparkling water; or club soda = 0 calories
● Sweetened, flavored seltzer or sparkling water = 70 to 85 calories
● Tonic water = 60 to 70 calories
● Diet tonic water = 2 calories

Water Chestnut A root vegetable with a crisp, white flesh and delicate flavor, commonly used in Oriental cooking. Because it remains firm and crunchy even after cooking, it is used in recipes to add texture. Fresh water chestnuts, available in specialty stores, have a brown husk that must be peeled away before using. Whole or sliced water chestnuts also are sold canned in most supermarkets. One-half cup of canned, sliced water chestnuts has about 35 calories.

Watercress A delicate salad green with small, round, dark green leaves on edible stems. Watercress leaves and stems have a lively, peppery tang. Watercress can be used in salads, sandwiches, and soups, and as a garnish.

Selecting:
Watercress is available year-round and usually is sold in small bunches. Choose healthy-looking stems with bright green leaves. Avoid any bunches with wilting or yellowing leaves.

Watercress

Storing: Wrap watercress in damp paper towels and refrigerate in a plastic bag for 1 or 2 days.

Nutrition information: Watercress has about 5 calories per cup.

Watermelon   A large, round, oval, or oblong fruit of the gourd family, with sweet, crisp, juicy meat. There are more than 50 watermelon varieties grown, and depending on the variety, the rind may be solid dark green, striped, or mottled. The meat can be anywhere from deep pink to red, and some varieties have yellow meat.

Regular watermelons can weigh from 10 to 50 pounds; smaller melons, called icebox melons (because they are designed to fit in the refrigerator), weigh from 5 to 10 pounds. Watermelons usually have flat, dark brown or black seeds, but seedless varieties are rapidly gaining in popularity.

Selecting: If you've heard about the thumping technique for choosing a whole watermelon, forget it. It does not accurately detect ripeness. Rely instead on the outer color, which should be even, dull, and pale to dark green with a creamy yellow area on the underside. A watermelon's shape should be symmetrical. Avoid ones with soft ends.

If you buy a cut piece, the flesh should look firm, brightly colored, and juicy. Avoid pieces with white streaks, holes, cracks, or a mealy appearance.

Storing: Wrap and keep cut melon pieces in the refrigerator. Whole watermelons can be stored in a cool place for up to a week.

Q: Do "seedless" watermelons have seeds?
A: Yes. Some seedless melons have tiny, soft white seeds that are not fully formed. These seeds are edible.

(See *Melon* for the Selecting Melons chart and preparation, nutrition, and other information.)

Watermelons

Weeping   An undesirable condition in which liquid separates out of a solid food. This type of leakage most commonly occurs with such foods as meringue pies (where the meringue and filling meet), custards, and jellies.

Q: How can weeping be avoided in a meringue pie?
A: Spread the meringue on top of the filled pie while the filling is still as hot as possible. The heat from the filling will help cook the underside of the meringue as it bakes and will minimize weeping.

Weights and Measures

Any of numerous means by which the quantity of a food is determined. Certain ingredients are listed in recipes by weight, usually as they would be found in the marketplace. Others are listed by liquid or dry measures. The use of these weights and measures in recipes and food preparation helps ensure accurate and consistent results. See the chart below for a listing of the most common weights and measures and their equivalents.

Weights and Measures

1 ounce = 28.35 grams
1 pound = 453.59 grams
1 gram = 0.035 ounce
1 kilogram = 2.2 pounds
3 teaspoons = 1 tablespoon
4 tablespoons = ¼ cup
5⅓ tablespoons = ⅓ cup
8 tablespoons = ½ cup
10⅔ tablespoons = ⅔ cup
12 tablespoons = ¾ cup
16 tablespoons = 1 cup
1 tablespoon = ½ fluid ounce
1 tablespoon = 14.79 milliliters
1 cup = 8 fluid ounces
1 cup = 236.6 milliliters
1 cup = ½ pint
2 cups = 1 pint
4 cups = 1 quart
2 pints = 1 quart
2 quarts = ½ gallon
4 quarts = 1 gallon
1 quart = 946.4 milliliters
1 liter = 1.06 quarts
8 quarts = 1 peck
2 gallons = 1 peck
4 pecks = 1 bushel

Wheat

The grain of a widely produced cereal grass. Wheat is a staple food to half of the population of the world and has a delicate, nutty flavor.

Wheat classes: Whether a class of wheat is better suited for making bread, pasta, or cake depends on the amount of protein and the gluten strength in that variety. Because protein contributes so much to a flour's characteristics, it is the basis for classifying the varieties of wheat.

Flour made from *Durum* wheat is very high in protein and often is used in pasta. Flour made from *Hard Red Spring* or *Winter* wheat is a high-protein, high-gluten flour used for bread making, and flour from *Soft Red Winter* or *Soft White* wheat contains less protein and gluten and is better suited to pastry making.

Q: What is semolina?
A: Semolina is milled from the endosperm of durum wheat kernels; it is a granular product. Semolina is used to make some pastas. It also is used to make Italian gnocchi. Buy semolina at Italian specialty shops and health food stores.

Market forms: There are a number of commercial wheat products.

☐ **Bulgur:** Precooked and dried, cracked wheat. Bulgur absorbs twice its volume in water and can be used in place of rice in many recipes. It needs to be soaked or cooked before eating.

☐ **Cracked Wheat:** The whole kernel broken into pieces. Add cracked wheat to baked goods or casseroles for a nutty flavor and crunchy texture, or cook it for a cereal.

☐ **Farina:** Coarse, granular particles milled from the endosperm (starchy interior) of hard wheats. It is cooked and served as a breakfast cereal.

☐ **Wheat Berry:** The whole wheat kernel with just the hull removed. The cooked whole wheat kernel is used as a substitute for rice or pasta, as a breakfast cereal, or as a replacement for beans in chili, salads, and baked dishes. Wheat berries also can be sprouted.

☐ **Wheat Bran:** The outer layer of the wheat kernel. It is an excellent source of dietary fiber and is used commercially in cereal products and baked goods and in home-baked goods. Wheat bran comes in plain and toasted forms.

☐ **Wheat Flour:** The finely ground or milled wheat kernel. Wheat flour is the most common type of flour available. Whole wheat flour is produced from the whole grain; all-purpose flour has the bran and germ removed. Flour is used in baked goods and as a thickener.

☐ **Wheat Germ:** The embryo or sprouting section of the wheat kernel. It has a nutty flavor and adds crunch to baked goods and casseroles. Wheat germ is sold both raw and toasted.

Storing: Store whole or cracked wheat in an airtight container in a cool, dry place for up to 6 months or freeze for up to a year. Store wheat bran in an airtight container in a cool, dry place for up to 1 month, refrigerate for up to 3 months, or freeze for up to 1 year. Because of its higher oil content, wheat germ is very perishable. Keep it in the refrigerator for up to 3 months. See *Flour* for storing information.

How to cook: See the Cooking Grains chart under *Grain.*

Nutrition information: A ¾-cup serving of cooked bulgur contains about 130 calories. The same-size serving of cooked farina contains about 100 calories. A ½-cup serving of cooked wheat berries contains about 40 calories.

Whip   To beat a food lightly and rapidly using a wire whisk, rotary beater, or electric mixer to incorporate air into the mixture and increase its volume.

Whitefish   A freshwater fish of the salmon and trout family, which lives in cold waters. The meat is very white with a mild, almost sweet flavor and firm texture.

Types: There are numerous types of whitefish. The most commercially important is the *Lake* whitefish, which rarely gets larger than 4 pounds. *Cisco* is another type. Cisco is

valuable for its roe, which is processed into a caviar substitute called golden caviar or whitefish caviar.

Market forms: Fresh whitefish is sold drawn or dressed and as fillets or steaks. Frozen whitefish most often is sold as fillets. Smoked whitefish also is available.

How to cook: Whitefish is good poached, baked, broiled, grilled, or panfried. For poaching, baking, broiling, and panfrying directions, see the Cooking Fish chart under *Fish.* For grilling directions, see the Direct-Grilling Fish chart under *Barbecue.*

Nutrition information: Baked lake whitefish has about 150 calories in a 3-ounce serving.

(See *Fish* for selecting, storing, thawing, and other information.)

White Sapote   *(suh PO dee)* A small, round, applelike fruit with a buttery, avocadolike texture and thin skin that can be green, yellow-green, or yellow. The cream-colored meat is sweet and juicy. It tastes like a blend of bananas and peaches and has shiny, inedible seeds.

Varieties: Although the *white* sapote is the most widely available sapote variety in the United States, other varieties, including the *black* sapote and the *Mamey* sapote, also can be found infrequently.

White sapotes

Selecting: White sapotes are available sporadically year-round. Choose fruit that is firm.

Storing: Allow white sapotes to ripen at room temperature until they yield to gentle pressure. Keep ripe fruit in the refrigerator for 3 to 5 days.

Nutrition information: White sapotes have about 300 calories per fruit.

White Sauce

White Sauce A basic cooking sauce made with margarine or butter, flour, and milk, cream, or stock. White sauces are quickly made by stirring together the flour and melted margarine or butter, then adding the liquid. The creamy mixture is cooked and stirred till it is thickened and bubbly. Sometimes cornstarch is used instead of flour for thickening.

There are two types of white sauce—béchamel and velouté. The only difference between them is the liquid. Béchamel uses milk, and velouté uses veal, chicken, or fish stock. White sauce is served with vegetables, poultry, fish, and meat and is the base for many other sauces.

Q: **What's the secret to a smooth white sauce?**

A: Prevent lumps in white sauce by stirring the flour or cornstarch into the melted margarine or butter. Then stir in the liquid all at once and combine. Finally, heat the mixture until bubbly, stirring constantly. If lumps do form, try beating the sauce briskly with a wire whisk or rotary beater.

White Sauce

- 1 **tablespoon margarine** *or* **butter**
- 1 **tablespoon all-purpose flour**
- ⅛ **teaspoon salt**
  Dash pepper
- ¾ **cup milk**

■ In a small saucepan melt margarine or butter. Stir in flour, salt, and pepper. Add milk all at once. Cook and stir over medium heat till thickened and bubbly. Cook and stir 1 minute more. Makes ¾ cup (twelve 1-tablespoon servings).

Nutrition information per tablespoon: 18 calories, 1 g protein, 1 g carbohydrate, 1 g fat (0 g saturated), 1 mg cholesterol, 41 mg sodium, 25 mg potassium.

Microwave directions: In a 2-cup microwave-safe measure micro-cook margarine or butter, uncovered, on 100% power (high) for 30 to 40 seconds or till melted. Stir in flour, salt, and pepper. Add ⅔ *cup* milk all at once

and stir to combine. Cook, uncovered, on high for 2 to 4 minutes or till thickened and bubbly, stirring every 30 seconds.

Nutrition information per tablespoon: 18 calories, 1 g protein, 1 g carbohydrate, 1 g fat (0 g saturated), 1 mg cholesterol, 40 mg sodium, 22 mg potassium.

Low-Calorie White Sauce: Prepare White Sauce as below left, *except* omit margarine or butter and substitute *skim milk* for the milk. In a screw-top jar combine flour, salt, pepper, and milk. Shake till blended. Cook as below left.

Nutrition information per tablespoon: 8 calories, 1 g protein, 1 g carbohydrate, 0 g fat, 0 mg cholesterol, 30 mg sodium, 26 mg potassium.

Cheese Sauce: Prepare White Sauce as below left, *except* omit salt. Over low heat, stir ¾ cup shredded process *Swiss, American, or Gruyère cheese* or ¼ cup crumbled *blue cheese* into the *cooked* sauce till melted. Serve with vegetables. Makes about 1 cup (sixteen 1-tablespoon servings).

Nutrition information per tablespoon: 32 calories, 2 g protein, 1 g carbohydrate, 2 g fat (1 g saturated), 6 mg cholesterol, 87 mg sodium, 30 mg potassium.

Whiting

Whiting A saltwater fish of the cod family with lean, white, fine flesh that falls apart easily. Whiting also is known as silver hake. Although caught off the New England coast, the biggest market for whiting is in the Midwest where it often is served at fish fries.

Market forms: You can buy fresh whiting dressed, drawn, and filleted. Frozen whiting is sold as fillets and in portions. Whiting also is sold smoked.

How to cook: Whiting can be poached, baked, broiled, or panfried. For cooking directions, see the Cooking Fish chart under *Fish.*

Nutrition information: A 3-ounce serving of baked whiting has about 100 calories.

(See *Fish* for selecting, storing, thawing, and other information.)

Whole Grain

The entire kernel, minus the hull, of any grain. Each tiny grain seed contains three distinct parts—the starchy endosperm; the high-fiber, nutrient-dense bran; and the nutrient-dense germ. A whole grain product includes all three parts; a refined product contains only part of the grain kernel.

Storing: Whole grains can become rancid relatively quickly, so store them in an airtight container in a cool, dry place for up to 1 month or in the refrigerator or freezer for 5 to 6 months.

Whole Grain Breads

Most breads made with whole grain ingredients have less volume and a more compact texture than those made with all-purpose or bread flour. For lighter, airier loaves, most whole grain breads (except for pumpernickels) are made from a combination of all-purpose or bread flour and whole grain flour.

Wiener Schnitzel *(VEE nuhr SHNIT suhl)* A main dish from Vienna for which thin slices of veal are dipped in egg, coated with bread crumbs, and deep-fat fried or panfried. Lemon wedges often are served as an accompaniment.

A Tip from Our Kitchen

When panfrying Wiener schnitzel, be sure to follow recipe cooking times and temperatures carefully. Otherwise, the crumbs may burn before the meat is done. Also, avoid overcrowding the skillet or the Wiener schnitzel may turn out soggy. If necessary, keep finished pieces warm in a heated oven while you're frying the remaining pieces or preparing a sauce.

Wiener Schnitzel

- 12 **ounces boneless veal leg top round steak *or* pork loin, cut about ½ to ¾ inch thick**
- 3 **tablespoons all-purpose flour**
- ¼ **teaspoon salt**
- ¼ **teaspoon pepper**
- 1 **beaten egg**
- 2 **tablespoons milk**
- ⅔ **cup fine dry bread crumbs**
- 2 **to 3 tablespoons margarine *or* butter Cream Sauce (optional)**
- 4 **lemon wedges**

■ Cut veal or pork into 4 pieces. Pound each piece between 2 pieces of plastic wrap to about ⅛-inch thickness. Remove the plastic wrap. Combine flour, salt, and pepper. Combine egg and milk. Coat veal with the flour mixture; shake gently to remove excess. Dip meat into the egg mixture, allowing excess to drip off. Coat with bread crumbs.
■ In a 12-inch skillet melt margarine or butter. Cook meat over medium-high heat for 1 to 2 minutes on each side or till light brown. Remove from skillet to heated serving platter. If desired, keep meat warm and prepare Cream Sauce. Serve meat with lemon wedges and Cream Sauce, if desired. Makes 4 servings.

Cream Sauce: Combine ½ cup *dairy sour cream* and 1 tablespoon *all-purpose flour*. Carefully pour ¾ cup *chicken broth* into the skillet in which meat was cooked. Stir sour cream mixture into chicken broth. Cook and stir till thickened and bubbly. Cook and stir for 1 minute more.

Nutrition information per serving (with sauce): 334 calories, 26 g protein, 21 g carbohydrate, 17 g fat (6 g saturated), 134 mg cholesterol, 547 mg sodium, 407 mg potassium.

Wild Rice

The long, dark brown or black, nutty-flavored seed of an annual marsh grass. Though early explorers dubbed it "rice" because it grows in water, it is not a rice at all and is the only cereal grain native to North America. *continued*   Wild rice

Storing: Uncooked wild rice keeps indefinitely stored in a cool, dry place or in the refrigerator. If it is cooked with no added ingredients, wild rice keeps, tightly covered, in the refrigerator for several weeks or in the freezer for several months.

Preparation hints: Rinse wild rice before using to remove tiny particles left after processing. To rinse, place rice in a pan of warm water. Stir, then remove any particles that float to the top; drain. Repeat.

How to cook: To prepare 2⅔ cups of cooked wild rice, in a medium saucepan bring 2 cups water to boiling. If desired, add ¼ teaspoon salt. Add 1 cup wild rice. Return to boiling. Reduce heat. Simmer, covered, about 40 minutes or till most of the water is absorbed. Drain, if necessary.

A Tip from Our Kitchen
To make expensive wild rice go further, combine a little of it with white or brown rice to make a flavorful pilaf. Combining wild rice with brown rice is especially easy because their cooking times are about the same.

Nutrition information: A ½-cup serving of cooked wild rice contains about 95 calories.

Wine The naturally fermented juice of ripe grapes or other fruit. Wine is used as a beverage and in cooking.

Types: Here are some different kinds of wines and how they're used.
☐ **Aperitif or Appetizer:** A wine usually served before a meal to stimulate the appetite. Aperitif wines range from sweet to very dry. Dry sherry, vermouth, and flavored wines are popular aperitifs. Aperitif wines contain between 15 and 20 percent alcohol.
☐ **Dessert:** A nonsparkling wine that's served after a meal. Dessert wines are full-bodied and usually sweet. Port, tokay, muscat, sweet vermouth, sweet sherry, and sauternes are some dessert wines. Dessert wines contain between 14 and 24 percent alcohol.
☐ **Dinner (table):** A nonsparkling red, white, or rosé wine that's traditionally served with dinner. Dinner wines range from sweet to dry and contain between 10 and 13.9 percent alcohol.

Most *red* dinner wines are dry and flavorful, and sometimes tart or astringent. Red burgundy, cabernet sauvignon, and chianti are some common examples.

White dinner wines range from dry and tart to sweet and fruity. Chardonnay, sauvignon blanc, chenin blanc, and riesling are some well-known types.

Rosé or *blush* dinner wines range from sweet to slightly tart or astringent.
☐ **Sparkling:** A bubbly wine that's naturally carbonated during fermentation. Sparkling wines can be served anytime. They range from slightly sweet to dry and usually are mild in flavor. Champagne and sparkling burgundy are two well-known sparkling wines. Sparkling wines contain about 14 percent alcohol or less.
☐ **Wine Cooler:** A bottled blend usually containing wine, carbonated water, sweeteners, and fruit flavoring. Wine coolers usually are served as cocktails or aperitifs. Two popular flavors are berry and citrus. Coolers contain from 4 to 9 percent alcohol.

Wine naming: What's in a name? Plenty, when it comes to wine. Here are some guidelines that manufacturers use when naming wines.
☐ **Varietal Wine:** A wine named for the grapes used to make it, such as zinfandel, chardonnay, gamay, or riesling. In the United States, at least 75 percent of the wine must come from the type of grape for which the wine is named.
☐ **Proprietary Wine:** A blended wine unique to a specific winery. Proprietary wines usually are sold under a brand name.
☐ **Generic Wine:** Any name, other than grape variety, given to American wines. Hearty Burgundy and Mountain Chablis are examples. A generic name does not give information about grape content.

Q: What's a vintage wine?
A: A vintage wine is a wine dated with the year in which the grapes were harvested. The vintage year appears on the label along with the generic, varietal, or proprietary name. In the United States, a vintage wine can be made from a single grape type or from a blend of wines as long as at least 95 percent of the wine in it was produced during the vintage year.

A nonvintage wine is a blend of wines produced in different years. These wines usually are blended to produce a wine of consistent style. A nonvintage wine label doesn't have a year on it.

Selecting: Here are some points to consider.
☐ Try to match wine and food intensities. For example, serve a spicy, robust wine with intensely flavored food. A mild wine could go unnoticed if paired with strong food.
☐ Try to match the level of sweetness of the wine to the food served with it. For example, serving a dry, tart wine with a sweet dish or a dessert could make the wine taste sour.
☐ Although the guideline "red wines with meat, white wines with fish or poultry" is not used as much as it once was, it is a good rule of thumb when you're unsure.

Tips from Our Kitchen
If you want to add a little wine to your cooking, here are a few hints to try.
● For a mild-flavored dish, use only a tablespoon or two of wine so that it enhances the flavor of the ingredients but doesn't dominate the dish's flavor.
● In most cases, add wine to a recipe while the dish is cooking briskly, or while it has at least 10 minutes to cook uncovered, so that the alcohol will "cook off" and the wine flavor will have a chance to blend with other flavors.
● Add full-bodied red wines to hearty dishes, such as stews, pot roasts, and brown sauces, and to meat marinades.
● Choose a dry white wine to add to delicate seafood and poultry dishes.

Q: What is a blush wine?
A: A blush wine is a fruity, often slightly sweet and light wine. It is actually a "white" wine made from red grapes. It has only a faint blush of red color because the skins are removed before fermentation. Since blush wine doesn't improve with age, drink it when it is young (usually in the year it is made). Serve it chilled as a cocktail or aperitif.

Storing: The length of time that wines should be stored can vary from wine to wine, but here are some general points.

For long-term storage, keep wine in a cool, humid, dark place. The ideal temperature is from 55° to 60°, but 10° higher or lower is acceptable. Don't let bottled wine get warmer than 70°. Wines sealed with corks must be stored on their sides so the corks don't dry out and let in too much air. Metal- or plastic-capped bottles can be stored upright.

Nutrition information: Wines vary in calorie content from about 25 calories per ounce for table and sparkling wines to about 40 calories per ounce for dessert wines.

Wine Math
With this chart, it is easy to figure out how much wine to buy when entertaining. First decide on what kind of wine and how many servings you'll need. Then look below for the size bottle that will give you that many servings. A serving of dinner or sparkling wine ranges from 4 to 6 ounces. A serving of aperitif or dessert wine ranges from 2 to 2½ ounces.

Bottle Size	Ounces	Servings (4 to 6 oz.)	(2 to 2½ oz.)
Full bottle (750 ml)	25.4	4–6	10–12
1-liter bottle (1,000 ml)	33.8	5–8	13–16
1.5-liter bottle (1,500 ml)	50.7	8–12	20–25
3-liter bottle (3,000 ml)	101.4	16–25	40–50

To seal a filled wonton, bring one end over the other, moistening it with a little water and pressing the ends together to seal. Moistening is the secret to making sure the ends stick together.

Wonton

Wonton *(WAHN tahn)* A thin square of dough with a small amount of filling, usually meat, seafood, or vegetable, wrapped inside. This versatile Oriental treat may be simmered in a soup or deep-fat fried and served as an appetizer. Sometimes fried wontons have a sweet filling and are served as a dessert.

A Tip from Our Kitchen

If you can't find wonton wrappers in the produce section of your local supermarket, substitute egg roll wrappers and cut them into quarters.

Wontons or Egg Rolls with Pork and Shrimp Filling

½ pound ground pork
1 teaspoon grated gingerroot
1 clove garlic, minced
1 cup finely chopped bok choy *or* cabbage
½ cup finely chopped onion
½ cup chopped water chestnuts
½ cup shredded carrot
2 tablespoons soy sauce
2 teaspoons cornstarch
½ teaspoon sugar
¼ teaspoon salt
1 4½-ounce can shrimp, rinsed, drained, and chopped
40 wonton wrappers *or* 8 egg roll wrappers
   Cooking oil for deep-fat frying
   Sweet-and-sour sauce

■ For filling, in a 12-inch skillet stir-fry pork, gingerroot, and garlic for 2 to 3 minutes or till meat is no longer pink. Drain off fat. Add bok choy, onion, water chestnuts, and carrot. Stir-fry 2 minutes more. In a bowl stir together soy sauce, cornstarch, sugar, and salt. Add to mixture in skillet. Cook and stir over medium heat till bubbly. Stir in shrimp. Cool slightly. Use to fill 40 wontons or 8 egg rolls.

■ **To shape wontons:** Place *1* wonton wrapper with 1 point toward you. Spoon *1 rounded teaspoon* filling just off-center of wonton wrapper. Fold the nearest point of wrapper over filling, tucking the point under the filling. Roll toward the center, leaving about 1 inch unrolled at the top. Moisten the right-hand corner with water. Lap the right-hand corner over the left-hand corner, pressing together to seal (see how-to photo at left). Repeat with remaining wrappers and filling.

■ **To shape egg rolls:** Place *1* egg roll wrapper with 1 point toward you. Spoon *about ⅓ cup* filling diagonally just off-center of wrapper. Fold the nearest point of wrapper over filling, tucking the point under the filling. Fold the side corners toward the center and roll up. Moisten the top point with water; press on roll to seal. Repeat with remaining wrappers and filling.

■ In deep-fat fryer or 2-quart saucepan, heat 1½ to 2 inches cooking oil to 365°. Fry wontons or egg rolls, a few at a time, in hot oil till golden brown, turning once. Allow 1½ to 2½ minutes for wontons and 2 to 4 minutes for egg rolls. Using a slotted spoon, remove from oil and drain on paper towels. Keep warm in a 300° oven while frying remaining wontons or egg rolls. Serve warm with sweet-and-sour sauce. Makes 40 wontons or 8 egg rolls.

Nutrition information per wonton: 42 calories, 2 g protein, 3 g carbohydrate, 2 g fat (0 g saturated), 9 mg cholesterol, 100 mg sodium, 39 mg potassium.

Nutrition information per egg roll: 176 calories, 11 g protein, 9 g carbohydrate, 11 g fat (2 g saturated), 47 mg cholesterol, 432 mg sodium, 193 mg potassium.

Worcestershire Sauce

Worcestershire Sauce *(WOOS tur sure)* A thin, pungent, dark brown sauce used to season meats, gravies, and soups. Because Worcestershire sauce is commercially made, its exact ingredients are kept secret, but it is generally made with soy sauce, vinegar, garlic, tamarind, onions, molasses, and various seasonings.

White wine Worcestershire sauce also is available. It has a milder flavor than the regular sauce and contains white wine in addition to the basic ingredients. It is used to season chicken, fish, and other foods that have a mild flavor.

Yam A starchy root vegetable that's not widely available in the United States and is often confused with sweet potatoes. The vegetables labeled yams in many U.S. supermarkets are a type of sweet potato. Throughout the rest of the world, yams are a tropically grown tuber with brownish skin and yellow to white starchy flesh.

Yeast A tiny, single-celled organism that makes bread dough rise. Yeast feeds on the sugar in a dough and produces carbon dioxide gas that makes doughs rise.

Market forms: Yeast for baking is available in these three forms.
☐ **Active Dry:** Dried granules of yeast. Active dry yeast comes in small, moistureproof, sealed packages and in jars.
☐ **Quick-Rising Active Dry:** A highly active strain of dry yeast that makes doughs rise faster than regular yeast.
☐ **Compressed:** Also known as fresh yeast. Moist and easily crumbled, compressed yeast comes in cakes. This form of yeast is more perishable than both types of active dry yeast.

Q: Can quick-rising yeast be used in recipes that call for active dry yeast?
A: Yes. Quick-rising yeast can replace active dry yeast in equal measures in practically any bread recipe (exceptions are breads using sourdough starter, Danish pastry, and croissants). The dough should rise in about a third less time. Be sure to follow manufacturer's directions for water temperatures to use because they differ from those used with active dry yeast.

Storing: Store packets of dry yeast in a cool, dry place and the yeast will stay fresh and retain its leavening power until the expiration date stamped on the package. Store jars of loose dry yeast in a cool, dry place till opened, then refrigerate tightly covered. Use before the expiration date printed on the jar.

Keep compressed yeast cakes refrigerated and use them within 2 weeks or keep them in the freezer for several months (once defrosted, use these yeast cakes right away).

Q: Does active dry yeast have to be dissolved in liquid before it is used?
A: Not always. The dry yeast can be combined with part of the flour before the *very warm* liquid (120° to 130°) is added. If your recipe is made by the traditional method, the yeast is dissolved in *warm* liquid (105° to 115°) before it is used in making a yeast product.

A Tip from Our Kitchen
Today, many bread recipes use a method where the dry yeast is combined with part of the flour, instead of the traditional method, where the yeast is softened in warm liquid. If you live in Canada, where the available yeast doesn't work well combining the yeast with flour, play it safe and use only recipes with the traditional method.

Yogurt A dairy product made by adding special bacterial cultures to milk (it can be whole milk, low-fat milk, or nonfat milk). Yogurt is thick and creamy with a tangy flavor.

Market forms: Many forms of yogurt are available, including plain yogurt, yogurt with fruit on the bottom, yogurt with fruit mixed throughout, artificially sweetened yogurts, flavored yogurts (made with fruit juice or natural flavors, such as lemon and vanilla), yogurt drinks, and frozen yogurt (see also *Yogurt, Frozen*). There also is yogurt cheese.
continued

Storing: Refrigerate yogurt as soon as possible after purchase. It will maintain its peak flavor for about 10 days after the expiration date stamped on the carton. Don't store yogurt in the freezer because large coarse ice crystals will develop.

A Tip from Our Kitchen

In cooking, yogurt can lose some of its body and become thin if it is overmixed. For best results, add it to products slowly and do not overstir. Unless your recipe calls for flour to be mixed into the yogurt, do not allow yogurt mixtures to boil.

Q: **Why do the yogurts that contain fruit have more calories than other yogurts?**
A: Many of the fruit yogurts have sugar or corn syrup added to them to help preserve the fruit. A smart calorie-saving tactic is to buy plain yogurt and stir in your own favorite fresh fruit.

Nutrition information: See the Yogurt Facts chart, below.

Yogurt Facts

The calories and fat in ½ cup of yogurt can vary greatly depending on the type you buy. Here's a comparison.

Type of Yogurt	Fat	Calories
Whole milk, plain	4 grams	70
Low-fat, plain	2 grams	72
Low-fat, flavored	2 grams	97
Low-fat with fruit	1 gram	115
Nonfat, plain	0 grams	64

Yogurt, Frozen A tangy frozen dessert similar to ice cream, but made with yogurt as the base. It often contains fruit or other flavors and a sweetener. It can be purchased or made at home in an ice-cream freezer.

Market forms: Commercial frozen yogurt is available in numerous flavors in hard-packed form from the frozen food section of the supermarket and in soft form dispensed from machines, much like soft-serve frozen desserts. Both types are sold at frozen-yogurt shops. The most common frozen yogurts are low-fat, with 2 to 4 percent fat content. Nonfat frozen yogurts, however, also are available.

Nutrition information: A ½-cup serving of vanilla frozen yogurt has about 120 calories and about 2 grams of fat. Nonfat yogurt has about 80 to 100 calories, and it contains less than 1 gram fat.

(See *Ice Cream* for storing information.)

Yorkshire Pudding (*YORK shir*) A breadlike accompaniment for roast beef that originated in the British Isles. It is made by pouring a batter similar to popover batter into a roasting pan after the beef has been roasted and removed. As the batter bakes, it puffs and is flavored by the pan drippings.

Zabaglione (*zahb uhl YO nee*) A light custardlike dessert made with egg yolks, wine, and sugar. The traditional wine used for zabaglione is marsala; however, sherry, port, brandy, and a liqueur also are common ingredients. The mixture is beaten while it cooks slowly in the top of a double boiler.

Zabaglione can be served warm or cold in small glasses. Sometimes it is served as a sauce over fruit or ice cream. It is called sabayon (*saa baa YONE*) in France.

impossible for a zucchini to be blemish-free, but look for small ones that are firm and free of cuts and soft spots. A canned zucchini and tomato mixture also is available. Frozen zucchini is sold as part of vegetable mixtures.

Storing: Refrigerate zucchini in a plastic bag for up to 5 days (up to 2 weeks if they are very fresh). Zucchini will keep better if they are dry, so make sure there is no moisture on the zucchini or in the plastic bag.

Zucchini

How to cook: See the Cooking Fresh Vegetables chart under *Vegetable.*

Nutrition information: A ½-cup serving of cooked sliced zucchini has about 15 calories.

Zuppa Inglese *(TSOO puh in GLAY zay)* A layered dessert made with sponge cake, a liquor, custard or whipped cream, and fruit. Zuppa inglese is an Italian dessert that resembles an English trifle. It differs from a trifle by using rum or kirsch for the liquor instead of sherry, wine, or brandy. Sometimes zuppa inglese is topped with a meringue.

Zwieback *(ZWI back)* A crisp, cracker-like product that is made from slightly sweetened yeast dough and often is flavored with cinnamon and lemon. After the dough is baked, cooled, and sliced, the slices are returned to the oven and toasted slowly till crisp and dry.

A Tip from Our Kitchen
Try zwieback crumbs instead of graham cracker crumbs when making dessert crusts for pies and cheesecakes. The crust made with zwieback will be slightly less sweet.

Nutrition information: One piece of zwieback (3¼x1⅛x½ inches) has about 30 calories.

---

m sherry

beat egg yolks combined. *boiling* water e water). Beat peed for 6 to s and emmed uit. Makes 6

ories, g saturated), g potassium.

n of the peel white n fruit oils, called

A Tip from Our Kitchen
To prepare the zest for use in cooking, rub the citrus fruit against a fine grater, being careful not to get any of the bitter white portion. Or, thinly slice it from the fruit with a knife, fruit zester, or vegetable peeler.

Zucchini Generally a slender, elongated member of the squash family that has thin, dark to light green skin, sometimes with yellow markings. The off-white meat has a very light and delicate flavor.

There are other zucchini varieties that are very different in color and shape. Some are bright yellow, some are fatter and paler green, and others are rounded.

Selecting: Zucchini is available year-round. Because of its tender skin, it is almost

Emergency Substitutions

For best recipe results, use the ingredients specified in the recipe. In an emergency, however, you can try one of the following.

If you don't have these ingredients	Substitute these ingredients
1 teaspoon baking powder	½ teaspoon cream of tartar *plus* ¼ teaspoon baking soda
1 tablespoon cornstarch (for thickening)	2 tablespoons all-purpose flour
1 cup cake flour	1 cup *minus* 2 tablespoons all-purpose flour
1 cup self-rising flour	1 cup all-purpose flour *plus* 1 teaspoon baking powder, ½ teaspoon salt, and ¼ teaspoon baking soda
1 package active dry yeast	1 cake compressed yeast
1 cup buttermilk	1 tablespoon lemon juice *or* vinegar *plus* enough whole milk to make 1 cup (let stand 5 minutes before using), *or* 1 cup plain yogurt
1 cup whole milk	½ cup evaporated milk *plus* ½ cup water, *or* 1 cup water *plus* ⅓ cup nonfat dry milk powder
1 cup dairy sour cream	1 cup plain yogurt
1 cup light cream	1 tablespoon melted butter *plus* enough whole milk to make 1 cup
1 cup whipping cream, whipped	2 cups whipped dessert topping
1 cup margarine	1 cup butter *or* 1 cup shortening *plus* ¼ teaspoon salt, if desired
1 square (1 ounce) semisweet chocolate	3 tablespoons semisweet chocolate pieces, *or* 1 square (1 ounce) unsweetened chocolate *plus* 1 tablespoon sugar
4 squares (4 ounces) sweet chocolate	¼ cup unsweetened cocoa powder *plus* ⅓ cup sugar and 3 tablespoons shortening
1 square (1 ounce) unsweetened chocolate	3 tablespoons unsweetened cocoa powder *plus* 1 tablespoon shortening *or* cooking oil
1 cup corn syrup	1 cup sugar *plus* ¼ cup liquid
1 cup dark corn syrup	¾ cup light corn syrup *plus* ¼ cup molasses, *or* 1 cup light corn syrup
1 cup honey	1¼ cups sugar *plus* ¼ cup liquid
1 cup molasses	1 cup honey
1 cup sugar	1 cup packed brown sugar *or* 2 cups sifted powdered sugar
1 slice crisp-cooked bacon, crumbled	1 tablespoon cooked bacon pieces
¼ cup fine dry bread crumbs	¾ cup soft bread crumbs *or* ¼ cup cracker crumbs *or* ¼ cup cornflake crumbs
1 cup beef broth *or* chicken broth	1 teaspoon *or* 1 cube instant beef *or* chicken bouillon *plus* 1 cup hot water
1 clove garlic	½ teaspoon bottled minced garlic *or* ⅛ teaspoon garlic powder
1 small onion, chopped (⅓ cup)	1 teaspoon onion powder *or* 1 tablespoon dried minced onion
1 teaspoon dry mustard (in cooked mixtures)	1 tablespoon prepared mustard
1 tablespoon prepared mustard	½ teaspoon dry mustard *plus* 2 teaspoons vinegar
1 teaspoon poultry seasoning	¾ teaspoon dried sage, crushed, *plus* ¼ teaspoon dried thyme, crushed, *or* dried marjoram, crushed
1 teaspoon apple pie spice	½ teaspoon ground cinnamon *plus* ¼ teaspoon ground nutmeg, ⅛ teaspoon ground allspice, and dash ground cloves *or* ginger
1 teaspoon pumpkin pie spice	½ teaspoon ground cinnamon *plus* ¼ teaspoon ground ginger, ¼ teaspoon ground allspice, and ⅛ teaspoon ground nutmeg
1 cup tomato juice	½ cup tomato sauce *plus* ½ cup water
2 cups tomato sauce	¾ cup tomato paste *plus* 1 cup water

Recipe Index

Angel Food Cake, 14
Appetizers
  Herbed Pork Pâté, 298
  Oysters Rockefeller, 288
  Wontons or Egg Rolls with Pork
    and Shrimp Filling, 442
Apple or Pear Filling, 110
Apricot Mousse, 263
Arroz con Pollo, 18

Baked Custard, 137
Baked Polenta, 321
Bean and Cheese Burritos, 64
Beef
  Beef Bourguignonne, 178
  Beef Goulash, 192
  Beef Pot Roast, 330
  Beef Stroganoff, 392
  Chili con Carne, 99
  German-Style Meatballs, 249
  Paella, 289
  Pepper Steak, 309
  Pizza, 318
  Sauerbraten, 189
  Sizzling Beef Fajitas, 158
  Steak au Poivre, 387
  Swiss Steak, 398
Beets, Harvard, 204
Berry Sherbet, 374
Beverages
  Cooked Eggnog, 153
  Eggnog for a Crowd, 153
Biscuits, 46
  Buttermilk Biscuits, 46
  Drop Biscuits, 47
  Garden Biscuits, 46
  Sour Cream Biscuits, 46
Blueberry Muffins, 264
Blueberry or Peach Filling, 110

Keep track of your daily nutrition needs by using the information we provide at the end of each recipe. We've analyzed the nutrition content of each recipe serving for you. When a recipe gives an ingredient substitution, we used the first choice in the analysis. If it makes a range of servings (such as 4 to 6), we used the smallest number. Ingredients listed as optional weren't included in the calculations.

Blueberry Sour Cream Pound
  Cake, 335
Boston Brown Bread, 51
Bread Pudding, 54
Breads
  Biscuits, 46
  Blueberry Muffins, 264
  Boston Brown Bread, 51
  Buttermilk Biscuits, 46
  Cheesy Corn Spoon Bread, 383
  Confetti Corn Bread, 121
  Corn Bread, 121
  Corn Sticks or Corn Muffins, 121
  Corny Corn Bread, 121
  Country Scones, 370
  Cranberry Muffins, 264
  Drop Biscuits, 47
  Dumplings, 150
  French Bread, 176
  Garden Biscuits, 46
  Green Chili Corn Bread, 121
  Herb Popovers, 324
  Hot Cross Buns, 213
  Mini French Bread Loaves, 176
  Muffins, 264
  Oat or Wheat Bran Muffins, 264
  Parmesan Popovers, 324
  Parmesan Spoon Bread, 324
  Sour Cream Biscuits, 46
  Spoon Bread, 382
Broiled Polenta, 321
Brownies, Rocky Road, 62
Burritos, Bean and Cheese, 64
Buttermilk Biscuits, 46

Caesar Salad, Today's, 69
Cakes
  Angel Food Cake, 14
  Blueberry Sour Cream Pound
    Cake, 335
  Chiffon Cake, 98
  Cocoa Angel Food Cake, 14
  Devil's Food Cake, 142
  Fruitcake, 181
  Fruit Jelly Roll, 221
  Gingerbread, 190
  Lemon-Poppy-Seed Pound
    Cake, 335
  Light Fruitcake, 181
  Sour Cream Pound Cake, 335

Candies
  Chocolate Truffles, 415
  Divinity, 145
  Mixed Nut Brittle, 58
  Nutty Truffles, 415
Cheese
  Bean and Cheese Burritos, 64
  Cheese French Omelet, 278
  Cheese-Herb Puffy Omelet, 279
  Cheese Sauce, 438
  Cheesy Corn Spoon Bread, 383
  Ham-and-Cheese Puffy
    Omelet, 279
  Spicy Cheese Manicotti, 217
Cheesecakes
  Cheesecake Supreme, 92
  Chocolate Swirl Cheesecake, 92
  Sour Cream Cheesecake, 92
Cherry or Rhubarb Filling, 110
Chicken
  Arroz con Pollo, 18
  Chicken and Dumplings, 150
  Chicken Chow Mein, 104
  Chicken Divan, 144
  Chicken Jambalaya, 220
  Chicken Saltimbocca, 363
  Chicken Tetrazzini, 407
  Chicken Tostadas, 412
  Moo Goo Gai Pan, 286
  Paella, 289
Chiffon Cake, 98
Chili con Carne, 99
Chocolate
  Chocolate Butter Frosting, 142
  Chocolate Pots de Crème, 331
  Chocolate Pudding, 339
  Chocolate Swirl Cheesecake, 92
  Chocolate Truffles, 415
  Devil's Food Cake, 142
  No-Cook Chocolate Ice Cream, 214
  Nutty Truffles, 415
  Rocky Road Brownies, 62
Chow Mein, Chicken, 104
Cioppino, 105
Clams
  Ciopppino, 105
  Manhattan Clam Chowder, 109
  New England Clam Chowder, 108
  Paella, 289
Classic Lasagna, 228
Classic Quiche Lorraine, 342
Cobbler, Fruit, 110
Cocoa Angel Food Cake, 14
Coleslaw, 115
Confetti Corn Bread, 121

Cooked Eggnog, 153
Corn
  Cheesy Corn Spoon Bread, 383
  Confetti Corn Bread, 121
  Corn Bread, 121
  Corn Relish, 123
  Corn Sticks or Corn Muffins, 121
  Corny Corn Bread, 121
  Green Chili Corn Bread, 121
Country Pork Ragout, 347
Country Scones, 370
Crab Louis, 126
Cranberry Muffins, 264
Crayfish Étouffée, 70
Cream Puffs, 130
Cream Sauce, 439
Creamy Potato Salad, 329
Crisp, Two-Fruit, 132
Crockery Cooker Recipes
  Beef Pot Roast, 330
  Swiss Steak, 398
Curried Shrimp Strata, 391
Custards
  Baked Custard, 137
  Stirred Custard, 137

Desserts
  Apple or Pear Filling, 110
  Apricot Mousse, 263
  Baked Custard, 137
  Berry Sherbet, 374
  Blueberry or Peach Filling, 110
  Bread Pudding, 54
  Cheesecake Supreme, 92
  Cherry or Rhubarb Filling, 110
  Chocolate Pots de Crème, 331
  Chocolate Pudding, 339
  Chocolate Swirl Cheesecake, 92
  Chocolate Truffles, 415
  Cream Puffs, 130
  Fruit Cobbler, 110
  Fruit Trifle, 414
  Meringue Shells, 253
  No-Cook Chocolate Ice Cream, 214
  No-Cook Strawberry Ice
    Cream, 214
  No-Cook Vanilla Ice Cream, 214
  Rocky Road Brownies, 62
  Sour Cream Cheesecake, 92
  Stirred Custard, 137
  Strawberry Shortcake, 374
  Two-Fruit Crisp, 132
  Vanilla Pudding, 339
  Zabaglione, 445

Devil's Food Cake, 142
Divinity, 145
Drop Biscuits, 47
Dumplings, 150

Eggnog, Cooked, 153
Eggnog for a Crowd, 153
Egg Rolls with Pork and Shrimp
  Filling, Wontons or, 442
Eggs
  Baked Custard, 137
  Cheese French Omelet, 278
  Cheese-Herb Puffy Omelet, 279
  Classic Quiche Lorraine, 342
  Eggs Benedict, 154
  French Omelet, 278
  Frittata, 179
  Greek Frittata, 179
  Ham-and-Cheese Puffy
    Omelet, 279
  Hollandaise Sauce, 210
  Meringue for Pie, 253
  Meringue Shells, 253
  Mushroom French Omelet, 278
  Oven Frittata, 179
  Puffy Omelet, 278
  Stirred Custard, 137
Enchiladas, Pork, 254

Fajitas, Sizzling Beef, 158
Fettuccine Alfredo, 162
Fillings
  Apple or Pear Filling, 110
  Blueberry or Peach Filling, 110
  Cherry or Rhubarb Filling, 110
Fish and Seafood
  Cioppino, 105
  Crab Louis, 126
  Crayfish Étouffée, 70
  Fish Chowder, 108
  Fish Fillets Amandine, 11
  Gumbo, 201
  Manhattan Clam Chowder, 109
  New England Clam Chowder, 108
  Oysters Rockefeller, 288
  Pompano en Papillote, 291
  Tempura, 406
  Trout Amandine, 11
  Wontons or Egg Rolls with Pork
    and Shrimp Filling, 442
French Bread, 176
French Omelet, 278
French Onion Soup, 282

French Vinaigrette, 429
Fried Polenta, 321
Frittata, 179
  Greek Frittata, 179
  Oven Frittata, 179
Frostings
  Chocolate Butter Frosting, 142
  Powdered Sugar Icing, 213
Fruitcake, 181
Fruitcake, Light, 181
Fruit Cobbler, 110
Fruit Jelly Roll, 221
Fruit Trifle, 414

Garden Biscuits, 46
Garlic Vinaigrette, 429
Gazpacho, 187
German-Style Meatballs, 249
German-Style Potato Salad, 329
Gingerbread, 190
Goulash, Beef, 192
Gravy, 197
Greek Frittata, 179
Green Chili Corn Bread, 121
Gumbo, 201

Ham
  Ham-and-Cheese Puffy
    Omelet, 279
  Pizza, 318
  Risotto, 354
  Veal Saltimbocca, 363
Harvard Beets, 204
Herbed Pork Pâté, 298
Herb Popovers, 324
Hollandaise Sauce, 210
Hot Cross Buns, 213

Ice Creams
  No-Cook Chocolate Ice Cream, 214
  No-Cook Strawberry Ice
    Cream, 214
  No-Cook Vanilla Ice Cream, 214
Indian Pilaf, 316
Irish Stew, 216
Italian Vinaigrette, 429

Jambalaya, Chicken, 220
Jelly Roll, Fruit, 221

Lamb
  Irish Stew, 216
  Moussaka, 262
Lasagna, Classic, 228
Lemon-Poppy-Seed Pound Cake, 335

449

Light Fruitcake, 181
Louis Dressing, 126
Low-Calorie White Sauce, 438
Low-Fat Tartar Sauce, 405

Main Dishes
　Arroz con Pollo, 18
　Bean and Cheese Burritos, 64
　Beef Bourguignonne, 178
　Beef Goulash, 192
　Beef Pot Roast, 330
　Beef Stroganoff, 392
　Cheese French Omelet, 278
　Cheese-Herb Puffy Omelet, 279
　Chicken and Dumplings, 150
　Chicken Chow Mein, 104
　Chicken Jambalaya, 220
　Chicken Saltimbocca, 363
　Chicken Tetrazzini, 407
　Chicken Tostadas, 412
　Chili con Carne, 99
　Cioppino, 105
　Classic Lasagna, 228
　Classic Quiche Lorraine, 342
　Country Pork Ragout, 347
　Crab Louis, 126
　Crayfish Étouffée, 70
　Curried Shrimp Strata, 391
　Eggs Benedict, 154
　Fettuccine Alfredo, 162
　Fish Chowder, 108
　Fish Fillets Amandine, 11
　French Omelet, 278
　Frittata, 179
　German-Style Meatballs, 249
　Greek Frittata, 179
　Gumbo, 201
　Ham-and-Cheese Puffy
　　Omelet, 279
　Irish Stew, 216
　Manhattan Clam Chowder, 109
　Moo Goo Gai Pan, 286
　Moussaka, 262
　Mushroom French Omelet, 278
　New England Clam Chowder, 108
　Oven Frittata, 179
　Paella, 289
　Pepper Steak, 309
　Pizza, 318
　Pompano en Papillote, 291
　Pork Enchiladas, 254
　Puffy Omelet, 278
　Sauerbraten, 189
　Sizzling Beef Fajitas, 158
　Spicy Cheese Manicotti, 217
　Steak au Poivre, 387

Main dishes *(continued)*
　Swiss Steak, 398
　Tempura, 406
　Trout Amandine, 11
　Turkey and Chorizo Mole, 261
　Veal Saltimbocca, 363
　Wiener Schnitzel, 439
Manhattan Clam Chowder, 109
Manicotti, Spicy Cheese, 217
Meatballs, German-Style, 249
Meringue for Pie, 253
Meringue Shells, 253
Microwave Recipes
　Chili con Carne, 99
　French Omelet, 278
　German-Style Potato Salad, 329
　Gingerbread, 191
　Harvard Beets, 204
　Hollandaise Sauce, 210
　Twice-Baked Potatoes, 420
　Vichyssoise, 429
　White Sauce, 438
Minestrone, 258
Mini French Bread Loaves, 176
Mixed Nut Brittle, 58
Mole, Turkey and Chorizo, 261
Moo Goo Gai Pan, 286
Moussaka, 262
Mousse, Apricot, 263
Muffins, 264
　Blueberry Muffins, 264
　Corn Sticks or Corn Muffins, 121
　Cranberry Muffins, 264
　Oat or Wheat Bran Muffins, 264
Mushroom French Omelet, 278

New England Clam Chowder, 108
No-Cook Chocolate Ice Cream, 214
No-Cook Strawberry Ice Cream, 214
No-Cook Vanilla Ice Cream, 214
Nutty Truffles, 415

Oat or Wheat Bran Muffins, 264
Omelets
　Cheese French Omelet, 278
　Cheese-Herb Puffy Omelet, 279
　French Omelet, 278
　Ham-and-Cheese Puffy
　　Omelet, 279
　Mushroom French Omelet, 278
　Puffy Omelet, 278
Onion Soup, French, 282
Oven Frittata, 179
Oysters Rockefeller, 288

Paella, 289
Pan Pizzas, 319
Parmesan Popovers, 324
Parmesan Spoon Bread, 383
Pasta
　Classic Lasagna, 228
　Fettuccine Alfredo, 162
　Spaetzle, 189
　Spicy Cheese Manicotti, 217
　Whole Wheat Spaetzle, 189
Pastry Shell, 342
Pâté, Herbed Pork, 298
Peach Filling, Blueberry or, 110
Pear Filling, Apple or, 110
Pepper Steak, 309
Pesto, 310
Pilaf, Indian, 316
Pilaf, Rice, 316
Pizza, 318
　Pan Pizzas, 319
　Thin Pizzas, 318
Polenta, 321
　Baked Polenta, 321
　Broiled Polenta, 321
　Fried Polenta, 321
Pompano en Papillote, 291
Popovers
　Herb Popovers, 324
　Parmesan Popovers, 324
Pork
　Chicken Chow Mein, 104
　Country Pork Ragout, 347
　Eggs Benedict, 154
　Herbed Pork Pâté, 298
　Pizza, 318
　Pork Enchiladas, 254
　Wiener Schnitzel, 439
　Wontons or Egg Rolls with Pork
　　and Shrimp Filling, 442
Potatoes
　Creamy Potato Salad, 329
　German-Style Potato Salad, 329
　Twice-Baked Potatoes, 420
　Vichyssoise, 428
Pot Roast, Beef, 330
Pots de Crème, Chocolate, 331
Poultry
　Arroz con Pollo, 18
　Chicken and Dumplings, 150
　Chicken Divan, 144
　Chicken Jambalaya, 220
　Chicken Saltimbocca, 363
　Chicken Tetrazzini, 407

450

Poultry *(continued)*
 Chicken Tostadas, 412
 Moo Goo Gai Pan, 286
 Paella, 289
 Turkey and Chorizo Mole, 261
Pound Cakes
 Blueberry Sour Cream Pound
  Cake, 335
 Lemon-Poppy-Seed Pound
  Cake, 335
 Sour Cream Pound Cake, 335
Powdered Sugar Icing, 213
Puddings
 Bread Pudding, 54
 Chocolate Pudding, 339
 Vanilla Pudding, 339
Puffy Omelet, 278

Quiche Lorraine, Classic, 342

Ragout, Country Pork, 347
Ratatouille, 348
Red Wine Vinaigrette, 429
Relish, Corn, 123
Rhubarb Filling, Cherry or, 110
Rice
 Indian Pilaf, 316
 Rice Pilaf, 316
 Risotto, 354
Risotto, 354
Rocky Road Brownies, 62

Salads
 Coleslaw, 115
 Crab Louis, 126
 Creamy Potato Salad, 329
 German-Style Potato Salad, 329
 Today's Caesar Salad, 69
 Vinaigrette Coleslaw, 115
 Waldorf Salad, 433
Salad Dressings
 French Vinaigrette, 429
 Garlic Vinaigrette, 429
 Italian Vinaigrette, 429
 Louis Dressing, 126
 Red Wine Vinaigrette, 429
 Vinaigrette, 429
Saltimbocca
 Chicken Saltimbocca, 363
 Veal Saltimbocca, 363
Sauces
 Cheese Sauce, 438
 Cream Sauce, 439
 Hollandaise Sauce, 210

Sauces *(continued)*
 Low-Calorie White Sauce, 438
 Low-Fat Tartar Sauce, 405
 Tartar Sauce, 405
 Tempura Dipping Sauce, 407
 White Sauce, 438
Sauerbraten, 189
Sausage
 Chicken Jambalaya, 220
 Classic Lasagna, 228
 Gumbo, 201
 Pizza, 318
 Turkey and Chorizo Mole, 261
Scones, Country, 370
Seasoning, Three-Pepper, 220
Sherbet, Berry, 374
Shortcake, Strawberry, 374
Shrimp
 Cioppino, 105
 Crayfish Étouffée, 70
 Curried Shrimp Strata, 391
 Gumbo, 201
 Paella, 289
 Tempura, 406
 Wontons or Egg Rolls with Pork
  and Shrimp Filling, 442
Sizzling Beef Fajitas, 158
Soups and Stews
 Beef Bourguignonne, 178
 Beef Goulash, 192
 Chicken Jambalaya, 220
 Chili con Carne, 99
 Cioppino, 105
 Fish Chowder, 108
 French Onion Soup, 282
 Gazpacho, 187
 Gumbo, 201
 Irish Stew, 216
 Manhattan Clam Chowder, 109
 Minestrone, 258
 New England Clam Chowder, 108
 Vichyssoise, 428
Sour Cream Biscuits, 46
Sour Cream Cheesecake, 92
Sour Cream Pound Cake, 335
Spaetzle, 189
Spaetzle, Whole Wheat, 189
Spicy Cheese Manicotti, 217
Spoon Bread, 382
 Cheesy Corn Spoon Bread, 383
 Parmesan Spoon Bread, 383
Steak au Poivre, 387
Stir-Fry, Vegetable-Stick, 390
Stirred Custard, 137

Strata, Curried Shrimp, 341
Strawberry Ice Cream, No-Cook, 214
Strawberry Shortcake, 374
Stroganoff, Beef, 392
Swiss Steak, 398

Tartar Sauce, 405
Tartar Sauce, Low-Fat, 405
Tempura, 406
Tempura Dipping Sauce, 407
Tetrazzini, Chicken, 407
Thin Pizzas, 318
Three-Pepper Seasoning, 220
Today's Caesar Salad, 69
Tostadas, Chicken, 412
Trifle, Fruit, 414
Trout Amandine, 11
Truffles
 Chocolate Truffles, 415
 Nutty Truffles, 415
Turkey
 Chicken Divan, 144
 Chicken Tetrazzini, 407
 Turkey and Chorizo Mole, 261
Twice-Baked Potatoes, 420
Two-Fruit Crisp, 132

Vanilla Ice Cream, No-Cook, 214
Vanilla Pudding, 339
Veal
 Veal Saltimbocca, 363
 Wiener Schnitzel, 439
Vegetables
 Harvard Beets, 204
 Ratatouille, 348
 Twice-Baked Potatoes, 420
 Vegetable-Stick Stir-Fry, 390
Vichyssoise, 428
Vinaigrette, 429
 French Vinaigrette, 429
 Garlic Vinaigrette, 429
 Italian Vinaigrette, 429
 Red Wine Vinaigrette, 429
Vinaigrette Coleslaw, 115

Waldorf Salad, 433
Wheat Bran Muffins, Oat or, 264
White Sauce, 438
White Sauce, Low-Calorie, 438
Whole Wheat Spaetzle, 189
Wiener Schnitzel, 439
Wontons or Egg Rolls with Pork
 and Shrimp Filling, 442

Zabaglione, 445

Text Index

When using the index, note the meanings of the following symbols.

A dagger (†) preceding the page number indicates that the information is located in a chart.

An asterisk (*) before the page number indicates that a recipe is provided.

Page numbers in italics indicate that there is a photo or illustration for the entry.

The indented information in parentheses directly below the index entry lists the subheads that you will find under the main entry in the book.

Abalone, 10
Ace plum, *319*
Acidophilus milk, 256, †257
Acini di pepe, *294*
  cooking, †296
Acorn squash, *385*, †386
  cooking, †427
Active dry yeast, 443
Additives, food, 172
Alcoholic beverage
  beer, 41
  bitters used in, 47
  cocktail, 110
  flaming, 168, *169*
  food group, †272
  imitating flavor of, 169
  liqueur, 234
  proof, 337
  punch, 340
  wassail, 434
  See also Wine
Al dente pasta, *10*
Alfalfa sprout, *383*
Alligator, 10
  (cooking hints, market forms, nutrition information, preparation hints)
Alligator pear. *See* Avocado
All-purpose flour, 170
Allspice, 10
  alternative for, 381
Almond, *10*–11, †270
  (storing, types)
  sliced vs. slivered, 10
  toasting, *11*
Almond bark (candy coating), 77

Almond paste, 11
Alphabet pasta, *295*
  cooking, †296
Alum, 11
Amandine style, *9*, *11
Amaranth, 12
  (nutrition information, storing)
Ambrosia, 12
American cheese, *12*, †88
American (Maine) lobster, 235
American (yellow) mustard, 267
American redfin (tilapia), 409
Anaheim pepper, †306, *307*
Ancho pepper, †306, *307*
Anchovy, 12
  (market forms, nutrition information)
  paste vs. fillet, 12
Anelli (ring pasta), *294*
  cooking, †296
Angel food cake, 12, *13*, *14, 71
  (nutrition information, preparation hints)
  dressing up, 12
  loosening from pan, *71*
  problem solving, 72
Angelica, 14
Angels on horseback, 14
Anise and aniseed, 14
  alternative for, 381
  leaves, using, 14
Anjou pear, 302, *303*
Antipasto, 15
Aperitif wine, 15, 440
Appetizer, 15
  angels on horseback, 14
  antipasto, 15
  canapé, 74
  crudités, 134
  dip, 143
  hors d'oeuvre, 212
    tapa, 404
  hummus, 214
Apple, 15, *16*–17
  (market forms, nutrition information, selecting, storing, varieties)
  for applesauce, 18
  browning, preventing, 15
  crab, *125*
  dried, cooking, †147
  equivalents, 15
  peeled, uses for, 15
  selecting, 15, †16
Apple-pear. *See* Asian pear

Apple pie spice, 17
  substitution for, emergency, †446
Applesauce, *17–18
  (how to cook, nutrition information)
  chunky vs. smooth, 17
  varieties of apples for, 18
Apricot, *18*
  (market forms, nutrition information, selecting, storing)
  dried, cooking, †147
  equivalents, 18
Arrowroot, 18
Arroz con pollo, *18–19
Artichoke, *19*
  (market forms, nutrition information, selecting, storing, types)
  cooking, †424
  eating, technique for, 19
  Jerusalem, *222*, †426
  preparing, *19*, †424
Arugula, *20*
  (nutrition information, preparation hints, selecting, storing)
Ascorbic acid color keeper, 20
  buying and storing, 20
Aseptic (shelf-stable) packaging, 372
Asiago cheese, †88
Asian pear, *20–21*
  (nutrition information, preparation hints, selecting, storing)
Asparagus, *21*
  (market forms, nutrition information, selecting, storing, types)
  cooking, †424
  grilling, †32
  scale removal, 21
Aspartame, 395
Aspic, 22
Atlantic salmon, 360
Au gratin, 22
Au jus, 22
Australian sole (orange roughy), †165, 283
Avocado, *22–23*
  (nutrition information, preparation hints, selecting, storing, varieties)
  browning, slowing, 23
  guacamole, 199
  ripeness, judging, 22
  seeding, *23*

452

Baba, 23
Baby vegetable, 423
  carrot, 80–81
    grilling, †32
  eggplant, *154*
  sunburst squash, *384*
Bacon, 23–24, *327*
    (market forms, nutrition
    information, selecting, types)
  Canadian-style, 74, *327*
    broiling, †246
    grilling, †29
    panbroiling, †248
  cooking, 24
  crumbled, 23
  panbroiling, †248
  storing, †245
Bacon bits, storing, †245
  substitution for, emergency, †446
Bagel, 24
  (nutrition information)
Baguette, 24
Baked Alaska, 24
Baked custard, *137
Baked ham, 203
Baked potato, pricking, *328*
Baker's ammonia (hartshorn
  powder), 204
Baking, 24
Baking (unsweetened) chocolate, *101*
Baking dish, 24
  measuring, 25
Baking pan, 25
  vs. baking dish, 24
  measuring, 25
Baking powder, 25
  high-altitude adjustments, †209
  potency, checking, 25
  substitution for, emergency, †446
Baking soda, 25
  in brittle, 58
  sunflower nuts, and, 395
  uses, 25
Baklava, 25
Balsamic vinegar, 429
Bamboo shoot, 25–26, *284*
  (market forms, nutrition
  information, storing)
Banana, *26–27*
    (market forms, nutrition
    information, selecting,
    storing, varieties)
  browning, preventing, 27
  cooking, 27
  equivalents, 27

Banana pepper, yellow, †306
Banana squash, *385*, †386
  cooking, †427
Barbecue, 27
Barbecuing, 27–32
  cleaning up from, 28
  direct grilling, 27
    fish, †31
    meat, †29
    poultry, †32
    vegetables, †32
  fire, starting, 27–28
  flare-ups, control of, 28
  indirect grilling, 27
    meat, †30–31
    poultry, †31
  smoke flavor, adding, 28
  temperature of coals
    adjusting for, 28
    testing, 28
Bar cookie, 117
  hints for making, 118
Barley, 33
  (market forms, nutrition
  information, storing)
  cooking, †193
  pearl, 33, †193, 304
Bartlett pear, 302, *303*
Basic Food Groups, †272
  in menu planning, 272–273
Basil, *33*
    (varieties)
  alternative for, 208
  in pesto, 33
Basmati rice, 352
Bass, 34, †165
  large- and smallmouth, 34, †165
  sea bass, 34, †165
Basting, 34
  kinds of foods for, 34
Batter, 34
  berries in, 43, 49
Bavarian cream, 34
Bay leaf, 34
  using, 34
Bean, dried, *36–37*
    (cooking hints, market forms,
    nutrition information, selecting,
    storing, varieties)
  black-eyed peas, †37, *48*, 299
  doneness, testing for, *37*
  refried, 350
  selecting and cooking, †37

Bean, fresh, 35–36
    (how to cook, market forms,
    nutrition information, selecting,
    storing, varieties)
  cooking, †424
  equivalents, 35
Bean curd (tofu), 285, 409–410
Bean noodle, 38, 100, *285*
Bean sprout, 38, *383*
    (nutrition information, selecting,
    storing)
  beans and roots on, 38
Bean thread, 38, 100, *285*
  cooking times, 38
Béarnaise sauce, 38
Beating, 38
Béchamel sauce, 38
Beef, 38–41
    (beef cuts, grading, how to
    cook, market forms, nutrition
    information, selecting,
    serving hints)
  broiling, †246
  carving, *81–82*
  corned, 121, †245
  cuts, 39, *40–41*
  doneness of steak, *39*
  dried, 146
  grilling, †29, †30
  ground. *See* Ground beef
  jerky, 222
  on low-fat diet, 39
  panbroiling, and panfrying, †248
  roasting, †247
  storing, †245
  variety meat, *421*
Beef salami, †366
Beef Wellington, 41
  simplifying, 41
Beer, 41
  (types)
Beet, *41–42*
    (market forms, nutrition
    information, selecting, storing)
  cooking, †424
  greens, 41, 42
    cooking, †425
  Harvard beets, *204, *205*
  soup (borscht), 51
Beet vs. cane sugar, 393
Beignet, 42
Belgian endive, 42–43, 156
  (nutrition information, preparation
  hints, selecting, storing)
Belgian waffle, 431

Bell pepper, †306, *307*
  cooking, †427
Belly clam, 107
Bel Paese cheese, †88
Benne. *See* Sesame seed
Berry, 43
    (selecting, storing, varieties)
  selecting, †43
  sinking in batter, 43
  See Selecting Berries
    chart, 43, for varieties
Betty, 44
  cubing bread for, 44
Beverage, 44
  amount for crowd, †341
  brewing, 57
  cocktail, 110
  eggnog, *139,* *153
  mulling, 265
  punch, 340
  soda, 378
  soda fountain, 44
  wassail, 434
  water, 434
  See also Alcoholic beverage; Coffee;
    Milk; Tea
Bias slicing, *44*
Bibb lettuce, †232
Binder and binding, 44
Bing cherry, *93*
Biscuit, 44, *45,* *46–47, 55
    (convenience products,
    storing, types)
  cutting, 46
  doneness, testing for, 46
  freezing, †175
  tips on making, 46
Bismarck, 47
Bisque, 47
Bitter (unsweetened) chocolate, *101*
Bitters, 47
Bittersweet (semisweet) chocolate,
  101
Black bean, *36,* †37
Blackberry, †43, *47*
  (market forms, varieties)
Black bottom pie, 47
Black Corinth grape, *194*
  dried currant, 136, 347
Blackened fish, 47
  smoke from, 47
Black-eyed pea, †37, *48,* 299
  (how to cook, nutrition information,
  selecting, storing)
Black Forest torte, 411

Black Mission fig, *163*
Black olive, 277
Black pepper, 304–305
Black radish, *346*
Blackstrap molasses, 260
Black tea, 405
Black walnut, †270, *433*
Blanching, 48
  timing, 48
Blancmange, 48
Bland food, 48
Blending, 48
Blintze, 48
Blitz torte, 411
Blond (white) fudge, 182
Blood orange, *282,* †283
Blood sausage, †366, *367*
Blueberry, †43, *49*
    (market forms, storing)
  bleeding in batter, 49
Blue cheese, *49,* †88
  (market forms, types)
Blue crab, 124
  cooking, †373
Bluefish, †165
Blush wine, 441
Bockwurst, †366
Boiled frosting, 180
Boiled ham, 203
Boiling, 50
  parboiling, 292
  rolling boil, 50, 220
Boiling (boiler) onion,
  279, *280*
Boiling-water canner, 77
Bok choy, *50,* 100
    (nutrition information,
    preparation hints, selecting,
    storing)
  other names for, 50
Bologna, †366, *367*
Bombe, 50
  unmolding, 50
Bone-in vs. boneless ham, 202,
  326, 327
  roasting, †247
Bone marrow, 242
Borage, †171
Bordeaux mustard, 267
Bordelaise sauce, 51
Borscht, 51
Bosc pear, 302, *303*
Boston brown bread, *51
Boston cream pie, 51
Boston lettuce, †232

Bouillabaisse, 51
Bouillon (broth), 51, 60
  court bouillon, 124
Bouquet garni, *52*
Bow tie, pasta, *295*
  cooking, †296
Boysenberry, †43, *52*
  (market forms)
Brain, 421
Braising, 52
  beef cuts for, *40–41*
  lamb cuts for, *227*
  pork cuts for, *326*
  veal cuts for, *422*
Bran, 52–53
    (nutrition information,
    storing, types)
  in baked foods, 52
  as fiber source, 52
  oat, 52, 53, 276
  in recipes, type for, 53
  rice, 52, 352
  wheat, 52, 437
Brandied food, 53
Bratwurst, †366, *367*
Braunschweiger, †366
Brazil nut, *53,* †270
  (storing)
  cracking, 53
Bread, 53
    (nutrition information)
  brown, 60
    Boston, *51
  crouton, 134
  crumb, 53–54, *134*
  cube, 44
  as food group, †272
  freezing, †175
  sourdough starter, 380
  spoon bread, *382–383
  sweet
    coffee cake, 114
    cruller, 134
    Sally Lunn, 360
    See also Doughnut
  unleavened
    matzo, 242
    pita, 318
    tortilla, 412
  whole grain, 439
  See also Quick bread; Sandwich;
    Toast; Yeast bread
Bread crumbs, 53
  cereal as substitute, 86
  making, 54, *134*
  substitution for, emergency, †446

Bread flour, 170
Breadfruit, 54
  (nutrition information, selecting,
  storing)
Breading, 54
  less messy method, 54
Bread pudding, *54
Breakfast cereal. See Cereal
Brewing, 57
  loose tea, 406
Brick cheese, 57, †88
Brie cheese, 58, †88
  (selecting)
Brine, 58
Brioche, 58
  hints for making, 58
Brittle, 9, *58–59
  baking soda in, 58
Broadleaf endive (escarole), 156, 157
Broccoli, 59
  (market forms, nutrition
  information, selecting, storing)
  amount for crowd, †341
  cooking, †424
  tough stems, 59
Broccoli raab (broccoli di rape), 60
  (how to cook, nutrition information,
  selecting, storing)
Broiler-fryer, 95
Broiling, 60, †246
  (nutrition hints)
  beef cuts for, 40–41
  fish, †167
  lamb cuts for, 227
  lobster, †373
  pork cuts for, 326–327
  poultry, †332
  preheating for, 60
  veal cuts for, 246
Broth (bouillon), 51, 60
  court bouillon, 124
  substitution for, emergency, †446
Brown bread, 60
  Boston, *51
Brownie, 60, 61, *62
Browning, 60
Brown mushroom, 265
Brown rice, 352, 353
  cooking, †352
    with wild rice, 440
Brown roux, 356
  making, 357
Brown sauce, 62, 364
  espagnole, 62
  piquant, 317

Brown sugar, 393
  measuring, 243
  softening, 394
Brown Turkey fig, 163
Brunch, 62
  (nutrition hints)
Brussels sprout, 62–63
  (market forms, nutrition
  information, selecting, storing)
  cooking, †424
Buckwheat, *63
  (how to cook, market forms,
  nutrition information, storing)
  cooking, †193
Bulgur, 63, 436
  (nutrition information, storing)
  cooking, †193
Bun, 63
Burger (hamburger), 204
  best ground beef for, 198
Burgoo, 63
Burnt (caramelized) sugar, 79
Burpless (English) cucumber, 135
Burrito, *64
Butter, 64–65, 159, 160
  (market forms, nutrition
  information, storing, types)
  amount for crowd, †341
  clarified, 64
  for croissant, 132
  equivalents, 65
  margarine substituted for, 240
  melting in microwave, 252
  for toffee, 409
  unsalted vs. regular, 64
Buttercup squash, 385, †386
  cooking, †427
Butterfat (milk fat), 65, 257
Butterfish, †165
Butterflying, 65
  shrimp, 376
Butter frosting, 180
Butterhead lettuce, 232, †232
Butter-margarine blend, 64, 240, 241
Buttermilk, 65, 256, †257
  (nutrition information)
  substitute for, 65, †446
Butternut squash, 385, †386
  cooking, †427
Butter sauce, 364
Butterscotch, 65
Button (red) radish, 346

Cabbage, 68
  (market forms, nutrition
  information, selecting, storing,
  varieties)
  Chinese, 68, 99–100
    bok choy, 50, 100
  coleslaw, *115
  cooking, 68, †424
  equivalents, 68
  kimchi, 223
  sauerkraut, 365
Cactus leaf, 69
  (preparation hints, selecting,
  storing)
Cactus pear. See Prickly pear
Caesar salad, *69
Café au lait, 113
Caffeine, 70
  in coffee, 113
Cajun cooking, *70
  (cuisine highlights, specialties)
  hotness of, 70
Cake, 71–72
  (baking hints, nutrition hints,
  storing, types)
  amount for crowd, †341
  angel food, 12, 13, *14, 71, 72
  baba, 23
  Boston cream pie, 51
  chiffon, 71, 72, 98
  cooling, 71
  cupcake, 135–136
  decorating, 73, 150
  devil's food, *142–143
  freezing, †175
  frosting, 180
  fruitcake, *181
  gingerbread, *190–191
  high-altitude adjustments, †209
  hints for making, 71
  Lady Baltimore, 226
  Lord Baltimore, 236
  one-bowl, 279
  petit four, 310
  pound, 275, 334–*335
  problem solving, 72
  removing from pan, 71
  sponge, 71, 72, 382
    jelly roll, 219, *221
    ladyfinger, 226
  torte, 411
    ground nuts for, 271
Cake decorating, 73
  dusted design, 150
  piping bag, simple, 73

Cake flour, 170
  substitution for, emergency, †446
Calamari (squid), 73, 387
  (nutrition information)
  preparing, 387
Calcium, †430
Calendula (pot marigold), †171
Calimyrna fig, 163
Calorie, 73
  needs, estimating, 73
  variation by type
    in milk, †257
    in water products, 434
    in yogurt, †444
  See also individual entries
Camembert cheese, 73, †88
Canadian-style bacon, 74, 327
  (nutrition information)
  broiling, †246
  grilling, †29
  panbroiling, †248
Canapé, 74
Candied fruit or peel, 74
Candied ginger, 190
Candy, 74–77
    (equipment, preparation hints,
      storing)
  brittle, 9, *58–59
  butterscotch, 65
  calibrating thermometer for, 76
  caramel, 79
  coating for dipping, 77
  cold water tests, 74, 75
  divinity, 139, 144–*145
    vs. nougat, 269
  fondant, 172
  fudge, 182–183
    penuche, 182, 304
  gumdrop, 201
  hints for making, 76
  humidity for, 76
  marshmallow, 242
  mint, 258
  nonpareil, 269
  nougat, 269
  praline, 335
  taffy, 402
  thermometer, 74, 76, 408
  toffee, 409
  truffle, *415
Cane vs. beet sugar, 393
Canned ham, 203
Cannelloni, 77
  shortcut, 77

Canners and canning, 77–78
    (equipment, using home-canned
      foods)
  high-altitude, 78
Canning salt, 361
Can sizes, †116
Cantaloupe, 78, †250, 251
  (nutrition information, selecting)
Capellini, 295
  cooking, †296
Caper, 78
Capon, 95
  roasting, †333
Cappuccino, 113
Carambola, 78–79
    (market forms, nutrition
      information, selecting, storing)
  preparing and using, 79
Caramel, 79
  shortcut for, 79
Caramelized sugar, 79
  preparing, 79
  working with, 79
Caraway, 79
Carbohydrate, 79–80
  See also Starch; Sugar
Cardaba banana, 26
Cardamom, 80
  alternative for, 381
  crushing, 80
Cardoon (cardoni), 80
    (nutrition information, preparation
      hints, selecting, storing)
Carob, 80
Carp, †165
Carrot, 80–81
    (market forms, nutrition
      information, selecting, storing,
      varieties)
  amount for crowd, †341
  cooking, †425
  equivalents, 81
  grilling, †32
  peeled vs. unpeeled, 81
Carving, 81–82
    (how to carve a bone-in roast,
      how to carve boneless meats, how
      to carve a turkey or other whole
      poultry)
  tips on, 81
Casaba, 82, †250, 251
  (nutrition information)
Cascabel pepper, †306, 307
Cashew, 82, †270
  (storing)

Casselman plum, 319
Casserole, 83
  freezing, †175
  size, determining, 83
Catfish, 83, †165
  (how to cook, market forms,
    nutrition information)
Catsup, 83
  (nutrition information)
Cauliflower, 83–84
    (market forms, nutrition
      information, selecting, storing,
      types)
  amount for crowd, †341
  cooking, †425
Cavatelli, 295
  cooking, †296
Cavendish banana, 26
Caviar, 84
  as appetizer, 84
Cayenne (ground red) pepper, 305,
  †306, 307
Celeriac, 84
    (nutrition information,
      preparation hint, selecting,
      storing)
  cooking, †425
Celery, 84–85
    (nutrition information, selecting,
      storing, types)
  amount for crowd, †341
  cooking, †425
  crispness, restoring, 85
  freezing, 85
Celery cabbage, 68, 100
Celery mustard. See Bok choy
Celery root. See Celeriac
Celery salt, 85
Celery seed, 85
Cellophane noodle, 38, 100, 285
Cereal, 85–86
    (market forms, nutrition hints,
      storing, varieties)
  for bread crumbs, 86
  as food group, †272
  granola, 194
  muesli, 263
Cereal grain. See Grain
Certified American lamb, 226
Cervelat, †366, 367
Champagne (Black Corinth)
    grape, 194
  dried currant, 136, 347
Chanterelle, 265
Chapman cherry, 93

Charcoal cooking. *See* Barbecuing
Chard (Swiss chard), *397*
Charlotte russe, 86
Chateaubriand, 86
Chayote, *86*
    (nutrition information, selecting, storing)
  cooking, †425
Cheddar cheese, *86*–87, †88
  (market forms, types)
Cheddaring, 86
Cheese, 87–90
    (from milk to cheese, nutrition hints, selecting, serving hints, storing, types of natural cheese, types of process and other cheese)
  chèvre, 95
  cottage, *123*
  cream, *129*
    Neufchâtel, 129, 269
  freezing, 90
  imitation, 87
  melting, 90
  natural vs. process, 87
  raclette, 346
  rarebit, 348
  ricotta, *353*–354
  selecting, †88–89
  string, 391–392
  See Selecting Cheese
    chart, 88–89, for varieties
Cheesecake, 90, *91, *92
  doneness, testing for, 92
  hints for making, 92
Cherimoya, *93*
    (nutrition information, selecting, storing)
  serving, 93
Cherries jubilee, 93
Cherry, *93*–94
    (market forms, nutrition information, preparation hint, selecting, storing, types)
  chokecherry, 103
  dried, cooking, †147
  equivalents, 94
  freezing, 94
Cherrystone clam, 107
Cherry tomato, 410, *411*
Chervil, 94
  alternative for, 208
Cheshire cheese, †88
Chess pie, 94

Chestnut, 95, †270
    (market forms, storing)
  dried, 95
  shelling, 95
Chèvre cheese, 95
Chicken, 95, *96,* 97
    (freezing, how to cook, market forms, nutrition hints, refrigerating, types)
  breast, skinning and boning, *96*
  broiling, †332
  cutting up
    cutting board for, 97
    whole chicken, *96*
  dark vs. light meat, 97
  doneness, testing for, *97*
  grilling, †31, †32
  roasting, †333
  See also Cornish game hen
Chicken-fried food, 97
Chick-pea (garbanzo bean), *36,* †37
  hummus, 214
Chicory (curly endive), *98,* 156
  red (radicchio), *346*
  witloof (Belgian endive), *42*–43, 156
Chiffon cake, 71, *98
  problem solving, 72
Chiffon pie, 98, 312
  hints for making, 313
Chili con carne, *67,* 98–*99
Chili paste, *285*
Chili pepper, 99, 305, †306, *307*
Chili powder, 99
  alternative for, 381
Chili sauce, 99
Chilled soufflé, 379
Chilling, 99
  cookie dough, 119
Chinese cabbage, *68,* 99–100
    (nutrition information, selecting, storing, varieties)
  bok choy, *50,* 100
Chinese chard cabbage. *See* Bok choy
Chinese cooking, *286–287
  See also Oriental ingredients
Chinese egg noodle, 100
Chinese gooseberry (kiwi fruit), *224*
Chinese long bean, *35,* 36
Chinese mustard (condiment), 267
Chinese mustard (vegetable). *See* Bok choy

Chinese noodle, 100
    (types)
  cellophane (bean thread), 38, 100, *285*
  rice stick, 100, 353
  substitution for, 100
Chinese orange (kumquat), †106, 225
Chinese parsley (cilantro), 105, *285*
Chinese pea pod (snow pea), *302*
Chinese pear. *See* Asian pear
Chinese white cabbage. *See* Bok choy
Chinook (King) salmon, †165, 360
Chipotle pepper, †306, *307*
Chipped (dried) beef, 146
Chitterling (chitlins), 421
Chive, *100*–101
    (market forms)
  alternative for, 208
  flower, †171
  using, 101
Chocolate, *101*–102
    (market forms, melting hints, nutrition information, storing, types)
  cocoa, 110–*111*
  gray color on, 102
  melted, unstiffening, 102
  substitutions, 102, 111
Chocolate-flavored syrup, 102, 399
Chocolate fudge, 182
Chocolatelike products, *101*–102
Chocolate milk, 256, †257
Chocolate pepper, †306
Chokecherry, 103
Cholesterol, 103, 159
  in egg recipes, reducing, 153
Chop, 103
  broiling, †246
  lamb, *227*
  panbroiling and panfrying, †248
  pork, *326, 327*
  storing, †245
  veal, *422*
Chopping, *103*
  vs. cubing, dicing, mincing, *103*
  in food processor, 103
  onion, *280*
Chop suey, 103
Chorizo, †366, *367*
Chou paste (choux), 103
  See also Cream puff
Chowchow, 104

Chowder, 104
  clam, *108–109
Chowder clam, 107
Chow mein, *104
Chow mein noodle, 104
Christmas (Santa Claus)
  melon, †250, *251*
Christmas (plum) pudding, 320
Chum (Keta, Dog) salmon, 360
Chutney, 104
Cider vinegar, 429
Cilantro, 105, *285*
  alternative for, 208
Cinnamon, 105
  alternative for, 381
  stick and oil forms, 105
Cioppino, *105
Cisco whitefish, 437
Citron, 105
Citrus fruit, 105–106
    (nutrition information, storing)
  freezing, 106
  juice from, 106
  peel
    candied, 74
    freezing, 106
    zest, 445
  sectioning, *371*
  selecting, †106
  See Selecting Citrus Fruit
      chart, 106, for varieties
Clam, *107–108*
    (market forms, nutrition
    information, preparation hints,
    selecting, storing, types)
  equivalents, 107
  preparing and cooking, †373
  shucking, *107*
Clam chowder, *108–109
Clarifying, 109
  butter, 64
Cling peach, 300
Cloud ear and wood ear, *285*
Clove, 109
  alternative for, 381
  pomander ball from, 109
Club (cold-pack) cheese, 87
Club soda, 434
Coagulation, 109
Coating, 109
Cobbler, 109–*110
  even cooking of, 109
Cockle, 110
Cocktail, 110
  fruit, 181

Cocktail avocado, *22*
Cocktail peanut, 301
Cocoa powder, 110–111
    (nutrition information,
    storing, types)
  substitution of, 111
Coconut, *111*–112
    (market forms, nutrition
    information, selecting, storing)
  cracking, 112
Cod, 112, †165
    (how to cook, market forms,
    nutrition information)
  scrod, 112, 370
Coddling (egg), 112
Coffee, 112–114
    (market forms, selecting,
    storing, types)
  amount for crowd, †341
  regular vs. decaffeinated, 113
  specialty beverages, 113
Coffee cake, 55, 114
    (convenience products, types)
Coffee (light) cream, 128
Coho (silver) salmon, †165, 360
Colby cheese, †88, *114*
Colby-Monterey Jack (Colby-Jack,
  Co-Jack) cheese, †88, *114*
Colcannon, 114
  easy, 114
Cold cut. *See* Luncheon meat
Cold-pack cheese and cheese food, 87
Coleslaw, *115
Collard greens, *115*
    (nutrition information, selecting,
    storing)
  cooking, 115, †425
Coloring, food, 172
Color keeper, ascorbic acid, 20
Comb honey, 211
Combining, 115
Comice pear, 302, *303*
Complete vs. incomplete
  protein, 337–338
Compote, 116
Compressed yeast, 443
Concentrating, 116
Conch, 116
Concord grape, *194,* 195
Condensed milk. *See* Sweetened
  condensed milk
Condiment, 116
    See also individual entries
Coney. *See* Frankfurter
Confectioner's (candy) coating, 77

Confectioners' sugar, 394
Conserve, 116
Consommé, 116
  cold, 116
Container size, †116
Cooked ham, 203
Cookie, 117–119
    (baking hints, preparation hints,
    storing, types)
  chilling dough for, 119
  decorating, 73
  freezing, †175
  frosting, 180
  gingersnap, 191
  hermit, 208
  hints for making, 118
  macaroon, 237
  margarine in, 117
  shortbread, 374
  snickerdoodle, 378
  spritz, 383
Cookie sheet or pan, 119
Cooking oil. *See* oil
Cooling, 119
  cakes, 71
  See also Chilling
Coq au vin, 119
Coquille, 119
  substitution for, 119
Cordon bleu, 119
Coriander, 120, *285*
  leaves, 105, *285*
Corkscrew noodle, *295*
  cooking, †296
Corn, *120*–121
    (market forms, nutrition
    information, selecting, storing,
    varieties)
  amount for crowd, †341
  bran, 52
  cooking, †425
  dried. *See* Hominy
  flour, 122
  freezing, 120
  with husks, buying, 120
  popcorn, 322
Corn bread, 55, *121
Corned beef, 121
    (how to cook, market forms,
    nutrition information)
  storing, †245
Cornish game hen, 122
    (how to cook, market forms,
    nutrition information)
  broiling, †332

458

Cornish game hen *(continued)*
  grilling, †31, †32
  halving, 122
  roasting, †333
Cornmeal, 122
    (nutrition information, storing)
  cooking, †193
  mush, 265
    polenta, *321
Corn pudding, 122
Corn relish, 122–*123
Cornstarch, 123
  lump-free cooking, 123
  substitution for, emergency, †446
  thickening power of, 123
Corn syrup, 399
  substitution for, emergency, †446
Corn tortilla, 412
Cortland apple, †16
Cos lettuce (romaine), *232,* †232, 355
Cottage cheese, *123*
    (nutrition information, types)
Cottage pudding, 124
Cotto salami, †366, *367*
Country ham, 203, *327*
Country-style sausage, †366
Court bouillon, 124
Couscous, 124
Cowpea. *See* Black-eyed pea
Crab, 124–125
    (how to cook, market forms,
    nutrition information, selecting,
    storing, types)
  cracking, *125*
  equivalents, 124
  preparing and cooking, †373
Crab apple, *125*
    (market forms, selecting, storing)
Crab boil, 126
Crab Louis, *126
Cracked rye, 357
Cracked wheat, 436
  cooking, †193
Cracker, 126
    (nutrition information,
    storing, types)
  crumbs, 126
    making, *134*
  graham, 192–193
  oyster, 288
Crackling, 126
Cranberry, †43, *127*
    (market forms, nutrition
    information, preparation hints,
    selecting, storing)
  dried, cooking, †147

Cranberry bean, *36,* †37
Crayfish (crawfish), 127
    (cooking hints, nutrition
    information)
  eating, *127*
  preparing and cooking, †373
Cream, 128
    (storing, types)
  crème fraîche, 130–131
  fat and calories in, 128
  freezing, whipped, 128
  substitution for half and half, 128
  whipping method, 128
Cream cheese, *129*
    (nutrition information,
    storing, types)
  frosting, 180
  Neufchâtel, 129, 269
Creamed cottage cheese, 123
Creaming, 129
Cream of tartar, 129
Cream pie, 129, 312, 313
  meringue on, 313
    baking time for, 129
    problems with, 253, 435
Cream puff, *67,* *130
  éclair, *150*
  procedure for making, *130*
  profiterole, 337
  tips on making, 130
Crème brûlée, 130
  tips on making, 130
Crème fraîche, 130–131
  substitute for, 131
Crenshaw melon, *131,* †250, *251*
Crepe, 131
  cooked in advance, 131
  folding, *131*
Cress, 131
  storing, 131
  watercress, *434*–435
Crimping, 131
Crisp, *132, *133*
Crispin apple, †16
Crisp-tender vegetable, *132*
Criterion apple, †16
Crockery cooker, 132
  tapioca, use in, 404
  tips on using, 132
Croissant, 132
  tips on making, 132
Crookneck squash, *384*
Croquette, 134
Crouton, 134

Cruciferous vegetables, 423
  See also individual entries
Crudités, 134
  advance preparation, 134
Cruller, 134
Crumb, 134
  bread, 53
    cereal substitute, 86
    making, 54, *134*
  cracker, 126, *134*
  equivalents, 134
  making, *134*
  zwieback, 445
Crumble and crumbling, 134
Crushing, 134
Crust, 134
  on rolls, 355
  See also Piecrust
Crustacean vs. mollusk, 372
Crystallized ginger, 190
Crystallized honey, dissolving, 211
Crystallized maple syrup
  dissolving, 240
  maple sugar, 239
Crystallizing, 134
Cubing, *103,* 134
  bread, 44
  meat, 245
Cucumber, *135*
    (nutrition information,
    preparation hint, selecting,
    storing, types)
  gherkin, 190
  peeling, optional, 135
  pickle, 311–312
Cumin, 135
  alternative for, 381
Cupcake, 135–136
    (baking hints)
  decorating, 73
  freezing, †175
  frosting, 180
Curdling, 136
  reducing risk of, 136
Curing, 136
Curly endive. *See* Chicory
Curly-leaf parsley, 293
Currant, †43, *136*
    (market forms)
Currant, dried, 136, 347
    (nutrition information)
  grape for, *194*
  as raisin substitute, 136
Curry, 136–137

Curry powder, 137
cooking, 137
Custard, *137
crème brûlée, 130
doneness, checking, *137*
flan, 169
floating island, 169
Custard apple. *See* Cherimoya
Custard cream (gelato), 188
Custard pie, 312
hints for making, 313
Cutlet, 137
Cutout cookie, 117
hints for making, 118
Cutting in, 137, *314*
with knives, 137

Daikon, 140, *346*
(nutrition information,
selecting, storing)
cooking, †425
Dandelion greens, 140
(nutrition information,
selecting, storing)
cooking, †425
Danish pastry, 140
Dark molasses, 260
Dark seedless raisin, 347
Dash, 140
Dashi-no-moto, *285*
Date, *140–141*
(market forms, nutrition
information, storing, types)
chopping, 141
prechopped, sugared, 141
softening, 141
Decaffeinated vs. regular coffee, 113
Decorating, cake 73, 150
Deep-fat frying, *182*
french frying, 179
hints on, 182, 406
thermometer, *182*, 408
Deep sea perch. *See* Orange roughy
Deer meat (venison), 428
Deglazing, 141
Deglet Noor date, *140*
Dehydration, 141
Delicata squash, *385*, †386
cooking, †427
Demitasse, 113
Dessert, 141–142
(selecting desserts for a menu)
amount for crowd, †341
health-conscious, 142
See also individual entries

Dessert topping, 142
(nutrition information)
Dessert wine, 440
Deveining shrimp, *142, 376*
Deviled food, 142
ham, 142
Devil's food cake, *142–143*
Dicing, *103,* 143
Diet. *See* Nutrition
Dieting tips, 273
Diet margarine, 240–241
Dijon mustard, 267
Dill, *143*
dill head, 143
Dill pickle, 311, 312
Diluting, 143
Dinner wine, 440
Dip and dipping, 143
Direct grilling. *See* Barbecuing
Dissolving, 143
Distilled vinegar, 430
Distilled water, 434
Ditalini (thimbles), *294*
cooking, †296
Divan, *144
Divinity, *139,* 144
making, *144–145*
critical factors, 144
hints for, 145
vs. nougat, 269
Dobos torte, 411
Dollop, 145
Dolphin fish. *See* Mahimahi
Dough, 145
kneading, 56, *57,* 224
sourdough, 380
See also Pastry
Doughnut, 145–146
(nutrition information)
bismarck, 47
greasiness, avoiding, 146
pan for frying, 146
Draining, 146
Drawn food, 64, 146, 168
Dredging, 146
Dressed food, 146, 168
Dressing. *See* Salad dressing; Stuffing
Dried beef, 146
(nutrition information)
saltiness of, 146
Dried chestnut, 95
Dried fruit, 147
(nutrition information,
preparation hints, storing, types)
cooking, †147

Dried fruit *(continued)*
prune, †147, 338
raisin or currant, 136, 347
Dried herb, 206, 207
Dried lily bud, *284*
Dried pepper, hot, †306, *307*
Drink. *See* Beverage
Drop biscuit, 44, *47*
Drop cookie, 117
hints for making, 118
Drum, red (redfish), †165, 350
Dry-curd cottage cheese, 123
Dry milk, 256
Dry (hard) Monterey Jack
cheese, 261
Dry mustard, 267
substitution for, emergency, †446
Dry-roasted peanut, 301
Dry/semidry sausage, 365–366, *367*
storing, †366
Dry sweet potato, 396
Duchess potatoes, 148
Duck and duckling, 148
(how to cook, market forms,
nutrition information, types)
greasiness, avoiding, 148
roasting, †333
Dumpling, 148, *149,* *150
cooking pointers, 148
gnocchi, 191
quenelle, 342
ravioli, *295,* †296, 350
spaetzle, *189, 295,* †296, 380
Dungeness crab, 124–*125*
Durum wheat, 436
Dusting, 150
cake decoration, 150
Dutch-process cocoa powder, 110

Éclair, 150
making, *150*
Edam cheese, †88, *150–151*
rind for serving, 151
Egg, 151–153
(cooking hints, grades and sizes,
how to cook, market forms,
nutrition information,
preparation hints, storing)
coddled, 69, 112
freezing, 152
poaching, 153, *320*
in pudding, adding, *338*
safe use of, 151

Egg *(continued)*
  white
    beating, 12, 14, 72, 252
    replacing whole eggs with, 153
    See also Meringue
  See also Omelet; Soufflé
Egg, fish (roe), 355
  caviar, 84
Egg cream, 44
Eggnog, *139,* *153
Egg pasta. *See* Noodle
Eggplant, *154*
  (nutrition information, selecting,
    storing, varieties)
  cooking, †425
  grilling, †32
Egg roll, 154, *442
Eggs Benedict, *154, *155*
Elephant garlic, *186,* 187
Emmentaler (Switzerland)
  Swiss cheese, 398
Emperor grape, 195
Empire apple, †*16*
Emulsion, 156
Enchilada, 156, *254
  advance preparation of, 156
Endive, 156
  (nutrition information, selecting,
    storing, varieties)
  escarole, 156, *157*
  See also Chicory
English cucumber, *135*
English muffin, 156
  splitting, 156
English mustard, 267
English (green) pea, 299
English walnut, †*270, 433*
Enoki mushroom, *265*
Entrée, 156
  See also individual names
Escargot (snail), 377
Escarole, 156, *157*
  using, 157
Espagnole sauce, 62
Espresso, 113
European (English) cucumber, *135*
European-style (Dutch-process) cocoa
  powder, 110
Evaporated milk, 157, 256
  (nutrition information, storing)
  nutritional comparison, †257
  vs. sweetened condensed milk, 157
Exotic grape, *194,* 195

Extract and oil, 157
  (storing)
  foods using, 157
  imitation (flavoring), 169
    vanilla, 421
  substitution for, 158
  vanilla, pure, 420

Fajita, *158
Fall/winter onion, 280
Farina, 158, 436
  (nutrition information, storing)
  cooking, †193
Fat, 159–160
  (cooking hints, market forms,
    nutrition information, selecting,
    storing, types)
  creaming, 129
  cutting in, 137, *314*
  as food group, †272
  frying in, 182
    See also Deep-fat frying
  lard, 160, 228
  lowering in diet, 273
  measuring, 243
  in milk, †257
  as nutrient, 158–159
    and cholesterol, 159
  removing from soup, 379
  shortening. *See* Shortening
  suet, 393
  in yogurt, †444
  See also Butter; Margarine
Fava bean, *36,* †37
Feijoa, *160*
  (nutrition information, preparation
    hints, selecting, storing)
Fell on lamb, 227
Fennel, *161*
  (nutrition information, selecting,
    storing)
  cooking, †425
  grilling, †32
Fennel seed, 161, 381
Fern, fiddlehead, *163*
Feta cheese, †88, *161*
  freezing, 161
Fettuccine, *139,* 161–*162, 294*
  cooking, †296
Fiber, 162
  (nutrition information, soluble
    and insoluble fiber)
  adding to diet, 162
  bran sources of, 52–53
Fiddlehead fern, *163*

Field pea, 299
Fig, *163–164*
  (nutrition information,
    preparation hints, selecting,
    storing, varieties)
  dried, cooking, †147
Filbert (hazelnut), *204,* †*270*
  (storing)
Filé powder, 164
Filet, 164
Fillet, 164, 168
Fines herbes, 164
Finnan haddie, 202
Finocchio. *See* Fennel
Fish, 164–168
  (how to cook, nutrition
    information, selecting, storing,
    thawing, types)
  amount per serving, 164
  blackened, 47
  cooking, †167
  doneness, testing for, *166*
  gefilte fish, 187
  grilling, †31
  hot-line number, 166
  market forms, common, 168
  roe, 355
    caviar, 84
  selecting, †165
  stews
    bouillabaisse, 51
    cioppino, *105
  surimi seafood, 396
  thawing in microwave, 166
  See Selecting Fish chart, 165, for
    types
Fish-and-chips, 168
Fish sauce, *284*
Five-spice powder, 168
  homemade, 168
Flake and flaking, 168
Flambé, 168
  flaming alcohol for, *169*
  best types, 168
Flame seedless grape, *194,* 195
Flan, 169
Flavor, 169
Flavoring, 169
  brandy and rum, 169
  vanilla, 421
Float, 44
Floating island, 169
Florence fennel. *See* Fennel

Florentine style, 169
Florida avocado variety, *22*
Florida pompano, 322
Flounder, †165, 169
    (how to cook, market forms,
     nutrition information, types)
  as sole, 169, 378
Flour, 169–171
    (market forms, nutrition
     information, storing, types)
  for bread, 56, 170
  buckwheat, 63
  for cakes, 71, 170
  corn, 122
  gluten in, 191, 436
  measuring, *243*
  oat, 276
  rice, 352
  rye, 357
  sifting, question of, 170, 377
  substitution for, emergency, †446
  tapioca, 404
  triticale, 414
  wheat, 436, 437
    whole wheat interchanged for
     all-purpose, 170
Flouring, 171
Flour tortilla, 412
Flower, edible, *171,* †171
    (selecting, storing)
  safety, determining, 171
  squash blossoms, †171, 386
Flummery, 172
Fluting, 172
  piecrust, *172*
Focaccia, 172
Foie gras, 172
Folding, 172
Fondant, 172
  ripening, 172
Fondue, 172
Fontina cheese, †89
Food additive, 172
Food coloring, 172
Food Groups, Basic, †272
  in menu planning, 272–273
Food processor, chopping in, 103
Food safety, 173
  egg, 151
  marinade, 241
  meat and poultry hot line, 173, 332
  poultry handling, 334
  seafood, raw, 287
  stuffing, 393, 418
  tips on, 173

Food storage, 173
    (how to store)
  See also Freezing and individual
    entries
Forelle pear, 302, *303*
Frankfurter (frank), 173–174, *367*
    (market forms, nutrition
     information, selecting)
  broiling, †246
  storing, †245, †366
Frappé, 174
Freestone and semifreestone
    peach, 300
Freeze-dried food, 174
Freezer burn, 175
Freezing, 174–175
    (freezer containers and
     wrappings, labeling, sealing
     packages, storing)
  cake, 71
  celery, 85
  cheese, 90, 161
  cherry, 94
  chicken, 97
  citrus fruit, 106
  corn, 120
  croissant, 132
  egg, 152
  freezer burn, 175
  herb, 206
  meat, †245
  pesto, 310
  poultry, 331–332
  prepared food, †175
    pie, †175, 312–313
  tips on, 174
  whipped cream, 128
French bread, *176, *177*
    (convenience products)
  baguette, 24
  vs. Italian bread, 176
  storing, 176
French Breakfast radish, *346*
French cooking, 176, *177, *178*
    (cuisine highlights, Paris
     specialties, regional specialties)
  nouvelle cuisine, 270
  See also individual entries
French (Belgian) endive, *42–43,* 156
French frying, 179
French omelet, 277, *278
  serving, *277*
French onion soup, 280, *281, *282
French prune, *319*

French toast, 179
  bread for, 179
Fresh bean curd (tofu), *285,* 409, 410
Freshwater fish, 164, †165
    See also individual entries
Fresh yeast, 443
Fresno pepper, †306
Friar plum, *319*
Fricassee, 179
Fried egg, 152
Fried pie, 179
Frijoles refritos (refried beans), 350
Frittata, *179
Fritter, 180
  beignet, 42
Frizzes (sausage), †366
Frog leg, 180
Frosting, 180
    (types)
  on cakes, hints for, 180
  decorating with, 73
Frozen pie, 312
  slicing, 313
Frozen yogurt, 444
    (market forms, nutrition
     information)
  amount for crowd, †341
Fructose, granulated, 394
Fruit, 180–181
    (market forms)
  amount for crowd, †341
  buying, in season, 181
  candied, 74
  cobbler, 109–*110
  cocktail, 181
  compote, 116
  conserve, 116
  crisp, 132, *133*
  dried, 147, †147
  as food group, †272
  jam and jelly, 220–221
  juice, 181
    citrus, 106
    nectar, 268
  marmalade, 242
  mincemeat, 258
  pectin in, 304
  pie, 312–313
  pit, 318
  preserve, 336
  salad, 358
    amount for crowd, †341
  soup, 182
  See also Berry; Citrus fruit; Melon;
    and individual entries

Fruitcake, *181
Fruit-flavored syrup, 399
Frying, 182
(methods)
See also Deep-fat frying
Fudge, 182–183
(types)
frosting, 180
penuche, 182, 304
prepared pan for, 183
shortcut, 183
tips on making, 183
Fuerte avocado, 22
Fuji apple, †16
Fungus
cloud ear and wood ear, 285
truffle, 415
Funnel cake, 183
Fusilli, 294
cooking, †296

Gala apple, †16
Galangal root, 285
Galia melon, †250, 251
Game, 186
(common forms, cooking hints, types)
preparation for cooking, 186
rabbit, 346
venison, 428
Game bird. *See* Pheasant; Quail
Game hen, Cornish. *See* Cornish game hen
Garbanzo bean, 36, †37
hummus, 214
Garden (green) pea, 299
Garlic, 186–187
(hint for using, market forms, storing, varieties)
elephant, 186, 187
equivalents, 187, †446
Garnish and garnishing, 187
Gazpacho, 185, *187
Gefilte fish, 187
Gelatin, 188
(preparation hints)
aspic, 22
not setting up, 188, 224
quick-chill method, 293
salad, 358
stages of setting, 188
partially set, 188, 293
reversing, 188
Gelato, 188

Gemelli, 295
cooking, †296
Generic wine, 440
Genoa salami, †366, 367
Geoduck clam, 107
Geranium, 171, †171
German cooking, 188–*189
(cuisine highlights, regional specialties)
See also individual entries
German mustard, 267
German (hard) sausage, †366
German-style mortadella (sausage), †366
Gherkin, 190
Giblet, 190
Ginger, 190
(market forms, selecting, storing)
alternative for, 381
grating, 190
Gingerbread, *190–191
Gingersnap, 191
Gjetost cheese, †89
Glacé food, 191
Glaze, 191
Gluten, 191, 436
Gnocchi, 191
Golden Bing cherry, 93
Golden Delicious apple, †16
Golden needle (dried lily bud), 284
Golden nugget squash, †386
cooking, †427
Golden pepper, †306, 307
Golden seedless raisin, 347
Goose, 191
(how to cook, market forms, nutrition information)
roasting, †333
Gooseberry, †43, 192
(market forms, storing)
cleaning, 192
Gorgonzola cheese, 49
Gouda cheese, †89, 192
Goulash, *192
Graham cracker, 192–193
(nutrition information)
crust
serving pie with, 192
zwieback for, 445
Graham (whole wheat) flour, 170
Grain, 193–194
(how to cook)
amaranth, 12
bran of. *See* Bran
cooking, †193

Grain *(continued)*
couscous, 124
finely ground. *See* Flour
as food group, †272
malt, 238
triticale, 414
whole, 439
wild rice, 439–440
See also Cereal; Rice; and Cooking Grains chart, 193, for varieties
Grain-fed veal, 422
Granadilla (passion fruit), 294
Granny Smith apple, †16
Granola, 194
(nutrition information, storing)
muesli, 263
Granulated sweetener, 394
Grape, 194–195
(market forms, nutrition information, selecting, storing, varieties)
dried, 136, 347
Grapefruit, †106, 195–196
(market forms, selecting, types)
knife for, 196
Grated peel (zest), 445
Grating, 196
ginger, 190
horseradish, 213
vs. shredding, 196
Gravy, 196–*197
smoother, 197
sour cream, adding, 380
Grease and greasing, 197
Great-headed (elephant) garlic, 186, 187
Great Northern bean, 36, †37
Green bean, 35–36
cooking, †424
Green cabbage, 68
Green chili (Anaheim) pepper, †306, 307
Greenhouse (English) cucumber, 135
Green olive, 277
Green onion, 280
Green pea, 299
Green pepper, †306, 307
cooking, †427
Green peppercorn, 305
Greens
beet, 41, 42
collard, 115
cooking, †425
dandelion, 140
kale, 223

462

Greens *(continued)*
  mustard, 267–268
  turnip, *419*
  See also Salad greens
Green tea, 405
Grenadine, 399
Grill and grilling, 197
  See also Barbecuing
Grinding, 197
  nuts, 271
Grits. *See* Hominy
Groats
  buckwheat, 63
    cooking, †193
  oat, 276
Ground beef, 197–198
    (how to cook, market forms,
    nutrition hints, nutrition
    information, preparation hints,
    selecting, types)
  broiling, †246
  burgers, 204
    best type for, 198
  doneness, determining, 198
  panbroiling, †248
  storing, †245
Ground red (cayenne) pepper, 305,
  †306
Gruyère cheese, †89, *198*–199
    (types)
  and Swiss, interchanged for, 199
Guacamole, 199
Guava, *199*
    (nutrition information, selecting,
    storing)
Guinea hen, 199
    (nutrition information)
Gumbo, 199, *200*, *201*
Gumdrop, 201
  snipping, 201
  storing, 201

Haddock, †165, 201–202
    (how to cook, market forms,
    nutrition information)
Hake, silver (whiting), †165, 438
Half and half, 128
Halibut, †165, 202
    (how to cook, market forms,
    nutrition information)

Ham, 202–203, *326–327*
    (ham cuts, how to cook, market
    forms, nutrition information,
    processing, selecting, storing)
  broiling, †246
  canned, storing, 203
  country, preparing, 203
  deviled, 142
  grilling, †29, †31
  panbroiling, †248
  prosciutto, 337
  roasting, †247
  storing, †245
Hamburger, 204
  See also Ground beef
Hard-cooked egg, 152
Hard Monterey Jack cheese, 262
Hard sauce, 204
Hard-shell clam, *107*
Hard vs. soft wheat, 436
Haricot verts, *35*, *36*
Hartshorn powder, 204
Harvard beets, *204*, *205*
Hash, 204
Hass avocado, *22*
Hazelnut, *204*, †270
    (storing)
Head cheese, 206
    (nutrition information)
Head lettuce, †232
  coring, 233
Heart, 421
Heart of palm, *206*
Heavy whipping cream, 128
Hen
  guinea, 199
  See also Cornish game hen
Herb, 206–208
    (cooking hints, market forms,
    nutrition information,
    preparation hints, selecting,
    storing)
  bouquet garni, *52*
  crushing, *207*
  drying or freezing, 206
  fines herbes, 164
  freshness, checking, 207
  growing, 207
  measuring dried, 244
  snipping, *378*
  substitutions, 207
    alternatives, 208
  See also individual entries
Herbal tea, 405
Hermit, 208

Herring, 208
    (market forms, nutrition
    information, types)
Hickory nut, *208*
High-altitude cooking, 209
  adjustments, 209
  cake, †209
  canning, 78
  further information source, 209
Hollandaise sauce, *210, 364*
  curdled, saving, 210
Hominy, 210–211
    (nutrition information, storing)
  cooking, †193
Homogenized milk, 257
Honey, 211
    (market forms, nutrition
    information, selecting, storing)
  crystallized, dissolving, 211
  substituting, for sugar, 211
  substitution for, emergency, †446
Honeydew, *212*, †250, *251*
Horned melon (kiwano), *223*
Hors d'oeuvre, 212
  number per person, 212
  tapa, 404
Horseradish, *212*–213
    (market forms, nutrition
    information, storing)
  grated, fumes from, 213
  Japanese (wasabi), 433
Hot cross bun, *185*, *213*
Hot dog. *See* Frankfurter
Hothouse (English) cucumber, *135*
Hot line
  fish, 166
  meat and poultry, 173, 332
Hot pepper, *305*, †306, *307*
Hot pepper sauce, 213
Hubbard squash, *385*, †386
  cooking, †427
Hull and hulling, 214
Hummus, 214
Hungarian paprika, 292
Hush puppy, 214

Ice, 214
Iceberg lettuce, †232
  coring, 233
Ice cream, *214–215*
    (nutrition information, storing,
    types)
  amount for crowd, †341
  sherbet vs., 372
  spumoni, 384

Ice cream *(continued)*
  sundae, 395
  tips for making, 215
  tortoni, 412
Ice-cream soda, 44
Ice milk, 214, 215
  (nutrition information)
Icicle radish, *346*
Icing, 180
Imitation food, 215
  cheese, 87
  difference from real, 215
  extract (flavoring), 169
    vanilla, 421
  maple syrup, 240
  shellfish (surimi seafood), 396
Incomplete vs. complete
  protein, 337–338
Indian pudding, 215
Indirect grilling. *See* Barbecuing
Infuser, tea, 406
Insoluble fiber, 162
Instant cocoa mix, *111*
Instant coffee, 113
Instant flour, 170
Instant oatmeal, 276
Iodine, †430
Irish coffee, 113
Irish oatmeal (steel-cut oats),
  †193, 276
Irish soda bread, 215
Irish stew, *216
Iron, †430
Italian bread, 216
  (convenience products, nutrition
  information)
  vs. French bread, 176
Italian cooking, 216–*217
  (cuisine highlights, local
  specialties, southern and northern
  cooking)
  See also individual entries
Italian green bean, *35*, 36
  cooking, †424
Italian parsley, 293
Italian prune, 320
Italian sausage, †366, *367*
Italian seasoning, 217
  alternative for, 208
Italian (plum) tomato, 410, *411*

Jackfruit, 54
Jalapeño pepper, †306, *307*

Jam, 220
  vs. jelly, preserves, 220
  pectin in, 220, 304
Jambalaya, *219,* *220
Japanese cooking, 286
  See also individual entries
Japanese eggplant, *154*
Japanese horseradish, 433
Japanese radish. *See* Daikon
Jarlsberg cheese, *398*
Jaune Canari (Juan Canary)
  melon, †250, *251*
Jelly, 220–221
  full rolling boil, 220
  pectin in, 220, 221, 304
  sheets off the spoon stage, 221
  tips on making, 221
Jelly roll, *219,* *221
  cracked, preventing, 221
Jelly-roll style, 355
Jerky, 222
Jerusalem artichoke, *222*
  (nutrition information, selecting,
  storing)
  cooking, †426
Jicama, *222*
  (nutrition information, selecting,
  storing)
  cooking, †426
Johnnycake, 222
Jonagold apple, †*16*
Jonathan apple, †16, *17*
Juan Canary melon, †250, *251*
Juice, 222
  fruit, 181
    citrus, 106
    nectar, 268
Julienne strips, cutting, 222
  quick method, 222

Kabob (kebab), 222–223
  chicken
    broiling, †332
    grilling, †32
  sate, 364
  seafood, †31
  skewers for, 377
  tips for making, 223
Kadota fig, 163
Kale, *223*
  (nutrition information, selecting,
  storing)
  collard greens, *115*
  cooking, †425

Kasha, 63
  cooking, †193
Kebab. *See* Kabob
Kelsey plum, *319,* 320
Ketchup (tomato catsup), 83
Key lime, *233*
Kidney bean, *36,* †37
Kielbasa (sausage), †366, *367*
Kimchi, 223
King crab, 124
Kirby (pickling cucumber), *135*
Kiszka (sausage), †366
Kitchen Bouquet, 223
Kiwano, *223*
  (nutrition information, selecting,
  storing)
Kiwi fruit, *224*
  (nutrition information,
  preparation hints, selecting,
  storing)
  gelatin, problem with, 224
Kneading, 56, 224
  technique, *57,* 224
Knockwurst, †366, *367*
Kohlrabi, *224–225*
  (nutrition information, selecting,
  storing)
  cooking, †426
  peeling, 225
Kolacky, 225
Korean cooking, 286
Kosher food, 225
Kosher salt, 361
Kosher sausage, †366
Krakow (sausage), †366
Kumquat, †106, 225
  (market forms, selecting, storing)

Labeling, 225–226
  (label language)
  light, lite, leaner, 233
  meat, 244
  sugar synonyms, 394
Lady Baltimore cake, 226
Ladyfinger, 226
Ladyfinger banana, *26*
Lake whitefish, *437*
Lamb, 226–228
  (certification, how to cook, lamb
  cuts, market forms, nutrition
  information, selecting)
  broiling, †246
  cuts, retail, *227*
  fell on, 227
  grilling, †29, †30

Lamb *(continued)*
  imported vs. domestic, 226
  Irish stew, *216
  panbroiling and panfrying, †248
  roasting, †247
  storing, †245
Lambert cherry, 93
Laos, *285*
Lard and larding, 160, 228
Lasagna (lasagne), *228, *229, 295*
  cooking, †296
Latke (potato pancake), 290
Lattice pie top, mock, 314
Layer-type cake, 71
  devil's food, *142–143
  gingerbread, *190–191
  Lady Baltimore, 226
  Lord Baltimore, 236
  one-bowl, 279
  problem solving, 72
  removing from pan, *71*
Leaf lettuce, *232,* †232
Leavening agent, 230
  air and steam as, 230
  See also individual entries
Lebanon bologna, †366
Leek, *230*
    (nutrition information, selecting,
    storing)
  cooking, †426
  grilling, †32
Legume, 230
  lentil, *231*
  See also Bean, dried; Pea; Peanut
Lemon, †106, *230–231*
    (market forms, selecting)
  equivalents, 231
Lemon curd, 231
Lemongrass, 231, *285*
  substitute for, 231
Lemon-pepper seasoning, 231
Lemon thyme, 408, 409
Lentil, *231*
    (how to cook, nutrition
    information, selecting, storing)
  sprout, *383*
Lettuce, *232–233*
    (nutrition information,
    preparation hints, selecting,
    storing)
  coring, 233
  romaine, *232,* †232, 355
  selecting, †232
Light cream, 128
  substitution for, emergency, †446

Light cream cheese (Neufchâtel),
    129, 269
Light cream cheese product, 129
Light food, 233
Light molasses, 260
Light whipping cream, 128
Lily bud, dried, *284*
Lima bean, 35, *36,* †37
Limburger cheese, †89, 233
  serving tray for, 233
Lime, †106, *233–234*
    (market forms, selecting, varieties)
  equivalents, 234
  Key lime pie, 233
Limequat, †106, *234*
    (nutrition information, selecting)
Limpa, 234
Linguine, *295*
  cooking, †296
Lipoprotein, 159
Liqueur, 234
Liquid margarine, 240, 241
Liquid smoke, 234
Litchi (lychee), *234*
    (nutrition information, selecting,
    storing)
Liter (litre), 234
Littleneck clam, 107
Liver, *421*
Liver loaf, †366
Liver sausage, †366, *367*
Lobster, 234–236
    (cooking hints, how to cook,
    market forms, nutrition
    information, selecting, storing,
    types)
  amount per person, 235
  preparing and cooking, †373
  tails, grilling, †31
  whole, removing meat from, *235,
    236*
Long grain rice, 352, *353*
  cooking, †352
  vs. medium and short, 352
Longhorn cheese, 86
Long-neck clam, 107
Long white potato, *327*
Loquat, *285*
Lord Baltimore cake, 236
Lotus root, *285*
Low-calorie, 226, 236
  sweetener, 394–395
Low-fat cottage cheese, 123
Low-fat milk, 256, †257

Lox, 236
Luau, 236
Luncheon meat, 237
    (nutrition information)
  head cheese, 206
  storing, †245
  turkey, *417*
Lychee (litchi), *234*
    (nutrition information, selecting,
    storing)
Lyonnaise style, 237
Lyons (sausage), †366

Macadamia nut, *237,* †270
  uses in cooking, 237
Macaroni, 237, *294, 295,* 381
  amounts needed, 297, †341
  cooking, †296
Macaroon, 237
Mace, 237
  alternate for, 381
Mackerel, †165, 238
    (how to cook, market forms,
    nutrition information, storing,
    types)
Mafalda, *295*
  cooking, †296
Mahimahi, †165, 238
    (how to cook, nutrition
    information)
Maki, 396
Malt, 238
Malted milk, 44
Mandarin, 238
  tangerines and tangelos, †106,
    238, *403*
Mango, *238–239*
    (nutrition information, preparation
    hints, selecting, storing)
Manhattan vs. New England clam
    chowder, *108–109
Manicotti, *217, 239, 294*
  cooking, †296
  stuffing, 239
Manzano banana, *26*
Maple cream or butter, 239
Maple sugar, 239
Maple syrup, 239–240
    (maple products, nutrition
    information, storing)
  crystallized or molded, 240
  pure
    standards for, 240
    taste difference, 240
Maraschino cherry, 94

Marbled (Colby-Monterey Jack)
cheese, †88, *114*
Margarine, 159, 160, 240–241
(market forms, nutrition hint,
nutrition information, preparation
hints, storing, types)
amount for crowd, †341
butter-margarine blend, 64, 240, 241
in cookies, 117
melting in microwave, 252
substituting for butter, 240
substitution for, emergency, †446
Marigold, pot, †171
Marinade; marinating, 241
(nutrition hint)
container for, 241
safety with, 241
Marjoram, *242*
alternative for, 208
vs. wild marjoram, 242, 284
Marmalade, 242
Marrow, 242
Marshmallow, 242
creme, 242
Marzipan, 242
Mashing, 242
Matzo (matzoh), 242
Mayonnaise, 243, 364
(nutrition information, types)
homemade, risk from, 243
McIntosh apple, †16, *17*
Meal, 243
one-dish, 279
Mealy food, 243
Measures. *See* Weights and measures
Measuring, *243–244*
(measuring techniques)
dry ingredients, *243*
flour, *243*
liquids, *243*
sugar, *243*
Meat, 244–248
(how to cook, inspection and
grading, labeling, market forms,
preparation hints)
bias slicing, *44*
broiling, †246
carving, *81–82*
chop. *See* Chop
cubing, 245
cutlet, 137
as food group, †272
grilling, †29–31
hot line, 173, 332
panbroiling and panfrying, †248

Meat *(continued)*
pounding, *334*
roasting, †247
thermometer use for, 246
servings per pound, 244
storing, †245
tenderizing, 245, 250, 407
thawing, 245
variety, *421*
See also Beef; Game; Lamb;
Luncheon meat; Pork;
Sausage; Veal
Meatball, *249*
shaping quickly, 249
Meat loaf, 250
doneness, testing for, 198, 250
Meat mallet, use of, 407
Meat tenderizer, 250
Meat thermometer, 408
using, 246
Medium grain rice, 352, 353
Medjool date, *140*
Medwurst, †366
Melba toast, 250
(nutrition information)
Mellorine, 214
Melon, 250–252, *251*
(market forms, nutrition
information, preparation hints,
selecting, storing)
selecting, †250
See Selecting Melons chart, 250,
for varieties
Melting, 252
cheese, 90
chocolate, 102
in microwave, 252
Menu planning, 272–273
dessert selection, 141
soup selection, 379
Meringue, 252–*253*
(preparation hints)
on baked Alaska, 24
on cream pie, 253, 313
baking time for, 129
egg-white pointers, 252
weeping, avoiding, 253, 435
Metric cooking hints, 480, †480
Mettwurst, †366
Metz (sausage), †366
Mexican cooking, *254*
(cuisine highlights, sauce
specialties)
Mexican green tomato (tomatillo), *410*
Mexican lime, 233
Key lime, *233*

Microwave cooking, 255
bacon, 24
brown sugar, softening, 394
cookware for, 255
fish, †167
thawing, 166
melting, 252
chocolate, 102
potato preparation, *328*
thermometer for, 408
tips on, 255
vegetables, †424–427
yeast bread, raising, 57
Milano (sausage), †366
Milk, 256–257
(nutrition hint, storing, types)
amount for crowd, †341
buttermilk, 65, 256, †257
for cheese, 87
evaporated, 157, 256, †257
vs. evaporated, 157
as food group, †272
homogenized, 257
nutrition comparison of
types, †257
pasteurization of, 256
"sell by" date, 257
substitutes for cup of, 257, †446
sweetened condensed, 79, 256,
†257, 396
Milk chocolate, *101*
Milk fat (butterfat), 65, 257
Milk-fed veal, 422
Millet, 257
(nutrition information, storing)
cooking, †193
Mincemeat, 258
Mincing, *103,* 258
Mineral, 430, †430
Mineral water, 434
Minestrone, *258, 259*
Mint (candy), 258
Mint (herb), 258, *260*
alternative for, 208
Mirliton. *See* Chayote
Miso, 260
Mixed grill, 260
Mixing and mixture, 260
Mocha, 260
Moistening, 260
Moist sweet potato, 396
Molasses, 260–261
(nutrition information, types)
light vs. dark, 260
substitution for, emergency, †446

Mold (fungus), 261
  on cheese, 90
  on maple syrup, 240
  on sour cream, 380
Mold (shaped food), 261
  gelatin salad, 358
  timbale, 409
Mole sauce, 254, 261
Mollusk vs. crustacean, 372
Monosodium glutamate (MSG), 261
Monounsaturated fat, 159
Monterey Jack cheese, †89, *261*
  (market forms)
  dried out, using, 261
Montmorency cherry, *93*
Morel, 265
Mornay sauce, 261
Mortadella (sausage), †366
Mortar and pestle, 262
Mostaccioli, *294*
  cooking, †296
Moussaka, *262
Mousse, 262–*263
Mozzarella cheese, †89, *263*
  (types)
  string cheese, *391*
  stringiness, 263
MSG (monosodium glutamate), 261
Muddling, 263
Muenster cheese, †89, *263*
Muesli, 263
  (storing)
Muffin, 55, *219,* *264
  (storing)
  doneness, testing for, 264
  English, 156
  ledges, avoiding, 264
  overmixing, avoiding, 264
Mull, 265
Mullet, †165
Mulligan stew, 265
Mulligatawny, 265
Munster (muenster) cheese, †89, *263*
Muscat grape, 195
  raisin from, 347
Mush, 265
  polenta, *321
Mushroom, *265–266*
  (how to cook, market forms,
  nutrition information, preparation
  hints, selecting, storing, varieties)
  cooking, †426
  dried, preparing, 266
  equivalents, 266
Muskellunge pike, 315

Muskmelon. *See* Cantaloupe
Mussel, 266–267
  (how to cook, market forms,
  nutrition information, selecting,
  storing, types)
  cleaning, *267*
  preparing and cooking, †373
Mustard, 267
  (market forms, nutrition
  information, preparation hints,
  prepared mustards)
Mustard greens, 267–*268*
  (nutrition information, selecting,
  storing)
  cooking, †425
Mutton, 226

Napa (Nappa) cabbage, *68,* 100
Napoleon, 268
Nashi pear. *See* Asian pear
Nasturtium, †*171*
Natural vs. process cheese, 87
  Gruyère, *198*–199
Navel orange, *282,* †*283*
Navy bean, *36,* †*37*
Nectar, 268
Nectarine, 268–269
  (nutrition information,
  preparation hints, selecting,
  storing, varieties)
  equivalents, 268
Nelis pear, 302, *303*
Neufchâtel cheese, 129, 269
Newburg, 269
New England sausage (Berliner), †366
New England vs. Manhattan clam
  chowder, *108–109
New potato, *327*
Newtown Pippin apple, †16
Niacin, †430
Nigiri, 396
Nonfat milk, 256, †*257*
Nonpareil, 269
Noodle and noodle dough, 269, 294,
  295, 297
  (market forms)
  cannelloni, 77
  chow mein noodle, 104
  cooking, †296
  fettuccine, *139,* 161–*162,* *294,* †296
  lasagna, *228,* *229,* *295,* †296
  manicotti, *217,* *239,* *294,* †296
  ravioli, *295,* †296, 350
  spaetzle, *189, *295,* †296, 380
  See also Chinese noodle

Nopal cactus
  fruit, 336–*337*
Northern pike, 315
Northern Spy apple, †16
Nougat, 269
  vs. divinity, 269
Nouvelle cuisine, 270
Nut, 270–271
  (market forms, nutrition hints,
  selecting, storing)
  brittle, *9,* *58–59
  ground for tortes, 271
  hickory, *208*
  selecting, †270
  substitution for, 271
  toasting, *11,* 271
  See also Peanut; Selecting Nuts
  chart, 270, for varieties
Nutmeg, 271
  alternative for, 381
  skin (mace), 237
Nutrition, 271–273
  (hints for losing weight,
  planning a balanced diet, steps
  to help plan daily menus)
  Basic Food Groups, †272
  carbohydrates, 79–80
    See also Starch; Sugar
  daily recommendations, 273
  dessert, health-conscious, 142
  fiber, 162
    bran sources of, 52–53
  label information about, 225–226
  protein, 337–338
  soup, health-conscious tips for, 379
  vitamins and minerals, †430,
    430–431
  water, 434
  See also Calorie; Fat

Oat, 276
  (market forms, nutrition
  information, storing)
  bran, 52, 53, 276
  cooking, †193
  flour, 276
Octopus, 276
  (market forms, nutrition
  information)
Oil, 159–160
  (cooking hints, market forms,
  nutrition information, selecting,
  storing, types)

Oil (continued)
  measuring, 243
  See also Deep-fat frying
Okra, 276–277
    (market forms, nutrition
    information, selecting, storing)
  cooking, †426
Old-fashioned (rolled) oat, †193, 276
Olive, 277
    (nutrition information, types)
  amount for crowd, †341
Omelet, 277–278, *278–279
    (cooking hints, preparation hints)
  fillings for, 278
  frittata, *179
  serving, 277
One-bowl cake, 279
  easy mixing of, 279
One-dish meal, 279
Onion, 279–280
    (market forms, nutrition
    information, preparation hints,
    selecting, storing, types)
  chopping, 280
  cooking, †426
  equivalents, 280
  green, using tops of, 280
  substitution for, emergency, †446
  See also Chive; Leek; Shallot
Onion soup, 280, 281, *282
Oolong tea, 405
Orange, †106, 282–283
    (market forms, preparation hints,
    selecting, varieties)
  equivalents, 283
  selecting, †283
Orange (golden) bell pepper,
  †306, 307
Orange roughy, †165, 283
  (how to cook, market forms,
  nutrition information)
Oregano, 284
  alternative for, 208
  as wild marjoram, 242, 284
Organ (variety) meat, 421
Oriental cooking, 284, *286–287
    (Chinese cooking, cuisine
    highlights, Japanese cooking,
    Korean cooking, Thai cooking,
    Vietnamese cooking)
  stir-frying, 182, 388, 389, *390
  See also Oriental ingredients
Oriental (elephant) garlic, 186, 187

Oriental ingredients, 284–285
  bamboo shoot, 25–26, 284
  bean sprout, 38, 383
  Chinese cabbage, 50, 68, 99–100
  cilantro and coriander, 105, 120, 285
  five-spice powder, 168
  lemongrass, 231, 285
  litchi, 234
  miso, 260
  monosodium glutamate, 261
  pea pod, 302, †426
  rice vinegar, 285, 430
  soy sauce, 285, 380
  Szechwan pepper, 305
  tofu, 285, 409–410
  wasabi, 433
  water chestnut, 434
  See also Chinese noodle
Oriental radish. See Daikon
Orzo (rosamarina), 287, 295
  cooking, †296
Osso buco, 287
Oven-frying, 287
Oven thermometer, 408
Oyster, 287–288
    (market forms, nutrition
    information, selecting, storing,
    types)
  preparing and cooking, †373
  raw
    vs. cooked, 288
    safety, question of, 287
  Rockefeller, 275, *288
  shucking, 287
Oyster cracker, 288
Oyster mushroom, 265
Oyster plant (salsify), 361

Paella, *289
  pan for, 289
Pak choi. See Bok choy
Panbroiling, †248, 289
  beef cuts for, 40–41
  lamb cuts for, 227
  pork cuts for, 326–327
Pancake, 55, 289–290
    (convenience products, nutrition
    information, preparation hints)
  batter, vs. waffle, 431
  blintze, 48
  crepe, 131
  evenly cooked, 289
  evenly shaped, 290
  keeping warm, 290
  potato, 290

Pandowdy, 290
Panfrying, 182, †248, 290
  beef cuts for, 40–41
  fish, †167
  lamb cuts for, 227
  pork cuts for, 326–327
  scallops, †373
  veal cuts for, 422
  Wiener schnitzel, 439
Pansy, 171, †171
Papain, 290
Papaw, 290
    (preparation hints, selecting,
    storing)
Papaya, 290–291
    (nutrition information, preparation
    hints, selecting, storing)
Paper bake cup, 291
Papillote, *291
Paprika, 292
  Hungarian, 292
Paraffin, 292
Parboiling, 292
Parfait, 292
  neat assembly of, 292
Paring, 292
Paris specialties, 178
Parmesan cheese, †89, 292
    (market forms)
  Romano for, 256
Parsley, 293
    (selecting and storing, types)
  alternative for, 208
  Chinese (cilantro), 105, 285
  snipping, 378
  wilted, saving, 293
Parsnip, 293
    (nutrition information, selecting,
    storing)
  cooking, †426
Partially set gelatin, 188, 293
  quick-chill method, 293
Pasilla pepper, †306, 307
Passion fruit, 294
    (nutrition information, selecting,
    storing)
Pasta, 294–297
    (how to cook, market forms,
    nutrition information,
    preparation hints, storing, types)
  al dente, 10
  amount for crowd, †341
  cooking, †296
  equivalents, 297

Pasta *(continued)*
  orzo (rosamarina), 287, *295,* †296
  shapes
    common, *294–295*
    and uses, 297
    See also Macaroni; Noodle
      and noodle dough
Pasta flour, 170
Paste, 297
  almond paste, 11
Pasteurization of milk, 256
Pasteurized process cheese product, 87
Pastrami, 297
  (nutrition information)
Pastry, 298
  chou paste, 103
  Danish, 140
  funnel cake, 183
  phyllo, 311
  puff, 339
    napoleon, 268
    patty shell, 299
  strudel, 392
  See also Piecrust
Pastry blender, *314*
  substitute for, 137
Pastry flour, 170
Pasty, 298
Pâté, *298–299*
  terrine, 298
Pattypan squash, *384,* †386
  cooking, †427
Patty shell, 299
Pea, *299*
  (how to cook, market forms,
    nutrition information, selecting,
    storing, varieties)
  amount for crowd, †341
  black-eyed, †37, *48*
  cooking, †426
Pea (navy) bean, *36,* †37
Peach, *300*
  (market forms, nutrition
    information, preparation hints,
    selecting, storing, varieties)
  dried, cooking, †147
  equivalents, 300
Peanut, 300–*301*
  (market forms, nutrition
    information, selecting, storing)
  cocktail vs. dry-roasted, 301
  raw, in cooking, 301
  roasting, 301

Peanut butter, 301–302
  (nutrition information, storing)
Pea pod, *302*
  (market forms, nutrition
    information, selecting, storing,
    varieties)
  cooking, †426
  stringing, *302*
Pear, 302–*303*
  (market forms, nutrition
    information, preparation hints,
    selecting, storing, varieties)
  dried, cooking, †147
  equivalents, 302
  peeling, question of, 303
  ripening, 303
Pearl barley, 33, 304
  (market forms, nutrition
    information, storing)
  cooking, †193
Pearl (creamer) onion,
  279, *280*
Pearl tapioca, 404
Pear-shaped tomato, 410
Pecan, †270, *304*
  (storing)
Pectin, 304
  difference in types, 304
  in jam and jelly, 220, 221, 304
Peel, 304
  candied, 74
  freezing, 106
  zest, 445
Penuche, 182, 304
Pepper (spice), 304–305
  (market forms, storing)
  black vs. ground red and
    Szechwan, 305
  white, use of, 305
Pepper (vegetable), 305–307
  (how to cook, market forms,
    nutrition information, preparation
    hints, selecting, storing)
  chili, 99, 305, †306, *307*
  cooking, †427
  grilling, †32
  paprika, 292
  pimiento, 316
  protection from oils, *305*
  roasting, 307
  sauce, hot pepper, 213
  selecting, †306
Peppermint, 258, *260*
Pepperoni, †366, *367*

Pepper steak, 307, *308,* *309
  steak au poivre, *387
Pequin pepper, †306, *307*
Perch, †165
  deep sea. *See* Orange roughy
  lake perch, †165
  ocean perch, †165
Persian lime, *233*
Persian melon, †250, *251, 309*
Persian (English) walnut, †270, 433
Persimmon, *309–310*
  (market forms, nutrition
    information, preparation hints,
    selecting, storing, varieties)
  dried, cooking, †147
Pestle, mortar and, 262
Pesto, 33, *310
  tips on storing, 310
Petit four, 310
Pheasant, 310–311
  (cooking hints, how to cook,
    market forms, nutrition
    information, storing)
  grilling, †31
  roasting, †333
Phosphorus, †430
Phyllo, 311
  keeping usable, 311
  for strudel dough, 392
Piccalilli, 311
Pickle, 311–312
  (nutrition information, market
    forms, types)
  amount for crowd, †341
  dill heads for, 143
  relish, 312, 351
Pickled ginger, 190
Pickling cucumber, *135*
Pickling salt, 361
Pickling spice, 312
Picnic, *326*
  vs. ham, 202
  roasting, †247
Pie, 312–313
  (storing, types)
  amount for crowd, †341
  black bottom, 47
  chess, 94
  chiffon, 98, 312, 313
  cream, 129, 312
    meringue, 129, 253, 313

Pie (continued)
  freezing, †175, 312–313
  fried, 179
  hints on making, 313
  Key lime, 233
  potpie, 330
  shepherd's, 372
  tart, 405
  weeping meringue, avoiding,
    253, 435
Piecrust, 314
    (market forms)
  fluting, 172
  graham cracker
    serving pie with, 192
    zwieback for, 445
  making, 314
  tips on, 314, 315
Pie plant (rhubarb), 351
Pigeon, young. See Squab
Pignolia (pine nut), †270, 317
Pike, †165, 315
  (how to cook, market forms,
    nutrition information, types)
Pilaf, 315–*316
  with wild rice, 440
Pimiento, 316
Pineapple, 316–317
    (market forms, nutrition
    information, preparation hints,
    selecting, storing)
  cutting, 317
Pineapple guava (feijoa), 160
Pine nut (piñon), †270, 317
  uses in cooking, 317
Pink (red) grapefruit, 195, 196
Pink (humpback) salmon, †165, 360
Pinto bean, 36, †37
Pinwheel, 317
Piping, 317
  bag, use of, 73
Piquant food, 317
Piquant sauce, 317
Pistachio nut, †270, 318
  red dye, 318
Pita bread, 318
    (nutrition information)
  homemade chips from, 318
Pit and pitting, 318
Pizza, *318–319
  amount for crowd, †341
Plantain, 319
    (nutrition information, selecting,
    storing)

Plum, 319–320
    (market forms, nutrition
    information, selecting, storing,
    varieties)
  dried (prune), †147, 338
  equivalents, 320
Plump food; plumping, 320
Plum pudding, 320
Plum tomato, 410, 411
Poaching, 320
  egg, 153, 320
  fish, †167
  shellfish, †373
  simmering vs. boiling liquid for, 320
Poblano pepper, †306, 307
Pocket (pita) bread, 318
Polenta, *321
Polished rice, 352
Polish sausage, †366, 367
Pollock, †165
Polyunsaturated fat, 159
Pomander ball, 109
Pomegranate, 321–322
    (market forms, nutrition
    information, selecting, storing)
  eating technique, 322
Pompano, †165, 322
  (how to cook, market forms,
    nutrition information)
Popcorn, 322
    (market forms, nutrition
    information, storing, types)
  cause of popping, 322
Popcorn (Colby-Monterey Jack)
    cheese, †88, 114
Popover, 55, 322, 323, *324
    (baking hints, storing)
  collapse, causes of, 324
  pan, substitutes for, 324
  versatility of, 324
Poppy seed, 325
    (storing)
Pork, 325–327
    (how to cook, market forms,
    nutrition information, pork
    doneness, selecting)
  broiling, †246
  chitterling, 421
  cracklings (rinds), 126
  cuts, retail, 326–327
  grilling, †29–31
  panbroiling and panfrying, †248
  roasting, †247

Pork (continued)
  sausage, †366, 367
  storing, †245
  tips on cooking, 325
  See also Bacon; Ham
Port du Salut cheese, †89
Potassium, †430
Potato, 327–328
    (market forms, nutrition
    information, preparation hints,
    selecting, storing, types)
  amount for crowd, †341
  cooking, †247
  Duchess, 148
  grilling, †32
  pancake, 290
  pricking, 328
  sweet, 396–397
    cooking, †427
    vs. yams, 396, 443
  twice-baked, *420
Potato salad, 328–*329
    (market forms, types)
Pot marigold, †171
Potpie, 330
Pot roast, *330
Pots de crème, 330–*331
Poultry, 331–334
    (cooking hints, freezing, how to
    cook, market forms,
    refrigerating, selecting, thawing)
  broiling, †332
  carving, 82
  giblet, 190
  grilling, †31–32
  guinea hen, 199
  handling safely, 334
  hot line, 173, 332
  pounding, 334
  roasting, †333
  stuffed. See Stuffing
  trussing, 416
  See also Chicken; Duck and
    duckling; Goose; Pheasant; Quail;
    Squab; Turkey
Poultry seasoning, 334
  alternative for, 208, †446
Pound cake, 275, 334–*335
    (preparation hints)
  crack on, 335
Pounding, 334
  covering meat for, 334
Powdered milk, 256
Powdered sugar, 394

Praline, 335
    pecans, temperature for, 335
Prasky (sausage), †366
Prawn, 335
    (how to cook)
    vs. shrimp, 335
Precooking, 336
Preheating, 336
    importance of, varied, 336
Premelted, unsweetened
    chocolate product, 101
Prepared mustard, 267
    substitution for, emergency, †446
Preservation methods, 336
    See also individual entries
Preserve, 336
    vs. jam and jelly, 220
Preserved ginger, 190
Pressure canner, 77
Pressure cooking, 336
    care of cooker, 336
Presweetened cocoa powder,
    110, 111
Pretzel, 336
    (nutrition hint)
    sodium, reducing, 336
Prickly pear, 336–337
    (nutrition information,
    preparation hints, selecting,
    storing)
    leaf of cactus, 69
    prickles, removing from fingers, 337
Process cheese, 87
    Gruyère, 198–199
Processing, 337
    canning, 77–78
Profiterole, 337
Proof, liquor's, 337
Proofing (raising) dough, 56, 337
    in microwave, 57
Proprietary wine, 440
Prosciutto ham, 337
Protein, 337–338
Provolone cheese, †89
Prune, 338
    (market forms, nutrition
    information)
    cooking, †147
    French, 319
    Italian, 320
Pudding, 338–*339
    (market forms)
    blancmange, 48
    bread, *54
    corn, 122

Pudding (continued)
    covering, 338
    Indian, 215
    plum, 320
    quick desserts using, 338–339
    stirring ingredients, 338
Puff pastry, 298, 339
    cutting dough for, 339
    napoleon, 268
    patty shell, 299
Puffy omelet, 277, *278–279
Pummelo, 195, 196
Pumpernickel, 339
Pumpkin, 340
    (nutrition information)
    homemade pulp from, 340
Pumpkin pie spice, 340
    substitution for, emergency, †446
Punch, 340
    wassail, 434
Puree and pureeing, 340
Purple bean, 35
    cooking, †424
Purple bell pepper, †306, 307
Purple potato, 327–328

Quahog, 107
Quail, 340
    (how to cook, nutrition
    information)
    grilling, †31
    roasting, †333
Quantity cooking, 340–342
    (cooking hints)
    amounts of food needed, †341
    multiplying recipes, 342
Queen Ann plum, 319, 320
Quenelle, 342
Quiche, 275, *342–343
    amount of additions to, 342
Quick bread, 55
    (preparation hints,
    storing, types)
    Boston brown bread, 51
    Irish soda bread, 215
    johnnycake, 222
    loaves, 55
        hints for making, 55
        slicing, 55
Quick-cooking grain
    cooking, †193
    oats, †193, 276
    rice, †352, 353
Quick-cooking tapioca, 404
Quick-rising yeast, 443

Quince, 343
    (nutrition information, selecting,
    storing)
Quinoa, 343
    (nutrition information, storing)
    cooking, †193

Rabbit, 346
Raclette, 346
Radicchio, 346
    (preparation hints, selecting,
    storing)
Radish, 346–347
    (nutrition information,
    preparation hints, selecting,
    storing, types)
    daikon, 140, 346
    cooking, †425
    sprout, 383
Ragout, *347
Rainier cherry, 93
Raisin, 347
    (nutrition information, varieties)
    dried currant, 136, 347
Ramekin, 348
Rape (broccoli raab, rapini), 60
    (how to cook, nutrition information,
    selecting, storing)
Rarebit, 348
Raspberry, †43, 348
    (market forms, varieties)
Ratatouille, *348, 349
Ravigote sauce, 350
Ravioli, 295, 350
    cooking, †296
Raw sugar, 394
Razor clam, 107
Recommended Dietary Allowances
    (RDAs), calorie estimates in, 73
Reconstituting, 350
Red banana, 26
Red Bartlett pear, 303
Red Beaut plum, 320
Red cabbage, 68
Red Delicious apple, †16, 17
Redfin, American (tilapia), 409
Redfish (red drum), †165, 350
Red grapefruit, 195, 196
Red onion, 280
Red pepper (cayenne), ground,
    305, 306
    alternative for, 208
Red pepper. See Pepper (vegetable)
Red radish, 346

Red snapper, †165, 350
  (how to cook, market forms,
  nutrition information)
Red-tip leaf lettuce, 232
Reducing, 350
Red vs. white wine, 440
Refried beans, 350
Refrigerator (sliced) cookie, 117
  hints for making, 118
Refrigerator thermometer, 408
Rehydrating, 350
  mushrooms, 266
  plumping, 320
Relish, 351
  amount for crowd, †341
  chowchow, 104
  chutney, 104
  corn, 122–*123
  piccalilli, 311
  pickle, 312, 351
Remoulade sauce, 351
Rennet, 351
Rhubarb, 351
  (how to cook, nutrition information,
  preparation hints, selecting, storing)
Rib
  beef, 40
  lamb, 227
  pork, 326
Ribier grape, 194, 195
Riboflavin, †430
Rice, 352–353
    (from long to short, market
    forms, nutrition information,
    storing)
  amount for crowd, †341
  bran, 52, 352
  cooking, †352
  doneness, testing for, 353
  extra, preparing, 352
  flour, 352
  pilaf, 315–*316
    with wild rice, 440
  risotto, 345, *354
  stickiness, 353
  sushi, 396
Rice, wild, 439–440
Rice stick (rice noodles,
    rice vermicelli), 100, 353
  storing, 353
Rice vinegar, 285, 430
Ricotta cheese, 353–354
  (nutrition information)

Rigatoni, 294
  cooking, †296
Rind, 354
  See also Peel
Ring pasta (anelli), 294
  cooking, †296
Ripening, 354
Risotto, 345, *354
Roast, 354
  carving, 81, 82
  grilling, †30–31
  kinds of, 40–41, 227, 326, 422
  pot roast, *330
  roasting, †247
  storing, †245
Roasting, 354
  meat, †247
    beef cuts for, 40–41
    lamb cuts for, 227
    pork cuts for, 326–327
    thermometer, using, 246
    veal cuts for, 422
  peanuts, 301
  peppers, 307
  poultry, †333
Roasting chicken, 95
Rock Cornish hen. See Cornish
  game hen
Rock crab, 124
Rocket (arugula), 20
Rockfish, †165
Rock salt, 361
Roe, 355
  (market forms, selecting)
  caviar, 84
Roll, 355
  (baking hints, convenience
  products)
  bagel, 24
  brioche, 58
  croissant, 132
  crust techniques, 355
  freezing, †175
  hot cross bun, 185, *213
Rolled oats, 276
  cooking, †193
Rolling, 355
  jelly-roll style, 355
Romaine, 232, †232, 355
  (nutrition information)
Romano cheese, †89, 356
  substitution for Parmesan, 356
Roma (plum) tomato, 410, 411
Rome Beauty apple, †16, 17
Roquefort cheese, 49

Roquette (arugula), 20
Rosamarina (orzo), 287, 295
  cooking, †296
Rose, †171
Rosemary, 356
    (preparation hints)
  alternative for, 208
  crushing, 356
Rosette, 356
Rotini, 295
  cooking, †296
Roughy. See Orange roughy
Roulade, 356
Round clam, 107
Round red and round white
  potato, 327, 328
Roux, 356
  brown, making, 357
    guidelines for, 357
Royal Ann cherry, 93
Ruby (red) grapefruit, 195, 196
Ruote (wagon wheels), 295
  cooking, †296
Rusk, 357
    (nutrition information)
  zwieback, 445
Russet potato, 327, 328
Rutabaga, 357
    (nutrition information, selecting,
    storing)
  cooking, †427
Rye, 357
  (market forms, nutrition
  information, storing)
Rye berry, 357
  cooking, †193
Rye bread
  limpa, 234
  pumpernickle, 339
Rye flour, 357

Sabayon (zabaglione), 444–*445
Sacher torte, 411
Safety, food. See Food safety
Saffron, 358
  alternative for, 381
  crushing, 358
  getting flavor from, 358
Sage, 358
  alternative for, 208
  rubbed and ground, 358
Salad, 358–359
    (market forms, nutrition hint,
    types)
  amount for crowd, †341

Salad (continued)
   Caesar, *69
   coleslaw, *115
   crab Louis, *126
   potato, 328–*329
   preparation hints, 359
   Waldorf, 431, 432, *433
Salad dressing, 146, 359
   (market forms, storing, types)
   mayonnaise, 243, 364
   vinaigrette, *429
Salad greens
   arugula, 20
   cress, 131
      watercress, 434–435
   mache, †359
   sorrel, 378–379
   Swiss chard, 397
   See also Endive; Lettuce
Salami, †366, 367
Salisbury steak, 360
Sally Lunn, 360
Salmon, †165, 360
   (how to cook, market forms,
      nutrition information, types)
   canned, handling, 360
   lox, 236
Salsa, 360
Salsify, 361
   (how to cook, nutrition information,
   selecting, storing)
Salt, 361
   (market forms, nutrition
   information, storing)
   celery, 85
Saltimbocca, 362, *363
Saltwater fish, 164, †165
   See also individual entries
Saltwater taffy, 402
Sandwich, 363
   (nutrition hint)
   canapé, 74
   freezing, †175
Santa Claus (Christmas) melon,
   †250, 251
Santa Rosa plum, 320
Sapodilla, 363
   (nutrition information, selecting,
   storing)
Sapote. See White sapote
Sapsago cheese, †89
Sardine, 364
   (market forms, nutrition
   information, types)
Sashimi, 364

Sassafras, 364
   filé powder, 164
Sate (satay), 364
Saturated fat, 159
   in margarine, 241
Sauce, 364–365
      (market forms, types)
   béarnaise, 38
   bordelaise, 51
   brown, 62, 364
      piquant, 317
   chili, 99
   cooking tips, 365
   fish, 284
   with foods, 364–365
   French use of, 176, 178
   gravy, 196–*197
   hard, 204
   hollandaise, *210, 364
   hot pepper, 213
   mayonnaise, 243, 364
   Mexican specialties, 254
      mole, 254, 261
      salsa, 360
   Mornay, 261
   ravigote, 350
   remoulade, 351
   sour cream, adding, 380
   soy, 380
      sweet, 285
   steak, 388
   sweet-and-sour, 397
   tartar, *405
   vinaigrette, 364, *429
   white, 364, *438
      béchamel, 38
      velouté, 428
   Worcestershire, 442–443
Sauerbraten, *189, 365
Sauerkraut, 365
   rinsing, 365
Sausage, 365–367
      (market forms, nutrition
      information, selecting,
      storing, types)
   cooking, 367
   head cheese, 206
   storing, †245, †366
   turkey, 417
   See also Frankfurter
Sautéing, 367
Savarin vs. baba, 23
Savory, 367–368
   alternative for, 208
Savoy cabbage, 68

Scalding, 368
Scale and scaling, 368
Scallion (green onion), 280
Scallop, 368
      (how to cook, market forms,
      nutrition information, selecting
      and storing, types)
   grilling, †31
   preparing and cooking, †373
Scalloped food, 368
Scallop flute, 172
Scaloppine, 368
Scamorze cheese, †89
Scampi, 368
Schaum torte, 411
Scone, 55, 368, 369, *370
Scoring, 370
Scottish oatmeal (steel-cut
   oats), †193, 276
Scrambled egg, 152
Scraper, rubber, stirring with, 388
Scraping, 370
   (nutrition hint)
Scrapple, 370
Scrod, 112, 202, 370
Seafood, 370
   alligator, 10
   surimi, 396
   See also Fish; Shellfish
Sea herring, 208
Searing, 370
Seasoning, 370–371
Seaweed, 371
Seckel pear, 302, 303
Section and sectioning, 371
Sectioned and formed ham, 203, 327
Seedless (English) cucumber, 135
Seedless grape, 194, 195
   raisins from, 347
Seedless watermelon, 435
Self-rising flour, 170
   substitution for, emergency, †446
Seltzer water, 434
Semi-boneless ham, 202
Semidry and dry sausage, 365–366, 367
   storing, †366
Semidry and semisoft date, 140
Semisoft Monterey Jack cheese, 261
Semisweet chocolate, 101
   substitution for, emergency, †446
Semolina, 436
Serrano pepper, †306, 307

Sesame seed, 371
  (storing)
  paste (tahini), 402
  toasting, 371
Seven-minute frosting, 180
Shake, 44
Shallot, *371*
  (how to cook, nutrition information, selecting, storing)
Shallow-frying, 182
Shaped cookie, 117
  gingersnap, 191
  hints for making, 118
  shortbread, 374
  snickerdoodle, 378
  spritz, 383
Shark, †165, 372
  (how to cook, nutrition information)
Sheets off the spoon stage of jelly, 221
Shelf-stable packaging, 372
  tofu, 409
Shell pasta, *295, 297*
  cooking, †296
Shellfish, 372
  (how to cook, market forms, nutrition information, storing, types)
  abalone, 10
  cockle, 110
  conch, 116
  cooking, †373
  grilling, †31
  imitation (surimi seafood), 396
  octopus, 276
  prawn, 335
  preparing, †373
  scampi, 368
  snail, 377
  squid (calamari), 73, *387*
  See Preparing and Cooking Shellfish chart, 373, for varieties
Shepherd's pie, 372
Sherbet, 372, *374
  (nutrition information)
  sorbet vs., 378
  tips for making, 215
Shiitake mushroom, *265*
Shortbread, 374
Shortcake, *345,* *374–375*
Shortening, 159, 160, 375
  cutting in, 137, *314*
  measuring, 243
  See also Deep-fat frying

Short food, 374
Short grain rice, 352, 353
Shredding, *375*
  vs. grating, 196
Shrimp, 375–376
  (cooking hints, how to cook, market forms, nutrition information, selecting, storing, types)
  boiling, †373
  butterflying, *376*
  deveining, *142, 376*
  equivalents, 375
  grilling, †31
  peeling, *376*
  vs. prawn, 335
  preparing, †373
  scampi, 368
Shrimp paste, *284*
Shrimp spice (crab boil), 126
Shucking, 376
Sieve and sieving, 376
  as substitute sifter, 376
Sifting, 377
  flour, question of, 170, 377
  with sieve, 376
Silver hake (whiting), †165, 438
Simmering, 377
Simple sugar syrup, 399
Skewer, 377
  spacing food on, 377
Skim milk, 256, †257
Skimming, 377
Slice, 377
Sliced cookie, 117
  hints for making, 118
Slicing, 377
  bias slicing, *44*
Slit, 377
Sliver and slivering, 377
Smoked pork, 325, *326–327*
  See also Bacon; Ham
Smoked sausage, 365, *367*
  storing, †366
Smoke flavor
  for barbecued foods, 28
  liquid, 234
Smorgasbord, 377
Snail, 377
Snapper, red, †165, 350
Snickerdoodle, 378
Snipping, *378*
Snow crab, 124
Snow pea, *302*
Sockeye (red) salmon, †165, 360

Soda, 378
  See also Baking soda
Soda bread, Irish, 215
Soda fountain beverage, 44
Soda water, 434
Sodium
  label terms, 226
Sodium chloride, †430
  as salt, 361
Soft vs. hard wheat, 436
Soft margarine, 240, 241
Soft-shell clam, 107
Sole, †165, 378
  (how to cook, market forms, nutrition information)
  Australian. *See* Orange roughy
  flounder as, 169, 378
Soluble fiber, 162
Sorbet, 378
Sorghum, 378
  (nutrition information)
Sorrel, *378–379*
  (nutrition information, selecting, storing)
Soufflé, 379
  (baking hints, preparation hints)
  chilled, 379
  collar for, *379*
  serving, 379
Soup, 379
  (selecting soups for a menu)
  amount for crowd, †341
  bisque, 47
  borscht, 51
  chowder, 104
    clam, *108–109
  freezing, †175
  fruit, 182
  gazpacho, *185,* *187
  health-conscious, 379
  minestrone, *258, 259*
  mulligatawny, 263
  onion, 280, *281,* *282
  vichyssoise, *428–429*
Sour cream, 380
  (nutrition information, storing)
  adding to hot mixtures, 380
  mold on, 380
  substitution for, emergency, †446
Sourdough, 380
  starter, tips on, 380
Sour milk, 51, 65
Southern pea, 299
  black-eyed, †37, *48*

Soybean, *36,* †37
Soybean curd (tofu), *285, 409–410*
Soy sauce, 380
　(varieties, nutrition information)
　sweet, *285*
Spaetzle, *189, 295,* 380
　cooking, †296
Spaghetti, *294, 297,* 381
　amount for crowd, †341
　cooking, †296
Spaghetti squash, *385,* †386
　cooking, †427
　serving, *386*
Spanish-style olive, 277
Sparkling water, 434
Sparkling wine, 440
Spearmint, 258, *260*
Spice, 381
　(market forms, nutrition
　　information, selecting, storing)
　alternatives, 381
　bag for, *381*
　freshness, judging, 381
　vs. oil, 158
　See also individual entries
Spinach, *382*
　(market forms, nutrition
　　information, preparation hints,
　　selecting, storing)
　cooking, †427
　Florentine dishes, 169
Spiny (Rock) lobster, 235
Split pea, *299*
Sponge cake, 71, 382
　(nutrition information)
　jelly roll, *219,* *221
　ladyfinger, 226
　problem solving, 72
Spoon bread, *382–383
Spread and spreading, 383
Sprig, 383
Spring/summer onion, 279–280
Sprinkling, 383
Spritz cookie, 383
Sprout, *383*
　(selecting, storing, varieties)
　bean, 38, *383*
　brussels, *62–63,* †424
Spumoni, 384
Spun honey, 211
Squab, 384
　(how to cook, nutrition
　　information)
　grilling, †31
　roasting, †333

Squash, *384–386*
　(market forms, nutrition
　　information, preparation hints,
　　selecting, storing, varieties)
　blossom, †171, 386
　chayote, *86,* †425
　cooking, †427
　pumpkin, *340*
　selecting, †386
　serving, *386*
　See also Zucchini
Squid (calamari), 73, 387
　(nutrition information)
　preparing, *387*
Squirt clam, 107
Stale food, 387
Star pasta, *295*
　cooking, †296
Starch, 387
　arrowroot, 18
　as carbohydrate, 80, 387
　cornstarch, 123
　tapioca, *404*
　See also Flour
Star fruit (carambola), *78–79*
Stayman apple, †16, *17*
Steak
　broiling, †246
　carving, *81*
　doneness, testing for, *39*
　grilling, †29
　kinds of, *40–41,* 326, 422
　panbroiling and panfrying, †248
　pepper steak, 307, *308,* *309
　　steak au poivre, *387
　storing, †245
　Swiss steak, *345,* *398
Steak au Poivre, *387
Steak Diane, 387
Steak sauce, 388
Steak tartare, 388
Steamer clam, 107
Steaming, 388
　shellfish, †373
　vegetables, †424–427
Steel-cut oat, 276
　cooking, †193
Steeping, 388
　tea, 406
Sterilization, 388
Stew, 388
　fish
　　bouillabaisse, 51
　　cioppino, *105
　freezing, †175

Stew *(continued)*
　goulash, *192
　gumbo, 199, *200,* *201
　Irish, *216
　jambalaya, *219,* *220
　mulligan, 265
　ragout, *347
Stewing chicken, 95
Stilton cheese, 49
Stir-fry and stir-frying, 182, 388,
　389, *390
　(stir-frying hints)
Stirred custard, *137*
Stirring, 388
　scraper for, 388
Stock, *390–391
　consommé, 116
Stone crab, 124
Storage, food, 173
　See also Freezing and individual
　　entries
Straightneck squash, *384*
Straining, 391
Strata, 391
　making ahead, 391
Strawberry, †43, *391*
　(market forms, preparation hints,
　　selecting)
Straw mushroom, 265
Streusel, 391
String cheese, *391–392*
Stroganoff, *392
　(nutrition hint)
Strudel, 392
　shortcut method for, 392
Stuffing, 146, 393
　adding, proper time for, 393, 418
　extra, cooking, 393
　turkey, *393,* 418
Substitutions, emergency, †446
Succotash, 393
Suet, 393
Sugar, 393–394
　(market forms, nutrition
　　information, storing)
　acidity blunted by, 394
　cane vs. beet, 393
　caramelizing, *79*
　as carbohydrate, 79
　crystallized, 134
　high-altitude adjustments, †209
　label synonyms, 394
　maple, 239

Sugar *(continued)*
  measuring, *243*
  softening, 394
  substitution for, emergency, †446
  vanilla, 421
Sugar snap pea, *302*
Sugar substitute, 394–395
    (types)
  replacing sugar with, 395
Sugar syrup, 399
Sukiyaki, 395
Sultana raisin, 347
Summer (candy) coating, 77
Summer sausage, †366, *367*
Summer savory, 367–368
Summer squash, *384*
  cooking, †427
  selecting, †386
  See also Zucchini
Sunburst squash, *384,* †386
  cooking, †427
Sunchoke (Jerusalem artichoke), *222*
  cooking, †426
Sundae, 395
Sunflower seed, 395
    (market forms)
  and baking soda, 395
Surf clam, 107
Surimi seafood, 396
  as precooked product, 396
Sushi, 396
Swamp cabbage (heart of palm), *206*
Sweet-and-sour sauce, 396
Sweetbread, *421*
Sweet (unsalted) butter, 64, 65
Sweet chocolate, *101*
  substitution for, emergency, †446
Sweet dumpling squash, †386
  cooking, †427
Sweetened condensed milk, 79, 256,
    †257, 396
    (nutrition information, storing)
  vs. evaporated milk, 157
Sweetener, 396
  low-calorie, 394–395
  See also Honey; Sugar; Syrup
Sweet marjoram. *See* Marjoram
Sweet pepper, 305, †306, *307*
  cooking, †427
  grilling, †32
Sweet pickle, 312

Sweet potato, 396–*397*
    (market forms, nutrition
    information, selecting, storing)
  cooking, †427
  vs. yam, 396, 443
Sweet soy sauce, *285*
Swiss chard, *397*
    (nutrition information, preparation
    hints, selecting, storing)
Swiss cheese, †89, *398*
    (types)
  Gruyère, †89, *198*–199
  substitution for, 199
Swiss steak, *345,* *398
Swordfish, †165, 399
    (how to cook, market forms,
    nutrition information)
Syrup, 399
    (nutrition information,
    preparation hints, storing, types)
  caramelized sugar, *79*
  maple, 239–240
  molasses, 260–261
  simple sugar syrups, 399
  sorghum, 378
Szechwan pepper, 305

Table (light) cream, 128
Table salt, 361
Table wine, 440
Taco, 402
Taffy, 402
  saltwater, 402
  testing mixture, 402
Tagliatelle, cooking, †296
Tahini, 402
Tamale, 402
  making extra, 402
Tamarillo, *402*–403
    (nutrition information, preparation
    hints, selecting, storing)
Tangelo, †106, 403
    (varieties)
  as mandarins, 238
Tangerine, †106, 403
    (selecting, varieties)
  as mandarin, 238
Tannin, 404
Tapa, 404
Tapioca, 404
    (market forms)
  clearness test for, *404*
  in crockery cooker, 404
Tapioca flour (tapioca starch), 404
Taro root, 404

Tarragon, *404*–405
  alternative for, 208
Tart, 405
Tartare, steak, 388
Tartarian cherry, 93
Tartar sauce, *405
Tea (beverage), 405–406
    (market forms, nutrition
    information, storing, types)
  amount for crowd, †341
  herbal, 405
  loose, brewing, 406
Tea (event), 406
Teawurst, †366
Temple orange, †283
Tempura, *401,* *406–407
  tips on making, 406
Tenderizing meat, 245, 250, 407
  meat mallet, use of, 407
Tepin (pequin) pepper, †306, *307*
Teriyaki, 407
  marinade, wine in, 407
Terrine, 298
Tetrazzini, *407
Thai cooking, 286
Thermometer, 408
    (types)
  candy, 74, 76, 408
  checking accuracy of, 76, 408
  deep-fat-frying, *182,* 408
  meat, 408
    for microwave, 408
    using, 246
Thiamin, †430
Thickening agent, 408
  roux, 356–*357*
  for soup, 379
  See also Gelatin; Starch
Thimble, pasta, *294*
  cooking, †296
Thompson seedless grape, *194,* 195
  raisins from, 347
Thuringer, †366
Thyme, *408*–409
  alternative for, 208
  foods compatible with, 409
Tientsin (Napa) cabbage, *68,* 100
Tiger lily bud, *284*
Tilapia, 409
Timbale, 409
Toast, 409
  French, 179
  melba, 250
  rusk, 357
    zwieback, 445

Toasting, 409
  nuts, *11,* 271
  sesame seeds, 371
Toffee, 409
  butter, use of, 409
Tofu, *285, 409–410*
  (market forms, nutrition
  information, storing)
Tokay grape, 195
Tomatillo, *410*
  (nutrition information, selecting,
  storing)
Tomato, *410–411*
  (market forms, nutrition
  information, preparation hints,
  selecting, storing, types)
  catsup, 83
  peeling, question of, 411
Tomato sauce, 364
  substitution for, emergency, †446
Tongue, *421*
Tonic water, 434
Torte, 411
  classic favorites, 411
  ground nuts for, 271
Tortellini, *295*
  cooking, †296
Tortilla, 412
    (nutrition information)
  corn vs. flour, 412
Tortoni, 412
Tossed salad, 358
  Caesar, *69
  hints for, 359
Tossing, 412
Tostada, *412, *413*
Tree ear (wood ear), *285*
Trifle, *401, *414*
Tripe, *421*
Tripolini, cooking, †296
Triticale, 414
    (storing)
  using flour, 414
Trout, †165, 414–415
    (how to cook, market forms,
    nutrition information, types)
  lake trout, †165, 414
  rainbow trout, †165, 414
  sea trout, †165
Truffle, *415
Trussing, 416
  alternative to, 416
Tuna, †165, 416
    (how to cook, market forms,
    nutrition information, types)

Turban squash, *385,* †386
  cooking, †427
Turkey, 416–418, *417*
    (how to cook, market forms,
    nutrition information, preparation
    hints, selecting, storing, types)
  amount per serving, 418
  broiling, †332
  carving, *82*
  doneness, testing for, 418
  grilling, †31, †32
  roasting, †333
  stuffing, *393,* 418
Turmeric, 418–419
Turnip, *419*
    (nutrition information, selecting,
    storing)
  cooking, †427
  greens, *419*
Turtle, 419
Tutti-frutti, 420
Twice-baked potato, *420
  preparing ahead, 420

Ultrapasteurized milk, 256
Unleavened bread
  matzo, 242
  pita, 318
  tortilla, 412
Unsalted butter, 64, 65
Unsaturated fat, 159
Unsweetened chocolate, *101*
  substitution for, emergency, †446
Unsweetened cocoa powder, 110, *111*

Vacuum-packed food, 420
Valencia orange, *282,* †283
Vanilla, 420–421
    (market forms, storing)
  sugar, making, 421
Vanilla bean, 421
Varietal wine, 440
Variety meat, *421*
    (nutrition information, types)
Veal, 422–423
    (how to cook, market forms,
    nutrition information, selecting,
    veal cuts)
  broiling, †246
  cuts, retail, *422*
  grilling, †29, †30
  milk-fed vs. grain-fed, 422
  panbroiling and panfrying, †248
  roasting, †247
  storing, †245

Vegetable, 423–427
    (how to cook, market forms,
    nutrition hints)
  amount for crowd, †341
  baby. *See* Baby vegetable
  cooking, preparation and, †424–427
  crisp-tender, *132*
  cruciferous, 423
    See also individual entries
  crudités, 134
  as food group, †272
  grilling, †32
  salad, 358
  scraping, 370
  soup (minestrone), *258, *259*
  stew (ratatouille), *348, *349*
  See Cooking Fresh Vegetables chart,
    424–427, for types
Velouté sauce, 428
Venison, 428
    (cooking hints, market forms,
    nutrition information, preparation
    hints, storing)
Vermicelli
  cooking, †296
  nested, *295*
  rice (rice sticks), 100, 353
Véronique style, 428
Vichyssoise, *428–429
Vienna bread, 429
Vienna sausage, †366
Vietnamese cooking, 286
Vinaigrette, 364, *429
Vinegar, 429–430
    (storing, types)
  rice, *285,* 430
Vintage wine, 441
Viola, †171
Violet, *171,* †171
Vitamin, 430, †430
  supplements, use of, 431

Wafer, 431
Waffle, 55, 431
    (convenience products, nutrition
    hint, nutrition information, waffle
    bakers)
  batter, vs. pancake, 431
  Belgian, 431
  keeping warm, 431
Wagon wheel pasta, *295*
  cooking, †296
Waldorf salad, 431, *432,* *433

Walnut, †270, *433*
    (storing)
    cracking, 433
Wasabi, 433
Wassail, 434
Water, 434
    (as a nutrient, types)
    calories in types, 434
    dehydration, 141
Water chestnut, 434
Watercress, *434–435*
    (nutrition information, selecting,
    storing)
Watermelon, †250, *251, 435*
    (selecting)
    seedless, seeds in, 435
Wax bean, yellow, *35, 36*
    cooking, †424
Weeping, 435
    in meringue pie, avoiding, 253, 435
Weight-loss hints, 273
Weights and measures, 436
    container sizes, †116
    dash, 140
    list of, 436
    liter, 234
Welsh rabbit (rarebit), 348
Western eggplant, *154*
Wheat, *436–437*
    (market forms, nutrition
    information, storing, wheat
    classes)
    bran, 52, 437
    bulgur, 63, †193, 436
    cooking, †193
    farina, 158, 436
    flour, 170, 436, 437
    semolina, 436
    sprout, 383
Wheat berry, †193, 436
Wheat germ, 437
Whipped butter, 64, 65
Whipped cream, 128
Whipped cream cheese, 129
Whipped honey, 211
Whipped margarine, 240–241
Whipping, 437
    cream, 128
Whipping cream, 128
    crème fraîche, 130–131
    substitution for, emergency, †446

White baking bars/pieces
    with cocoa butter, *101*–102
White eggplant, *154*
Whitefish, †165, 437
    (how to cook, market forms,
    nutrition information, types)
White (blond) fudge, 182
White grapefruit, 195, *196*
White mushroom, *265*
White onion, *280*
White pattypan squash, *384*
White pepper, 305
White sapote, *437*
    (nutrition information, selecting,
    storing, varieties)
White sauce, 364, *438
    béchamel, 38
    lumps, preventing, 438
    velouté, 428
White vinegar, 430
White vs. red wine, 440
White wine Worcestershire
    sauce, 443
Whiting, †165, 438
    (how to cook, market forms,
    nutrition information)
Whole grain, 439
    (storing)
    using, in bread, 439
Whole milk, 256, †257
Whole wheat flour, 170
Wiener. *See* Frankfurter
Wiener schnitzel, *439
    panfrying, tips on, 439
Wild marjoram, 242, 284
Wild rice, *439–440*
    (how to cook, nutrition
    information, preparation hints,
    storing)
    combined in pilaf, 440
Wine, 440–441
    (nutrition information, selecting,
    storing, types, wine naming)
    amount to buy, †441
    aperitif, 15, 440
    blush, 441
    cooking tips, 441
    teriyaki marinade, 407
    vintage, 441

Wine cooler, 440
Winesap apple, †16, *17*
Wine vinegar, 430
Winter and summer savory, 367–368
Winter squash, *385*
    cooking, †427
    selecting, †386
    serving, *386*
Witloof chicory. *See* Belgian endive
Wonton, *401,* *442
    sealing, *442*
    substitute wrappers, 442
Wood ear and cloud ear, *285*
Wood for smoke flavor, 28
Worcestershire sauce, 442–443

Yachtwurst, †366
Yam, 443
    sweet potato vs., 396, 443
Yard (Chinese long) bean, *35, 36*
Yearling, 226
Yeast, 443
    (market forms, storing)
    dissolving methods, 443
    quick-rising, use of, 443
    substitution for, emergency, †446
Yeast bread, 56
    (baking hints, storing, types)
    batter vs. kneaded, 56
    buns, 63
        hot cross, *185,* *213
        kolacky, 225
    Danish pastry, 140
    English muffin, 156
    flour for, choosing, 56
    focaccia, 172
    French bread, *176, *177*
        baguette, 24
    high-altitude cooking, 209
    Italian bread, 176, 216
    kneading dough for, 224
    limpa, 234
    making, *57*
        hints for, 57
    pumpernickel, 339
    raising
        best place for, 56
        in microwave, 57
    Vienna bread, 429
    yeast for, 443
    See also Roll

Yellow banana pepper, †306
Yellow Bartlett pear, *303*
Yellow bell pepper, †306, *307*
 cooking, †427
Yellow (American) mustard, 267
Yellow onion, *280*
Yellow potato, *327, 328*
Yellow squash, *384,* †386
 cooking, †427
Yellow wax bean, *35,* 36
 cooking, †424
Yogurt, 443–444
  (market forms, storing)
 cooking with, 444
 fat and calories in, by type, †444
 frozen, 444
  amount for crowd, †341
 fruit, 444
York Imperial apple, †16
Yorkshire pudding, 444

Zabaglione, 444–*445
Zahidi date, *140*
Zante currant, 347
 grape for, *194*
Zest, 445
 preparing, 445
Ziti, *295*
 cooking, †296
Zucchini, *384,* †386, *445*
  (nutrition information, selecting, storing)
 cooking, †427
 grilling, †32
Zuppa inglese, 445
Zwieback, 445
  (nutrition information)
 for crumb crusts, 445

Acknowledgments

We would like to express our gratitude and appreciation to the individuals and associations whose help was invaluable in producing this book.

Almond Board of California,
 San Francisco, California
The American Dairy Association,
 Rosemont, Illinois
American Egg Board,
 Park Ridge, Illinois
American Lamb Council,
 Englewood, Colorado
American Soybean Association,
 St. Louis, Missouri
American Spice Trade Association,
 New York, New York
Michelle C. Bing, MLIS
David Brenner, Agronomy Department,
 Iowa State University, Ames, Iowa
J. R. Brooks & Son,
 Homestead, Florida
Charles R. Burnham
California Tree Fruit Agreement,
 Sacramento, California
Calorie Control Council,
 Atlanta, Georgia
Chocolate Manufacturers Association of
 U.S.A., McLean, Virginia
Driscoll's, Watsonville, California
Karen K. Fabian, Home Economics
 Consultant
Kenneth Fry, Agronomy Department,
 Iowa State University, Ames, Iowa
The Green House Fine Herbs,
 Encinitas, California
Marilyn Hotchkiss
International Apple Institute,
 McLean, Virginia
Barbara Jean Martell
National Broiler Council,
 Washington, D.C.
The National Buckwheat Institute,
 Penn Yan, New York
National Coffee Association of U.S.A.,
 Inc., New York, New York
National Fisheries Institute,
 Arlington, Virginia
National Honey Board,
 Longmont, Colorado
National Live Stock and Meat Board,
 Chicago, Illinois
National Pasta Association,
 Arlington, Virginia
National Pork Producers Council,
 Des Moines, Iowa
National Turkey Federation,
 Reston, Virginia
Peanut Advisory Board,
 Atlanta, Georgia
Pickle Packers International,
 New York, New York
The Popcorn Institute,
 Chicago, Illinois
Ruetenik Gardens,
 Brooklyn Heights, Ohio
T. Jackie Runyan, Nu-Trends
 Consulting, Ames, Iowa
Cindy Slobaszewski
John Strait, Professor Emeritus of
 Agricultural Engineering,
 University of Minnesota
The Sugar Association, Inc.,
 Washington, D.C.
Tea Council of the U.S.A.,
 New York, New York
USA Rice Council, Houston, Texas
Vermont Maple Industry Council,
 Colchester, Vermont
The Vinegar Institute,
 Atlanta, Georgia
The Walnut Marketing Board,
 Sacramento, California
Wheat Foods Council,
 Washington, D.C.
Wine Institute,
 San Francisco, California
Wisconsin Milk Marketing Board,
 Madison, Wisconsin

Some of the photographs used in the book were previously printed in other *Better Homes and Gardens*® publications. We would like to thank the following photographers:

Ron Crofoot
Sean Fitzgerald
Bill Hopkins, Hopkins Associates
Scott Little
Tim Schultz

Metric Cooking Hints

By making a few conversions, cooks in Australia, Canada, and the United Kingdom can use the recipes in Better Homes and Gardens® *Complete Guide to Food and Cooking* with confidence. The charts on this page provide a guide for converting measurements from the U.S. customary system, which is used throughout this book, to the imperial and metric systems. There also is a conversion table for oven temperatures to accommodate the differences in oven calibrations.

Volume and Weight: Americans traditionally use *cup* measures for liquid and solid ingredients. The chart (top right) shows the approximate imperial and metric equivalents. If you are accustomed to weighing solid ingredients, here are some helpful approximate equivalents:

- 1 cup butter, caster sugar, or rice = 8 ounces = about 250 grams
- 1 cup flour = 4 ounces = about 125 grams
- 1 cup icing sugar = 5 ounces = about 150 grams

Spoon measures are used for smaller amounts of ingredients. Although the size of the teaspoon is the same, the size of the tablespoon varies slightly among countries. However, for practical purposes and for recipes in this book, a straight substitution is all that's necessary.

Measurements made using cups or spoons always should be *level,* unless stated otherwise.

Product Differences: Most of the ingredients called for in the recipes in this book are available in English-speaking countries. However, some are known by different names. Here are some common American ingredients and their possible counterparts:

- Sugar is granulated or caster sugar.
- Powdered sugar is icing sugar.
- All-purpose flour is plain household flour or white flour. When self-rising flour is used in place of all-purpose flour in a recipe that calls for leavening, omit the leavening (baking soda or baking powder) and salt.
- Light corn syrup is golden syrup.
- Cornstarch is cornflour.
- Baking soda is bicarbonate of soda.
- Vanilla is vanilla essence.

Useful Equivalents

⅛ teaspoon = 0.5ml	⅔ cup = 5 fluid ounces = 150ml
¼ teaspoon = 1ml	¾ cup = 6 fluid ounces = 175ml
½ teaspoon = 2ml	1 cup = 8 fluid ounces = 250ml
1 teaspoon = 5ml	2 cups = 1 pint
¼ cup = 2 fluid ounces = 50ml	2 pints = 1 litre
⅓ cup = 3 fluid ounces = 75ml	½ inch = 1 centimetre
½ cup = 4 fluid ounces = 125ml	1 inch = 2 centimetres

Baking Pan Sizes

American	Metric
8x1½-inch round baking pan	20x4-centimetre sandwich or cake tin
9x1½-inch round baking pan	23x3.5-centimetre sandwich or cake tin
11x7x1½-inch baking pan	28x18x4-centimetre baking pan
13x9x2-inch baking pan	32.5x23x5-centimetre baking pan
12x7½x2-inch baking dish	30x19x5-centimetre baking pan
15x10x2-inch baking pan	38x25.5x2.5-centimetre baking pan (Swiss roll tin)
9-inch pie plate	22x4- or 23x4-centimetre pie plate
7- or 8-inch springform pan	18- or 20-centimetre springform or loose-bottom cake tin
9x5x3-inch loaf pan	23x13x6-centimetre or 2-pound narrow loaf pan or pâté tin
1½-quart casserole	1.5-litre casserole
2-quart casserole	2-litre casserole

Oven Temperature Equivalents

Fahrenheit Setting	Celsius Setting*	Gas Setting
300°F	150°C	Gas Mark 2
325°F	160°C	Gas Mark 3
350°F	180°C	Gas Mark 4
375°F	190°C	Gas Mark 5
400°F	200°C	Gas Mark 6
425°F	220°C	Gas Mark 7
450°F	230°C	Gas Mark 8
Broil		Grill (watch time and heat)

Electric and gas ovens may be calibrated using Celsius. However, increase the Celsius setting 10 to 20 degrees when cooking above 160°C with an electric oven. For convection or forced-air ovens (gas or electric), lower the temperature setting 10°C when cooking at all heat levels.